Readings in
Managerial
Psychology

Edited by
Harold J.
Leavitt,
Louis R.
Pondy,
and
David M.
Boje

Readings in Managerial Psychology

Third Edition

The University of Chicago Press
Chicago and London

The University of Chicago Press, Chicago 60637
The University of Chicago Press, Ltd., London
© 1964, 1973, 1980 by The University of Chicago
All rights reserved. Published 1964. Second Edition 1973
Third Edition 1980
Printed in the United States of America

90 89 88 87 86 85 84 83   2 3 4 5 6

Library of Congress Cataloging in Publication Data

Leavitt, Harold J.   ed.
  Readings in managerial psychology.

  Includes bibliographical references.
    1. Psychology, Industrial—Addresses, essays,
lectures.   2. Industrial management—Addresses, essays,
lectures.   I. Pondy, Louis R.   II. Boje, David M.
III. Title.
HF5548.8.L36   1980   658   79–21587
ISBN: 0–226–46986–7
ISBN: 0–226–46987–5 pbk.

Contents

Preface ix

Section 1

**1 Motivation: The
Driving Force**

Introduction 3
A Theory of Human Motivation 5
A. H. Maslow

Intrinsic and Extrinsic Motivation 23
Barry M. Staw

Power is the Great Motivator 62
David C. McClelland and
David H. Burnham

A New Strategy for Job Enrichment 80
J. Richard Hackman, Greg Oldham,
Robert Janson, and Kenneth Purdy

**2 Mind: Thinking,
Creating, Analyzing**

Introduction 104

Two Sides of the Brain 106
Robert E. Ornstein

How Managers' Minds Work 126
James L. McKenney and
Peter G. W. Keen

The Science of "Muddling
Through" 144
Charles E. Lindblom

Emotional Blocks 161
James L. Adams

3 Opinions, Beliefs, and Attitudes: The Balancing Act

Introduction 171

The Rationalizing Animal 173
Elliot Aronson

Achieving Change in People: Some Applications of Group Dynamics Theory 184
Darwin Cartwright

Training the Woman to Know Her Place: The Power of a Nonconscious Ideology 197
Sandra L. Bem and Daryl J. Bem

Behavior Modification: A Contingency Approach to Employee Performance 210
C. Ray Gullett and Robert Reisen

4 The Whole Person and the Whole Situation: Putting it Together

Introduction 221

Personality vs. Organization 223
Chris Argyris

A Therapist's View of the Good Life: The Fully Functioning Person 240
Carl R. Rogers

Management and the Art of Chinese Baseball 251
Ralph G. H. Siu

Section 2

**5 Communicating:
Listening and Being
Heard**

Introduction 261

Defensive Communication 263
Jack R. Gibb

On the Dynamics of the Helping
Relationship 270
David A. Kolb and Richard E. Boyatzis

Intercultural Communication: A Guide
to Men of Action 290
Edward T. Hall and William Foote Whyte

**6 Leading: Inspiration
and Direction**

Introduction 308

The Human Side of Enterprise 310
Douglas M. McGregor

A Normative Model of Leadership
Style 322
Victor H. Vroom and Philip Yetton

Female Leadership in Formal
Organizations: Must the Female
Leader Go Formal? 341
Jean Lipman-Blumen

**7 Power: Over and
Under the Table**

Introduction 363

Power Tactics 365
Norman H. Martin and
John Howard Sims

Who Gets Power—And How They Hold
on to It: A Strategic-contingency
Model of Power 373
Gerald R. Salancik and Jeffrey Pfeffer

Sources of Power of Lower Participants
in Complex Organizations 396
David Mechanic

Section 3

**8 Groups: Pressures
and Decisions**

Introduction 410

Management Development as a Process
of Influence 412
Edgar H. Schein

Groupthink 432
Irving L. Janis

Making a Horse Out of a Camel:
A Contingency Model for Managing
the Problem Solving Process in
Groups 445
David M. Boje

**9 Conflict
Management:
Friends and Enemies**

Introduction 471

Organizational Conflict: Concepts
and Models 473
Louis R. Pondy

The Absorption of Protest 493
Ruth Leeds Love

How the Top Is Different 522
Rosabeth Moss Kanter

Section 4

**10 Organizational
Decision Making:
Analysis, Intuition,
Judgment**

Introduction 535

The Bureaucratic Paradox: The Efficient
Organization Centralizes in Order to
Decentralize 537
Charles Perrow

Managerial Work: Analysis from
Observation 551
Henry Mintzberg

The Technology of Foolishness 570
James G. March

**11 Organizational
Design: Size, Shape,
Function and Beauty**

Introduction 581

On the Design Part of Organizational
Design 584
Harold J. Leavitt

Organization Design: Organizations as
Self-designing Systems 592
Karl E. Weick

The Organizational Saga in
Higher Education 604
Burton R. Clark

**12 Organizational
Change: Moving the
Mountain**

Introduction 614

Optimizing Team-building Efforts 616
Richard Beckhard

Improving Organizational
Communication Through Long-term
Intergroup Intervention 628
Clayton P. Alderfer

Symbols, Patterns, and Settings:
An Optimistic Case for Getting
Things Done 646
Thomas J. Peters

Stories Managers Tell: A New Tool
for Organizational Problem Solving 666
Ian I. Mitroff and Ralph H. Kilmann

**13 Organizations and
Their Environments:
There's a Real World
Out There**

Introduction 677

Type Z Organization: Stability in
the Midst of Mobility 679
William G. Ouchi and Alfred M. Jaeger

Linking Pins between Organizations
and Environment: Individuals Do the
Interacting 693
Dennis W. Organ

Beyond Management and the Worker:
The Institutional Function of
Management 704
Jeffrey Pfeffer

Strategies for Survival: How
Organizations Cope with Their
Worlds 720
Harold J. Leavitt, William R. Dill, and
Henry B. Eyring

Preface

This third edition of *Readings in Managerial Psychology* is almost an entirely new book. Most of the structure remains the same. As before, we build from the individual to larger units—to groups and large organizations. And this time, much more than before, we include (in keeping with the flows of both managerial concerns and contemporary research) material on the relationship between the organization and the world "out there."

There are thirty-two new (to this book) articles in this edition, and only eleven old ones. All of the old ones appear in the first nine chapters, on individuals and groups. Everything in chapters 10 through 13 is entirely new, reflecting a major shift in recent research and practice toward treating the organization itself as a unit for study and for change. In those last chapters the reader will find more "macro-level" papers, looking at organizational design, organizational change, and organization-environment relationships.

But the early parts of the book include a lot of new material too, reflecting new developments in research and application in motivation, in cognition, and in attitude formation and change. And we have included much more on issues of leadership and power in the organization.

Some of the "new" material is really old. Some old pieces turn out now to be more valuable than they seemed when they were young. And once again we have tried to include as many as possible of those scarce and valuable writings that are both lucid and solid. We have sometimes been forced to sacrifice some lucidity to guarantee solidity, but never, we believe, the other way around.

The reader may find more "soft stuff" in this edition—more on values, on intuition and imagination, on organizational legends and sagas. That shift does not, we propose, represent any abandonment of the hard, the analytic, the scientific. On the contrary, it reflects an awareness now widely shared in the profession, that there is more going on in large human organizations than meets the naively analytic eye.

Readers familiar with the fourth edition (1978) of Leavitt's *Managerial Psychology* will find that these readings roughly parallel that volume so that the two can be used together.

HJL, LRP, DMB

Acknowledgments

We would like to acknowledge the contributions of several students who provided helpful comments and criticisms in the selection of the articles in the third edition: Linda Azarone, Terry Blake, Robyn Gill, and Michael Passaloqua.

1

1 Motivation: The Driving Force

Introduction

Perhaps more than any other question, managers ask: "How do I moti-vate my people?" "What does one do with someone who's lost his motivation?" "How does one motivate young people these days?" The word "motivation is used commonly in the vocabulary of managers. Interestingly enough though, it was not common a few decades ago. Managers in those days apparently didn't think much in terms of what motivates people; they probably thought much more in terms of work specifications and specialization. The notion that people search, work, learn in response to some kinds of "wants" or deficiencies" or "needs" is a *relatively* new notion. It is also a very "soft" notion, still subject to great controversy within the discipline of psychology. But contro-versial or not, it is important for the manager to try to understand the nature of human motivation, just as it is for the psychologist. The more we understand the human being, the more effectively we can design organizations in which human beings can live and work productively.

We have included four papers in this first chapter. The first is a classic by Abraham Maslow, whose name more than that of any other American psychologist is associated with the concept of motivation. Maslow was a clinician who observed individuals over extended peri-ods of time and with great care and sensitivity. He evolved the idea of a *hierarchy of needs,* the notion that people tend to move from one level of motivation onward and upward to triple levels as each level achieves some degree of satisfaction. So, satisfying an existing set of needs becomes not the end but the beginning, the opening of a new level of motives. Thus humans are "growth" oriented, with old achievements forever triggering higher-level interests. The validity of Maslow's theory is debated constantly, but its utility to the manager as a tool for thinking seems beyond question.

The second paper, by Staw, is a more contemporary piece, dealing with a motivational problem that has important implications for the managing process. The issue is intrinsic vs. extrinsic motivation. Some behavioral people like to say (with good reason) that one should not ask the question "How do I motivate people?" You cannot motivate people, only God can motivate. The more proper question would be something like: "What are the conditions under which people's intrinsic God-given motivation can be nurtured to grow and bloom?" By that view, motivation is an *intrinsic* phenomonon, bubbling up out of the human soul. But of course we all know that to some degree we can get more work out of people if we pay them more, or if we offer them other *extrinsic* incentives. Staw reviews what is known about those two interacting aspects of motivation, for they are interactive—and not always harmonious. Sometimes, for example, when we add extrinsic motivation we kill intrinsic motivation. If I paid you to do something you now do for fun, would the two motivating forces simply sum? Or would they conflict?

We move then to a third great contributor in our understanding of motivation, David McClelland. McClelland has for many years been concerned with cross-cultural as well as individual differences in motivation. In the paper included here, a recent one, McClelland shows his growing conviction that power, more than motives like achievement or affiliation, is most closely related to managerial success. But he divides power into two types, so that the reader who is turned off by a term like "power motivation" should hold his fire until after he has examined that article.

Finally, the paper by Hackman et al. takes us into some applications of motivational theory in managerial practice. It looks at the new popular notion of job enrichment as a mechanism for generating greater motivational energy at work. While theories of motivation differ widely, the job enrichment idea, providing wider variety and greater control, fits almost all theoretical perspectives as a sensible route to providing room on the job for human motivation to evolve.

So the papers in this chapter move from theory to practice, and this pattern will be observed in several of the chapters that follow. We have not, of course, either covered all major theories of motivation or all major practices that have been extrapolated from them. But these four papers are relevant and we believe useful for the manager and the student of management.

A Theory of Human Motivation
A. H. Maslow

Dynamics of the basic needs

The "physiological" needs

The needs that are usually taken as the starting point for motivation theory are the so-called physiological drives. Two recent lines of research make it necessary to revise our customary notions about these needs: first, the development of the concept of homeostasis, and second, the finding that appetites (preferential choices among foods) are a fairly efficient indication of actual needs or lacks in the body.

Homeostasis refers to the body's automatic efforts to maintain a constant, normal state of the blood stream. Cannon[1] has described this process for (1) the water content of the blood, (2) salt content, (3) sugar content, (4) protein content, (5) fat content, (6) calcium content, (7) oxygen content, (8) constant hydrogen-ion level (acid-base balance), and (9) constant temperature of the blood. Obviously this list can be extended to include other minerals, the hormones, vitamins, and so on.

Young in a recent article[2] has summarized the work on appetite in its relation to body needs. If the body lacks some chemical, the individual will tend to develop a specific appetite or partial hunger for that food element.

Thus it seems impossible as well as useless to make any list of fundamental physiological needs for they can come to almost any number one might wish, depending on the degree of specificity of description.

Abridged from A. H. Maslow, "A Theory of Human Motivation," *Psychological Review* 50 (1943): 370–96. Copyright 1943 by the American Psychological Association, and reproduced by permission.

1. W. B. Cannon, *Wisdom of the Body* (New York: Norton, 1932).
2. P. T. Young, "The Experimental Analysis of Appetite," *Psychological Bulletin* 38 (1941): 129–64.

We cannot identify all physiological needs as homeostatic. That sexual desire, sleepiness, sheer activity, and maternal behavior in animals are homeostatic has not yet been demonstrated. Furthermore, this list would not include the various sensory pleasures (tastes, smells, tickling, stroking) which are probably physiological and which may be come the goals of motivated behavior.

In a previous paper[3] it has been pointed out that these physiological drives or needs are to be considered unusual rather than typical because they are isolable and because they are localized somatically. That is to say, they are relatively independent of each other, of other motivations, and of the organism as a whole, and, in many cases, it is possible to demonstrate a localized, underlying somatic base for the drive. This is true less generally than has been thought (exceptions are fatigue, sleepiness, maternal responses), but it is still true in the classic instances of hunger, sex, and thrist.

It should be pointed out again that any of the physiological needs and the consummatory behavior involved with them serve as channels for all sorts of other needs as well. The person who thinks he is hungry may actually be seeking more for comfort or dependence than for vitamins or proteins. Conversely, it is possible to satisfy the hunger need in part by other activities such as drinking water or smoking cigarettes. In other words, these physiological needs are only relatively isloable.

Undoubtedly these physiological needs are the most prepotent of all needs. What this means specifically is that, in the human being who is missing everything in life in an extreme fashion, it is most likely that the major motivation would be the physiological needs rather than any others. A person who is lacking food, safety, love, and esteem would most probably hunger for food more strongly than for anything else.

If all the needs are unsatisfied, and the organism is then dominated by the physiological needs, all other needs may become simply non-existent or be pushed into the background. It is then fair to characterize the whole organism by saying that it is hungry, for consciousness is almost completely preempted by hunger. All capacities are put into the service of hunger-satisfaction, and the organization of these capacities is almost entirely determined by the one purpose of satisfying hunger. The receptors and effectors, the intelligence, memory, habits, all may now be defined simply as hunger-gratifying tools. Capacities that are not useful for this purpose lie dormant or are pushed into the

3. A. H. Maslow, "A Preface of Motivation Theory," *Psychosomatic Medicine* 5 (1943): 85–92.

background. The urge to write poetry, the desire to acquire an automobile, the interest in American history, the desire for a new pair of
shoes are, in the extreme case, forgotten or become of secondary
importance. For the man who is extremely and dangerously hungry,
no other interests exist but food. He dreams food, he remembers food,
he thinks about food, he emotes only about food, he perceives only
food, and he wants only food. The more subtle determinants that
ordinarily fuse with the physiological drives in organizing even feeding, drinking, or sexual behavior, may now be so completely overwhelmed as to allow us to speak at this time (but *only* at this time) of
pure hunger drive and behavior, with the one unqualified aim of relief.

Another peculiar characteristic of the human organism when it is
dominated by a certain need is that the whole philosophy of the future
tends also to change. For our chronically and extremely hungry man,
utopia can be defined very simply as a place where there is plenty of
food. He tends to think that, if only he is guaranteed food for the rest
of his life, he will be perfectly happy and will never want anything
more. Life itself tends to be defined in terms of eating. Anything else
will be defined as unimportant. Freedom, love, community feeling,
respect, philosophy may all be waved aside as fripperies which are
useless, since they fail to fill the stomach. Such a man may fairly be
said to live by bread alone.

It cannot possibly be denied that such things are true, but their *generality* can be denied. Emergency conditions are, almost by definition,
rare in the normally functioning peaceful society. That this truism can
be forgotten is due mainly to two reasons. First, rats have few motivations other than physiological ones, and since so much of the research
on motivation has been made with these animals, it is easy to carry the
rat-picture over to the human being. Second, it is too often not realized
that culture itself is an adaptive tool, one of whose main functions is
to make the physiological emergencies come less and less often. In
most of the known societies, chronic extreme hunger of the emergency
type is rare rather than common. In any case, this is still true in the
United States. The average American citizen is experiencing appetite
rather than hunger when he says, "I am hungry." He is apt to experience sheer life-and-death hunger only by accident and then only a few
times through his entire life.

Obviously a good way to obscure the "higher" motivations, and to
get a lopsided view of human capacities and human nature, is to make
the organism extremely and chronically hungry or thirsty. Anyone who
attempts to make an emergency picture into a typical one and who will
measure all of man's goals and desires by his behavior during extreme
physiological deprivation is certainly being blind to many things. It is

quite true that man lives by bread alone—when there is no bread. But
what happens to man's desires when there *is* plenty of bread and when
his belly is chronically filled?

At once other (and "higher") needs emerge and these, rather than
physiological hungers, dominate the organism. And when these in turn
are satisfied, again new (and still "higher") needs emerge, and so on.
This is what we mean by saying that the basic human needs are organized into a hierarchy of relative prepotency.

One main implication of this phrasing is that gratification becomes
as important a concept as deprivation in motivation theory, for it releases the organism from the domination of a relatively more physiological need, permitting thereby the emergence of other more social
goals. The physiological needs, along with their partial goals, when
chronically gratified cease to exist as active determinants or organizers
of behavior. They now exist only in a potential fashion in the sense
that they may emerge again to dominate the organism if they are
thwarted. But a want that is satisfied is no longer a want. The organism
is dominated and its behavior organized only by unsatisfied needs. If
hunger is satisfied, it becomes unimportant in the current dynamics of
the individual.

This statement is somewhat qualified by a hypothesis to be discussed
more fully later, namely, that it is precisely those individuals in whom
a certain need has always been satisfied who are best equipped to
tolerate deprivation of that need in the future; furthermore, those who
have been deprived in the past will react to current satisfactions differently from the one who has never been deprived.

The safety needs

If the physiological needs are relatively well gratified, there then
emerges a new set of needs, which we may categorize roughly as the
safety needs. All that has been said of the physiological needs is equally
true, although in lesser degree, of these desires. The organism may
equally well be wholly dominated by them. They may serve as the
almost exclusive organizers of behavior, recruiting all the capacities
of the organism in their service, and we may then fairly describe the
whole organism as a safety-seeking mechanism. Again we may say of
the receptors, the effectors, of the intellect and the other capacities that
they are primarily safety-seeking tools. Again, as in the hungry man,
we find that the dominating goal is a strong determinant not only of his
current world-outlook and philosophy but also of his philosophy of
the future. Practically everything looks less important than safety
(even sometimes the physiological needs which, being satisfied, are
now underestimated). A man, in this state, if it is extreme enough and
chronic enough, may be characterized as living almost for safety alone.

Although in this paper we are interested primarily in the needs of the adult, we can approach an understanding of his safety needs perhaps more efficiently by observation of infants and children, in whom these needs are much more simple and obvious. One reason for the clearer appearance of the threat or danger reaction in infants is that they do not inhibit this reaction at all, whereas adults in our society have been taught to inhibit it at all costs. Thus even when adults do feel their safety to be threatened, we may not be able to see this on the surface. Infants will react in a total fashion and as if they were endangered, if they are disturbed or dropped suddenly, startled by loud noises, flashing light, or other unusual sensory stimulation, by rough handling, by general loss of support in the mother's arms, or by inadequate support.[4]

In infants we can also see a much more direct reaction to bodily illnesses of various kinds. Sometimes these illnesses seem to be immediately and per se threatening and seem to make the child feel unsafe. For instance, vomiting, colic, or other sharp pains seem to make the child look at the whole world in a different way. At such a moment of pain, it may be postulated that, for the child, the appearance of the whole world suddenly changes from sunniness to darkness, so to speak, and becomes a place in which anything at all might happen, in which previously stable things have suddenly become unstable. Thus a child who because of some bad food is taken ill may, for a day or two, develop fear, nightmares, and a need for protection and reassurance never seen in him before his illness.

Another indication of the child's need for safety is his preference for some kind of undisrupted routine or rhythm. He seems to want a predictable, orderly world. For instance, injustice, unfairness, or inconsistency in the parents seems to make a child feel anxious and unsafe. This attitude may be not so much because of the injustice per se or any particular pains involved, but rather because this treatment threatens to make the world look unreliable or unsafe or unpredictable. Young children seem to thrive better under a system which has at least a skeletal outline of rigidity, in which there is a schedule of a kind, some sort of routine, something that can be counted upon, not only for the present, but also far into the future. Perhaps one could express this more accurately by saying that the child needs an organized world rather than an unorganized or unstructured one.

The central role of the parents and the normal family setup are in-

4. As the child grows up, sheer knowledge and familiarity as well as better motor development make these "dangers" less and less dangerous and more and more manageable. Throughout life it may be said that one of the main conative functions of education is this neutralizing of apparent dangers through knowledge, e.g., I am not afraid of thunder because I know something about it.

disputable. Quarreling, physical assault, separation, divorce, or death within the family may be particularly terrifying. Also parental outbursts of rage or threats of punishment directed to the child, calling him names, speaking to him harshly, shaking him, handling him roughly, or actual physical punishment sometimes elicit such total panic and terror in the child that we must assume more is involved than the physical pain alone. While it is true that in some children this terror may represent also a fear of loss of parental love, it can also occur in completely rejected children, who seem to cling to the hating parents more for sheer safety and protection than because of hope of love.

Confronting the average child with new, unfamiliar, strange, unmanageable stimuli or situations will too frequently elicit the danger or terror reaction, as, for example, getting lost or even being separated from the parents for a short time, being confronted with new faces, new situations, or new tasks, the sight of strange, unfamiliar, or uncontrollable objects, illness, or death. Particularly at such times, the child's frantic clinging to his parents is eloquent testimony to their role as protectors (quite apart from their roles as food-givers and love-givers).

From these and similar observations, we may generalize and say that the average child in our society usually prefers a safe, orderly, predictable, organized world which he can count on and in which unexpected, unmanageable, or other dangerous things do not happen and in which, in any case, he has all-powerful parents who protect and shield him from harm.

That these reactions may so easily be observed in children is in a way a proof of the fact that children in our society feel too unsafe (or, in a world, are badly brought up). Children who are reared in an unthreatening, loving family do *not* ordinarily react as we have described above.[5] In such children the danger reactions are apt to come mostly to objects or situations that adults too would consider dangerous.[6]

The healthy, normal, fortunate adult in our culture is largely satis-

5. M. Shirley, "Children's Adjustments to a Strange Situation," *Journal of Abnormal and Social Psychology* 37 (1942): 201–17.

6. A "test battery" for safety might be confronting the child with a small exploding firecracker or with a bewhiskered face, having the mother leave the room, putting him upon a high ladder, giving him a hypodermic injection, having a mouse crawl up to him, and so on. Of course I cannot seriously recommend the deliberate use of such "tests," for they might very well harm the child being tested. But these and similar situations come up by the score in the child's ordinary day-to-day living and may be observed. There is no reason why these stimuli should not be used with, for example, young chimpanzees.

fied in his safety needs. The peaceful, smoothly running, "good" society ordinarily makes its members feel safe enough from wild animals, extremes of temperature, criminals, assault and murder, tyranny, and so on. Therefore, in a very real sense, they no longer have any safety needs as active motivators. Just as a sated man no longer feels hungry, a safe man no longer feels endangered. If we wish to see these needs directly and clearly we must turn to neurotic or near-neurotic individuals, and to the economic and social underdogs. In between these extremes, we can perceive the expressions of safety needs only in such phenomena as, for instance, the common preference for a job with tenure and protection, the desire for a savings account, and for insurance of various kinds (medical, dental, unemployment, disability, old age).

Other broader aspects of the attempt to seek safety and stability in the world are seen in the very common preference for familiar rather than unfamiliar things, or for the known rather than the unknown. The tendency to have some religion or world-philosophy that organizes the universe and the men in it into some sort of satisfactorily coherent, meaningful whole is also in part motivated by safety-seeking. Here too we may list science and philosophy in general as partially motivated by the safety needs (we shall see later that there are also other motivations to scientific, philosophical, or religious endeavor).

Otherwise the need for safety is seen as an active and dominant mobilizer of the organism's resources only in emergencies, e.g., war, disease, natural catastrophes, crime waves, societal disorganization, neurosis, brain injury, chronically bad situations.

Some neurotic adults in our society are, in many ways, like the unsafe child in their desire for safety, although in the former it takes on a somewhat special appearance. Their reaction is often to unknown, psychological dangers in a world that is perceived to be hostile, overwhelming, and threatening. Such a person behaves as if a great catastrophe were almost always impending, i.e., he is usually responding as if to an emergency. His safety needs often find specific expression in a search for a protector, or a stronger person on whom he may depend, or perhaps a *Führer*.

The neurotic individual may be described in a slightly different way with some usefulness as a grown-up person who retains his childish attitudes toward the world. That is to say, a neurotic adult may be said to behave "as if" he were actually afraid of a spanking or of his mother's disapproval or of being abandoned by his parents or of having his food taken away from him. It is as if his childish attitudes of fear and threat reaction to a dangerous world had gone underground and, untouched by the growing up and learning processes, were now ready to be called out by any stimulus that would make a child feel endangered and threatened.[7]

The neurosis in which the search for safety takes its clearest form is in the compulsive-obsessive neurosis. Compulsive-obsessives try frantically to order and stabilize the world so that no unmanageable, unexpected, or unfamiliar dangers will ever appear.[8] They hedge themselves about with all sorts of ceremonials, rules, and formulas so that every possible contingency may be provided for and so that no new contingencies may appear. They are much like the brain-injured cases, described by Goldstein,[9] who manage to maintain their equilibrium by avoiding everything unfamiliar and strange and by ordering their restricted world in such a neat, disciplined, orderly fashion that everything in the world can be counted upon. They try to arrange the world so that anything unexpected (dangers) cannot possibly occur. If, through no fault of their own, something unexpected does occur, they go into a panic reaction as if this unexpected occurrence constituted a grave danger. What we can see only as a none-too-strong preference in the healthy person, e.g., preference for the familiar, becomes a life-and-death necessity in abnormal cases.

The love needs

If both the physiological and the safety needs are fairly well gratified, then there will emerge the love and affection and belongingness needs, and the whole cycle already described will repeat itself with this new center. Now the person will feel keenly, as never before, the absence of friends or a sweetheart or a wife or children. He will hunger for affectionate relations with people in general, namely, for a place in his group, and he will strive with great intensity to achieve this goal. He will want to attain such a place more than anything else in the world and may even forget that once, when he was hungry, he sneered at love.

In our society the thwarting of these needs is the most commonly found core in cases of maladjustment and more severe psychopathology. Love and affection, as well as their possible expression in sexuality, are generally looked upon with ambivalence and are customarily hedged about with many restrictions and inhibitions. Practically all theorists of psychopathology have stressed thwarting of the love needs as basic in the picture of maladjustment. Many clinical studies have

7. Not all neurotic individuals feel unsafe. Neurosis may have at its core a thwarting of the affection and esteem needs in a person who is generally safe.
8. A. H. Maslow and B. Mittelmann, *Principles of Abnormal Psychology* (New York: Harper & Bros., 1941).
9. K. Goldstein, *The Organism* (New York: American Book Co., 1939).

therefore been made of this need and we know more about it perhaps than any of the other needs except the physiological ones.[10]

One thing that must be stressed at this point is that love is not synonymous with sex. Sex may be studied as a purely physiological need. Ordinarily sexual behavior is multidetermined, that is to say, determined not only by sexual but also by other needs, chief among which are the love and affection needs. Also not to be overlooked is the fact that the love needs involve both giving *and* receiving love.[11]

The esteem needs

All people in our society (with a few pathological exceptions) have a need or desire for a stable, firmly based, (usually) high evaluation of themselves, for self-respect, or self-esteem, and for the esteem of others. By firmly based self-esteem, we mean that which is soundly based on real capacity, achievement, and respect from others. These needs may be classified into two subsidiary sets. These are, first, the desire for strength, for achievement, for adequacy, for confidence in the face of the world, and for independence and freedom.[12] Second, we have what we may call the desire for reputation or prestige (defining it as respect or esteem from other people), recognition, attention, importance, or appreciation.[13] These needs have been relatively stressed by Alfred Adler and his followers, and have been relatively neglected by Freud and the psychoanalysts. More and more today, however, there is appearing widespread appreciation of their central importance.

Satisfaction of the self-esteem need leads to feelings of self-confidence, worth, strength, capability, and adequacy, of being useful and

10. Maslow and Mittelmann, *Principles of Abnormal Psychology.*

11. For further details see A. H. Maslow, "The Dynamics of Psychological Security-Insecurity," *Character and Personality* 10 (1942): 331–44, and J. Plant, *Personality and the Cultural Pattern* (New York: Commonwealth Fund, 1937), chap. 5.

12. Whether or not this particular desire is universal we do not know. The crucial question, especially important today, is, "Will men who are enslaved and dominated inevitably feel dissatisfied and rebellious?" We may assume on the basis of commonly known clinical data that a man who has known true freedom (not paid for by giving up safety and security but rather built on the basis of adequate safety and security) will not willingly or easily allow his freedom to be taken away from him. But we do not know that this is true for the person born into slavery. The events of the next decade should give us our answer. See discussion of this problem in E. Fromm, *Escape from Freedom* (New York: Farrar & Rinehart, 1941), chap. 5.

13. Perhaps the desire for prestige and respect from others is subsidiary to the desire for self-esteem or confidence in one's self. Observation of children seems to indicate that this is so, but clinical data give no clear support of such a conclusion.

necessary in the world. But thwarting of these needs produces feelings of inferiority, of weakness, and of helplessness. These feelings in turn give rise to either basic discouragement or else compensatory or neurotic trends. An appreciation of the necessity of basic self-confidence and an understanding of how helpless people are without it can be easily gained from a study of severe traumatic neurosis.[14]

The need for self-actualization

Even if all these needs are satisfied, we may still often (if not always) expect that a new discontent and restlessness will soon develop, unless the individual is doing what he is fitted for. A musician must make music, an artist must paint, a poet must write, if he is to be ultimately happy. What a man *can* be, he *must* be. This need we may call self-actualization.

This term, first coined by Kurt Goldstein, is being used in this paper in a much more specific and limited fashion. It refers to the desire for self-fulfillment, namely, to the tendency for one to become actualized in what one is potentially. This tendency might be phrased as the desire to become more and more what one is, to become everything that one is capable of becoming.

The specific form that these needs take will of course vary greatly from person to person. In one individual it may be expressed maternally, as the desire to be an ideal mother, in another athletically, in still another aesthetically, in the painting of pictures, and in another inventively, in the creation of new contrivances. It is not necessarily a creative urge, although in people who have any capabilities for creation it will take this form.

The clear emergence of these needs rests upon prior satisfaction of the physiological, safety, love, and esteem needs. We shall call people who are satisfied in these needs, basically satisfied people, and it is from these that we may expect the fullest (and healthiest) creativeness.[15] Since, in our society, basically satisfied people are the ex-

---

14. A. Kardiner, *The Traumatic Neuroses of War* (New York: Hoeber, 1941). For more extensive discussion of normal self-esteem, as well as for reports of various researches, see A. H. Maslow, "Dominance, Personality, and Social Behavior in Women," *Journal of Social Psychology* 10 (1939): 3–39.

15. Clearly creative behavior, like painting, is like any other behavior in having multiple determinants. It may be seen in "innately creative" people whether they are satisfied or not, happy or unhappy, hungry or sated. Also, it is clear that creative activity may be compensatory, ameliorative, or purely economic. It is my impression (as yet unconfirmed) that it is possible to distinguish the artistic and intellectual products of basically satisfied people from those of basically unsatisfied people by inspection alone. In any case, here too we must distinguish, in a dynamic fashion, the overt behavior itself from its various motivations or purposes.

ception, we do not know much about self-actualization, either experimentally or clinically. It remains a challenging problem for
research.

The preconditions for the basic need satisfactons

There are certain conditions which are immediate prerequisites for the
basic need satisfactions. Danger to these is reacted to almost as if it
were a direct danger to the basic needs themselves. Such conditions as
freedom to speak, freedom to do what one wishes so long as no harm
is done to others, freedom to express one's self, freedom to investigate
and seek for information, freedom to defend one's self, justice, fairness,
honesty, orderliness in the group are examples of such preconditions
for basic need satisfactions. Thwarting in these freedoms will be reacted to with a threat or emergency response. These conditions are not
ends in themselves but they are *almost* so, since they are so closely related to the basic needs, which are apparently the only ends in themselves. These conditions are defended because without them the basic
satisfactions are quite impossible, or, at least, very severely endangered.

If we remember that the cognitive capacities (perceptual, intellectual, learning) are a set of adjustive tools, which have, among other
functions, that of satisfaction of our basic needs, then it is clear that any
danger to them, any deprivation or blocking of their free use, must also
be indirectly threatening to the basic needs themselves. Such a statement is a partial solution of the general problems of curiosity, the
search for knowledge, truth, and wisdom, and the ever-persistent urge
to solve the cosmic mysteries.

We must therefore introduce another hypothesis and speak of degrees of closeness to the basic needs, for we have already pointed out
that *any* conscious desires (partial goals) are more or less important
as they are more or less close to the basic needs. The same statement
may be made for various behavior acts. An act is psychologically important if it contributes directly to satisfaction of basic needs. The less
directly it contributes, or the weaker this contribution is, the less important this act must be conceived to be from the point of view of
dynamic psychology. A similar statement may be made for the various
defense or coping mechanisms. Some are very directly related to the
protection or attainment of the basic needs, others are only weakly and
distantly related. Indeed, if we wished, we could speak of more basic
and less basic defense mechanisms and then affirm that danger to the
more basic defenses is more threatening than danger to less basic defenses (always remembering that this is so only because of their relationship to the basic needs).

The desires to know and to understand

So far, we have mentioned the cognitive needs only in passing. Acquiring knowledge and systematizing the universe have been considered as, in part, techniques for the achievement of basic safety in the world, or, for the intelligent man, expressions of self-actualization. Also freedom of inquiry and expression have been discussed as preconditions of satisfactions of the basic needs. True though these formulations may be, they do not constitute definitive answers to the question as to the motivation role of curiosity, learning, philosophizing, experimenting, and so on. They are, at best, no more than partial answers.

This question is especially difficult because we know so little about the facts. Curiosity, exploration, desire for the facts, desire to know may certainly be observed easily enough. The fact that they often are pursued even at great cost to the individual's safety is an earnest of the partial character of our previous discussion. In addition, the writer must admit that, though he has sufficient clinical evidence to postulate the desire to know as a very strong drive in intelligent people, no data are available for unintelligent people. It may then be largely a function of relatively high intelligence. Rather tentatively, then, and largely in the hope of stimulating discussion and research, we shall postulate a basic desire to know, to be aware of reality, to get the facts, to satisfy curiosity, or as Wertheimer phrases it, to see rather than to be blind.

This postulation, however, is not enough. Even after we know, we are impelled to know more and more minutely and microscopically, on the one hand, and, on the other, more and more extensively in the direction of a world philosophy, religion, and so on. The facts that we acquire, if they are isolated or atomistic, inevitably get theorized about, and either analyzed or organized or both. This process has been phrased by some as the search for "meaning." We shall then postulate a desire to understand, to systematize, to organize, to analyze, to look for relations and meanings.

Once these desires are accepted for discussion, we see that they too form themselves into a small hierarchy in which the desire to know is prepotent over the desire to understand. All the characteristics of a hierarchy of prepotency that we have described above seem to hold for this one as well.

We must guard ourselves against the too-easy tendency to separate these desires from the basic needs we have discussed above, i.e., to make a sharp dichotomy between "cognitive" and "conative" needs. The desire to know and to understand are themselves conative, i.e., have a striving character, and are as much personality needs as the "basic needs" we have already discussed.[16]

Further characteristics of the basic needs

The degree of fixity of the hierarchy of basic needs

We have spoken so far as if this hierarchy were a fixed order but actually it is not nearly as rigid as we may have implied. It is true that most of the people with whom we have worked have seemed to have these basic needs in about the order that has been indicated. However, there have been a number of exceptions.

1. There are some people in whom, for instance, self-esteem seems to be more important than love. This most common reversal in the hierarchy is usually due to the development of the notion that the person who is most likely to be loved is a strong or powerful person, one who inspires respect or fear and who is self-confident or aggressive. Therefore, such people who lack love and seek it, may try hard to put on a front of aggressive, confident behavior. But essentially they seek high self-esteem and its behavior expressions more as a means-to-an-end than for its own sake; they seek self-assertion for the sake of love rather than for self-esteem itself.

2. There are other, apparently innately creative people in whom the drive to creativeness seems to be more important than any other counterdeterminant. Their creativeness might appear as self-actualization released not by basic satisfaction but in spite of lack of basic satisfaction.

3. In certain people the level of aspiration may be permanently deadened or lowered. That is to say, the less prepotent goals may simply be lost and may disappear forever, so that the person who has experienced life at a very low level, i.e., chronic unemployment, may continue to be satisfied for the rest of his life if only he can get enough food.

4. The so-called psychopathic personality is another example of permanent loss of the love needs. There are people who, according to the best data available,[17] have been starved for love in the earliest months of their lives and have simply lost forever the desire and the ability to give and to receive affection (as animals lose sucking or pecking reflexes that are not exercised soon enough after birth).

16. M. Wertheimer, unpublished lectures at the New School for Social Research.
17. D. M. Levy, "Primary Affect Hunger," *American Journal of Psychiatry* 94 (1937): 643–52.

5. Another cause of reversal of the hierarchy is that when a need has been satisfied for a long time, this need may be underevaluated. People who have never experienced chronic hunger are apt to underestimate its effects and to look upon food as a rather unimportant thing. If they are dominated by a higher need, this higher need will seem to be the most important of all. It then becomes possible, and indeed does actually happen, that they may, for the sake of this higher need, put themselves into the position of being deprived in a more basic need. We may expect that after a long-time deprivation of the more basic need there will be a tendency to reevaluate both needs so that the more prepotent need will actually become consciously prepotent for the individual who may have given it up very lightly. Thus, a man who has given up his job rather than lose his self-respect, and who then starves for six months or so, may be willing to take his job back even at the price of losing his self-respect.

6. Another partial explanation of *apparent* reversals is seen in the fact that we have been talking about the hierarchy of prepotency in terms of consciously felt wants or desires rather than of behavior. Looking at behavior itself may give us the wrong impression. What we have claimed is that the person will *want* the more basic of two needs when deprived in both. There is no necessary implication here that he will act upon his desires. Let us say again that there are many determinants of behavior other than needs and desires.

7. Perhaps more important than all these exceptions are the ones that involve ideals, high social standards, high values, and the like. With such values people become martyrs; they will give up everything for the sake of a particular ideal or value. These people may be understood, at least in part, by reference to one basic concept (or hypothesis) which may be called "increased frustration-tolerance through early gratification." People who have been satisfied in their basic needs throughout their lives, particularly in their earlier years, seem to develop exceptional power to withstand present or future thwarting of these needs simply because they have strong, healthy character structure as a result of basic satisfaction. They are the "strong" people who can easily weather disagreement or opposition, who can swim against the stream of public opinion, and who can stand up for the truth at great personal cost. It is just the ones who have loved and been well loved and who have had many deep friendships who can hold out against hatred, rejection, or persecution.

I say all this in spite of the fact that there is a certain amount of sheer habituation which is also involved in any full discussion of frustration tolerance. For instance, it is likely that those persons who have been accustomed to relative starvation for a long time are partially enabled thereby to withstand food deprivation. What sort of balance must be made between these two tendencies, of habituation on the one hand, and of past satisfaction breeding present frustration tolerance on the other hand, remains to be worked out by further research. Meanwhile we may assume that they are both operative, side by side, since they do not contradict each other. In respect to this phenomenon of increased frustration tolerance, it seems probable that the most important gratifications come in the first two years of life. That is to say, people who have been made secure and strong in the earliest years tend to remain secure and strong thereafter in the face of whatever threatens.

Degrees of relative satisfaction

So far, our thoretical discussion may have given the impression that these five sets of needs are somehow in a stepwise, all-or-none relationship to one another. We have spoken in such terms as the following "If one need is satisfied, then another emerges." This statement might give the false impression that a need must be satisfied 100 percent before the next need emerges. In actual fact, most members of our society who are normal are partially satisfied in all their basic needs at the same time. A more realistic description of the hierarchy would be in terms of decreasing percentages of satisfaction as we go up the hierarchy of prepotency. For instance, if I may assign arbitrary figures for the sake of illustration, it is as if the average citizen is satisfied perhaps 85 percent in his physiological needs, 70 percent in his safety needs, 50 percent in his love needs, 40 percent in his self-esteem needs, and 10 percent in his self-actualization needs.

As for the concept of emergence of a new need after satisfaction of the prepotent need, this emergence is not a sudden, saltatory phenomenon but rather a gradual emergence by slow degrees from nothingness. For instance, if prepotent need A is satisfied only 10 percent then need B may not be visible at all. However, as this need A becomes satisfied 25 percent, need B may emerge 5 percent; as need A becomes satisfied 75 percent, need B may emerge 90 percent; and so on.

Unconscious character of needs

These needs are neither necessarily conscious nor unconscious. On the whole, however, in the average person, they are more often unconscious. It is not ncessary at this point to overhaul the tremendous mass of evidence which indicates the crucial importance of unconscious motivation. It would by now be expected, on a priori grounds alone, that unconscious motivations would on the whole be rather more im-

portant than the conscious motivations. What we have called the basic
needs are very often largely unconscious although they may, with suitable techniques and with sophisticated people, become conscious.

The role of gratified needs

It has been pointed out above several times that our higher needs
usually emerge only when more prepotent needs have been gratified.
Thus gratification has an important role in motivation theory. Apart
from this, however, needs cease to play an active determining or
organizing role as soon as they are gratified.

What this means, for example, is that a basically satisfied person
no longer has the needs for esteem, love, safety, and so on. The only
sense in which he might be said to have them is in the almost meta-
physical sense that a sated man has hunger or a filled bottle has emptiness. If we are interested in what *actually* motivates us and not in what
has, will, or might motivate us, then a satisfied need is not a motivator.
It must be considered for all practical purposes simply not to exist,
to have disappeared. This point should be emphasized because it has
been either overlooked or contradicted in every theory of motivation
I know.[18] The perfectly healthy, normal, fortunate man has no sex
needs or hunger needs, or needs for safety or for love or for prestige
or for self-esteem, except in stray moments of quickly passing threat.
If we were to say otherwise, we should also have to aver that every
man had all the pathological reflexes, e.g., Babinski, etc., because if
his nervous system were damaged, these would appear.

It is such considerations as these that suggest the bold postulation
that a man who is thwarted in any of his basic needs may fairly be en-
visaged simply as a sick man. This is a fair parallel to our designation
as "sick" of the man who lacks vitamins or minerals. Who is to say
that a lack of love is less important than a lack of vitamins? Since we
know the pathogenic effects of love starvation, who is to say that we
are invoking value-questions in an unscientific or illegitmate way, any
more than the physician does who diagnoses and treats pellagra or
scurvy? If I were permitted this usage, I should then say simply that a
healthy man is primarily motivated by his needs to develop and actual-
ize his fullest potentialities and capacities. If a man has any other basic
needs in any active, chronic sense, then he is simply an unhealthy man.
He is as surely sick as if he had suddenly developed a strong salt-
hunger or calcium hunger.[19]

18. Note that acceptance of this theory necessitates basic revision of the
Freudian theory.
19. If we were to use the "sick" in this way, we should then also have to face
squarely the relations of man to his society. One clear implication of our defini-

If this statement seems unusual or paradoxical, the reader may be assured that this is only one among many such paradoxes that will appear as we revise our ways of looking at man's deeper motivations. When we ask what man wants of life, we deal with his very essence.

Summary

1. There are at least five sets of goals which we may call basic needs. These are briefly physiological, safety, love, esteem, and self-actualization. In addition, we are motivated by the desire to achieve or maintain the various conditions upon which these basic satisfactions rest and by certain more intellectual desires.

2. These basic goals are related to one another, being arranged in a hierarchy of prepotency. This means that the most prepotent goal will monopolize consciousness and will tend of itself to organize the recruitment of the various capacities of the organism. The less prepotent needs are minimized, even forgotten or denied. But when a need is fairly well satisfied, the next prepotent ("higher") need emerges, in turn to dominate the conscious life and to serve as the center of organization of behavior, since gratified needs are not active motivators.

Thus man is a perpetually wanting animal. Ordinarily the satisfaction of these wants is not altogether mutually exclusive but only tends to be. The average member of our society is most often partially satisfied and partially unsatisfied in all of his wants. The hierarchy principle is usually empirically observed in terms of increasing percentages of nonsatisfaction as we go up the hierarchy. Reversals of the average order of the hierarchy are sometimes observed. Also it has been observed that an individual may permanently lose the higher wants in the hierarchy under special conditions. There are not only ordinarily multiple motivations for usual behavior but, in addition, many determinants other than motives.

3. Any thwarting or possibility of thwarting of these basic human goals, or danger to the defenses which protect them or to the conditions upon which they rest, is considered to be a psychological threat. With a few exceptions, all psychopathology may be partially traced to such threats. A basically thwarted man may actually be defined as a "sick" man.

---

tion would be that (1) since a man is to be called sick who is basically thwarted, and (2) since such basic thwarting is made possible ultimately only by forces outside the individual, the (3) sickness in the individual must come ultimately from a sickness in the society. The "good" or healthy society would then be defined as one that permitted man's highest purposes to emerge by satisfying all his prepotent basic needs.

4. It is such basic threats which bring about the general emergency reactions.

5. Certain other basic problems have not been dealt with because of limitations of space. Among these are (a) the problem of values in any definitive motivation theory, (b) the relation between appetites, desires, needs, and what is "good" for the organism, (c) the etiology of the basic needs and their possible derivation in early childhood, (d) redefinition of motivational concepts, i.e., drive, desire, wish, need, goal, (e) implication of our theory for hedonistic theory, (f) the nature of the uncompleted act, of success and failure, and of aspiration-level, (g) the role of association, habit, and conditioning, (h) relation to the theory of interpersonal relations, (i) implications for psychotherapy, (j) implication for theory of society, (k) the theory of selfishness, (l) the relation between needs and cultural patterns, (m) the relation between this theory and Allport's theory of functional autonomy. These as well as certain other less important questions must be considered as motivation theory attempts to become definitive.

Intrinsic and Extrinsic Motivation
Barry M. Staw

The study of motivation is not only a specialized research area within the field of psychology, but also an important pursuit for nearly everyone. People engage widely in the art of untangling the causes of human behavior and stand ready to predict the future actions of others. The scientific study of motivation is an organized effort to go beyond these native skills or common sense in explaining, predicting, and possibly controlling, individual behavior.

Typically, explantions of motivational phenomena attempt to answer such questions as, "Why does this worker spend so much time at his job?" or "Why did that student write a fifty-page term paper when everyone else stopped at ten?" To the layman these questions are often answered, or the behavior is "explained," by verbally linking a given action with a recognized goal or desirable outcome (Koch 1956; Lawler 1973). For example, if Person X performs a given act y, his behavior can be made intelligible to the lay person by completing the sentence. "X did y in order to . . ." Thus, acceptable commonsense explanations of a worker's behavior would include such reasons as "in order to increase his salary" or "to be promoted to a better job," while a student's high level of performance could be explained by such goals as "to receive the highest grade" or "to please others."

Commonsense theorizing, however, rarely constitutes a scientific explanation of behavior. It does not specify why a particular goal or end state was valued by an individual or why particular behaviors were chosen to reach the goal. As noted by Vroom (1964), the study of motivation by psychologists has been in large part directed toward filling in this missing empirical content of commonsense reasoning. The

Barry M. Staw, *Intrinsic and Extrinsic Motivation*. © 1976 Silver Burdett Company (Morristown, N.J.: General Learning Press). Reprinted by permission of Silver Burdett Company.

scientific effort basically has been one of specifying which objects or outcomes have value to the individual (e.g., those which reduce primary, biologically based drives or accomplish ends ultimately related to these basic needs), how attraction to various end states undergoes change (e.g., via deprivation, satiation, stimulus generalization), and how behavior directed toward particular outcomes is acquired, refined, and persists over time.

In this module we would like to emphasize, as Koch (1956) has done earlier, that there is an important similarity between common-sense reasoning and scientific theories of motivation. Both are based on an assumption of instrumentalism such that individuals are considered to be doing things for specifiable ends. For example, two of the most dominant approaches to the study of motivation—drive theory (Hull 1943; Spence 1956) and expectancy × value theory (Lewin 1938; Tolman 1932)—include the notion of a reward or desired outcome and posit a learned connection within the organism. For drive theory this learned connection is an S-R habit strength; for expectancy × value theory it is a behavior-outcome expectancy which is perceived by the individual (Campbell et al. 1970). In sum, the instrumentalism present in scientific theories of motivation is not far removed from the layman's "in order to . . ." explanation.

The instrumental view of human behavior is most readily apparent in several formulations of the expectancy × value theory of motivation. As shown in table 1, the formal statements of expectancy × value theory specify that motivation is a product of the utility or valence of a particular goal and the probability of achieving the desired outcome. For each theoretical formulation, the individual is assumed to take the shortest or most direct path toward a valued goal. However, it is important to recognize that in each case the valued goal is also considered to be *external* to the process of "doing." That is, in analyzing behavior, an individual will probably be considered to be performing an act for some goal independent of the activity itself (e.g., higher pay, promotion to a better job). Unfortunately, these expectancy × value formulations (like many others in motivational psychology) do not easily allow for the fact that a worker may be highly productive simply because he enjoys working hard or is satisfied by good work. Likewise, the theories do not readily lead one to an explanation that a student's work is due to a sheer love of writing or a desire to get something fully explained regardless of the grade or praise to be received from others.

Viewed as a whole, the expectancy × value theories outlined in table 1 can be classified as theories of extrinsic motivation, since each assumes a specific goal that provides satisfaction independent of the activity itself.[1] But, actions may sometimes be valued for their own sake, and they may be self-sustained without any external inducement. In these situations, behavior can be said to be intrinsically motivated. Thus whereas extrinsic motivation emphasizes the value an individual places on the ends of an action and the probability of reaching these ends, intrinsic motivation refers to the pleasure or value associated with the activity itself. Let us examine more closely the theoretical and empirical basis of intrinsic motivation so that we may explicitly build this factor into a revised theory of motivation that takes both factors into account.

The basis of intrinsic motivation

Value inherent in behavior

There is strong evidence that many activities such as manipulation, exploration, and information processing provide satisfaction in and of themselves. For example, in some early studies on animal behavior, Harlow and his associates (Harlow et al., 1950; Harlow and McClearn 1954) demonstrated that monkeys will learn to disassemble puzzles for no reward other than the opportunity to manipulate things. Similarly, Montgomery (1954) showed that rats will systematically select the path in a maze which leads to an opportunity to explore additional mazes. Also, in studies using human subjects it has been shown that the absence of stimulation and environmental change can lead to extreme discomfort. In one of the most vivid demonstrations of the need for stimulation, Bexton et al. (1954) employed college students to lie on a cot for 24 hours a day in a sound-deadened room (with time out for meals and toilet needs). In this study visual and tactile stimulation was also minimized since subjects were required to wear translucent goggles and special gloves. Although the participants were paid extremely well for their time ($20 in 1954 currency), few could tolerate the experiment for as long as two or three days.

In general, research has shown that in the absence of either external pleasureful-painful stimulation or basic homeostatic needs, an individual is not quiescent. In fact, there is some evidence that it is precisely when external pressures (e.g., hunger, thirst, sex) are minimized that play, exploration, manipulation, and curiosity behaviors are most

1. Although Lewin's construct of "resultant force" emphasized the goal-directed nature of motivation, its formulation did actually include the intrinsic valence associated with a behavioral path as well as the extrinsic ends of an action.

Table 1. Summary of Expectancy × Value Theories.

Theorist	Major Motivational Constructs			Resultant
Lewin et al. (1944)	Subjective probability of achieving desired outcome	× (Valence) value of desired outcome		→ Force
Tolman (1955)	Expectation of achieving desired outcome	× Demand level for given outcome	× Level of given outcome	→ Performance vector
Edwards (1955)	Subjective probability of achieving desired outcome	× Utility of desired outcome		→ Behavior choice
Rotter (1954)	Expectancy of achieving desired reinforcement	× Value of reinforcement		→ Behavior potential
Atkinson (1966)	Probability of achieving desired outcome	× Motive level for achieving desired outcome	× Incentive level of desired outcome	→ Resultant motivation
Vroom (1964)	Expectancy of achieving desired outcome	× (Valence) value of desired outcome		→ Force

SOURCE: Abraham K. Korman, *The Psychology of Motivation.* © 1974. Reprinted by permission of Prentice-Hall, Inc., Englewood Cliffs, N.J.

likely to be manifested (Hunt 1965). As a result of these findings, several psychologists have gone so far as to posit new human needs for manipulation (Harlow and McClearn 1954), exploration (Montgomery 1954), and curiosity (Berlyne 1960). Tasks engaging these needs can be considered intrinsically motivating, since the activity provides value to the individual independent of any external sources of satisfaction.

Value inherent in accomplishment

In addition to the value an individual may derive from the physical or mental activities involved in a task, he may also gain satisfaction from knowing that his efforts have led to a completed product or accomplishment. McClelland (1951, 1961) has conceptualized this source of satisfaction as the fulfillment of a need for achievement. Using a projective test (the TAT) to assess the strength of achievement motivation, it has been shown that situations involving competition or the testing of individual abilities produce the greatest motive arousal (McClelland 1971). A learned drive to achieve is thought to be activated when performance can be readily evaluated as a success or failure, and the affect potentially associated with a task (the incentive value of success) is hypothesized to be a function of both the strength of this achievement need and the probability of success. The greatest satisfaction or pride in accomplishment would therefore be derived by persons with high need for achievement who are successful in performing a difficult task (see Litwin [1966] and Cook [1970] for empirical tests of this hypothesis).

Also consistent with the notion that many people seek out or value accomplishment are the theoretical statements of White (1959) and Maslow (1954, 1970). White posits that individuals are motivated toward competence or mastery over their environments—that they not only manipulate and explore their surroundings but strive to master them through higher levels of motor and mental coordination. In a similar vein, Maslow states that many individuals possess active higher-order needs for esteem and self-actualization. Esteem needs include a need for personal feelings of achievement or success, while a self-actualization need is considered to be a striving for personal growth and development through one's *own* actions. Thus like McClelland's formulation of achievement motivation, both White's and Maslow's theoretical statements suggest that individuals may be motivated to perform certain tasks without an apparent need for external reward. If a task involves the opportunity for one to use new skills or is challenging to one's ability, it may therefore provide satisfaction in and of itself.

A revised expectancy × value theory

Although expectancy × value theories were originally conceived as models of extrinsic motivation, they can be amended to include intrinsic factors. As we have seen, it is important to recognize two sources of individual satisfaction that are not generally included in an expectancy × value model. First, a person may work on a task merely for the activity and stimulation involved regardless of whether his actions lead to a specific accomplishment or tangible rewards provided by others. Second, individual accomplishments may provide satisfaction regardless of whether they lead to external rewards such as money, praise, or increased status. We may thus think of task performance as involving three distinct sources of value to an individual: (1) value associated with a behavior itself, (2) value associated with accomplishment, and (3) value associated with rewards presented by others, the first two sources of value are mediated by the individual and can be considered intrinsic to his performance, while the third comprises an extrinsic source of satisfaction.

Several recent formulations of task motivation within organizational settings have incorporated intrinsic as well as extrinsic factors into the expectancy × value framework. Galbraith and Cummings (1967), Porter and Lawler (1967), and Lawler (1971, 1973) have each noted that task accomplishment can be rewarding to an individual independent of any externally mediated rewards. However, their models of motivation have each defined intrinsic rewards as those derived only from achievement, and they have not specifically considered the intrinsic rewards associated with behavior irrespective of task accomplishment. A recent expectancy model put forth by House and his associates (House 1971; House et al., 1974) is most inclusive in that it specifies both these potential sources of intrinsic motivation. A slightly amended version of the model is presented below.

$$M = IV_a + (P_1)(IV_b) + [\sum_{i=1}^{n}(P_{2i})(EV_i)]$$

where

M = task motivation

IV_a = intrinsic valence associated with task behavior

IV_b = intrinsic valence associated with task accomplishment

EV_i = extrinsic valences associated with task accomplishment

P_1 = perceived probability that one's behavior will lead to accomplishment of the task

P_{2i} = perceived probabilities that one's task accomplishment will lead to extrinsic valences

House's theory of task motivation posits that the individual estimates the instrumentality of his behavior, P_1, for accomplishing a task goal and also the likelihood, P_2, that a task accomplishment will lead to valued extrinsic rewards. In assessing P_1 the individual may take into consideration such factors as the level of his abilities relevant to the task, barriers to work goal accomplishment in the environment (e.g., not getting sufficient materials to finish a job correctly), and the help or support he will receive from others in the work setting. In assessing P_2 the individual may consider the likelihood that his supervisor will recognize good performance through praise, favoritism, a salary raise, or promotion to a better job. In addition, the individual is assumed to place some subjective value upon the behaviors involved in task performance, task accomplishment, and the extrinsic rewards potentially available through work performance. Thus a worker who is bored at home may possess a high IV_a, a worker who has a high need for achievement will be high on IV_b, while the person in dire need of a bigger paycheck should have a high EV_i. We will make use of this revised version of expectancy × value theory in predicting individual task motivation and formulating specific strategies for changing motivation.[2]

Methods of increasing task motivation

Extrinsic factors

Probably the most common action individuals take to change another's task behavior is to alter extrinsic motivation. From the expectancy × value model presented above, we can see that extrinsic motivation can be increased by changing either the extrinsic valences associated with task accomplishment (EV_i) or the perceived probabilities linking accomplishment to rewards (P^{2i}).

One procedure by which the valence of extrinsic rewards can be altered is through deprivation. Numerous laboratory studies have shown that by depriving a subject of a valued commodity (e.g., food,

2. Clearly, any effort to change the motivation or behavior of another individual implies certain ethical considerations. For example, as a change agent, one must assess the likely consequences of a change intervention; the results of not intervening; and the rights, both legal and ethical, of the "target" individual. In the sections that follow, several motivational strategies are described in terms of increasing another person's intrinsic and/or extrinsic motivation to perform a task. The examples that illustrate these strategies consider the change agent to be someone in control of resources or other sources of social power, such as a task supervisor, educational instructor, or group leader. Obviously, there may be alternative initiators of change interventions (workers, students, outside consultants), and some of the strategies illustrated here may be (justifiably) rejected by a change agent on the basis of local values and social norms.

water, sex), motivation can be increased for any task which leads to its attainment. The same principle no doubt holds in everyday life, but the use of deprivation to motivate someone to perform a task is considered an ethically undesirable way to change behavior. Fortunately, few allocators of rewards have the amount of control over the lives of others necessary to use it successfully. At present, for example, if an industrial firm chose to restrict workers' pay, it would, in addition to increasing the perceived value of money, cause workers to transfer quickly to another job. Only when the workers' options are extremely limited (e.g., during periods of high unemployment or a government-controlled labor market) would deprivation be an effective motivational tool.

A preferable way to increase extrinsic motivation is to assess the desires or needs of the individuals performing a task and to make available those extrinsic rewards with the greatest utility. For instance, one purpose of periodic meetings between supervisors and subordinates within small task groups and attitude surveys within large organizations could be to assess regularly the changing needs of employees. Ideally, extrinsic rewards could be tailored to groups of individuals with similar needs (e.g., for security, money, verbal praise) or provided on an individual basis. By simply restructuring the mix of rewards to achieve the greatest extrinsic valences, motivation to perform a task could thus be increased (see Lawler [1971] for a discussion of "cafeteria-style" pay schemes as applied to industry).

In addition to the valences associated with extrinsic rewards, considerable attention should also be given to the perceived probability that task accomplishment will lead to rewards. The most effective procedure in terms of increasing motivation is to make rewards contingent upon performance. As shown in figure 1, dramatic changes in behavior can result from tying extrinsic rewards to behavior. Depicted in the figure is the level of desired behavior emitted by patients of a mental hospital when rewards are both contingent and noncontingent on behavior. The extrinsic rewards used in the study were tokens which could be exchanged for food, cigarettes, or other valued commodities.

In practice, there are many ways of designing a contingent reward system. When task accomplishments are easily defined and measurable, it is often feasible to institute some sort of piece-rate incentive system. In these cases, the level of extrinsic rewards is based upon the quantity and/or quality of performance. Often, however, task accomplishments are neither clearly defined nor easily measured. In these cases, a judgment of the individual's performance is required by a supervisor or allocator of rewards. Obviously, any error in evalua-

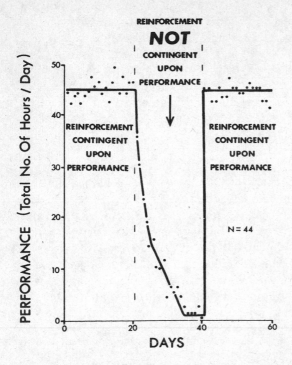

SOURCE: Allyon, T. and Azrin N. H. "The Measurement and Reinforcement of Behavior of Psychotics." *Journal of the Experimental Analysis of Behavior,* 1965, 8, 357–383. Copyright 1965 by the Society for the Experimental Analysis of Behavior, Inc. (Additional information and related research can be found in *The Token Economy: A Motivational System for Therapy and Rehabilitation* by T. Allyon and N. Azrin, published by Appleton-Century-Crofts, 1968.)

Figure 1. Total number of hours of onward performance by a group of 44 patients under contingent and noncontingent reinforcement schemes.

tion or sudden change in the criteria of performance will sharply reduce the individual's perception that task accomplishment leads to rewards. As a consequence, the perceived objectivity or fairness of the appraisal system can be as important a determinant of the individual's task motivation as the actual contingency between rewards and performance.

Making valued extrinsic rewards contingent upon performance is generally an effective motivational strategy. However, it is not without some problems. First, it requires that a supervisor possess a sufficient quantity of extrinsic rewards to motivate workers to complete a task. Although most formal organizations (e.g., industry, government) can afford literally to purchase a worker's services, a lack of valued extrinsic rewards can present a motivational problem in many informal work settings (e.g., social clubs, volunteer organizations, home environment). Also, as discussed, an effective strategy of extrinsic motivation requires that performance be accurately assessed by supervisors so that rewards can be dispensed on a contingent basis. Although this is no problem on a routine task for which the supervisor can clearly set the criteria of performance and measure it, frequently (on tasks involving a great deal of skill and creativity) the supervisor may actually know less about the job than the worker and be in a very poor position to evaluate his performance.

Intrinsic factors

From the revised expectancy $\times$ value model we can see that intrinsic motivation results from the perception of rewards inherent in either task behavior (IV_a) or accomplishment (IV_b). Several factors can be expected to account for the intrinsic valences associated with both behavior and accomplishment, but not all of them are easily alterable. For example, it would be most difficult to change individual needs for activity, manipulation, or exploration, except on a temporary basis. McClelland and his associates have had some success in increasing an individual's achievement needs and motivating entrepreneurial behavior through intensive training sessions (McClelland and Winter 1969). However, it is doubtful that achievement motivation can, by itself, affect the performance of persons on routine organizational tasks or other activities which are not highly achievement oriented (McClelland 1973a, 1973b).

Perhaps the most practical method of increasing a person's intrinsic motivation to perform a task is to purposely alter the characteristics of his work activities. Assuming that individuals possess at least a moderate need for activity and achievement, many tasks can be changed so that individuals derive greater satisfaction from either task behavior or accomplishment. Many industrial firms have, in effect, followed these principles in programs of job enlargement and job enrichment. For example, it would be most difficult to change individual needs for often improved by increasing the variety of skills necessary to perform a task or by rotating workers among several different tasks. Similarly, the intrinsic rewards associated with task accomplishment can be improved by increasing the responsibility of workers or the importance of the tasks they perform.

Increasing intrinsic motivation has several advantages as a motivational strategy. When individuals can derive satisfaction from task behaviors or accomplishment, there may, for example, be a reduced need for extrinsic rewards to motivate behavior. This may be especially important in cases where supervisors have a limited supply of extrinsic inducements or where individuals do not value those that are readily available. A second advantage of intrinsic motivation is that the need to monitor another's task behavior is reduced. With intrinsic motivation, it may not be necessary to rely totally upon piece-rate incentive systems or periodic performance appraisals to induce a high level of task performance. Instead, a task can be designed so that the quantity and/or quality of performance fulfills the individual's needs for achievement. When this is done, the worker who values achievement can monitor his own task accomplishment and reward himself on a completely contingent basis.

There are a number of ways a task can be changed to increase intrinsic motivation and some of the most important ones are listed in figure 2. The job characteristics shown in the figure are based heavily upon

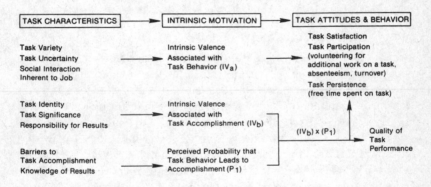

Figure 2. Task determinants of intrinstic motivation.

the recent research and theory of Hackman and Oldham (1975), but are framed within the expectancy × value model of motivation discussed earlier. It should be noted that the research underlying the model presented here has been conducted largely within industrial organizations. However, the characteristics of tasks are stated in rather general terms and may be applicable to many other settings (e.g., educational organizations). A brief consideration of each of these task characteristics and how they might be altered follows.

Task variety

In order to increase the intrinsic valence associated with task behavior (IV$_3$), greater variety can often be introduced into a job. A greater assortment of tasks can be performed by the individual on a single job or, if this is impossible, he can be rotated periodically from job to job. Many industrial firms have followed this procedure to reduce boredom, and increases in task satisfaction commonly result from such changes. Within educational organizations, a similar increase in the variety of learning tasks can often be used to maintain student interest.

Task uncertainty

Very mechanistic tasks, even if they comprise a varied set of activities, may not be totally satisfying to most individuals. Because of our needs for exploration and cognitive stimulation, a task that involves information processing and/or the resolution of uncertainty may be of greater intrinsic interest (e.g., Hune [1971], Lanzetta [1971]). Obviously, there may be some upper limit to the degree of uncertainty satisfying to an individual. Both the individual's level of task-relevant skills needed to resolve uncertainty and his personal tolerance for ambiguity may therefore determine the optimal task design.

Social interaction inherent to the job

The fact that individuals generally derive satisfaction from interacting with others can be an important inducement for working. For most persons, the intrinsic valence associated with task behavior is greater when social interaction is an integral part of the job. The formation of task groups and exchange of information are techniques used by schools for increasing the intrinsic interest of students. Also, within industry, there are now experiments in which prevously isolated workers can increase their contact with the ultimate users of their services as well as with their co-workers (Hackman et al. in press).

Task identity

Another way to improve the intrinsic valence associated with task accomplishment might be to increase the "wholeness" or identity of a person's work output. At present, within industry, many jobs are so specialized that the worker cannot see the relationship between his small task and the final finished product. In order to increase task identity, jobs can often be redesigned. The individual can be allowed to produce a larger module of work, or a small team of workers can be formed to complete an entire assembly process.

Task significance

The intrinsic valence associated with task accomplishment (IV_b) can often be improved by increasing the perceived significance of a person's work output. This can be done either by changing the individual to a more important job or by increasing the salience of his present work output. An example of the latter course of action would be to emphasize the usefulness of the person's work or to place the person in direct contact with the ultimate users of his product. Within the educational setting, an increase of task significance may translate itself into a stress for "relevance" in learning activities.

Responsibility for results

If an individual does not feel responsible for his work output, it is doubtful that he will place a high value on task accomplishment. Only when the person can experience success or failure on a task is he likely to value the intrinsic rewards associated with accomplishment. Therefore, to increase intrinsic motivation, the person might be given a larger amount of discretion over his task activities and held more accountable for his results. In industry, the autonomy of workers is often increased by allowing them to schedule their own work activities, decide on work methods, and check the quantity of their own output. Quite similar procedures could be devised within a school environment in order to increase the felt responsibility of students for their own learning.

Barriers to task accomplishment

Within any task setting (e.g., industrial, educational, etc.) the perceived probability that behavior leads to accomplishment (P_2) may depend on the extent to which there are barriers to task accomplishment. Some of these barriers may be internal to the individual such as his ability or training to perform a task; others may be related to his immediate task environment (e.g., not getting the necessary material or social support to complete the job). Restructuring a job (or educational task) to remove external barriers to accomplishment and providing requisite training and supervision may thus serve to increase an individual's intrinsic motivation.

Knowledge of results

Knowledge of results can also be expected to affect a person's intrinsic motivation to perform a task. Clearly, if the individual receives no feedback on the quality of his performance, it will be difficult for him to derive satisfaction from accomplishment. Thus it is important for supervisors to relate to workers exactly how they are doing. This feedback should be on a continuous basis so that the individual can quickly change his behavior, and not merely on a periodic review basis. Ideally, a feedback system should be built into the work itself. At present many industrial tasks do contain their own quality checks which can be performed by the worker, and within the educational context, computerized instruction provides a good example of learning tasks in which immediate feedback is provided so that changes in behavior can be effected by the individual.

Effects of intrinsic motivation

Figure 2 shows that intrinsic motivation can influence both an individual's task attitudes and his behavior. If the individual values the behaviors associated with a task actively (IV_a), he can be expected to participate in the task, be satisfied with it, and perhaps even to volunteer for additional tasks of a similar nature. If the individual values task accomplishment and perceives a strong link between his behavior and accomplishment $[(IV_b) (P_1)]$, he can also be expected to produce high-quality work. Empirical support for these hypotheses is derived from research on both task design and work effectiveness within organizational settings (see Hackman and Lawler 1971; Hackman and Oldham 1975; House 1971; Oldham 1974).

Combining intrinsic and extrinsic motivation

It is apparent from our discussion that both intrinsic and extrinsic motivation can be effective methods of energizing behavior. Either of these motivational strategies can be used to get an individual to perform a task, and both intrinsic and extrinsic rewards can bring satisfaction to the individual. The question remains, however, whether these two sources of motivation can be combined effectively to yield overall positive effects on the individual's task attitudes and behavior.

In the expectancy × value model presented above, intrinsic and extrinsic factors are added to form an overall measure of motivation. This model, like those of Galbraith and Cummings (1967), Porter and Lawler (1967), and Lawler (1971, 1973), *assumes* that the perception of intrinsic rewards and the perception of extrinsic rewards are additive in their effect on anticipated work satisfaction. It assumes that intrinsic motivation $[(IV_a) + (P_1) (IV_b)]$ and extrinsic motivation

$$[\sum_{i=1}^{n} (P_{2i}) (EV_i)]$$

summate to produce overall motivation and that intrinsic and extrinsic motivation are separate, independent factors.

Whether or not intrinsic and extrinsic sources of motivation are independent or do in fact have an effect upon each other is a question of considerable practical as well as theoretical significance. For example, if they are positively interrelated, we might expect extrinsic rewards to increase a person's intrinsic interest in a task, whereas if they are negatively interrelated, the administration of an extrinsic reward could drive out intrinsic motivation. This issue is of importance to any setting (e.g., industrial organizations, schools, or voluntary work situations) in which extrinsic rewards are administered and the allocator of the rewards is interested in the individual's resultant task attitudes and behavior.

The interrelationship of intrinsic and extrinsic motivation

Historically, the interrelationship of intrinsic and extrinsic motivation has been the subject of considerable controversy. In fact, it can be said that there exist psychological theories which will predict either a positive relationship between intrinsic and extrinsic motivation, a negative relationship, or no relationship at all. As a consequence, we will examine each of these theoretical positions in some detail and, in the light of recent empirical research, attempt to formulate a unified view of the interrelationship between intrinsic and extrinsic factors.

Long ago, Woodworth (1918) suggested that in the process of acquiring a set of skills toward some end, the skills themselves could develop their own motivating force that might endure even after the end is no longer sought. He made the point in the following context:

> . . . while a man may enter a certain line of business from a purely external economic motive, he develops an interest in the business for its own sake . . . and the motive force that drives him in the daily task, provided of course this does not degenerate into mere automatic routine, is precisely an interest in the problems confronting him and in the processes by which he is able to deal with those problems. The end furnishes the motive force for the search for means but once the means are found, they are apt to become interesting on their own account. [P. 104]

Allport (1937) has argued in a similar vein that certain behaviors develop their own motive power or "functional autonomy." He noted that while many activities, such as making money and solving problems, originally may have served some other motive, their persistence in the absence of external force necessitates their having developed a value on their own.

The notion that an activity or task behavior can become valued by an individual through its continued association with an external reward can be explained by the process of *secondary reinforcement*. Secondary reinforcement refers to a process by which an originally neutral stimulus acquires reinforcing properties through its pairing with a primary reinforcer (Ferster and Skinner 1957; Uhl and Young 1967). Thus in these terms it is possible to assert that an intrinsically motivating activity is simply one in which the reinforcement value of an extrinsic goal has associatively rubbed off on the behavior. Irrespective of temporal considerations (i.e., how long it might take for an activity to acquire reinforcing properties on its own), we can therefore predict, through secondary reinforcement, that there will be a positive relationship between intrinsic and extrinsic motivation. In short, no matter what a person's original reaction to a task, secondary reinforcement predicts that it may improve over time if it leads to valued extrinsic rewards.

Other psychologists, as we have seen, might disagree with the notion that all activities currently valued by individuals are merely those which have previously led to positive external outcomes. As noted by Harlow (1950). Montgomery (1954), and Berlyne [1960], an intrinsically motivated activity may stem from an innate human need for stimulation, information, or knowledge and is not necessarily dependent upon external reinforcement. Since certain activities may be valued independently of homeostatic needs or acquired drives based upon them, we might therefore posit that there is no clear relationship between intrinsic and extrinsic motivation.

A new approach to the problem

Recently, investigations have been undertaken into the relationship between intrinsic and extrinsic motivation from an entirely different perspective. Instead of asking how intrinsic motivation might be derived from extrinsic reward contingencies or independent human motives, several researchers have concluded that both intrinsic and extrinsic motivation may be more usefully studied as perceptions on the part of individuals. From a perceptual approach it is not necessary to know how specific behaviors originally acquired reinforcing properties, but only that an individual at a given point in time may perceive a task to be rewarding in and of itself. That is, if individuals *think* they are intrinsically motivated, this self-perception alone may be enough to influence future behavior and attitudes. This new approach is consistent with our expectancy × value formulation of motivation, since in that model individuals are assumed to hold perceptions of rewards to be derived from their actions, and behavior is assumed to be based on the direction and magnitude of these perceptual states.

Within the area of interpersonal perception, it has been noted (Heider 1958) that an individual may infer the causes of another's actions to be a function of personal and environmental force:

$$\text{Action} = f(\text{personal force} + \text{environmental force})$$

This is quite close to saying that individuals attempt to determine whether another person is intrinsically motivated to perform an activity (action due to personal force), or extrinsically motivated (action due to environmental force), or both. The extent to which an individual will infer intrinsic motivation on the part of another is predicted to be affected by the clarity and strength of external forces within the situation (Kelley 1967; Jones and Davis 1965; Jones and Nisbett 1971). When there are strong forces bearing on the individual to perform an activity, there is little reason to assume that a behavior is self-determined, whereas a high level of intrinsic motivation might be inferred if environmental force is minimal. Several studies dealing with interpersonal perception have supported this general conclusion (Jones et al. 1961; Thibaut and Riecken 1955; Jones and Harris 1967; Strickland 1958).

Bem (1967*a*, 1967*b*) extrapolated this interpersonal theory of causal attribution to the study of self-perception or how one views his *own* behavior within a social context. Bem hypothesized that the extent to which external pressures are sufficiently strong to account for one's behavior will determine the likelihood that a person will attribute his own actions to internal causes. Thus if a person acts under strong external rewards or punishments, he is likely to assume that his behavior is under external control. However, if extrinsic contingencies are not strong or salient, the individual is likely to assume that his behavior is due to his own interest in the activity or that his behavior is intrinsically motivated. De Charms has made a similar point in his discussion of individuals' perceptions of personal causation (1968, p. 328):

> As a first approximation, we propose that whenever a person experiences himself to be the locus of causality for his own behavior (to be an Origin), he will consider himself to be intrinsically motivated. Conversely, when a person perceives the locus of causality for his behavior to be external to himself (that he is a Pawn), he will consider himself to be extrinsically motivated.

De Charms emphasized that the individual may attempt psychologically to label his actions on the basis of whether or not he has been instrumental in affecting his own behavior; that is, whether his behavior has been intrinsically or extrinsically motivated.

The case for a negative relationship between intrinsic and extrinsic motivation

The self-perception approach to intrinsic and extrinsic motivation leads to the conclusion that there may be a negative interrelationship between these two motivational factors. The basis for this prediction stems from the assumption that individuals may work backward from their own actions in inferring sources of causation (Bem 1967*a*, 1967*b*,

1972). For example, if external pressures on an individual are so high that they would ordinarily cause him to perform a given task regardless of the internal characteristics of the activity, then the individual might logically infer that he is extrinsically motivated. In contrast, if external reward contingencies are extremely low or nonsalient, the individual might then infer that his behavior is intrinsically motivated. What is important is the fact that a person, in performing an activity, may *seek out* the probable cause of his own actions. Since behavior has no doubt been caused by something, it makes pragmatic, if not scientific, sense for the person to conclude that the cause is personal (intrinsic) rather than extrinsic if he can find no external reasons for his actions.

Two particular situations provide robust tests of the self-perception prediction. One is a situation in which there is insufficient justification for a person's actions, a situation in which the intrinsic rewards for an activity are very low (e.g., a dull task) and there are no compensating extrinsic rewards (e.g., monetary payment, verbal praise). Although rationally, one ordinarily tries to avoid these situations, there are occasions when one is faced with the difficult question of "why did I do that?" The self-perception theory predicts that in situations of insufficient justification, the individual may cognitively reevaluate the intrinsic characteristics of an activity in order to justify or explain his own behavior. For example, if the individual performed a dull task for no external reward, he may "explain" his behavior by thinking that the task was not really so bad after all.

Sometimes a person may also be fortunate enough to be in a situation in which his behavior is oversufficiently justified. For example, a person may be asked to perform an interesting task and at the same time be lavishly paid for his efforts. In such situations, the self-perception theory predicts that the individual may actually reevaluate the activity in a downward direction. Since the external reward would be sufficient to motivate behavior by itself, the individual may mistakenly infer that he was extrinsically motivated to perform the activity. He may conclude that since he was forced to perform the task by an external reward, the task probably was not terribly satisfying in and of itself.

Figure 3 graphically depicts the situations of insufficient and overly sufficient justification. From the figure, we can see that the conceptual framework supporting self-perception theory raises several interesting issues. First, it appears from this analysis that there are only two fully stable attributions of behavior: (1) the perception of extrinsically motivated behavior in which the internal rewards associated with performing an activity are low while external rewards are high, and (2) the perception of intrinsically motivated behavior in which the task is

LEVEL OF EXTRINSIC REWARDS

	LOW	HIGH
LOW	Insufficient Justification (unstable perception)	Perception of Extrinsically Motivated Behavior
HIGH	Perception of Intrinsically Motivated Behavior	Overly Sufficient Justification (unstable perception)

(Row labels on far left: LEVEL OF INTRINSIC REWARDS, with LOW and HIGH)

Figure 3. A conceptual framework of self-perception theory.

inherently rewarding but external rewards are low. Furthermore, it appears that situations of insufficient justification (where intrinsic and extrinsic rewards are both low) and oversufficient justification (where intrinsic and extrinsic rewards are both high) involve unstable attribution states. As shown in figure 4, individuals apparently resolve this attributional instability by altering their perceptions of intrinsic rewards associated with the task.

An interesting question posed by the self-perception analysis is why

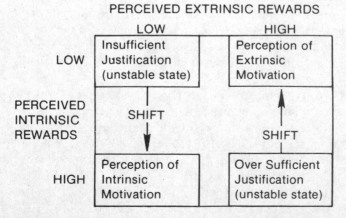

PERCEIVED EXTRINSIC REWARDS

	LOW	HIGH
LOW	Insufficient Justification (unstable state)	Perception of Extrinsic Motivation
HIGH	Perception of Intrinsic Motivation	Over Sufficient Justification (unstable state)

(Row labels on far left: PERCEIVED INTRINSIC REWARDS, with LOW and HIGH; SHIFT arrows point from upper-left to lower-left and from lower-right to upper-right)

Figure 4. A schematic analysis of the self-perception of intrinsic and extrinsic motivation.

individuals are predicted to resolve an unstable attribution state by cognitively reevaluating a task in terms of its intrinsic rewards rather than changing their perceptions of extrinsic factors. The answer to this question may lie in the relative clarity of extrinsic as compared with intrinsic rewards, and the individual's relative ability to distort the two aspects of the situation. Within many settings (and especially within laboratory experiments) extrinsic rewards are generally quite salient and specific, whereas an individual must judge the intrinsic nature of a task for himself. Any shifts in the perception of intrinsic and extrinsic rewards may therefore be more likely to occur in the intrinsic factor. As shown in figure 4, it is these predicted shifts in perceived intrinsic rewards that may theoretically underlie a negative relationship between intrinsic and extrinsic motivation.

Empirical evidence

Insufficient justification

Several studies have shown that when an individual is induced to commit an unpleasant act for little or no external justification, he may subsequently conclude that the act was not so unpleasant after all. Actually, the first scientific attempt to account for this phenomenon was the theory of cognitive dissonance (Festinger 1957). It was predicted by dissonance theorists (Festinger 1957; Aronson 1966) that, since performing an unpleasant act for little or no reward would be an inconsistent (and seemingly irrational) thing to do, an individual might subsequently change his attitude toward the act in order to reduce the inconsistency or to appear rational. Bem's self-perception theory yields the same predictions but does not require one to posit that there is a motivating state such as dissonance reduction or self-rationalization. To Bem, since the individual examines his own behavior in light of the forces around him, he is simply more likely to come to the conclusion that his actions were intrinsically satisfying if they were performed under minimal external force.

In general, two types of experiments have been designed to assess the consequences of insufficient justification. One type of design has involved the performance of a dull task with varied levels of reward (Brehm and Cohen 1962; Weick 1964; Freedman 1963; Weick and Penner 1965). A second and more popular design has involved some form of counterattitudinal advocacy, either in terms of lying to a fellow subject about the nature of an experiment or writing an essay against one's position on an important issue (Festinger and Carlsmith 1959; Carlsmith et al. 1966; Linder et al. 1967). Fundamentally, the two types of designs are not vastly different. Both require subjects to perform an intrinsically dissatisfying act under varied levels of external inducement, and both predict that, in the low payment condition, the subject will change his attitude toward the activity (i.e., think more favorably of the task or begin to believe the position advocated).

The most well-known experiment designed to test the insufficient justification paradigm was conducted by Festinger and Carlsmith (1959). Subjects participated in a repetitive and dull task (putting spools on trays and turning pegs) and were asked to tell other waiting subjects that the experiment was enjoyable, interesting, and exciting. Half the experimental subjects were paid \$1 and half were paid \$20 for the counterattitudinal advocacy (and to be "on call" in the future), while control subjects were not paid and did not perform the counter-attitudinal act. As predicted, the smaller the reward used to induce subjects to perform the counterattitudinal act, the greater the positive change in their attitudes toward the task. Although the interpretation of the results of this study have been actively debated (e.g., between dissonance and self-perception theorists) the basic findings have been replicated by a number of different researchers. It should be noted, however, that several mediating variables have also been isolated as being necessary for the attainment of this dissonance or self-perception effect: free choice (Linder et al. 1967), commitment or irrevocability of behavior (Brehm and Cohen 1962), and substantial adverse consequences (Calder et al. 1973; Collins and Hoyt 1972).

Recently, a strong test of the insufficient justification paradigm was also conducted outside the laboratory (Staw 1974a). A natural field experiment was made possible by the fact that many young men had joined an organization (Army ROTC) in order to avoid being drafted, *and* these same young men subsequently received information (a draft lottery number) that changed the value of this organizational reward. Of particular relevance was the fact that those who joined ROTC did so not because of their intrinsic interest in the activities involved (drills, classes, and summer camp), but because they anticipated a substantial extrinsic reward (draft avoidance). As a result, those who received draft numbers that exempted them from military service subsequently faced a situation of low extrinsic as well as intrinsic rewards, a situation of insufficient justification. In contrast, persons who received draft numbers that made them vulnerable to military call-up found their participation in ROTC perfectly justified—they were still successfully avoiding the draft by remaining in the organization. To test the insufficient justification effect, both the attitudes and the performance of ROTC cadets were analyzed by draft number before and after the national draft lottery. The results showed that those in the insufficient justification situation enhanced their perception of ROTC and even performed somewhat better in ROTC courses after the lottery. It should be recognized, however, that this task enhancement occurred only under circumstances very similar to those previously found necessary for the dissonance or self-perception effect (i.e., high commitment, free choice, and adverse consequences).

Overly sufficient justification

There have been several empirical studies designed to test the self-perception prediction within the context of overly sufficient justification. Generally, a situation in which an extrinsic reward is added to an intrinsically rewarding task has been experimentally contrived for this purpose. Following self-perception theory, it is predicted that an increase in external justification will cause individuals to lose confidence in their intrinsic interest in the experimental task. Since dissonance theory cannot make this prediction (it is neither irrational nor inconsistent to perform an activity for too many rewards), the literature on overly sufficient justification provides the most important data on the self-perception prediction. For this reason, we will examine the experimental evidence in some detail.

In an experiment specifically designed to test the effect of overly sufficient justification on intrinsic motivation, Deci (1971) enlisted a number of college students to participate in a problem-solving study. All the students were asked to work on a series of intrinsically interesting puzzles for three experimental sessions. After the first session, however, half of the students (the experimental group) were told that they would also be given an extrinsic reward (money) for correctly solving the second set of puzzles, while the other students (the control group) were not told anything about the reward. In the third session, neither the experimental nor the control subjects were rewarded. This design is schematically outlined below:

	Time 1	Time 2	Time 3
Experimental group	No payment	Payment	No payment
Control group	No payment	No payment	No payment

Deci had hypothesized that the payment of money in the second experimental session might decrease subjects' intrinsic motiation to perform the task. That is, the introduction of an external force (money) might cause participants to alter their self-perception about why they were working on the puzzles. Instead of being intrinsically motivated to solve the interesting puzzles, they might find themselves working primarily to get the money provided by the experimenter. Thus Deci's goal in conducting the study was to compare the changes in subjects' intrinsic motivation from the first to third sessions for both the experimental and control groups. If the self-perception hypothesis was correct, the intrinsic motivation of the previously paid experimental subjects would decrease in the third session, whereas the intrinsic motivation of the unpaid controls should remain unchanged.

As a measure of intrinsic motivation, Deci used the amount of free time participants spent on the puzzle task. To obtain this measure, the experimenter left the room during each session, supposedly to feed some data into the computer. As the experimenter left the room, he told the subjects they could do anything they wanted with their free time. In addition to the puzzles, current issues of *Time, The New Yorker,* and *Playboy* were placed near the subjects. However, while the first experimenter was out of the laboratory, a second experimenter, unknown to the subjects, observed their behavior through a one-way mirror. It was reasoned that if the subject worked on the puzzles during this free time period, he must be intrinsically motivated to perform the task. As shown in table 2, the amount of free time spent on the task decreased for those who were previously paid to perform the activity, while there was a slight increase for the unpaid controls. Although the difference between the experimental and control groups was only marginally significant, the results are suggestive of the fact that an overly sufficient extrinsic reward may decrease one's intrinsic motivation to perform a task.

Table 2. Mean Number of Seconds Spent Working on the Puzzles during the Free Time Periods.

Group	Time 1	Time 2	Time 3	Time 3 — Time 1
Experimental (n = 12)	248.2	313.9	198.5	−49.7
Control (n = 12)	213.9	202.7	241.8	27.9

SOURCE: Deci, E. L., "The Effects of Externally Mediated Rewards on Intrinsic Motivation." *Journal of Personality and Social Psychology.* 1971, 18: 105–115. Copyright 1971 by the American Psychological Association. Reprinted by permission.

Lepper et al. (1973) also conducted a study that tested the self-perception prediction in a situation of overly sufficient justification. Their study involved having nursery school children perform an interesting activity (playing with Magic Markers) with and without the expectation of an additional extrinsic reward. Some children were induced to draw pictures with the markers by promising them a Good Player Award consisting of a big gold star, a bright red ribbon, and a place to print their name. Other children either performed the activity without any reward or were told about the reward only after completing the activity. Children who participated in these three experimental conditions (expected reward, no reward, unexpected reward) were then covertly observed during the following week in a free-play period. As in the Deci (1971) study, the amount of time children spent on the activity when they could do other interesting things (i.e., playing with other toys) was taken to be an indicator of intrinsic motivation.

The findings of the Lepper et al. study showed that the introduction of an extrinsic reward for performing an already interesting activity caused a significant decrease in intrinsic motivation. Children who played with Magic Markers with the expectation of receiving the external reward did not spend as much subsequent free time on the activity as did children who were not given a reward or those who were unexpectedly offered the reward. Moreover, the rated quality of drawings made by children with the markers was significantly poorer in the expected reward group than either the no-reward or unexpected reward groups.

The results of the Lepper et al. study help to increase our confidence in the findings of the earlier Deci experiment. Not only are the earlier findings replicated with a different task and subject population, but an important methodological problem is minimized. By reexamining table 2, we can see that the second time period in the Deci experiment was the period in which payment was expected by subjects for solving the puzzles. However, we can also see that in time 2 there was a whopping increase in the free time subjects spent on the puzzles. Deci explained this increase as an attempt by subjects to practice puzzle solving to increase their chances of earning money. However, what Deci did not discuss is the possibility that the subsequent decrease in time 3 was due not to the prior administration of rewards but to the effect of satiation or fatigue. One contribution of the Lepper et al. study is that its results are not easily explained by this alternative. In the Lepper et al. experiment, there was over one week's time between the session in which an extrinsic reward was administered and the final observation period.

Although both the Deci and Lepper et al. studies support the notion that the expectation of an extrinsic reward may decrease intrinsic interest in an activity, there is still one important source of ambiguity in both these studies. You may have noticed that the decrease in intrinsic motivation follows not only the prior administration of an extrinsic reward, but also the withdrawal of this reward. For example, in the Deci study, subjects were not paid in the third experimental session in which the decrease in intrinsic motivation was reported. Likewise, subjects were not rewarded when the final observation of intrinsic motivation was taken by Lepper et al. It is therefore difficult to determine whether the decrease in intrinsic interest is due to a change in the self-perception of motivation following the application of an extrinsic reward or merely to frustration following the removal of the reward. An experiment by Kruglanski et al. (1971) helps to resolve this ambiguity.

Kruglanski et al. induced a number of teenagers to volunteer for some creativity and memory tasks. To manipulate extrinsic rewards, the experimenters told half the participants that because they had volunteered for the study, they would be taken on an interesting tour of the psychology laboratory; the other participants were not offered this extrinsic reward. The results showed that teenagers offered the reward were less satisfied with the experimental tasks and were less likely to volunteer for future experiments of a similar nature than were teenagers who were not offered the extrinsic reward. In addition, the extrinsically rewarded group did not perform as well on the experimental task (in terms of recall, creativity, and the Zeigarnik effect) as the nonrewarded group. These findings are similar to those of Deci (1971) and Lepper et al. (1973), but they cannot be as easily explained by a frustration effect. Since in the Kruglanski et al. study the reward was never withdrawn for the experimental group, the differences between the experimental (reward) and control (no reward) conditions are better explained by a change in self-perception than by a frustration effect.

The designs of the three overly sufficient justification studies described above have varying strengths and weaknesses (Calder and Staw 1975a), but taken together, their results can be interpreted as supporting the notion that extrinsic rewards added to an already interesting task can decrease intrinsic motivation. This effect, if true, has important ramifications for educational, industrial, and other work settings. There are many situations in which people are offered extrinsic rewards (grades, money, special privileges) for accomplishing a task which may already be intrinsically interesting. The self-perception effect means that, by offering external rewards, we may sometimes be sacrificing an important source of task motivation and not necessarily increasing either the satisfaction or the performance of the participant. Obviously, because the practical implications of the self-perception effect are large, we should proceed with caution. Thus, in addition to scrutinizing the validity of the findings themselves (as we have done above), we should also attempt to determine the exact conditions under which they might be expected to hold.

Earlier, Deci (1971, 1972) had hypothesized that only rewards contingent on a high level of task performance are likely to have an adverse effect on intrinsic motivation. He had reasoned that a reward contingent upon specific behavioral demands is most likely to cause an individual to infer that his behavior is extrinsically rather than intrinsically motivated and that a decrease in intrinsic motivation may result from this change in self-perception. Although this assumption seems reasonable, there is not a great deal of empirical support for it. Certainly in the Kruglanski et al. and Lepper et al. studies all that was necessary to cause a decrease in intrinsic motivation was for rewards to be contingent upon the completion of an activity. In each of these studies what seemed to be important was the cognition that one was performing an activity *in order to get an extrinsic reward* rather than a prescribed goal for a particular level of output. Thus as long as it is salient, a reward contingency based upon the completion of an activity may decrease intrinsic motivation just like a reward contingency based on the quality or quantity of performance.

Ross (in press) recently conducted two experiments that dealt specifically with the effect of the salience of rewards on changes in intrinsic motivation. In one study, children were asked to play a musical instrument (drums) for either no reward, a nonsalient reward, or a salient reward. The results showed that intrinsic motivation, as measured by the amount of time spent on the drums versus other activities in a free play situation, was lowest for the salient reward condition. Similar results were found in a second study in which some children were asked to think either of the reward (marshmallows) while playing a musical instrument, think of an extraneous object (snow), or not think of anything in particular. The data for this second study showed that intrinsic motivation was lowest when children consciously thought about the reward while performing the task.

In addition to the salience of an external reward, there has been empirical research on one other factor mediating the self-perception effect, the existing norms of the task situation. In examining the prior research using situations of overly sufficient justification, Staw et al. (1975) reasoned that there is one common element which stands out. Always, the extrinsic reward appears to be administered in a situation in which persons are not normally paid or otherwise reimbursed for their actions. For example, students are not normally paid for laboratory participation, but the Deci (1971) and Kruglanski et al. (1971) subjects were. Likewise, nursery school children are not normally enticed by special recognition or rewards to play with an interesting new toy, but both the Lepper et al. (1973) and Ross (in press) subjects were. Thus Staw et al. (1975) manipulated norms for payment as well as the actual payment of money for performing an interesting task. They found an interaction of norms and payment such that the introduction of an extrinsic reward decreased intrinsic interest in a task only when there existed a situational norm for no payment. From these data and the findings of the Ross study, it thus appears that an extrinsic reward must be both salient and situationlly inappropriate for there to be a reduction in intrinsic interest.

Reassessing the self-perception effect

At present there is growing empirical support for the notion that intrinsic and extrinsic motivation *can* be negatively interrelated. The effect of extrinsic rewards on intrinsic motivation has been replicated by several researchers using different classes of subjects (males, females, children, college students) and different activities (puzzles, toys), and the basic results appear to be internally valid. As we have seen, however, the effect of extrinsic rewards is predicated on certain necessary conditions (e.g., situational norms and reward salience), as is often the case with psychological findings subjected to close examination.

To date, the primary data supporting the self-perception prediction have come from situations of insufficient and overly sufficient justification. Empirical findings have shown that individuals may cognitively reevaluate intrinsic rewards in an upward direction when their behavior is insufficiently justified and in a downward direction when there is overly sufficient justification. In general, it can be said that the data of these two situations are consistent with the self-perception hypothesis. Still, theoretically, it is not immediately clear why previous research has been restricted to these two particular contexts. No doubt it is easier to show an increase in intrinsic motivation when intrinsic interest is initially low (as under insufficient justification) or a decrease when intrinsic interest is initially high (as under overly sufficient justification). Nevertheless, the theory should support a negative interrelationship of intrinsic and extrinsic factors at *all levels,* since it makes the rather general prediction that the greater the extrinsic rewards, the less likely is the individual to infer that he is intrinsically motivated.

One recent empirical study has tested the self-perception hypothesis by manipulating *both* intrinsic and extrinsic motivation. Calder and Staw (1975*b*) experimentally manipulated both the intrinsic characteristics of a task as well as extrinsic rewards in an attempt to examine the interrelationship of these two factors at more than one level. In the study male college students were asked to solve one of two sets of puzzles identical in all respects except the potential for intrinsic interest. One set of puzzles contained an assortment of pictures highly rated by students (chiefly from *Life* magazine but including several *Playboy* centerfolds); another set of puzzles was blank and rated more neutrally. To manipulate extrinsic rewards, half the subjects were promised $1 for their 20 minutes of labor (and the dollar was placed prominently in view), while for half of the subjects, money was neither mentioned nor displayed. After completing the task, subjects were asked to fill out a questionnaire on their reactions to the puzzle-solving activity. The two primary dependent variables included in the questionnaire were a measure of task satisfaction and a measure of subjects' willingness to volunteer for additional puzzle-solving exercises. The latter consisted of a sign-up sheet on which subjects could indicate the amount of time they would be willing to spend (without pay or additional course credit) in future experiments of a similar nature.

The results of the Calder and Staw experiment showed a significant interaction between task and payment on subjects' satisfaction with the activity and a marginally significant interaction on subjects' willingness to volunteer for additional work without extrinsic reward. These data provided empirical support for the self-perception effect in a situation of overly sufficient justification, but not under other conditions. Specifically, when the task was initially interesting (i.e., using the picture puzzle activity), the introduction of money caused a reduction of task satisfaction and volunteering. However, when the task was initially more neutral (i.e., using the blank puzzle activity), the introduction of money increased satisfaction and subjects' intentions to volunteer for additional work. Thus if we consider Calder and Staw's dependent measures as indicators of intrinsic interest, the first finding is in accord with the self-perception hypothesis, while the latter result is similar to what one might predict from a reinforcement theory. The implications of these data, together with previous findings, are graphically depicted in figure 5.

As shown in the figure, self-perception effects have been found *only*

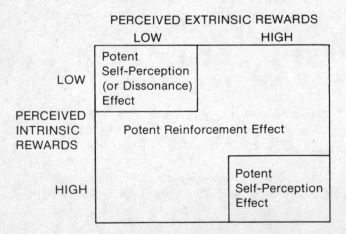

Figure 5. The relative potency of self-perception and reinforcement mechanisms.

at the extremes of insufficient and overly sufficient justification. Thus it may be prudent to withhold judgment on the general hypothesis that there is a uniformly negative relationship between intrinsic and extrinsic motivation. Perhaps we should no longer broadly posit that the greater external rewards and pressures, the weaker the perception of intrinsic interest in an activity; and the lower external pressures, the stronger intrinsic interest. Certainly, under conditions other than insufficient and overly sufficient justification, reinforcement effects of extrinsic rewards on intrinsic task satisfaction have readily been found (Cherrington et al. 1971; Cherrington 1973; Greene 1974).

At present it appears that only in situations of insufficient or overly sufficient reward will there be attributional instability of such magnitude that shifts will occur in the perception of intrinsic rewards. We might therefore speculate that either no attributional instability is evoked in other situations or it is just not strong enough to overcome a countervailing force. I would place my confidence in the latter theoretical position. It seems likely that both self-perception *and* reinforcement mechanisms holds true, but that their relative influence over an individual's task attitudes and behavior varies according to the situational context. For example, only in situations with insufficient or overly sufficient justification will the need to resolve attributional instability probably be strong enough for external rewards to produce a decrease in intrinsic motivation. In other situations we might reasonably expect a more positive relationship between intrinsic and extrinsic factors, as predicted by reinforcement theory.

Although this new view of the interrelationship between intrinsic and extrinsic motivation remains speculative, it does seem reasonable in light of recent theoretical and empirical work. Figure 6 graphically elaborates this model and shows how the level of intrinsic and extrinsic motivation may depend on the characteristics of the situation. In the figure, secondary reinforcement is depicted to be a general force for producing a positive relationship between intrinsic and extrinsic motivation. However, under situations of insufficient and oversufficient justification, self-perception (and dissonance) effects are shown to provide a second but still potentially effective determinant of a negative interrelationship between intrinsic and extrinsic motivation. Figure 6 shows the joint operation of these two theoretical mechanisms and illustrates their ultimate effect on individuals' satisfaction, persistence, and performance on a task.

Implications of intrinsic and extrinsic motivation

In this discussion we have noted that the administration of both intrinsic and extrinsic rewards can have important effects on a person's task attitudes and behavior. Individually, extrinsic rewards may direct

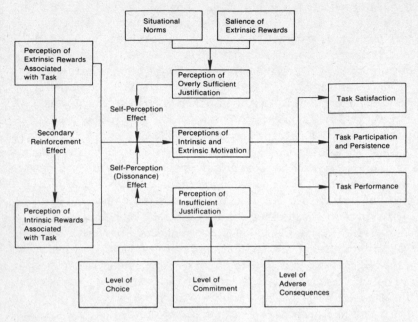

Figure 6. The interrelationship of intrinsic and extrinsic motivation as a function of situational characteristics.

and control a person's activity on a task and provide an important source of satisfaction. By themselves, intrinsic rewards can also motivate task-related behavior and bring gratification to the individual. As we have seen, however, the joint effect of intrinsic and extrinsic rewards may be quite complex. Not only may intrinsic and extrinsic factors not be additive in their overall effect on motivation and satisfaction, but the interaction of intrinsic and extrinsic factors may under some conditions be positive and under other conditions negative. As illustrated in figures 5 and 6, a potent reinforcement effect will often cause intrinsic and extrinsic motivation to be positively interrelated, although on occasion a self-perception mechanism may be so powerful as to create a negative relationship between these two factors.

The reinforcement predictions of figures 5 and 6 are consistent with our common sense. In practice, extrinsic rewards are relied upon heavily to induce desired behaviors, and most allocators of rewards (administrators, teachers, parents) operate on the theory that extrinsic rewards will positively affect an individual's intrinsic interest in a task. We should therefore concentrate on those situations in which our common sense may be in error—those situations in which there may in fact be a negative relationship between intrinsic and extrinsic motivation.

Motivation in educational organizations

One of the situations in which intrinsic and extrinsic motivation may be negatively interrelated is our schools. As Lepper and Greene (in press) have noted, many educational tasks are inherently interesting to students and would probably be performed without any external force. However, when grades and other extrinsic inducements are added to the activity, we may, via overly sufficient justification, be converting an interesting activity into work. That is, by inducing students to perform educational tasks with strong extrinsic rewards or by applying external force, we may be converting learning activities into behaviors that will not be performed in the future without some additional outside pressure or extrinsic force.

Within the educational context, a negative relationship between intrinsic and extrinsic motivation poses a serious dilemma for teachers who allocate external rewards. For example, there is no doubt that grades, gold stars, and other such incentives can alter the direction and vigor of specific "in school" behaviors (e.g., getting students to complete assigned exercises by a particular date). But because of their effect on intrinsic motivation, extrinsic rewards may also weaken a student's general interest in learning tasks and decrease voluntary learning behavior that extends beyond the school setting. In essence, then, the extrinsic forces that work so well at motivating and controlling specific task behaviors may actually cause the extinction of these same behaviors within situations devoid of external reinforcers. This is an important consideration for educational organizations, since most of an individual's learning activity will no doubt occur outside the highly regulated and reinforced setting of the classroom.[3]

In order to maintain students' intrinsic motivation in learning activities it is recommended that the use of extrinsic rewards be carefully controlled. As a practical measure, it is recommended that when a learning task is inherently interesting (and would probably be performed without any external force) all external pressures on the individual be minimized. Only when a task is so uninteresting that individuals would not ordinarily perform it should extrinsic rewards be applied. In addition, it is suggested that the student role be both en-

3. It is interesting to note that Kazdin and Bootzen (1972) have made a quite similar point in their recent review of research on token economies. They noted that while operant conditioning procedures have been quite effective in altering focal behaviors within a controlled setting, seldom have changes been found to generalize to natural, nonreinforcing environments.

larged and enriched to increase rather directly the level of intrinsic motivation. The significance of learning tasks, responsibility for results, feedback, and variety in student activities are all areas of possible improvement.

Motivation in work organizations

Voluntary work organizations are very much like educational organizations; their members are often intrinsically motivated to perform certain tasks and extrinsic rewards are generally not necessary to induce the performance of many desired behaviors. Moreover, if for some reason extrinsic rewards were to be offered to voluntary workers for performing their services, we would expect to find, as in the educational setting, a decrease in intrinsic motivation. As in the educational context, we would expect an external reward to decrease self-motivated (or voluntary) behavior in settings free from external reinforcement, although the specific behaviors which are reinforced might be increased. As a concrete example, let us imagine a political candidate who decides to "motivate" his volunteer campaign workers by paying them for distributing fliers to prospective voters. In this situation, we might expect that the administration of an extrinsic reward will increase the number of fliers distributed. However, the political workers' subsequent interest in performing other campaign activities *without pay* may subsequently be diminished. Similarly, the volunteer hospital worker who becomes salaried may no longer have the same intrinsic interest in his work. Although the newly professionalized worker may exert a good deal of effort on the job and be relatively satisfied with it, his satisfaction may stem from extrinsic rather than intrinsic sources of reward.

Let us now turn to the implications of intrinsic and extrinsic motivation for nonvoluntary work organizations. Deci (1972), in reviewing his research on intrinsic motivation, cautioned strongly against the use of contingent monetary rewards within industrial organizations. He maintained that paying people contingently upon the performance of specific tasks may reduce intrinsic motivation for these activities, and he recommended noncontingent reinforcers in their stead. As we have seen, however, a decrease in intrinsic motivation does not always occur following the administration of extrinsic rewards; certain necessary conditions must be present before there is a negative relationship between intrinsic and extrinsic motivation. Generally, industrial work settings do not meet these necessary conditions.

First, within industrial organizations, a large number of jobs are not inherently interesting enough to foster high intrinsic motivation. Persons would not ordinarily perform many of the tasks of the industrial world (e.g., assembly-line work) without extrinsic inducements, and this initial lack of intrinsic interest will probably preclude the effect of overly sufficient justification. Second, even when an industrial job is inherently interesting, there exists a powerful norm for extrinsic payment. Not only do workers specifically join and contribute their labor in exchange for particular inducements, but the instrumental relationship between task behavior and extrinsic rewards is supported by both social and legal standards. Thus the industrial work situation is quite unlike that of either a voluntary organization or an educational system. In the former cases, participants may be initially interested in performing certain tasks without external force, and the addition of overly sufficient rewards may convey information that the task is not intrinsically interesting. Within industrial organizations, on the other hand, extrinsic reinforcement *is* the norm, and tasks may often be perceived to be even more interesting when they lead to greater extrinsic rewards.

The very basic distinction between nonvoluntary work situations and other task settings (e.g., schools and voluntary organizations) is that, without extrinsic rewards, nonvoluntary organizations would be largely without participants. The important question for industrial work settings is therefore not one of payment versus nonpayment, but of the recommended degree of contingency between reward and performance. On the basis of current evidence, it would seem prudent to suggest that, within industrial organizations, rewards continue to be made contingent upon behavior. This could be accomplished through performance evaluation, profit sharing, or piece-rate incentive schemes. In addition, intrinsic motivation should be increased directly via the planned alteration of specific job characteristics (e.g., by increasing task variety, complexity, social interaction, task identity, significance, responsibility for results, and knowledge of results).

A final comment

Although the study of the interaction of intrinsic and extrinsic motivation is a relatively young area within psychology, it has been the intent of this paper to outline a theoretical model and provide some practical suggestions based upon the research evidence available to date. As we have seen, the effects of intrinsic and extrinsic motivation are not always simple, and several mediating variables must often be taken into account before specific predictions can be made. Thus in addition to providing "answers" to theoretical and practical problems, this paper may illustrate the complexities involved in drawing conclusions from a limited body of research data. The main caution for the reader is to regard these theoretical propositions and practical recommendations as working statements subject to the influence of future empirical evidence.

Bibliography

G. W. Allport, *Personality, A Psychological Interpretation.* Holt, 1937.

E. Aronson, "The Psychology of Insufficient Justification: An Analysis of Some Conflicting Data." In S. Feldman, ed., *Cognitive Consistency: Motivational Antecedents and Behavior Consequences.* Academic Press, 1966.

J. W. Atkinson, *An Introduction to Motivation.* Van Nostrand, 1964.

T. Ayllon and N. H. Azrin, "The Measurement and Reinforcement of Behavior of Psychotics." *Journal of Experimental Analysis of Behavior,* 1965, 8:357–383.

D. J. Bem, "Self-perception: An Alternative Interpretation of Cognitive Dissonance Phenomena." *Psychological Review,* 1967a, 74: 183–200.

———, "Self-perception: The Dependent Variable of Human Performance." *Organizational Behavior and Human Performance,* 1967b, 2:105–121.

———, "Self-perception Theory." In L. Berkowitz, ed., *Advances in Experimental Social Psychology,* Vol. 6, Academic Press, 1972.

D. E. Berlyne, *Conflicts, Arousal, and Curiosity.* McGraw-Hill, 1960.

W. H. Bexton, W. Heron, and T. H. Scott, "Effects of Decreased Variation in the Sensory Environment." *Canadian Journal of Psychology,* 1954, 8:70–76.

J. W. Brehm and A. R. Cohen, *Explorations in Cognitive Dissonance.* Wiley, 1962.

B. J. Calder, M. Ross, and C. A. Insko, "Attitude Change and Attitude Attribution: Effects of Incentive, Choice, and Consequences." *Journal of Personality and Social Psychology,* 1973, 25:84–100.

B. J. Calder and B. M. Staw, "The Interaction of Intrinsic and Extrinsic Motivation: Some Methodological Notes." *Journal of Personality and Social Psychology,* 1975a, 31:76–80.

———, "Self-perception of Intrinsic and Extrinsic Motivation." *Journal of Personality and Social Psychology,* 1975b, 31:599–605.

J. P. Campbell, M. D. Dunnette, E. E. Lawler, and K. E. Weick, *Managerial Behavior, Performance, and Effectiveness.* McGraw-Hill, 1970.

J. M. Carlsmith, B. E. Collins, and R. L. Helmreich, "Studies in Forced Compliance: The Effect of Pressure for Compliance on Attitude Change Produced by Face-to-Face Role Playing and Anonymous

Essay Writing." *Journal of Personality and Social Psychology,* 1966, 4:1–13.

D. J. Cherrington, "The Effects of a Central Incentive-Motivational State on Measures of Job Satisfaction." *Organizational Behavior and Human Performance,* 1973, 10:271–289.

D. J. Cherrington, H. J. Reitz, and W. E. Scott, "Effects of Reward and Contingent Reinforcement on Satisfaction and Task Performance." *Journal of Applied Psychology,* 1971, 55:531–536.

B. E. Collins and M. F. Hoyt, "Personal Responsibility-for-Consequences: An Integration and Extension of the Forced Compliance Literature." *Journal of Experimental Social Psychology,* 1972, 8:558–594.

R. E. Cook, "Relation of Achievement Motivation and Attribution to Self-reinforcement." Ph.D. dissertation. University of California, 1970.

R. de Charms, *Personal Causation: The Internal Affective Determinants of Behavior.* Academic Press, 1968.

E. L. Deci, "The Effects of Externally Mediated Rewards on Intrinsic Motivation." *Journal of Personality and Social Psychology,* 1971, 18:105–115.

————, "The Effects of Contingent and Noncontingent Rewards and Controls on Intrinsic Motivation." *Organizational Behavior and Human Peformance,* 1972, 8:217–229.

W. Edwards, "The Prediction of Decision among Bets." *Journal of Experimental Psychology,* 1955, 50:201–214.

C. B. Ferster and B. F. Skinner, *Schedules of Reinforcement.* Appleton-Century-Crofts, 1957.

L. Festinger, *A Theory of Cognitive Dissonance,* Stanford University Press, 1957.

L. Festinger and J. M. Carlsmith, "Cognitive Consequences of Forced Compliance." *Journal of Abnormal and Social Psychology,* 1959, 58:203–210.

J. L. Freedman, "Attitudinal Effects of Inadequate Justification." *Journal of Personality,* 1963, 31:371–385.

J. Galbraith and L. L. Cummings, "An Emprical Investigation of the Motivational Determinants of Task Performance: Interactive Effects Between Instrumentality-Valence and Motivation-Ability." *Organizational Behavior and Human Performance,* 1967, 2:237–257.

C. N. Greene, "Causal Connections among Managers' Merit Pay, Job Satisfaction, and Performance." *Journal of Applied Psychology,* 1974, 58:95–100.

J. R. Hackman and E. E. Lawler, "Employee Reactions to Job Characteristics." *Journal of Applied Psychology,* 1971, 55:259–286.

J. R. Hackman and G. R. Oldham, "Development of the Job Diagnostic Survey." *Journal of Applied Psychology,* 1975, 60:159–170.

———, "Motivation through the Design of Work." *Organizational Behavior and Human Performance,* in press.

J. R. Hackman, G. R. Oldham, R. Janson, and K. Purdy, "A New Strategy for Job Enrichment." *California Management Review,* in press, 1975.

H. F. Harlow, "Learning and Satiation of Response in Intrinsically Motivated Complex Puzzle Performance by Monkeys." *Journal of Comparative and Physiological Psychology,* 1950, 43:289–294.

H. F. Harlow, M. K. Harlow, and D. R. Meyer, "Learning Motivated by a Manipulation Drive." *Journal of Experimental Psychology,* 1950, 40:228–234.

H. F. Harlow and G. E. McClearn, "Object Discrimination Learned by Monkeys on the Basis of Manipulation Motives." *Journal of Comparative and Physiological Psychology,* 1954, 47:73–76.

F. Heider, *The Psychology of Interpersonal Relations.* Wiley, 1958.

R. J. House, "A Path-Goal Theory of Leader Effectiveness." *Administrative Science Quarterly,* 1971, 16:321–338.

R. J. House, H. J. Shapiro, and M. A. Wahba, "Expectancy Theory as a Predictor of Work Behavior and Attitude: A Reevaluation of Empirical Evidence." *Decision Sciences,* 1974, 5:481–506.

C. L. Hull, *Principles of Behavior,* Appleton-Century-Crofts, 1943.

J. McV. Hunt, "Intrinsic Motivation and Its Role in Psychological Development." In D. Levine, ed., *Nebraska Symposium on Motivation.* University of Nebraska Press, 1965.

———, "Toward a History of Intrinsic Motivation." In H. I. Day, D. E. Berlyne, and D. E. Hunt, eds., *Intrinsic Motivation: A New Direction in Education.* Holt, Rinehart, and Winston of Canada, 1971.

E. E. Jones and K. E. Davis, "From Acts to Dispositions: The Attribution Process in Person Perception." In L. Berkowitz, ed., *Advances in Experimental Psychology,* Vol. 2, Academic Press, 1965.

E. E. Jones, K. E. Davis, and K. E. Gergen, "Role Playing Variations and Their Informational Value for Person Perception." *Journal of Abnormal and Social Psychology,* 1961, 63:302–310.

E. E. Jones and V. A. Harris, "The Attribution of Attitudes," *Journal of Experimental Social Psychology,* 1967, 3:1–24.

E. E. Jones and R. E. Nisbett, *The Actor and the Observer: Divergent Perceptions of the Causes of Behavior.* General Learning Press, 1971.

A. E. Kazdin and R. R. Bootzen, "The Token Economy: An Evaluative Review," *Journal of Applied Behavior Analysis,* 1972, 5:343–372.

F. S. Keller, *Learning: Reinforcement Theory,* 2d ed. Random House, 1969.

H. H. Kelley, "Attribution Theory in Social Psychology." In D. Levine, ed., *Nebraska Symposium on Motivation,* Vol. 15. University of Nebraska Press, 1967.

―――, *Attribution in Social Interaction.* General Learning Press, 1971.

S. Koch, "Behavior as 'Intrinsically' Regulated: Work Notes towards a Pretheory of Phenomena Called Motivational." In M. R. Jones, ed., *Nebraska Symposium on Motivation.* University of Nebraska Press, 1956.

A. K. Korman, *The Psychology of Motivation.* Prentice-Hall, 1974.

A. W. Kruglanski, I. Freedman, and G. Zeevi, "The Effects of Extrinsic Incentives on Some Qualitative Aspects of Task Performance." *Journal of Personality,* 1971, 39:606–617.

J. T. Lanzetta, "The Motivational Properties of Uncertainty." In H. I. Day, D. E. Berlyne, and D. E. Hunt, eds., *Intrinsic Motivation: A New Direction in Education.* Holt, Rinehart, and Winston of Canada, 1971.

E. E. Lawler, *Pay and Organizational Effectiveness: A Psychological View.* McGraw-Hill, 1971.

―――, *Motivation in Work Organizations.* Brooks/Cole, 1973.

M. R. Lepper and D. Greene, "Turning Play into Work: Effects of Adult Surveillance and Extrinsic Rewards on Children's Intrinsic Motivation." *Journal of Personality and Social Psychology,* in press.

M. R. Lepper, D. Greene, and R. E. Nisbett, "Undermining Children's Intrinsic Interest with Extrinsic Rewards: A Test of the 'Overjustification' Hypothesis." *Journal of Personality and Social Psychology,* 1973, 28:129–137.

K. Lewin, *The Conceptual Representation and the Measurement of Psychological Forces.* Duke University Press, 1938.

K. Lewin, T. Dembo, L. Festinger, and P. W. Sears, "Level of Aspiration." In J. McV. Hunt, ed., *Personality and the Behavior Disorders,* Vol. 1. Ronald Press, 1944.

D. E. Linder, J. Cooper, and E. E. Jones, "Decision Freedom as a Determinant of the Role of Incentive Magnitude in Attitude Change." *Journal of Personality and Social Psychology,* 1967, 6:245–254.

G. H. Litwin, "Motives and Expectancies as Determinants of Preference for Degrees of Risk." In J. W. Atkinson and N. T. Feather, eds., *A Theory of Achievement Motivation.* Wiley, 1966.

A. H. Maslow, *Motivation and Personality*. Harper and Row, 1954.

————, *Motivation and Personality,* 2d ed. Harper and Row, 1970.

D. C. McClelland, "Measuring Motivation in Phantasy: The Achievement Motive." In H. Guetzkow, ed., *Groups, Leadership, and Man.* Carnegie Press, 1951.

————, *The Achieving Society*. Van Nostrand, 1961.

————, *Assessing Human Motivation*. General Learning Press, 1971.

————, "The Role of Educational Technology in Developing Achievement Motivation." In D. C. McClelland R. W. Steele, eds., *Human Motivation: A Book of Readings*. General Learning Press, 1973a.

————, "What Is the Effect of Achievement Motivation Training in the Schools?" In D. C. McClelland and R. S. Steele, eds., *Human Motivation: A Book of Readings*. General Learning Press, 1973b.

D. C. McClelland and D. G. Winter, *Motivating Economic Achievement*. Free Press, 1969.

K. C. Montgomery, "The Role of the Exploratory Drive in Learning." *Journal of Comparative Physiological Psychology,* 1954, 47:60–64.

G. R. Oldham, "Intrinsic Motivation: Relationship to Job Characteristics and Performance." Paper presented at Eastern Psychological Association, 1974.

L. W. Porter and E. E. Lawler, *Managerial Attitudes and Performance*. Irwin Dorsey Press, 1967.

M. Ross, "Salience of Reward and Intrinsic Motivation." *Journal of Personality and Social Psychology,* in press.

J. B. Rotter, "Generalized Expectancies for Internal Versus External Control of Reinforcement." *Psychological Monographs,* 1966, 80: (1), 1–28.

K. W. Spence, *Behavior Theory and Conditioning,* Yale University Press, 1956.

B. M. Staw, "Attitudinal and Behavioral Consequences of Changing a Major Organizational Reward: A Natural Field Experiment." *Journal of Personality and Social Psychology,* 1974a, 6:742–751.

————, "Notes toward a Theory of Intrinsic and Extrinsic Motivation." Paper presented at Eastern Psychological Association. 1974b.

————, "Attribution of the 'Causes' of Performance: A New Alternative Interpretation of Cross-sectional Research on Organizations." *Organizational Behavior and Human Performance,* 1975, 13:414–432.

B. M. Staw, B. J. Calder, and R. Hess, "Intrinsic Motivation and Norms about Payment." Working paper, Northwestern University, 1975.

L. H. Strickland, "Surveillance and Trust." *Journal of Personality,* 1958, 26:200–215.

J. W. Thibaut and H. W. Riecken, "Some Determinants and Consequences of the Perception of Social Causality." *Journal of Personality,* 1955, 24:113–133.

E. C. Tolman, *Purposive Behavior in Animals and Men.* Appleton-Century-Crofts, 1932.

———, "Principles of Performance." *Psychological Review,* 1955, 62:315–326.

C. N. Uhl and A. G. Young, "Resistance to Extinction as a Function of Incentive, Percentage of Reinforcement, and Number of Non-reinforced Trials." *Journal of Experimental Psychology,* 1967, 73: 556–564.

V. H. Vroom, *Work and Motivation.* Wiley, 1964.

K. E. Weick, "Reduction of Cognitive Dissonance through Task Enhancement and Effort Expenditure." *Journal of Abnormal and Social Psychology,* 1964, 68:533–539.

K. E. Weick and D. D. Penner, "Justification and Productivity." Unpublished manuscript, University of Minnesota, 1965.

R. W. White, "Motivation Reconsidered: The Concept of Competence." *Psychological Review,* 1959, 66:297–333.

R. S. Woodworth, *Dynamic Psychology.* Columbia University Press, 1918.

Power is the Great Motivator
David C. McClelland
and David H. Burnham

What makes or motivates a good manager? The question is so enormous in scope that anyone trying to answer it has difficulty knowing where to begin. Some people might say that a good manager is one who is successful; and by now most business researchers and businessmen themselves know what motivates people who successfully run their own small businesses. They key to their success has turned out to be what psychologists call "the need for achievement," the desire to do something better or more efficiently than it has been done before. Any number of books and articles summarize research studies explaining how the achievement motive is necessary for a person to attain success on his own.[1]

But what has achievement motivation got to do with good management? There is no reason on theoretical grounds why a person who has a strong need to be more efficient should make a good manager. While it sounds as if everyone ought to have the need to achieve, in fact, as psychologists define and measure achievement motivation, it leads people to behave in very special ways that do not necessarily lead to good management.

For one thing, because they focus on personal improvement, on doing things better by themselves, achievement-motivated people want to do things themselves. For another, they want concrete short-term feedback on their performance so that they can tell how well they are doing. Yet a manager, particularly one of or in a large complex organization,

Author's note: All the case material in this article is disguised.

Reprinted from the *Harvard Business Review,* March-April, pp. 100–110, by permission of the authors and the publisher. © 1976 by the President and Fellows of Harvard College; all rights reserved.

1. For instance, see my books *The Achieving Society* (New York: Van Nostrand, 1961) and (with David Winter) *Motivating Economic Achievement* (New York: Free Press, 1969).

cannot perform all the tasks necessary for success by himself or herself. He must manage others so that they will do things for the organization. Also, feedback on his subordinate's performance may be a lot vaguer and more delayed than it would be if he were doing everything himself.

The manager's job seems to call more for someone who can influence people than for someone who does things better on his own. In motivational terms, then, we might expect the successful manager to have a greater "need for power" than need to achieve. But there must be other qualities besides the need for power that go into the makeup of a good manager. Just what these qualities are and how they interrelate is the subject of this article.

To measure the motivations of managers, good and bad, we studied a number of individual managers from different large U.S. corporations who were participating in management workshops designed to improve their managerial effectiveness. (The workshop techniques and research methods and terms used are described in the insert on pp. 74–75.

The general conclusion of these studies is that the top manager of a company must possess a high need for power, that is, a concern for influencing people. However, this need must be disciplined and controlled so that it is directed toward the benefit of the institution as a whole and not toward the manager's personal aggrandizement. Moreover, the top manager's need for power ought to be greater than his need for being liked by people.

Now let us look at what these ideas mean in the context of real individuals in real situations and see what comprises the profile of the good manager. Finally, we will look at the workshops themselves to determine how they go about changing behavior.

Measuring managerial effectiveness

First off, what does it mean when we say that a good manager has a greater need for "power" than for "achievement"? To get a more concrete idea, let us consider the case of Ken Briggs, a sales manager in a large U.S. corporation who joined one of our managerial workshops (see p. 74). Some six or seven years ago, Ken Briggs was promoted to a managerial position at corporate headquarters, where he had responsibility for salesmen who service his company's largest accounts.

In filling out his questionnaire at the workshop, Ken showed that he correctly perceived what his job required of him, namely, that he should influence others' success more than achieve new goals himself or socialize with his subordinates. However, when asked with other members of the workshop to write a story depicting a managerial situation, Ken unwittingly revealed through his fiction that he did not share those concerns. Indeed, he discovered that his need for achievement was very high—in fact over the 90th percentile—and his need for power was very low, in about the 15th percentile. Ken's high need to achieve was no surprise—after all, he had been a very successful salesman—but obviously his motivation to influence others was much less than his job required. Ken was a little disturbed but thought that perhaps the measuring instruments were not too accurate and that the gap between the ideal and his score was not as great as it seemed.

Then came the real shocker. Ken's subordinates confirmed what his stories revealed: he was a poor manager, having little positive impact on those who worked for him. Ken's subordinates felt that they had little responsibility delegated to them, that he never rewarded but only criticized them, and that the office was not well organized, but confused and chaotic. On all three of these scales, his office rated in the 10th to 15th percentile relative to national norms.

As Ken talked the results over privately with a workshop leader, he became more and more upset. He finally agreed, however, that the results of the survey confirmed feelings he had been afraid to admit to himself or others. For years, he had been miserable in his managerial role. He now knew the reason: he simply did not want to nor had he been able to influence or manage others. As he thought back, he realized that he had failed every time he had tried to influence his staff, and he felt worse than ever.

Ken had responded to failure by setting very high standards—his office scored in the 98th percentile on this scale—and by trying to do most things himself, which was close to impossible; his own activity and lack of delegation consequently left his staff demoralized. Ken's experience is typical of those who have a strong need to achieve but low power motivation. They may become very successful salesmen and, as a consequence, may be promoted into managerial jobs for which they, ironically, are unsuited. If achievement motivation does not make a good manager, what motive does? It is not enough to suspect that power motivation may be important; one needs hard evidence that people who are better managers than Ken Briggs do in fact possess stronger power motivation and perhaps score higher in other characteristics as well. But how does one decide who is the better manager?

Real-world performance measures are hard to come by if one is trying to rate managerial effectiveness in production, marketing, finance, or research and development. In trying to determine who the better managers were in Ken Briggs's company, we did not want to rely only on the opinions of their superiors. For a variety of reasons, superiors' judgments of their subordinates' real-world performance may be inaccurate. In the absence of some standard measure of performance, we decided that the next best index of a manager's effectiveness would be the climate he or she creates in the office, reflected in the morale of subordinates.

Almost by definition, a good manager is one who, among other things, helps subordinates feel strong and responsible, who rewards them properly for good performance, and who sees that things are organized in such a way that subordinates feel they know what they should be doing. Above all, managers should foster among subordinates a strong sense of team spirit, of pride in working as part of a particular team. If a manager creates and encourages this spirit, his subordinates certainly should perform better.

In the company Ken Briggs works for, we have direct evidence of a connection between morale and performance in the one area where performance measures are easy to come by—namely, sales. In April 1973, at least three employees from this company's 16 sales districts filled out questionnaires that rated their office for organizational clarity and team spirit (see p. 75). Their scores were averaged and totaled to give an overall morale score for each office. The percentage gains or losses in sales for each district in 1973 were compared with those for 1972. The difference in sales figures by district ranged from a gain of nearly 30% to a loss of 8%, with a median gain of around 14%. Figure 1 shows the average gain in sales performance plotted against the increasing averages in morale scores.

In figure 1 we can see that the relationship between sales and morale is surprisingly close. The six districts with the lowest morale early in the year showed an average sales gain of only around 7% by year's end (although there was wide variation within this group), whereas the two districts with the highest morale showed an average gain of 28%. When morale scores rise above the 50th percentile in terms of national norms, they seem to lead to better sales performance. In Ken Briggs's company, at least, high morale at the beginning is a good index of how well the sales division actually performed in the coming year.

And it seems very likely that the manager who can create high morale among salesmen can also do the same for employees in other areas (production, design, and so on), leading to better performance. Given that high morale in an office indicates that there is a good manager present, what general characteristics does he possess?

A Need for Power

In examining the motive scores of over 50 managers of both high and low morale units in all sections of the same large company, we found that most of the managers—over 70%—were high in power motivation compared with men in general. This finding confirms the fact that

Average percent gain in sales by district from 1972 to 1973

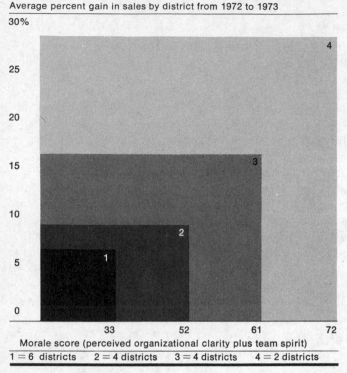

Figure 1. Correlation between morale score and sales performance for a large U.S. corporation.

power motivation is important for management. (Remember that as we use the term "power motivation," it refers not to dictatorial behavior, but to a desire to have impact, to be strong and influential.) The better managers, as judged by the morale of those working for them, tended to score even higher in power motivation. But the most important determining factor of high morale turned out not to be how their power motivation compared to their need to achieve but whether it was higher than their need to be liked. This relationship existed for 80% of the better sales managers as compared with only 10% of the poorer managers. And the same held true for other managers in nearly all parts of the company.

In the research, product development, and operations divisions, 73% of the better managers had a stronger need for power than a need to be liked (or what we term "affiliation motive") as compared with only 22% of the poorer managers. Why should this be so? Sociologists have long argued that, for a bureaucracy to function effectively, those who manage it must be universalistic in applying rules. That is, if they make exceptions for the particular needs of individuals, the whole system will break down.

The manager with a high need for being liked is precisely the one who wants to stay on good terms with everybody, and, therefore, is the one most likely to make exceptions in terms of particular needs. If a male employee asks for time off to stay home with his sick wife to help look after her and the kids, the affiliative manager agrees almost without thinking, because he feels sorry for the man and agrees that his family needs him.

When President Ford remarked in pardoning ex-President Nixon that he had "suffered enough," he was responding as an affiliative manager would, because he was empathizing primarily with Nixon's needs and feelings. Sociological theory and our data both argue, however, that the person whose need for affiliation is high does not make a good manager. This kind of person creates poor morale because he or she does not understand that other people in the office will tend to regard exceptions to the rules as unfair to themselves, just as many U.S. citizens felt it was unfair to let Richard Nixon off and punish others less involved than he was in the Watergate scandal.

Socialized power

But so far our findings are a little alarming. Do they suggest that the good manager is one who cares for power and is not at all concerned about the needs of other people? Not quite, for the good manager has other characteristics which must still be taken into account.

Above all, the good manager's power motivation is not oriented toward personal aggrandizement but toward the institution which he or she serves. In another major research study, we found that the signs of controlled action or inhibition that appear when a person exercises his or her imagination in writing stories tell a great deal about the kind of power that person needs.[2] We discovered that, if a high power motive score is balanced by high inhibition, stories about power tend to be altruistic. That is, the heroes in the story exercise power on behalf of someone else. This is the "socialized" face of power as distinguished from the concern for personal power, which is characteristic of individuals whose stories are loaded with power imagery but which show no sign of inhibition or self-control. In our earlier study, we found ample evidence that these latter individuals exercise their power impulsively. They are more rude to other people, they drink too much,

2. David C. McClelland, William N. Davis, Rudolf Kalin, and Eric Warner, *The Drinking Man* (New York: The Free Press, 1972).

they try to exploit others sexually, and they collect symbols of personal prestige such as fancy cars or big offices.

Individuals high in power and in control, on the other hand, are more institution minded; they tend to get elected to more offices, to control their drinking, and to want to serve others. Not surprisingly, we found in the workshops that the better managers in the corporation also tend to score high on both power and inhibition.

Profile of a good manager

Let us recapitulate what we have discussed so far and have illustrated with data from one company. The better managers we studied are high in power motivation, low in affiliation motivation, and high in inhibition. They care about institutional power and use it to stimulate their employees to be more productive. Now let us compare them with affiliative managers—those in whom the need for affiliation is higher than the need for power—and with the personal power managers—those in whom the need for power is higher than for affiliation but whose inhibition score is low.

In the sales division of our illustrative company, there were managers who matched the three types fairly closely. Figure 2 shows how their subordinates rated the offices they worked in on responsibility, organizational clarity, and team spirit. There are scores from at least three subordinates for each manager, and several managers are represented for each type, so that the averages shown in the exhibit are quite stable. Note that the manager who is concerned about being liked by people tends to have subordinates who feel that they have very little personal responsibility, that organizational procedures are not clear, and that they have little pride in their work group.

In short, as we expected, affiliative managers make so many ad hominem and ad hoc decisions that they almost totally abandon orderly procedures. Their disregard for procedure leaves employees feeling weak, irresponsible, and without a sense of what might happen next, of where they stand in relation to their manager, or even of what they ought to be doing. In this company, the group of affiliative managers portrayed in figure 2 were below the 30th percentile in morale scores.

The managers who are motivated by a need for personal power are somewhat more effective. They are able to create a greater sense of responsibility in their divisions and, above all, a greater team spirit. They can be thought of as managerial equivalents of successful tank commanders such as General Patton, whose own daring inspired admiration in his troops. But notice how in figure 2 these men are still only in the 40th percentile in the amount of organizational clarity they

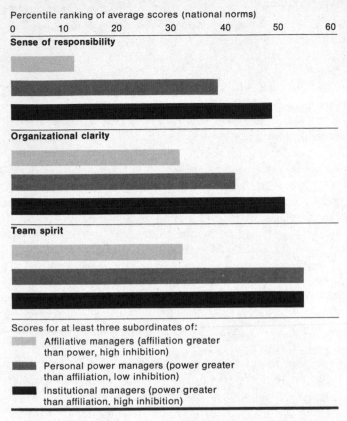

Figure 2. Average scores on selected climate dimensions by subordinates of managers with different motive profiles.

create, as compared to the high power, low affiliation, high inhibition managers, whom we shall term "institutional."

Managers motivated by personal power are not disciplined enough to be good institution builders, and often their subordinates are loyal to them as individuals rather than to the institution they both serve. When a personal power manager leaves, disorganization often follows. His subordinates' strong group spirit, which the manager has personally inspired, deflates. The subordinates do not know what to do for themselves.

Of the managerial types, the "institutional" manager is the most successful in creating an effective work climate. Figure 2 shows that his subordinates feel that they have more responsibility. Also, this kind of manager creates high morale because he produces the greatest

sense of organizational clarity and team spirit. If such a manager
leaves, he or she can be more readily replaced by another manager, because the employees have been encouraged to be loyal to the institution
rather than to a particular person.

Managerial styles

Since it seems undeniable from figure 2 that either kind of power
orientation creates better morale in subordinates than a "people" orientation, we must consider that a concern for power is essential to
good management. Our findings seem to fly in the face of a long and
influential tradition of organizational psychology, which insists that
authoritarian management is what is wrong with most businesses in
this country. Let us say frankly that we think the bogeyman of authoritarianism has in fact been wrongly used to downplay the importance
of power in management. After all, management is an influence game.
Some proponents of democratic management seem to have forgotten
this fact, urging managers to be primarily concerned with people's
human needs rather than with helping them to get things done.

But a good deal of the apparent conflict between our findings and
those of other behavioral scientists in this area arises from the fact
that we are talking about *motives,* and behaviorists are often talking
about *actions.* What we are saying is that managers must be interested
in playing the influence game in a controlled way. That does not necessarily mean that they are or should be authoritarian in action. On the
contrary, it appears that power-motivated managers make their subordinates feel strong rather than weak. The true authoritarian in action
would have the reverse effect, making people feel weak and powerless.

Thus another important ingredient in the profile of a manager is his
or her managerial style. In the illustrative company, 63% of the better
managers (those whose subordinates had higher morale) scored higher
on the democratic or coaching styles of management as compared with
only 22% of the poorer managers, a statistically significant difference.
By contrast, the latter scored higher on authoritarian or coercive management styles. Since the better managers were also higher in power
motivation, it seems that, in action, they express their power motivation in a democratic way, which is more likely to be effective.

To see how motivation and style interact, let us consider the case
of George Prentice, a manager in the sales division of another company. George had exactly the right motive combination to be an institutional manager. He was high in the need for power, low in the need
for affiliation, and high in inhibition. He exercised his power in a controlled, organized way. His stories reflected this fact. In one, for instance, he wrote, "The men sitting around the table were feeling pretty

good; they had just finished plans for reorganizing the company; the company has been beset with a number of organizational problems. This group, headed by a hard driving, brilliant young executive, has completely reorganized the company structurally with new jobs and responsibilities. . . ."

This described how George himself was perceived by the company, and shortly after the workshop he was promoted to vice-president in charge of all sales. But George was also known to his colleagues as a monster, a tough guy who would "walk over his grandmother" if she stood in the way of his advancement. He had the right motive combination and, in fact, was more interested in institutional growth than in personal power, but his managerial style was all wrong. Taking his cue from some of the top executives in the corporation, he told people what they had to do and threatened them with dire consequences if they didn't do it.

When George was confronted with his authoritarianism in a workshop, he recognized that this style was counterproductive—in fact, in another part of the study we found that it was associated with low morale—and he subsequently changed to acting more like a coach, which was the scale on which he scored the lowest initially. George saw more clearly that his job was not to force other people to do things but to help them to figure out ways of getting their job done better for the company.

The institutional manager

One reason it was easy for George Prentice to change his managerial style was that in his imaginative stories he was already having thoughts about helping others, characteristic of men with the institution-building motivational pattern. In further examining institution builders' thoughts and actions, we found they have four major characteristics:

1. They are more organization-minded, that is, they tend to join more organizations and to feel responsible for building up these organizations. Furthermore, they believe strongly in the importance of centralized authority.

2. They report that they like to work. This finding is particularly interesting because our research on achievement motivation has led many commentators to argue that achievement motivation promotes the "Protestant work ethic." Almost the precise opposite is true. People who have a high need to achieve like to get out of work by becoming more efficient. They would like to see the same result obtained in less time or with less effort. But managers who have a need for institutional power actually seem to like the discipline of work. It satisfies their need for getting things done in an orderly way.

3. They seem quite willing to sacrifice some of their own self-interest for the welfare of the organization they serve. For example, they are more willing to make contributions to charities.

4. They have a keen sense of justice. It is almost as if they feel that if a person works hard and sacrifices for the good of the organization, he should and will get a just reward for his effort.

It is easy to see how each of these four concerns helps a person become a good manager, concerned about what the institution can achieve.

Maturity

Before we go on to look at how the workshops can help managers to improve their managerial style and recognize their own motivations, let us consider one more fact we discovered in studying the better managers at George Prentice's company. They were more mature (see pp. 74–75). Mature people can be most simply described as less egotistic. Somehow their positive self-image is not at stake in what they are doing. They are less defensive, more willing to seek advice from experts, and have a longer-range view. They accumulate fewer personal possessions and seem older and wiser. It is as if they have awakened to the fact that they are not going to live forever and have lost some of the feeling that their own personal future is all that important.

Many U.S. businessmen fear this kind of maturity. They suspect that it will make them less hard-driving, less expansion-minded, and less committed to organizational effectiveness. Our data do not support their fears. These fears are exactly the ones George Prentice had before he went to the workshop. Afterward he was a more effective manager, not despite his loss of some of the sense of his own importance, but because of it. The reason is simple: his subordinates believed afterward that he genuinely was more concerned about the company than about himself. Where once they respected his confidence but feared him, they now trust him. Once he supported their image of him as a "big man" by talking about the new Porsche and the new Honda he had bought; when we saw him recently he said, almost as an aside, "I don't buy things anymore."

Changing managerial style

George Prentice was able to change his managerial style after learning more about himself in a workshop. But does self-knowledge generally improve managerial behavior?

Some people might ask, "What good does it do to know, if I am a manager, that I should have a strong power motive, not too great a concern about being liked, a sense of discipline, a high level of maturity, and a coaching managerial style? What can I do about it?" The answer is that workshops for managers that give information to them in a supportive setting enable them to change.

Consider the results shown in figure 3, where "before" and "after" scores are compared. Once again we use the responses of subordinates to give some measure of the effectiveness of managers. To judge by their subordinates' responses, the managers were clearly more effective afterward. The subordinates felt that they were given more responsibility, that they received more rewards, that the organizational procedures were clearer, and that morale was higher. These differences are all statistically significant.

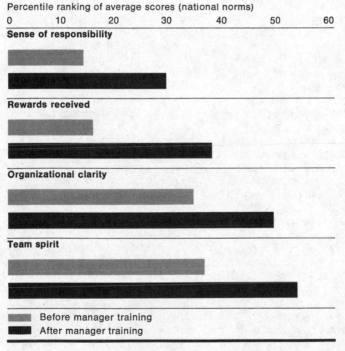

Figure 3. Average scores on selected climate dimensions by over 50 salesmen before and after their managers were trained.

But what do these differences mean in human terms? How did the managers change? Sometimes they decided they should get into another line of work. This happened to Ken Briggs, for example, who found that the reason he was doing so poorly as a manager was because he had almost no interest in influencing others. He understood how he would have to change if he were to do well in his present job, but in

Workshop techniques

The case studies and data on companies used in this article were derived from a number of workshops we conducted where executives came to learn about their managerial styles and abilities as well as how to change them. The workshops had a dual purpose, however. They provided an opportunity for us to study which motivation pattern, whether it be a concern for achievement, power, people, or a combination thereof, makes the best managers.

When the managers first arrived at the workshops, they were asked to fill out a questionnaire about their job. Each participant analyzed his job, explaining what he or she thought it required of him. The managers were asked to write a number of stories to pictures of various work situations. The stories were coded for the extent to which an individual was concerned about achievement, affiliation, or power, as well as for the amount of inhibition or self-control they revealed. The results were then matched against national norms. The differences between a person's job requirements and his or her motivational patterns can often help assess whether the person is in the right job, whether he is a candidate for promotion to another job, or whether he is likely to be able to adjust to fit his present position.

At the workshops and in this article, we use the technical terms "need for achievement," "need for power," and "need for affiliation" as defined in the books *The Achieving Society* and *Power: The Inner Experience*. The terms refer to measurable factors in groups and individuals. Briefly, these characteristics are measured by coding an individual's spontaneous thoughts for the frequency with which he thinks about doing something better or more efficiently than before (need for achievement), about establishing or maintaining friendly relations with others (need for affiliation), or about having impact on others (need for power). (When we talk about power, we are not talking about dictatorial power, but about the need to be strong and influential.) As used here, therefore, the motive labels are precise terms, referring to a particular method of defining and measuring, much as "gravity" is used in physics, or "gross national product" is used in economics.

To find out what kind of managerial style the participants had, we gave them a questionnaire in which they had to choose how they would handle various realistic work situations in office settings. Their answers were coded for six different management styles or ways of dealing with work situations. The styles depicted were democratic, affiliative, pace-setting, coaching, coercive, and authoritarian. The managers were asked to comment on the effectiveness of each style and to name the style that they prefer.

One way to determine how effective managers are is to ask the people who work for them. Thus, to isolate the characteristics that good managers have, we surveyed at least three subordinates of each manager at the workshop to see how they answered questions about their work situations that revealed characteristics of their supervisors along several dimensions, namely: (1) the amount of conformity to rules required, (2) the responsibility they feel they are given, (3) the emphasis the department places on standards of performance, (4) the degree to which they feel rewards are given for good work as opposed to punishment for something that goes wrong, (5) the degree of organizational clarity in the office, and (6) its team spirit.* The managers who received the highest morale scores (organizational clarity plus team spirit) from their subordinates were determined to be the best managers, possessing the most desirable motive patterns.

The subordinates were also surveyed six months after the managers returned to their offices to see if the morale scores rose after the workshop.

One other measure was obtained from the participants to find out which managers had another characteristic deemed important for good management: maturity. Scores were obtained for four stages in the progress toward maturity by coding the stories which the managers wrote for such matters as their attitudes toward authority and the kinds of emotions displayed over specific issues.

People in stage 1 are dependent on others for guidance and strength. Those in stage 2 are interested primarily in autonomy, in controlling themselves. In stage 3, people want to manipulate others; in stage 4, they lose their egotistic desires and wish to selflessly serve others.† The conclusions presented in this article are based on workshops attended by over 500 managers from over 25 different U.S. corporations. However, the data in the exhibits are drawn from just one of these companies for illustrative purposes.

* Based on G. H. Litwin and R. A. Stringer's *Motivation and Organizational Climate* (Boston: Division of Research, Harvard Business School, 1966).

† Based on work by Abigail Stewart reported in David C. McClelland's *Power: The Inner Experience* (New York: Irvington Publishers, 1975).

the end decided, with the help of management, that he would prefer to work back into his first love, sales.

Ken Briggs moved into "remaindering," to help retail outlets for his company's products get rid of last year's stock so that they could take on each year's new styles. He is very successful in this new role; he has cut costs, increased dollar volume, and in time has worked himself into an independent role selling some of the old stock on his own in a way that is quite satisfactory to the business. And he does not have to manage anybody anymore.

In George Prentice's case, less change was needed. He was obviously a very competent person with the right motive profile for a top managerial position. When he was promoted, he performed even more successfully than before because he realized the need to become more positive in his approach and less coercive in his managerial style.

But what about a person who does not want to change his job and discovers that he does not have the right motive profile to be a manager?

The case of Charlie Blake is instructive. Charlie was as low in power motivation as Ken Briggs, his need to achieve was about average, and his affiliation motivation was above average. Thus he had the affiiliative manager profile, and, as expected, the morale among his subordinates was very low. When Charlie learned that his subordinates' sense of responsibility and perception of a reward system were in the 10th percentile and that team spirit was in the 30th, he was shocked. When shown a film depicting three managerial climates, Charlie said he preferred what turned out to be the authoritarian climate. He became angry when the workshop trainer and other members in the group pointed out the limitations of this managerial style. He became obstructive in the group process and objected strenuously to what was being taught.

In an interview conducted much later, Charlie said, "I blew my cool. When I started yelling at you for being all wrong, I got even madder when you pointed out that, according to my style questionnaire, you bet that was just what I did to my salesmen. Down underneath I knew something must be wrong. The sales performance for my division wasn't so good. Most of it was due to me anyway and not to my salesmen. Obviously their reports that they felt very little responsibility was delegated to them and that I didn't reward them at all had to mean something. So I finally decided to sit down and try to figure what I could do about it. I knew I had to start being a manager instead of trying to do everything myself and blowing my cool at others because they didn't do what I thought they should. In the end, after I calmed down on the way back from the workshop, I realized that it is not so bad to make a mistake; it's bad not to learn from it."

After the course, Charlie put his plans into effect. Six months later, his subordinates were asked to rate him again. He attended a second workshop to study these results and reported, "On the way home I was very nervous. I knew I had been working with those guys and not selling so much myself, but I was very much afraid of what they were going to say about how things were going in the office. When I found out that the team spirit and some of those other low scores had jumped from around 30th to the 55th percentile, I was so delighted and relieved that I couldn't say anything all day long."

When he was asked how he acted differently from before, he said, "In previous years when the corporate headquarters said we had to make 110% of our original goal, I had called the salesmen in and said, in effect, 'This is ridiculous; we are not going to make it, but you know perfectly well what will happen if we don't. So get out there and work your tail off.' The result was that I worked 20 hours a day and they did nothing.

"This time I approached it differently. I told them three things. First, they were going to have to do some sacrificing for the company. Second, working harder is not going to do much good because we are already working about as hard as we can. What will be required are special deals and promotions. You are going to have to figure out some new angles if we are to make it. Third, I'm going to back you up. I'm going to set a realistic goal with each of you. If you make that goal but don't make the company goal, I'll see to it that you are not punished. But if you do make the company goal, I'll see to it that you will get some kind of special rewards."

When the salesmen challenged Charlie saying he did not have enough influence to give them rewards, rather than becoming angry Charlie promised rewards that were in his power to give—such as longer vacations.

Note that Charlie has now begun to behave in a number of ways that we found to be characteristic of the good institutional manager. He is, above all, higher in power motivation, the desire to influence his salesmen, and lower in his tendency to try to do everything himself. He asks the men to sacrifice for the company. He does not defensively chew them out when they challenge him but tries to figure out what their needs are so that he can influence them. He realizes that his job is more one of strengthening and supporting his subordinates than of criticizing them. And he is keenly interested in giving them just rewards for their efforts.

The changes in his approach to his job have certainly paid off. The sales figures for his office in 1973 were up more than 16% over 1972 and up still further in 1974 over 1973. In 1973 his gain over the previous year ranked seventh in the nation; in 1974 it ranked third. And he wasn't the only one in his company to change managerial styles. Overall sales at his company were up substantially in 1973 as compared with 1972, an increase which played a large part in turning the overall company performance around from a $15 million loss in 1972 to a $3 million profit in 1973. The company continued to improve its performance in 1974 with an 11% further gain in sales and a 38% increase in profits.

Of course not everyone can be reached by a workshop. Henry Carter managed a sales office for a company which had very low morale (around the 20th percentile) before he went for training. When morale was checked some six months later, it had not improved. Overall sales gain subsequently reflected this fact since it was only 2% above the previous year's figures.

Oddly enough, Henry's problem was that he was so well liked by everybody that he felt little pressure to change. Always the life of the party, he is particularly popular because he supplies other managers with special hard-to-get brands of cigars and wines at a discount. He uses his close ties with everyone to bolster his position in the company, even though it is known that his office does not perform well compared with others.

His great interpersonal skills became evident at the workshop when he did very poorly at one of the business games. When the discussion turned to why he had done so badly and whether he acted that way on the job, two prestigious participants immediately sprang to his defense, explaining away Henry's failure by arguing that the way he did things was often a real help to others and the company. As a result, Henry did not have to cope with such questions at all. He had so successfully developed his role as a likeable, helpful friend to everyone in management that, even though his salesmen performed badly, he did not feel under any pressure to change.

Checks and balances

What have we learned from Ken Briggs, George Prentice, Charlie Blake, and Henry Carter? Principally, we have discovered what motive combination makes an effective manager. We have also seen that change is possible if a person has the right combination of qualities.

Oddly enough, the good manager in a large company does not have a high need for achievement, as we define and measure that motive, although there must be plenty of that motive somewhere in his organization. The top managers shown here have a high need for power and an interest in influencing others, both greater than their interest in being liked by people. The manager's concern for power should be socialized—controlled so that the institution as a whole, not only the individual, benefits. Men and nations with this motive profile are empire builders; they tend to create high morale and to expand the organizations they head.

But there is also danger in this motive profile; empire building can lead to imperialism and authoritarianism in companies and in countries.

The same motive pattern which produces good power management can also lead a company or a country to try to dominate others, ostensibly in the interests of organizational expansion. Thus it is not surprising that big business has had to be regulated from time to time by federal agencies. And it is most likely that international agencies will perform the same regulative function for empire-building countries.

For an individual, the regulative function is performed by two characteristics that are part of the profile of the very best managers: a greater emotional maturity, where there is little egotism, and a democratic, coaching managerial style. If an institutional power motivation is checked by maturity, it does not lead to an aggressive, egotistic expansiveness.

For countries, this checking means that they can control their destinies beyond their borders without being aggressive and hostile. For individuals, it means they can control their subordinates and influence others around them without resorting to coercion or to an authoritarian management style. Real disinterested statesmanship has a vital role to play at the top of both countries and companies.

Summarized in this way, what we have found out through empirical and statistical investigations may just sound like good common sense. But the improvement over common sense is that now the characteristics of the good manager are objectively known. Managers of corporations can select those who are likely to be good managers and train those already in managerial positions to be more effective with more confidence.

A New Strategy for Job Enrichment

J. Richard Hackman, Greg Oldham, Robert Janson, and Kenneth Purdy

Practitioners of job enrichment have been living through a time of excitement, even euphoria. Their craft has moved from the psychology and management journals to the front page and the Sunday supplement. Job enrichment, which began with the pioneering work of Herzberg and his associates, originally was intended as a means to increase the motivation and satisfaction of people at work—and to improve productivity in the bargain. (1–5) Now it is being acclaimed in the popular press as a cure for problems ranging from inflation to drug abuse.

Much current writing about job enrichment is enthusiastic, sometimes even messianic, about what it can accomplish. But the hard questions of exactly what should be done to improve jobs, and how, tend to be glossed over. Lately, because the harder questions have not been dealt with adequately, critical winds have begun to blow. Job enrichment has been described as yet another "management fad," as "nothing new," even as a fraud. And reports of job-enrichment failures are beginning to appear in management and psychology journals.

This article attempts to redress the excesses that have characterized some of the recent writings about job enrichment. As the technique increases in popularity as a management tool, top managers inevitably will find themselves making decisions about its use. The intent of this paper is to help both managers and behavioral scientists become better able to make those decisions on a solid basis of fact and data.

Succinctly stated, we present here a new strategy for going about the redesign of work. The strategy is based on three years of collaborative work and cross-fertilization among the authors— two of whom are academic researchers and two of whom are active practitioners in job enrichment. Our approach is new, but it has been tested in many organizations. It draws on the contributions of both management practice and psychological theory, but it is firmly in the middle ground between them. It builds on and complements previous work by Herzberg and others, but provides for the first time a set of tools for *diagnosing* existing jobs—and a map for translating the diagnostic results into specific action steps for change.

What we have, then, is the following:

1. A theory that specifies when people will get personally "turned on" to their work. The theory shows what kinds of jobs are most likely to generate excitement and commitment about work, and what kinds of employees it works best for.

2. A set of action steps for job enrichment based on the theory, which prescribe in concrete terms what to do to make jobs more motivating for the people who do them.

3. Evidence that the theory holds water and that it can be used to bring about measurable—and sometimes dramatic—improvements in employee work behavior, in job satisfaction, and in the financial performance of the organizational unit involved.

The theory behind the strategy

What makes people get turned on to their work?

For workers who are really prospering in their jobs, work is likely to be a lot like play. Consider, for example, a golfer at a driving range, practicing to get rid of a hook. His activity is *meaningful* to him; he has chosen to do it because he gets a "kick" from testing his skills by playing the game. He knows that he alone is *responsible* for what happens when he hits the ball. And he has *knowledge of the results* within a few seconds.

Behavioral scientists have found that the three "psychological states" experienced by the golfer in the above example also are critical in determining a person's motivation and satisfaction on the job.

Experienced meaningfulness

The individual must perceive his work as worthwhile or important by some system of values he accepts.

Experienced responsibility

He must believe that he personally is accountable for the outcomes of his efforts.

Knowledge of results

He must be able to determine, on some fairly regular basis, whether or not the outcomes of his work are satisfactory.

When these three conditions are present, a person tends to feel very good about himself when he performs well. And those good feelings will prompt him to try to continue to do well—so he can continue to earn the positive feelings in the future. That is what is meant by "internal motivation"—being turned on to one's work because of the positive internal feelings that are generated by doing well, rather than being dependent on external factors (such as incentive pay or compliments from the boss) for the motivation to work effectively.

What if one of the three psychological states is missing? Motivation drops markedly. Suppose, for example, that our golfer has settled in at the driving range to practice for a couple of hours. Suddenly a fog drifts in over the range. He can no longer see if the ball starts to tail off to the left a hundred yards out. The satisfaction he got from hitting straight down the middle—and the motivation to try to correct something whenever he didn't—are both gone. If the fog stays, it's likely that he soon will be packing up his clubs.

The relationship between the three psychological states and on-the-job outcomes is illustrated in figure. 1. When all three are high, then internal work motivation, job satisfaction, and work quality are high, and absenteeism and turnover are low.

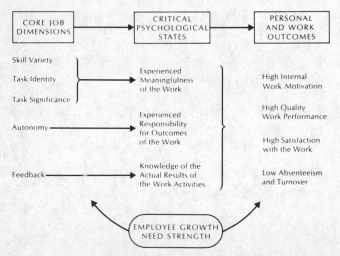

Figure 1. Relationships among core job dimensions, critical psychological states, and on-the-job outcomes.

What job characteristics make it happen?

Recent research has identified five "core" characteristics of jobs that elicit the psychological states described above. (6–8) These five core job dimensions provide the key to objectively measuring jobs and to changing them so that they have high potential for motivating people who do them.

Toward meaningful work. Three of the five core dimensions contribute to a job's meaningfulness for the worker:

1. Skill Variety—the degree to which a job requires the worker to perform activities that challenge his skills and abilities. When even a single skill is involved, there is at least a seed of potential meaningfulness. When several are involved, the job has the potential of appealing to more of the whole person, and also of avoiding the monotony of performing the same task repeatedly, no matter how much skill it may require.

2. Task Identity—the degree to which the job requires completion of a "whole" and identifiable piece of work—doing a job from beginning to end with a visible outcome. For example, it is clearly more meaningful to an employee to build complete toasters than to attach electrical cord after electrical cord, especially if he never sees a completed toaster. (Note that the whole job, in this example, probably would involve greater skill variety as well as task identity.)

3. Task Significance—the degree to which the job has a substantial and perceivable impact on the lives of other people, whether in the immediate organization or the world at large. The worker who tightens nuts on aircraft brake assemblies is more likely to perceive his work as significant than the worker who fills small boxes with paper clips— even though the skill levels involved may be comparable.

Each of these three job dimensions represents an important route to experienced meaningfulness. If the job is high in all three, the worker is quite likely to experience his job as very meaningful. It is not necessary, however, for a job to be very high in all three dimensions. If the job is low in any one of them, there will be a drop in overall experienced meaningfulness. But even when two dimensions are low the worker may find the job meaningful if the third is high enough.

Toward personal responsibility. A fourth core dimension leads a worker to experience increased responsibility in his job. This is *autonomy,* the degree to which the job gives the worker freedom, independence, and discretion in scheduling work and determining how he will carry it out. People in highly autonomous jobs know that they are personally responsible for successes and failures. To the extent that their autonomy is high, then, how the work goes will be felt to depend more on the individual's own efforts and initiatives rather than on detailed instructions from the boss or from a manual of job procedures.

Toward knowledge of results. The fifth and last core dimension is *feedback*. This is the degree to which a worker, in carrying out the work activities required by the job, gets information about the effectiveness of his efforts. Feedback is most powerful when it comes directly from the work itself—for example, when a worker has the responsibility for gauging and otherwise checking a component he has just finished, and learns in the process that he has lowered his reject rate by meeting specifications more consistently.

The overall "motivating potential" of a job. Figure 1 shows how the five core dimensions combine to affect the psychological states that are critical in determining whether or not an employee will be internally motivated to work effectively. Indeed, when using an instrument to be described later, it is possible to compute a "motivating potential score" (MPS) for any job. The MPS provides a single summary index of the degree to which the objective characteristics of the job will prompt high internal work motivation. Following the theory outlined above, a job high in motivating potential must be high in at least one (and hopefully more) of the three dimensions that lead to experienced meaningfulness and high in both autonomy and feedback as well. The MPS provides a quantitative index of the degree to which this is in fact the case* As will be seen later, the MPS can be very useful in diagnosing jobs and in assessing the effectiveness of job-enrichment activities.

Does the theory work for everybody?

Unfortunately not. Not everyone is able to become internally motivated in his work, even when the motivating potential of a job is very high indeed.

Research has shown that the *psychological needs* of people are very important in determining who can (and who cannot) become internally motivated at work. Some people have strong needs for personal

---

* For the algebraically inclined, the Motivating Potential Score is computed as follows

$$\text{MPS} = \left[\frac{\text{Skill Variety} + \text{Task Identity} + \text{Task Significance}}{3} \right] \text{X Autonomy} \quad \text{X Feedback}$$

It should be noted that in some cases the MPS score can be *too* high for positive job satisfaction and effective performance—in effect overstimulating the person who holds the job. This paper focuses on jobs which are toward the low end of the scale—and which potentially can be improved through job enrichment.

accomplishment, for learning and developing themselves beyond where they are now, for being stimulated and challenged, and so on. These people are high in "growth-need strength."

Figure 2 shows diagrammatically the proposition that individual growth needs have the power to moderate the relationship between the characteristics of jobs and work outcomes. Many workers with high growth needs will turn on eagerly when they have jobs that are high in the core dimensions. Workers whose growth needs are not so strong may respond less eagerly—or, at first, even balk at being "pushed" or "stretched" too far.

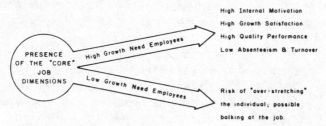

Figure 2. The moderating effect of employee growth-need strength.

Psychologists who emphasize human potential argue that everyone has within him at least a spark of the need to grow and develop personally. Steadily accumulating evidence shows, however, that unless that spark is pretty strong, chances are it will get snuffed out by one's experiences in typical organizations. So, a person who has worked for twenty years in stultifying jobs may find it difficult or impossible to become internally motivated overnight when given the opportunity.

We should be cautious, however, about creating rigid categories of people based on their measured growth-need strength at any particular time. It is true that we can predict from these measures who is likely to become internally motivated on a job and who will be less willing or able to do so. But what we do not know yet is whether or not the growth-need "spark" can be rekindled for those individuals who have had their growth needs dampened by years of growth-depressing experience in their organizations.

Since it is often the organization that is responsible for currently low levels of growth desires, we believe that the organization also should provide the individual with the chance to reverse that trend whenever possible, even if that means putting a person in a job where he may be "stretched" more than he wants to be. He can always move back later to the old job—and in the meantime the embers of his growth needs just might burst back into flame, to his surprise and pleasure, and for the good of the organization.

From theory to practice: a technology for job enrichment

When job enrichment fails, it often fails because of inadequate *diagnosis* of the target job and employees' reactions to it. Often, for example, job enrichment is assumed by management to be a solution to "people problems" on the job and is implemented even though there has been no diagnostic activity to indicate that the root of the problem is in fact how the work is designed. At other times, some diagnosis is made—but it provides no concrete guidance about what specific aspects of the job require change. In either case, the success of job enrichment may wind up depending more on the quality of the intuition of the change agent—or his luck—than on a solid base of data about the people and the work.

In the paragraphs to follow, we outline a new technology for use in job enrichment which explicitly addresses the diagnostic as well as the action components of the change process. The technology has two parts: (1) a set of diagnostic tools that are useful in evaluating jobs and people's reactions to them prior to change—and in pinpointing exactly what aspects of specific jobs are most critical to a successful change attempt; and (2) a set of "implementing concepts" that provide concrete guidance for action steps in job enrichment. The implementing concepts are tied directly to the diagnostic tools; the output of the diagnostic activity specifies which action steps are likely to have the most impact in a particular situation.

The diagnostic tools

Central to the diagnostic procedure we propose is a package of instruments to be used by employees, supervisors, and outside observers in assessing the target job and employees' reactions to it. (9) These instruments gauge the following:

1. The objective characteristics of the jobs themselves, including both an overall indication of the "motivating potential" of the job as it exists (that is, the MPS score) and the score of the job on each of the five core dimensions described previously. Because knowing the strengths and weaknesses of the job is critical to any work-redesign effort, assessments of the job are made by supervisors and outside observers as well as the employees themselves—and the final assessment of a job uses data from all three sources.

2. The current levels of motivation, satisfaction, and work performance of employees on the job. In addition to satisfaction with the work itself, measures are taken of how people feel about other aspects of the work setting, such as pay, supervision, and relationships with co-workers.

3. The level of growth-need strength of the employees. As indicated earlier, employees who have strong growth needs are more likely to be more responsive to job enrichment than employees with weak growth needs. Therefore, it is important to know at the outset just what kinds of satisfactions the people who do the job are (and are not) motivated to obtain from their work. This will make it possible to identify which persons are best to start changes with, and which may need help in adapting to the newly enriched job.

What, then, might be the actual steps one would take in carrying out a job diagnosis using these tools? Although the approach to any particular diagnosis depends upon the specifics of the particular work situation involved, the sequence of questions listed below is fairly typical.

Step 1. Are motivation and satisfaction central to the problem? Sometimes organizations undertake job enrichment to improve the work motivation and satisfaction of employees when in fact the real problem with work performance lies elsewhere—for example, in a poorly designed production system, in an error-prone computer, and so on. The first step is to examine the scores of employees on the motivation and satisfaction portions of the diagnostic instrument. (The questionnaire taken by employees is called the job diagnostic survey and will be referred to hereafter as the JDS.) If motivation and satisfaction are problematic, the change agent would continue to step 2; if not, he would look to other aspects of the work situation to identify the real problem.

Step 2. Is the job low in motivating potential? To answer this question, one would examine the motivating potential score of the target job and compare it to the MPSs of other jobs to determine whether or not *the job itself* is a probable cause of the motivational problems documented in step 1. If the job turns out to be low on the MPS, one would continue to step 3; if it scores high, attention should be given to other possible reasons for the motivational difficulties (such as the pay system, the nature of supervision, and so on).

Step 3. What specific aspects of the job are causing the difficulty? This step involves examining the job on each of the five core dimensions to pinpoint the specific strengths and weaknesses of the job as it is currently structured. It is useful at this stage to construct a "profile" of the target job, to make visually apparent where improvements need to be made. An illustrative profile for two jobs (one "good" job and one job needing improvement) is shown in figure 3.

Job A is an engineering maintenance job and is high on all of the core dimensions; the MPS of this job is a very high 260. (MPS scores can range from 1 to about 350; an "average" score would be about 125.)

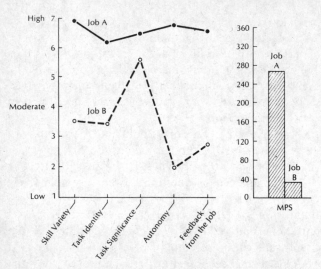

Figure 3. The JDS diagnostic profile for a "good" and a "bad" job.

Job enrichment would not be recommended for this job; if employees working on the job were unproductive and unhappy, the reasons are likely to have little to do with the nature or design of the work itself.

Job B, on the other hand, has many problems. This job involves the routine and repetitive processing of checks in the "back room" of a bank. The MPS is 30, which is quite low—and indeed, would be even lower if it were not for the moderately high task significance of the job. (Task significance is moderately high because the people are handling large amounts of other people's money, and therefore the quality of their efforts potentially has important consequences for for their unseen clients.) The job provides the individuals with very little direct feedback about how effectively they are doing it: the employees have little autonomy in how they go about doing the job; and the job is moderately low in both skill variety and task identity.

For Job B, then, there is plenty of room for improvement—and many avenues to examine in planning job changes. For still other jobs, the avenues for change often turn out to be considerably more specific: for example, feedback and autonomy may be reasonably high, but one or more of the core dimensions that contribute to the experienced meaningfulness of the job (skill variety, task identity, and task significance) may be low. In such a case, attention would turn to ways to increase the standing of the job on these latter three dimensions.

Step 4. How "ready" are the employees for change? Once it has been documented that there is need for improvement in the job and the particularly troublesome aspects of the job have been identified then it is time to begin to think about the specific action steps which will be taken to enrich the job. An important factor in such planning is the level of growth needs of the employees, since employees high on growth needs usually respond more readily to job enrichment than do employees with little need for growth. The JDS provides a direct measure of the growth-need strength of the employees. This measure can be very helpful in planning how to introduce the changes to the people (for instance, cautiously versus dramatically), and in deciding who should be among the first group of employees to have their jobs changed.

In actual use of the diagnostic package, additional information is generated which supplements and expands the basic diagnostic questions outlined above. The point of the above discussion is merely to indicate the kinds of questions which we believe to be most important in diagnosing a job prior to changing it. We now turn to how the diagnostic conclusions are translated into specific job changes.

The implementing concepts

Five "implementing concepts" for job enrichment are identified and discussed below. (10) Each one is a specific action step aimed at improving both the quality of the working experience for the individual and his work productivity. They are: (1) forming natural work units; (2) combining tasks; (3) establishing client relationships; (4) vertical loading; (5) opening feedback channels.

The links between the implementing concepts and the core dimensions are shown in figure 4—which illustrates our theory of job enrichment, ranging from the concrete action steps through the core dimensions and the psychological states to the actual personal and work outcomes.

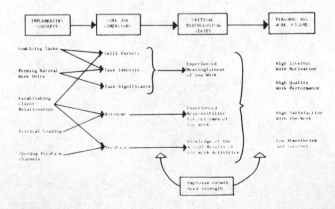

Figure 4. The full model: how use of the implementing concepts can lead to positive outcomes.

After completing the diagnosis of a job, a change agent would know which of the core dimensions were most in need of remedial attention. He could then turn to figure 4 and select those implementing concepts that specifically deal with the most troublesome parts of the existing job. How this would take place in practice will be seen below.

Forming natural work units. The notion of distributing work in some logical way may seem to be an obvious part of the design of any job. In many cases, however, the logic is one imposed by just about any consideration except job-holder satisfaction and motivation. Such considerations include technological dictates, level of worker training or experience, "efficiency" as defined by industrial engineering, and current workload. In many cases the cluster of tasks a worker faces during a typical day or week is natural to anyone *but* the worker.

For example, suppose that a typing pool (consisting of one supervisor and ten typists) handles all work for one division of a company. Jobs are delivered in rough draft or dictated form to the supervisor, who distributes them as evenly as possible among the typists. In such circumstances the individual letters, reports, and other tasks performed by a given typist in one day or week are randomly assigned. There is no basis for identifying with the work or the person or department for whom it is performed, or for placing any personal value upon it.

The principle underlying natural units of work, by contrast, is "ownership"—a worker's sense of continuing responsibility for an identifiable body of work. Two steps are involved in creating natural work units. The first is to identify the basic work items. In the typing pool, for example, the items might be "pages to be typed." The second step is to group the items in natural categories. For example, each typist might be assigned continuing responsibility for all jobs requested by one or several specific departments. The assignments should be made, of course, in such a way that workloads are about equal in the long run. (For example, one typist might end up with all the work from one busy department, while another handles jobs from several smaller units.)

At this point we can begin to see specifically how the job-design principles relate to the core dimensions (cf. figure 4). The ownership fostered by natural units of work can make the difference between a feeling that work is meaningful and rewarding and the feeling that it is irrelevant and boring. As the diagram shows, natural units of work are directly related to two of the core dimensions: task identity and task significance.

A typist whose work is assigned naturally rather than randomly— say, by departments—has a much greater chance of performing a whole job to completion. Instead of typing one section of a large report, the individual is likely to type the whole thing, with knowledge of exactly what the product of the work is (task identity). Furthermore, over time the typist will develop a growing sense of how the work affects co-workers in the department serviced (task significance).

Combining tasks. The very existence of a pool made up entirely of persons whose sole function is typing reflects a fractionalization of jobs that has been a basic precept of "scientific management." Most obvious in assembly-line work, fractionalization has been applied to non-manufacturing jobs as well. It is typically justified by efficiency, which is usually defined in terms of either low costs or some time-and-motion type of criteria.

It is hard to find fault with measuring efficiency ultimately in terms of cost-effectiveness. In doing so, however, a manager should be sure to consider *all* the costs involved. It is possible, for example, for highly fractionalized jobs to meet all the time-and-motion criteria of efficiency, but if the resulting job is so unrewarding that performing it day after day leads to high turnover, absenteeism, drugs and alcohol, and strikes, then productivity is really lower (and costs higher) than data on efficiency might indicate.

The principle of combining tasks, then, suggests that whenever possible existing and fractionalized tasks should be put together to form new and larger modules of work. At the Medfield, Massachusetts, plant of Corning Glass Works the assembly of a laboratory hot plate has been redesigned along the lines suggested here. Each hot plate now is assembled from start to finish by one operator, instead of going through several separate operations that are performed by different people.

Some tasks, if combined into a meaningfully large module of work, would be more than an individual could do by himself. In such cases, it is often useful to consider assigning the new, larger task to a small *team* of workers—who are given great autonomy for its completion. At the Racine, Wisconsin, plant of Emerson Electric, the assembly process for trash disposal appliances was restructured this way. Instead of a sequence of moving the appliance from station to station, the assembly now is done from start to finish by one team. Such teams include both men and women to permit switching off the heavier and more delicate aspects of the work. The team responsible is identified on the appliance. In case of customer complaints, the team often drafts the reply.

As a job-design principle, task combination, like natural units of work, expands the task identity of the job. For example, the hot-plate assembler can see and identify with a finished product ready for shipment, rather than a nearly invisible junction of solder. Moreover, the

more tasks that are combined into a single worker's job, the greater
the variety of skills he must call on in performing the job. So task
combination also leads directly to greater skill variety—the third
core dimension that contributes to the overall experienced meaningfulness of the work.

Establishing client relationships. One consequence of fractionalization is that the typical worker has little or no contact with (or even
awareness of) the ultimate user of his product or service. By encouraging and enabling employees to establish direct relationships with the
clients of their work, improvements often can be realized simultaneously on three of the core dimensions. Feedback increases, because of
additional opportunities for the individual to receive praise or criticism
of his work outputs directly. Skill variety often increases, because of
the necessity to develop and exercise one's interpersonal skills in maintaining the client relationship. And autonomy can increase because the
individual often is given personal responsibility for deciding how to
manage his relationships with the clients of his work.

Creating client relationships is a three-step process. First, the client
must be identified. Second, the most direct contact possible between
the worker and the client must be established. Third, criteria must be
set up by which the client can judge the quality of the product or service he receives. And whenever possible, the client should have a means
of relaying his judgments directly back to the worker.

The contact between worker and client should be as great as possible
and as frequent as necessary. Face-to-face contact is highly desirable,
at least occasionally. Where that is impossible or impractical, telephone and mail can suffice. In any case, it is important that the performance criteria by which the worker will be rated by the client must
be mutually understood and agreed upon.

Vertical loading. Typically the split between the "doing" of a job
and the "planning" and "controlling" of the work has evolved along
with horizontial fractionalization. Its rationale, once again, has been
"efficiency through specialization." And once again, the excess of specialization that has emerged has resulted in unexpected but significant
costs in motivation, morale, and work quality. In vertical loading, the
intent is to partially close the gap between the doing and the controlling
parts of the job—and thereby reap some important motivational advantages.

Of all the job-design principles, vertical loading may be the single
most crucial one. In some cases, where it has been impossible to implement any other changes, vertical loading alone has had significant
motivational effects.

When a job is vertically loaded, responsibilities and controls that formerly were reserved for higher levels of management are added to the job. There are many ways to accomplish this:

Return to the job holder greater discretion in setting schedules, deciding on work methods, checking on quality, and advising or helping to train less experienced workers.

Grant additional authority. The objective should be to advance workers from a position of no authority or highly restricted authority to positions of reviewed, and eventually, near-total authority for their own work.

Time management. The job holder should have the greatest possible freedom to decide when to start and stop work, when to break, and how to assign priorities.

Troubleshooting and crisis decisions. Workers should be encouraged to seek problem solutions on their own, rather than calling immediately for the supervisor.

Financial controls. Some degree of knowledge and control over budgets and other financial aspects of a job can often be highly motivating. However, access to this information frequently tends to be restricted. Workers can benefit from knowing something about the costs of their jobs, the potential effect upon profit, and various financial and budgetary alternatives.

When a job is vertically loaded it will inevitably increase in *autonomy*. And as shown in figure 4, this increase in objective personal control over the work will also lead to an increased feeling of personal responsibility for the work, and ultimately to higher internal work motivation.

Opening feedback channels. In virtually all jobs there are ways to open channels of feedback to individuals or teams to help them learn whether their performance is improving, deteriorating, or remaining at a constant level. While there are numerous channels through which information about performance can be provided, it generally is better for a worker to learn about his performance *directly as he does his job* —rather than from management on an occasional basis.

Job-provided feedback usually is more immediate and private than supervisor-supplied feedback, and it increases the worker's feelings of personal control over his work in the bargain. Moreover, it avoids many of the potentially disruptive interpersonal problems that can develop when the only way a worker has to find out how he is doing is through direct messages or subtle cues from the boss.

Exactly what should be done to open channels for job-provided feedback will vary from job to job and organization to organization.

Yet in many cases the changes involve simply removing existing blocks that isolate the worker from naturally occurring data about performance—rather than generating entirely new feedback mechanisms. For example:

Establishing direct client relationships often removes blocks between the worker and natural external sources of data about his work.

Quality-control efforts in many organizations often eliminate a natural source of feedback. The quality check on a product or service is done by persons other than those responsible for the work. Feedback to the workers—if there is any—is belated and diluted. It often fosters a tendency to think of quality as "someone else's concern." By placing quality control close to the worker (perhaps even in his own hands), the quantity and quality of data about performance available to him can dramatically increase.

Tradition and established procedure in many organizations dictate that records about performance be kept by a supervisor and transmitted up (not down) in the organizational hierarchy. Sometimes supervisors even check the work and correct any errors themselves. The worker who made the error never knows it occurred—and is denied the very information that could enhance both his internal work motivation and the technical adequacy of his performance. In many cases it is possible to provide standard summaries of performance records directly to the worker (as well as to his superior), thereby giving him personally and regularly the data he needs to improve his performance.

Computers and other automated operations sometimes can be used to provide the individual with data now blocked from him. Many clerical operations, for example, are now performed on computer consoles. These consoles often can be programmed to provide the clerk with immediate feedback in the form of a CRT display or a printout indicating that an error has been made. Some systems even have been programmed to provide the operator with a positive feedback message when a period of error-free performance has been sustained.

Many organizations simply have not recognized the importance of feedback as a motivator. Data on quality and other aspects of performance are viewed as being of interest only to management. Worse still, the *standards* for acceptable performance often are kept from workers as well. As a result, workers who would be interested in following the daily or weekly ups and downs of their performance, and in trying accordingly to improve, are deprived of the very guidelines they need to do so. They are like the golfer we mentioned earlier, whose efforts to correct his hook are stopped dead by fog over the driving range.

The strategy in action: how well does it work?

So far we have examined a basic theory of how people get turned on to their work; a set of core dimensions of jobs that create the conditions for such internal work motivation to develop on the job; and a set of five implementing concepts that are the action steps recommended to boost a job on the core dimensions and thereby increase employee motivation, satisfaction, and productivity.

The remaining question is straightforward and important: *Does it work?* In reality, that question is twofold. First, does the theory itself hold water, or are we barking up the wrong conceptual tree? And second, does the change strategy really lead to measurable differences when it is applied in an actual organizational setting?

This section summarizes the findings we have generated to date on these questions.

Is the job-enrichment theory correct?

In general, the answer seems to be yes. The JDS instrument has been taken by more than 1,000 employees working on about 100 diverse jobs in more than a dozen organizations over the last two years. These data have been analyzed to test the basic motivational theory—and especially the impact of the core job dimensions on worker motivation, satisfaction, and behavior on the job. An illustrative overview of some of the findings is given below. (8)

1. People who work on jobs high on the core dimensions are more motivated and satisfied than are people who work on jobs that score low on the dimensions. Employees with jobs high on the core dimensions (MPS scores greater than 240) were compared to those who held unmotivating jobs (MPS scores less than 40). As shown in figure 5, employees with high MPS jobs were higher on (*a*) the three psychological states, (*b*) internal work motivation, (*c*) general satisfaction, and (*d*) "growth" satisfaction.

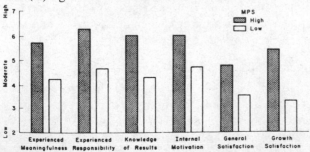

Figure 5. Employee reactions to jobs high and low in motivating potential for two banks and a steel firm.

2. Figure 6 shows that the same is true for measures of actual behavior at work—absenteeism and performance effectiveness—although less strongly so for the performance measure.

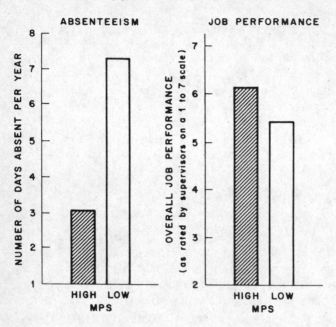

Figure 6. Absenteeism and job performance for employees with jobs high and low in motivating potential.

3. Responses to jobs high in motivating potential are more positive for people who have strong growth needs than for people with weak needs for growth. In figure 7 the linear relationship between the motivating potential of a job and employees' level of internal work motivation is shown, separately for people with high versus low growth needs as measured by the JDS. While both groups of employees show increases in internal motivation as MPS increases, the *rate* of increase is significantly greater for the group of employees who have strong needs for growth.

How does the change strategy work in practice?

The results summarized above suggest that both the theory and the diagnostic instrument work when used with real people in real organizations. In this section, we summarize a job-enrichment project conducted at The Travelers Insurance Companies, which illustrates how the change procedures themselves work in practice.

The Travelers project was designed with two purposes in mind.

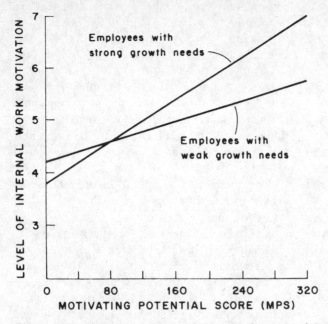

Figure 7. Relationship between the motivating potential of a job and the internal work motivation of employees. (Shown separately for employees with strong versus weak growth-need strength.)

One was to achieve improvements in morale, productivity, and other indicators of employee well-being. The other was to test the general effectiveness of the strategy for job enrichment we have summarized in this article.

The work group chosen was a keypunching operation. The group's function was to transfer information from printed or written documents onto punched cards for computer input. The work group consisted of ninety-eight keypunch operators and verifiers (both in the same job classification), plus seven assignment clerks. All reported to a supervisor who, in turn, reported to the assistant manager and manager of the data-input division.

The size of individual punching orders varied considerably, from a few cards to as many as 2,500. Some work came to the work group with a specified delivery date, while other orders were to be given routine service on a predetermined schedule.

Assignment clerks received the jobs from the user departments. After reviewing the work for obvious errors, omissions, and legibility problems, the assignment clerk parceled out the work in batches expected to take about one hour. If the clerk found the work not suitable for punching it went to the supervisor, who either returned the work to the user department or cleared up problems by phone. When work went to operators for punching, it was with the instruction, "Punch only what you see. Don't correct errors, no matter how obvious they look."

Because of the high cost of computer time, key-punched work was 100 percent verified—a task that consumed nearly as many man-hours as the punching itself. Then the cards went to the supervisor, who screened the jobs for due dates before sending them to the computer. Errors detected in verification were assigned to various operators at random to be corrected.

The computer output from the cards was sent to the originating department, accompanied by a printout of errors. Eventually the printout went back to the supervisor for final correction.

A great many phenomena indicated that the problems being experienced in the work group might be the result of poor motivation. As the only person performing supervisory functions of any kind, the supervisor spent most of his time responding to crisis situations, which recurred continually. He also had to deal almost daily with employees' salary grievances or other complaints. Employees frequently showed apathy or outright hostility toward their jobs.

Rates of work output, by accepted work-measurement standards, were inadequate. Error rates were high. Due dates and schedules frequently were missed. Absenteeism was higher than average, especially before and after weekends and holidays.

The single, rather unusual exception was turnover. It was lower than the companywide average for similar jobs. The company has attributed this fact to a poor job market in the base period just before the project began, and to an older, relatively more settled work force—made up, incidentally, entirely of women.

The diagnosis

Using some of the tools and techniques we have outlined, a consulting team from the Management Services Department and from Roy W. Walters & Associates concluded that the keypunch-operator's job exhibited the following serious weaknesses in terms of the core dimensions.

Skill variety: there was none. Only a single skill was involved—the ability to punch adequately the data on the batch of documents.

Task identity: virtually nonexistent. Batches were assembled to provide an even workload, but not whole identifiable jobs.

Task significance: not apparent. The keypunching operation was a necessary step in providing service to the company's customers. The individual operator was isolated by an assignment clerk and a supervisor from any knowledge of what the operation meant to the using department, let alone its meaning to the ultimate customer.

Autonomy: none. The operators had no freedom to arrange their daily tasks to meet schedules, to resolve problems with the using department, or even to correct, in punching, information that was obviously wrong.

Feedback: none. Once a batch was out of the operator's hands, she had no assured chance of seeing evidence of its quality or inadequacy.

Design of the experimental trial

Since the diagnosis indicated that the motivating potential of the job was extremely low, it was decided to attempt to improve the motivation and productivity of the work group through job enrichment. Moreover, it was possible to design an experimental test of the effects of the changes to be introduced: the results of changes made in the target work group were to be compared with trends in a control work group of similar size and demographic makeup. Since the control group was located more than a mile away, there appeared to be little risk of communication between members of the two groups.

A base period was defined before the start of the experimental trial period, and appropriate data were gathered on the productivity, absenteeism, and work attitudes of members of both groups. Data also were available on turnover; but since turnover was already below average in the target group, prospective changes in this measure were deemed insignificant.

An educational session was conducted with supervisors, at which they were given the theory and implementing concepts and actually helped to design the job changes themselves. Out of this session came an active plan consisting of about twenty-five change items that would significantly affect the design of the target jobs.

The implementing concepts and the changes

Because the job as it existed was rather uniformly low on the core job dimensions, all five of the implementing concepts were used in enriching it.

Natural units of work. The random batch assignment of work was replaced by assigning to each operator continuing responsibility for certain accounts—either particular departments or particular recurring jobs. Any work for those accounts now always goes to the same operator.

Task combination. Some planning and controlling functions were combined with the central task of keypunching. In this case, however, these additions can be more suitably discussed under the remaining three implementing concepts.

Client relationships. Each operator was given several channels of direct contact with clients. The operators, not their assignment clerks, now inspect their documents for correctness and legibility. When problems arise, the operator, not the supervisor, takes them up with the client.

Feedback. In addition to feedback from client contact, the operators were provided with a number of additional sources of data about their performance. The computer department now returns incorrect cards to the operators who punched them, and operators correct their own errors. Each operator also keeps her own file of copies of her errors. These can be reviewed to determine trends in error frequency and types of errors. Each operator receives weekly a computer printout of her errors and productivity, which is sent to her directly, rather than given to her by the supervisor.

Vertical loading. Besides consulting directly with clients about work questions, operators now have the authority to correct obvious coding errors on their own. Operators may set their own schedules and plan their daily work, as long as they meet schedules. Some competent operators have been given the option of not verifying their work and making their own program changes.

Results of the trial

The results were dramatic. The number of operators declined from ninety-eight to sixty. This occurred partly through attrition and partly through transfer to other departments. Some of the operators were promoted to higher-paying jobs in departments whose cards they had been handling—something that had never occurred before. Some details of the results are given below.

Quantity of work. The control group, with no job changes made, showed an increase in productivity of 8.1 percent during the trial period. The experimental group showed an increase of 39.6 percent.

Error rates. To assess work quality, error rates were recorded for about forty operators in the experimental group. All were experienced, and all had been in their jobs before the job-enrichment program began. For two months before the study, these operators had a collective error rate of 1.53 percent. For two months toward the end of the study, the collective error rate was 0.00 percent. By the end of the study the number of operators with poor performance had dropped from 11.1 percent to 5.5 percent.

Absenteeism. The experimental group registered a 24.1 percent decline in absences. The control group, by contrast, showed a 29 percent *increase*.

Attitudes toward the job. An attitude survey given at the start of the project showed that the two groups scored about average, and nearly identically, in nine different areas of work satisfaction. At the end of the project the survey was repeated. The control group showed an insignificant 0.5 percent improvement, while the experimental group's overall satisfaction score rose 16.5 percent.

Selective elimination of controls. Demonstrated improvements in operator proficiency permitted them to work with fewer controls. Travelers estimates that the reduction of controls had the same effect as adding seven operators—a saving even beyond the effects of improved productivity and lowered absenteeism.

Role of the supervisor. One of the most significant findings in the Travelers experiment was the effect of the changes on the supervisor's job, and thus on the rest of the organization. The operators took on many responsibilities that had been reserved at least to the unit leaders and sometimes to the supervisor. The unit leaders, in turn, assumed some of the day-to-day supervisory functions that had plagued the supervisor. Instead of spending his days supervising the behavior of subordinates and dealing with crises, he was able to devote time to developing feed-back systems, setting up work modules, and spearheading the enrichment effort—in other words, managing. It should be noted, however, that helping supervisors change their own work activities when their subordinates' jobs have been enriched is itself a challenging task. And if appropriate attention and help are not given to supervisors in such cases, they rapidly can become disaffected— and a job-enrichment "backlash" can result. (11)

Summary

By applying work-measurement standards to the changes wrought by job enrichment—attitude and quality, absenteeism, and selective administration of controls—Travelers was able to estimate the total dollar impact of the project. Actual savings in salaries and machine rental charges during the first year totaled $64,305. Potential savings by further application of the changes were put at $91,937 annually. Thus, by almost any measure used—from the work attitudes of individual employees to dollar savings for the company as a whole—the Travelers test of the job-enrichment strategy proved a success.

Conclusions

In this article we have presented a new strategy for the redesign of work in general and for job enrichment in particular. The approach has four main characteristics:

1. It is grounded in a basic psychological theory of what motivates people in their work.
2. It emphasizes that planning for job changes should be done on

the basis of *data* about the jobs and the people who do them—and a set of diagnostic instruments is provided to collect such data.

3. It provides a set of specific implementing concepts to guide actual job changes, as well as a set of theory-based rules for selecting *which* action steps are likely to be most beneficial in a given situation.

4. The strategy is buttressed by a set of findings showing that the theory holds water, that the diagnostic procedures are practical and informative, and that the implementing concepts can lead to changes that are beneficial both to organizations and to the people who work in them.

We believe that job enrichment is moving beyond the stage where it can be considered "yet another management fad." Instead, it represents a potentially powerful strategy for change that can help organizations achieve their goals for higher-quality work—and at the same time further the equally legitimate needs of contemporary employees for a more meaningful work experience. Yet there are pressing questions about job enrichment and its use that remain to be answered.

Prominent among these is the question of employee participation in planning and implementing work redesign. The diagnostic tools and implementing concepts we have presented are neither designed nor intended for use only by management. Rather, our belief is that the effectiveness of job enrichment is likely to be enhanced when the tasks of diagnosing and changing jobs are undertaken *collaboratively* by management and by the employees whose work will be affected.

Moreover, the effects of work redesign on the broader organization remain generally uncharted. Evidence now is accumulating that when jobs are changed, turbulence can appear in the surrounding organization—for example, in supervisory-subordinate relationships, in pay and benefit plans, and so on. Such turbulence can be viewed by management either as a problem with job enrichment, or as an opportunity for further and broader organizational development by teams of managers and employees. To the degree that management takes the latter view, we believe, the oft-espoused goal of achieving basic organizational change through the redesign of work may come increasingly within reach.

The diagnostic tools and implementing concepts we have presented are useful in deciding on and designing basic changes in the jobs themselves. They do not address the broader issues of who plans the changes, how they are carried out, and how they are followed up. The way these broader questions are dealt with, we believe, may determine whether job enrichment will grow up—or whether it will die an early and unfortunate death, like so many other fledgling behavioral-science approaches to organizational change.

References

1. F. Herzberg, B. Mausner and B. Snyderman, *The Motivation to Work* (New York: John Wiley & Sons, 1959).

2. F. Herzberg, *Work and the Nature of Man* (Cleveland: World, 1966).

3. F. Herzberg, "One More Time: How Do You Motivate Employees?" *Harvard Business Review* (1968), pp. 53–62.

4. W. J. Paul, Jr.; K. B. Robertson and F. Herzberg, "Job Enrichment Pays Off," *Harvard Business Review* (1969), pp. 61–78.

5. R. N. Ford, *Motivation through the Work Itself* (New York: American Management Association, 1969).

6. A. N. Turner and P. R. Lawrence, *Industrial Jobs and the Worker* (Cambridge, Mass.: Harvard Graduate School of Business Administration, 1965).

7. J. R. Hackman and E. E. Lawler, "Employee Reactions to Job Characteristics," *Journal of Applied Psychology Monograph* (1971), pp. 259–286.

8. J. R. Hackman and G. R. Oldham, *Motivation through the Design of Work: Test of a Theory,* Technical Report No. 6, Department of Administrative Sciences, Yale University, 1974.

9. J. R. Hackman and G. R. Oldham, "Development of the Job Diagnostic Survey," *Journal of Applied Psychology* (1975), pp. 159–170.

10. R. W. Walters and Associates, *Job Enrichment for Results* (Cambridge, Mass.: Addison-Wesley, 1975).

11. E. E. Lawler III, J. R. Hackman, and S. Kaufman, "Effects of Job Redesign: A Field Experiment," *Journal of Applied Social Psychology* (1973), pp. 49–62.

2

Mind: Thinking,
Creating, Analyzing

Introduction

In chapter 1 we treated man as an emotionally motivated critter, pushed by his needs and wants and pulled by the carrots of incentives and rewards. But we had better not forget that the human being is also a thinking being, a reasoner, an imaginer, an analyzer. The four papers in this chapter focus on the way human beings think, create, solve problems. We have selected from this large field some work that seems especially relevant to the managing process, perhaps particularly relevant at this time in history. What managers ought to be thinking about and how they ought to be thinking about those things is one of the major questions that Western society is pressing its contemporary managers to reconsider.

The reader will, we feel sure, find the first article, by Ornstein, both enlightening and stimulating. For a very long time observers of human nature have noticed two contrasting ways of thinking. Different words have been used for the two styles. Sometimes we have talked about *analytic* versus *intuitive* thinking; sometimes *rational* versus *emotional;* or *convergent* versus *divergent*. Ornstein describes some fairly recent research on the two hemispheres of the brain. That research suggests that different thinking functions are performed by the two hemispheres, and Ornstein suggests that those two functions grossly parallel those earlier dichotomies of analytic versus intuitive and the like. The reader should be cautioned that the evidence for clearly different thinking in the two hemispheres is limited and not yet well validated. Given that caution, the implications of this perspective for managerial decision making are unquestionably important.

The McKenney-Keen piece is concerned with "cognitive styles," the characteristic styles people choose when confronted with problems. Just as individuals may be said to show characteristics and durable patterns of motivation, it can be argued that people also show characteristic ways of thinking about problems. McKenney and Keen administered a selected set of pencil-and-paper tests to several categories of managers. They do indeed find different cognitive patterns that seem to be particularly relevant to different aspects of the managing process; and some of the patterns, the reader will notice, are not unlike those described by Ornstein.

The third article, by Lindblom, is another classic. It may be a little harder to follow than some of the other papers in this book, but it is very much worth reading. Lindblom, a senior political scientist, makes a strong and sensible challenge to the notion that the only "right" way to think is the logical, analytic, systematic way. He raises questions about alternative strategies that may be messier, more contingent, and more "muddling," but nevertheless more effective than puristic advanced planning. Indeed, Lindblom's article represents the start of a strong and growing literature that challenges analytic, logical, planful models of the managing process. This more "muddling" kind of orientation, this argument that managing requires flexibility and adjustment and intuition as well as analytic skills will recur in section 4 of this book in the articles by Mintzberg, March, Leavitt, and Weick.

The last paper in this section, by James Adams, is almost a how-to-do-it article about creative thinking. It is taken from Adams' book, *Conceptual Blockbusting*. Adams is an engineer with interests in design and ways of finding original and unusual solutions to difficult and complex problems. He offers a set of rules of thumb or heuristics for escaping from traditional constrained ways of thinking. He advocates looking at problems upside down, backward, with a microscope, and with a telescope to find new ways to break through old thought barriers.

So the focal point in this chapter is problem solving and how people can and do use their heads, and how they might use them better.

Two Sides of the Brain
Robert E. Ornstein

Never know when it might come in useful

Nasrudin sometimes took people for trips in his boat. One day a pedagogue hired him to ferry him across a very wide river. As soon as they were afloat, the scholar asked whether it was going to be rough.

"Don't ask me nothing about it," said Nasrudin.
"Have you never studied grammar?"
"No," said the Mulla.
"In that case, half your life has been wasted."
The Mulla said nothing.
Soon a terrible storm blew up. The Mulla's crazy cockleshell was filling with water. He leaned over toward his companion. "Have you ever learned to swim?"
"No," said the pedant.
"In that case, schoolmaster, *all* your life is lost for we are sinking." (1)

The two characters in this story represent two major modes of consciousness: the verbal, rational mode is portrayed by the pedagogue, who is involved in and insists on neat and tidy perfection; the other mode is represented here by the skill of swimming, which involves movement of the body in space, a mode often devalued by the neat, rational mind of the pedagogue.

On one level, these two characters represent different types of people. The verbal-logical grammarian can also be the scientist, the logician, the mathematician who is committed to reason and "correct" proof. The boatman, ungraceful and untutored in formal terms, repre-

From *The Psychology of Consciousness,* 2d ed., © 1977 by Robert E. Ornstein. Reprinted by permission of Harcourt Brace Jovanovich, Inc.

sents the artist, the craftsman, the dancer, the dreamer whose output is often unsatisfactory to the purely rational mind.

But other interpretations of this story are possible. These two characters can also represent major modes of consciousness which exist across cultures (comparing the Trobrianders with the West) and which simultaneously coexist within each person. Try the following exercise. Close your eyes and attempt to sense each side of your body separately. Try to get in touch with the feelings of the left and of the right side, their strengths, their weaknesses. When you are finished, open your eyes for a moment and reflect on one of these questions. Close your eyes and sense inside for the answer, then repeat the process with the next question.

1. Which side of you is more feminine?
2. Which is more masculine?
3. Which do you consider the "dark" side of yourself?
4. Which side is the "lighter"?
5. Which is more active?
6. Which is more passive?
7. Which side is more logical?
8. Which more "intuitive"?
9. Which side of you is the more mysterious?
10. Which side is the more artistic?

If you are right-handed, most likely you felt the right side of your body as more masculine, lighter, active, and logical, the left side as more feminine, dark, passive, intuitive, mysterious, and artistic. The psychologist William Domhoff asked a large number of people to rate the concepts *left* and *right* on several dimensions. His sample regarded *left* as "bad," "dark," "profane," and "female," while *right* was considered the opposite. (2)

The difference between the left and right sides of the body may provide a key to open our understanding of the psychological and physiological mechanisms of the two major modes of consciousness. The cerebral cortex of the brain is divided into two hemispheres, joined by a large bundle of interconnecting fibers called the "corpus callosum." The left side of the body is mainly controlled by the right side of the cortex, and the right side of the body by the left side of the cortex. When we speak of *left* in ordinary speech, we are referring to that side of the body, and to the *right* hemisphere of the brain.

Both the structure and the function of these two "halfbrains" in some part underlie the two modes of consciousness which simultaneously coexist within each one of us. Although each hemisphere shares the potential for many functions, and both sides participate in most activities, in the normal person the two hemispheres tend to specialize. The left hemisphere (connected to the right side of the body) is predominantly involved with analytic, logical thinking, especially in verbal and mathematical functions. Its mode of operation is primarily linear. This hemisphere seems to process information sequentially. This mode of operation of necessity must underlie logical thought, since logic depends on sequence and order. Language and mathematics, both left-hemisphere activities, also depend predominantly on linear time.

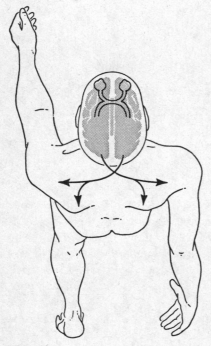

Figure 1.

If the left hemisphere is specialized for analysis, the right hemisphere (again, remember, connected to the left side of the body) seems specialized for holistic mentation. Its language ability is quite limited. This hemisphere is primarily responsible for our orientation in space, artistic endeavor, crafts, body image, recognition of faces. It processes information more diffusely than does the left hemisphere, and its responsibilities demand a ready integration of many inputs at once. If the left hemisphere can be termed predominantly analytic and sequential in its operation, then the right hemisphere is more holistic and relational, and more simultaneous in its mode of operation.*

For over a century, neurological evidence has been slowly accumulating on the differential specialization of man's two cerebral hemispheres. A very valuable part of this evidence has come from the study of people whose brains have been damaged by accident or illness, and from the surgery performed on them. It is, then, in the work of clinical neurology, and especially in the review paper of Joseph Bogen, that the primary indications of our hemispheric specialization are to be found. (3)

In 1864, the great neurologist Hughlings Jackson considered the left hemisphere to be the seat of the "faculty of expression," and noted of a patient with a tumor in the right hemisphere, "She did not know objects, persons, and places." Since Hughlings Jackson, many other neurologists, neurosurgeons, and psychiatrists have confirmed that two modes of consciousness seem to be lateralized in the two cerebral hemispheres of man. In hundreds of clinical cases, it has been found that damage to the left hemisphere very often interferes with, and can in some cases completely destroy, language ability. Often patients cannot speak after such left-hemisphere lesions, a condition known as "aphasia." An injury to the right hemisphere may not interfere with language performance at all, but may cause severe disturbance in spatial awareness, in musical ability, in recognition of other people, or in awareness of one's own body. Some patients with right-hemisphere damage cannot dress themselves adequately, although their speech and reason remain unimpaired.

Throughout the clinical and neurological reports, there exists a tendency to term the left and right hemispheres the "major" and the "minor," respectively. This seems more a societal than a neurological distinction. The dominant or major mode of our culture is verbal and intellectual, and this cultural emphasis can bias observations. If an injury to the right hemisphere is not found to affect speech or reason, then this damage has often been considered minor. Injury to the left hemisphere affects verbal functions; thus it has often been termed the major hemisphere. However, the conception of the function of the two

---

* This right-left specialization is based on right-handers. Left-handers, who are about 5 percent of the population, are less consistent; some have reversed specialization of the hemispheres, but some have mixed specialization—e.g., language in both sides. Some are specialized in the same way as right-handers. And even in right-handers these differences are not binary, but are specializations of each "half-brain." At least in very young people, each side does possess the potential for both modes; e.g., brain damage to the left hemisphere in young children often results in the development of language in the right side.

hemispheres is changing, largely because of the superb work of Bogen and the increasing evidence of the brain's lateral specialization. The position of the fussy pedagogue who devalues the nonverbal boatman becomes less and less tenable.

Each hemisphere is the major one, depending on the mode of consciousness under consideration. If one is a wordsmith, a scientist, or a mathematician, damage to the left hemisphere may prove disastrous. If one is a musician, a craftsman, or an artist, damage to the left hemisphere often does not interfere with one's capacity to create music, crafts, or arts, yet damage to the right hemisphere may well obliterate a career.

In more precise neuropsychological studies, Brenda Milner and her associates at McGill University in Montreal have attempted to correlate disorders in specific kinds of tasks with lesions in specific areas of the brain. For example, a lobectomy of the right temporal lobe severely impairs the performance of visual and tactile mazes, whereas left temporal-lobe lesions of equal extent produce little deficit. These researchers also report that lesions in specific areas of the left hemisphere are associated with specific kinds of language disorders: an impairment of verbal memory is associated with lesions in the anterior (front) left temporal lobe; speech impairment seems to result from lesions in the posterior (rear) left temporal lobe. (4) On less empirical grounds, the Russian physiologist Luria has reported that mathematical function is also disturbed by lesions of the left side. (5) Milner and her associates also report that the recognition of musical pitch seems to be in the province of the right hemisphere.

The clinical neurological research is intriguing, correlating the different functions of the hemispheres which are impaired by brain damage. More intriguing still is the research of Roger Sperry of the California Institute of Technology, and his associates, notably Joseph Bogen and Michael Gazzaniga. The two cerebral hemispheres communicate through the corpus callosum, which joins the two sides anatomically. Professor Sperry and his colleagues had for some years experimentally severed the corpus callosum in laboratory animals. This led to the adoption of a radical treatment for severe epilepsy in several human patients of Drs. Vogel and Bogen of the California College of Medicine. (6)

This treatment involved an operation on humans similar to Sperry's experimental surgery on animals—a severing of the interconnections between the two cerebral hemispheres, effectively isolating one side from the other. The hope of this surgery was that when a patient had a seizure in one hemisphere, the other would still be available to take control of the body. With this control available, it was hoped that the patient could ingest the proper medication or perhaps inform the doctor of his attack. In many cases, the severely disturbed patients were improved enough to leave the hospital.

In day-to-day living, these "split-brain" people exhibit almost no abnormality, which is somewhat surprising in view of the radical surgery. However, Roger Sperry and his associates have developed many subtle tests which uncovered evidence that the operation had clearly separated the specialized functions of the two cerebral hemispheres.

If, for instance, the patient felt a pencil (hidden from sight) in his right hand, he could verbally describe it, as would be normal. But if the pencil was in his left hand, he could not describe it at all. Recall that the left hand informs the right hemisphere, which does not possess any capability for speech. With the corpus callosum cut, the verbal (left) hemisphere is no longer connected to the right hemisphere, which largely communicates with the left hand; so the verbal apparatus literally does not know what is in the left hand. If, however, the patient was offered a selection of objects—a key, book, pencil, etc.—and was asked to choose the previously given object with his left hand, he could choose correctly, although he still could not state verbally just what he was doing. This situation resembles closely what might happen if I were privately requested to perform an action and you were expected to discourse on it.

Another experiment tested the lateral specialization of the two hemispheres using visual input. The right half of each eye sends its messages to the right hemisphere, the left half to the left hemisphere. In this experiment the word "heart" was flashed to the patient, with the "he" to the left of the eyes' fixation point, and "art" to the right. Normally if any person were asked to report this experience, he would say that he saw "heart." But the split-brain patients responded differently, depending on which hemisphere was responding. When the patient was asked to *name* the word just presented, he or she replied "art," since this was the portion projected to the left hemisphere, which was answering the question. When, however, the patient was asked to point with the left hand to one of two cards on which were written "he" and "art," the left hand pointed to "he." The simultaneous experiences of each hemisphere seemed unique and independent of each other in these patients. The verbal hemisphere gave one answer, the nonverbal hemisphere another.

Although most right-handed people write and draw with the right hand, most can to some extent write and draw with their left. After surgery, Dr. Bogen tested the ability of the split-brain patients to write and draw with either hand. The ability to write English remained in the right hand after surgery, but this hand could no longer draw very well. It seemed to have lost its ability to work in a relational, spatial manner. Given a square to copy with the right hand, the patient might draw four corners stacked together: he could draw *only* the corners; the hand seemed no longer able to link the disconnected segments. The left hemisphere, which controls the right hand, seems to be able to operate well in an analytic manner, yet poorly in a relational mode. The performance of the left hand reversed that of the right. The left could draw and could copy spatial figures, but could not copy a written word. It can operate holistically, but does not have very much capacity for verbal-analytic information processing. In these split-brain patients, the right hemisphere can understand some simple speech, though it has no capacity for verbal expression; we do not know whether this is an artifact of the surgery or whether it represents a rudimentary right-hemisphere capability in normal people.

A common test of spatial mentation requires the construction of a two-dimensional geometric figure using a set of cubes, each face painted with a different color or combination of colors. The patient's left hand could perform this task quite well; the right hand could not. Professor Sperry often shows an interesting film clip of the right hand attempting to solve the problem and failing, whereupon the patient's left hand cannot restrain itself and "corrects" the right—as when you may know the answer to a problem and watch me making mistakes, and cannot refrain from telling me the answer.

The split-brain surgery most dramatically delineates the two major modes of consciousness which seem normally to coexist within each person. Recent research with experimental split-brain monkeys indicates that the two hemispheres can function simultaneously as well as independently. At the same moment, a split-brain monkey can be trained on one learning problem with one eye-brain pair (the optic chiasm in monkeys is severed as part of the experimental procedure) and a second problem with the other eye-brain pair. (7) One experiment with the split-brain people has also indicated that their two hemispheres can simultaneously process more information than can those of a normal person. Dr. Sperry writes of the effect of the operation in humans: "Everything we have seen so far indicated that the surgery has left each of these people with two separate minds, that is, with two separate spheres of consciousness." (8)

The recognition that we possess two cerebral hemispheres which are specialized to operate in different modes may allow us to understand much about the fundamental duality of our consciousness. This duality has been reflected in classical as well as modern literature as between reason and passion, or between mind and intuition. Perhaps the most famous of these dichotomies in psychology is that proposed by Sigmund Freud, of the split between the "conscious" mind and the "un-conscious." The workings of the "conscious" mind are held to be accessible to language and to rational discourse and alteration; the "unconscious" is much less accessible to reason or to the verbal analysis. Some aspects of "unconscious" communication are gestures, facial and body movements, tone of voice.

There are moments in each of our lives when our verbal-intellect suggests one course and our "heart" or intuition another. Because of psychosurgery which has physically separated the hemispheres, the split-brain patients provide a clear example of dual response to certain situations. In one experimental test, Roger Sperry attempted to deter-mine whether the right hemisphere could learn to respond verbally to different colors. Either a red or a green light was flashed to the left visual field of the patient, which is received on the right half of the retina and sent to the right hemisphere (see figure 2). Sperry then asked the split-brain patients to guess verbally which color was flashed to them. Since the left hemisphere controls the verbal output and the color information was sent to the right hemisphere, it was ex-pected that the patients would not be able to guess the answer beyond chance, no matter how many guesses were allowed. The side which was doing the guessing, after all, was disconnected from the side which knew the answer.

After a few trials, however, the patients' scores improved whenever the examiner allowed a second guess. What happened was this. If a red light was flashed and the patient guessed correctly by chance, this terminated the trial. If the patient guessed incorrectly, he might frown, shake his head, and then "correct" his answer verbally. The right hemisphere had seen the light, then heard the left make an incorrect answer. Having no access to verbal output, the right hemisphere used the means at its disposal, and caused a frown and a headshake, which informed the left hemisphere that its answer was incorrect.

In a loose way, this is an analogue of the conflict between "con-scious" and "unconscious" processes which Freud so compellingly de-scribed. In the split-brain patients, the verbal, rational processing sys-tem disconnected from the source of information, was countermanded by gestures and tone of voice, as when a person may insist "I am *not* angry," yet his tone of voice and facial expression simultaneously in-dicate exactly the opposite feeling.

A similar situation occurred when emotion-laden information was given to the right hemisphere while the verbal hemisphere remained unaware of it. A photograph of a nude woman was shown to the right hemisphere of a patient in the course of a series of otherwise dull laboratory tests. At first, the woman viewing the nude on the screen

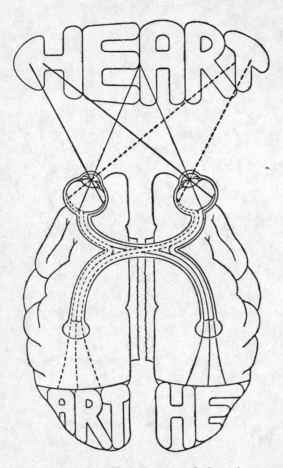

Figure 2. A simplified diagram of visual input to the two hemispheres of the brain. Images in the left visual field are projected to the right hemisphere, images in the right visual field to the left hemisphere. This schematic drawing illustrates one experiment performed on split-brain patients: note that the corpus callosum is cut. The "HE" and "ART" projections are, of course, fanciful, not anatomically correct.

said that she saw nothing, then immediately flushed, alternately squirmed, smiled, and looked uncomfortable and confused. But her "conscious" or verbal half was *still* unaware of what had caused the emotional turmoil. All that was accessible to the verbal apparatus was that *something* unusual was occurring in her body. Her words reflected that the emotional reaction had been "unconscious," unavailable to her language apparatus. To paraphrase her, "What a funny machine you have there, Dr. Sperry."

In this instance a clear split was observed between the two independent consciousnesses which are normally in communication and collaboration. In such an experiment with split-brain patients, we can accurately localize the split of information in the system. A similar process, although much more difficult to localize, may underlie the classic Freudian symptoms of repression and denial, both situations in which the verbal mechanism has no access to emotional information in other parts of the system. In less pathological instances, when we perform an action "intuitively," our words often make no sense, perhaps because the action has been initiated by a part of the brain little involved in language.

But these spectacular split-brain and lesion studies are not the only evidence for the physiological duality in consciousness. In general, caution should be exercised in drawing inferences on normal functioning from pathological and surgical cases alone. In dealing with these cases we must recall that we are investigating disturbed, not normal, functioning, from which inference to how normal people function may be a bit tenuous. In cases of brain damage, it is never fully clear that one hemisphere has not taken over a function from the other to an unusual degree because of the injury. It is necessary to seek out evidence from normally functioning people, even if that evidence is more indirect, since we don't go poking inside the brains of our friends. In this, we are fortunate that recent research with normal people has confirmed much of the neurosurgical explorations.

If the right hemisphere operates predominantly in a simultaneous manner, it could integrate diverse input quickly. This mode of information-processing would be advantageous for spatial orientation, when the person must quickly integrate visual, muscular, and kinesthetic cues. In a carefully controlled experiment with normal people, the right hemisphere was found to be superior in depth perception to the left. (9)

When a tachistoscope is used to introduce information to only the right hemisphere and either a nonverbal or a verbal response is required, the nonverbal response comes more quickly than the verbal one. A verbal response requires the information to be sent across the callosum to the left hemisphere, which takes some time. This indicates that the normal brain does indeed make use of the lateral specialization, selecting the appropriate area for differential information processing. (10)

Another experiment which confirms the differential specialization of the two hemispheres uses eye movements as an indicator. Ask a friend a question such as, "How do you spell Mississippi?" The chances are that he will shift his gaze off to one side while reflecting. Marcel Kinsbourne of Duke University, and Katherine Kocel, David Galin, Edward Merrin, and myself of our research group at the Langley Porter Neuropsychiatric Institute, have found that which direction a person gazes in is affected by the kind of question asked. If the question is verbal-analytical (such as "Divide 144 by 6, and multiply the answer by 7"), more eye-movements are made to the right than if the question involves spatial mentation (such as "Which way does an Indian face on the nickel?"). (11)

Kinsbourne has performed another experiment which deserves special mention. Ask a friend to balance a wooden dowel on the index finger of each hand, one hand at a time. Generally, the preferred hand is more adept at this balancing. Ask the person then to speak while balancing this dowel, and time the length of the balancing. In Kinsbourne's experiment, the balancing time of the right hand decreased, as would be expected, since the addition of a task interferes with performance in most situations. But the balancing time of the left hand *increased* with concurrent verbalization. (12)

The right hand, recall, is predominantly controlled by the left hemisphere. When the left hemisphere is engaged in speech, its control of the right hand suffers. While the left hand is balancing, the left hemisphere may still intrude on its performance. When the left hemisphere is occupied in speech, it no longer seems to interfere with the left hand and the balancing time of the left improves.

The normal brain constantly exhibits electrical activity, in the form of very low voltages, as recorded at the scalp by the electroencephalograph or EEG. If the EEG is recorded from both hemispheres of a normal person during the performance of verbal or spatial information-processing tasks, different "brain-wave" patterns result. During a verbal task, the alpha rhythm in the right hemisphere increases relative to the left, and in a spatial task the alpha rhythm increases in the left hemisphere relative to the right. The appearance of the alpha rhythm indicates a "turning off" of information processing in the area involved. As if to reduce the interference between the two conflicting modes of operation of its two cerebral hemispheres, the brain tends to turn off its unused side in a given situation. (13)

But how do these two modes interact in daily life? My opinion, and that of David Galin, is that in most ordinary activities we simply alternate between the two modes, selecting the appropriate one and inhibiting the other. It is not at all clear how this process occurs. Do the two systems work continuously in parallel, and merely alternate control of the body, or do they truly time-share the control? Clearly each of us can work in both modes—we all speak, we all can move in space, we all can do both at once; yet in skiing, for instance, an attempt to verbally encode each bodily movement would lead to disaster. The two modes of operation *complement* each other, but do not readily substitute for one another. Consider describing a spiral staircase. Most would begin using words and quickly begin to gesture in the air. Or consider attempting to ride a bicycle purely from a verbal instruction.

This lateral specialization of the brain seems to be unique to humans and related to the evolution of language. There is no evidence that the two cerebral hemispheres of other primates are specialized, although it would be reasonable to assume some evolutionary precursor of man's hemispheric asymmetry. Jerre Levy-Agresti and Roger Sperry have suggested that humans have evolved in this manner because the sequential information-processing which must underlie language, mathematics, and "rational" thought is not readily compatible with the more simultaneous mode of information-processing which underlies relational perception, orientation in space, and what our verbal intellect can only term "intuition." (14)

Within each person the two polarities seem to exist simultaneously as two semi-independent information-processing units with different specialties. There is some suggestive evidence that the modes of physiological organization may be different in the two hemispheres. Josephine Semmes, of the National Institute of Mental Health, has found that damage to the left hemisphere results in quite localized disturbance of function, whereas damage to the right interferes less focally with performance. Semmes and her co-workers studied 124 war veterans who had incurred brain injuries. They tested the effects of brain injury on simple motor reactions, somatosensory thresholds, and object discrimination—testing each hand-hemisphere pair separately. Studying the right hand, they found that injuries in quite specific areas of the left hemisphere interfered with performance of specific tasks, but no such focus of localization could be found with right-hemisphere lesions. (15) This evidence seems to indicate that the left hemisphere is more anatomically specialized for the discrete, focal information-processing underlying logic, and that the right hemisphere is more diffusely organized, which is advantageous for orientation in space and for other situations which require simultaneous processing of many inputs.

It is the polarity and the integration of these two modes of consciousness, the complementary workings of the intellect and the intuitive, which underlie our highest achievements. However, it has often been noticed that some persons habitually prefer one mode over the other, for example, our pedagogue at the beginning of this chapter. The exclusively verbal, logical scientist manifests a similar dominance, and may often forget and even deny that he possesses another side; he may find it difficult to work in the areas of the right hemisphere, in art, crafts, dance, sports. But this other mode, although less logical and clear, is important for creativity: "combinatory play" was Einstein's phrase. "Have you ever learned to swim?" asks the boatman.

This duality in human consciousness has long been recognized in other cultures. For instance, the Hopi Indians of the American Southwest distinguish the function of the two hands, one for writing, one for making music. The French word for Law, that most linear and rational of human pursuits, is *droit,* which literally means "right." For the Mojave Indians, the left hand is the passive, maternal side of the person, the right, the active father. William Domhoff concludes his interesting survey of the myth and symbolism of *left* and *right* by noting that the left is often the area of the taboo, the sacred, the unconscious, the feminine, the intuitive, and the dreamer. And we do find that the symbolism of the two sides of the body is quite often in agreement with these ideas. In myth, the feminine side is most often on the left, the masculine on the right. (16)

On this right-left duality, we have scientific evidence only for dreaming, and it is not too strong. In a report on three cases, Humphrey and Zangwill have found that damage to the right parietal lobe of the brain seems to interfere with dreaming. Bogen notes that his split-brain patients tend to report the absence of dreams after the operation, perhaps because of the disconnection of the verbal output from the right hemisphere. In a study with normal subjects, Austin reports that people who tend to specialize in analytic thinking (convergers) are less likely to recall dreams than those with the opposite bias (divergers), whom he characterized as more imaginative and more able to deal with the nonrational. (17)

In Vedanta, the duality in consciousness is said to be between intellect (Buddhi) and mind (manas). Such a distinction may be hard for us to state clearly, for when we say, "This person has a fine mind," we are usually referring only to the verbal and intellectual portion of the mind. The Chinese Yin-Yang symbol neatly encapsulates the duality and complementarity of these two poles of consciousness.

Facing out, on the figure's left is the "night," the dark side named *K'un* in the *I Ching.* On the figure's right is the "day," the light, *Ch'ien,* the creative, sometimes translated as the active or the originating principle. Here are the two polarities of man (and all creation) as represented in the Wilhelm-Baynes translation of the *I Ching:*

Ch'ien, The Creative

The first hexagram is made up of six unbroken lines. These unbroken lines stand for the primal power, which is light-giving, active, strong, and of the spirit. The hexagram is consistently

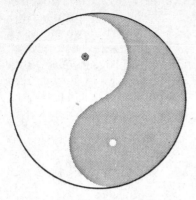

Figure 3. The Yin-Yang symbol.

strong in character, and since it is without weakness, its essence is power or energy. Its image is heaven. Its energy is represented as unrestricted by any fixed conditions in space and is therefore conceived of as motion. Time is regarded as the basis of this motion. Thus, the hexagram includes also the power of time and the power of persisting in time, that is, duration.

K'un, The Receptive

This hexagram is made up of broken lines only. The broken line represents the dark, yielding, receptive primal power of yin. The attribute of the hexagram is devotion; its image is the earth. It is the perfect complement of *The Creative*—the complement, not the opposite, for the Receptive does not combat the creative but completes it. It represents nature in contrast to spirit, earth in contrast to heaven, space as against time, the female-maternal as against the male-paternal. However, as applied to human affairs, the principle of this complementary relationship is found not only in the relation between man and woman, but also in that between prince and minister and between father and son. Indeed, even in the individual this duality appears in the coexistence of the spiritual world and the world of the senses. (18)

Note that one pole is in time, the other in space; one is light, one dark; one active, one receptive; one male, one female.

It is the complementarity of these two modes of consciousness which is a central consideration of this book, as they manifest themselves on several levels simultaneously—within each person, between different persons, within different disciplines such as scientific inquiry (psychology in particular), and in the organization of cultures. In his review on the "other" side of the brain, Joseph Bogen clarified the concept by presenting a set of dichotomies between the two modes of consciousness. Following him, I present one such table, but only for purposes of suggestion and clarification in an intuitive sort of way, not as a final categorical statement of the conception. Many of the poles are, of course, tendencies and specializations, not at all binary classifications. Examination of the table may also make the day-night metaphor I am using a bit clearer.

The two modes of consciousness: a tentative dichotomy

Who Proposed It?		
Many Sources	Day	Night
Blackburn	Intellectual	Sensuous
Oppenheimer	Time, History	Eternity, Timelessness
Deikman	Active	Receptive
Polanyi	Explicit	Tacit
Levy, Sperry	Analytic	Gestalt
Domhoff	Right (side of body)	Left (side of body)
Many sources	Left hemisphere	Right hemisphere
Bogen	Propositional	Appositional
Lee	Lineal	Nonlineal
Luria	Sequential	Simultaneous
Semmes	Focal	Diffuse
I Ching	The Creative: heaven masculine, Yang	The Receptive: earth feminine, Yin
I Ching	Light	Dark
I Ching	Time	Space
Many sources	Verbal	Spatial
Many sources	Intellectual	Intuitive
Vedanta	Buddhi	Manas
Jung	Causal	Acausal
Bacon	Argument	Experience

Many different occupations and disciplines involve a concentration in one of the major modes of consciousness. Science and law are heavily involved in linearity, duration, and verbal logic. Crafts, the "mystical" disciplines, music are more present-centered, aconceptual, intuitive. A complete human consciousness involves the polarity and integration of the two modes, as a complete day includes the daylight and the darkness.

The first chapter of this book restated the idea that even scientific knowledge, largely a linear and rational pursuit, also relies heavily on intuition for completeness. W. I. B. Beveridge, in his *The Art of Scientific Investigation,* stresses the need for the development of the intuitive side in scientists. He defines "intuition" in science as "a clarifying idea which comes suddenly to mind." Intuitive knowledge complements the normal, rational scientific knowledge, much as the paradigm change is the complement to the normal progress of scientific thought. (19)

According to Beveridge, intuitions have most often come to scientific investigators when the normal rational processes are temporarily suspended. The French mathematician Poincaré, after dismissing his work from his rational mind, went for a drive in the country. "Just as I put my foot on the brake, the idea came to me." Many others have stressed this point, that reason in science must be complemented by the "other" mode. Albert Einstein, for instance, said of his own creative processes, "The really valuable thing is intuition." The realm of the paradigm maker is the "other" side of science. The complete scientific endeavor, then, involves working in both modes.

To take a similar example quite close to hand. In the writing of this book, I have had vague idea after idea at different times: on the beach, in the mountains, in discussion, even while writing. These intuitions are sparse images—perhaps a connection which allows a new gestalt to form—but they are never fully clear, and never satisfactory by themselves. They are incomplete realizations, not a finished work. For me, it is only when the intellect has worked out these glimpses of form that the intuition becomes of any use to others. It is the very linearity of a book which enables the writer to refine his own intuitions, and clarify them, first to himself, and then, if possible, to the reader.

The process of building a house provides another example. At first, there may be a sudden inspiration of the gestalt of the finished house, but this image must be brought to completion, slowly, by linear methods, by plans and contracts, and then by the actual construction, sequentially, piece by piece.

The idea of the complementarity of two major modes of consciousness is hardly new. It antedates the *I Ching* and is found in many forms of philosophical, religious, and psychological endeavor. It was emphasized in physics by Robert Oppenheimer and in metaphysics by many. What is new now is a recognition that these modes operate physiologically as well as mentally and culturally. With a recognition of the physiological basis of the dual specializations of consciousness, we may be able to redress the balance in science and in psychology, a balance which has in recent years swung a bit too far to the right, into a strict insistence on verbal logic that has left context and perspective undeveloped. Two contemporary psychologists stress this same integrative view, although neither refers to the two modes of the brain. The Italian psychiatrist, Roberto Assagioli, discusses the articulation of the two modes.

We will consider intuition mainly in its cognitive function, i.e., as a psychic organ or means to apprehend reality. It is a synthetic function in the sense that it apprehends the totality of a given situation or psychological reality. It does not work from the part to the whole—as the analytical mind does—but apprehends a totality directly in its living existence. As it is a normal function of the human psyche, its activation is produced chiefly by eliminating the various obstacles preventing its activity. . . .

The most important combination is that with a controlled mental activity and mental discrimination. To use an analogy, it is a necessary and difficult marriage. Often it is a stormy marriage which sometimes ends in divorce. First, there is a good number of those who do not even contemplate such a marriage. They are content to either use only the intuition or only the intellect. Even when this attempt at matrimony is begun, there are various difficulties: in some cases one of the partners is too imperative and devaluates and keeps in subjection the other—and it can be either one that makes this mistake, with all the drawbacks of repression, of overt or covert rebellion. In other cases there is an oscillation, a fight between the two in which temporarily the one or the other predominates.

Many intellectuals are to a certain extent afraid when an intuition intrudes into their thought processes; they are diffident and treat it very gingerly; consciously or unconsciously, in most cases they repress it.

To speak more directly, and without metaphor, of the true relationship between intuition and intellect, intuition is the creative advance toward reality. Intellect [needs, first, to perform] the valuable and necessary function of interpreting, i.e., of translating, verbalizing in acceptable mental terms, the results of the intuition; second, to check its validity; and third, to coordinate and to include it into the body of already accepted knowledge. These functions are the rightful activity of the intellect, without its trying to assume functions which are not its province. A really fine and harmonious interplay between the two can work perfectly in a successive rhythm: intuitional insight, interpretation, further insight and its interpretation, and so on. (20)

The American Jerome Bruner, who has contributed much to our understanding of individual consciousness, elegantly summarizes the interplay of the two modes. He relates them both to the current problem in psychology and science, and to the two sides of the body.

Since childhood, I have been enchanted by the fact and the symbolism of the right hand and the left—the one the doer, the other the dreamer. The right is order and lawfulness, *le droit*. Its beauties are those of geometry and taut implication. Reaching for knowledge with the right hand is science. Yet to say only that much of science is to overlook one of its excitements, for the great hypotheses of science are gifts carried in the left.

Of the left hand we say that it is awkward and, while it has been proposed that art students can seduce their proper hand to more expressiveness by drawing first with the left, we nonetheless suspect this function. The French speak of the illegimate descendant as being *à main gauche,* and, though the heart is virtually at the center of the thoracic cavity, we listen for it on the left. Sentiment, intuition, bastardy. And should we say that reaching for knowledge with the left hand is art? Again it is not enough, for as surely as the recital of a daydream differs from the well-wrought tale, there is a barrier between undisciplined fantasy and art. To climb the barrier requires a right hand adept at technique and artifice. . . .

One thing has become increasingly clear in pursuing the nature of knowing. It is that the conventional apparatus of the psychologist—both his instruments of investigation and the conceptual tools he uses in the interpretation of his data—leaves one approach unexplored. It is an approach whose medium of exchange seems to be the metaphor paid out by the left hand. It is a way that grows happy hunches and "lucky" guesses, that is stirred into connective activity by the poet and the necromancer looking sidewise rather than directly. Their hunches and intuitions generate a grammar of their own—searching out connections, suggesting similarities, weaving ideas loosely in a trial web. . . .

The psychologist, for all his apartness, is governed by the same constraints that shape the behavior of those whom he studies. He too searches widely and metaphorically for his hunches. He reads novels, looks at and even paints pictures, is struck by the power of myth, observes his fellow men intuitively and with wonder. In doing so, he acts only part-time like a proper psychologist, racking up cases against the criteria derived from a hypothesis. Like his fellows, he observes the human scene with such sensibility as he can muster in the hope that his insight will be deepened. If he is lucky or if he has subtle psychological intuition, he will from time to time come up with hunches, combinatorial products of his metaphoric activity. If he is not fearful of these products of his own subjectivity, he will go so far as to tame the metaphors that have produced the hunches, tame them in the sense of shifting them from the left hand to the right hand by rendering them into notions that can be tested. It is my impression from observing myself and my colleagues that the forging of metaphoric hunch into testable hypothesis goes on all the time. And I am inclined to think that this process is the more evident in psychology, where the theoretical apparatus is not so well developed that it lends itself readily to generating interesting hypotheses.

Yet because our profession is young and because we feel insecure, we do not like to admit our humanity. We quite properly seek a distinctiveness that sets us apart from all those other who ponder about man and the human condition—all of which is worthy, for thereby we forge an intellectual discipline. But we are not satisfied to forge distinctive methods of our own. We must reject whoever has been successful in the task of understanding man—if he is not one of us. We place a restrictive covenant on our domain. Our articles, submitted properly to the appropriate psychological journal, have about them an aseptic quality designed to proclaim the intellectual purity of our psychological enterprise. Perhaps this is well, though it is not enough.

It is well, perhaps because it is economical to report the products of research and not the endless process that constitutes the research itself. But it is not enough in the deeper sense that we may be concealing some of the most fruitful sources of our ideas from one another. (21)

References

1. From Idries Shah, *The Exploits of the Incomparable Mulla Nasrudin* (New York: E. P. Dutton, 1972), p. 18.

2. G. William Domhoff, "But Why Did They Sit on the King's Right in the First Place?" *Psychoanalytic Review,* 56 (1969–70), 586–596.

3. Perhaps the best review of right-hemisphere functions is Joseph E. Bogen, "The Other Side of the Brain, I, II, II," *Bulletin of the Los Angeles Neurological Societies,* vol. 34, No. 3 (July 1969). Reprinted in part in Robert Ornstein, ed., *The Nature of Human Consciousness* (San Francisco, W. H. Freeman & Co.; New York, The Viking Press, 1973).

4. Brenda Milner, "Brain Mechanisms Suggested by Studies of Temporal Lobes" in F. L. Darley and C. H. Millikan, eds., *Brain Mechanisms Underlying Speech and Language* (New York: Grune & Stratton, 1965). Also Brenda Milner, "Interhemispheric Differences in the Localization of Psychological Processes in Man," *British Medical Bulletin,* 27, no. 3 (1971), 272–277.

5. A. R. Luria, *Higher Cortical Functions in Man* (New York: Basic Books, 1966).

6. R. W. Sperry, "The Great Cerebral Commissure," *Scientific American* (Jan. 1964), pp. 42–52. Offprint no. 174. Michael S. Gazzaniga, "The Split Brain in Man," *Scientific American* (Aug. 1967), pp. 24–29. Offprint no. 508.

7. *Ibid.*

8. Roger Sperry, "Problems Outstanding in the Evolution of Brain Function," James Arthur Lecture, American Museum of Natural History, New York, 1964.

9. Margaret Durnford and Doreen Kimura, "Right-Hemisphere Specialization for Depth Perception Reflected in Visual Field Differences," *Nature,* 231 (June 11, 1971), 394–395.

10. R. A. Filbey and Michael Gazzaniga, "Splitting the Normal Brain with Reaction Time," *Psychonomic Science,* 17 (1969), 335–336.

11. Marcel Kinsbourne, unpublished manuscript, Duke University, 1971. Katherine Kocel, David Galin, Robert Ornstein, and Edward Merrin, "Lateral Eye Movements and Cognitive Mode," *Psychonomic Science* (1972), in press.

12. Marcel Kinsbourne and Jay Cook, "Generalized and Lateralized Effects of Concurrent Verbalization on a Unimanual Skill," *Quarterly Journal of Experimental Psychology,* 23 (1971), 341-345.

13. David Galin and Robert Ornstein, "Lateral Specialization of Cognitive Mode: An EEG Study," *Psychophysiology* (1972), in press.

14. J. Levy-Agresti and Roger Sperry, "Differential Perceptual Capacities in Major and Minor Hemispheres," *Proceedings of the National Academy of Sciences,* 61 (1968), 1151.

15. Josephine Semmes, "Hemispheric Specialization: A Possible Clue to Mechanism," *Neuropsychologia,* 6 (1968), 11–16.

16. Domhoff, *op. cit.*

17. M. E. Humphrey and O. L. Zangwill, "Cessation of Dreaming after Brain Injury," *Journal Neurol. Neurosurg. Psychiatry,* 14 (1951), 322–325. Bogen, "The Other Side of the Brain, II," *loc. cit.* M. D. Austin, "Dream Recall and the Bias of Intellectual Ability," *Nature,* 231 (May 7, 1971), 59.

18. R. Wilhelm, trans., and C. F. Baynes, ed., *I Ching* (Princeton University Press, 1950), pp. 3, 10–11.

19. W. I. B. Beveridge, *The Art of Scientific Investigation* (New York: Random House, 1950).

20. Roberto Assagioli, *Psychosynthesis* (New York: The Viking Press, 1971), pp. 217-224.

21. Jerome Bruner, *On Knowing: Essays for the Left Hand* (Cambridge, Mass.: Harvard University Press, 1962), pp. 2–5.

How
Managers' Minds
Work
James L. McKenney and
Peter G. W. Keen

A common topic in management literature over the past few years has been the difference between managers and management scientists, usually in relation to the argument that their association has not been a productive one. For example, a recent article by C. Jackson Grayson, Jr., compares the situation with C. P. Snow's famous notion of the two cultures of science and humanities:

> Managers and management scientists are operating as two separate cultures, each with its own goals, languages, and methods. Effective cooperation—and even communication—between the two is just about minimal.[1]

Perhaps this is an overpessimistic viewpoint, but it is one that is expressed often and by individuals who have substantial experience with the use of analytic methods in management.

Management science techniques have been very successful in such areas of business as logistics planning, resource allocation, financial forecasting, and so forth. It appears that, on the whole, these techniques have found the applications for which they are best suited, and managers make substantial and continued use of them.

However, in other areas of business they have been unable to gain any real foothold. Most obviously, they have had little impact on areas of decision making where the management problems do not lend themselves to explicit formulation, where there are ambiguous or overlapping criteria for action, and where the manager operates through intuition.

The major issue for management science as a discipline now seems

Reprinted from the *Harvard Business Review,* May-June, pp. 79–90, by permission of the authors and the publisher. © 1974 by the President and Fellows of Harvard College; all rights reserved.

1. "Management Science and Business Practice," HBR July-August 1973, p. 41.

to be to get managers in such situations to make use of the formal techniques that can clearly be so helpful to them but have not yet been so in practice. There seem to be two main factors affecting this problem.

One concerns the actual techniques available. Obviously, process chemists use linear programming because it suits the constraints and natures of the problems they deal with.

The primary factor, however, is the differences in approach and behavior between the two cultures. A feature under little control by either manager or scientist is that each has a distinctive style of thinking and problem solving. In its own context, each style is highly effective but not easily communicated to the other. The differences in thinking are neither "good" nor "bad"; they simply exist.

In a way, it is platitudinous to state that managers and scientists are different, but a reason for focusing explicitly on this factor is to examine the argument, maintained by management writers, that to bridge the gap between the two groups each should become a little more like the other. In this view, the differences themselves are the problem, and education is generally recommended as the solution: the manager should be trained in elementary quantitative techniques, and the scientist, in interpersonal and managerial skills.

Yet it is this very differentiation of thinking style that makes each of them successful in his chosen specialization. But the cost of differentiation is the increased difficulty it presents in integration. Therefore, the issue for both manager and scientist is complex: how to communicate with each other; how to complement each other's strengths without sacrificing too much of one's own.

In this article, we are explicitly concerned with these differences in thinking between the two cultures. We shall offer suggestions as to how the manager and the scientist can best work together in the development and use of analytic models and decision aids.

We suggest that such aids must be designed to amplify the user's problem-solving strategies. Thus it seems that the central factor determining whether a manager will use a model to reach a decision is the extent to which it "fits" his style of thinking. The main body of this paper largely defines what we mean by "fit."

Over the past four years, we have developed and tested a model of cognitive style, drawing on the developmental psychology that has in recent years reinvigorated the whole study of thinking and problem solving.[2] Our main aim has been to better understand the cognitive aspects of the decision-making process.

2. See Jerome S. Bruner, Jacqueline J. Goodnow, and George A. Austin, *A Study of Thinking* (New York, John Wiley & Sons, 1956).

In the first section of this article, we shall provide a statement of our model in terms applicable to problem solving and decision making in general, rather than just to analytic techniques. Next, we shall discuss the experimental data we have gathered in validating the model. Finally, we shall extend our findings to the implications of cognitive style for implementing formal analytic models.

Model of cognitive style

We view problem solving and decision making in terms of the processes through which individuals organize the information they perceive in their environment, bringing to bear habits and strategies of thinking. Our model is based on the dual premise that consistent modes of thought develop through training and experience and that these modes can be classified along two dimensions, information gathering and information evaluation, as shown in figure 1.

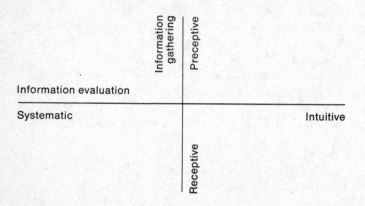

Figure 1. Model of cognitive style.

Information gathering relates to the essentially perceptual processes by which the mind organizes the diffuse verbal and visual stimuli it encounters. The resultant "information" is the outcome of a complex coding that is heavily dependent on mental set, memory capacity, and strategies—often unconscious ones—that serve to ease "cognitive strain." Of necessity, information gathering involves rejecting some of the data encountered, and summarizing and categorizing the rest.

Perceptive individuals bring to bear concepts to filter data; they focus on relationships between items and look for deviations from or conformities with their expectations. Their precepts act as cues for both gathering and cataloging the data they find.

Receptive thinkers are more sensitive to the stimulus itself. They focus on detail rather than relationships and try to derive the attributes of the information from direct examination of it instead of from fitting it to their precepts.

Each mode of information gathering has its advantages in specific situations; equally, each includes risks of overlooking the potential meaning of data. The perceptive individual too easily ignores relevant detail, while the receptive thinker may fail to shape detail into a coherent whole. In management positions, the former will be more successful in many marketing or planning roles, and the latter in tasks such as auditing.

Information evaluation refers to processes commonly classified under problem solving. Individuals differ not only in their method of gathering data but also in their sequence of analysis of those data. These differences are most pronounced in relation to formal planning.

Systematic individuals tend to approach a problem by structuring it in terms of some method which, if followed through, leads to a likely solution.

Intuitive thinkers usually avoid committing themselves in this way. Their strategy is more one of solution testing and trial-and-error. They are much more willing to jump from one method to another, to discard information, and to be sensitive to cues that they may not be able to identify verbally.

Here again, each mode of information evaluation has advantages and risks. In tasks such as production management, the systematic thinker can develop a method of procedure that utilizes all his experience and economizes on effort. An intuitive thinker often reinvents the wheel each time he deals with a particular problem. However, the intuitive person is better able to approach ill-structured problems where the volume of data, the criteria for solution, or the nature of the problem itself do not allow the use of any predetermined method.

Focus on Problem Finding

Most modern theories of the decision process stress "rationality." Mathematical decision theory and game theory, for example, are both mainly concerned with defining the basics of rational behavior. Accounting for the discrepancies between it and observed behavior is only a secondary aim. Other theories, particularly those concerning organizational decision making, include factors of motivation, personality, and social forces but still treat decision making as essentially equivalent to problem solving.

In our model of cognitive style, we focus on problem solving, but our central argument is that decision making is above all situational and, therefore, includes problem finding. The manager scans his environment and organizes what he perceives. His efforts are as much geared to clarifying his values and intents as to dealing with predefined problems.

Obviously, some problems do force themselves on his awareness; this is particularly true in crisis situations. Nonetheless, he generally has some discretion in the selection of problems to deal with and in the level of aspiration he sets for himself. (His aspiration often determines the extent to which he involves himself in terms of effort and risk.)

The manager's activities are bounded not only by the formal constraints of his job, but also by the more informal traditions and expectations implicit in his role. Because of this, the decision-making activity is strongly influenced by his perception of his position. A decision "situation" exists when he sees some event or cue in his environment that activates him into a search-analyze-evaluate sequence that results in a decision. This sequence is initiated by and depends on his environment assessment.

Our cognitive-style model provides some explanation of the processes affecting the manager's assessment of his environment. It thus includes an important aspect of behavior omitted in most theories on decision making—namely, that of problem finding, problem recognition, and problem definition. Generally, other theories assume that the situation has already been defined; the manager is presented with a neatly packaged problem and instructions on what he should try to do.

Implicit in the focus on problem finding is the concept that particular modes of cognition are better suited to certain contexts than others. As we mentioned earlier, the central argument of our study is that there needs to be a fit between the decision maker's cognitive style and the information-processing constraints of his task. Given this fit, the manager is more likely to gather environmental information that leads to successful (or at least comfortable) problem finding. He should also be able to evaluate that information in a way that facilitates successful problem solving. Perhaps the implications of a misfit are easier to indicate.

We mentioned earlier that a receptive thinker focuses on detail rather than pattern. But a receptive field sales manager who receives a wide range of information may well be flooded by it. He probably cannot examine all the sales reports, orders, phone calls, and so on. Instead, he should try to filter his information and be alert to trends and discrepancies. Thus a combination of the sales pattern in a particular region and a recent salesman's report of several customers' comments may lead him to recognize signs of change in consumer taste.

The preceptive individual is particularly suited to those tasks where he must have a concept of his environment. A preceptive manager would not be very successful in a task such as editing.

Similarly, it is easy to envisage tasks in which the intuitive thinker cannot come to terms with the data that are required in his decision making because he is unable to think in terms of a methodical sequence of analysis.

We have chosen the term "style" rather than the more common one of "structure" to stress the fact that modes of thinking relate more to propensity than to capacity. An individual's style develops out of his experience. For example, there is a tendency, particularly in late high school and college, for a student to increasingly choose courses that build on his strengths. This reinforcing pattern further develops those strengths and perhaps atrophies the skills in which he is less confident.

This suggests not only that tasks exist that are suited to particular cognitive styles, but also that the capable individual will *search out* those tasks that are compatible with his cognitive propensities. In addition, he will generally approach tasks and problems using his most comfortable mode of thinking.

Our model indicates some important differences in the ways in which individuals of particular styles approach problems and data. The accompanying list summarizes the main characteristics of each style:

Systematic thinkers tend to—

. . . look for a method and make a plan for solving a problem.
. . . be very conscious of their approach.
. . . defend the quality of a solution largely in terms of the method.
. . . define the specific constraints of the problem early in the process.
. . . discard alternatives quickly.
. . . move through a process of increasing refinement of analysis.
. . . conduct an ordered search for additional information.
. . . complete any discrete step in analysis that they begin.

Intuitive thinkers tend to—

. . . keep the overall problem continuously in mind.
. . . redefine the problem frequently as they proceed.
. . . rely on unverbalized cues, even hunches.
. . . defend a solution in terms of fit.
. . . consider a number of alternatives and options simultaneously.
. . . jump from one step in analysis or search to another and back again.
. . . explore and abandon alternatives very quickly.

Receptive thinkers tend to—

. . . suspend judgment and avoid preconceptions.

. . . be attentive to detail and to the exact attributes of data.

. . . insist on a complete examination of a data set before deriving conclusions.

Preceptive thinkers tend to—

. . . look for cues in a data set.

. . . focus on relationships.

. . . jump from one section of a data set to another, building a set of explanatory precepts.

Our research supports the concept that particular tasks and roles are more suited to one cognitive style than to another. Figure 2 shows careers that seem to be especially compatible with the skills and predispositions implicit in each of the cognitive modes of style.

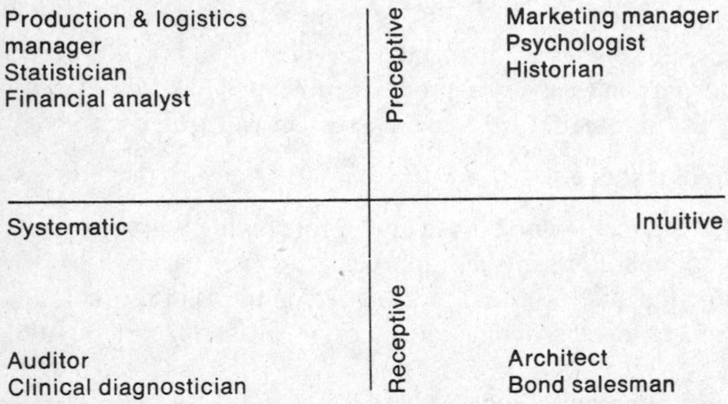

	Preceptive	
Production & logistics manager Statistician Financial analyst		Marketing manager Psychologist Historian
Systematic		Intuitive
Auditor Clinical diagnostician	Receptive	Architect Bond salesman

Figure 2. Tasks and roles compatible with each cognitive style.

Experimental results

We have carried out a range of experiments over the past four years aimed at validating the assertions made in the preceding statements.[3] The main effort in the experiments has been to identify and measure cognitive style. In the spring of 1972, a set of 12 standard reference tests for cognitive factors, developed by the Educational Testing Service, was administered to 107 MBA students. Each test was specifically

3. These experiments are described in detail in Peter G. W. Keen, "The Implications of Cognitive Style for Individual Decision Making," unpublished doctoral dissertation, Harvard Business School, 1973.

chosen to fit one particular mode or style. The results confirmed most of the main characteristics of each style summarized earlier.

Initial tests

In our first set of experiments, 70% of the sample showed distinct differences in performance level between the systematic and the intuitive tests or between the receptive and the preceptive. This supports our basic contention that individuals tend to have a definite style.

We chose a conservative approach for our tests, classifying a subject as "intuitive," "systematic," and so on, only when the scores on tests requiring, say, an intuitive response were substantially different from those measuring capacity for the other mode of style along the same dimension. The comparisons focused on relative, not absolute, performance. The numeric scores were converted to a 1 to 7 scale, with a "1" indicating that the subject scored in the lowest seventh of the sample and a "7" corresponding to the top seventh.

From our main sample of 107 MBA students, we selected 20 whose test results indicated a distinct cognitive style for a follow-up experiment. This made use of a "cafeteria" set of 16 problems from which the subjects were asked to choose any 5 to answer. In individual sessions, which were tape recorded, the subjects were invited, though not required, to talk aloud as they dealt with each problem. The results pointed to distinct differences in the ways in which individuals of particular styles respond to problems.

As expected, the systematic subjects tended to be very concerned with getting into a problem by defining how to solve it. They were conscious of their planning and often commented on the fact that there were other specific ways of answering the problem.

In contrast, the intuitive subjects tended to jump in, try something, and see where it led them. They generally showed a pattern of rapid solution testing, abandoning lines of exploration that did not seem profitable.

More important, each mode of response was effective in solving different kinds of problems. In one instance, which required the decoding of a ciphered message, the intuitive subjects solved the problem—sometimes in a dazzling fashion—while none of the systematics were able to do so. In this particular case, there seemed to be a pattern among the intuitives: a random testing of ideas, followed by a necessary incubation period in which the implications of these tests were assimilated, and then a sudden jump to the answer.

There were often unexplained shifts in the reasoning of the intuitives, who were also much more likely to answer the problems orally. The latter tendency provided some confirmation for the idea that intuitive individuals use their own talking aloud to cue their activities and to alert themselves to possible lines of analysis.

There were distinct differences in the problems chosen by each of the groups, and their ratings of which problems they enjoyed most were remarkably consistent. The systematics preferred program-type problems, while the intuitives liked open-ended ones, especially those that required ingenuity or opinion.

The overall results of the initial experiments provided definite evidence to support both our model of cognitive style and the classification methods we developed through the main-sample test scores. The verbal answers in particular highlighted the degree to which these subjects consistently and distinctively respond to problems. There seems little doubt that, in these extreme cases at least, the individual maps himself onto the problem, rather than matching his behavior to the constraints and demands of the particular task.

Secondary sampling

In another set of tests, again using the main sample of 107 subjects, we examined the relationship between cognitive style and personality. We did this through comparisons of our test results with the Myers-Briggs scales used to classify individuals in relation to Jungian theories of psychological type.[4]

The most striking result of our experiment was that, while the scores on the Myers-Briggs scales showed virtually no correlation with absolute performance on our tests, there was a relationship between cognitive style and those scales. In particular, the systematic subjects were very likely to be of the "thinking" type and the intuitives much more likely to be at the other end of the scale, "feeling." R. O. Mason and I. I. Mitroff provide a useful summary of the difference between the thinking-feeling types:

> A thinking individual is the type who relies primarily on cognitive processes. His evaluations tend to run along the lines of abstract true/false judgments and are based on formal systems of reasoning. A preference for Feeling, on the other hand implies the type of individual who relies primarily on affective processes. His evaluations tend to run along personalistic lines of good/bad, pleasant/unpleasant, and like/dislike. Thinking types systematize; feeling types take moral stands and are interested in and concerned with moral judgments.[5]

4. See Isabel Briggs Myers and Katharine C. Briggs, "The Myers-Briggs Type Indicator," Educational Testing Service, New Jersey, 1957.
5. "A Program for Research on Management Information Systems," *Management Science,* January 1973, p. 475.

We found a more modest relationship between systematic style and "introversion" and, similarly, between intuitive style and "extroversion." Thus our findings mesh well with Mason and Mitroff's predictions (they did not report any experimental data) about psychological type and information systems.

Final study

A year after the first two sets of experiments, we examined the relationship between style and career choice, using a sample of 82 MBA students. The results showed consistent differentiations between systematic and intuitive subjects. We compared the career preferences of the two groups and also looked at the test scores of those individuals who showed strong preference for particular careers.

In this experiment, the systematic students were attracted to administrative careers, to the military and to occupations involving production, planning, control, and supervision. The intuitive group's choices centered around the more open-ended business functions; they preferred careers in psychology, advertising, library science, teaching, and the arts.

The overall result of the three sets of student experiments supports the validity of our conceptual model as a useful and insightful framework for examining the role of cognitive processes in decision making. More important, now that we have established such proof, we plan to extend our research to the study of business managers and especially to model builders and model users.

Analytic models

One of our major conjectures, which partly underlay the whole development of our model, has been that computer systems in general are designed by systematic individuals for systematic users. Although management science has lost its early tones of missionary zeal, of bringing "right" thinking to the ignorant, the implementation of analytic techniques not unreasonably reflects the scientist's own distinctive approach to problem solving.

Model building, from the viewpoint of the management scientist, involves making the causal relationships in a particular situation explicit and articulating the problem until he gets a reasonably predictive model; he will then generally refine that model. He has a faith in his own plan and process, and his specialized style of thinking enables him to literally build a model, shaping ideas and concepts into a methodological whole, and above all articulating relationships that the manager may understand but may not be able to make explicit.

The management scientist's skill is indeed a specialized one; the powerful organizing and systematizing capacity he brings to model building is his special contribution. But, obviously, that can be a vice rather than a virtue in specific situations. What Donald F. Heany calls the "have technique, will travel"[6] banner really amounts to the rigorously systematic individual's preference for a methodical approach to all problems in all contexts.

Fortunately, there are many systematic managers. Our assumption is that most general managers who use management science techniques are likely to be systematic in style. The techniques match their own innate approach to problems, and they gravitate to occupations that are suited to their style.

For example, since inventory control is a task that can be systematized, it will attract systematic managers, and it will therefore be an area in which management science techniques will find fruitful ground.

However, there are just as many management positions not filled by systematic thinkers. For example, advertising, which is not so easily systematized, will attract intuitive people. If management scientists want their techniques used in these more loosely structured business areas, they must try both to make their models less awesome to the intuitive managers they will be working with and to support the managers in their decision-making processes.

This requires understanding the intuitive approach to problem solving in general and developing models which will amplify and complement that approach.

Classes of problems

We have found it useful to categorize tasks—and problems in general—in terms of the problem solver's assessment of his ability to first recognize and then act on relevant information.[7] This process provides four basic classes of problems, as in figure 3.

The classes are easily illustrated. If, for example, a manager encounters a problem of inventory control in which he feels that he knows both what data are relevant and what mental operations and analysis are required to deal with those data, the problem is one of planning (type 1 in figure 3). His whole effort then involves merely arranging the data into a form which can be used as input to a defined sequence of evaluation.

Another class of problem (type 2) exists when the required operations and methods are known, but the data involved are not. Price forecasting in complex markets is an example of this situation. Before a

6. See "Is TIMS Talking to Itself?" *Management Science,* December 1965, p. B-156.
7. See James L. McKenney, "A Taxonomy of Problem Solving," working paper, Harvard Business School, 1973.

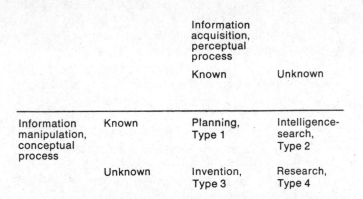

Figure 3. Classification of tasks and problems.

forecast can be made, a mass of data on economic, price, and market variables must be organized and sifted. Once this has been done, the forecasting procedure is simple.

A very different state of affairs exists when the individual understands the data but does not know how to manipulate them. Many production-scheduling problems fall into this class, invention (type 3). The relevant data are known and the problem consists of finding a way to achieve the desired end.

The fourth class of problem exists when both information and operations are unknown. In this situation, there is a conscious search for cues and a generation of explanatory concepts, together with the development of a method for manipulating the data thus organized. The development of new products is a typical research problem.

Specialized Styles

Many management-science projects start as resarch. For example, modeling a complex environment such as the housing market in order to make industry or demand forecasts generally requires a complicated first step in which two areas of the problem are worked on in parallel: (1) the generation of concepts to "explain" reality and identify the most relevant variables, and (2) the definition of the outputs, aims, and implementation of the model.

Systematic Individual

In our cafeteria experiment, the one problem rated most enjoyable by well over half the systematic group was a basic planning task. The systematic management scientist can often take a research problem and shift it to one of planning. The methodological formalization he provides helps translate unknown states of perception and conception into known ones.

However, there is sometimes the danger that he will force the translation; he may insist on some objective function that does not really fit the situation, partly because his preference for planning leaves him unwilling to accept "unknown" states. He needs to make the implicit explicit.

Intuitive Manager

Just as the systematic management scientist's specialized style of thinking provides very definite strengths in specialized tasks, so too does the intuitive manager's. It is important to again stress that the intuitive mode is not sloppy or loose; it seems to have an underlying discipline at least as coherent as the systematic mode, but is less apparent because it is largely unverbalized.

There are many situations where the volume of information, the lack of structure in the task, and the uncertainty of the environment defy planning and programming. In such situations the intuitive manager's style can be highly effective.

For example, there is no way for any manager to systematically forecast consumer tastes for furniture styles. He can, however, build a set of cues and flexible premises that may alert him to shifts in taste. He may also use the rapid scanning and testing (the main characteristic of the intuitive) for a sense of fit among disparate items of information. More important, he need never make his concepts and methods explicit.

Unlike the model builder, the intuitive manager can act without making any conscious articulation of his premises. An amusing instance of this fact occurred in many of the early efforts to use process-control computers in paper making. The computer experts "knew" that paper makers knew how to make paper; the experts' only problem was articulating the decision processes that the paper makers used, which turned out to depend mainly upon the operators' "tasting the broth" and controlling the paper flow.

For a long time, this well-established and highly effective human decision process defied conversion into formal and explicit terms. The operators were not too helpful. They "knew" what worked; they had built up out of their experience a clear but not conscious sense of the process, but this sense often varied with the individual. Thus, when a shift changed, the new crew chief, for example, might reset the valves and modify the whole operation, asserting that the changes were needed because of the time of day. There was no articulated set of concepts or methods by which this assertion could even be tested.

The decision makers here—and they merit the term, since controlling the paper-making process is a constant series of evaluations, assessments, and actions—were able to act efficiently even though they could not articulate their own procedures. This lack of articulation became a problem only when it was necessary for the computer experts to build a model of that process.

Approach differences

Systematic and intuitive individuals often treat the same project as two entirely different problems. The systematic management scientist may try to structure the problem to reduce the unknowns and to define very explicitly all the constraints in the situation. He aims at a model that is complete and has predictive power, which he can then improve and refine. That, essentially, is how he regards problem solving.

However, consciously or not, the intuitive manager is most concerned with using the model to give him a better sense of the problem. He focuses on and enjoys playing with the unknowns until he gets a feeling for the necessary steps for completion. Then he is ready to delegate the process of dealing with the problem to some individual in his organization who can systematically handle it in a more routine fashion.

The intuitive manager may also approach a task for which a model is to be built not with a need to understand the analytic process, but with a desire to discover what he can trust in order to make useful predictions. This can be of value to the systematic scientist, in that, if he can build a model which "works," the manager may well be ready to use it even though he does not understand it.

The central issue, however, is the validation of the model. The scientist validates his model formally and methodologically; he can test it in relation to known inputs and outputs. In general, he will have faith in his plan and in his own systematic process. The manager will validate the model experimentially and test it against some of his own concepts and expectations. He places much less faith in external "authority."

Recommendations for action

If our line of argument is valid, it is clear that the solution to the difficulties intuitive managers and systematic management scientists have in working together will not be obtained by trying to blur the differences. The intuitive manager may learn what network optimization is, but that is unlikely to make him think in the same systematic mode as the management scientist, who, in turn, is unlikely to develop intuitive responses through any form of education.

(This is not to assert that cognitive style is fixed, but to reinforce the point that individuals with very distinctive styles in specialized areas of activity have strengths that are directly related to their syles. It seems unlikely that the cognitive specialist will change easily—or that he should do so in any case.)

The real solution seems to lie in two areas: (1) in defining the model's role within the larger decision-making process of the particular situation, and (2) in determining how to validate the model.

From this, the manager and scientist together can better control both the process of building the model structure and their mutual expectations and actions. At the root of both these areas of concern is the whole question of trust and communication, less in the interpersonal than in the cognitive sense.

Role definition

The management scientist's role can be one of either product or service. It is important that he decide which it is in a particular situation.

On the one hand, if his model will mainly help clarify a manager's sense of the issues and options, then there is no point in the scientist's trying to provide a meticulous and complex simulation. The manager does not intend to use the model as the basis for any decision. In fact, the model may simply help him decide what the problem is and can then be thrown away.

On the other hand, the manager may need a product rather than a service; for example, a financial forecasting model, once validated, may be used by a manager as the main basis for ongoing decisions.

The degree and direction of the scientist's efforts will be very different, depending on how he perceives the manager's needs in the situation. The scientist can only identify those needs by asking questions: How does this manager approach problems? How does he define his problem, given the four different classifications in figure 3? Does he want the model to further his own learning or to help him make a specific decision?

The answer to each question has distinct consequences. For example, if the manager's response to problems is systematic, the model should explicitly reflect this fact. The scientist should explain to him the underlying assumptions as to method; the two can afford to invest substantial time and discussion on how to deal with the problem. Here, the manager is essentially looking for a technique and the scientist is the expert, with a catalog of methods.

However, if the manager is intuitive in style, the scientist should recognize that the model must allow the manager to range over alternatives and test solutions in the fashion that fits his natural mode of problem solving.

In this context, J. W. Botkin has used the paradigm of cognitive style in designing an interactive computer system for intuitive subjects.[8] He has identified five necessary features for such a model:

1. The user should have the ability to create an arbitrary order of processing, the system should not impose a "logical" or step-by-step sequence on him. In Botkin's words, "This lack of set sequence allows the intuitive user to follow his instinct for developing his ill-defined information plan directly from environmental cues."

2. The user should be able to define, explore, and play out "scenarios" that may either generate cues or test solutions.

3. The user should be able to shift between levels of detail and generality.

4. The user should have some control over the forms of output and should be able to choose visual, verbal, and numeric displays at varying levels of detail.

5. The user should be able to extend his programming, providing input in an irregular and unspecific form (i.e., he should be able to provide commands such as, "Repeat the last step, increasing X by 10%").

Botkin's experiment showed fairly clearly that intuitive and systematic subjects used his model in greatly differing ways. The differences corresponded on the whole to those found in our cafeteria experiment. The intuitive group seemed to learn from the system and to enjoy using it as much as the systematic group.

Even though Botkin's model was a special case, his results suggest that an effort on the part of the model builder to consider how the manager will use the model—in terms of process rather than output—will provide large dividends.

Here again, there is a distinction between service and product. Where the manager is most concerned with the recommendations he can derive from the model, the sort of cognitive amplifiers Botkin provides are unnecessary. However, where the manager wants the model to help him clarify his own understanding of the situation, it may well be essential to build them into the formal structure of the model.

Thus the management scientist needs to consider what a "good" model is. For himself, goodness is largely a quality of predictive power and technical elegance. For the manager, it is more a concern of com-

8. "An Intuitive Computer System: A Cognitive Approach to the Management Learning Process," unpublished doctoral dissertation, Harvard Business School, 1973.

patibility and comfort—that is, the fit between how he approaches the problem and how the model allows him to do so.

Model validation

Perhaps even more important than either recognizing the relevance of the user's own problem-solving process or determining how that person will use the model is the whole question of trust. Often, the manager does not get involved in the model itself; he simply asks for the outputs. He may well wish to validate the model by testing out some scenarios for which he has some expectations of the outcome.

However, John S. Hammond suggests that the model builder should recognize that in a large and complex model the user will have neither the desire nor the ability to understand its mechanics. The designer must, therefore, provide the user with some other way of testing out— of building trust in—the model. Hammond recommends, therefore, that the management scientist should aim—

> . . . to get something simple and useful up and running as soon as possible. By skillfully manipulating the resultant model, the management scientist should be able to obtain results that will give great insights about the problem, its nature, and its alternatives to the manager. These insights should cue the mind of the manager and cause him to perceive the problems and alternatives differently, which will in turn affect the priorities and direction of the management effort. . . .
>
> Thus the management scientist, too, will learn about the nature of the problem and also about the nature of the manager's perception of it.[9]

This recommendation seems particularly relevant in cases where the manager can obtain the initial exploration and trial testing that effort and minimal commitment to a particular definition and design, the manager can obtain the initial exploration and trial testing that may enable him to articulate his assessments of the problem—or, better, that may enable the scientist to deduce them for him.

Our recommendations are fairly modest. Essentially, they argue that if both manager and scientist alike will look at the process instead of the output, the techniques will look after themselves. It seems of central importance for the manager and scientist to recognize that each has a distinctive style of problem solving, and that each should accept the other's difference.

9. "The Roles of the Manager and Analyst in Successful Implementation," paper presented to the XX International Meeting of the Institute of Management Sciences, Tel Aviv, Israel, 1973.

If the management scientist can anticipate the fact that the manager may not use in his decision-making process the conscious planning that is so natural for the scientist himself, he will be less likely to assume that the manager's reluctantly given statement of what the problem is has any permanent force. The intuitive manager can recognize a good plan, if he can validate it at some point on his own terms; the scientist's responsibility is to provide the plan and also the validation.

The manager's responsibility is to make very clear, first to himself and then to the scientist, what he wants the model to do and to be. If he asks for an optimization program for a facilities planning project, he should decide well in advance what he will do with the results. If he knows that he will not make his decision on the basis of the model's output, he should make sure that the design process and the model structure allow him to use the model to amplify his own thinking.

The intuitive manager is very happy to relinquish the mechanics of formal analytic techniques to the expert, but only after he has developed confidence and trust in that expert. It is in this sense that the common recommendation of educating the manager in quantitative skills seems so inadequate. The intuitive manager will learn to make use of these skills supplied by others; but this learning is internal, experiential, and informal.

More than anything, the manager needs to learn how to tell a good model from a bad one. For him, a good model is one that he can, by testing his own scenarios, make sense of. However sloppy this may seem to the systematic scientist, his model will be used only if it allows the manager to make such tests or if the process of designing it has done so on a more ongoing basis.

Concluding note

People in general tend to assume that there is some "right" way of solving problems. Formal logic, for example, is regarded as a correct approach to thinking, but thinking is always a compromise between the demands of comprehensiveness, speed, and accuracy. There is no best way of thinking. If the manager and the management scientist can recognize first that each has a different cognitive style, and thus a different way of solving the same problem, then their dialogue seems more likely to bear fruit.

Our model of cognitive style is not necessarily either complete or precise. We suggest, however, that it does provide a useful way of focusing on the implementation of analytic models for decision making and of developing strategies of action that are much more likely to succeed than those based on concepts of technique, education, and salesmanship.

The Science of
"Muddling Through"
Charles E. Lindblom

Suppose an administrator is given responsibility for formulating policy with respect to inflation. He might start by trying to list all related values in order of importance, e.g., full employment, reasonable business profit, protection of small savings, prevention of a stock market crash. Then all possible policy outcomes could be rated as more or less efficient in attaining a maximum of these values. This would of course require a prodigious inquiry into values held by members of society and an equally prodigious set of calculations on how much of each value is equal to how much of each other value. He could then proceed to outline all possible policy alternatives. In a third step, he would undertake systematic comparison of his multitude of alternatives to determine which attains the greatest amount of values.

In comparing policies, he would take advantage of any theory available that generalized about classes of policies. In considering inflation, for example, he would compare all policies in the light of the theory of prices. Since no alternatives are beyond his investigation, he would consider strict central control and the abolition of all prices and markets on the one hand and elimination of all public controls with reliance completely on the free market on the other, both in the light of whatever theoretical generalizations he could find on such hypothetical economies. Finally, he would try to make the choice that would in fact maximize his values.

An alternative line of attack would be to set as his principal objective, either explicitly or without conscious thought, the relatively simple goal of keeping prices level. This objective might be compromised or complicated by only a few other goals, such as full employment. He would in fact disregard most other social values as beyond his present

Reprinted from the *Public Administration Review* 19, no. 2 (1959): 78–88, by permission of the author and the American Society for Public Administration.

interest, and he would for the moment not even attempt to rank the few values that he regarded as immediately relevant. Were he pressed, he would quickly admit that he was ignoring many related values and many possible important consequences of his policies.

As a second step, he would outline those relatively few policy alternatives that occurred to him. He would then compare them. In comparing his limited number of alternatives, most of them familiar from past controversies, he would not ordinarily find a body of theory precise enough to carry him through a comparison of their respective consequences. Instead he would rely heavily on the record of past experience with small policy steps to predict the consequences of similar steps extended into the future.

Moreover, he would find that the policy alternatives combined objectives or values in different ways. For example, one policy might offer price level stability at the cost of some risk of unemployment; another might offer less price stability but also less risk of unemployment. Hence, the next step in his approach—the final selection—would combine into one the choice among values and the choice among instruments for reaching values. It would not, as in the first method of policy making, approximate a more mechanical process of choosing the means that best satisfied goals that were previously clarified and ranked. Because practitioners of the second approach expect to achieve their goals only partially, they would expect to repeat endlessly the sequence just described, as conditions and aspirations changed and as accuracy of prediction improved.

By root or by branch

For complex problems, the first of these two approaches is of course impossible. Although such an approach can be described, it cannot be practiced except for relatively simple problems and even then only in a somewhat modified form. It assumes intellectual capacities and sources of information that men simply do not possess, and it is even more absurd as an approach to policy when the time and money that can be allocated to a policy problem are limited, as is always the case. Of particular importance to public administrators is the fact that public agencies are in effect usually instructed not to practice the first method. That is to say, their prescribed functions and constraints—the politically or legally possible—restrict their attention to relatively few values and relatively few alternative policies among the countless alternatives that might be imagined. It is the second method that is practiced.

Curiously, however, the literatures of decision making, policy formulation, planning, and public administration formalize the first approach rather than the second, leaving public administrators who handle complex decisions in the position of practicing what few preach. For emphasis I run some risk of overstatement. True enough, the literature is well aware of limits on man's capacities and of the inevitability that policies will be approached in some such style as the second. But attempts to formalize rational policy formulation—to lay out explicitly the necessary steps in the process—usually describe the first approach and not the second.[1]

The common tendency to describe policy formulation even for complex problems as though it followed the first approach has been strengthened by the attention given to, and successes enjoyed by, operations research, statistical decision theory, and systems analysis. The hallmarks of these procedures, typical of the first approach, are clarity of objective, explicitness of evaluation, a high degree of comprehensiveness of overview, and, wherever possible, quantification of values for mathematical analysis. But these advanced procedures remain largely the appropriate techniques of relatively small-scale problem solving where the total number of variables to be considered is small and value problems restricted. Charles Hitch, head of the Economics Division of RAND Corporation, one of the leading centers for application of these techniques, has written:

> I would make the empirical generalization from my experience at RAND and elsewhere that operations research is the art of suboptimizing, i.e., of solving some lower-level problems, and that difficulties increase and our special competence diminishes by an order of magnitude with every level of decision making we attempt to ascend. The sort of simple explicit model which operations researchers are so proficient in using can certainly reflect most of the significant factors influencing traffic control on the George Washington Bridge, but the proportion of the relevant reality which we can represent by any such model or models in studying, say, a major foreign-policy decision, appears to be almost trivial.[2]

Accordingly, I propose in this paper to clarify and formalize the

---

1. James G. March and Herbert A. Simon similarly characterize the literature. They also take some important steps, as have Simon's other recent articles, to describe a less heroic model of policy making. See *Organizations* (New York: John Wiley & Sons, 1958), p. 137.

2. "Operations Research and National Planning—a Dissent." *Operations Research 5* (October 1957): 718. Hitch's dissent is from particular points made in the article to which his paper is a reply; his claim that operations research is for low-level problems is widely accepted.

For examples of the kind of problems to which operations research is applied see C. W. Churchman, R. L. Ackoff, and E. L. Arnoff, *Introduction to Operations Research* (New York: John Wiley & Sons, 1957); and J. F. McCloskey and J. M. Coppinger, eds., *Operations Research for Management*, vol. 2 (Baltimore: Johns Hopkins Press, 1956).

second method, much neglected in the literature. This might be described as the method of *successive limited comparisons*. I will contrast it with the first approach, which might be called the rational-comprehensive method.[3] More impressionistically and briefly—and therefore generally used in this article—they could be characterized as the "branch method" and "root method," the former continually building out from the current situation, step-by-step and by small degrees; the latter starting from fundamentals anew each time, building on the past only as experience is embodied in a theory, and always prepared to start completely from the ground up.

Let us put the characteristics of the two methods side by side in simplest terms.

Rational-Comprehensive *(Root)*	*Successive Limited* *Comparisons* *(Branch)*
1*a*. Clarification of values or objectives distinct from and usually prerequisite to empirical analysis of alternative policies.	1*b*. Selection of value goals and empirical analysis of the needed action not distinct from one another but closely intertwined.
2*a*. Policy-formulation is therefore approached through means-end analysis: First the ends are isolated, then the means to achieve them are sought.	2*b*. Since means and ends are not distinct, means-end analysis is often inappropriate or limited.
3*a*. The test of a "good" policy is that it can be shown to be the most appropriate means to desired ends.	3*b*. The test of a "good" policy is typically that various analysts find themselves directly agreeing on a policy (without their agreeing that it is the most appropriate means to an agreed objective).
4*a*. Analysis is comprehensive; every imporatnt relevant factor is taken into account.	4*b*. Analysis is drastically limited: (i) Important possible outcomes are neglected. (ii) Important alternative potential policies are neglected. (iii) Important affected values are neglected.
5*a*. Theory is often heavily relied upon.	5*b*. A succession of comparisons greatly reduces or eliminates reliance on theory.

3. I am assuming that administrators often make policy and advise in the making of policy and am treating decision making and policy making as synonymous for purposes of this paper.

Assuming that the root method is familiar and understandable, we proceed directly to clarification of its alternative by contrast. In explaining the second, we shall be describing how most administrators do in fact approach complex questions, for the root method, the "best" way as a blueprint or model, is in fact not workable for complex policy questions, and administrators are forced to use the method of successive limited comparisons.

Intertwining evaluation and empirical analysis (1b)

The quickest way to understand how values are handled in the method of successive limited comparisons is to see how the root method often breaks down in *its* handling of values or objectives. The idea that values should be clarified, and in advance of the examination of alternative policies, is appealing. But what happens when we attempt it for complex social problems? The first difficulty is that on many critical values or objectives, citizens disagree, congressmen disagree, and public administrators disagree. Even where a fairly specific objective is prescribed for the administrator, there remains considerable room for disagreement on subobjectives. Consider, for example, the conflict with respect to locating public housing, described in Meyerson and Banfield's study of the Chicago Housing Authority[4]—disagreement which occurred despite the clear objective of providing a certain number of public housing units in the city. Similarly conflicting are objectives in highway location, traffic control, minimum wage administration, development of tourist facilities in national parks, or insect control.

Administrators cannot escape these conflicts by ascertaining the majority's preference, for preferences have not been registered on most issued; indeed, there often *are* no preferences in the absence of public discussion sufficient to bring an issue to the attention of the electorate. Furthermore, there is a question of whether intensity of feeling should be considered as well as the number of persons preferring each alternative. By the impossibility of doing otherwise, administrators often are reduced to deciding policy without clarifying objectives first.

Even when an administrator resolves to follow his own values as a criterion for decisions, he often will not know how to rank them when they conflict with one another, as they usually do. Suppose, for example, that an administrator must relocate tenants living in tenements scheduled for destruction. One objective is to empty the buildings fairly promptly, another is to find suitable accommodation for persons displaced, another is to avoid friction with residents in other areas in

4. Martin Meyerson and Edward C. Banfield, *Politics, Planning, and the Public Interest* (Glencoe, Ill.: Free Press, 1955).

which a large influx would be unwelcome, another is to deal with all concerned through persuasion if possible, and so on.

How does one state even to himself the relative importance of these partially conflicting values? A simple ranking of them is not enough; one needs ideally to know how much of one value is worth sacrificing for some of another value. The answer is that typically the administrator chooses—and must choose—directly among policies in which these values are combined in different ways. He cannot first clarify his values and then choose among policies.

A more subtle third point underlies both the first two. Social objectives do not always have the same relative values. One objective may be highly prized in one circumstance, another in another circumstance. If, for example, an administrator values highly both the dispatch with which his agency can carry through its projects *and* good public relations, it matters little which of the two possibly conflicting values he favors in some abstract or general sense. Policy questions arise in forms which put to administrators such a question as: Given the degree to which we are or are not already achieving the values of dispatch and the values of good public relations, is it worth sacrificing a little speed for a happier clientele, or is it better to risk offending the clientele so that we can get on with our work? The answer to such a question varies with circumstances.

The value problem is, as the example shows, always a problem of adjustments at a margin. But there is not practicable way to state marginal objectives or values except in terms of particular policies. That one value is preferred to another in one decision situation does not mean that it will be preferred in another decision situation in which it can be had only at great sacrifice of another value. Attempts to rank or order values in general and abstract terms so that they do not shift from decision to decision end up by ignoring the relevant marginal preferences. The significance of this third point thus goes very far. Even if all administrators had at hand an agreed set of values, objectives, and constraints, and an agreed ranking of these values, objectives, and constraints, their marginal values in actual choice situations would be impossible to formulate.

Unable consequently to formulate the relevant values first and then choose among policies to achieve them, administrators must choose directly among alternative policies that offer different marginal combinations of values. Somewhat paradoxically, the only practicable way to disclose one's relevant marginal values even to oneself is to describe the policy one chooses to achieve them. Except roughly and vaguely, I know of no way to describe—or even to understand—what my relative evaluations are for, say, freedom and security, speed and accuracy in governmental decisions, or low taxes and better schools than to describe my preferences among specific choices that might be made between the alternatives in each of the pairs.

In summary, two aspects of the process by which values are actually handled can be distinguished. The first is clear: evaluation and empirical analysis are intertwined; that is, one chooses among values and among policies at one and the same time. Put a little more elaborately, one simultaneously chooses a policy to attain certain objectives and chooses the objectives themselves. The second aspect is related but distinct: the administrator focuses his attention on marginal or incremental values. Whether he is aware of it or not, he does not find general formulations of objectives very helpful and in fact makes specific marginal or incremental comparisons. Two policies, X and Y, confront him. Both promise the same degree of attainment of objectives *a, b, c, d,* and *e.* But X promises him somewhat more of *f* than does Y, while Y promises him somewhat more of *g* than does X. In choosing between them, he is in fact offered the alternative of a marginal or incremental amount of *f* at the expense of a marginal or incremental amount of *g.* The only values that are relevant to his choice are these increments by which the two policies differ; and, when he finally chooses between the two marginal values, he does so by making a choice between policies.[5]

As to whether the attempt to clarify objectives in advance of policy selection is more or less rational than the close intertwining of marginal evaluation and empirical analysis, the principal difference established is that for complex problems the first is impossible and irrelevant, and the second is both possible and relevant. The second is possible because the administrator need not try to analyze any values except the values by which alternative policies differ and need not be concerned with them except as they differ marginally. His need for information on values or objectives is drastically reduced as compared with the root method; and his capacity for grasping, comprehending, and relating values to one another is not strained beyond the breaking point.

Relations between means and ends (2*b*)

Decision making is ordinarily formalized as a means-ends relationship: means are conceived to be evaluated and chosen in the light of ends finally selected independently of and prior to the choice of means. This is the means-ends relationship of the root method. But it follows from all that has just been said that such a means-ends relationship is

5. The line of argument is, of course, an extension of the theory of market choice, especially the theory of consumer choice, to public policy choices.

possible only to the extent that values are agreed upon, are reconcilable, and are stable at the margin. Typically, therefore, such a means-ends relationship is absent from the branch method, where means and ends are simultaneously chosen.

Yet any departure from the means-ends relationship of the root method will strike some readers as inconceivable. For it will appear to them that only in such a relationship is it possible to determine whether one policy choice is better or worse than another. How can an administrator know whether he has made a wise or foolish decision if he is without prior values or objectives by which to judge his decisions? The answer to this question calls up the third distinctive difference between root and branch methods: how to decide the best policy.

The test of "good" policy (3b)

In the root method, a decision is "correct," "good," or "rational" if it can be shown to attain some specified objective, where the objective can be specified without simply describing the decision itself. Where objectives are defined only through the marginal or incremental approach to values described above, it is still sometimes possible to test whether a policy does in fact attain the desired objectives; but a precise statement of the objectives takes the form of a description of the policy chosen or some alternative to it. To show that a policy is mistaken one cannot offer an abstract argument that important objectives are not achieved; one must instead argue that another policy is more to be preferred.

So far, the departure from customary ways of looking at problem solving is not troublesome, for many administrators will be quick to agree that the most effective discussion of the correctness of policy does take the form of comparison with other policies that might have been chosen. But what of the situation in which administrators cannot agree on values or objectives, either abstractly or in marginal terms? What then is the test of "good" policy? For the root method, there is no test. Agreement on objectives failing, there is no standard of "correctness." For the method of successive limited comparisons, the test is agreement on policy itself, which remains possible even when agreement on values is not.

It has been suggested that continuing agreement in Congress on the desirability of extending old-age insurance stems from liberal desires to strengthen the welfare programs of the federal government and from conservative desires to reduce union demands for private pension plans. If so, this is an excellent demonstration of the ease with which individuals of different ideologies often can agree on concrete policy. Labor mediators report a similar phenomenon; the contestants cannot agree on criteria for settling their disputes but can agree on specific proposals. Similarly, when one administrator's objective turns out to be another's means, they often can agree on policy.

Agreement on policy thus becomes the only practicable test of the policy's correctness. And for one administrator to seek to win the other over to agreement on ends as well would accomplish nothing and create quite unnecessary controversy.

If agreement directly on policy as a test for "best" policy seems a poor substitute for testing the policy against its objectives, it ought to be remembered that objectives themselves have no ultimate validity other than that they are agreed upon. Hence agreement is the test of "best" policy in both methods. But where the root method requires agreement on what elements in the decision constitute objectives and on which of these objectives should be sought, the branch method falls back on agreement wherever it can be found.

In an important sense, therefore, it is not irrational for an administrator to defend a policy as good without being able to specify what it is good for.

Noncomprehensive analysis (4b)

Ideally, rational-comprehensive analysis leaves out nothing important. But it is impossible to take everything important into consideration unless "important" is so narrowly defined that analysis is in fact quite limited. Limits on human intellectual capacities and on available information set definite limits to man's capacity to be comprehensive. In actual fact, therefore, no one can practice the rational-comprehensive method for really complex problems, and every administrator faced with a sufficiently complex problem must find ways drastically to simplify.

An administrator assisting in the formulation of agricultural economic policy cannot in the first place be competent on all possible policies. He cannot even comprehend one policy entirely. In planning a soil bank program, he cannot successfully anticipate the impact of higher or lower farm income on, say, urbanization—the possible consequent loosening of family ties, the possible consequent need for revisions in social security and further implications for tax problems arising out of new federal responsibilities for social security and municipal responsibilities for urban services. Nor, to follow another line of repercussions, can he work through the soil bank program's effects on prices for agricultural products in foreign markets and consequent implications for foreign relations, including those arising out of economic rivalry between the United States and the USSR.

In the method of successive limited comparisons, simplification is systematically achieved in two principal ways. First, it is achieved through limitation of policy comparisons to those policies that differ in relatively small degree from policies presently in effect. Such a limitation immediately reduces the number of alternatives to be investigated and also drastically simplifies the character of the investigation of each. For it is not necessary to undertake fundamental inquiry into an alternative and its consequences; it is necessary only to study those respects in which the proposed alternative and its consequences differ from the status quo. The empirical comparison of marginal differences among alternative policies that differ only marginally is, of course, a counterpart to the incremental or marginal comparison of values discussed above.[6]

Relevance as well as realism

It is a matter of common observation that in Western democracies public administrators and policy analysts in general do largely limit their analyses to incremental or marginal differences in policies that are chosen to differ only incrementally. They do not do so, however, solely because they desperately need some way to simplify their problems; they also do so in order to be relevant. Democracies change their policies almost entirely through incremental adjustments. Policy does not move in leaps and bounds.

The incremental character of political change in the United States has often been remarked. The two major political parties agree on fundamentals; they offer alternative policies to the voters only on relatively small points of difference. Both parties favor full employment, but they define it somewhat differently; both favor the development of water power resources, but in slightly different ways; and both favor unemployment compensation, but not the same level of benefits. Similarly, shifts of policy within a party take place largely through a series of relatively small changes, as can be seen in their only gradual acceptance of the idea of governmental responsibility for support of the unemployed, a change in party positions beginning in the early thirties and culminating in a sense in the Employment Act of 1946.

Party behavior is in turn rooted in public attitudes, and political theorists cannot conceive of democracy's surviving in the United States in the absence of fundamental agreement on potentially disruptive issues, with consequent limitation of policy debates to relatively small differences in policy.

6. A more precise definition of incremental policies and a discussion of whether a change that appears "small" to one observer might be seen differently by another is to be found in my "Policy Analysis," *American Economic Review* 48(June 1958): 298.

Since the policies ignored by the administrator are politically impossible and so irrelevant, the simplification of analysis achieved by concentrating on policies that differ only incrementally is not a capricious kind of simplification. In addition, it can be argued that, given the limits on knowledge within which policy makers are confined, simplifying by limiting the focus to small variations from present policy makes the most of available knowledge. Because policies being considered are like present and past policies, the administrator can obtain information and claim some insight. Nonincremental policy proposals are therefore typically not only politically irrelevant but also unpredictable in their consequences.

The second method of simplification of analysis is the practice of ignoring important possible consequences of possible policies, as well as the values attached to the neglected consequences. If this appears to disclose a shocking shortcoming of successive limited comparisons, it can be replied that, even if the exclusions are random, policies may nevertheless be more intelligently formulated than through futile attempts to achieve a comprehensiveness beyond human capacity. Actually, however, the exclusions, seeming arbitrary or random from one point of view, need be neither.

Achieving a degree of comprehensiveness

Suppose that each value neglected by one policy-making agency were a major concern of at least one other agency. In that case, a helpful division of labor would be achieved, and no agency need find its task beyond its capacities. The shortcomings of such a system would be that one agency might destroy a value either before another agency could be activated to safeguard it or in spite of another agency's efforts. But the possibility that important values may be lost is present in any form of organization, even where agencies attempt to comprehend in planning more than is humanly possible.

The virtue of such a hypothetical division of labor is that every important interest or value has its watchdog. And these watchdogs can protect the interests in their jurisdiction in two quite different ways: first, by redressing damages done by other agencies; and, second, by anticipating and heading off injury before it occurs.

In a society like that of the United States in which individuals are free to combine to pursue almost any possible common interest they might have and in which government agencies are sensitive to the pressures of these groups, the system described is approximated. Almost every interest has its watchdog. Without claiming that every interest has a sufficiently powerful watchdog, it can be argued that our system often can assure a more comprehensive regard for the values of the whole society than any attempt at intellectual comprehensiveness.

In the United States, for example, no part of government attempts a comprehensive overview of policy on income distribution. A policy nevertheless evolves, and one responding to a wide variety of interests. A process of mutual adjustment among farm groups, labor unions, municipalities and school boards, tax authorities, and government agencies with responsibilities in the fields of housing, health, highways, national parks, fire, and police accomplishes a distribution of income in which particular income problems neglected at one point in the decision processes become central at another point.

Mutual adjustment is more pervasive than the explicit forms it takes in negotiation between groups; it persists through the mutual impacts of groups upon one another even where they are not in communication. For all the imperfections and latent dangers in this ubiquitous process of mutual adjustment, it will often accomplish an adaptation of policies to a wider range of interests than could be done by one group centrally.

Note, too, how the incremental pattern of policy making fits with the multiple pressure pattern. For when decisions are only incremental—closely related to known policies, it is easier for one group to anticipate the kind of moves another might make and easier too for it to make correction for injury already accomplished.[7]

Even partisanship and narrowness, to use pejorative terms, will sometimes be assets to rational decision making, for they can doubly insure that what one agency neglects, another will not; they specialize personnel to distinct points of view. The claim is valid that effective rational coordination of the federal administration, if possible to achieve at all, would require an agreed set of values[8]—if "rational" is defined as the practice of the root method of decision making. But a high degree of administrative coordination occurs as each agency adjusts its policies to the concerns of the other agencies in the process of fragmented decision making I have just described.

For all the apparent shortcomings of the incremental approach to policy alternatives with its arbitrary exclusion coupled with fragmentation, when compared to the root method, the branch method often looks far superior. In the root method, the inevitable exclusion of

7. The link between the practice of the method of successive limited comparisons and mutual adjustment of interests in a highly fragmented decision-making process adds a new facet to pluralist theories of government and administration.

8. Herbert Simon, Donald W. Smithburg, and Victor A. Thompson, *Public Administration* (New York: Alfred A. Knopf, 1950), p. 434.

factors is accidental, unsystematic, and not defensible by any argument so far developed, while in the branch method the exclusions are deliberate, systematic, and defensible. Ideally, of course, the root method does not exclude; in practice it must.

Nor does the branch method necessarily neglect long-run considerations and objectives. It is clear that important values must be omitted in considering policy, and sometimes the only way long-run objectives can be given adequate attention is through the neglect of short-run considerations. But the values omitted can be either long-run or short-run.

Succession of comparisons (5*b*)

The final distinctive element in the branch method is that the comparisons, together with the policy choice, proceed in a chronological series. Policy is not made once and for all; it is made and remade endlessly. Policy making is a process of successive approximation to some desired objectives in which what is desired itself continues to change under reconsideration.

Making policy is at best a very rough process. Neither social scientists nor politicians nor public administrators yet know enough about the social world to avoid repeated error in predicting the consequences of policy moves. A wise policy maker consequently expects that his policies will achieve only part of what he hopes and at the same time will produce unanticipated consequences he would have preferred to avoid. If he proceeds through a *succession* of incremental changes, he avoids serious lasting mistakes in several ways.

In the first place, past sequences of policy steps have given him knowledge about the probable consequences of further similar steps. Second, he need not attempt big jumps toward his goals that would require predictions beyond his or anyone else's knowledge, because he never expects his policy to be a final resolution of a problem. His decision is only one step, one that if successful can quickly be followed by another. Third, he is in effect able to test his previous predictions as he moves on to each further step. Lastly, he often can remedy a past error fairly quickly—more quickly than if policy proceeded through more distinct steps widely spaced in time.

Compare this comparative analysis of incremental changes with the aspiration to employ theory in the root method. Man cannot think without classifying, without subsuming one experience under a more general category of experiences. The attempt to push categorization as far as possible and to find general propositions which can be applied to specific situations is what I refer to with the word "theory." Where root analysis often leans heavily on theory in this sense, the branch method does not.

The assumption of root analysts is that theory is the most systematic and economical way to bring relevant knowledge to bear on a specific problem. Granting the assumption, an unhappy fact is that we do not have adequate theory to apply to problems in any policy area, although theory is more adequate in some areas—monetary policy, for example —than in others. Comparative analysis, as in the branch method, is sometimes a systematic alternative to theory.

Suppose an administrator must choose among a small group of policies that differ only incrementally from each other and from present policy. He might aspire to "understand" each of the alternatives—for example, to know all the consequences of each aspect of each policy. If so, he would indeed require theory. In fact, however, he would usually decide that, *for policy-making purposes,* he need know, as explained above, only the consequences of each of those aspects of the policies in which they differed from one another. For this much more modest aspiration, he requires no theory (although it might be helpful, if available), for he can proceed to isolate probable differences by examining the differences in consequences associated with past differences in policies, a feasible program because he can take his observations from a long sequence of incremental changes.

For example, without a more comprehensive social theory about juvenile delinquency than scholars have yet produced, one cannot possibly understand the ways in which a variety of public policies— say on education, housing, recreation, employment, race relations, and policing—might encourage or discourage delinquency. And one needs such an understanding if he undertakes the comprehensive overview of the problem prescribed in the models of the root method. If, however, one merely wants to mobilize knowledge sufficient to assist in a choice among a small group of similar policies—alternative policies on juvenile court procedures, for example—he can do so by comparative analysis of the results of similar past policy moves.

Theorists and practitioners

This difference explains—in some cases at least—why the administrator often feels that the outside expert or academic problem solver is sometimes not helpful and why they in turn often urge more theory on him. And it explains why an administrator often feels more confident when "flying by the seat of his pants" than when following the advice of theorists. Theorists often ask the administrator to go the long way round to the solution of his problems, in effect ask him to follow the best canons of the scientific method, when the administrator knows that the best available theory will work less well than more modest incremental comparisons. Theorists do not realize that the administrator is often in fact practicing a systematic method. It would be foolish to push this explanation too far, for sometimes practical decision makers are pursuing neither a theoretical approach nor successive comparisons, nor any other systematic method.

It may be worth emphasizing that theory is sometimes of extremely limited helpfulness in policy making for at least two rather different reasons. It is greedy for facts; it can be constructed only through a great collection of observations. And it is typically insufficiently precise for application to a policy process that moves through small changes. In contrast, the comparative method both economizes on the need for facts and directs the analyst's attention to just those facts that are relevant to the fine choices faced by the decision maker.

With respect to precision of theory, economic theory serves as an example. It predicts that an economy without money or prices would in certain specified ways misallocate resources, but this finding pertains to an alternative far removed from the kind of policies on which administrators need help. Yet it is not precise enough to predict the consequences of policies restricting business mergers, and this is the kind of issue on which the administrators need help. Only in relatively restricted areas does economic theory achieve sufficient precision to go far in resolving policy questions; its helpfulness in policy making is always so limited that it requires supplementation through comparative analysis.

Successive comparison as a system

Successive limited comparisons is, then, indeed a method or system; it is not a failure of method for which administrators ought to apologize. Nonetheless, its imperfections, which have not been explored in this paper, are many. For example, the method is without a built-in safeguard for all relevant values, and it also may lead the decision maker to overlook excellent policies for no other reason than that they are not suggested by the chain of successive policy steps leading up to the present. Hence, it ought to be said that under this method, as well as under some of the most sophisticated variants of the root method—operations research, for example—policies will continue to be as foolish as they are wise.

Why then bother to describe the method in all the above detail? Because it is in fact a common method of policy formulation, and is, for complex problems, the principal reliance of administrators as well as of other policy analysts.[9] And because it will be superior to any

9. Elsewhere I have explored this same method of policy formation as practiced by academic analysts of policy ("Policy Analysis," *American Economic*

other decision-making method available for complex problems in many circumstances, certainly superior to a futile attempt at super-human comprehensiveness. The reaction of the public administrator to the exposition of method doubtless will be less a discovery of a new method than a better acquaintance with an old. But by becoming more conscious of their practice of this method, administrators might practice it with more skill and know when to extend or constrict its use. (That they sometimes practice it effectively and sometimes not may explain the extremes of opinion on "muddling through," which is both praised as a highly sophisticated form of problem solving and denounced as no method at all. For I suspect that insofar as there is a system in what is known as "muddling through," this method is it.)

One of the noteworthy incidental consequences of clarification of the method is the light it throws on the suspicion an administrator sometimes entertains that a consultant or adviser is not speaking relevantly and responsibly when in fact by all ordinary objective evidence he is. The trouble lies in the fact that most of us approach policy problems within a framework given by our view of a chain of successive policy choices made up to the present. One's thinking about appropriate policies with respect, say, to urban traffic control is greatly influenced by one's knowledge of the incremental steps taken up to the present. An administrator enjoys an intimate knowledge of his past sequences that "outsiders" do not share, and his thinking and that of the "outsider" will consequently be different in ways that may puzzle both. Both may appear to be talking intelligently, yet each may find the other unsatisfactory. The relevance of the policy chain of succession is even more clear when an American tries to discuss, say, antitrust policy with a Swiss, for the chains of policy in the two countries are strikingly different and the two individuals consequently have organized their knowledge in quite different ways.

If this phenomenon is a barrier to communication, an understanding of it promises an enrichment of intellectual interaction in policy

Review, vol. 48). Although it has been here presented as a method for public administrators, it is no less necessary to analysts more removed from immediate policy questions, despite their tendencies to describe their own analytical efforts as though they were the rational-comprehensive method with an especially heavy use of theory. Similarly, this same method is inevitably resorted to in personal problem solving, where means and ends are sometimes impossible to separate, where aspirations or objectives undergo constant development, and where drastic simplification of the complexity of the real world is urgent if problems are to be solved in the time that can be given to them. To an economist accustomed to dealing with the marginal or incremental concept in market processes, the central idea in the method is that both evaluation and empirical analysis are incremental. Accordingly I have referred to the method elsewhere as "the incremental method."

formulation. Once the source of difference is understood, it will sometimes be stimulating for an administrator to seek out a policy analyst whose recent experience is with a policy chain different from his own.

This raises again a question only briefly discussed above on the merits of like-mindedness among government administrators. While much of organization theory argues the virtues of common values and agreed organizational objectives, for complex problems in which the root method is inapplicable, agencies will want among their own personnel two types of diversification: administrators whose thinking is organized by reference to policy chains other than those familiar to most members of the organization and, even more commonly, administrators whose professional or personal values or interests create diversity of view (perhaps coming from different specialties, social classes, geographical areas) so that, even within a single agency, decision making can be fragmented and parts of the agency can serve as watchdogs for other parts.

Emotional Blocks
James L. Adams

This chapter will begin with a game—a game which requires a group of people, the larger the better, so try it at a party. It was, I think, invented by Bob McKim and is called "Barnyard."

Exercise

Divide your group and assign them to be various animals as follows:

If their last names begin with:	they are:
A-E	sheep
F-K	pigs
L-R	cows
S-Z	turkeys

Now tell each person to find a partner (preferably someone he does not know too well) and to look this partner in the eye. You will then count to three, at which time everyone is to make the sound of his animal as loudly as he possibly can. See how loud a barnyard you can build.

The participants in this game will be able to experience a common emotional block to conceptualization—namely, that of feeling like an ass. If you did not play the game and want to experience the feeling, merely stand alone on any busy corner (or wherever you are right now) and loudly make the sound of one of the animals.

As mentioned in the previous chapter, conceptualization is risky and new ideas are hard to evaluate. The expression of a new idea, and especially the process of trying to convince someone else it has value, sometimes makes one feel like an ass, since you are doing something that possibly exposes your imperfections. In order to avoid this feel-

Selection is reprinted from CONCEPTUAL BLOCKBUSTING by James L. Adams, with the permission of W. W. Norton & Company, Inc. Copyright © 1974, 1976 by James L. Adams. This book was published originally as a part of The Portable Stanford, a series of books published by the Stanford Alumni Association, Stanford, California.

ing, people will often avoid conceptualization, or at least avoid publicizing the output.

Before we discuss specific emotional blocks, let me make a few comments about psychological theory. Although, as I stated earlier, psychological theory does not offer a complete model for explaining the conceptual process, many theories exist and have commonalities which are pertinent to understanding emotional blocks. Of particular importance are the theories of Freud and his followers and of the contemporary humanistic psychologists (Rogers, Maslow et al.).

Freud

Much of Freudian theory is based upon conflicts between the *id* (the instinctive animal part of ourselves) and the *ego* (the socially aware and conscious aspect) and *superego* (the moralistic portion of ourselves that forbids and prohibits). The motive force in the Freudian model is the id, which resides in the unconscious and is concerned with satisfying our needs. According to Freud, ideas originating in the unconscious must be subjected to the scrutiny of the ego (which may reject them because we cannot realistically carry them out), and the superego (which may reject them because we should not have let ourselves have such ideas in the first place). If these ideas are rejected, they will either be completely repressed or they will contribute to neurotic behavior because of unresolved conflict. If they are accepted, they will be admitted to the conscious mind. (This acceptance may be accompanied by anxiety, since once the ego and superego identify with an idea one can be hurt by its rejection.) If the ego and superego are overly selective, relatively few creative ideas will reach the conscious mind. If they are not selective enough, a torrent of highly innovative but extremely impractical ideas will emerge.

Since the time of Freud, his theory has been elaborated upon by his followers. A good example of this can be seen in Lawrence S. Kubie's book *Neurotic Distortion of the Creative Process*. Kubie utilizes the Freudian concept of *preconscious* in his model of creative thinking. He relegates the subconscious portions of creative thought and problem-solving to this preconscious, reserving the unconscious for unsettled conflicts and repressed impulses. In this model, the preconscious mental processes are hindered both by the conscious and the unconscious processes. As Kubie states in *Neurotic Distortion:*

Preconscious processes are assailed from both sides. From one
side they are nagged and prodded into rigid and distorted symbols
by unconscious drives which are oriented away from reality and
which consist of rigid compromise formations, lacking in fluid

inventiveness. From the other side they are driven by literal conscious purpose, checked and corrected by conscious retrospective critique.

Like Freud, Kubie has a model of the mind in which creative thinking is inhibited by the conscious ego and superego and in which creativity occurs at least partly below the conscious level. However, neuroses play a much more villainous role in Kubie's model than in Freud's.

The Humanistic psychologists

Although humanistic psychologists agree that creativity is a response to basic inner needs in people, they have a somewhat broader hierarchy of needs than the Freudians. They maintain that people create in order to grow and to fulfill themselves, as well as to solve conflicts and to answer the cravings of the id. They are more concerned with reaching upward and outward. Carl Rogers, in an article entitled "Toward a Theory of Creativity" in *Creativity and its Cultivation* (edited by Harold Anderson) explains:

> The mainspring of creativity appears to be the same tendency which we discover so deeply as the curative force in psychotherapy— man's tendency to actualize himself, to become his potentialities. By this I mean the directional trend which is evident in all organic and human life—the urge to expand, extend, develop, mature— the tendency to express and activate all the capacities of the organism, to the extent that such activation enhances the organism or the self. This tendency may become deeply buried under layer after layer of encrusted psychological defenses; it may be hidden behind elaborate façades which deny its existence; it is my belief, however, based on my experience, that it exists in every individual and awaits only the proper conditions to be released and expressed.

The humanistic psychologists feel that the creative person is emotionally healthy and sensitive both to the needs and the capabilities of his unconscious to produce creative ideas. Like Freud's creative person, he possesses a strong ego and a realistic superego which allow him to be a prolific conceptualizer and relatively free of distracting neuroses.

We can now come to several interesting and believable conclusions, based upon our brief psychoanalytic discussion:

1. Man creates for reasons of inner drive, whether it be for purposes of conflict resolution, self-fulfillment, or both. He can, of course, also create for other reasons, such as money.
2. At least part of creativity occurs in a part of the mind which is below the conscious level.

3. Although creativity and neuroses may stem from the same source, creativity tends to flow best in the absence of neuroses.
4. The conscious mind, or ego, is a control valve on creativity.
5. Creativity can provoke anxieties.

Now I will continue with our discussion of emotional blocks.

Emotional blocks may interfere with the freedom with which we explore and manipulate ideas, with our ability to conceptualize fluently and flexibly—and prevent us from communicating ideas to others in a manner which will gain them acceptance. Let me list a few of them, which I will then discuss:

1. Fear to make a mistake, to fail, to risk
2. Inability to tolerate ambiguity; overriding desires for security, order; "no appetite for chaos"
3. Preference for judging ideas, rather than generating them
4. Inability to relax, incubate, and "sleep on it"
5. Lack of challenge; problem fails to engage interest
6. Excessive zeal; overmotivation to succeed quickly
7. Lack of access to areas of imagination
8. Lack of imaginative control
9. Inability to distinguish reality from fantasy

Fear of taking a risk

Fear to make a mistake, to fail, or to take a risk is perhaps the most general and common emotional block. Most of us have grown up rewarded when we produce the "right" answer and punished if we make a mistake. When we fail we are made to realize that we have let others down (usually someone we love). Similarly we are taught to live safely (a bird in the hand is worth two in the bush, a penny saved is a penny earned) and avoid risk whenever possible. Obviously, when one produces and tries to sell a creative idea he is taking a risk: of making a mistake, failing, making an ass of himself, losing money, hurting himself, or whatever.

This type of fear is to a certain extent realistic. Something new is usually a threat to the status quo, and is therefore resisted with appropriate pressure upon its creator. The risks involved with innovation often can result in real hardship. Far be it from me to suggest that people should not be realistic in assessing the costs of creativity. For instance, I spend a great amount of time attempting to explain to students that somehow the process of making money out of a commercially practical idea seems to require at least eight years, quite a bit of physical and emotional degradation, and often the sacrifice of such things as marriages and food. However, as I also try to explain to students, the fears which inhibit conceptualization are often *not* based upon a realistic assumption of the consequences. Certainly, a slightly "far-out" idea submitted as an answer to a class assignment is not going to cost the originator his life, his marriage, or even financial ruin. The only possible difficulty would arise if I, the teacher, were annoyed with his answer (and I happen to like such responses from students). The fear which is involved here is a more generalized fear of taking a chance.

One of the better ways of overcoming such a block is to realistically assess the possible negative consequences of an idea. As is sometimes asked, "What are your catastrophic expectations?" If one has an idea for a better bicycle lock and is considering quitting a job and founding a small business based upon the lock and a not-yet-conceived product line to go with it, the risks are considerable (unless the innovator happens to have large sums of money and important commercial contacts). If one invents a new method of flight (say, wings of feathers held together with wax) the risks may also be considerable in perfecting the product. However, if one thinks of a new way to schedule his day, paint his bathroom, or relate to others in his dormitory, the risks are considerably less.

In my experience, people do not often realistically assess the probable consequences of a creative act. Either they blithely ignore any consequences, or their general fear of failure causes them to attach excessive importance to any "mistake," no matter how minor it will appear in the eyes of future historians. Often the potential negative consequences of exposing a creative idea can be easily endured. If one has an idea which seems risky, it is well worth the time to do a brief study of the possible consequences. During the study, one should include "catastrophic expectations" (assume everything goes badly) and look at the result. By doing this, it will become apparent whether you want to take the risk or not.

Exercise

Next time you are having difficulty deciding whether to push a "creative" idea, write a short (two-page) "catastrophic expectations" report. In it detail as well as you can precisely what would happen to you *if everything went wrong.* By making such information explicit and facing it, you swap your analytical capability for your fear of failure—a good trade.

No appetite for chaos

The fear of making a mistake is, of course, rooted in insecurity, which most people suffer from to some extent. Such insecurities are also responsible for the next emotional block, the "inability to tolerate ambiguity; overriding desire for order; 'no appetite for chaos.'" Once again, some element of this block is rational. I am not suggesting that in order to be creative one should shun order and live in a totally chaotic situation. I am talking more of an excessive fondness for order in all things. The solution of a complex problem is a messy process. Rigorous and logical techniques are often necessary, but not sufficient. One must usually wallow in misleading and ill-fitting data, hazy and difficult-to-test concepts, opinions, values, and other such untidy quantities. In a sense, problem-solving is *bringing order to chaos*. A desire for order is therefore necessary. However, the ability to tolerate chaos is a must.

We all know compulsive people, those who must have everything always in its place and who become quite upset if the order of their physical lives is violated. If this trait carries over into a person's mental process, he is severely impaired in his ability to work with certain types of problems. One reason for extreme ordering of the physical environment is efficiency. Another may be the aesthetic satisfaction of precise physical relationships. However, another reason is insecurity. If one's underwear is precisely folded and "dressed right," one has precise control over one's underwear, and thus there is one less thing out of control to be threatening. I do not actually care how your underwear is stored. However, if your thoughts are precisely folded and dressed right you are probably a fairly limited problem-solver. The process of bringing widely disparate thoughts together cannot work too well because your mind is not going to allow widely disparate thoughts to coexist long enough to combine.

Judging rather than generating ideas

The next emotional block, the "preferencing for judging ideas, rather than generating them," is also the "safe" way to go. Judgment, criticism, tough-mindedness, and practicality are of course essential in problem-solving. However, if applied too early or too indiscriminately in the problem-solving process, they are extremely detrimental to conceptualization. In the Design Division, we often speak of analysis, judgment, and synthesis as three distinct types of thinking. In *analysis,* there is usually a right answer. I am an engineer: if you pay me to tell you how large a beam is needed to hold up a patio roof, you rightly expect *the* answer. Fortunately, I know how to analyze such things mathematically and can give it to you. *Judgment* is generally used in a problem where there are several answers and one must be chosen. A court case (the Angela Davis trial) is a good example. A situation such as Watergate is another. Judgments are made by sensible people as to guilt or innocence, and the situation is sufficiently complex that disagreements can occur. *Synthesis* is even more of a multianswer situation. A design problem (design a better way to serve ice cream) has an infinitude of answers, and there are few rigorous techniques to help in deciding between them.

If one analyzes or judges too early in the problem-solving process, he will reject many ideas. This is detrimental for two reasons. First of all, newly formed ideas are fragile and imperfect—they need time to mature and acquire the detail needed to make them believable. Secondly, as we will discuss later, ideas often lead to other ideas. Many techniques of conceptualization, such as brainstorming, depend for their effectiveness on maintaining "way-out" ideas long enough to let them mature and spawn other more realistic ideas. It is sometimes difficult to hold onto such ideas because people generally do not want to be suspected of harboring impractical thoughts. However, in conceptualization one should not judge too quickly.

The judgment of ideas, unfortunately, is an extremely popular and rewarded pastime. One finds more newspaper space devoted to judgment (critic columns, political analyses, editorials, etc.) than to the *creation* of ideas. In the university, much scholarship is devoted to judgment, rather than creativity. One finds that people who heap negative criticism upon all ideas they encounter are often hearalded for their practical sense and sophistication. Bad-mouthing everyone else's concepts is in fact a cheap way to attempt to demonstrate your own mental superiority.

If you are a professional idea-haver, your criticism tends to be somewhat more friendly. Professional designers are often much more receptive to the ideas of our students than non-design-oriented faculty members. Professional problem-solvers have a working understanding of the difficulty in having ideas and a respect for ideas, even if they are flawed. If you are a compulsive idea-judger you should realize that this is a habit which may exclude ideas from your own mind before they have had time to bear fruit. You are taking little risk (unless you are excluding ideas that could benefit you) and are perhaps feeding your ego somewhat with the thrill of being able to judge the outputs of others, but you are sacrificing some of your own creative potential.

Inability to incubate

The "inability to relax, incubate, and 'sleep on it'" is also a somewhat common emotional block. There is general agreement that the unconscious plays an extremely important role in problem solving. Everyone has had the experience of having the answer to a problem suddenly occur in his mind. One maddeningly familiar phenomenon to many people is a late answer to an important problem. One may work for days or weeks on a problem, complete it, and go on to other activities. Then, at some seemingly random point in time, a better answer "appears." Since the original problem was probably completed in order to reach a deadline, this "better" answer often only serves to annoy one that he did not think of it sooner. This better answer came straight from the unconscious as a result of the "incubation" process it was going through. I have found in my own case that this "incubation" process works and is reliable. I have the confidence to think hard about a problem (charging up my unconscious) and then forget about it for a period of time. When I begin work on it again, new answers are usually present.

Many "symptoms" of incubation are common. There is a widespread belief among students that they do their best work just before deadlines. If, in fact, they worked on the material when they received it long enough to store the data in their unconscious, then incubation can occur, and a better solution may emerge at a later time. Incubation does often seem to produce the right answer at the appropriate time. Students often claim to have come up with a winning idea the morning that it is due, after struggling futilely with the problem for days.

One must allow the unconscious to struggle with problems. Incubation is important in problem-solving. It is poor planning not to allow adequate time for incubation in the solution of an important problem. It is also important to be able to relax in the midst of problem-solving. One's overall compulsiveness is less fanatical when he is relaxed, and the mind is more likely to deal with seemingly "silly" combinations of thoughts. If one is never relaxed, his mind is usually on guard against nonserious activities, with resulting difficulties in the type of thinking necessary for fluent and flexible conceptualization.

Lack of challenge and excessive zeal

"Lack of challenge" and "excessive zeal" are opposite villians. One cannot do his best on a problem unless he is motivated. Professional problem-solvers learn to be motivated somewhat by money and future work which may come their way if they succeed. However, challenge must be present for at least some of the time, or the process ceases to be rewarding. On the other hand, an excessive motivation to succeed, especially to succeed quickly, can inhibit the creative process. The tortoise-and-the-hare phenomenon is often apparent in problem-solving. The person who thinks up the simple elegant solution, although he may take longer in doing so, often wins. As in the race, the tortoise depends upon an inconsistent performance from the rabbit. And if the rabbit spends so little time on conceptualization that he merely chooses the first answers that occur, such inconsistency is almost guaranteed.

Reality and fantasy

"Lack of access to areas of imagination," "lack of imaginative control," and "inability to distinguish reality from fantasy" will be discussed in more detail in chapter 7. In brief, the imagination attempts to create objects and events. The creative person needs to be able to control his imagination and needs complete access to it. If all senses are not represented (not only sight, but also sound, smell, taste, and touch (his imagination cannot serve him as well as it otherwise could. All senses need representation not only because problems involving all senses can be attacked, but also because imagery is more powerful if they are all called upon. If one thinks purely verbally, for instance, there will be little imagery available for the solving of problems concerning shapes and forms. If visual imagery is also present, the imagination will be much more useful, but still not as potent as if the other senses are also present. One can usually imagine a ball park much more vividly if one is able to recall the smell of the grass, the taste of the peanuts and beer, the feel of the seats and the sunshine, and the sounds of the crowd.

The creative person must be able not only to vividly form complete images, but also to manipulate them. Creativity requires the *manipulation* and *recombination* of experience. An imagination which cannot manipulate experience is limiting to the conceptualizer. One should be able to imagine a volcano being born in his ball park, or an airplane landing in it, or the ball park shrinking as the grass simultaneously turns purple, if one is to make maximum use of his imagination. Chapter 7 will contain some exercises to allow you to gauge your ability to control your imagination as well as discussions on how to strengthen the "mental muscle" used in imagining.

"The inability to distinguish reality from fantasy" is a more unusual, but equally severe, block. The creative person needs the ability to fantasize freely and vividly. Yet, if his fantasies become too realistic, they may be less controllable. If you cannot go through the following exercise without a sense of acute physical discomfort, you may have difficulty distinguishing reality from fantasy. This exercise is taken from *Put Your Mother on the Ceiling* by Richard de Mille. Stay with each fantasy (marked off by slashes) until you have it fully formed in your imagination. This game is called *breathing*.

Let us imagine that we have a goldfish in front of us. Have the fish swim around. / Have the fish swim into your mouth. / Take a deep breath and have the fish go down into your lungs, into your chest. / Have the fish swim around in there. / Let out your breath and have the fish swim out into the room again. /

Now breath in a lot of tiny goldfish. / Have them swim around in your chest. / Breathe them all out again. /

Let's see what kind of things you can breathe in and out of your chest. / Breathe in a lot of rose petals. / Breathe them

out again. / Breathe in a lot of water. / Have it gurgling in
your chest. / Breathe it out again. / Breathe in a lot of dry
leaves. / Have them blowing around in your chest. / Breathe
them out again. / Breathe in a lot of raindrops. / Have them
pattering in your chest. / Breathe them out again. / Breathe
in a lot of sand. / Have it blowing around in your chest. /
Breathe it out again. / Breathe in a lot of little firecrackers. /
Have them all popping in your chest. / Breathe out the smoke
and bits of them that are left. / Breathe in a lot of little
lions. / Have them all roaring in your chest. / Breathe them
out again. /

Breathe in some fire. / Have it burning and crackling in your
chest. / Breathe it out again. / Breathe in some logs of
wood. / Set fire to them in your chest. / Have them roaring
as they burn up. / Breathe out the smoke and ashes. /

Have a big tree in front of you. / Breathe fire on the tree and
burn it all up. / Have an old castle in front of you. / Breathe
fire on the castle and have it fall down. / Have an ocean in
front of you. / Breathe fire on the ocean and dry it up. /

What would you like to breathe in now? / All right. / Now
what? / All right. / What would you like to burn up by
breathing fire on it? / All right. /

Be a fish. / Be in the ocean. / Breathe the water of the ocean,
in and out. / How do you like that? / Be a bird. / Be high
in the air. / Breathe the cold air, in and out. / How do you
like that? / Be a camel. / Be on the desert. / Breathe the hot
wind of the desert, in and out. / How does that feel? / Be an
old-fashioned steam locomotive. / Breathe out steam and
smoke all over everything. / How is that? / Be a stone. /
Don't breathe. / How do you like that? / Be a boy (girl). /
Breathe the air of this room, in and out. How do you like that?

It would certainly be uncomfortable to inhale sand. Whether you
can imagine the feeling of inhaling sand depends somewhat upon your
ability to fantasize. No danger exists from imagining such an act, and
any pain felt is imagined, not real. However, if one's fantasies are confused with reality, it can be very difficult to fantasize such things. The
imagination is extremely powerful because it can go beyond reality.
But in order to do this, the imagination must be set free of the constraints placed upon *real* acts and events.

3

Opinions, Beliefs, and Attitudes: The Balancing Act

Introduction

In the first chapter of this section we looked at human motivation. In the second chapter we looked at the thinking and reasoning side of human beings. In this one we try to bring the two together; to look at that realm of human behavior that combines the emotional and the rational, the realm of attitudes, beliefs, and values.

Most readers are probably familiar with culture shock. In a few hours we can fly from a Western culture to the Orient and are immediately beset with a host of new sights and smells and customs. The shock part of culture shock seems to come from our initial inability to straighten out and simplify this jungle of new stimulation.

Because human beings are unable to cope with massive numbers of discrete inputs from the outside world, they need to find ways of simplifying, filtering, stabilizing, and classifying their information about the world. This chapter is about those simplifying, filtering, stabilizing, and classifying processes.

Consider the following statements: "A woman's place is in the home." "Smoking pot won't lead to using the hard stuff." "Whites don't have soul." "People should be objective in dealing with others on the job, and not let personal considerations enter into their decisions." "It's not right for public employees to strike." Each of those statements expresses an attitude either about some factual matter or about rights and wrongs. Each of those attitudes, true or not, justified or not, helps its holder to simplify part of the world. The woman who believes that her place *is* in the home doesn't have to spend time deciding which career to pursue. The person who believes that pot won't lead to harder stuff will find it easier to decide whether or not to accept the offer of a stick. Attitudes (and stereotypes and values), by simplifying and categorizing chunks of the world, enable one to deal more easily with it. But while simplifying, our attitudes may also partially blind us; for some of the simplification is brought about by filtering out some of

171

what is really out there. And there is no guarantee that the filter will only filter out the irrelevant facts.

This chapter is about attitudes and perceptions, about how attitudes are formed, how they influence our behavior, and how we can change them, and how and why what we perceive may be different from what is really there. Like needs and motivations, attitudes are a state of mind. But whereas needs and motives provide the driving force for behavior, attitudes provide the *premises* for behavior. They play a vital role both in influencing our perceptions and providing cues for behavior. Indeed attitudes provide the meeting place of the emotional and the reasoning sides of people.

The first paper in this chapter, by Aronson, is about the dynamics of just such processes, the processes by which we balance our feelings, our cognitions, our perceptions to maintain some kind of total integrity as human beings. That paper pulls together a large amount of theorizing and researching on the dynamics of human attitude formation and decision making. It treats human beings as simplifying self-balancing creatures, not tolerant of large amounts of inconsistent information; as organisms who must reduce, simplify, clarify, rationalize in a continuous effort to stay together.

The next paper, by Cartwright, picks up the same theme, but this time from the perspective of trying to change or modify peoples' behavior. For clearly if people are dynamic balancers rather than just reasoners, it does not make sense to try to change them through reason alone. Emotionality must also enter the equation.

And the Bem and Bem article goes even further in showing how some of our most central attitudes and values are initiated during early childhood and infancy. Once formed, such attitudes and values become the screens through which we filter and access new information. The Bems show the extent to which the attitudes held by many women in our culture, at least until recently, were inculcated early in life and served to shape a great range of rules and regulations about what women were or were not permitted to do.

And finally in this chapter, a more applied paper, the piece by Gullett and Reisen on behavior modification and employee performance. That paper is concerned, of course, specifically with trying to change the attitudes, beliefs, and opinions of people in organizations by using some rather simple and direct methods that have emerged from American learning theory. The reader can examine the implications of this paper and of reinforcement theory in general for the practice of management. Behavior modification is in an expanding mode and is likely to be seen more and more in the organizational world, not only in the training of new employees, but in day-to-day efforts to shape and direct worker behavior.

The Rationalizing Animal
Elliot Aronson

Man likes to think of himself as a rational animal. However, it is more true that man is a *rationalizing* animal, that he attempts to appear reasonable to himself and to others. Albert Camus even said that man is a creature who spends his entire life in an attempt to convince himself that he is not absurd.

Some years ago a woman reported that she was receiving messages from outer space. Word came to her from the planet Clarion that her city would be destroyed by a great flood on December 21. Soon a considerable number of believers shared her deep commitment to the prophecy. Some of them quit their jobs and spent their savings freely in anticipation of the end.

On the evening of December 20, the prophet and her followers met to prepare for the event. They believed that flying saucers would pick them up, thereby sparing them from disaster. Midnight arrived, but no flying saucers. December 21 dawned, but no flood.

What happens when prophecy fails? Social psychologists Leon Festinger, Henry Riecken, and Stanley Schachter infiltrated the little band of believers to see how they would react. They predicted that persons who had expected the disaster, but awaited it alone in their homes, would simply lose faith in the prophecy. But those who awaited the outcome in a group, who had thus admitted their belief publicly, would come to believe even more strongly in the prophecy and turn into active proselytizers.

This is exactly what happened. At first the faithful felt despair and shame because all their predictions had been for naught. Then, after waiting nearly five hours for the saucers, the prophet had a new vision. The city had been spared, she said, because of the trust and faith of her devoted group. This revelation was elegant in its simplicity, and the

Reprinted from *Psychology Today,* May 1973, by permission of Psychology Today Magazine. © 1973 Ziff-Davis Publishing Company.

believers accepted it enthusiastically. They now sought the press that they had previously avoided. They turned from believers into zealots.

Living on the fault

In 1957 Leon Festinger proposed his theory of *cognitive dissonance,* which describes and predicts man's rationalizing behavior. Dissonance occurs whenever a person simultaneously holds two inconsistent cognitions (ideas, beliefs, opinions). For example, the belief that the world will end on a certain day is dissonant with the awareness, when the day breaks, that the world has not ended. Festinger maintained that this state of inconsistency is so uncomfortable that people strive to reduce the conflict in the easiest way possible. They will change one or both cognitions so that they will "fit together" better.

Consider what happens when a smoker is confronted with evidence that smoking causes cancer. He will become motivated to change either his attitudes about smoking or his behavior. And as anyone who has tried to quit knows, the former alternative is easier.

The smoker may decide that the studies are lousy. He may point to friends ("If Sam, Jack, and Harry smoke, cigarettes can't be all that dangerous"). He may conclude that filters trap all the cancer-producing materials. Or he may argue that he would rather live a short and happy life with cigarettes than a long and miserable life without them.

The more a person is committed to a course of action, the more resistant he will be to information that threatens that course. Psychologists have reported that the people who are least likely to believe the dangers of smoking are those who tried to quit—and failed. They have become more committed to smoking. Similarly, a person who builds a $100,000 house astride the San Andreas Fault will be less receptive to arguments about imminent earthquakes than would a person who is renting the house for a few months. The new homeowner is committed; he doesn't want to believe that he did an absurd thing.

When a person reduces his dissonance, he defends his ego, and keeps a positive self-image. But self-justification can reach startling extremes; people will ignore danger in order to avoid dissonance, even when that ignorance can cause their deaths. I mean that literally.

Suppose you are Jewish in a country occupied by Hitler's forces. What should you do? You could try to leave the country; you could try to pass as "Aryan"; you could do nothing and hope for the best. The first two choices are dangerous: if you are caught you will be executed. If you decide to sit tight, you will try to convince yourself that you made the best decision. You may reason that while Jews are indeed being treated unfairly, they are not being killed unless they break the law.

Now suppose that a respected man from your town announces that he has seen Jews being butchered mercilessly, including everyone who has recently been deported from your village. If you believe him, you might have a chance to escape. If you don't believe him, you and your family will be slaughtered.

Dissonance theory would predict that you will not listen to the witness, because to do so would be to admit that your judgment and decisions were wrong. You will dismiss his information as untrue, and decide that he was lying or hallucinating. Indeed, Elie Wiesel reported that this happened to the Jews in Sighet, a small town in Hungary, in 1944. Thus people are not passive receptacles for the deposit of information. The manner in which they view and distort the objective world in order to avoid and reduce dissonance is entirely predictable. But one cannot divide the world into rational people on one side and dissonance reducers on the other. While people vary in their ability to tolerate dissonance, we are all capable of rational or irrational behavior, depending on the circumstances—some of which follow.

Dissonance because of effort

Judson Mills and I found that if people go through a lot of trouble to gain admission to a group, and the group turns out to be dull and dreary, they will experience dissonance. It is a rare person who will accept this situation with an "Oh, pshaw. I worked hard for nothing. Too bad." One way to resolve the dissonance is to decide that the group is worth the effort it took to get admitted.

We told a number of college women that they would have to undergo an initiation to join a group that would discuss the psychology of sex. One third of them had severe initiation: they had to recite a list of obscene words and read some lurid sexual passages from novels in the presence of a male experimenter (in 1959, this really was a "severe" and embarrassing task). One third went through a mild initiation in which they read words that were sexual but not obscene (such as "virgin" and "petting"); and the last third had no initiation at all. Then all of the women listened to an extremely boring taped discussion of the group they had presumably joined. The women in the severe initiation group rated the discussion and its drab participants much more favorably than those in the other groups.

I am not asserting that people enjoy painful experiences, or that they enjoy things that are associated with painful experiences. If you got hit on the head by a brick on the way to a fraternity initiation, you would not like that group any better. But if you volunteered to get hit with a brick *in order to join* the fraternity, you definitely would like the group more than if you had been admitted without fuss.

After a decision—especially a difficult one that involves much time, money, or effort—people almost always experience dissonance. Awareness of defects in the preferred object is dissonant with having chosen it; awareness of positive aspects of the unchosen object is dissonant with having rejected it.

Accordingly, researchers have found that *before* making a decision, people seek as much information as possible about the alternatives. Afterward, however, they seek reassurance that they did the right thing, and do so by seeking information in support of their choice or by simply changing the information that is already in their heads. In one of the earliest experiments on dissonance theory, Jack Brehm gave a group of women their choice between two appliances, such as a toaster or a blender, that they had previously rated for desirability. When the subjects reevaluated the appliances after choosing one of them, they increased their liking for the one they had chosen and downgraded their evaluation of the rejected appliance. Similarly, Danuta Ehrlich and her associates found that a person about to buy a new car does so carefully, reading all ads and accepting facts openly on various makes and models. But after he buys his Volvo, for instance, he will read advertisements more selectively, and he will tend to avoid ads for Volkswagens, Chevrolets, and so on.

The decision to behave immorally

Your conscience, let us suppose, tells you that it is wrong to cheat, lie, steal, seduce your neighbor's husband or wife, or whatever. Let us suppose further that you are in a situation in which you are sorely tempted to ignore your conscience. If you give in to temptation, the cognition "I am a decent, moral person" will be dissonant with the cognition "I have committed an immoral act." If you resist, the cognition "I want to get a good grade (have that money, seduce that person)" is dissonant with the cognition "I could have acted so as to get that grade, but I chose not to."

The easiest way to reduce dissonance in either case is to minimize the negative aspects of the action one has chosen, and to change one's attitude about its immorality. If Mr. C. decides to cheat, he will probably decide that cheating isn't really so bad. It hurts no one; everyone does it; it's part of human nature. If Mr. D. decides not to cheat, he will no doubt come to believe that cheating is a sin, and deserves severe punishment.

The point here is that the initial attitudes of these men is virtually the same. Moreover, their decisions could be a hairs breadth apart. But once the action is taken, their attitudes diverge sharply.

Judson Mills confirmed these speculations in an experiment with sixth-grade children. First he measured their attitudes toward cheating, and then put them in a competitive situation. He arranged the test so that it was impossible to win without cheating, and so it was easy for the children to cheat, thinking they would be unwatched. The next day, he asked the children again how they felt about cheating. Those who had cheated on the test had become more lenient in their attitudes; those who had resisted the temptation adopted harsher attitudes.

The data are provocative. They suggest that the most zealous crusaders are not those who are removed from the problem they oppose. I would hazard to say that the people who are most angry about "the sexual promiscuity of the young" are *not* those who have never dreamed of being promiscuous. On the contrary, they would be persons who had been seriously tempted by illicit sex, who came very close to giving in to their desires, but who finally resisted. People who almost live in glass houses are the ones who are most likely to throw stones.

Insufficient justification

If I offer George $20 to do a boring task, and offer Richard $1 to do the same thing, which one will decide that the assignment was mildly interesting? If I threaten one child with harsh punishment if he does something forbidden, and threaten another child with mild punishment, which one will transgress?

Dissonance theory predicts that when people find themselves doing something and they have neither been rewarded adequately for doing it nor threatened with dire consequences for not doing it, they will find *internal* reasons for their behavior.

Suppose you dislike Woodrow Wilson and I want you to make a speech in his favor. The most efficient thing I can do is to pay you a lot of money for making the speech, or threaten to kill you if you don't. In either case, you will probably comply with my wish, but you won't change your attitude toward Wilson. If that were my goal, I would have to give you a *minimal* reward or threat. Then, in order not to appear absurd, you would have to seek additional reasons for your speech—this could lead you to find good things about Wilson and hence, to conclude that you really do like Wilson after all. Lying produces great attitude change only when the liar is undercompensated.

Festinger and J. Merrill Carlsmith asked college students to work on boring and repetitive tasks. Then the experimenters persuaded the students to lie about the work, to tell a fellow student that the task would be interesting and enjoyable. They offered half of their subjects $20 for telling the lie, and they offered the others only $1. Later they asked all subjects how much they had really liked the tasks.

The students who earned $20 for their lies rated the work as deadly dull, which it was. They experienced no dissonance: they lied, but they were well paid for that behavior. By contrast, students who got $1 decided that the tasks were rather enjoyable. The dollar was apparently enough to get them to tell the lie, but not enough to keep them from feeling that lying for so paltry a sum was foolish. To reduce dissonance, they decided that they hadn't lied after all; the task was fun.

Similarly, Carlsmith and I found that mild threats are more effective than harsh threats in changing a child's attitude about a forbidden object, in this case a delightful toy. In the severe-threat condition, children refrained from playing with the toys and had a good reason for refraining—the very severity of the threat provided ample justification for not playing with the toy. In the mild-threat condition, however, the children refrained from playing with the toy but when they asked themselves, "How come I'm not playing with the toy?" they did not have a superabundant justification (because the threat was not terribly severe). Accordingly, they provided additional justification in the form of convincing themselves that the attractive toy was really not very attractive and that they didn't really want to play with it very much in the first place. Jonathan Freedman extended our findings, and showed that severe threats do not have a lasting effect on a child's behavior. Mild threats, by contrast, can change behavior for many months.

Perhaps the most extraordinary example of insufficient justification occurred in India, where Jamuna Prasad analyzed the rumors that were circulated after a terrible earthquake in 1950. Prasad found that people in towns that were *not* in immediate danger were spreading rumors of impending doom from floods, cyclones, or unforeseeable calamities. Certainly the rumors could not help people feel more secure; why then perpetrate them? I believe that dissonance helps explain this phenomenon. The people were terribly frightened—after all, the neighboring villages had been destroyed—but they did not have ample excuse for their fear, since the earthquake had missed them. So they invented their own excuse; if a cyclone is on the way, it is reasonable to be afraid. Later, Durganand Sinha studied rumors in a town that had actually been destroyed. The people were scared, but they had good reason to be; they didn't need to seek additional justification for their terror. And their rumors showed no predictions of impending disaster and no serious exaggerations.

The decision to be cruel

The need for people to believe that they are kind and decent can lead them to say and do unkind and indecent things. After the National

Guard killed four students at Kent State, several rumors quickly spread: the slain girls were pregnant, so their deaths spared their families from shame; the students were filthy and had lice on them. These rumors were totally untrue, but the townspeople were eager to believe them. Why? The local people were conservative, and infuriated at the radical behavior of some of the students. Many had hoped that the students would get their comeuppance. But death is an awfully severe penalty. The severity of this penalty outweighs and is dissonant with the "crimes" of the students. In these circumstances, any information that put the victims in a bad light reduces dissonance by implying, in effect, that it was good that the young people died. One high-school teacher even avowed that anyone with "long hair, dirty clothes, or [who goes] barefooted deserves to be shot."

Keith Davis and Edward Jones demonstrated the need to justify cruelty. They persuaded students to help them with an experiment, in the course of which the volunteers had to tell another student that he was a shallow, untrustworthy, and dull person. Volunteers managed to convince themselves that they didn't like the victim of their cruel analysis. They found him less attractive than they did before they had to criticize him.

Similarly, David Glass persuaded a group of subjects to deliver electric shocks to others. The subjects, again, decided that the victim must deserve the cruelty; they rated him as stupid, mean, etc. Then Glass went a step further. He found that a subject with high self-esteem was most likely to derogate the victim. This led Glass to conclude, ironically, that it is precisely because a person thinks he is nice that he decides that the person he has hurt is a rat. "Since nice guys like me don't go around hurting innocent people," Glass's subjects seemed to say, "you must have deserved it." But individuals who have *low* self-esteem do not feel the need to justify their behavior and derogate their victims; it is *consonant* for such persons to believe they have behaved badly. "Worthless people like me do unkind things."

Ellen Berscheid and her colleagues found another factor that limits the need to derogate one's victim: the victim's capacity to retaliate. If the person doing harm feels that the situation is balanced, that his victim will pay him back in coin, he had no need to justify his behavior. In Berscheid's experiment, which involved electric shocks, college students did not derogate or dislike the persons they shocked if they believed the victims could retaliate. Students who were led to believe that the victims would not be able to retaliate *did* derogate them. Her work suggests that soldiers may have a greater need to disparage civilian victims (because they can't retaliate) than military victims. Lt. William L. Calley, who considered the "gooks" at My Lai to be something less than human, would be a case in point.

Dissonance and the self-concept

On the basis of recent experiments, I have reformulated Festinger's original theory in terms of the self-concept. That is, dissonance is most powerful when self-esteem is threatened. Thus the important aspect of dissonance is not, "I said one thing and I believe another," but "I have misled people—and I am a truthful, nice person." Conversely, the cognitions, "I believe the task is dull," and "I told someone the task was interesting," are not dissonant for a psychopathic liar.

David Mettee and I predicted in a recent experiment that persons who had low opinions of themselves would be more likely to cheat than persons with high self-esteem. We assumed that if an average person gets a temporary blow to his self-esteem (by being jilted, say, or not getting a promotion), he will temporarily feel stupid and worthless, and hence do any number of stupid and worthless things—cheat at cards, bungle an assignment, break a valuable vase.

Mettee and I temporarily changed 45 female students' self-esteem. We gave one third of them positive feedback about a personality test they had taken (we said that they were interesting, mature, deep, etc.); we gave one third negative feedback (we said that they were relatively immature, shallow, etc.); and one third of the students got no information at all. Then all the students went on to participate in what they hought was an unrelated experiment, in which they gambled in a competitive game of cards. We arranged the situation so that the students could cheat and thereby win a considerable sum of money, or not cheat, in which case they were sure to lose.

The results showed that the students who had received blows to their self-esteem cheated far more than those who had gotten positive feedback about themselves. It may well be that low self-esteem is a critical antecedent of criminal or cruel behavior.

The theory of cognitive dissonance has proved useful in generating research; it has uncovered a wide range of data. In formal terms, however, it is a very sloppy theory. Its very simplicity provides both its greatest strength and its most serious weakness. That is, while the theory has generated a great deal of data, it has not been easy to define the limits of the theoretical statement, to determine the specific predictions that can be made. All too often researchers have had to resort to the very unscientific rule of thumb, "If you want to be sure, ask Leon."

Logic and psychologic

Part of the problem is that the theory does not deal with *logical* inconsistency, but *psychological* inconsistency. Festinger maintains that two cognitions are inconsistent if the opposite of one follows from the other. Strictly speaking, the information that smoking causes cancer does not make it illogical to smoke. But these cognitions produce dissonance because they do not make sense psychologically, assuming that the smoker does not want cancer.

One cannot always predict dissonance with accuracy. A man may admire Franklin Roosevelt enormously and discover that throughout his marriage FDR carried out a clandestine affair. If he places a high value on fidelity and he believes that great men are not exempt from this value, then he will experience dissonance. Then I can predict that he will either change his attitudes about Roosevelt or soften his attitudes about fidelity. But, he may believe that marital infidelity and political greatness are totally unrelated; if this were the case, he might simply shrug off these data without modifying his opinions either about Roosevelt or about fidelity.

Because of the sloppiness in the theory, several commentators have criticized a great many of the findings first uncovered by dissonance theory. These criticisms have served a useful purpose. Often, they have goaded us to perform more precise research, which in turn has led to a clarification of some of the findings which, ironically enough, has eliminated the alternative explanations proposed by the critics themselves.

For example, Alphonse and Natalia Chapanis argued that the "severe initiation" experiment could have completely different causes. It might be that the young women were not embarrassed at having to read sexual words, but rather were aroused, and their arousal in turn led them to rate the dull discussion group as interesting. Or, to the contrary, the women in the severe-initiation condition could have felt much sexual anxiety, followed by relief that the discussion was so banal. They associated relief with the group, and so rated it favorably.

So Harold Gerard and Grover Mathewson replicated our experiment, using electric shocks in the initiation procedure. Our original findings were supported—subjects who underwent severe shocks in order to join a discussion group rated that group more favorably than subjects who had undergone mild shocks. Moreover, Gerard and Mathewson went on to show that merely linking an electric shock with the group discussion (as in a simple conditioning experiment) did not produce greater liking for the group. The increase in liking for the group occurred only when subjects volunteered for the shock *in order* to gain membership in the group—just as dissonance theory would predict.

Routes to consonance

In the real world there is usually more than one way to squirm out of inconsistency. Laboratory experiments carefully control a person's alternatives, and the conclusions drawn may be misleading if applied to everyday situations. For example, suppose a prestigious university rejects a young Ph.D. for its one available teaching position. If she feels that she is a good scholar, she will experience dissonance. She can then decide that members of that department are narrow-minded and senile, sexist, and wouldn't recognize talent if it sat on their laps. Or she could decide that if they could reject someone as fine and intelligent as she, they must be extraordinarily brilliant. Both techniques will reduce dissonance, but note that they leave this woman with totally opposite opinions about professors at the university.

This is a serious conceptual problem. One solution is to specify the conditions under which a person will take one route to consonance over another. For example, if a person struggles to reach a goal and fails, he may decide that the goal wasn't worth it (as Aesop's fox did) or that the effort was justified anyway (the fox got a lot of exercise in jumping for the grapes). My own research suggests that a person will take the first means when he has expended relatively little effort. But when he has put in a great deal of effort, dissonance will take the form of justifying the energy.

This line of work is encouraging. I do not think that it is very fruitful to demand to know that *the* mode of dissonance reduction is; it is more instructive to isolate the various modes that occur, and determine the optimum conditions for each.

Ignorance of absurdity

No dissonance theorist takes issue with the fact that people frequently work to get rewards. In our experiments, however, small rewards tend to be associated with greater attraction and greater attitude change. Is the reverse ever true?

Jonathan Freedman told college students to work on a dull task after first telling them (*a*) their results would be of no use to him, since his experiment was basically over, or *(b)* their results would be of great value to him. Subjects in the first condition were in a state of dissonance, for they had unknowingly agreed to work on a boring chore that apparently had no purpose. They reduced their dissonance by deciding that the task was enjoyable.

Then Freedman ran the same experiment with one change. He waited until the subjects finished the task to tell them whether their work would be important. In this study he found incentive effects: students told that the task was valuable enjoyed it more than those who were told that their work was useless. In short, dissonance theory does not apply when an individual performs an action in good faith without having any way of knowing it was absurd. When we agree to participate in an experiment we naturally assume that it is for a purpose. If we are informed afterward that it *had* no purpose, how were we to have known? In this instance we like the task better if it had an important purpose. But if we agreed to perform it *knowing* that it had no purpose, we try to convince ourselves that it is an attractive task in order to avoid looking absurd.

Man cannot live by consonance alone

Dissonance reduction is only one of several motives, and other powerful drives can counteract it. If human beings had a pervasive, all-encompassing need to reduce all forms of dissonance, we would not grow, mature, or admit to our mistakes. We would sweep mistakes under the rug or, worse, turn the mistakes into virtues; in neither case would we profit from error.

But obviously people do learn from experience. They often do tolerate dissonance because the dissonant information has great utility. A person cannot ignore forever a leaky roof, even if that flaw is inconsistent with having spent a fortune on the house. As utility increases, individuals will come to prefer dissonance-arousing but useful information. But as dissonance increases, or when commitment is high, future utility and information tend to be ignored.

It is clear that people will go to extraordinary lengths to justify their actions. They will lie, cheat, live on the San Andreas Fault, accuse innocent bystanders of being vicious provocateurs, ignore information that might save their lives, and generally engage in all manner of absurd postures. Before we write off such behavior as bizarre, crazy, or evil, we would be wise to examine the situations that set up the need to reduce dissonance. Perhaps our awareness of the mechanism that makes us so often irrational will help turn Camus' observation on absurdity into a philosophic curiosity.

Achieving Change in People: Some Applications Of Group Dynamics Theory
Darwin Cartwright

I

We hear all around us today the assertion that the problems of the twentieth century are problems of human relations. The survival of civilization, it is said, will depend upon man's ability to create social inventions capable of harnessing, for society's constructive use, the vast physical energies now at man's disposal. Or, to put the matter more simply, we must learn how to change the way in which people behave toward one another. In broad outline, the specifications for a good society are clear, but a serious technical problem remains: How can we change people so that they neither restrict the freedom nor limit the potentialities for growth of others; so that they accept and respect people of different religion, nationality, color, or political opinion; so that nations can exist in a world without war, and so that the fruits of our technological advances can bring economic well-being and freedom from disease to all the people of the world? Although few people would disagree with these objectives when stated abstractly, when we become more specific, differences of opinion quickly arise. How is change to be produced? Who is to do it? Who is to be changed? These questions permit no ready answers.

Before we consider in detal these questions of social technology, let us clear away some semantic obstacles. The word "change" produces emotional reactions. It is not a neutral word. To many people it is threatening. It conjures up visions of a revolutionary, a dissatisfied idealist, a troublemaker, a malcontent. Nicer words referring to the process of changing people are education, training, orientation, guidance, indoctrination, therapy. We are more ready to have others "educate" us than to have them "change" us. We, ourselves, feel less

Reprinted from *Human Relations,* vol. 4, no. 4, © 1951 by the Plenum Publishing Corporation.

guilty in "training" others than in "changing" them. Why this emotional response? What makes the two kinds of words have such different meanings? I believe that a large part of the difference lies in the fact that the safer words (like education or therapy) carry the implicit assurance that the only changes produced will be good ones, acceptable within a currently held value system. The cold, unmodified word "change," on the contrary, promises no respect for values; it might even tamper with values themselves. Perhaps for this very reason it will foster straight thinking if we use the word "change" and thus force ourselves to struggle directly and self-consciously with the problems of value that are involved. Words like education, training, or therapy, by the very fact that they are not so disturbing, may close our eyes to the fact that they too inevitably involve values.

Another advantage of using the word "change" rather than other related words is that it does not restrict our thinking to a limited set of aspects of people that are legitimate targets of change. Anyone familiar with the history of education knows that there has been endless controversy over what it is about people that "education" properly attempts to modify. Some educators have viewed education simply as imparting knowledge—others mainly as providing skills for doing things, still others as producing healthy "attitudes," and some have aspired to instill a way of life. Or if we choose to use a word like "therapy," we can hardly claim that we refer to a more clearly defined realm of change. Furthermore, one can become inextricably entangled in distinctions and vested interests by attempting to distinguish sharply between, let us say, the domain of education and that of therapy. If we are to try to take a broader view and to develop some basic principles that promise to apply to all types of modifications in people, we had better use a word like "change" to keep our thinking general enough.

The proposal that social technology may be employed to solve the problems of society suggests that social science may be applied in ways no different from those used in the physical sciences. Does social science, in fact, have any practically useful knowledge which may be brought to bear significantly on society's most urgent problems? What scientifically based principles are there for guiding programs of social change: In this paper we shall restrict our considerations to certain parts of a relatively new branch of social science known as "group dynamics." We shall examine some of the applications for social action which stem from research in this field of scientific investigation.

What is "group dynamics"? Perhaps it will be most useful to start by looking at the derivation of the word "dynamics." It comes from a Greek word meaning force. In careful usage of the phrase, "group dynamics" refers to the forces operating in groups. The investigation of group dynamics, then, consists of a study of these forces: what gives rise to them, what conditions modify them, what consequences they have, etc. The practical application of group dynamics (or the technology of group dynamics) consists of the utilization of knowledge about these forces for the achievement of some purpose. In keeping with this definition, then, it is clear that group dynamics, as a realm of investigation, is not particularly novel, nor is it the exclusive property of any person or institution. It goes back at least to the outstanding work of men like Simmel, Freud, and Cooley.

Although interest in groups has a long and respectable history, the past 15 years have witnessed a new flowering of activity in this field. Today, research centers in several countries are carrying out substantial programs of research designed to reveal the nature of groups and of their functioning. The phrase "group dynamics" has come into common usage during this time and intense efforts have been devoted to the development of the field, both as a branch of social science and as a form of social technology.

In this development the name of Kurt Lewin has been outstanding. As a consequence of his work in the field of individual psychology and from his analysis of the nature of the pressing problems of the contemporary world, Lewin became convinced of society's urgent need for a *scientific approach* to the understanding of the dynamics of groups. In 1945 he established the Research Center for Group Dynamics to meet this need. Since that date the Center has been devoting its efforts to improving our scientific understanding of groups through laboratory experimentation, field studies, and the use of techniques of action research. It has also attempted in various ways to help get the findings of social science more widely used by social management. Much of what I have to say in this paper is drawn from the experiences of this Center in its brief existence of a little more than five years. (1)

II

For various reasons we have found that much of our work has been devoted to an attempt to gain a better understanding of the ways in which people change their behavior or resist efforts by others to have them do so. Whether we set for ourselves the practical goal of improving behavior or whether we take on the intellectual task of understanding why people do what they do, we have to investigate processes of communication, influence, social pressure—in short, problems of change.

In this work we have encountered great frustration. The problems have been most difficult to solve. Looking back over our experience, I have become convinced that no small part of the trouble has resulted from an irresistible tendency to conceive of our problems in terms of the individual. We live in an individualistic culture. We value the individual highly, and rightly so. But I am inclined to believe that our political and social concern for the individual has narrowed our thinking as social scientists so much that we have not been able to state our research problems properly. Perhaps we have taken the individual as the unit of observation and study when some larger unit would have been more appropriate. Let us look at a few examples.

Consider first some matters having to do with the mental health of an individual. We can all agree, I believe, that an important mark of a healthy personality is that the individual's self-esteem has not been undermined. But on what does self-esteem depend? From research on this problem we have discovered that, among other things, repeated experiences of failure or traumatic failures on matters of central importance serve to undermine one's self-esteem. We also know that whether a person experiences success or failure as a result of some undertaking depends upon the level of aspiration which he has set for himself. Now, if we try to discover how the level of aspiration gets set, we are immediately involved in the person's relationships to groups. The groups to which he belongs set standards for his behavior which he must accept if he is to remain in the group. If his capacities do not allow him to reach these standards, he experiences failure, he withdraws or is rejected by the group and his self-esteem suffers a shock.

Suppose, then, that we accept a task of therapy, of rebuilding his self-esteem. It would appear plausible from our analysis of the problem that we should attempt to work with variables of the same sort that produced the difficulty, that is to work with him either in the groups to which he now belongs or to introduce him into new groups which are selected for the purpose and to work upon his relationships to groups as such. From the point of view of preventive mental health, we might even attempt to train the groups in our communities—classes in schools, work groups in business, families, unions, religious and cultural groups—to make use of practices better designed to protect the self-esteem of their members.

Consider a second example. A teacher finds that in her class she has a number of troublemakers, full of aggression. She wants to know why these children are so aggressive and what can be done about it. A foreman in a factory has the same kind of problem with some of his workers. He wants the same kind of help. The solution most tempting to both the teacher and the foreman often is to transfer the worst troublemakers to someone else, or if facilities are available, to refer them for counseling. But is the problem really of such a nature that it can be solved by removing the troublemaker from the situation or by working on his individual motivations and emotional life? What leads does research give us? The evidence indicates, of course, that there are many causes of aggressiveness in people, but one aspect of the problem has become increasingly clear in recent years. If we observe carefully the amount of aggressive behavior and the number of troublemakers to be found in a large collection of groups, we find that these characteristics can vary tremendously from group to group even when the different groups are composed essentially of the same kinds of people. In the now-classic experiments of Lewin et al. (2) on the effects of different styles of leadership, it was found that the same group of children displayed markedly different levels of aggressive behavior when under different styles of leadership. Moreover, when individual children were transferred from one group to another, their levels of aggressiveness shifted to conform to the atmosphere of the new group. Efforts to account for one child's aggressiveness under one style of leadership merely in terms of his personality traits could hardly succeed under these conditions. This is not to say that a person's behavior is entirely to be accounted for by the atmosphere and structure of the immediate group, but it is remarkable to what an extent a strong, cohesive group can control aspects of a member's behavior traditionally thought to be expressive of enduring personality traits. Recognition of this fact rephrases the problem of how to change such behavior. It directs us to a study of the sources of the influence of the group on its members.

Let us take an example from a different field. What can we learn from efforts to change people by mass media and mass persuasion? In those rare instances when educators, propagandists, advertisers, and others who want to influence large numbers of people have bothered to make an objective evaluation of the enduring changes produced by their efforts, they have been able to demonstrate only the most negligible effects. (3) The inefficiency of attempts to influence the public by mass media would be scandalous if there were agreement that it was important or even desirable to have such influences strong exerted. In fact, it is no exaggeration to say that all of the research and experience of generations has not improved the efficiency of lectures or other means of mass influence to any noticeable degree. Something must be wrong with our theories of learning, motivation, and social psychology.

Within very recent years some research data have been accumulating which may give us a clue to the solution of our problem. In one series of experiments directed by Lewin, it was found that a method of group decision, in which the group as a whole made a decision to have its members change their behavior, was from two to ten times as effective in producing actual change as was a lecture presenting exhortation to change. (4) We have yet to learn precisely what produces these differences of effectiveness, but it is clear that by introducing group forces into the situation a whole new level of influence has been achieved.

The experience has been essentially the same when people have attempted to increase the productivity of individuals in work settings. Traditional conceptions of how to increase the output of workers have stressed the individual; select the right man for the job; simplify the job for him; train him in the skills required; motivate him by economic incentives; make it clear to whom he reports; keep the lines of authority and responsibility simple and straight. But even when all these conditions are fully met we are finding that productivity is far below full potential. There is even good reason to conclude that this individualistic conception of the determinants of productivity actually fosters negative consequences. The individual, now isolated and subjected to the demands of the organization through the commands of his boss, finds that he must create with his fellow employees informal groups, not shown on any table of organization, in order to protect himself from arbitrary control of his life, from the boredom produced by the endless repetition of mechanically sanitary and routine operations, and from the impoverishment of his emotional and social life brought about by the frustration of his basic needs for social interaction, participation, and acceptance in a stable group. Recent experiments have demonstrated clearly that the productivity of work groups can be greatly increased by methods of work organization and supervision which give more responsibility to work groups, which allow for fuller participation in important decisions, and which make stable groups the firm basis for support of the individual's social needs (5) I am convinced that future research will also demonstrate that people working under such conditions become more mature and creative individuals in their homes, in community life, and as citizens.

As a final example, let us examine the experience of efforts to train people in workshops, institutes, and special training courses. Such efforts are common in various areas of social welfare, intergroup relations, political affairs, industry, and adult education generally. It is an unfortunate fact that objective evaluation of the effects of such training efforts has only rarely been undertaken, but there is evidence for those who will look that the actual change in behavior produced is most disappointing. A workshop not infrequently develops keen interest among the participants, high morale and enthusiasm, and a firm resolve on the part of many to apply all the wonderful insights back home. But what happens back home? The trainee discovers that his colleagues don't share his enthusiasm. He learns that the task of changing others' expectations and ways of doing things is discouragingly difficult. He senses, perhaps not very clearly, that it would make all the difference in the world if only there were a few other people sharing his enthusiasm and insights with whom he could plan activities, evaluate consequences of effort, and from whom he could gain emotional and motivational support. The approach to training which conceives of its task as being merely that of changing the individual probably produces frustration, demoralization, and disillusionment in as large a measure as it accomplishes more positive results.

A few years ago the Research Center for Group Dynamics undertook to shed light on this problem by investigating the operation of a workshop for training leaders in intercultural relations. (6) In a project, directed by Lippitt, we set out to compare systematically the different effects of the workshop upon trainees who came as isolated individuals in contrast to those who came as teams. Since one of the problems in the field of intercultural relations is that of getting people of good will to be more active in community efforts to improve intergroup relations, one goal of the training workshop was to increase the activity of the trainees in such community affairs. We found that before the workshop there was no difference in the activity level of the people who were to be trained as isolates and of those who were to be trained as teams. Six months after the workshop, however, those who had been trained as isolates were only slightly more active than before the workshop whereas those who had been members of strong training teams were now much more active. We do not have clear evidence on the point, but we could be quite certain that the maintenance of heightened activity over a long period of time would also be much better for members of teams. For the isolates the effect of the workshop had the characteristic of a "shot in the arm" while for the team member it produced a more enduring change because the team provided continuous support and reinforcement for its members.

III

What conclusions may we draw from these examples? What principles of achieving change in people can we see emerging? To begin with the most general proposition, we may state that the behavior, attitudes, beliefs, and values of the individual are all firmly grounded in the groups to which he belongs. How aggressive or cooperative a person is, how much self-respect and self-confidence he has, how energetic and productive his work is, what he aspires to, what he believes to be true and good, whom he loves or hates, and what beliefs and prejudices he holds— all these characteristics are highly determined by the individual's group memberships. In a real sense, they are properties of groups and of the relationships between people. Whether they change or resist change will, therefore, be greatly influenced by the nature of these groups. Attempts to change them must be concerned with the dynamics of groups.

In examining more specifically how groups enter into the process of change, we find it useful to view groups in at least three different ways. In the first view, the group is seen as a source of influence over its members. Efforts to change behavior can be supported or blocked by pressures on members stemming from the group. To make constructive use of these pressures the group must be used *as a medium of change*. In the second view, the group itself becomes the *target of change*. To change the behavior of individuals it may be necessary to change the standards of the group, its style of leadership, its emotional atmosphere, or its stratification into cliques and hierarchies. Even though the goal may be to change the behavior of *individuals,* the target of change becomes the group. In the third view, it is recognized that many changes of behavior can be brought about only by the organized efforts of groups *as agents of change*. A committee to combat intolerance, a labor union, an employers association, a citizens group to increase the pay of teachers—any action group will be more or less effective depending upon the way it is organized, the satisfaction it provides to its members, the degree to which its goals are clear, and a host of other properties of the group.

An adequate social technology of change, then, requires at the very least a scientific understanding of groups viewed in each of these ways. We shall consider here only the first two aspects of the problem; the group as a medium of change and as a target of change.

The Group as a Medium of Change

Principle No. 1. If the group is to be used effectively as a medium of change, these people who are to be changed and those who are to exert influence for change must have a strong sense of belonging to the same group.

Kurt Lewin described this principle well: "The normal gap between teacher and student, doctor and patient, social worker and public, can . . . be a real obstacle to acceptance of the advocated conduct." In other words, in spite of whatever status differences there might be between them, the teacher and the student have to feel as members of one group in matters involving their sense of values. The chances for reeducation seem to be increased whenever a strong we-feeling is created. (7) Recent experiments by Preston and Heintz have demonstrated greater changes of opinions among members of discussion groups operating with participatory leadership than among those with supervisory leadership (8). The implications of this principle for classroom teaching are far-reaching. The same may be said of supervision in the factory, army, or hospital.

Principle No. 2. The more attractive the group is to its members the greater is the influence that the group can exert on its members.

This principle has been extensively documented by Festinger and his co-workers. (9) They have been able to show in a variety of settings that in more cohesive groups there is a greater readiness of members to influence others, a greater readiness to be influenced by others, and stronger pressures toward conformity when conformity is a relevant matter for the group. Important for the practitioner wanting to make use of this principle is, of course, the question of how to increase the attractiveness of groups. This is a question with many answers. Suffice it to say that a group is more attractive the more it satisfies the needs of its members. We have been able to demonstrate experimentally an increase in group cohesiveness by increasing the liking of members for each other as persons, by increasing the perceived importance of the group goal, and by increasing the prestige of the group among other groups. Experienced group workers could add many other ways to this list.

Principle No. 3. In attempts to change attitudes, values, or behavior, the more relevant they are to the basis of attraction to the group, the greater will be the influence that the group can exert upon them.

I believe this principle gives a clue to some otherwise puzzling phenomena. How does it happen that a group, like a labor union, seems to be able to exert such strong discipline over its members in some matters (let us say in dealings with management), while it seems unable to exert nearly the same influence in other matters let us say in political action? If we examine why it is that members are attracted to the group. I believe we will find that a particular reason for belonging seems more related to some of the group's activities than to others. If a man joins a union mainly to keep his job and to improve his working conditions, he may be largely uninfluenced by the union's attempt to modify his attitudes toward national and international affairs. Groups differ tremendously in the range of matters that are relevant to them and hence over which they have influence. Much of the inefficiency of adult education could be reduced if more attention were paid to the need that influence attempts be appropriate to the groups in which they are made.

Principle No. 4. The greater the prestige of a group member in the eyes of the other members, the greater the influence he can exert.

Polansky et al. (10) have demonstrated this principle with great care and methodological ingeunity in a series of studies in children's summer camps. From a practical point of view it must be emphasized that the things giving prestige to a member may not be those characteristics most prized by the official management of the group. The most prestige-carrying member of a Sunday school class may not possess the characteristics most similar to the minister of the church. The teacher's pet may be a poor source of influence within a class. This principle is the basis for the common observation that the official leader and the actual leader of a group are often not the same individual.

Principle No. 5. Efforts to change individuals or subparts of a group which, if successful, would have the result of making them deviate from the norms of the group will encounter strong resistance.

During the past few years a great deal of evidence has been accumulated showing the tremendous pressures which groups can exert upon members to conform to the group's norms. The price of deviation in most groups is rejection or even expulsion. If the member really wants to belong and be accepted, he cannot withstand this type of pressure. It is for this reason that efforts to change people by taking them from the group and giving them special training so often have disappointing results. This principle also accounts for the finding that people thus trained sometimes display increased tension, aggressiveness toward the group, or a tendency to form cults or cliques with others who have shared their training.

These five principles concerning the group as a medium of change would appear to have readiest application to groups created for the purpose of producing changes in people. They provide certain specifications for building effective training or therapy groups. They also point, however, to a difficulty in producing change in people in that they show how resistant an individual is to changing in any way contrary to group pressures and expectations. In order to achieve many kinds of changes in people, therefore, it is necessary to deal with the group as a target of change.

The group as a target of change

Principle No. 6. Strong pressure for changes in the group can be established by creating a shared perception by members of the need for change, thus making the source of pressure for change lie within the group.

Marrow and French (11) report a dramatic case study which illustrates this principle quite well. A manufacturing concern had a policy against hiring women over 30 because it was believed that they were slower, more difficult to train, and more likely to be absent. The staff psychologist was able to present to management evidence that this belief was clearly unwarranted at least within their own company. The psychologist's facts, however, were rejected and ignored as a basis for action because they violated accepted beliefs. It was claimed that they went against the direct experience of the foremen. Then the psychologist hit upon a plan for achieving change which differed drastically from the usual one of argument, persuasion, and pressure. He proposed than management conduct its own analysis of the situation. With his help management collected all the facts which they believed were relevant to the problem. When the results were in they were now their own facts rather than those of some "outside" expert. Policy was immediately changed without further resistance. The important point here is that facts are not enough. The facts must be the accepted property of the group if they are to become an effective basis for change. There seems to be all the difference in the world in changes actually carried out between those cases in which a consulting firm is hired to do a study and present a report and those in which technical experts are asked to collaborate with the group in doing its own study.

Principle No. 7. Information relating to the need for change, plans for change, and consequences of change must be shared by all relevant people in the group.

Another way of stating this principle is to say that change of a group ordinarily requires the opening of communication channels. Newcomb (12) has shown how one of the first consequences of mistrust and hostility is the avoidance of communicating openly and freely about the things producing the tension. If you look closely at a pathological group (that is, one that has trouble making decisions or effecting coordinated efforts of its members), you will certainly find strong restraints in that group against communicating vital information among its members. Until these restraints are removed there can be little hope for any real and lasting changes in the group's functioning. In passing it should be pointed out that the removal of barriers to communication will ordinarily be accompanied by a sudden increase in the communication of hostility. The group may appear to be falling apart, and it will certainly be a painful experience to many of the members. This pain and the fear that things are getting out of hand often stop the process of change once begun.

Principle No. 8. Changes in one part of a group produce strain in other related parts which can be reduced only by eliminating the change or by bringing about readjustments in the related parts.

It is a common practice to undertake improvements in group functioning by providing training programs for certain classes of people in the organization. A training program for foremen, for nurses, for teachers, or for group workers is established. If the content of the training is relevant for organizational change, it must of necessity deal with the relationships these people have with other subgroups. If nurses in a hospital change their behavior significantly, it will affect their relations both with the patients and with the doctors. It is unrealistic to assume that both these groups will remain indifferent to any significant changes in this respect. In hierarchical structures this process is most clear. Lippitt has proposed on the basis of research and experience that in such organizations attempts at change should always involve three levels, one being the major target of change and the other two being the one above and the one below.

IV

These eight principles represent a few of the basic propositions emerging from research in group dynamics. Since research is constantly going on and since it is the very nature of research to revise and reformulate our conceptions, we may be sure that these principles will have to be modified and improved as time goes by. In the meantime they may serve as guides in our endeavors to develop a scientifically based technology of social management.

In social technology, just as in physical technology, invention plays a crucial role. In both fields progress consists of the creation of new mechanisms for the accomplishment of certain goals. In both fields inventions arise in response to practical needs and are to be evaluated by how effectively they satisfy these needs. The relation of invention to scientific development is indirect but important. Inventions cannot proceed too far ahead of basic scientific development, nor should they be allowed to fall too far behind. They will be more effective the more they make good use of known principles of science, and they often make new developments in science possible. On the other hand, they are in no sense logical derivations from scientific principles.

I have taken this brief excursion into the theory of invention in order to make a final point. To many people "group dynamics" is know only for the social inventions which have developed in recent years in work with groups. Group dynamics is often thought of as certain techniques to be used with groups. Role playing, buzz groups, process observers, post-meeting reaction sheets, and feedback of group observations are devices popularly associated with the phrase "group dynamics." I trust I have been able to show that group dynamics is more than a collection of gadgets. It certainly aspires to be a science as well as a technology.

This is not to underplay the importance of these inventions nor of the function of inventing. As inventions they are all mechanisms designed to help accomplish important goals. How effective they are will demand upon how skillfully they are used and how appropriate they are to the purposes to which they are put. Careful evaluative research must be the ultimate judge of their usefulness in comparison with alternative inventions. I believe that the principles enumerated in this paper indicate some of the specifications that social inventions in this field must meet.

References

1. Cartwright, D. *The Research Center for Group Dynamics: A Report of Five Years' Activities and a View of Future Needs*. Ann Arbor: Institute for Social Research, 1950.

2. Lewin, K., Lippitt, R., and White, R. K. Patterns of aggressive behavior in experimentally created "social climates." *Journal of Social Psychology,* 1939, 10, 271–99.

3. Cartwright, D. Some principles of mass persuasion: Selected findings of research on the sale of United States war bonds. *Human Relations,* 1949, 2(3), 253–67.

4. Lewin, K. *Field Theory in Social Science,* pp. 229–36. New York: Harper & Bros., 1951.

5. Coch, L. and French, J. T. P. Jr. Overcoming resistance to change. *Human Relations,* 1948, 1(4), 512–32.

6. Lippitt, R. *Training in Community Relations.* New York: Harper & Bros., 1949.

7. Lewin, K. *Resolving Social Conflicts,* p. 67. New York: Harper & Bros., 1948.

8. Preston, M. G. and Heintz, R. K. Effects of participatory vs. supervisory leadership on group judgment. *Journal of Abnormal and Social Psychology,* 1949, 44, 345–55.

9. Festinger, L., et al. *Theory and Experiment in Social Communication: Collected Papers.* Ann Arbor: Institute for Social Research, 1950.

10. Polansky, N., Lippitt, R., and Redl, F. An investigation of behavorial contagion in groups. *Human Relations,* 1950, 3(4), 319–48.

11. Marrow, A. J. and French, J. R. P. Changing a stereotype in industry. *Journal of Social Issues,* 1945, 1(3), 33–37.

12. Newcomb, T.M. Autistic hostility and social reality. *Human Relations,* 1947, 1(1), 69–86.

Training the Woman to Know Her Place: The Power of a Nonconscious Ideology

Sandra L. Bem and Daryl J. Bem

In the beginning God created the heaven and the earth. . . . And God said, Let us make man in our image, after our likeness; and let them have dominion over the fish of the sea, and over the fowl of the air, and over the cattle, and over all the earth. . . . And the rib, which the Lord God had taken from man, made he a woman and brought her unto the man. . . . And the Lord God said unto the woman, What is this that thou has done? And the woman said, The serpent beguiled me, and I did eat. . . . Unto the woman He said, I will greatly multiply thy sorrow and thy conception; in sorrow thou shalt bring forth children; and thy desire shall be to thy husband, and he shall rule over thee. [Gen. 1, 2, 3]

And lest anyone fail to grasp the moral of this story, Saint Paul provides further clarification:

For a man . . . is the image and glory of God; but the woman is the glory of the man. For the man is not of the woman, but the woman of the man. Neither was the man created for the woman, but the woman for the man. [1 Cor. 11]

Let the woman learn in silence with all subjection. But I suffer not a woman to teach, nor to usurp authority over the man, but to be in silence. For Adam was first formed, then Eve. And Adam was not deceived, but the woman, being deceived, was in the transgression. Notwithstanding, she shall be saved in childbearing, if they continue in faith and charity and holiness with sobriety. [1 Tim. 2]

Adapted from S. L. Bem and D. J. Bem, "Case Study of a Nonconscious Ideology: Training the Woman to Know Her Place," in D. J. Bem. *Beliefs, Attitudes, and Human Affairs.* © 1970 by Wadsworth Publishing Company, Inc. Reprinted by permission of the publisher, Brooks/Cole Publishing Company, Monterey, California.
Order of authorship determined by the flip of a coin.

And lest it be thought that only Christians have this rich heritage of ideology about women, consider the morning prayer of the Orthodox Jew:

Blessed art Thou, oh Lord our God, King of the Universe, that I was not born a gentile.
Blessed art Thou, oh Lord our God, King of the Universe, that I was not born a slave.
Blessed art Thou, oh Lord our God, King of the Universe, that I was not born a woman.

Or the Koran, the sacred text of Islam:

Men are superior to women on account of the qualities in which God has given them preeminence.

Because they think they sense a decline in feminine "faith, charity, and holiness with sobriety," many people today jump to the conclusion that the ideology expressed in these passages is a relic of the past. Not so. It has simply been obscured by an equalitarian veneer, and the ideology has now become nonconscious. That is, we remain unaware of it because alternative beliefs and attitudes about women go unimagined. We are like the fish who is unaware that his environment is wet. After all, what else could it be? Such is the nature of all nonconscious ideologies. Such is the nature of America's ideology about women. For even those Americans who agree that a black skin should not uniquely qualify its owner for janitorial or domestic service continue to act as if the possession of a uterus uniquely qualifies *its* owner for precisely that.

Consider, for example, the 1968 student rebellion at Columbia University. Students from the radical left took over some administration buildings in the name of equalitarian principles which they accused the university of flouting. Here were the most militant spokesmen one could hope to find in the cause of equalitarian ideals. But no sooner had they occupied the buildings than the male militants blandly turned to their sisters-in-arms and assigned them the task of preparing the food, while they—the menfolk—would presumably plan further strategy. The reply these males received was the reply they deserved, and the fact that domestic tasks behind the barricades were desegregated across the sex line that day is an everlasting tribute to the class consciousness of the ladies of the left.

But these conscious coeds are not typical, for the nonconscious assumptions about a woman's "natural" talents (or lack of them) are at least as prevalent among women as they are among men. A psychologist named Philip Goldberg[1] demonstrated this by asking female college students to rate a number of professional articles from each of six fields. The articles were collated into two equal sets of booklets, and the names of the authors were changed so that the identical article was attributed to a male author (e.g., John T. McKay) in one set of booklets and to a female author (e.g., Joan T. McKay) in the other set. Each student was asked to read the articles in her booklet and to rate them for value, competence, persuasiveness, writing style, and so forth.

As he had anticipated, Goldberg found that the identical article received significantly lower ratings when it was attributed to a female author than when it was attributed to a male author. He had predicted this result for articles from professional fields generally considered the province of men, like law and city planning, but to his surprise, these coeds also downgraded articles from the fields of dietetics and elementary school education when they were attributed to female authors. In other words, these students rated the male authors as better at everything, agreeing with Aristotle that "we should regard the female nature as afflicted with a natural defectiveness." We repeated this experiment informally in our own classrooms and discovered that male students show the same implicit prejudice against female authors that Goldberg's female students showed. Such is the nature of a nonconscious ideology!

It is significant that examples like these can be drawn from the college world, for today's students have challenged the established ways of looking at almost every other issue, and they have been quick to reject those practices of our society which conflict explicitly with their major values. But as the above examples suggest, they will find it far more difficult to shed the more subtle aspects of a sex-role ideology which—as we shall now attempt to demonstrate—conflicts just as surely with their existential values as any of the other societal practices to which they have so effectively raised objection. And as we shall see, there is no better way to appreciate the power of a society's nonconscious ideology than to examine it within the framework of values held by that society's avant-garde.

Individuality and self-fulfillment

The dominant values of today's students concern personal growth on the one hand, and interpersonal relationships on the other. The

1. P. Goldberg, "Are Women Prejudiced against Women?" *Transaction 5* (April 1968): 28–30.

first of these emphasizes individuality and selffulfillment; the second stresses openness, honesty, and equality in all human relationships.

The values of individuality and self-fulfillment imply that each human being, male or female, is to be encouraged to "do his own thing." Men and women are no longer to be stereotyped by society's definitions. If sensitivity, emotionality, and warmth are desirable human characteristics, then they are desirable for men as well as for women. (John Wayne is no longer an idol of the young, but their pop-art satire.) If independence, assertiveness, and serious intellectual commitment are desirable human characteristics, then they are desirable for women as well as for men. The major prescription of this college generation is that each individual should be encouraged to discover and fulfill his own unique potential and identity, unfettered by society's presumptions.

But society's presumptions enter the scene much earlier than most people suspect, for parents begin to raise their children in accord with the popular stereotypes from the very first. Boys are encouraged to be aggressive, competitive, and independent, whereas girls are rewarded for being passive and dependent.[2] In one study, six-month-old infant girls were already being touched and spoken to more by their mothers while they were playing than were infant boys. When they were thirteen months old, these same girls were more reluctant than the boys to leave their mothers; they returned more quickly and more frequently to them; and they remained closer to them throughout the entire play period. When a physical barrier was placed between mother and child, the girls tended to cry and motion for help; the boys made more active attempts to get around the barrier.[3] No one knows to what extent these sex differences at the age of thirteen months can be attributed to the mothers' behavior when the child was six months, but it is hard to believe that the two are unconnected.

As children grow older, more explicit sex-role training is introduced. Boys are encouraged to take more of an interest in mathematics and science. Boys, not girls, are given chemistry sets and microscopes for Christmas. Moreover, all children quickly learn that mommy is proud to be a moron when it comes to mathematics and science, whereas daddy knows all about these things. When a young boy returns from

2. H. Barry III, M. K. Bacon, and I. L. Child, "A Cross-cultural Survey of Some Sex Differences in Socialization," *Journal of Abnormal and Social Psychology 55* (1957): 327—32; R. R. Sears, E. E. Maccoby, and H. Levin, *Patterns of Child Rearing* (Evanston, Ill.: Row, Peterson, 1957).
3. S. Goldberg and M. Lewis, "Play Behavior in the Year-old Infant: Early Sex Differences," *Child Development* 40(1969): 21–31.

school all excited about biology, he is almost certain to be encouraged to think of becoming a physician. A girl with similar enthusiasm is told that she might want to consider nurse's training later so she can have "an interesting job to fall back upon in case—God forbid—she ever needs to support herself." A very different kind of encouragement. And any girl who doggedly persists in her enthusiasm for science is likely to find her parents as horrified by the prospect of a permanent love affair with physics as they would be by the prospect of an interracial marriage.

These socialization practices quickly take their toll. By nursery school age, for example, boys are already asking more questions about how and why things work.[4] In first and second grade, when asked to suggest ways of improving various toys, boys do better on the fire truck and girls do better on the nurse's kit, but by the third grade, boys do better regardless of the toy presented.[5] By the ninth grade, 25 percent of the boys, but only 3 percent of the girls, are considering careers in science or engineering.[6] When they apply for college, boys and girls are about equal on verbal aptitude tests, but boys score significantly higher on mathematical aptitude tests—about sixty points higher on the College Board examinations, for example.[7] Moreover, girls improve their mathematical performance if problems are reworded so that they deal with cooking and gardening, even though the abstract reasoning required for their solutions remains the same.[8] Clearly, not just ability, but motivation too, has been affected.

But these effects in mathematics and science are only part of the story. A girl's long training in passivity and dependence appears to exact an even higher toll from her overall motivation to achieve, to search for new and independent ways of doing things, and to welcome the challenge of new and unsolved problems. In one study, for example, elementary school girls were more likely to try solving a puzzle by imitating an adult, whereas the boys were more likely to search for

4. M. E. Smith, "The Influence of Age, Sex, and Situation on the Frequency of Form and Functions of Questions Asked by Preschool Children," *Child Development* 3 (1933): 201–13.

5. E. P. Torrance, *Guiding Creative Talent* (Englewood Cliffs, N. J.: Prentice-Hall, 1962).

6. J. C. Flanagan, "Project Talent," unpublished manuscript; cited by J. Kagan, "Acquisition and Significance of Sex Typing and Sex Role Identity," in M. L. Hoffman, eds., *Review of Child Development Research* (New York: Russell Sage Foundation, 1964), I: 137–67.

7. R. Brown. *Social Psychology* (New York: Free Press, 1965), p. 162.

8. G. A. Milton, *Five Studies of the Relation between Sex Role Identification and Achievement in Problem Solving,* Technical Report no. 3, Department of Industrial Administration. Department of Psychology, Yale University, December 1958.

a novel solution not provided by the adult.[9] In another puzzle-solving study, young girls asked for help and approval from adults more frequently that the boys; and, when given the opportunity to return to the puzzles a second time, the girls were more likely to rework those they had already solved, whereas the boys were more likely to try puzzles they had been unable to solve previously.[10] A girl's sigh of relief is almost audible when she marries and retires from the outside world of novel and unsolved problems. This, of course, is the most conspicuous outcome of all: the majority of American women become full-time homemakers. Such are the consequences of a nonconscious ideology.

But why does this process violate the values of individuality and self-fulfillment? It is *not* because some people may regard the role of homemaker as inferior to other roles. That is not the point. Rather, the point is that our society is managing to consign a large segment of its population to the role of homemaker solely on the basis of sex just as inexorably as it has in the past consigned the individual with a black skin to the role of janitor or domestic. It is not the quality of the role itself which is at issue here, but the fact that in spite of their unique identities, the majority of America's women end up in the *same* role.

Even so, however, several arguments are typically advanced to counter the claim that America's homogenization of its women subverts individuality and self-fulfillment. The three most common arguments invoke, respectively, (1) free will, (2) biology, and (3) complementarity.

1. The free will argument proposes that a twenty-one-year-old woman is perfectly free to choose some other role if she cares to do so; no one is standing in her way. But this argument conveniently overlooks the fact that the society which has spent twenty years carefully marking the woman's ballot for her has nothing to lose in that twenty-first year by pretending to let her cast it for the alternative of her choice. Society has controlled not her alternatives, but her motivation to choose any but one of those alternatives. The so-called freedom to choose is illusory and cannot be invoked to justify the society which controls the motivation to choose.

2. The biological argument suggests that there may really be inborn differences between men and women in, say, independence or mathematical ability. Or that there may be biological factors beyond the fact

9. J. W. McDavid, "Imitative Behavior in Preschool Children," *Psychological Monographs,* vol. 73, whole no. 486 (1959).
10. V. J. Crandall and A. Rabson, "Children's Repetition Choices in an Intellectual Achievement Situation Following Success and Failure," *Journal of Genetic Psychology* 97 (1960): 161–68.

that women can become pregnant and nurse children which uniquely dictate that they, but not men, should stay home all day and shun serious outside commitment. Maybe female hormones really are responsible somehow. One difficulty with this argument, of course, is that female hormones would have to be different in the Soviet Union, where one-third of the engineers and 75 percent of the physicians are women. In America, women constitute less than 1 percent of the engineers and only 7 percent of the physicians.[11] Female physiology *is* different, and it may account for some of the psychological differences between the sexes, but America's sex-role ideology still seems primarily responsible for the fact that so few women emerge from childhood with the motivation to seek out any role beyond the one that our society dictates.

But even if there really were biological differences between the sexes along these lines, the biological argument would still be irrelevant. The reason can best be illustrated with an analogy.

Suppose that every black American boy were to be socialized to become a jazz musician on the assumption that he has a "natural" talent in that direction, or suppose that his parents should subtly discourage him from other pursuits because it is considered "inappropriate" for black men to become physicians or physicists. Most liberal Americans, we submit, would disapprove. But suppose that it *could* be demonstrated that black Americans, *on the average,* did possess an inborn better sense of rhythm than white Americans. Would *that* justify ignoring the unique characteristics of a *particular* black youngster from the very beginning and specifically socializing him to become a musician? We don't think so. Similarly, as long as a woman's socialization does not nurture her uniqueness, but treats her only as a member of a group on the basis of some assumed *average* characteristic, she will not be prepared to realize her own potential in the way that the values of individuality and self-fulfillment imply she should.

The irony of the biological argument is that it does not take biological differences seriously enough. That is, it fails to recognize the range of biological differences between individuals of the same sex. Thus, recent research has revealed that biological factors help determine many personality traits. Dominance and submissiveness, for example, have been found to have large inheritable components; in other words, biological factors *do* have the potential for partially determining how dominant or submissive an individual, male or female, will turn out to be. But the effects of this biological potential could be

11. N. D. Dodge, *Women in the Soviet Economy* (Baltimore: The Johns Hopkins Press, 1966).

detected only in males.[12] This implies that only the males in our culture are raised with sufficient flexibility, with sufficient latitude given to their biological differences, for their "natural" or biologically determined potential to shine through. Females, on the other hand, are subjected to a socialization which so ignores their unique attributes that even the effects of biology seem to be swamped. In sum, the biological argument for continuing America's homogenization of its women gets hoisted with its own petard.

3. Many people recognize that most women do end up as full-time homemakers because of their socialization and that these women do exemplify the failure of our society to raise girls as unique individuals. But, they point out, the role of the homemaker is not inferior to the role of the professional man: it is complementary but equal.

This argument is usually bolstered by pointing to the joys and importance of taking care of small children. Indeed, mothers *and* fathers find childrearing rewarding, and it is certainly important. But this argument becomes insufficient when one considers that the average American woman now lives to age seventy-four and has her *last* child at about age twenty-six; thus, by the time the woman is thirty-three or so, her children all have more important things to do with their daytime hours than to spend them entertaining an adult woman who has nothing to do during the second half of her life span. As for the other "joys" of homemaking, many writers[13] have persuasively argued that the role of the homemaker has been glamorized far beyond its intrinsic worth. This charge becomes plausible when one considers that the average American homemaker spends the equivalent of a man's working day, 7.1 hours, in preparing meals, cleaning house, laundering, mending, shopping, and doing other household tasks. In other words, 43 percent of her waking time is spent in activity that would command an hourly wage on the open market well below the federally set minimum for menial industrial work.

The point is not how little she would earn if she did these things in someone else's home, but that this use of time is virtually the same for homemakers with college degrees and for those with less than a grade school education, for women married to professional men and for women married to bluecollar workers. Talent, education, ability, interests, motivations: all are irrelevant. In our society, being female uniquely qualifies an individual for domestic work.

It is true, of course, that the American homemaker, has, on the

12. I. I. Gottesman, "Heritability of Personality: A Demonstration," *Psychological Monographs*, vol. 77, whole no. 572 (1963).
13. B. Friedan, *The Feminine Mystique* (New York: Norton, 1963).

average 5.1 hours of leisure time per day, and it is here, we are told, that each woman can express her unique identity. Thus, politically interested women can join the League of Women Voters; women with humane interests can become part-time Gray Ladies; women who love music can raise money for the symphony. Protestant women play canasta; Jewish women play Mah-Jongg; brighter women of all denominations and faculty wives play bridge; and so forth.

But politically interested *men* serve in legislatures; *men* with humane interests become physicians or clinical psychologists; *men* who love music play in the symphony; and so forth. In other words, why should a woman's unique identity determine only the periphery of her life rather than its central core?

Again, the important point is not that the role of homemaker is necessarily inferior, but that the woman's unique identity has been rendered irrelevant. Consider the following "predictability test." When a boy is born, it is difficult to predict what he will be doing twenty-five years later. We cannot say whether he will be an artist, a doctor, or a college professor because he will be permitted to develop and to fulfill his own unique potential, particularly if he is white and middle-class. But if the newborn child is a girl, we can usually predict with confidence how she will be spending her time twenty-five years later. Her individuality doesn't have to be considered; it is irrelevant.

The socialization of the American male has closed off certain options for him too. Men are discouraged from developing certain desirable traits such as tenderness and sensitivity just as surely as women are discouraged from being assertive and, alas, "too bright." Young boys are encouraged to be incompetent at cooking and child care just as surely as young girls are urged to be incompetent at mathematics and science.

Indeed, one of the errors of the early feminist movement in this country was that it assumed that men had all the goodies and that women could attain self-fulfillment merely by being like men. But that is hardly the utopia implied by the values of individuality and self-fulfillment. Rather, these values would require society to raise its children so flexibly and with sufficient respect for the integrity of individual uniqueness that some men might emerge with the motivation, the ability, and the opportunity to stay home and raise children without bearing the stigma of being peculiar. If homemaking is as glamorous as the women's magazines and television commercials portray it, then men, too, should have that option. Even if homemaking isn't all that glamorous, it would probably still be more fulfilling for some men than the jobs in which they now find themselves.

And if biological differences really do exist between men and women in "nurturance," in their inborn motivations to care for children, then this will show up automatically in the final distribution of men and women across the various roles: relatively fewer men will choose to stay at home. The values of individuality and self-fulfillment do not imply that there must be equality of outcome, an equal number of men and women in each role, but that there should be the widest possible variation in outcome consistent with the range of individual differences among people, regardless of sex. At the very least, these values imply that society should raise its males so that they could freely engage in activities that might pay less than those being pursued by their wives without feeling that they were "living off their wives." One rarely hears it said of a woman that she is "living off her husband."

Thus, it is true that a man's options are limited by our society's sex-role ideology, but as the "predictability test" reveals, it is still the woman in our society whose identity is rendered irrelevant by America's socialization practices. In 1954, the United States Supreme Court declared that a fraud and hoax lay behind the slogan "separate but equal." It is unlikely that any court will ever do the same for the more subtle motto that successfully keeps the woman in her place: "complementary but equal."

Interpersonal equality

> Wives, submit yourselves unto your own husbands, as unto the
> Lord. For the husband is the head of the wife, even as Christ is
> the head of the church; and he is the savior of the body. Therefore,
> as the church is subject unto Christ, so let the wives be to their own
> husbands in everything. [Eph. 5]

As this passage reveals, the ideological rationalization that men and women hold complementary but equal positions is a recent invention of our modern "liberal" society, part of the equalitarian veneer which helps to keep today's version of the ideology nonconscious. Certainly those Americans who value open, honest, and equalitarian relationships generally are quick to reject this traditional view of the male-female relationship; and, an increasing number of young people even plan to enter "utopian" marriages very much like the following hypothetical example:

> Both my wife and I earned Ph.D. degrees in our respective
> disciplines. I turned down a superior academic post in Oregon and
> accepted a slightly less desirable position in New York where my
> wife could obtain a part-time teaching job and do research at one
> of the several other colleges in the area. Although I would have
> preferred to live in a suburb, we purchased a home near my wife's

college so that she could have an office at home where she would
be when the children returned from school. Because my wife earns
a good salary, she can easily afford to pay a maid to do her major
household chores. My wife and I share all other tasks around the
house equally. For example, she cooks the meals, but I do the
laundry for her and help her with many of her other household tasks.

Without questioning the basic happiness of such a marriage or its
appropriateness for many couples, we can legitimately ask if such a
marriage is, in fact, an instance of interpersonal equality. Have all the
hidden assumptions about the woman's "natural" role really been
eliminated? Has the traditional ideology really been exorcised? There
is a very simple test. If the marriage is truly equalitarian, then its
description should retain the same flavor and tone even if the roles of
the husband and wife were to be reversed:

Both my husband and I earned Ph.D. degrees in our respective
disciplines. I turned down a superior academic post in Oregon and
accepted a slightly less desirable position in New York where my
husband could obtain a part-time teaching job and do research at
one of the several other colleges in the area. Although I would have
preferred to live in a suburb, we purchased a home near my
husband's college so that he could have an office at home where
he would be when the children returned from school. Because my
husband earns a good salary, he can easily afford to pay a maid to
do his major household chores. My husband and I share all other
tasks around the house equally. For example, he cooks the meals,
but I do the laundry for him and help him with many of his other
household tasks.

It seems unlikely that many men or women in our society would mistake the marriage *just* described as either equalitarian or desirable,
and thus it becomes apparent that the ideology about the woman's
"natural" role nonconsciously permeates the entire fabric of such
"utopian" marriages. It is true that the wife gains some measure of
equality when her career can influence the final place of residence, but
why is it the unquestioned assumption that the husband's career
solely determines the initial set of alternatives that are to be considered? Why is it the wife who automatically seeks the parttime position?
Why is it *her* maid instead of *their* maid? Why *her* laundry? Why *her*
household tasks. And so forth throughout the entire relationship.

The important point here is not that such marriages are bad or that
their basic assumptions of inequality produce unhappy, frustrated
women. Quite the contrary. It is the very happiness of the wives in such

marriages that reveals society's smashing success in socializing its women. It is a measure of the distance our society must yet traverse toward the goals of self-fulfillment and interpersonal equality that such marriages are widely characterized as utopian and fully equalitarian. It is a mark of how well the woman has been kept in her place that the husband in such a marriage is often idolized by women, including his wife, for "permitting" her to squeeze a career into the interstices of their marriage as long as his own career is not unduly inconvenienced. Thus is the white man blessed for exercising his power benignly while his "natural" right to that power forever remains unquestioned.

Such is the subtlety of a nonconscious ideology!

A truly equalitarian marriage would permit both partners to pursue careers or outside commitments which carry equal weight when all important decisions are to be made. It is here, of course, that the "problem" of children arises. People often assume that the woman who seeks a role beyond home and family would not care to have children. They assume that if she wants a career or serious outside commitment, then children must be unimportant to her. But of course no one makes this assumption about her husband. No one assumes that a father's interest in his career necessarily precludes a deep and abiding affection for his children or a vital interest in their development. Once again America applies a double standard of judgment. Suppose that a father of small children suddenly lost his wife. No matter how much he loved his children, no one would expect him to sacrifice his career in order to stay home with them on a full-time basis—*even if he had an independent source of income.* No one would charge him with selfishness or lack of parental feeling if he sought professional care for his children during the day. An equalitarian marriage simply abolishes this double standard and extends the same freedom to the mother, while also providing the framework for the father to enter more fully into the pleasures and responsibilities of child rearing. In fact, it is the equalitarian marriage which has the most potential for giving children the love and concern of two parents rather than one.

But few women are prepared to make use of this freedom. Even those women who have managed to finesse society's attempt to rob them of their career motivations are likely to find themselves blocked by society's trump card: the feeling that the raising of the children is their unique responsibility and—in time of crisis—ultimately theirs alone. Such is the emotional power of a nonconscious ideology.

In addition to providing this potential for equalized child care, a truly equalitarian marriage embraces a more general division of labor which satisfies what might be called "the roommate test." That is, the labor is divided just as it is when two men or two women room together in college or set up a bachelor apartment together. Errands and domestic chores are assigned by preference, agreement, flipping a coin, given to hired help, or—as is sometimes the case—left undone.

It is significant that today's young people, many of whom live this way prior to marriage, find this kind of arrangement within marriage so foreign to their thinking. Consider an analogy. Suppose that a white male college students decided to room or set up a bachelor apartment with a black male friend. Surely the typical white student would not blithely assume that his black roommate was to handle all the domestic chores. Nor would his conscience allow him to do so even in the unlikely event that his roommate would say: "No, that's okay. I like doing housework. I'd be happy to do it." We suspect that the typical white student would still not be comfortable if he took advantage of this offer, if he took advantage of the fact that his roommate had been socialized to be "happy" with such an arrangement. But change this hypothetical black roommate to a female marriage partner, and somehow the student's conscience goes to sleep. At most it is quickly tranquilized by the thought that "she is happiest when she is ironing for her loved one." Such is the power of a nonconscious ideology.

Of course, it may well be that she *is* happiest when she is ironing for her loved one.

Such, indeed, is the power of a nonconscious ideology!

Behavior Modification:
A Contingency Approach to
Employee Performance
C. Ray Gullett, and
Robert Reisen

All "principles" of management are based upon man's conceptions and beliefs about himself. Classical theory, represented by such notables as Taylor, Weber, and Fayol, stressed improvements in productivity and economic performance by providing employees with well-defined and often narrowly structured work environments linked with economic rewards for desired performance. Early human relations theory stressed social satisfactions through cohesive work groups and participation in decision making. (1, 2) Contemporary writers, such as Likert, have continued this tradition in relatively current works dealing with the importance of effective and interlocking work teams. (3) More recently, increased emphasis has been placed on individual autonomy, greater development of a person's talents, and recognition of individual accomplishments. (4, 5) The job enrichment movement and management by objectives have become popular vehicles for implementing these ideas. (6, 7)

Human needs as an explanation of approaches to motivation

Analyses of both past and current motivational prescriptions often employ the Maslow need hierarchy to explain the rationale behind these prescriptions. Taylor's scientific management has been exhaustively discussed in terms of its tacit assumption that individuals are "economic men" operating at the first two need hierarchy levels. Much of the writings on human relations center on the social needs level, while Herzberg's satisfiers-dissatisfiers concept and McGregor's Theory Y have been compared to the esteem and self-actualization need levels.(8) While the formulators of the theories, themselves, have typically made no mention of the hierarchy concept, they, nevertheless, share the tacit assumption with Maslow that a given internal state is the dominant factor determining most employees' behavior at a point in history. Thus, as is true of Maslow's model, these are inner-directed theories of why organization members behave as they do.

But, as others have observed, the problem with human needs lies in our inability to observe them directly. (9) At best, we can only infer their existence through indirect measures. And, perhaps more importantly, we must assume the hierarchy's validity as a way of describing the internal state of most individuals. Even Maslow, himself, had doubts about this. As he explained, "My work on motivation came from the clinic, from a study of neurotic people. The carry-over of this theory to the industrial situation has some support from industrial studies, but, certainly, I would like to see many more studies of this kind, before feeling convinced that this carry-over from the study of neurosis to the study of labor in factories is legitimate (10) (p. 55). In a recent review of the literature of motivation, Miner and Dachler found that need importance varies among individuals. Important variables affecting employee needs included span of control, whether one holds a line or staff position, and a person's cultural background. They further concluded that the available evidence either fails to support the need hierarchy concept or it has not been sufficiently formulated to be tested. (11)

On a related note, criticisms of Herzberg's two-factor theory are well known, raising questions as to the validity of his methodology, as well as to the success of the job enrichment prescription on a carte blanche basis. And experience has indeed shown that not all employees desire enriched jobs. (12)

The one best way to approach motivation

Implicit in the need hierarchy schema and in most popular theories of motivation is the assumption that there is a "best" way to motivate persons in an organization. If one assumes that a given need is dominant in all or virtually all organization members, then payoffs, geared to that need, can be provided as rewards for productivity or inducements to contribute. Thus, scientific management emphasized economic rewards, human relationists stressed social satisfactions, and well-known contemporary behavorial theories put emphasis upon opportunities for self-control and development of latent abilities. The need that is stressed is usually linked to the historical point in time of the theorey's development.

To an extent, the assumption of a dominant need is undoubtedly justified. In the early years of this century, large masses of workers were unskilled, poorly educated, and primarily concerned with finding and holding a job. In terms of the need hierarchy, they were operating at the physiological and safety need levels. By contrast, today's employees are relatively well educated, more highly skilled, and more likely to be secure financially. Unemployment holds less terror than it did in Taylor's time. In today's environment, employees are more likely to respond to management and organization configurations that allow job enrichment, Theory Y management, and management by objectives.

Contingency of situational views of motivation

Clearly, however, a great deal of organizational research has been provided in the last few years that indicates the success of varying sorts of organizational and job configurations. (13–15) Such factors as type of technology and rate of change in the environment are often major determinants of effective organization and job design. From the standpoint of individual satisfaction, it is becoming clear that not all persons view rewards in the same preference ordering. Intuitively, we can agree with Vroom that, "Lists of motives which are supposedly common to all persons, such as the ones proposed by Maslow (1954), fail to do justice to . . . individual differences." (16)

Vroom's approach to motivation recognized the differences in motives or needs of individuals. By linking motivation to the perceived desirability of various outcomes, the likelihood of these outcomes occurring, as perceived by the individual, and the individual's perception of his ability to influence outcomes, Vroom built a motivational model based on individual differences. (17)

Although theoretically correct, the model share a deficiency with the Maslow need hierarchy concept: the necessity for determining a person's internal perceptual state to predict his behavior, knowing external contingencies. The model is basically cognitive because as with the Maslow model, it requires the researcher or practitioner to determine individual anticipation. Thus, environmental variables become inner-directed occurrences, assuming varying degrees of importance relative to different persons.

Nevertheless, Vroom's model of motivation broke dramatically with one of the best approaches dominanting management thinking and writing since the time of Taylor. By specifically modeling the importance of individual goals and perceptions upon behavior. Vroom moved motivation research in the direction of contingency thinking.

Operant conditioning and reinforcement

Independent of introspective and inner-directed theories of motivation, operant conditioning has emerged, whose best known advocate is B.

F. Skinner. (18, 19) The essence of this approach is that behavior can be changed by the consequences of that behavior. The operant model, unlike other behavioral approaches, avoids concern with the inner motivation of the individual. It does not dwell on man's drives and needs, nor does it hypothesize concerning his aspirations. Rather, it is founded upon the observable; that is, the behaviors or responses which can be seen, measured, and modified.

An operant can be described as a "class of responses, the subsequent likelihood of which may be modified by its consequences." (20) Operant behavior refers to any response "the properties of which may be modified by its effect on the environment." (20) The purpose of the operant conditioning process, then, is to develop contingencies of reinforcement that will increase the probability that certain behaviors (responses) will result. These contingencies are the relationships that exist between the occasion upon which a response occurs, the response itself, and the reinforcing consequences.

Identifying desired behavior

An applicant of operant conditioning begins wit the identification of desired behaviors of organization members. For programmed and relatively routine work, this task is not greatly difficult. Job analysis, methods and motion study, and engineered time standards may often be employed. Less routine tasks, such as those performed by management and professional employees, become more difficult to define, in terms of desired behavior. Management by objectives offers, however, the potential for identifying desirable end results that members are to pursue. Accomplishment, or lack of accomplishment of objectives, can be evaluated at a later date.

Determining positive reinforcers

When desired behaviors are identified, reinforcers must be determined. Positive reinforcers are rewards sought by the individual; negative reinforcers are forms of punishment that a person seeks to avoid. Although some support the use of negative reinforcement, most advocates of operant conditioning maintain that the unanticipated consequences of punishment far outweigh its advantages in influencing behavior. Thus, emphasis is placed, instead, upon the granting or withholding of positive reinforcers. (19)

Potential reinforcers are many and varied, ranging from monetary rewards, to social acceptance, to praise by superiors. Important reinforcers and their potential effect upon behavior are shown in figure 1. With the exception of such primary reinforcers as water, food, and air, external stimuli become reinforcers through learning. These

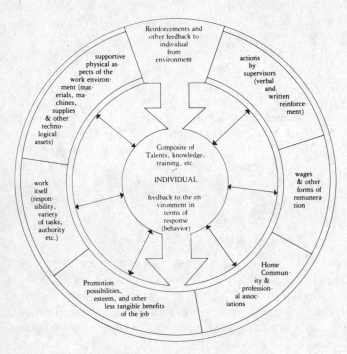

Figure 1. Potential Reinforcers of Behavior

stimuli, such as praise, promotion, and tasks requiring complex responses are called secondary reinforcers. Almost all the rewards used in organizations are secondary in nature.

Two limitations are placed on the effective use of these rewards: their availability in the organization and the extent to which organization members will work to achieve them. Not all jobs, for example, lead to promotions or wage increases. However, when these rewards are available, some employees may be unwilling to work harder to achieve them.

The task then becomes one of identifying those available rewards which employees will work to achieve. Most thories of motivation have predetermined what employees want (i.e., enriched jobs or more money) and thus circumvent this issue. The operant approach, however, emphasizes controlled experimentation to determine which rewards best reinforce desired behavior. Lower error rates, higher work volume, and fewer absences are examples of positive responses to one or more reinforcers.

Effective reinforcers are thus identified through trial and error. At

Emery Air Freight, where positive reinforcement has been used with striking success, the point is made this way: "The best test (of a reward's effectiveness): observe the behavior after a reward is offered. Does performance change? If not, try another reward" (20) (p. 171). Implicit in this approach is the lack of prejudgment concerning the desirability of one kind of reward over another that is often made in other motivational approaches.

As soon as effective reinforcers are identified, the frequency of their availability should be determined. Rewards can be offered in a number of sequences: continuous, fixed ratio, variable ratio, fixed interval, or variable interval. These sequences are summarized in figure 2.

The choice among these schedules of reinforcement has a profound effect upon the rate of response and its immunity to extinction. For example, continuous reinforcement works well during a learning period when a person is acquiring new knowledge. The principle of feedback, utilized in programmed instruction, is an example of continuous reinforcement.

For teaching complex tasks, the shaping concept is often used. Here, initially complex material is broken down into smaller modules. By reinforcing the successful completion of these relatively simple responses, which do not in themselves accomplish the ultimate objective, we enhance the probability of moving behavior in the desired direction. In one such approach, a bedframe manufacturer used the shaping concept to train hard-core unemployeds to produce finished bedframes. As each part of the job was learned, rewards were granted until the entire job cycle was mastered. (22)

As soon as desired job behaviors are learned, noncontinuous rein-reinforcement schedules are more effective for maintaining the desired behavior. Both the fixed and variable ratio and interval schedules

Figure 2. Schedules for reinforcement.

Type of Schedule Continuous Partial

Rate of Reinforcement
After every desired response

Ratio: A function of the number of responses		Interval: A function of time elapsed	
Fixed	Variable	Fixed	Variable
Reinforcement provided after the same number of responses every time	Different numbers of desired responses must be made to elicit reinforcement	Reinforcement provided after a fixed amount of of time	Reinforcement provided after varying amounts of of time

summarized in figure 2 are noncontinuous. Variable ratio schedules often provide the highest behavior rates. Here, a reinforcer is provided after an average number of responses. For example, a supervisor might praise a worker's performance on the average of once every twenty nondefective units produced. While the average would be set at twenty, praise might occur after the completion of thirty, twenty-five, fifteen, and ten units.

Variable schedules of reinforcement may allow previously non-effective rewards to stimulate productivity. Pay-checks, for example, while noncontinuous, are fixed interval, occurring weekly, monthly, or after some other predictable period of time. The provision of pay on a predictable interval schedule may reinforce only the picking up of the paycheck at the end of the period. Thus, more performance-based monetary rewards such as bonuses, commissions, or special awards may be more effective in linking monetary payments to level of productivity. Praise may become more effective when not linked only to annual or semi-annual performance appraisals.

Perhaps the best known success of positive reinforcement is at Emery Air Freight. To improve larger container utilization, which stood initially at 45%, management instituted a checklist program, whereby a worker checked a sheet each time he used the larger container for shipping. At the end of his shift the worker totaled his usage to determine if he had achieved the 90% goal announced by the company. Employees who showed any increase in usage were praised by supervisors and regional managers. The result was that, in a number of the company's offices, usage rose from 45% to 95% in a single day. Savings were estimated at $44,000 a month or $520,000 a year. (15)

One interesting application of position reinforcement is the use of a lottery by a hardware store's management to reduce tardiness and absenteeism. Employees with perfect attendance records were given chances in a lottery for cash prizes. Employee tardiness and absenteeism dropped dramatically as a result. (23) (p. 396). The bedframe manufacturer, previously mentioned, awarded points to employees who successfully mastered job skills. Points could later be traded for various prizes. (22)

At the managerial level, two researchers developed a training program to teach supervisors how to use positive reinforcement. Supervisors were taught how to define employee problems in terms of observable events, how to measure the frequencies of behavior, how to determine the probable stimuli that evoked the behavior, and techniques of positive reinforcement to change employee behavior in the desired direction. As a result of the training, participating supervisors increased their effectiveness ratings by a minimum of 5% with significant cost savings to the company. (24)

In a nonindustry experiment, a researcher gave a group of 106 children a series of addition problems to perform each day for five days. At the end of each day one group was praised for its performance. A second group, matched with the first in age, sex, and initial performance, was publicly reproved for its performance. A third matched group was ignored, but allowed to observe the praise and reproach given the other groups. A control group was also tested in a different room and given no feedback whatever. The results after five days showed the praised group with the most improved performance, followed by the reproved group, the ignored group, and finally the control group. While some evidence is provided here for the value of negative reinforcement, positive feedback shows a stronger relationship to productivity improvement (19) (p. 217).

In another experiment, four researchers offered small cash payments to workers in a Mexican manufacturing plant for each day they arrived at work on time. A control group that was not allowed to participate in the program showed an increase in tardiness over the test period. (25)

Although operant conditioning through positive reinforcement has shown promise for modifying behavior in organizations, problems in implementation, nevertheless, exist. Most of the experiments reported have occurred at the operative level, where desired behaviors are relatively easy to identify and reinforce. At managerial and professional levels, role complexity greatly complicates the task of identifying desired behaviors and developing appropriate behavior modification techniques. As mentioned previously, management by objectives offers promise at these levels.

A second problem with behavior modification involves conflicting reinforcements. While managements may be capable of granting or withholding certain desired rewards, there are, typically, other desired reinforcements which are largely, or totally, outside of management's control. As figure 1 points out, home, community, and professional associations provide rewards and punishments for certain behavior. Social rewards from co-workers may be granted or withheld on the basis of behaviors contrary to formal organization goals. Thus, the problem of providing proper reinforcements to induce desired behaviors widens in scope. To design an effective program of positive reinforcement, the possibility of reinforcers outside the direct control of management must be acknowledged. In some instances, these reinforcers may conflict with organizational goals and may thus nullify, or reduce, the effectiveness of organizational rewards. Where possible, these reinforcements should be made compatible with organizational rewards. One interpretation of the success of Scanlon plans is the combination of monetary rewards and work group approval provided to those whose suggestions for improving productivity are accepted (23) (p. 394).

A final, but perhaps short-term, problem is unfamiliarity of practicing managers in the theory and practice of operant conditioning. Not only are the majority unfamiliar with techniques of reinforcement, they are also unfamiliar with methods of observation of responses. For the most part, management thinking continues to analyze behavior on the basis of internal states, such as those in the Maslow need hierarchy. When a person exhibits inappropriate responses, the tendency may be to rely on theories that try to explain behavior in terms of internal motivations. Dealing with the behavior itself, rather than theorizing about motivations that caused it, would appear to be both more practical and more effective in many instances. Widespread acceptance and understanding of operant conditioning is, however, a necessary precondition to its use in most organizations.

Several suggestions can be made for the implementation of the operant approach. A necessary beginning is the identification of desired performance at all organization levels. This is especially critical for positions above the operative level. Just what is "good performance"? And just as important, when it has been defined, how will we measure it? Management by objectives may often be useful in answering these questions.

Further, our managers must be trained to better understand the relationship between a worker's behavior and the environmental influences which affect it. They should be more attuned to recognizing the relationship between changes in responses and fluctuations in the work, peer group, or supervisory contingencies.

Programmed learning techniques should be applied to training programs wherever possible. Not only are they highly reinforcing to correct responses, they have proven to be one of the fastest methods of instruction, while freeing supervisors to attend to other operations or problems.

Design of compensation plans which operate on variable schedules should be encouraged. Stable periodic payment/bonus plans are not conducive to increased performance. As mentioned earlier, there are many lottery and bonus programs available to management. Their application is limited only by the lack of creativity or imagination of the manager. And these suggestions are meant to neither eliminate nor minimize the value of such practices as employee participation or varied and more complex job content. But as with other rewards, they should be used selectively if there is evidence that employees will respond positively to them.

Finally, we need to convince ourselves of the value and utility of the operant approach to motivation. It has proven its usefulness, but it can only succeed if we study it, understand it, and have the courage to apply it. No change of any kind can be instituted in business, today, which lacks the conviction and support of its management. And this can only be achieved through an understanding and acceptance of the tangible benefits provided by operant conditioning.

For many persons, behavior modification, or operant conditioning, has evoked feelings of mistrust, fear of the loss of individuality, and other negative reactions. Since time began, however, modification of people's behavior has been our way of life. During the socialization process, in our learning institutions, in business organizations, everywhere, we are changing or trying to change the behavior of others. Much of this effort is misguided and, in the end, produces little tangible benefit.

Operant conditioning takes these efforts and improves upon them. Instead of a rule-of-thumb approach, the operant approach stresses goals, achievement, and direction. It stresses the utility of effort; the avoidance of nonconstructive or inappropriate behavior. It is philosophically compatible with contingency theories of management, offering varied rewards that best suit the situation.

The concept of behavior modification is still in an embryonic stage of development. There are, however, indications that it will progress. The observations and suggestions made here will hopefully provide some insight for those who wish to pursue the subject further. With proper utilization, behavior modification may be an important means of implementing a contingency approach to organizational behavior.

References

1. Mayo, Elton. *The Human Problems of Industrial Civilization.* New York: Macmillan, 1933.

2. Roethlisberger, Fritz J. and Dickson, William J. *Management and the Worker.* Cambridge, Mass.: Harvard University Press, 1939.

3. Likert, Rensis. *The Human Organization.* New York: McGraw-Hill Book Company.

4. Herzberg, Frederick. *Work and the Nature of Man.* Cleveland: World Publishing Company, 1966.

5. McGregor, Douglas. *The Professional Manager.* New York: McGraw-Hill Book Company, 1967.

6. Carrol, Stephun J. Jr. and Josi, Henri L. Jr. *Management by Objectives.* New York: Macmillan, 1973.

7. Ford, Robert. *Motivation through the Work Itself.* New York: American Management Association, 1969.

8. Donnelly, James H. Jr., Gibson, James L., and Ivancevich, John

M. *Fundamentals of Management*. Austin, Texas: Business Publications, Inc., 1971.

9. Hicks, Herbert G. and Gullett, C. Ray. *Organizations: Theory and Behavior*. New York: McGraw-Hill Book Company, 1975.

10. Maslow, Abraham. *Eupaychian Management: A Journal*. Homewood, Ill.: Irwin/Dorsey, 1965.

11. Miner, John B. and Dachler, H. P. "Personnel Attitudes and Motivation," in P. H. Mussen and M. R. Rosenweig (eds.) *Annual Review of Psychology* (Vol. 24, 1973).

12. Morse, John J. "A Contingency Look at Job Design." *California Management Review* (Fall 1973):67–73.

13. Lawrence, Paul R. and Lorsch, Jay W. *Organization and Environment: Managing Differentiation and Integration*. Boston: Division of Research, Harvard Business School, 1967.

14. Thompson, James D. *Organizations in Action*. New York: McGraw-Hill Book Company, 1967.

15. "Where Skinner's Theories Work." *Business Week* (Dec. 2, 1972):64–65.

16. Vroom, Victor H. *Motivation in Management*. New York: American Foundation for Management Research, 1965.

17. Vroom, Victor H. *Work and Motivation*. New York: John Wiley and Sons, Inc., 1964.

18. Skinner, B. F. *Beyond Freedom and Dignity*. New York: Bantam Books, 1971.

19. Skinner, B. F. *Contingencies of Reinforcement, A Theoretical Analysis*. New York: Appleton-Century-Crofts, 1969.

20. Catania, Charles. *Contemporary Research in Operant Behavior*. Glenview, Ill.: Scott, Foresman, and Company, 1968.

21. *Positive Reinforcement*. Emery Air Freight System Performance Department, 1970.

22. Schneider, C. E. "Behavior Modification: Training the Hard Core Unemployed." *Personnel* (May-June, 1973):65–69.

23. Nord, Walter R. "Beyond the Teaching Machine: The Neglected Area of Operant Conditioning in the Theory and Practice of Management." *Organization Behavior and Human Performance* (4, 1969):375–401.

24. Luthans, Fred and Lyman, David. "Training Supervisors to Use Organization Behavior Modification." *Personnel* (Sept.-Oct. 1973):38–44.

25. Hermann, J. A., de Montes, Ana I., Dominguez, B., Montes, F., and Hopkins, B. L. "Effects of Bonuses for Punctuality on the Tardiness of Industrial Workers." *Journal of Applied Behavior Analysis* (6, 1973):563–572.

4

The Whole Person
And The
Whole Situation:
Putting It Together

Introduction

The three preceding chapters were more about people that about managing. They were about what pushes and motivates people, about how people think, and about how they put their feelings and thoughts together to form opinions, beliefs, and attitudes. But so far we have said very little about the settings, the situations in which people live and work. We haven't talked about differences in job, in rank, in family situations. We have said nothing of the here-and-now pressures and forces that shape and mold the behavior of the whole person, at any point in time.

The "situation" is terribly important for one simple reason: it is usually much easier to change the situation than it is to change the person. We can modify jobs, we change locations, we can join different groups than the ones we were in last week. It is mighty hard to change human motives or thinking styles quickly and easily. And while opinions, beliefs, and attitudes can certainly change one time, they are often changed more readily by working on the situation than by working on the person directly.

The first paper in this chapter, the Argyris paper, raises the whole question of the compatibility of the human with organized institutions. Every reader surely has thought at some time about the question of individual freedom versus organizational constraint. Some have argued that incompatability is basic and irreconcilable; that people cannot be free within organized settings; that the whole concept of organization is by definition restrictive of human behavior. Argyris, perhaps more than any other recent student of organizations, has worried about that issue. The Argyris paper examines the person-organization interface in meaningful detail.

The second paper, by Rogers, is a personal statement by one of the leading psychologists of our era. Carl Rogers tries to describe what the "good life" and what a "fully functioning" person looks like to him. Note that he does not talk about a "normal" person, or even a "healthy" one. The question of what is a "normal" or "healthy" person is a surprisingly elusive one. And one of the reasons it is elusive is because people can never be observed except in complicated situations. Is it "normal" or "healthy" for a person to "give in" in a severe torture situation? Is it "abnormal" or "unhealthy" for a person to become so frustrated by a large bureaucratic situation that he or she just quits and walks out? Rogers, instead of using words like 'health" and "normality," speaks about the process of living, about functioning fully. As a leading clinician and theoretician of human personality, Rogers' optimistic assessment of the fully functioning person is well worth the reader's time.

The third paper in this set, by Siu, on Chinese baseball, is different from the others but not as different as it looks at first. It too is concerned with the fully functioning person, but this time with an emphasis on human thinking. Siu is concerned with the total use of the total mind; with intuition and sensitivity, as well as with logic and rationality. And he is concerned with the total use of mind in the managerial siuation. Perhaps when managers can come close to using the total information-processing capacities of their minds they will function better in the kinds of uncertain, disorderly, and deadline situations they so often face.

Personality vs. Organization
Chris Argyris

Approximately every seven years we develop the itch to review the relevant literature and research in personality and organization theory, to compare our own evolving theory and reasearch with those of our peers—an exercise salutary, we trust, in confirmation and also confrontation. We're particularly concerned to measure our own explicit model of man with the complementary or conflicting models advanced by other thinkers. Without an explicit normative model, personality and organization theory (P. and O. theory) tends to settle for a generalized description of behavior as it is observed in existing institutions —at best, a process that embalms the status quo; at worst, a process that exalts it. Current behavior becomes the prescription for future actions.

By contrast, I contend that behavioral science research should be normative, that it is the mission of the behavioral scientist to intervene selectively in the organization whenever there seems a reasonable chance of improving the quality of life within the organization without imperiling its viability. Before surveying the P. and O. landscape, however, let's review the basic models of man and formal organization.

Fundamentals of man and organization

The following steps indicate how the worlds of man and formal organization have developed:

1. Organizations emerge when the goals they seek to achieve are too complex for any one man. The actions necessary to achieve the goals are divided into units manageable by individuals—the more complex the goals, other things being equal, the more people are required to meet them.

2. Individuals themselves are complex organizations with diverse needs. They contribute constructively to the organization only if *on balance,* the organization fulfills these needs and their sense of what is just.

3. What are the needs that individuals seek to fulfill? Each expert has his own list and no two lists duplicate priorities. We have tried to bypass this intellectual morass by focusing on some relatively reliable predispositions that remain valid irrespective of the situation. Under any circumstances individuals seek to fulfill these predispositions; at the same time, their exact nature, potency, and the degree to which they must be fulfilled are influenced by the organizational context—for example, the nature of the job. In their attempt to live, to grow in competence, and to achieve self-acceptance, men and women tend to program themselves along the lines of the continua depicted in figure 1.

Figure 1. Developmental continua.

Infants begin as	Adults strive toward
(1) being dependent and submissive to parents (or other significant adult)	(1) relative independence, autonomy, relative control over their immediate world
(2) having few abilities	(2) developing many abilities
(3) having skin-surfaced or shallow abilities	(3) developing a few abilities in depth
(4) having a short time perspective	(4) developing a longer time perspective

Together, these continua represent a developmental logic that people ignore or suppress with difficulty, the degree of difficulty depending on the culture and the context, as well as the individual's interactions with the key figures in his or her life. The model assumes that the thrust of this developmental program is from left to right, but nothing is assumed about the location of any given individuals along these continua.

A central theme of P. and O. theory has been the range of differences between individuals and how it is both necessary and possible to arrange a match between the particular set of needs an individual brings to the job situation and the requirements—technical and psychological—of the job itself, as well as the overall organizational climate.

We have written four studies that highlighted an individual's interrelationship with the work context. In each study, a separate analysis was made of each participant that included (1) the predispositions that he or she desired to express, (2) the potency of each predisposition, (3) the inferred probability that each would be expressed, and (4) a final score that indicated the degree to which the individual was able to express his or her predispositions.

A personal expression score enabled us to make specific predictions as to how individuals would react to the organization. We had expected individuals with low scores, for example, to state that they were frustrated and to have poorer attendance records and a higher quitting rate—expectations that also showed how individual differences in predispositions were differentially rewarded in different types of departments. Bank employees with a need to distrust and control others, for example, instinctively opted for positions in the internal audit department of the bank.

So much for the model of man. Now to organizations, which have a life of their own, in the sense that they have goals that unfortunately may be independent of or antagonistic to individual needs. The next step was to determine if there was a genetic logic according to which organizations were programmed.

Observation and reading combined to suggest that most organizations had pyramidal structures of different sizes. The logic behind each of these pyramids—great or small—was first, to centralize information and power at the upper levels of the structure; second, to specialize work. According to this logic, enunciated most clearly by Frederick Winslow Taylor and Max Weber, management should be high on the six organizational activities summarized in figure 2.

Figure 2. Continua of organizational activities.

Designing specialized and fractionalized work

low	high

Designing production rates and controlling speed of work

low	high

Giving orders

low	high

Evaluating performance

low	high

Rewarding and punishing

low	high

Perpetuating membership

low	high

This model assumed that the closer an organization approached the right ends of the continua, the closer it approached the ideal of formal organization. The model assumed nothing, however, about where any given organization would be pinpointed along these continua.

Personality vs. Organization

Given the dimensions of the two models, the possibilities of interaction are inevitable and varied; so is the likelihood of conflict between the

needs of individuals and the structured configuration of the formal
organization. The nature of the interaction between the individual and
the organization and the probability of conflict vary according to the
conditions depicted in figure 3.

Figure 3. Conditions of interaction.

If the individual aspired toward	And the organization (through its jobs, technology, controls, leadership, and so forth) required that the individual aspire toward
(1) adulthood dimensions	(1) infancy dimensions
(2) infancy dimensions	(2) adulthood dimensions
(3) adulthood dimensions	(3) adulthood dimensions
(4) infancy dimensions	(4) infancy dimensions

From this model, we can hypothesize that the more the organization approaches the model of the formal organization, the more individuals will be forced to behave at the infant ends of the continua.
What if—still operating at the level of an intellectual exercise—the
individuals aspired toward the adult ends of the continua? What would
the consequences be? Wherever there is an incongruence between the
needs of individuals and the requirements of a formal organization,
individuals will tend to experience frustration, psychological failure,
short time perspective, and conflict.

What factors determine the extent of the incongruence? The chief
factors are as follows: first, the lower the employee is positioned in
the hierarchy, the less control he has over his working conditions and
the less he is able to employ his abilities; second, the more directive the
leadership, the more dependent the employee; and last, the more uni-
lateral the managerial controls, the more dependent the employee will
feel.

We have said that individuals find these needs difficult to ignore or
suppress, and if they are suppressed, frustration and conflict result.
These feelings, in turn, are experienced in several ways:

The employee fights the organization and tries to gain more control
—for example, he may join a union.

The employee leaves the organization, temporarily or permanently.

The employee leaves it psychologically, becoming a half-worker, un-
involved, apathetic, indifferent.

The employee downgrades the intrinsic importance of work and
substitutes higher pay as the reward for meaningless work. Barnard
observed almost 40 years ago that organizations emphasized financial
satisfactions because they were the easiest to provide. He had a point—
then and now.

We want to emphasize several aspects about these propositions. The personality model provides the base for predictions as to the impact of any organizational variable upon the individual, such as organizational structure, job content, leadership style, group norms, and so on. The literature has concentrated on employee frustration expressed in fighting the organization, because it's the most common form of response, but we shouldn't ignore the other three responses.

In a study of two organizations in which technology, job content, leadership, and managerial controls confined lower-skilled employees to the infancy ends of the continua, their response was condition 3—no union, almost no turnover or absenteeism, but also apathy and indifference.

Last, we believe that the model holds regardless of differences in culture and political ideology. The fundamental relationships between individuals and organizations are the same in the United States, England, Sweden, Yugoslavia, Russia, or Cuba, a drastic statement but, we think, a true one.

Research that tests the model

Several studies in the past six years designed specifically to test the validity of the model all bore it out, to a greater or lesser extent. One study involved a questionnaire that measured self-expression as defined by our model. In a random sample of 332 U.S. salaried managers, hourly paid workers, and self-employed businessmen, it was found that the lower the self-actualization, the more likely employees were to exhibit the following behavior: To daydream, to have aggressive feelings toward their superiors, to have aggressive feelings toward their co-workers, to restrict output or make avoidable errors, to postpone difficult tasks or decisions, to emphasize money as the reward for service, and to be dissatisfied with their current jobs and think about another job.

A study in a different culture—Brazil—dealt with 189 employees in 13 banks. It revealed that 86 percent of the employees registered a discrepancy between their own felt needs and the formal goals of the organization. All agreed that the organizational goals were important, but only the top managers felt an absence of conflict between their own needs and the goals of the organization.

A second U. S. study involving 329 respondents—104 businessmen, 105 managers, and 120 workers—confirmed the model, but not in most cases to a degree that was statistically significant. On balance, however, the respondents supported the proposition that employees who perceive their work situations as highly bureaucratic feel more isolated, alienated, and powerless.

Research that supports the model

Additional studies with no formal relationship to the model nevertheless tend to underwrite it. A national sample of 1,533 employees in
1972, for example, showed that among all age groups interesting work
was more important than money in providing job satisfaction.

Bertil Gardell, a Swedish psychologist, examined four plants in mass
production and process industries, seeking to relate production technology to alientation and mental health. Among his findings were
these:

The more skilled the task and the more control the individual feels
over how he performs it, the more independence and the less stress
he experiences.

There is a big discrepancy between people as to which jobs they
deem interesting; some employees, for example, describe jobs with
low discretion as interesting—this is a contradiction of our model, but
they account for only 8 percent of the employees surveyed.

In come is not a factor in determining alienation. A high-income
employee with little control over his job feels just as alienated as the
man laboring for a pittance.

Gardell concluded:

Severe restrictions in worker freedom and control and in skill
level required are found to be related to increased work alienation
and lowered level of mental health even after control is made for
age, sex, income, type of leadership, and satisfaction with pay. The
relation between task organization and mental health is valid,
however, only after allowance is made for work alienation. In both
industries certain people regard jobs of low discretion and skill level
as interesting and free from constraint, but these groups amount to
only 8 percent in each industry and are strongly overrepresented
as to workers above 50 years of age.
Within the mass-production industry, restrictions in discretion and
skill level are found to go together with increased feelings of
psychological stress and social isolation. People working under piece
rate systems—compared with hourly paid workers—find their work
more monotonous, constrained, and socially isolating, as well as
having lower social status. . . .
High self-determination and job involvement are found to be related
to high demands for increased worker influence on work and
company decisions in the process industries, while in the mass-
production industries demand for increased worker influence is
greatest among those who feel their work to be monotonous and

constrained. Perceptions of strong worker influence by collective arrangements are accompanied by increased demands for individual decision-power as well as increased job satisfaction and decreased alienation.

A batch of studies reaffirmed the relationship between job specialization and feelings of powerlessness on the job and of frustration and alienation. One that compared craftsmen, monitors, and assemblers found that job satisfaction varied dramatically according to the degree of specialization: Job satisfaction was lowest among the assemblers —14 percent; next were the monitors—52 percent; and last were the craftsmen—87 percent. The same study found a strong relationship between job specialization and powerlessness on the job. Thus, 93 percent of the assemblers and 57 percent of the monitors, but only 19 percent of the craftsmen, experienced a lack of freedom and control.

Still other studies related job levels to the degree of dissatisfaction with the jobs. A comparison of 15 managers with 26 supervisors and 44 workers showed that the degree of satisfaction paralleled their position in the hierarchy, with managers the most satisfied and workers the least satisfied.

Frederick Herzberg reported a study of 2,665 Leningrad workers under 30 that again correlated job level with job satisfaction. Researchers who have concentrated on the higher levels of the organization typically have found a systematic tendency—the higher the positions held by the individuals in the organization, the more positive their attitudes tended to be.

An unusual study by Allan Wicker compared undermanned situations in which participants assumed more responsibility and performed larger tasks with overmanned situations in which the tasks were small and the responsibilities minute. Not surprisingly, in the overmanned situations employees reported less meaningful tasks and less sense of responsibility.

Can we reduce powerlessness at work, a factor closely linked to job alienation? One suggestive article points up three possibilities: Employees should allocate their own tasks; crews should be allowed to select themselves through sociometric procedures; the members of the group should select the group leaders.

Finally, research throws light on the question of whether time is the great reconciler. How long do dissatisfaction and frustration with the job persist? The answer appears to be—indefinitely. An interesting comparison of an old and a new assembly plant found that after 14 years the presumably acclimated employees were more dissatisfied and less involved with the product and the company than the new employees. Familiarity breeds frustration, alienation, and contempt.

Research results explained by the model

If employees are predisposed toward greater autonomy and formal organizations are designed to minimize autonomy, at least at the lower levels, we would expect to find a significant correlation between job status and job satisfaction—the lower the job, the less the job satisfaction. This has been found in a number of studies. Harold Wilensky, for example, reported in one of his studies the proportion of satisfied employees ranged from 90 percent for professors and mathematicians to 16 percent for unskilled auto workers. Furthermore, he found that the percentage of people who would go into similar work if they could start over again varied systematically with the degree of autonomy, control, and the chance to use their abilities that they experienced in their current jobs.

Several studies focused on the relationship between control and job satisfaction. An analysis of 200 geographically separate systems that were parts of larger organizations—for example, automotive dealers, clerical operations, manufacturing plants, and power plants in the same company—revealed that the greatest discrepancy between actual and ideal control occurred at the level of the rank-and-file employee. Ninety-nine percent of the work groups wanted more control over their immediate work area. Still another study found that employees became more dissatisfied after moving to a new, more efficient plant because of the reduction of their control over work. These studies were in the United States. Similar research in Yugoslavia and Norway further buttressed the point that employees want to enlarge the degree of their control over their immediate work world.

What about the impact of control upon turnover? The logic of the model leads us to predict that employees would be more likely to quit an organization when they experienced too much control by the organization or its representatives. Once again, research supports the hypothesis. One study found that the authoritarian foreman was a major factor in labor turnover; a second showed that there was a close relationship between the supervisor's inequitable treatment—he could not be influenced, did not support his subordinates, and did not attempt to redress employee grievances—and the turnover rate. Employees, in short, fled from unfair treatment.

One assemblage of studies would appear at first glance to contradict the model. We refer to those studies that show that lower-skilled workers appear to be more interested in how much money they make than they are in how interesting their jobs are. As John Goldthorpe and others demonstrate, however, they are merely being realists. Goldthorpe, in particular, points out repeatedly and documents in detail the fact that workers do desire intrinsically satisfying jobs, but find such aspirations to be unrealistic. In the long run, however great the reluctance and the pain, they adapt.

His research dealt with British workers but a number of studies in the United States replicate his findings. As you move up the job hierarchy, employees consistently assign a higher value to job characteristics that potentially fulfill growth needs. Medium- and high-status white-collar workers, for example. placed primary emphasis on work-content factors as a source of job satisfaction, while low-status white-collar workers and blue-collar workers tended to play them down. As our model would predict, employees seek out job satisfactions they feel are second-rate, because higher-level satisfactions are unattainable —certainly in their current jobs.

In summary, this research demonstrates first, that the overall impact of the formal organization on the individual is to decrease his control over his immediate work area, decrease his chance to use his abilities, and increase his dependence and submissiveness; second, that to the extent to which the individual seeks to be autonomous and function as an adult he adapts by reactions ranging from withdrawal and noninterest, to agression, or perhaps to the substitution of instrumental money rewards for intrinsic rewards. The weight of the deprivations and the degree of adaptation increase as we descend the hierarchy. Formal organizations, alas, are unintentionally designed to discourage the autonomous and involved worker.

Job enlargement or enrichment

Job enlargement in the true sense, not the multiplication of meaningless tasks, but quite literally the enrichment of the job either by adding tasks that provide intrinsic satisfactions or increasing the worker's control over the tasks he already performs, obviously conforms to our models. And we would expect that employees whose jobs were enriched would be more satisfied with their jobs and less likely to manifest their dissatisfaction in ways that undermine the organization. Looking at the other side of the coin, we also would expect that more positive attitudes would be accompanied by increased productivity.

And we would not be disappointed. No fewer than eight studies testify that designing that permit more self-regulation, self-evaluation, self-adjustment, and participation in goal-setting both improved attitudes and increased productivity.

Of particular importance is a study by Hackman and Lawler that correlated the core dimensions of jobs—variety, autonomy, task identity, and feedback—with motivation, satisfaction, performance, and attendance. The principal findings of their study are these:

The higher the jobs are on core dimensions, the higher the employees are rated by their supervisors as doing better quality work and being more effective performers.

When jobs rank high on the core dimensions, employees report feeling more intrinsically motivated to perform well.

Core dimensions are strongly and positively related to job satisfaction and involvement.

The job satisfaction items that strongly correlate with the job core dimension are related to control over one's own work, feeling of worth-while accomplishment, and self-esteem.

The strength of the relationships described above increases with those employees who seek to meet higher-order needs. This finding is significant because research seldom examines individual differences in this way.

Hackman and Lawler differentiate between horizontal enlargement —increasing the number of things an employee does—and vertical enlargement—increasing the degree to which an employee is responsible for making most major decisions about his work. They would argue and we would concur that a combination of both types of enlargement —what we have earlier called role enlargement—is optimal.

What about practice? The concept of job enrichment isn't new. A study of IBM published in 1948 included an assessment of job enrichment and its benefits.

We would expect a concept so fulfilling, so helpful in meeting the goals of both the employee and the organization to be widely adopted. And we would be disappointed. A recent survey of 300 of the top 1,000 *Fortune* industrials showed that only 4 percent had made any formal, systematic attempt to enrich jobs. And even they had enriched only a very small percentage of their total jobs.

What accounts for the lag in adopting job enrichment? Two factors seem to be at work and to reinforce each other. First, most managements are convinced that job enrichment doesn't pay off economically. This belief, in turn, leads them to exhibit signs of the ostrich syndrome —they ignore the accumulating body of evidence as to the substantial psychic dividends that employees derive from job enrichment.

Let me quote from just two of the voluminous research studies that demonstrate the efficiency of job enrichment. The first is the ambitious and significant attempt by the Gaines dog food division of General Foods to design an entire plant using horizontal and vertical enlargement of work. They key features of the design are the following:

(1) Autonomous work groups that develop their own production

schedules, manage production problems, screen and select new members, maintain self-policing activities, and decide questions such as who gets time off and who fills which work station.

(2) Integrated support functions. Each work team performs its own maintenance, quality control, and industrial engineering functions—plus challenging job assignments.

(3) Job mobility and rewards for learning. People are paid not on the basis of the job they are doing, but on the basis of the number of jobs that they are prepared to do.

(4) Self-government for the plant community.

The transition from a work environment on the infant ends of our continua to the adult ends was not easy for the people involved. Drastic change never is, even when the participants benefit from the change. The results to date, however, are impressive. A similar plant, organized along traditional lines, would require 110 employees; this one was manned by 70. The plant has met or exceeded production goals. Employees reported greater opportunities for learning and self-actualization. And team leaders and plant managers were more involved in community affairs than foremen and managers of comparable plants.

A second significant experiment in job enlargement is taking place at Volvo's new auto assembly plant in Kalmar, Sweden. Volvo faced serious problems—wildcat strikes, absenteeism, and turnover that were getting out of hand. Turnover in the old car assembly plant was over 40 percent annually. Absenteeism was running 20 to 25 percent. Now, assembly has been divided among teams of 15 to 25 workers, who will decide how to distribute the job of car assembly among themselves. Each team determines its own work pace, subject to meeting production standards that are set for them. Each team selects its own boss, and deselects him if it's unhappy with him.

The new plant cost approximately 10 percent more than it would have if it had been constructed along traditional lines. Will the benefits justify the extra expense? Time alone will tell—the plant has been on stream for only a matter of months—but Pehr Gyllenhammar, the managing director Volvo, hopes that it will realize both his economic and social objectives: "A way must be found to create a workplace that meets the needs of the modern working man for a sense of purpose and satisfaction in his daily work. A way must be found of attaining this goal without an adverse effect on productivity."

The model of man and the design or organization

Organizations depend on people. Thus, many organizational variables are designed around an explicit or implicit model of man. Taylor's molecularized jobs, for example, took a one-dimensional view of man and assumed that one could hire a hand; by contrast, the champions of vertical and horizontal job enrichment assume that one hires a whole human being.

Then there are the theorists who take the sociological viewpoint and impoverish their theories by ignoring the psychological element and treating man as a black box.

In each case the complexity of organizational reality leads them into contradictions, the significance of which they either play down or ignore altogether. Crozier, for example, although lacking an explicit model of man, also concluded that his data did not confirm the inhumanity of organizations toward individuals—but how can one define inhumanity without a concept of man? Nevertheless, in the same work he stated that monotonous and repetive work produces nervous tension in workers, that apathy and social isolation are great, and that work loads produce pressure.

Charles Perrow is a technological determinist who argues that the structure of organization depends on the requirements of the technology. An electronics plant making components should have a different structure from one making inertial guidance system components because of differences in the kind of research required by their technology, unanalyzable versus analyzable, or the number of exceptions it requires—few or many. Perrow's insight, valid but partial, is an inadequate concept to explain the total relationship between man and organization, an inadequacy that Perrow himself is coming to recognize. He concedes that "personality factors can have a great deal of influence upon the relations between coordination and subordinate power," that Robert McNamara, for example, was the key factor in changes in the Defense Department.

To elevate any one as *the* defining characteristic of organizations as Perrow did with technology and make all other characteristics dependent variables only leads to poor theory and inadequate and incomplete explanations of behavior in organizations. An error of equal magnitude is to ignore either the sociological or the psychological view in studying organizations.

We need a synthesis of the sociological and psychological views in studying man and a recognition that there are no fewer than four sets of independent but interacting characteristics that determine the behavior of any organization—structure and technology, leadership and interpersonal relations, administrative controls and regulations, and human controls. The strength of each of the four will vary from organization to organization, vary within different parts of the same organization, and vary over time within the same parts of each organization. However, any major change in an organization's structure is

doomed to failure unless major changes take place in all four characteristics.

Rational man decision theorists

In addition to those with no explicit model of man we have the rational
man decision theorists such as Simon, Cyert, and March, whose partial
view of man focuses on the concept of man as a finite information-
processing system striving to be rational and to "satisfice" in his
decision making. What this model neglects are the issues stressed by
P. and O. theory, such as dependence, submissiveness, the need for
psychological success, confirmation, and feelings of essentiality. As we
have written elsewhere, "Simon saw management's task as designing
organizational structures and mechanisms of organization influence
which ingrained into the nervous system of every member what the
organization required him to do. Intendedly, rational man was expected to follow authority, but he was also given appropriate and indirect inducements to produce."

Cyert and March retain the basic perspectives of the pyramidal
structure—specialization of tasks and centralization of power and information—but they add elements of reality and sophistication. By
cranking into their models the concepts of people as members of
coalitions politicking against each other for scarce resources and
settling for the quasi-reduction of conflicts between them, they were
able to predict more accurately how the organization was going to
behave, for example, in setting prices.

That the rational man thinkers have indeed helped managers to
make more effective decisions in some situations—those in which the
factors involved corresponded to their model—shouldn't lead us to
ignore the more frequent situations in which the rational man theories
were either a poor predictive tool or acted themselves to exacerbate
the situation. Recent research suggests that managers may resist the
management informations systems designed by the rational man theorists precisely because they work well—for example, accomplish the
desired objective of reducing uncertainty. What accounts for the apparent paradox? Man is not primarily rational, or rather he reacts in
response to what we like to call the rationality of feelings. He dislikes
being dependent and submissive toward others; he recognizes the increased probability that when management information systems work
best he will tend to experience psychological failure. The organization's goals are being met at the expense of his own. Management
information systems, in consequence, have become to managers at
many levels what time-study people were to the rank and file years
ago—an object of fear commingled with hatred and aggression.

Another trend that totally escapes the rational man theorists is the increasing hostility of an increasing number of young people toward the idea that organizations should be able to buy off people to be primarily rational, to submit to the mechanisms of organizational influence, and to suppress their feelings.

A third trend flows from the combined impact of the first two. Given the inability to predict the relationship of emotionality versus rationality in any particular context, and the reaction against rational man and organizational mechanisms of influence, add to these elements the largely unintended support of the status quo, and the use of "satisficing" to rationalize incompetence, and we end up with an interaction of forces that makes change in organizations seem almost impossible.

Hard to follow or accept? The line of argument is as follows:

1. To the degree that man accepts inducements to behave rationally, he acts passively in relation to the way power, information, and work are designed in the organization.

2. Over time, such individuals sterilize their self-actualizing tendencies by any one or a combination of approaches: They suppress them, deny them, or distort them. Eventually, they come to see their legitimate role in the organization—at least, as it bears on the design of power, information, and tasks—as pawns rather than as initiators.

3. A little further down the road, individuals come to view being passive and controlled as good, natural, and necessary. Eventually, they may define responsibility and maturity in these terms.

4. Individuals soon create managerial cultures—some have already done so—in which the discussion of self-actualizing possibilities is viewed as inappropriate.

5. The youth who because of the very success of the system are able to focus more on the self-actualizing needs will attempt to change things. They will come up, however, against facts 1 to 4 and end up terribly frustrated.

6. The frustration will tend to lead to regression, with two probable polarized consequences—withdrawal into communes or militancy.

7. Because we know very little about how to integrate self-actualizing activities with rational activities, older people will resent the hostility of youth or look upon their withdrawal as a cop-out.

The last and most important point is that the rational man theory, unlike P. and O. theory, could not predict the single most important trend about public and private organizations—their increasing internal deterioration and lack of effectiveness in producing services or products. As citizen, consumer, and presumably an organization man, you either feel it or you don't. We do feel strongly on this score. And we cite that while 25 years ago 75 percent of the respondents in a national survey felt that public and private organizations performed well, only 25 percent had the same opinion in 1972. How many believe that the percentage would be higher today?

The case for normative research

Most of the research that we have reviewed has been descriptive research that contents itself with describing, understanding, and predicting human behavior within organizations. In our research the emphasis is normative and based upon the potentialities of man. We're interested in studying man in terms of what he is capable of, not merely how he currently behaves within organizations.

Looked at from this normative viewpoint, the most striking fact about most organizations is the limited opportunities they afford most employees to fulfill their potential. We can show empirically that the interpersonal world of most people in ongoing organizations is characterized by much more distrust, conformity, and closedness than trust, individuality, and openness. This world—we call it Pattern A—fits with, if indeed it isn't derived from, the values about effective human behavior endemic in the pyramidal structure or in what Simon calls the mechanisms of organizational influence. Thus, findings based on descriptive research will tend to opt for the status quo.

Moreover, unless we conduct research on new worlds, scholars will tend to use data obtained in the present world as evidence that people do not want to change. Many of them are doing so already. What they forget is how human beings can desire or even contemplate worlds that they have learned from experience to view as unrealistic.

Take a recent publication by Ernest Gross in which he suggests that concepts like individual dignity and self-development probably reflect academic values instead of employee desires, because employees rarely report the need to express such values. The question still remains whether this state of affairs implies that people should accept them and should be trained to adapt to them. Gross appears to think so. He stated that there is little one can do by way of providing opportunities for self-actualization and, if it were possible, providing them would frighten some people. Furthermore, he noted that assembly-line jobs didn't require a worker to demonstrate initiative or to desire variety. "One wants him (the worker) simply to work according to an established pace. Creativity, then, is not always desirable."

Note the logic. Gross starts by asserting that the P. and O. theorists cannot state that one *should* (his italics) provide workers with more challenge or autonomy in accordance with their values because to do so would be to rest their case not on a scientific theory, but on a program for organizations. Then he suggests that no one has proved how harmful dissatisfaction, anxiety, dependency, and conformity are to the individual—which is probably correct. He goes on to argue that these conditions are, to a degree, both unavoidable and helpful, although offering no empirical data to support his assertion. Then he concludes that employees should be educated to live within this world:

> Perhaps the most general conclusion we can draw is that since organizations appear to be inevitable . . . a major type of socialization of the young ought to include methods for dealing with the organization. . . . [For example] an important consideration in the preparation of individuals for work should include training for the handling of or adjustment to authority.

At this point Gross has taken a normative position, but one with which I vigorously dissent.

I am very concerned about those who hold that job enrichment may not be necessary because workers in an automobile factory have about the same attitude toward their jobs as do workers in jobs with greater freedom and job variety. But what is the meaning of the response to a question such as "How satisfied would you say you are with your present job?" if the man is working under conditions of relative deprivation? We think that what it means is that workers recognize that they are boxed in, that few opportunities are available to them for better paid or more interesting work; in consequence, they become satisfied with the jobs they have because the jobs they want are unobtainable. It is frequently observed that the greatest dissatisfaction on a routine job occurs during the first years. After three to five years, the individual adapts to the job and feels satisfied. On the other hand, Neil Herrick in a recent book with the catchy title *Where Have All the Robots Gone?* reported that for the first time, there was a major drop in the number of Americans expressing job satisfaction.

That most jobs as currently designed are routine and provide few opportunities for self-actualization, that the social norms and the political actions that support these norms tend to produce mostly individuals who simultaneously value and fear growth and who strive for security and safety, tell only part of the unfortunate tale of the present industrial conditions. Employees perceive—and the perception is accurate—that few men at the top want to increase their opportunities for self-actualization; even fewer men at the top are competent to do the job.

Make no mistake—employees are conservative on this issue. They have no interest in seeing their physiological and security needs frustrated or denied because their organization collapsed while trying to increase their chances for self-actualization. And the possibility of such a collapse is a real one. Our own experience and the published research combine to suggest that there now does not exist a top-management group so competent in meeting the requirements of the new ethic that they do not lose their competence under stress. With expert help and heavy emphasis on top-management education, one such group was still encountering great difficulties after five years of attempting to raise the quality of life within its organization.

If the ethic, as employees themselves recognize, is so difficult to realize in practice, is the effort worthwhile? Is a game with so many incompetent players worth the playing?

On two counts we feel strongly that it is: First, on normative grounds we feel that social science research has an obligation to help design a better world. Second, we feel that the game is worth the playing because eventually some people and some organizations can be helped to play it effectively. Take the case of job enrichment. Let us assume that all jobs can be enriched. The assumption is probably unrealistic; many jobs in fact, can never be enriched. If we opt for the world that is psychologically richer, however, we will induce employees at every level into developing whatever opportunities for enrichment exist in each job situation.

I believe with Maslow in taking the behavior that characterizes rare peak experiences and making it the behavior toward which all employees should aspire. The skeptic argues that such behavior is so rare that it is useless to try to achieve it. I agree that the behavior is rare, but go on to plead for systematic research that will tell us how the behavior may be made more frequent. Twenty years ago no one had pole-vaulted higher than 16 feet. Yet no one took this as a given. Today the 16-foot mark is broken continually because people refused to view the status quo as the last word and focused on enhancing the potentiality of man. Over time, a similar focus on enhancing the potentiality of man-on-the job should produce similar breakthroughs.

A Therapist's View of the Good Life: The Fully Functioning Person
Carl R. Rogers

My views regarding the meaning of the good life are largely based upon my experience in working with people in the very close and intimate relationship which is called psychotherapy. These views thus have an empirical or experiential foundation, as contrasted perhaps with a scholarly or philosophical foundation. I have learned what the good life seems to be by observing and participating in the struggle of disturbed and troubled people to achieve that life.

I should make it clear from the outset that this experience I have gained comes from the vantage point of a particular orientation to psychotherapy which has developed over the years. Quite possibly all psychotherapy is basically similar, but since I am less sure of that than I once was, I wish to make it clear that my therapeutic experience has been along the lines that seem to me most effective, the type of therapy termed "client-centered."

Let me attempt to give a very brief description of what this therapy would be like if it were in every respect optimal, since I feel I have learned most about the good life from therapeutic experiences in which a great deal of movement occurred. If the therapy were optimal, intensive as well as extensive, then it would mean that the therapist has been able to enter into an intensely personal and subjective relationship with the client—relating not as a scientist to an object of study, not as a physician expecting to diagnose and cure, but as a person to a person. It would mean that the therapist feels this client to be a person of unconditional self-worth: of value no matter what his condition, his behavior, or his feelings. It would mean that the therapist is genuine, hiding behind no defensive façade, but meeting the client with the feelings which organically he is experiencing. It would mean that the therapist is able to let himself go in understanding this client; that no inner barriers keep him from sensing what it feels like to be the client at each moment of the relationship; and that he can convey something of his empathic understanding to the client. It means that the therapist has been comfortable in entering this relationship fully, without know-ing cognitively where it will lead, satisfied with providing a climate which will permit the client the utmost freedom to become himself.

For the client, this optimal therapy would mean an exploration of increasingly strange and unknown and dangerous feelings in him-self, the exploration proving possible only because he is gradually realizing that he is accepted unconditionally. Thus he becomes ac-quainted with elements of his experience which have in the past been denied to awareness as too threatening, too damaging to the structure of the self. He finds himself experiencing these feelings fully, com-pletely, in the relationship, so that for the moment he *is* his fear, or his anger, or his tenderness, or his strength. And as he lives these widely varied feelings, in all their degrees of intensity, he discovers that he has experienced *himself,* that he *is* all these feelings. He finds his behavior changing in constructive fashion in accordance with his newly experienced self. He approaches the realization that he no longer needs to fear what experience may hold, but can welcome it freely as a part of his changing and developing self.

This is a thumbnail sketch of what client-centered therapy comes close to, when it is at its optimum. I give it here simply as a brief picture of the context in which I have formed my views of the good life.

A negative observation

As I have tried to live understandingly in the experiences of my clients, I have gradually come to one negative conclusion about the good life. It seems to me that the good life is not any fixed state. It is not, in my estimation, a state of virtue, or contentment, or nirvana, or happiness. It is not a condition in which the individual is adjusted, or fulfilled, or actualized. To use psychological terms, it is not a state of drive-reduction, or tension-reduction, or homeo-stasis.

I believe that all of these terms have been used in ways which imply that if one or several of these states is achieved, then the goal of life has been achieved. Certainly, for many people happiness, or adjustment, are seen as states of being which are synonymous with the good life. And social scientists have frequently spoken of the reduction of tension, or the achievement of homeostasis or equilib-rium as if these states constituted the goal of the process of living.

So it is with a certain amount of surprise and concern that I realize

that my experience supports none of these definitions. If I focus on
the experience of those individuals who seem to have evidenced the
greatest degree of movement during the therapeutic relationship, and
who, in the years following this relationship, appear to have made
and to be making real progress toward the good life, then it seems to
me that they are not adequately described at all by any of these terms
which refer to fixed states of being. I believe they would consider
themselves insulted if they were described as "adjusted," and they
would regard it as false if they were described as "happy" or "contented," or even "actualized." As I have known them I would regard
it as most inaccurate to say that all their drive tensions have been reduced, or that they are in a state of homeostasis. So I am forced to
ask myself whether there is any way in which I can generalize about
their situation, any definition which I can give of the good life which
would seem to fit the facts as I have observed them. I find this not at all
easy, and what follows is stated very tentatively.

A postive observation

If I attempt to capture in a few words what seems to me to be true
of these people, I believe it will come out something like this:

The good life is a *process,* not a state of being.

It is a direction, not a destination.

The direction which constitutes the good life is that which is selected
by the total organism, when there is psychological freedom to move in
any direction.

This organismically selected direction seems to have certain discernible general qualities which appear to be the same in a wide
variety of unique individuals.

So I can integrate these statements into a definition which can at
least serve as a basis for consideration and discussion. The good life,
from the point of view of my experience, is the process of movement
in a direction which the human organism selects when it is inwardly
free to move in any direction, and the general qualities of this selected
direction appead to have a certain universality.

The characteristics of the process

Let me now try to specify what appear to be the characteristic
qualities of this process of movement, as they crop up in person after
person in therapy.

An increasing openness to experience

In the first place, the process seems to involve an increasing oppen-
ness to experience. This phrase has come to have more and more

meaning for me. It is the polar opposite of defensiveness. Defensiveness I have described in the past as being the organism's response to experiences which are perceived or anticipated as threatening, as incongruent with the individual's existing picture of himself, or of himself in relationship to the world. These threatening experiences are temporarily rendered harmless by being distorted in awareness, or being denied to awareness. I quite literally cannot see, with accuracy, those experiences, feelings, reactions in my self which are significantly at variance with the picture of myself which I already possess. A large part of the process of therapy is the continuing discovery by the client that he is experiencing feelings and attitudes which heretofore he has not been able to be aware of, which he has not been able to "own" as being a part of himself.

If a person could be fully open to his experience, however, every stimulus—whether orginating within the organism or in the environment—would be freely relayed through the nervous system without being distorted by any defensive mechanism. There would be no need of the mechanism of "subception" whereby the organism is forewarned of any experience threatening to the self. On the contrary, whether the stimulus was the impact of a configuration of form, color, or sound in the environment on the sensory nerves, or a memory trace from the past, or a visceral sensation of fear or pleasure or disgust, the person would be "living" it, would have it completely available to awareness.

Thus, one aspect of this process which I am naming "the good life" appears to be a movement away from the pole of defesiveness toward the pole of openness to experience. The individual is becoming more able to listen to himself, to experience what is going on within himself. He is more open to his feelings of fear and discouragement and pain. He is also more open to his feelings of courage, and tenderness, and awe. He is free to live his feelings subjectively, as they exist in him, and also free to be aware of these feelings. He is more able fully to live the experiences of his organism rather than shutting them out of awareness.

Increasingly existential living

A second characteristic of the process which for me is the good life is that it involves an increasing tendency to live fully in each moment. This is a thought which can easily be misunderstood, and which is perhaps somewhat vague in my own thinking. Let me try to explain what I mean.

I believe it would be evident that for the person who was fully open to his new experience, completely without defensiveness, each moment would be new. The complex configuration of inner and outer stimuli which exists in this moment has never existed before in just this fashion. Consequently such a person would realize that "What I will be in the next moment, and what I will do, grows out of that moment, and cannot be predicted in advance either by me or by others." Not infrequently we find clients expressing exactly this sort of feeling.

One way of expressing the fluidity which is present in such existential living is to say that the self and personality emerge *from* experience, rather than experience being translated or twisted to fit preconceived self-structure. It means that one becomes a participant in and an observer of the ongoing process of organismic experience, rather than being in control of it.

Such living in the moment means an absence of rigidity, of tight organization, of the imposition of structure on experience. It means instead a maximum of adaptability, a discovery of structure *in* experience, a flowing, changing organization of self and personality.

It is this tendency toward existential living which appears to me very evident in people who are involved in the process of the good life. One might almost say that it is the most essential quality of it. It involves discovering the structure of experience in the process of living the experience. Most of us, on the other hand, bring a preformed structure and evaluation to our experience and never relinquish it, but cram and twist the experience to fit our preconceptions, annoyed at the fluid qualities which make it so unruly in fitting our carefully constructed pigeonholes. To open one's spirit to what is going on *now,* and to discover in that present process whatever structure it appears to have—this to me is one of the qualities of the good life, the mature life, as I see clients approach it.

An increasing trust in his organism

Still another characteristic of the person who is living the process of the good life appears to be an increasing trust in his organism as a means of arriving at the most satisfying behavior in each existential situation. Again let me try to explain what I mean.

In choosing what course of action to take in any situation, many people rely upon guiding principles, upon a code of action laid down by some group or institution, upon the judgment of others (from wife and friends to Emily Post), or upon the way they have behaved in some similar past situation. Yet as I observe the clients whose experiences in living have taught me so much, I find that increasingly such individuals are able to trust their total organismic reaction to a new situation because they discover to an ever-increasing degree that if they are open to their experience, doing what "feels right" proves to be a competent and trustworthy guide to behavior which is truly satisfying.

As I try to understand the reason for this, I find myself following this line of thought. The person who is fully open to his experience would have access to all of the available data in the situation, on which to base his behavior; the social demands, his own complex and possibly conflicting needs, his memories of similar situations, his perception of the uniqueness of this situation, etc., etc. The data would be very complex indeed. But he could permit his total organism, his consciousness participating, to consider each stimulus, need, and demand, its relative intensity and importance, and out of this complex weighing and balancing discover that course of action which would come closest to satisfying all his needs in the situation. An analogy which might come close to a description would be to compare this person to a giant electronic computing machine. Since he is open to his experience, all of the data from his sense impressions, from his memory, from previous learning, from his visceral and internal states are fed into the machine. The machine takes all of these multitudinous pulls and forces which are fed in as data, and quickly computes the course of action which would be the most economical vector of need satisfaction in this existential situation. This is the behavior of our hypothetical person.

The defects which in most of us make this process untrustworthy are the inclusion of information which does *not* belong to this present situation, or the exclusion of information which *does*. It is when memories and previous learnings are fed into the computations as if they were *this* reality, and not memories and learnings, that erroneous behavioral answers arise. Or when certain threatening experiences are inhibited from awareness, and hence are withheld from the computation or fed into it in distorted form, this too produces error. But our hypothetical person would find his organism thoroughly trustworthy, because all of the available data would be used, and they would be present in accurate rather than distorted form. Hence his behavior would come as close as possible to satisfying all his needs—for enhancement, for affiliation with others, and the like.

In this weighing, balancing, and computation, his organism would not by any means be infallible. It would always give the best possible answer for the available data, but sometimes data would be missing. Because of the element of openness to experience, however, any errors, any following of behavior which was not satisfying, would be quickly corrected. The computations, as it were, would always be in process of being corrected, because they would be continually checked in behavior.

Perhaps you will not like my analogy of an electronic computing machine. Let me return to the clients I know. As they become more open to all of their experiences, they find it increasingly possible to trust their reactions. If they "feel like" expressing anger they do so and find that this comes out satisfactorily, because they are equally alive to all of their desires for affection, affiliation, and relationship. They are surprised at their own intuitive skill in finding behavioral solutions to complex and troubling human relationships. It is only afterward that they realize how surprisingly trustworthy their inner reactions have been in bringing about satisfactory behavior.

The process of functioning more fully

I should like to draw together these three threads describing the process of the good life into a more coherent picture. It appears that the person who is psychologically free moves in the direction of becoming a more fully functioning person. He is more able to live fully in and with each and all of his feelings and reactions. He makes increasing use of all his organic equipment to sense, as accurately as possible, the existential situation within and without. He makes use of all of the information his nervous system can thus supply, using it in awareness, but recognizing that his total organism may be, and often is, wiser than his awareness. He is more able to permit his total organism to function freely in all its complexity in selecting, from the multitude of possibilities, that behavior which in this moment of time will be most generally and genuinely satisfying. He is able to put more trust in his organism in this functioning not because it is infallible, but because he can fully open to the consequences of each of his actions and correct them if they prove to be less than satisfying.

He is more able to experience all of his feelings, and is less afraid of any of his feelings; he is his own sifter of evidence, and is more open to evidence from all sources; he is completely engaged in the process of being and becoming himself, and thus discovers that he is soundly and realistically social; he lives more completely in this moment, but learns that this is the soundest living for all time. He is becoming a more fully functioning organism, and because of the awareness of himself which flows freely in and through his experience, he is becoming a more fully functioning person.

Some implications

Any view of what constitutes the good life carries with it many implications, and the view I have presented is no exception. I hope that these implications may be food for thought. There are two or three of these about which I would like to comment.

A new perspective on freedom vs determinism

The first of these implications may not immediately be evident. It has to do with the age-old issue of "free will." Let me endeavor to spell out the way in which this issue now appears to me in a new light.

For some time I have been perplexed over the living paradox which exists in psychotherapy between freedom and determinism. In the therapeutic relationship some of the most compelling subjective experiences are those in which the client feels within himself the power of naked choice. He is *free*—to become himself or to hide behind a façade; to move forward or to retrogress; to behave in ways which are destructive of self and others, or in ways which are enhancing; quite literally free to live or die, in both the physiological and psychological meaning of those terms. Yet as we enter this field of psychotherapy with objective research methods, we are, like any other scientist, committed to a complete determinism. From this point of view every thought, feeling, and action of the client is determined by what preceded it. There can be no such thing as freedom. The dilemma I am trying to describe is no different than that found in other fields—it is simply brought to sharper focus, and appears more insoluble.

This dilemma can be seen in a fresh perspective, however, when we consider it in terms of the definition I have given of the fully functioning person. We could say that in the optimum of therapy the person rightfully experiences the most complete and absolute freedom. He wills or chooses to follow the course of action which is the most economical vector in relationship to all the internal and external stimuli, because it is that behavior which will be most deeply satisfying. But this is the same course of action which from another vantage point may be said to be determined by all the factors in the existential situation. Let us contrast this with the picture of the person who is defensively organized. He wills or chooses to follow a given course of action, but finds that he *cannot* behave in the fashion that he chooses. He is determined by the factors in the existential situation, but these factors include his defensiveness, his denial or distortion of some of the relevant data. Hence it is certain that his behavior will be less than fully satisfying. His behavior is determined, but he is not free to make an effective choice. The fully functioning person, on the other hand, not only experiences, but utilizes, the most absolute freedom when he spontaneously, freely, and voluntarily chooses and wills that which is also absolutely determined.

I am not so naive as to suppose that this fully resolves the issue between subjective and objective, between freedom and necessity. Nevertheless it has meaning for me that the more the person is living the good life, the more he will experience a freedom of choice, and the more his choices will be effectively implemented in his behavior.

Creativity as an element of the good life

I believe it will be clear that a person who is involved in the directional process which I have termed "the good life" is a creative person. With his sensitive openness to his world, his trust of his own ability to form new relationships with his environment, he would be the type of person from whom creative products and creative living emerge. He would not necessarily be "adjusted" to his culture, and he would almost certainly not be a conformist. But at any time and in any culture he would live constructively, in as much harmony with his culture as a balanced satisfaction of needs demanded. In some cultural situations he might in some ways be very unhappy, but he would continue to move toward becoming himself, and to behave in such a way as to provide the maximum satisfaction of his deepest needs.

Such a person would, I believe, be recognized by the student of evolution as the type most likely to adapt and survive under changing environmental conditions. He would be able creatively to make sound adjustments to new as well as old conditions. He would be a fit vanguard of human evolution.

Basic trustworthiness of human nature

It will be evident that another implication of the view I have been presenting is that the basic nature of the human being, when functioning freely, is constructive and trustworthy. For me this is an inescapable conclusion from a quarter-century of experience in psychotherapy. When we are able to free the individual from defensiveness, so that he is open to the wide range of his own needs, as well as the wide range of environmental and social demands, his reactions may be trusted to be positive, forward-moving, constructive. We do not need to ask who will socialize him, for one of his own deepest needs is for affiliation and communication with others. As he becomes more fully himself, he will become more realistically socialized. We do not need to ask who will control his aggressive impulses; for as he becomes more open to all of his impulses, his need to be liked by others and his tendency to give affection will be as strong as his impulses to strike out or to seize for himself. He will be aggressive in situations in which aggression is realistically appropriate, but there will be no runaway need for aggression. His total behavior, in these and other areas, as he moves toward being open to all his experience, will be more balanced and realistic, behavior which is appropriate to the survival and enhancement of a highly social animal.

I have little sympathy with the rather prevalent concept that man is basically irrational, and that his impulses, if not controlled, will lead to destruction of others and self. Man's behavior is exquisitely rational, moving with subtle and ordered complexity toward the goals his organism is endeavoring to achieve. The tragedy for most of us is that our defenses keep us from being aware of this rationality, so that consciously we are moving in one direction, while organismically we are moving in another. But in our person who is living the process of the good life there would be a decreasing number of such barriers, and he would be increasingly a participant in the rationality of his organism. The only control of impulses which would exist, or which would prove necessary, is the natural and internal balancing of one need against another, and the discovery of behaviors which follow the vector most closely approximating the satisfaction of all needs. The experience of extreme satisfaction of one need (for aggression, or sex, etc.) in such a way as to do violence to the satisfaction of other needs (for companionship, tender relationship, etc.)— an experience very common in the defensively organized person— would be greatly decreased. We would participate in the vastly complex self-regulatory activities of his organism—the psychological as well as physiological thermostatic controls—in such a fashion as to live in increasing harmony with himself and with others.

The greater richness of life

One last implication I should like to mention is that this process of living in the good life involves a wider range, greater richness, than the constricted living in which most of us find ourselves. To be a part of this process means that one is involved in the frequently frightening and frequently satisfying experience of a more sensitive living, with greater range, greater variety, greater richness. It seems to me that clients who have moved significantly in therapy live more intimately with their feelings of pain, but also more vividly with their feelings of ecstasy; that anger is more clearly felt, but so also is love; that fear is an experience they know more deeply, but so is courage. And the reason they can thus live fully in a wider range is that they have this underlying confidence in themselves as trustworthy instruments for encountering life.

I believe it will have become evident why, for me, adjectives such as happy, contented, blissful, enjoyable do not seem quite appropriate to any general description of this process I have called the good life, even though the person in this process would experience each one of these feelings at appropriate times. But the adjectives which seem more generally fitting are adjectives such as enriching, exciting, rewarding, challenging, meamingful. This process of the good life is not, I am convinced, a life for the faint-hearted. It involves the stretching and growing of becoming more and more of one's potentialities. It involves the courage to be. It means launching oneself fully into the stream of life. Yet the deeply exciting thing about human beings is that when the individual is inwardly free, he chooses as the good life this process of becoming.

Management
and the Art
of Chinese Baseball
Ralph G. H. Siu

The crux of effective management is getting the desired things done by acting, quasi-acting, and nonacting. To be sure, acting and nonacting include the *science of management*—the objective, the verbalizable, the systems analytical, and all of the other quantifiable factors that have been so well covered in the thoughtful pages of SMR. But they also include the *art of management*—the subjective, the ineffable, the holistic synthetic, and the infinite concatenations of cascading sensed-unknowables. Small executive decisions are weighted toward the scientific polarity; BIG executive decisions are weighted toward the artistic.

This little opinion in a somewhat light vein proposes to spotlight the artistic and intuitive facets of executive life. Without intending to detract from the essential scientific and objective inputs, it seeks to depict the reality of what actually goes on and to encourage a richer amalgam of the two polarities than has been evident in the relatively one-sided, scientifically dominated management literature of the last two decades.

The singularly essential art

By way of background, let us refresh ourselves as to the kind of milieu in which BIG decisions are made by referring to two current examples. The first example is from international trade. For over a decade, the giant transatlantic commercial airlines have been eying each other and gingerly lowering their respective fares a little at a time to obtain a higher fraction of the total passenger business. Just about the time when some semblance of competitive price equilibrium was about to be reached, Britain's Laker Airways suddenly launched a no-frills, no-

Reprinted from *Sloan Management Review* 19, no. 3: 83–89. © 1978. Used by permission.

reservation air service between New York City and London at drastically reduced rates in late 1977 and began steps to start a similar service between Los Angeles and London in late 1978. The round-trip ticket in the latter case would be less than half that charged by TWA and British Airways, covering the same route. Overnight, as it were, the carefully calculated projections of the major carriers had to be recalibrated.

The second case is taken from domestic politics. During the early stages of congressional debate over the energy bill in 1977, the Senate majority was pushing toward a version to which the president said he was unalterably opposed. Several of the loyal Democratic senators took the signal and launched a filibuster to defeat the measure. Just as they felt that their maneuver was succeeding, as everyone was being worn to a frazzle, the vice-president and the majority leader pulled a parliamentary move that resulted in the passage of the controversial bill. This left the erstwhile filibustering stalwarts, as the American vernacular puts it, "fit to be tied."

We can readily see from these sketches why it is that the singularly essential skill among senior executives lies in the art of Chinese baseball. Chinese baseball, by the way, is played almost exactly like American baseball. It uses the same players, same field, same bats and balls, same method of keeping score, and so on. The batter stands in the batter's box, as usual. The pitcher stands on the pitcher's mound, as usual. He winds up, as usual, and zips the ball down the alley. There is one and only one difference—after the ball leaves the pitcher's hand and as long as the ball is in the air, anyone can move any of the bases anywhere.

In other words, everything is continually changing—not only the events themselves, but also the very rules governing those events. This kind of arena is alien to the scientific tradition of fixed boundary conditions, clearly defined variables, nonsubjective assessments, and rational consistency within a closed system. In the ball game of competitive actualities, everything is in flux, and all systems are open.

Five management principles

From the strategic artistry of Chinese baseball flow five basic management principles.

1. Act from an instantaneous apprehension of the totality.
This principle pertains to what many Chinese regard as the mark of a wise man. The key word is "apprehending," as contrasted to "understanding." It is important, of course, to understand things. But that is not enough. An effective chief executive must be able to reach into a mass of conflicting data and opinions and pull out the right thing to

do at the right moment of need. He or she does not get trapped in the double bind of riding the train of logic too long. Such a fix is exemplified by the King of the Alligators, who captured a beautiful maiden when she fell out of her canoe. The mother begged for her return. Touched by the streaming tears, the King of the Alligators offered her a sporting proposition. He would return the daughter, if the mother could make one true statement. Without thinking, the old lady replied: "You're going to keep my daughter."

Effective CEOs are seldom sprung in this manner. They are aware that rationality and the scientific method provide critical inputs to only one of three crucial questions overarching key decisions. These are (a) Does it add up? (b) Does it sound okay? and (c) Does it feel right? Logic and science contribute primarily to the first question, less to the second, and even less to the third. The master executive always massages his or her critical decisions in such a way that the responses to all three questions are positive. This can never be realized through understanding alone but only through apprehending.

The second important word in the first management principle is "totality." There is no need to belabor the familiar moral behind the story of the blind men and the elephant. But a comment or two on the contrast between the wholist and the partist strategies in resolving issues may be cogent.

The *wholist strategy* begins with the totality of a situation, whereby all possible factors are included within the net of consideration. The unnecessary and less relevant components are then successively eliminated until the desired equilibrium is attained. In this case, the tentative resolution at any given time is always relatively correct but imprecise due to the varying degrees of extraneous chaff until the end point is reached.

The *partist strategy* begins with a small collection of factors assumed to be necessary and sufficient for the case at hand. Different combinations and permutations of increasing complexity are then successively tested. In this case, the tentative resolution at any given time is always precisely stated but relatively wrong until the end point is reached.

Some time ago some researchers conducted a preliminary comparison of the two approaches in the solution of problems. The results suggested that given infinite time, either technique would deliver the correct resolution. Given only limited time, however, the wholist strategy was found to be superior. When the game of Chinese baseball is taken into consideration, the odds would be overwhelmingly in favor of the wholist strategy. Furthermore, as any professional football player knows so well, the BIG games are decided more often than not on the mistakes committed rather than on the yardage gained. Although the wholist strategy may not make as much yardage in any one play or any one game, it is relatively invulnerable to fatal mistakes. In contrast, although the partist strategy may make a spectacular yardage in any one play or any one game, it is invariably susceptible to fatal mistakes over time.

2. *Subsume yourself and resonate.*

This principle pertains to the social meaning of one's own operations. In applying the principle, the executive will first have to clearly define both his or her operational concern and the context in which his or her operations are imbedded. In the case of a chief executive officer, the operational concern is the corporation and the context is the community at large. The executive imparts social significance and value to the operations (the corporation) by subsuming it in the larger context (the community) and then by looking at them separately from the two perspectives: from his or her position of responsibility in the corporation and from the interest and viewpoint of the community. By continually resonating one against the other, the executive can then draw unto the corporation a broader-based strength from the community and at the same time given the community the full benefit of the corporation's operations.

An example of how the subsuming-and-resonating principle works is the way in which accomplished utility executives are able to gain their requested rate increases from utility commissions. They intuitively sense the fact that the decisive factor in winning them is not the company's need for the higher rates per se but the community's perception of whether its overall requirements can be met better by granting the rate increases rather than by spending its monies elsewhere. By being sensitive to the feelings of the people in the subsuming context and their regulator-representatives and by continually resonating the corporation's interest against the commuity's throughout the year, the accomplished utility executive brings about a shared mutuality. The more congruent the perceived overlapping interests, the closer the executive is targeting the requisite resonance.

3. *Maintain multiple tactical targets within attainable reach until the moment of final commitment.*

This principle pertains to competitive effectiveness. What is being assured is the freedom of tactical movement within a strategic thrust. One should not be a slave to a single tactical target from the very beginning. This would lock the individual into a rigid course of advance, which can be much more readily frustrated by the inevitable vicissitudes of life. Instead, the executive should have at least two alternative targets, committing himself or herself to a specific one at the last moment. This reference to alternative tactical targets in no way implies a prime target with fallback substitutes. For although this is often the best that can be achieved, it is preferable to have all alternatives equally feasible until the final closure.

The AMK Company's takeover of United Fruit a decade or so ago illustrates the principle. Up to the last move, AMK could have either clinched control of United Fruit by acquiring more shares or made money by selling the shares it held. It chose to gain control.

Another example of multiple tactical targets is contained in the story of the prisoner in ancient Persia. He and his cellmate had been condemned to death by the sultan. Knowing how much the sultan loved his stallion, the prisoner offered to teach the horse to fly in a year in exchange for his life. The sultan, fancying himself as the rider of the only flying horse in the world, agreed. The other prisoner looked on in disbelief. "You *know* horses don't fly. You're only postponing the inevitable." "Not so," said the clever tactician. "I have actually given myself *four* chances for freedom. First, the sultan might die during the year. Second, I might die. Third, the horse might die. And fourth, you know, I might just teach that horse to fly."

4. Be propitious.

This principle pertains to elegance and style in getting things done. Everyone talks at length about timing: lead time, lag time, critical path in planning schedules, and so on. But relatively few exhibit a native feel for the instrument of time in practice. Most people allow wishful thinking to distort their estimates of incubation time, of time to build up a psychological head of steam, of time for infractions to be forgiven, and of time for people to become bored and impatient. They do not anticipate the time it takes for different acts to come to fruition, or match this against the development time available. They fail to lay the basis for the resolution of conflicts before their actual onset. The net result is a lifelong staccato of crisis after crisis. They never glide with the art of de-existing them.

A common manifestation of inept timing, especially among more aggressive junior executives, is premature closure. They want to arrive at an answer as soon as possible, instead of when required. As a consequence, they do not reconnoiter the problem thoroughly. They do not probe the more complex alternatives, which might prove more remunerative. They do not even allow sufficient time for the dilemma to go away on its own, when such might well happen. When victory seems within sight, they often launch into the final push before making certain that the psychological momentum is in their favor. A favorable outcome, if attained under such circumstances, may be extra costly. And they may very well fail.

Many executives just cannot seem to get the sequencing of their actions straight in the implementation of a well-drawn-up plan. They are reminiscent of the Texan who wanted to become an Alaskan. When Alaska was admitted as a state, the Texan moved up there because he wanted to continue living in the largest state of the Union. Even after spending quite some time there, however, he did not seem to be accepted by the natives as a real sourdough. In his deep discouragement sitting at the bar one day, he bemoaned his troubles to the bartender. The man took pity on him and finally told him the secret. "What you need to do to become accepted as one of us are three things. First, drink a fifth of whiskey in one swig. Second make love to an eskimo girl. And third, shoot an Alaskan bear." The Texan grabbed the bottle of whiskey, downed it in one long gurgle, then stalked out of the saloon. Eight hours later the Texan staggered back through the swinging doors, all bloodied and battered, clothes torn to shreds, but still undaunted. He beat his chest and bellowed forth: "Noaaw, where's that eskimo gal ah'm s'pposed to shoot?"

5. Orchestrate the virtual presences.

This principle pertains to the essence of leadership. The creation of and response to virtual presences are unique to the human species among animals. A virtual presence is something which is not real in the space-time sense, yet it exerts a practical effect as if it were. An example of a virtual presence in mathematics is the square root of minus one. There is no such thing even by its own rules. It cannot be plus one, because plus one times plus one equals one—not minus one. It cannot be minus one, because minus one times minus one equals plus one—not minus one. Yet this purely imaginary number is used very effectively in calculations involving real events, producing very worthwhile and practical answers that cannot be obtained in any other way. There would not have been any modern physics in the sense we know it today had not the virtual presence of the square root of minus one been invented.

Much of man's psychological well-being is a function of virtual presences. There would not have been such mental anguish, had not the capacity for producing virtual presences of hallucinations, delusions, and schizophrenic selves been engendered through the unfortunate confluence of genetic endowments and environmental influences.

Our social activities are driven by virtual presences. There would not have been such rapid cultural progress of the kind we know today had not the virtual presences of all kinds of myths been blandished before the young by their elders. There would not have been wars of the massive destructiveness we experience today had not the virtual presences of patriotism and other fanciful propaganda been drummed into the citizenry by its leaders.

In this connection, one of the most prevalent deficiencies among the inexperienced and immature is the disdain with which they view ceremonies. Men and women of great power, however, know all too well that ceremonies constitute the lubricant of social processes and the seal of community approval. They are always creatively nimble in the adaptation of ceremonial stratagems.

The master of action

It may be well, in closing, to remind ourselves that the various facets of management have been dissected into distinct topics only for discussion purposes. It seems that we can think and talk about things only in an abstract and analytical mode. Of course, this is not the way that phenomena occur in nature. Happenings do not stand still for our slow-witted thinking. To be in control of the situation is to ride the moment on the wing in an agglomerate gut-feeling fitness. Science and art, cause and effect, plans and operations, means and ends—all merge in the instant of the act. This is the hallmark of the Master of Action.

Ten day-to-day guidelines

Five proverbs for planning:

1. The shrike hunting the locust is unaware of the hawk hunting him.
2. The mouse with but one hole is easily taken.
3. In shallow waters, shrimps make fools of dragons.
4. Do not try to catch two frogs with one hand.
5. Give the bird room to fly.

Five proverbs for operations:

6. Do not insult the crocodile until you have crossed the river.
7. It is better to struggle with a sick jackass than carry the wood yourself.
8. Do not throw stone at mouse and break precious vase.
9. It is not the last blow of the ax that fells the tree.
10. The great executive not only brings home the bacon but also the applesauce.

2

5

Communicating:
Listening and Being Heard

Introduction

Throughout the four chapters in part 1, our focus was on the individual human being. In the three chapters in part 2, our attention shifts. Now we look at the space between people, at the *interactions* between individuals, especially the processes by which people try to *communicate* with, and *influence* one another. In chapters 6 and 7 which follow this one, a good deal of emphasis will be placed on the influence process. But influence requires, as a precondition, communication among the people involved. This first chapter of part 2, therefore, deals specifically with communication processes.

There is more to communication than words alone. Important messages are often conveyed by means other than the written or spoken word. Gibb's paper, on defensive communication, is rapidly becoming a classic in the field. He describes how the whole climate of a relationship between people can be shaped by subtle, often nonverbal communications. He shows how frequently and how easily a climate of defensiveness is generated by communication methods of participants and how such a climate then sets obstacles in the path of further communication. One can easily generate defensiveness without even knowing that one is doing so; by unintentionally evaluating someone else's behavior, for instance, or by appearing to prescribe what's the "right" course of action for someone else.

The second paper, by Kolb and Boyatzis, neatly complements the first. They are concerned with how to set up a helping relationship, with the problem of giving effective help to other persons. Giving help requires much more than advice or information. It requires communication which enables the "helpee" to use the counsel or information or support that he or she is being given. In effect, Kolb and Boyatzis are looking at methods of non-defense-generating communication.

The third article, by Hall and Whyte, points out the cultural differences in communication, differences that frequently lead to misunderstandings across cultures. The style of communicating used by an American manager in dealing with a subordinate may seem strange and disturbing when transplanted to Japan. Attitudes toward authority, toward time and space, toward the display of emotion, and toward physical contact all differ from culture to culture.

Some of these cultural differences are only differences in the meanings assigned to common symbols. For example, the North American gesture for "okay," made by forming a circle with the thumb and index finger, carries an entirely different and quite insulting connotation in Latin America. One of us, during a trip to Brazil, discovered this difference to his horror after the damage had been done.

But it is fairly easy to learn the local meanings of such specific symbols and gestures. It is much more difficult to learn the meaning associated not with specific actions but with whole patterns of behavior. In the Hall and Whyte piece the reader will find many pithy examples.

But we would like to add a postscript to the Hall and Whyte article. Despite the homogenizing influences of television and the other mass media, there are still significant cultural differences in the meanings of words and behavioral patterns *within* the United States, even between organizations. Not only is the ghetto vocabulary different from the suburban one; but almost every occupational and professional group, indeed almost every social group, develops a verbal and behavioral jargon of its own. The same English word can have two very different meaning in two related discussion groups, and representatives of the two groups may not discover the difference for quite some time. For example, in most of the social and physical sciences the word "model" means "abstract representation." But in the very closely related field of academic medicine, the word typically means "prototype," that is, a working demonstration rather than some abstraction. This very subtle difference in the meaning of one word, lying unknown, delayed for several days the resolution of a problem in a research team of our acquaintance made up jointly of management scientists and academic physicians.

The rough rules of thumb that seem to emerge from all this are these: If you want to increase your chances of influencing someone in your direction, (*a*) keep two-way communication channels open by avoiding actions that generate a defensive climate, and (*b*) watch out for the hidden pitfalls of unrecognized intercultural differences.

Defensive Communication
Jack R. Gibb

One way to understand communication is to view it as a people process rather than as a language process. If one is to make fundamental improvement in communication, he must make changes in interpersonal relationships. One possible type of alteration—and the one with which this paper is concerned—is that of reducing the degree of defensiveness.

Definition and significance

"Defensive behavior" is behavior which occurs when an individual perceives threat or anticipates threat in the group. The person who behaves defensively, even though he also gives some attention to the common task, devotes an appreciable portion of his energy to defending himself. Besides talking about the topic, he thinks about how he appears to others, how he may be seen more favorably, how he may win, dominate, impress, or escape punishment, and/or how he may avoid or mitigate a perceived or an anticipated attack.

Such inner feelings and outward acts tend to create similarly defensive postures in others; and, if unchecked, the ensuing circular response becomes increasingly destructive. Defensive behavior, in short, engenders defensive listening, and this in turn produces postural, facial, and verbal cues which raise the defense level of the original communicator.

Defensive arousal prevents the listener from concentrating upon the message. Not only do defensive communicators send off multiple value, motive, and affect cues, but also defensive recipients distort what they receive. As a person becomes more and more defensive, he becomes less and less able to perceive accurately the motives, the

Reprinted from the *Journal of Communication* 11, no. 3 (September 1961): 141–48, by permission of the author and the publisher.

values, and the emotions of the sender. My analyses of tape-recorded discussions revealed that increases in defensive behavior were correlated positively with losses in efficiency in communication.[1] Specifically, distortions became greater when defensive states existed in the groups.

The converse also is true. The more "supportive" or defense-reductive the climate, the less the receiver reads into the communication-distorted loadings which arise from projections of his own anxieties, motives, and concerns. As defenses are reduced, the receivers become better able to concentrate upon the structure, the content, and the cognitive meanings of the message.

Categories of defensive and supportive communication

In working over an eight-year period with recordings of discussions occurring in varied settings, I developed the six pairs of defensive and supportive categories presented in table 1. Behavior which a listener perceives as possessing any of the characteristics listed in the

Table 1. Categories of Behavior Characteristics of
Supportive and Defensive Climates in Small Groups

Defensive Climates	Supportive Climates
1. Evaluation	1. Description
2. Control	2. Problem orientation
3. Strategy	3. Spontaneity
4. Neutrality	4. Empathy
5. Superiority	5. Equality
6. Certainty	6. Provisionalism

left-hand column arouses defensiveness, whereas that which he interprets as having any of the qualities designated as supportive reduces defensive feelings. The degree to which these reactions occur depends upon the personal level of defensiveness and upon the general climate in the group at the time.[2]

Evaluation and description

Speech or other behavior which appears evaluative increases defensiveness. If by expression, manner of speech, tone of voice, or verbal content the sender seems to be evaluating or judging the listener, then

1. J. R. Gibb, "Defense Level and Influence in Small Groups," in *Leadership and Interpersonal Behavior,* ed. L. Petrullo and B. M. Bass (New York: Holt, Rinehart & Winston, 1961), pp. 66–81.

2. J. R. Gibb, "Sociopsychological Processes of Group Instruction," in *The Dynamics of Instructional Groups,* ed. N. B. Henry (Fifty-ninth Yearbook of the National Society for the Study of Education, part 2, 1960), pp. 115–35.

the receiver goes on guard. Of course, other factors may inhibit the reaction. If the listener thinks that the speaker regards him as an equal and is being open and spontaneous, for example, the evaluativeness in a message will be neutralized and perhaps not even perceived. This same principle applies equally to the other five categories of potentially defense-producing climates. The six sets are interactive.

Because our attitudes toward other persons are frequently, and often necessarily, evaluative, expressions which the defensive person will regard as non judgmental are hard to frame. Even the simplest question usually conveys the answer that the sender wishes or implies the response that would fit into his value system. A mother, for example, immediately following an earth tremor that shook the house, sought for her small son with the question: "Bobby, where are you?" The timid and plaintive "Mommy, I didn't do it" indicated how Bobby's chronic mild defensiveness predisposed him to react with a projection of his own guilt and in the context of his chronic assumption that questions are full of accusation.

Anyone who has attempted to train professionals to use information-seeking speech with neutral effect appreciates how difficult it is to teach a person to say even the simple "Who did that?" without being seen as accusing. Speech is so frequently judgmental that there is a reality base for the defensive interpretations which are so common.

When insecure, group members are particularly likely to place blame, to see others as fitting into categories of good or bad, to make moral judgments of their colleagues, and to question the value, motive, and affect loadings of the speech which they hear. Since value loadings imply a judgment of others, a belief that the standards of the speaker differ from his own causes the listener to become defensive.

Descriptive speech, in contrast to that which is evaluative, tends to arouse a minimum of uneasiness. Speech acts which the listener perceives as genuine requests for information or as material with neutral loadings is descriptive. Specifically, presentations of feelings, events, perceptions, or processes which do not ask or imply that the receiver change behavior or attitude are minimally defense-producing. The difficulty in avoiding overtone is illustrated by the problems of news reporters in writing stories about unions, communists, Negroes, and religious activities without tipping off the "party" line of the newspaper. One can often tell from the opening words in a news article which side the newspaper's editorial policy favors.

Control and problem orientation

Speech which is used to control the listener evokes resistance. In most of our social intercourse someone is trying to do something to someone else—to change an attitude, to influence behavior, or to restrict the field of activity. The degree to which attempts to control produce defensiveness depends upon the openness of the effort, for a suspicion that hidden motives exist heightens resistance. For this reason attempts of nondirective therapists and progressive educators to refrain from imposing a set of values, a point of view, or a problem solution upon the receivers meet with many barriers. Since the norm is control, non-controllers must earn the perceptions that their efforts have no hidden motives. A bombardment of persuasive "messages" in the fields of politics, education, special causes, advertising, religion, medicine, industrial relations, and guidance has bred cynical and paranoidal responses in listeners.

Implicit in all attempts to alter another person is the assumption by the change agent that the person to be altered is inadequate. That the speaker secretly views the listener as ignorant, unable to make his own decisions, uninformed, immature, unwise, or possessed of wrong or inadequate attitudes is a subconscious perception which gives the latter a valid base for defensive reactions.

Methods of control are many and varied. Legalistic insistence on detail, restrictive regulations and policies, conformity norms, and all laws are among the methods. Gestures, facial expressions, other forms of nonverbal communication, and even such simple acts as holding a door open in a particular manner are means of imposing one's will upon another and hence are potential sources of resistance.

Problem orientation, on the other hand, is the antithesis of persuasion. When the sender communicates a desire to collaborate in defining a mutual problem and in seeking its solution, he tends to create the same problem orientation in the listener; and, of greater importance, he implies that he has no predetermined solution, attitude, or method to impose. Such behavior is permissive in that it allows the receiver to set his own goals, make his own decisions, and evaluate his own progress—or to share with the sender in doing so. The exact methods of attaining permissiveness are not known, but they must involve a constellation of cues, and they certainly go beyond mere verbal assurances that the communicator has no hidden desires to exercise control.

Strategy and spontaneity

When the sender is perceived as engaged in a stratagem involving ambiguous and multiple motivations, the receiver becomes defensive. No one wishes to be a guinea pig, a role player, or an impressed actor, and no one likes to be the victim of some hidden motivation. That which is concealed, also, may appear larger than it really is, with the degree of defensiveness of the listener determining the perceived size of the suppressed element. The intense reaction of the reading audience to the material in the *Hidden Persuaders* indicates the prevalence of defensive reactions to multiple motivations behind strategy. Group members who are seen as "taking a role," as feigning emotion, as toying with their colleagues, as withholding information, or as having special sources of data are especially resented. One participant once complained that another was "using a listening technique" on him!

A large part of the adverse reaction to much of the so-called human relations training is a feeling against what are perceived as gimmicks and tricks to fool or to "involve" people, to make a person think he is making his own decision, or to make the listener feel that the sender is genuinely interested in him as a person. Particularly violent reactions occur when it appears that someone is trying to make a stratagem appear spontaneous. One person has reported a boss who incurred resentment by habitually using the gimmick of "spontaneously" looking at his watch and saying, "My gosh, look at the time—I must run to an appointment." The belief was that the boss would create less irritation by honestly asking to be excused.

Similarly, the deliberate assumption of guilelessness and natural simplicity is especially resented. Monitoring the tapes of feedback and evaluation sessions in training groups indicates the surprising extent to which members perceive the strategies of their colleagues. This perceptual clarity may be quite shocking to the strategist, who usually feels that he has cleverly hidden the motivational aura around the "gimmick."

This aversion to deceit may account for one's resistance to politicians who are suspected of behind-the-scenes planning to get his vote; to psychologists whose listening apparently is motivated by more than the manifest or content-level interest in his behavior, or to the sophisticated, smooth, or clever person whose "one-upmanship" is marked with guile. In training groups the role-flexible person frequently is resented because his changes in behavior are perceived as strategic maneuvers.

Conversely, behavior which appears to be spontaneous and free of deception is defense-reductive. If the communicator is seen as having a clean id, as having uncomplicated motivations, as being straightforward and honest, and as behaving spontaneously in response to the situation, he is likely to arouse minimal defense.

Neutrality and empathy

When neutrality in speech appears to the listener to indicate a lack of concern for his welfare, he becomes defensive. Group members usually desire to be perceived as valued persons, as individuals of special worth, and as objects of concern and affection. The clinical, detached, person-is-an-object-of-study attitude on the part of many psychologist-trainers is resented by group members. Speech with low affect that communicates little warmth or caring is in such contrast with the affect-laden speech in social situations that it sometimes communicates rejection.

Communication that conveys empathy for the feelings and respect for the worth of the listener, however, is particularly supportive and defense-reductive. Reassurance results when a message indicates that the speaker identifies himself with the listener's problems, shares his feelings, and accepts his emotional reactions at face value. Abortive efforts to deny the legitimacy of the receiver's emotions by assuring the receiver that he need not feel bad, that he should not feel rejected, or that he is overly anxious, though often intended as support-giving, may impress the listener as lack of acceptance. The combination of understanding and empathizing with the other person's emotions with no accompanying effort to change him apparently is supportive at a high level.

The importance of gestural behavorial cues in communicating empathy should be mentioned. Apparently spontaneous facial and bodily evidences of concern are often interpreted as especially valid evidence of deep-level acceptance.

Superiority and equality

When a person communicates to another that he feels superior in position, power, wealth, intellectual ability, physical characteristics, or other ways, he arouses defensiveness. Here, as with the other sources of disturbance, whatever arouses feelings of inadequacy causes the listener to center upon the affect loading of the statement rather than upon the cognitive elements. The receiver then reacts by not hearing the message, by forgetting it, by competing with the sender, or by becoming jealous of him.

The person who is perceived as feeling superior communicates that he is not willing to enter into a shared problem-solving relationship, that he probably does not desire feedback, that he does not require help, and/or that he will be likely to try to reduce the power, the status, or the worth of the receiver.

Many ways exist for creating the atmosphere that the sender feels himself equal to the listener. Defenses are reduced when one perceives the sender as being willing to enter into participative planning with mutual trust and respect. Differences in talent, ability, worth, appearance, status, and power often exist, but the low-defense communicator seems to attach little importance to these distinctions.

Certainty and provisionalism

The effects of dogmatism in producing defensiveness are well known. Those who seem to know the answers, to require no additional data, and to regard themselves as teachers rather than as co-workers tend to put others on guard. Moreover, in my experiment, listeners often perceived manifest expressions of certainty as connoting inward feelings of inferiority. They saw the dogmatic individual as needing to be right, as wanting to win an argument rather than solve a problem, and as seeing his ideas as truths to be defended. This kind of behavior often was associated with acts which others regarded as attempts to exercise control. People who were right seemed to have low tolerance for members who were "wrong"—i.e., who did not agree with the sender.

One reduces the defensiveness of the listener when he communicates that he is willing to experiment with his own behavior, attitudes, and ideas. The person who appears to be taking provisional attitudes, to be investigating issues rather than taking sides on them, to be problem solving rather than debating, and to be willing to experiment and explore tends to communicate that the listener may have some control over the shared quest or the investigation of the ideas. If a person is genuinely searching for information and data, he does not resent help or company along the way.

Conclusion

The implications of the above material for the parent, the teacher, the manager, the administrator, or the therapist are fairly obvious. Arousing defensiveness interferes with communication and thus makes it difficult—and sometimes impossible—for anyone to convey ideas clearly and to move effectively toward the solution of therapeutic, educational, or managerial problems.

On the Dynamics of
The Helping Relationship
David A. Kolb, and
Richard E. Boyatzis

Most of us as teachers, managers, parents, or friends find ourselves increasingly involved in giving and receiving help. This process of sharing wealth, knowledge, or skill with one who happens to have less of these valuable commodities is far from being a simple exchange, easily accomplished. Rather we find that the way to an effective helping relationship is fraught with many psychological difficulties that can either sidetrack or destroy the relationship. Carl Rogers, in his classic article, "The Characteristics of a Helping Relationship" defines a helping relationship as one "in which at least one of the parties has the intent of promoting the growth, development, maturity, improved functioning, improved coping with life of the other" (Rogers, 1961, pp. 39–40). This definition would include parent and child, teacher and students, manager and subordinates, therapist and patient, consultant and client, and many other less formally defined relationships.

The purpose of this paper and the program of research of which it is a part is to understand more fully the dynamics of helping relationships in order to discover how these relationships may be made more effective. The first part of the paper describes the model that has guided our investigations and the second part reports an experiment which tests some of the propositions implied by the model.

The model of the helping relationship at this point is unfortunately not a precise set of mathematical interrelationships among operationally defined variables, but rather is a preliminary attempt to translate case observations and empirical findings from studies of helping relationships in education, welfare, assistance, and therapy programs into a single theoretical framework which will eventually allow operational definitions of variables and tests of interrelationship. The model itself, depicted in figure 1, emphasizes five key elements in the helping relationship: (1) the task or problem around which the helping relationship develops, (2) the helper with his motives (achievement motivation, power motivation, and affiliation motivation) and his self-image, (3) the receiver of help and his motives and self-image, (4) the environment and psychological climate in which the helping activities occur, and (5) the information feedback which occurs during the helping process.

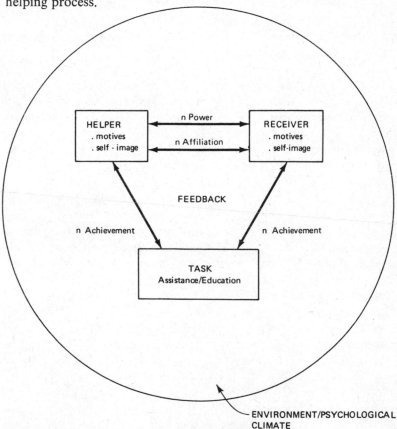

Figure 1. A model for analysis of the helping relationship.

The task

The tasks around which helping relationships develop are widely varied—they range from tying a shoe to changing attitudes about birth control to improving the effectiveness of an organization. It is possible to classify all tasks on a single dimension, namely, the extent to which it is required that the receiver of help be capable of accomplishing the task independently when the helper is no long present. At one end of this dimension are tasks defined as assistance; situations where there is no emphasis on the client's independent task perforance. Giving a vagrant a dime for a cup of coffee is a good example of this end of the continuum. Many welfare and foreign aid programs are close to this end of the dimension. The emphasis is on the solution of an immediate problem with no provision for handling recurrences of that problem or similar problems. This type of assistance aimed only at symptom relief is likely to induce a dependency on the helper, making termination of the relationship difficult. When the relationship has been concluded, the client may blame the helper for inadequate help if he cannot replicate a successful result.

The other end of the continuum is education. Here the emphasis is on increasing the client's ecological wisdom, i.e., on developing the client's ability to solve problems like his present problem when they occur by using the resources of his natural environment. The helper avoids using the special knowledge, skills, or other resources he may command to relieve the client's immediate need, but instead works with the client, in the client's frame of reference, to increase his problem-solving ability. The "felt needs" approach to community development is perhaps the purest example of an educational helping relationship.

While the educational approach in most cases holds the greatest potential for the client's long-term benefit, it can cause great frustration to a client with strong needs for symptom relief. In addition the educational approach will in some cases be seen by the client as an intrusion on his privacy and an escalation of his problem. India, for example, was quite willing to receive assistance in the form of surplus food, but grew resentful at U.S. insistence that such assistance be coupled with an educational program to solve their basic problems of food production.

The helper and receiver of help

The personal characteristics of the helper and receiver of help are major factors influencing the process and outcome of the helping relationship. Two types of characteristics are particularly important—the motives and self-image of helper and client. At least three motives seem necessary to understand the dynamics of the helping relationship—power motivation (n Power), affiliation motivation (n Affiliation), and achievement motivation (n Achievement.) These motives are important because they determine how the helper and client will orient themselves to one another and to their task.

The helper's and the client's power motivations determine how much they will be concerned about influencing and controlling one another. By asking for and/or receiving help offered, the client places himself in a dependent position, where he often feels weaker than and vulnerable to the source of help. The helper at the same time must deal with tendencies to feel superior, thereby letting the satisfactions of power and control overshadow the sometimes elusive goal of acting in the client's best interest. If the helper and client are unable to re-solve power struggles and bring about a situation of power equaliza-tion, the relationship can degenerate into rebellion or passivity by the client or rejection by the helper ("He doesn't appreciate what I am trying to do for him"). One empirical example of the detrimental effects of a helper's overconcern with power can be seen in Prakash's (1968) study of effective and ineffective organization change agents. He found that ineffective change agents were more concerned with their own personal goals and with their political position within the organization than were the effective change agents, who were more concerned about task accomplishment.

The helper's and receiver's affiliation motivations determine how much they will be concerned about intimacy and understanding. To be helpful, the helper must know his client and understand how he per-ceives his problem. The intimacy required for effective understanding is hard to come by in situations where the helper has impossible de-mands on his time, and yet a lack of intimacy can leave the helper and client in two different worlds speaking two different languages. Too great a concern about affiliation by the helper and his client, on the other hand, can produce pressure toward conformity and mutual sympathy which may cause the helper to lose his perspective on the client's problem and the client to lose his respect for the helper's expertise.

The achievement motivation of the helper and receiver of help determines how concerned they will be about accomplishing their task or solving their problem. A major question here is—How is the goal of the helping relationship defined? Does the helper decide "what's good for" the client or does the client retain the power to decide what help he wants? In the first case the client is likely to have little motiva-tion to accomplish the helper's task and in the second the helper's motivation is likely to be reduced. Only when the interpersonal issues of influence and intimacy have been resolved does it appear possible that the helper and client can agree on a goal to which they are mu-tually committed. Even if this is accomplished there is still a problem of what are often strong desires to achieve the goal of the helping relationship. Help is often so late in coming that both helper and client feel strong needs to accomplish *something*. The result is usually assistance programs designed to eliminate the client's immediate desperation rather than programs of education designed to help the client diagnose the causes of the problem and learn to solve the problem himself.

There is an interaction among motives in any helping relationship. It is possible for the helper and client to be so highly power motivated that they become preoccupied with controlling one another at the expense of understanding one another and/or accomplishing their task. Similarly, as we have suggested, high achievement motivation can cause the helper and receiver to orient themselves to accomplishing the task without attending to the interpersonal processes of influence and understanding necessary for having the receiver of help learn to solve the problem on his own. In a case like this, the offer of "Here, let me help you," by the helper is often his cue to push the client aside and do the task himself, leaving the client nearly as ignorant about how to solve the problem as before. And finally, high affiliation motivation can lead to concerns about intimacy and understanding that prejudice attempts to influence others and to accomplish tasks.

The implication of this analysis for helping relationships is that moderate levels of achievement, affiliation, and power motivation in the helper and client are optimal for effective help to take place. The dynamics of the helping relationship are such that influence, intimacy and understanding, and a concern for task accomplishment are all necessary for effective help to take place; yet excess concern in any one area can lead to the deterioration of an effective helping relationship.

The self-image and attitudes of the helper and client are also important defining variables in a helping relationship. The client must see himself as capable of improvement and willing to receive help. If this is not so, a major portion of helping activity must center on building self-confidence and optimism before learning can take place. The helper on the other hand must see himself as capable of helping and yet at the same time must not feel himself to be the "know-it-all" expert who has never experienced his own ignorance. This latter point is related to the issues of influence and intimacy discussed earlier. The helper must be willing to influence and at the same time have empathy with the feelings of the person he is helping.

The environment and psychological climate

It is a truism in contemporary social psychology that behavior is a function of both the person and the environment. While one could imagine many environmental variables which could influence the process of helping such as comfort of surroundings, freedom from distraction, etc., we have limited ourselves for the present time to a consideration of those environmental factors which are related to influence, intimacy and understanding, and task accomplishment. Atkinson (1964) and Atkinson and Feather (1966) and Litwin (1961) have argued that the tendency (T) to act in these three ways can be predicted by the strength of the individual's motivation (M) power, affiliation, and achievement; times the individual's perceived probability (P) that action in terms of one or more of these motives will be rewarded; times the amount (I) of power, affiliation, and achievement rewards he expects to get. Thus, the individual acts to maximize his satisfaction following the formula $T = M \times P \times I$ for three motives: power, affiliation, and achievement. While M refers to the individual's motivation, P and I refer to the individual's perception of the environment.

This analysis has important implications for predictions about effective helping, for if the environment tends to reward one motive disproportionately it can alter the behavior of an otherwise moderately motivated helper and client. One example of this occurs in the Peace Corps, where volunteers who might otherwise establish very effective relationships with host country nationals become bogged down in issues of power and control because the host country people (and sometimes the volunteer himself) perceive the Peace Corps to be a political agent of U. S. foreign policy.

Feedback

The last element of the model is the information feedback which occurs during the helping process. Two aspects of information feedback are important here. First, there is the source which controls information. Feedback can be controlled by the task as in the case of programmed instruction, or by the receiver of help as in self-research methods (Kolb et al. 1968; Schwitzgebel 1964) or by the helper as in traditional teaching methods.

The second aspect of information feedback is the characteristic of the information itself, whether it is accurate or distorted, intense or mild, positive or negative, and so on. This second aspect of feedback has been the subject of a great deal of theoretical speculation, especially among students of sensitivity training. For example, Schein and Bennis (1965) suggest the following criteria for valid, helpful feedback: (1) The feedback should be based on publicly observed behavior in the T-group, (2) it should be contiguous in time to the experience it refers to, and (3) it should be modified through all the data sources (i.e., group members) available.

A major question about the characteristics of helpful feedback concerns whether this feedback should be positive (pleasant for the client to hear) or negative (unpleasant). While there are those who feel that negative feedback is sometimes helpful in that it serves to unfreeze" the client's self-satisfied concept of himself and increase his motivation to change (cf. Bennis et al., most learning theorists have concluded that in the long run reward is more effective than punishment. One example of reward-centered feedback is found in the programmed instruction technique of "error-free learning." Rogers, too, places heavy emphasis on the importance of positive feedback to the client in his concept of unconditional positive regard. "I find that the more acceptance and liking I feel toward this individual, the more I will be creating a relationship which he can use. By acceptance I mean a warm regard for him as a person of unconditional self-worth—of value no matter what his condition, or his feelings. . . . This acceptance of each fluctuating aspect of this other person makes it for him a relationship of warmth and safety, and the safety of being liked and prized as a person seems a highly important element in a helping relationship" (Rogers, 1961, p. 34). To support his conclusion Rogers cites psychotherapy research by Halkides (1958) which showed that therapists who demonstrated a high degree of unconditional positive regard for their clients were more successful than those who did not.

An experimental study of effective helpers, ineffective helpers and nonhelpers

To test some of the hypotheses implied in the model presented above we designed an experiment to study helping as it took place in self-analytic groups (T-groups, see Schein and Bennis [1965] for full description). We decided in this study to focus on the characteristics of effective helpers, leaving aside for the time being questions about the characteristics of effective receivers of help. More specifically we were interested in studying the motives and self-image of helpers and describing the kind of feedback they gave to those they were trying to help.

The first step was to define what constituted help in a T-group situation. *We defined an effective helper as one who, in an environment where giving help is seen as appropriate (the T-group), attempts to help others while the others see this help as significant and important to them.* This definition implies two comparison groups—ineffective helpers who attempt to give others help but these others do not regard the help as important, and nonhelpers who do not attempt to help. While this definition of help has some problems in that it is based on the receiver's subjective judgment of how important the information given by the helper was, it nonetheless seems an important aspect of any helping process. If the client does not regard the information that he receives from his helper to be significant it seems unlikely that he will use this information to modify his behavior. Thus this definition of help can be seen as necessary but possibly not a sufficient aspect of the helping process. What we learn about giving help here can be considered necessary for effective help in situations where the relationship is based on information exchange, but other factors may be important in relationships where the client is required to act on the basis of information he has received from the helper.

Hypotheses

The following hypotheses were made about differences among effective helpers, ineffective helpers, and nonhelpers:

Hypothesis IA: Effective helpers will have moderate scores on power affiliation and achievement motivation.

Hypothesis IB: Ineffective helpers will have high scores on power and achievement motivation and low scores on affiliation motivation.

Hypothesis IC: Nonhelpers will have high scores on affiliation motivation and low scores on power and achievement motivation.

Hypothesis IA is an application of the model of the helping relationship to this experimental situation. Hypothesis IB is based on the notion that what ineffective helpers had to say was not regarded as significant because receivers of help felt that the helper was trying to control them (high power motivation) and that he did not understand them (low affiliation motivation). We also predicted that the ineffective helpers would be less effective because they were overconcerned with the group's task accomplishment (high achievement motivation). We predicted in hypothesis IC that nonhelpers would not try to influence others (low power motivation) or try to accomplish the group's task of helping others (low achievement motivation), but would be highly concerned about understanding and empathy with other group members (high affiliation motivation).

Hypothesis II: There will be significant differences in self-image among effective helpers, ineffective helpers, and nonhelpers.

Since so little is known about the relationship between self-image and the process of giving help, no specific hypotheses were made here.

Hypothesis IIIA: Receivers of help will perceive more positive feedback from effective helpers and more negative feedback from ineffective helpers.

Hypothesis IIIB: Receivers of help will perceive more affection-related feedback from effective helpers and more control-related feedback from ineffective helpers.

Due to limitations of the experimental design which will be described next in the procedure section, it was only possible to test differences between the types of feedback given by effective and ineffective helpers since nonhelpers gave very few feedback that was recorded by the receivers of help. In addition, since the type of feedback was described by the receivers of help rather than independent observers, differences between feedback received from effective and ineffective helpers may be due to (1) the type of feedback the helper gave (2) the type of feedback the receiver heard, or (3) some combination of 1 and 2. Thus, any results concerning hypotheses IIIA and IIIB must be cautiously interpreted with this in mind.

Hypothesis IIIA is based on our earlier reasoning that positive feedback is generally more helpful than negative feedback. Hypothesis IIIB is based on the differential motive patterns that we predicted for helpers and ineffective helpers, i.e., ineffective helpers will be higher in need for power and lower in the need for affiliation than effective helpers. Thus they will give more feedback related to control (power) and less feedback related to affection (affiliation). (No data were collected about feedback related to task accomplishment.)

Procedure

The setting for the experiment was a semester-long course in psychology and human organization, required of master's candidates in management at the M. I. T. Sloan School. As part of the course 111 students participated in 30 hours of T-group training usually divided into two two-hour sessions each week. There were 8 groups of approximately 15 students each. These groups were structured differently from the traditional T-group method (see Schein and Bennis, 1965, chapter 3) in that they were focused around a task—helping one another achieve personal change goals. The method used was the self-directed change method developed by Kolb et al., (1968). With this approach students chose, at the beginning of the T-group, individual change goals which they wanted to achieve. They picked goals like having more empathy, being a more effective leader, and talking more; and customarily they shared these goals with other group members, asking them for feedback on their progress. This procedure served to define clearly the group's task as one of helping others achieve their goals.

The students were about half undergraduates and half master's candidates in management. There were two females. About 10% of the students were foreign nationals with varying degrees of fluency in the English language. Subjects ranged in age from 19 to 35, with most in their early twenties.

Data collection

At the beginning of the course students filled out a 60-item semantic differential to describe their self-image and took the standard six-picture Thematic Apperception Test (TAT) described by Atkinson (1958). This test was scored for *n* Achievement, *n* Power, and *n* Affiliation by expert scorers who had demonstrated their scoring reliability according to the procedures specified by Atkinson (1958). The *n* Power scores were obtained by using Winter's (1967) improved and modified version of Veroff's (Atkinson 1968) power motivation scoring system. The expert scorer demonstrated scoring reliability using practice stories by Winter.

Data feedback on helping was gathered from group members themselves at the end of each session. Each individual at the end of each session filled out the form shown in figure 2. This form asked group members to indicate to whom they had given feedback and from whom they had received feedback during the session. In addition it asked them to describe up to three pieces of feedback which had been most significant to them and to indicate from which group member it had come. The definitions of the feedback description categories are described below as they were given to the group members. The descriptive categories were chosen to represent a wide variety of theoretical notions about what constitutes help and nonhelpful feedback.

Description of Feedback Dimensions

Category of Dimension	*Explanation or Description*
Like-Dislike Neutral	Do you like the *person* who gave you this feedback? Do you dislike him? Are you neutral toward him? Rate on scale −2 to +2.
Verbal-Nonverbal	Was this feedback *spoken* to you (VERBAL), or was it communicated through gestures, facial expressions, nods, etc. (NONVERBAL)? Check one or the other.
Strong-Weak	This dimension refers to the intensity of the feedback. Was it emphatic and vigorous, or was it expressed mildly? Check one or the other.
Here-and-Now	This dimension refers to the content of the feedback. Did it refer to events or behavior taking place now or recently in the group (HERE-AND-NOW), or did it refer to things in the past not shared by other group members (THERE-AND-THEN)? Check one or the other.
Positive-Negative	Did the feedback agree with you or encourage you? Did you like to hear it (POSITIVE)? Or did it dis-

agree with you, discourage you? Was it "painful" to hear (NEGATIVE)? Check one or the other.

Supported

This dimension refers to the reaction of other group members to the feedback. Did they corroborate, agree with or support it, or did they disagree or remain silent about it (NONSUPPORTED)? Check one or the other.

**Owned-
Not-Owned**

This dimension refers to the person giving you the feedback. Did he attach himself personally to the feedback; did he make it clear that it was his own opinion or feeling (OWNED)? Or was it not clear that the feedback represented the giver's own opinion (NOT OWNED)? *Examples:* Owned—"I think you talk too much." (or) "Nobody in this group listens to me." Not-owned—"Does the group feel that John talks too much?; (or) "Isn't this group supposed to listen to people?" Check one or the other. Hint—not-owned feedback is often in question form.

**Directed-
Nondirected**

This dimension refers to *you* as the receiver of feedback. Was the feedback directed or applied to you personally; did it have your "name" on it (DIRECTED)? Or did you have to make the application to yourself from a general statement (NONDIRECTED)? *Examples:* Directed—"John Smith is not sensitive to my feelings." Nondirected—"Some people in this group are not sensitive to my feelings." Check one or the other.

**Evaluative-
Nonevaluative**

This dimension applies to the pressure of an implicit or explicit value judgment *in* the feedback. *Example:* Evaluative—"I think it's wrong that you should try to control the group." Nonevaluative—"I think you are trying to control the group." Check one or the other. Hint—value judgments are often expressed by tone of voice as well as in words.

**Spontaneous-
Solicited**

Solicited feedback is feedback that you specifically asked for. Spontaneous feedback is feedback that someone gives you without being asked. Check one or the other.

Inclusion-Directed

Was the feedback related to any aspect of your participation or nonparticipation in the group, acceptance or rejection by the group, interaction with the group, etc.?

Control-Directed

Did the feedback pertain to any aspect of your influence, lack of influence, leadership, control in the group, etc.?

Affection-Directed

Was the feedback related to your warmth, friendliness, unfriendliness, openness, etc.?

**Related to Your
Self-Change Project**

Was the feedback related to the self-change project you have chosen?

Name_____   Date _____

I. List below in boxes 1, 2, and 3, the three pieces of feedback from today's session that stand out most in your mind. Do this by recording in these boxes the initials of the giver of the feedback. You may also record here the central theme of the feedback if you wish. Try to put the feedback that stands out most in your mind in box 1, etc. A piece of feedback is defined here as a piece of information from one individual. A giver may be listed as many times as appropriate.

II. Beginning with column 1, go down the column checking those categories which describe the feedback you received. Descriptions of each category appear on the cover sheet. When you have completed column 1, continue in the same fashion in columns 2 and 3.

	1	2	3
Using a −2 to +2 scale, indicate your feelings about the person who gave you the feedback. −2 = dislike very much; −1 = dislike slightly; 0 = neutral to; +1 = like somewhat; +2 = like very much.			
VERBAL (spoken feedback) NON-VERBAL (gestured feedback)			
STRONG (intense, vigorous feedback) WEAK (mild feedback)			
HERE-AND-NOW (feedback about event or behavior in group) THERE-AND-THEN (about event outside of group experience)			
POSITIVE (pleasant to hear) NEGATIVE (unpleasant)			
SUPPORTED (corroborated by others) NON-SUPPORTED (not corroborated)			
OWNED (giver makes it clear that feedback represents his own opinion) NOT OWNED (not clear that feedback represents the giver's own opinion)			
DIRECTED (giver applies remark directly to you) NON-DIRECTED (from general statement, you make application to yourself)			
EVALUATIVE (giver is making value judgment) NON-EVALUATIVE (giver is not making value judgment)			
SOLICITED (you requested feedback) SPONTANEOUS (you did not request feedback)			
Feedback refers to your participation, non-participation, interaction, etc. (INCLUSION)			
Feedback refers to your leadership, influence, lack of influence, etc. (CONTROL)			
Feedback refers to your friendliness, unfriendliness, etc. (AFFECTION)			
Related to your self change project			

III. Check below the names of the people you gave feedback to (G) and received feedback from (R) in today's session.

Name	G	R		Name	G	R

IV. How close are you to your goal today? Rate on a scale 1 to 9 with 1 being farthest from your goal and 9 being closest to it. _____

Figure 2. Feedback form.

Definition of effective, ineffective and nonhelper

The above procedure yielded approximately 15 forms per group session with each group having about 11 sessions. With the exception of one group, all of the groups submitted complete data. The group with incomplete data had to be eliminated from our analysis.

The procedure for defining effective, ineffective, and nonhelping was simple. To begin with each group was analyzed separately, since different groups developed somewhat differently due to different trainer styles and member needs. Thus a member was classified as an effective, ineffective, or nonhelper in relation to other group members who shared the same climate as he did, not in relation to the total experimental population. For each member of the group, the investigators totaled the number of times he had been mentioned as a giver of a significant feedback, i.e., his initials had been placed on the top of one of the three columns in figure 2. The investigators also totaled the number of times the member indicated that he had given feedback to other group members, i.e., the number of checks he placed in the "G" box after members' names in figure 2. With these two variables—for each member the number of significant feedbacks members had received from him and the number of feedbacks he reported giving—a matrix of the group members was plotted as shown in figure 3.

Subjects who were above the group median in number of feed-

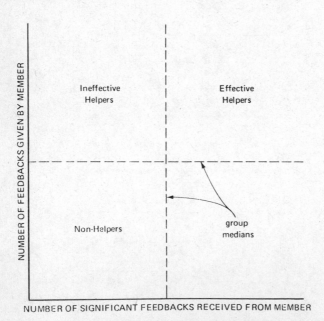

Figure 3. Definition of effective, ineffective, and non-helpers.

backs given and below the group median in number of significant feedbacks received were classed as ineffective helpers, i.e., they gave a
lot of feedback but few people regarded this feedback as significant.
Subjects who were below the group median on both variables were
classed as nonhelpers. Those who were above both medians were
classed as effective helpers, i.e., they gave a lot of feedback and many
members reported receiving significant feedback from them. As might
be expected few subjects (12 out of 98) fell into the fourth quadrant.
Those that did were classed as effective helpers since they in all cases
came very close to the median of number of feedbacks given. (We
assumed that many of those who fell in this quadrant did so because
they failed to check the names of all of the people to whom they had
given feedback.) The effective, ineffective, and nonhelpers from each
group were then combined to form a total sample of 98 subjects—47
effective helpers, 24 ineffective helpers, and 27 nonhelpers.

Results and discussion

Motivation

The *n* Achievement, *n* Power, and *n* Affiliation scores for the three
groups are shown in table 1, and portrayed graphically in figure 4. As

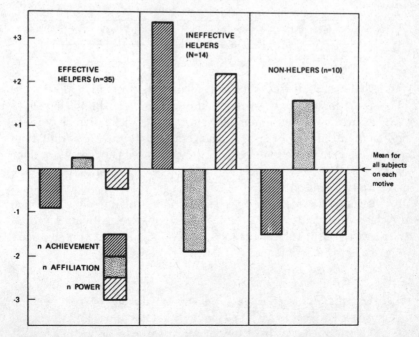

Figure 4. Helpers' motives expressed as deviations from the mean of all
subjects.

figure 4 indicates, the results for all three motives were in the direction predicted, although in several cases difference did not reach the .05 level of significance. The most clearcut differences were shown on *n* Affiliation and *n* Power. Ineffective helpers scored much lower on *n* Affiliation than did effective helpers or nonhelpers. The difference in *n* Affiliation scores between nonhelpers and effective helpers, however, was not significant. Ineffective helpers scored much higher on *n* Power than did effective helpers or nonhelpers. There was no significant difference between the *n* Power scores of effective helpers and nonhelpers. The *n* Achievement scores were significantly higher for ineffective helpers than for effective helpers, but again the difference between effective helpers and nonhelpers was not statistically meaningful.

Table 1. Motive Scores of Effective Helpers, Ineffective Helpers, and Nonhelpers

Gp	A n=35	B n=14	C n=10	P value*		
Motive	Effective Helpers	Ineffective Helpers	Nonhelpers	A v. B	A v. C	B v. C
n Achievement	9.20	13.50	8.64	.04	NS	.09
n Power	4.51	7.14	3.50	.01	NS	.001
n Affiliation	5.37	3.29	6.64	.03	NS	.02

* Mann Whitney U. Test 1 tail, NS = P > .10.

Viewed overall, these results can generally be seen as supporting the hypothesis that effective helpers are moderately motivated in *n* Achievement, *n* Power, and *n* Affiliation, while ineffective helpers are high in the need for power and achievement and low on *n* Affiliation, and nonhelpers are low in needs for power and achievement and high on *n* Affiliation. However, a more cautious conclusion based only on statistically significant differences would suggest that ineffective helpers are differentiated from effective helpers and nonhelpers by very high *n* Achievement and *n* Power scores and very low *n* Affiliation scores. In this experiment none of the three motives significantly differentiates effective helpers and nonhelpers.

Self image

The semantic differential data on the self-image of effective, ineffective, and nonhelpers is shown in table 2. Only those adjective pairs which differentiated at least two of the three groups beyond the .05

level (2-tail) are shown in the table. While no specific hypotheses were made about self-image, these data are interesting in that they seem to support the conception of effective helpers, ineffective helpers, and nonhelpers suggested by the motivation results. The nonhelpers are different from both the effective and ineffective helpers in that they describe themselves as more passive, democratic, not cynical, submissive, followers, guarded, quiet, timid, not influential, inarticulate, self-conscious, and preferring to listen. The general picture that emerges from these adjectives is that of an accepting, democratic person who lacks the self-confidence to influence others.

Ineffective helpers, on the other hand, describe themselves differently from nonhelpers (P < .05 2-tail) and effective helpers (P < .10 2-tail)—seeing themselves as organized, impatient, open, and superior. These adjectives seem to portray an extreme self-confidence with impatience and lack of interest in others.

The most interesting part of table 2 is that the effective helpers consistenly (with three exceptions) place themselves between the ineffective and nonhelpers. They are, it appears, self-confident without being overbearing—a moderation which is suggested by their moderate motive scores in achievement, affiliation, and power.

The above results, while only suggestive, are extremely useful in that they help to sharpen our mental image of two types of help that are doomed to failure—the brash, overconfident, superior approach which places the client on the defensive, and the timid, hesitant, passive approach which may raise questions about the helper's qualifications and lead to a lack of confidence in the helper. The description of the successful helper is somewhat vague from the self-descriptions in table 2 because no adjectives significantly differentiate effective helpers from the other two groups.

Feedback

The types of feedback given by effective and ineffective helpers is shown in table 3. The figures after each category represent the percent of the total number of significant feedbacks received from each group. Totals equal greater than 100% because more than one characteristic was checked on each piece of feedback. The hypothesis that receivers would report more control feedback from ineffective helpers was supported (33% vs. 26% P < .03 1-tail). The hypothesis that less affection feeback would be received from them was not supported, however.

The hypothesis that effective helpers would give more positive feedback and ineffective helpers more negative feedback was also supported by the data. It is difficult, however, to assess the implication of this result. We cannot say conclusively that effective helpers *gave* more

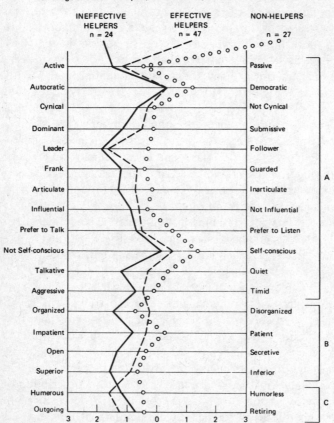

Self-image of Effective Helpers, Ineffective Helpers, and Non-helpers

Table 2. A = These adjectives differentiate Non-helpers from both Effective
and Ineffective Helpers (Mann-Whitney U-Test p < .05 2 tail)
B = These adjectives differentiate Non-helpers from Ineffective
Helpers (p < .05 2 tail) and Effective Helpers from Ineffective
Helpers (p < .10 2 tail)
C = These adjectives differentiate Effective from Ineffective Helpers only
(p < .05)
No adjectives differentiate Effective from Ineffective Helpers at the .05
level 2-tail.

positive than negative feedback—we can only say that more positive
feedback was heard from effective helpers. This can either be due to
the fact that effective helpers did give more positive feedback or due
to the fact that negative feedback given by effective helpers was
ignored by receivers of help.

Table 3. Comparison of Types of Feedback Given by
Effective (n = 47) and Ineffective Helpers (n = 24)

Feedback Category	Effective Helpers*	Ineffective Helpers*	P of Difference†
Verbal	92	96	.007
Nonverbal	6	3	.008
Strong	63	59	NS
Weak	34	40	NS
Here-and-Now	87	86	NS
There-and-Then	10	13	NS
Positive	55	45	.04 1 tail
Negative	42	54	.04 1 tail
Supported	64	66	NS
Nonsupported	33	33	NS
Owned	90	96	.002
Not Owned	8	3	.002
Directed	83	86	NS
Nondirected	14	13	NS
Evaluative	71	71	NS
Nonevaluative	26	27	NS
Solicited	27	33	NS
Spontaneous	70	65	NS
Inclusion	47	44	NS
Control	26	33	.03 1 tail
Affection	22	20	.12 1 tail
Related to Self-Change Project	52	52	NS

* Figures represent % of total significant feedback received from each group.
These total greater than 100% because more than one characteristic was checked
on each piece of feedback.

† Probabilities marked 1-tail were predicted in advance, all others are 2-tail.
(NS = 7.10)

The other unpredicted results are difficult to explain. A greater percentage of nonverbal feedback (6% vs. 3%) and not-owned feedback (8% vs. 3%) was received from effective helpers than from ineffective helpers. The most plausible explanation seems to be that the ineffective helpers were unable to communicate so subtly—using nonverbal expressions or opinions they did not clearly identify as their own—because they lacked the empathy to time such or because their controlling behavior caused receivers defensively to block out such communications.

Summary

The results of this experiment suggest that the helping relationship is best viewed as one involving a complex interaction of at least three motives—*n* Achievement, *n* Affiliation, and *n* Power. Effective helpers appear to be those individuals who score moderately on these three motives. A similar moderation appears in the self-image of effective helpers. They are not as brash and overconfident as ineffective helpers nor as timid and self-concious as nonhelpers. The feedback that is received from effective helpers tends to be more positive and less related to control issues than feedback from ineffective helpers. Also, receivers of help get more nonverbal and not-owned feedback from effective helpers.

In future research, other implications of the model of the helping relationship should be explored. We are currently involved in investigating the characteristics of effective receivers of help following the same research paradigm described here. The generality of the model should at some point be tested by research in a situation where the task is not an interpersonal one. Also, the impact of different psychological climates on the helping process should be investigated.

Bibliography

Atkinson, J. (ed.) *Motives in fantasy, action and society,* Princeton, New Jersey: Van Nostrand, 1958.

Atkinson, J. *An introduction to motivation, Princeton,* New Jersey: Van Nostrand, 1964.

Atkinson, J. and Feather, N. T. *A theory of achievement motivation,* New York: John Wiley and Sons, 1966.

Bennis, W.; Schein, E.; Berlew, D.; and Steele, F. *Interpersonal dynamics.* Homewood, Illinois: Dorsey Press, 1964.

Halkides, G. *An experimental study of four conditions necessary for therapeutic change.* Unpublished doctoral dissertation, University of Chicago, 1958.

Kolb, D. Winter, S.; Berlew, D. Self-directed change: Two studies. *Journal of Applied Behavioral Science,* 1968, Vol. 4, 453–473.

Prakash, S. *Some characteristics of an effective organization develop- ment agent.* Unpublished master's thesis, Sloan School of Management. Massachusetts Institute of Technology, 1968.

Rogers, C. *On becoming a person.* Cambridge, Massachusetts: Riverside Press, 1961.

Schein, E. and Bennis, W. *Personal and organizational change through group methods.* New York: John Wiley and Sons, 1965.

Schwitzgebel, R. *A simple behavorial system for recording and implementing change in natural settings.* Unpublished doctoral thesis. Harvard University, 1964.

Winter, David G. *Power motivation in thought and action.* Unpublished doctoral thesis, Harvard University, 1967.

Intercultural Communication: A Guide to Men of Action

Edward T. Hall and William Foote Whyte

How can anthropological knowledge help the man of action in dealing with people of another culture? We shall seek to answer that question by examining the process of intercultural communication.

Anthropologists have long claimed that a knowledge of culture is valuable to the administrator. More and more people in business and government are willing to take this claim seriously, but they ask that we put culture to them in terms they can understand and act upon.

When the layman thinks of culture, he is likely to think in terms of (1) the way people dress, (2) the beliefs they hold, and (3) the customs they practice—with an accent upon the esoteric. Without undertaking any comprehensive definition, we can concede that all three are aspects of culture, and yet point out that they do not get us very far, either theoretically or practically.

Dress is misleading, if we assume that differences in dress indicate differences in belief and behavior. If that were the case, then we should expect to find people dressed like ourselves to be thinking and acting like ourselves. While there are still peoples wearing "colorful" apparel quite different from ours, we find in many industrializing societies that the people with whom we deal dress much as we do—and yet think and act quite differently.

Knowledge of beliefs may leave us up in the air because the connections between beliefs and behavior are seldom obvious. In the case of religious beliefs, we may know, for example, that the Mohammedan must pray to Allah a certain number of times a day and that therefore the working day must provide for praying time. This is important, to be sure, but the point is so obvious that it is unlikely to be overlooked by anyone. The administrator must also grasp the less dramatic as-

Reproduced with the permission of the Society for Applied Anthropology from *Human Organization* 19, no. 1 (1960): 5–12.

pects of everyday behavior, and here a knowledge of beliefs is a very imperfect guide.

Customs provide more guidance, providing we do not limit ourselves to the esoteric and also search for the pattern of behavior into which a given custom fits. The anthropolist, in dealing with customary behavior, is not content with identifying individual items. To him, these items are not miscellaneous. They have meaning only as they are fitted together into a pattern.

But even assuming that the pattern can be communicated to the administrator, there is still something important lacking. The pattern shows how the people act—when among themselves. The administrator is not directly concerned with that situation. Whatever background information he has, he needs to interpret to himself how the people act *in relation to himself*. He is dealing with a cross-cultural situation. The link between the two cultures is provided by acts of communication between the administrator, representing one culture, and people representing another. If communication is effective, then understanding grows with collaborative action. If communication is faulty, then no book knowledge of culture can assure effective action.

This is not to devalue the knowledge of culture that can be provided by the anthropologist. It is only to suggest that the point of implementation of the knowledge must be in the communication process. Let us therefore examine the process of intercultural communication. By so doing we can accomplish two things. (*a*) broaden knowledge of ourselves by revealing some of our own unconscious communicative acts, and (*b*) clear away heretofore almost insurmountable obstacles to understanding in the cross-cultural process. We also learn that communication, as it is used here, goes far beyond words and includes many other acts upon which judgments of what is transpiring are based and from which we draw conclusions as to what has occurred in the past.

Culture affects communication in various ways. It determines the time and timing of interpersonal events, the places where it is appropriate to discuss particular topics, the physical distance separating one speaker from another, the tone of voice that is appropriate to the subject matter. Culture, in this sense, delineates the amount and type of physical contact, if any, which convention permits or demands, and the intensity of emotion which goes with it. Culture includes the relationship of *what is said to what is meant*—as when "no" means "maybe" and "tomorrow" means "never." Culture, too, determines whether a given matter—say, a business contract—should be initially discussed between two persons or hacked out in a daylong conference which includes four or five senior officials from each side, with perhaps an assist from the little man who brings in the coffee.

These are important matters which the businessman who hopes to trade abroad ignores at his peril. They are also elusive, for every man takes his own culture for granted. Even a well-informed national of another country is hard put to explain why, in his own land, the custom is thus-and-so rather than so-and-thus; as hard put, indeed, as you would probably be asked what is the "rule" which governs the precise time in a relationship that you begin using another man's first name. One "just knows." In other words, you do not know and cannot explain satisfactorily because you learn this sort of thing unconsciously in your upbringing, in your culture, and you take such knowledge for granted. Let the impact of culture on communication can be observed and the lessons taught.

Since the most obvious form of communication is by language, we will first consider words, meanings, voice tones, emotions, and physical contact; then take up, in turn, the cultural impact of time, place, and social class relations on business situations in various lands. Finally, we will suggest what the individual administrator may do to increase his effectiveness abroad, and what students of culture may do to advance this application of anthropology.

Beyond language

Americans are often accused of not being very good at language, or at least not very much interested in learning foreign languages. There is little evidence that any people are inherently "better" at languages than any other, given the opportunity and incentive to learn. The West and Central European who has since childhood been in daily contact with two or three languages learns to speak them all, and frequently to read and write them as well. Under similar conditions, American children do the same. Indeed, a not uncommon sight on the backroads of Western Europe is a mute, red-faced American military family lost on a Sunday drive while the youngest child, barely able to lisp his own English, leans from the window to interpret the directions of some gnarled farmer whose dialect is largely unintelligible to most of his own countrymen.

We should not underestimate the damage our lack of language facility as a nation has done to our relations all over the world. Obviously, if you cannot speak a man's language, you are terribly handicapped in communicating with him.

But languages can be learned and yet most, if not all, of the disabling errors described in this article could still be made. Vocabulary, grammar, even verbal facility are not enough. Unless a man understands the subtle cues that are implicit in language, tone, gestures, and expression, he will not only consistently misinterpret what is said to him, but he may offend irretrievably without knowing how or why.

Do they mean what they say?

Can't you believe what a man says? We all recognize that the basic honesty of the speaker is involved. What we often fail to recognize, however, is that the question involves cultural influences that have nothing to do with the honesty or dependability of the individual.

In the United States we put a premium on direct expression. The "good" American is supposed to say what he means and to mean what he says. If, on important matters, we discover that someone spoke deviously or evasively, we would be inclined to regard him thereafter as unreliable if not out-and-out dishonest.

In some other cultures, the words and their meanings do not have such a direct connection. People may be more concerned with the emotional context of the situation than with the meaning of particular words. This leads them to give an agreeable and pleasant answer to a question when a literal, factual answer might be unpleasant or embarrassing.

This situation is not unknown in our culture, of course. How many times have you muttered your delighted appreciation for a boring evening? We term this simple politness and understand each other perfectly.

On the other hand, analogous "polite" behavior on a matter of factory production would be incomprehensible. An American businessman would be most unlikely to question another businessman's word if he were technically qualified and said that his plant could produce 1,000 gross of widgets a month. We are "taught" that it is none of our businss to inquire too deeply into the details of his production system. This would be prying and might be considered an attempt to steal his operational plans.

Yet this cultural pattern has trapped many an American into believing that when a Japanese manufacturer answered a direct question with the reply that he could produce 1,000 gross of widgets, he meant what he said. If the American had been escorted through the factory and had seen quite clearly that its capacity was, at the most, perhaps 500 gross of widgets per month, he would be likely to say to himself: "Well, this fellow probably has a brother-in-law who has a factory who can make up the difference. He isn't telling the whole story because he's afraid I might try to make a better deal with the brother-in-law. Besides, what business is it of mine, so long as he meets the schedule?"

The cables begin to burn after the American returns home and only 500 gross of widgets arrive each month.

What the American did not know was that in Japanese culture one avoids the direct question unless the questioner is absolutely certain that the answer will not embarras the Japanese businessman in any way whatsoever. In Japan for one to admit being unable to perform a given operation or measure up to a given standard means a bitter loss of face. Given a foreigner who is so stupid, ignorant, or insensitive as to ask an embarrassing question, the Japanese is likely to choose what appears to him the lesser of two evils.

American caught in this cross-cultural communications trap are apt to feel doubly deceived because the Japanese manufacturer may well be an established and respected member of the business community.

Excitable people?

Man communicates not by words alone. His tone of voice, his facial expressions, his gestures all contribute to the infintely varied calculus of meaning. But the confusion of tongues is more than matched by the confusion of gesture and other culture cues. One man's nod is another man's negative. Each culture has its own rich array of meaningful signs, symbols, gestures, emotional connotations, historical references, traditional responses, and—equality significant—pointed silences. These have been built up over the millennia as (who can say?) snarls, growls, and love murmurs gathered meaning and dignity with long use, to end up perhaps as the worn coinage of trite expression.

Consider the Anglo-Saxon tradition of preserving one's calm. The American is taught by his culture to suppress his feelings. He is conditioned to regard emotion as generally bad (except in weak women who can't help themselves) and a stern self-control as good. The more important a matter, the more solem and outwardly dispassionate he is likely to be. A cool head, granite visage, dispassionate logic—it is no accident that the Western story hero consistently displays these characteristics.

In the Middle East it is otherwise. From childhood, the Arab is permitted, even encouraged, to express his feelings without inhibition. Grown men can weep, shout, gesture expressively and violently, jump up and down—and be admired as sincere.

The modulated, controlled Anglo-Saxon is likely to be regarded with suspicion—he must be hiding something, practicing to deceive.

The exuberant and emotional Arab is likely to disturb the Anglo-Saxon, cause him to write inwardly with embarrassment—for isn't this childish behavior? And aren't things getting rather out of hand?

Then, again, there is the matter of how loudly one should talk.

In the Arab world, in discussions among equals, the men attain a decibel level that would be considered aggressive, objectionale and obnoxious in the United States. Loudness connotes strength and sincerity among Arabs; a soft tone implies weakness, deviousness. This is so "right" in the Arab culture that several Arabs have told us they discounted anything heard over the "Voice of America" because the signal was so weak!

Personal status modulates voice tone, however, even in Arab society. The Saudi Arab shows respect to his superior—to a sheik, say—by lowering his voice and mumbling. The affluent American may also be addressed in this fasion, making almost impossible an already difficult situation. Since in the American culture one unconsciously "asks" another to raise his voice by raising one's own, the American speaks louder. This lowers the Arab's tone more and increases the mumble. This triggers a shouting response in the American—which cues the Arab into a frightened "I'm not being respectful enough" tone well below audibility.

They are not likely to part with much respect for each other.

To touch or not to touch?

How much physical contact should appropriately accompany social or business conversation?

In the United States we discourage physical contact, particularly between adult males. The most common physical contact is the handshake and, compared to Europeans, we use it sparingly.

The handshake is the most detached and impersonal form of greeting or farewell in Latin America. Somewhat more friendly is the left hand placed on another man's shoulder during a handshake. Definitely more intimate and warm is the *double abrazo* in which two men embrace by placing their arms around each other's shoulders.

These are not difficult conventions to live with, particularly since the North American can easily permit the Latin American to take initiative in any form of contact more intimate than the handshake. Far more difficult for the North American to learn to live with comfortably are the less stylized forms of physical contact such as the hand on one's arm during conversation. To the North American this is edging toward what in his culture is an uncomfortable something— possibly sexual—which inhibits his own communication.

Yet there are cultures which restrict physical contact far more than we do. An American at a cocktail party in Java tripped over the invisible ropes which mark the boundaries of acceptable behavior. He was seeking to develop a business relationship with a prominent Javanese and seemed to be doing very well. Yet, when the cocktail party ended, so apparently did a promising beginning. For the North American spent nearly six months trying to arrange a second meeting. He finally learned, through pitying intermediaries, that at the cocktail party he had momentarily placed his arm on the shoulder of the Javanese—and in the presence of other people. Humiliating! Almost unpardonable in traditional Javanese etiquette.

In this particular case, the unwitting breach was mended by a graceful apology. It is worth noting, however, that a truly cordial business relationship never did develop.

The five dimensions of time

If we peel away a few layers of cultural clothing, we begin to reach almost totally unconscious reactions. Our ideas of time, for example, are deeply instilled in us when we are children. If they are contradicted by another's behavior, we react with anger, not knowing exactly why. For the businessman, five important temporal concepts are appointment time, discussion time, acquaintance time, visiting time, and time schedules.

Anyone who has traveled abroad or dealt at all extensively with non-Americans learns that punctuality is variously interpreted. It is one thing to recognize this with the mind; to adjust to a different kind of *appointment time* is quite another.

In Latin America, you should expect to spend hours waiting in outer offices. If you bring your American interpretation of what constitutes punctuality to a Latin-American office, you will fray your temper and elevate your blood pressure. For a forty-five-minute wait is not unusual—no more than a five-minute wait would be in the United States. No insult is intended, no arbitrary pecking order is being established. If, in the United States, you would not be outraged by a five-minute wait, you should not be outraged by the Latin American's forty-five-minute delay in seeing you. The time pie is differently cut, that's all.

Further, the Latin American doesn't usually schedule individual appointments to the exclusion of other appointments. The informal clock of his upbringing ticks more slowly and he rather enjoys seeing several people on different matters at the same time. The three-ring circus atmosphere which results, if interpreted in the American's scale of time and propriety, seems to signal him to go away, to tell him that he is not being properly treated, to indicate that his dignity is under attack. Not so. The clock on the wall may look the same but it tells a different sort of time.

The cultural error may be compounded by a further miscalculation. In the United States, a consistently tardy man is likely to be considered undependable, and by our cultural clock this is a reasonable conclusion. For you to judge a Latin American by your scale of time values is to risk a major error.

Suppose you have waited forty-five minutes and there is a man in his office, by some miracle alone in the room with you. Do you now get down to business and stop "wasting time"?

If you are not forewarned by experience or a friendly advisor, you may try to do this. And it would usually be a mistake. For in the American culture, *discussion* is a means to an end: the deal. You try to make your point quickly, efficiently, neatly. If your purpose is to arrange some major affairs, your instinct is probably to settle the major issues first, leave the details for later, possibly for the technical people to work out.

For the Latin American, the discussion is a part of the spice of life. Just as he tends not to be overly concerned about reserving you your specific segment of time, he tends not as rigidly to separate business from nonbusiness. He runs it all together and wants to make something of a social event out of what you, in your culture, regard as strictly business.

The Latin American is not alone in this. The Greek businessman, partly for the same and partly for different reasons, does not lean toward the "hit-and-run" school of business behavior, either. The Greek businessman adds to the social element, however, a feeling about what length of discussion time constitutes good faith. In America, we show good faith by ignoring the details. "Let's agree on the main points. The details will take care of themselves. "

Not so the Greek. He signifies good will and good faith by what may seem to you an interminable discussion which includes every conceivable detail. Otherwise, you see, he cannot help but feel that the other man might be trying to pull the wool over his eyes. Our habit, in what we feel to be our relaxed and friendly way, of postponing details until later smacks the Greek between the eyes as a maneuver to flank him. Even if you can somehow convince him that this is not the case, the meeting must still go on a certain indefinite—but, by our standards, long—time or he will feel disquieted.

The American desire to get down to business and on with other things works to our disadvantage in other parts of the world, too; and not only in business. The head of a large, successful Japanese firm commented: "You Americans have a terrible weakness. We Japanese know about it and exploit it every chance we get. You are impatient. We have learned that if we just make you wait long enough, you'll agree to anything."

Whether this is literally true or not, the Japanese executive singled out a trait of American culture which most of us share and which, one may assume from the newspapers, the Russians have not overlooked, either.

By *acquaintance time* we mean how long you must know a man before you are willing to do business with him.

In the United States, if we know that a salesman represents a well-known, reputable company, and if we need his product, he may walk away from the first meeting with an order in his pocket. A few minutes' conversation to decide matters or price, delivery, payment, model of product—nothing more is involved. In Central America, local custom does not permit a salesman to land in town, call on the customer, and walk away with an order, no matter how badly your prospect wants and needs your product. It is traditional there that you must see your man at least three times before you can discuss the nature of your business.

Does this mean that the South American businessman does not recognize the merits of one product over another? Of course it doesn't. It is just that the weight of tradition presses him to do business within a circle of friends. If a product he needs is not available within his circle, he does not go outside it so much as he enlarges the circle itself to include a new friend who can supply the want. Apart from his cultural need to "feel right" about a new relationship, there is the logic of his business system. One of the realities of his life is that it is dangerous to enter into business with someone over whom you have no more than formal, legal "control." In the past decades, his legal system has not always been as firm as ours and he has learned through experience that he needs the sanctions implicit in the informal system of friendship.

Visiting time involves the question of who sets the time for a visit. George Coelho, a social psychologist from India, gives an illustrative case. A U.S. businessman received this invitation from an Indian businessman: "Won't you and your family come and see us? Come anytime." Several weeks later, the Indian repeated the invitation in the same words. Each time the American replied that he would certainly like to drop in—but never did. The reason is obvious in terms of our culture. Here "come anytime" is just an expression of friendliness. You are not really expected to show up unless your host proposes a specific time. In India, on the contrary, the words are meant literally—that the host is putting himself at the disposal of his guest and really expects him to come. It is the essence of politeness to leave it to the guest to set a time at his convenience. If the guest never comes, the Indian naturally assumes that he does not want to come. Such a misunderstanding can lead to a serious rift between men who are trying to do business with each other.

Time schedules present Americans with another problem in many parts of the world. Without schedules, deadlines, priorities, and time-tables, we tend to feel that our country could not run at all. Not only are they essential to getting work done, but they also play an important role in the informal communication process. Deadlines indicate priorities and priorities signal the relative importance of people and the processes they control. These are all so much a part of our lives that a day hardly passes without some reference to them. "I have to be there by 6:30." "If I don't have these plans out by 5:00 they'll be useless." "I told J. B. I'd be finished by noon tomorrow and now he tells me to drop everything and get hot on the McDermott account. What do I do now?"

In our system, there are severe penalties for not completing work on time and important rewards for holding to schedules. One's integrity and reputation are at stake.

You can imagine the fundamental conflicts that arise when we attempt to do business with people who are just as strongly oriented away from time schedules as we are toward them.

The Middle Eastern peoples are a case in point. Not only is our idea of time schedules no part of Arab life but the mere mention of a deadline to an Arab is like waving a red flag in front of a bull. In his culture, your emphasis on a deadline has the emotional effect on him that his backing you into a corner and threatening you with a club would have on you.

One effect of this conflict of unconscious habit patterns is that hundreds of American-owned radio sets are lying on the shelves of Arab radio repair shops, untouched. The Americans made the serious cross-cultural error of asking to have the repair completed by a certain time.

How do you cope with this? How does the Arab get another Arab to do anything? Every culture has its own ways of bringing pressure to get results. The usual Arab way is one which Americans avoid as "bad manners." It is needling.

An Arab businessmen whose car broke down explained it this way:

First, I go to the garage and tell the mechanic what is wrong with my car. I wouldn't want to give him the idea that I didn't know. After that, I leave the car and walk around the block. When I come back to the garage, I ask him if he has started to work yet. On my way home from lunch I stop in and ask him how things are going. When I go back to the office I stop by again. In the evening, I return and peer over his shoulder for a while. If I didn't keep this up, he'd be off working on someone else's car.

If you haven't been needled by an Arab, you just haven't been needled.

A place for everything

We say that there is a time and place for everything, but compared to other countries and cultures we give very little emphasis to place distinctions. Business is almost a universal value with us; it can be discussed almost anywhere, except perhaps in church. One can even talk business on the church steps going to and from the service. Politics is only slightly more restricted in the places appropriate for its discussion.

In other parts of the world, there are decided place restrictions on the discussion of business and politics. The American who is not conscious of the unwritten laws will offend if he abides by his own rather than by the local rules.

In India, you should not talk business when visiting a man's home. If you do, you prejudice your chances of ever working out a satisfactory business relationship.

In Latin America, although university students take an active interest in politics, tradition decrees that a politician should avoid political subjects when speaking on university grounds. A Latin American politician commented to anthropologist Allan Holmberg that neither he nor his fellow politicians would have dared attempt a political speech on the grounds of the University of San Marcos in Peru—as did Vice-President Nixon.

To complicate matters further, the student body of San Marcos, anticipating the visit, had voted that Mr. Nixon would not be welcome. The university rector had issued no invitation, presumably because he expected what did, in fact, happen.

As a final touch, Mr. Nixon's interpreter was a man in full military uniform. In Latin American countries, some of which had recently overthrown military dictators, the symbolism of the military uniform could hardly contribute to a cardial atmosphere. Latin Americans need no reminder that the United States is a great military power.

Mr. Nixon's efforts were planned in the best traditions of our own culture: he hoped to improve relations through a direct, frank, and face-to-face discussion with students—the future leaders of their country. Unfortunately, this approach did not fit in at all with the culture of the host country. Of course, elements hostile to the United States did their best to capitalize upon this cross-cultural misunderstanding.

However, even Latin Americans friendly to us, while admiring the vice-president's courage, found themselves acutely embarrassed by the behavior of their people and ours in the ensuing difficulties.

Being comfortable in space

Like time and place, differing ideas of space traps for the uninformed. Without realizing it, almost any person raised in the United States is likely to give an unintended snub to a Latin American simply in the way we handle space relationships, particularly during conversations.

In North America, the "proper" distance to stand when talking to another adult male you do not know well is about two feet, at least in a formal business conversation. (Naturally, at a cocktail party, the distance shrinks, but anything under eight to ten inches is likely to provoke an apology or an attempt to back up.)

To a Latin American, with his cultural traditions and habits, a distance of two feet seems to him approximately what five feet would to us. To him, we seem distant and cold. To us, he gives an impression of pushiness.

As soon as a Latin American moves close enough for him to feel comfortable, we feel uncomfortable and edge back. We once observed a conversation between a Latin and a North American which began at one end of a forty-foot hall. At intervals we noticed them again, finally at the other end of the hall. This rather amusing displacement had been accomplished by an almost continual series of small backward steps on the part of the American, trying unconsciously to reach a comfortable talking distance, and an equal closing of the gap by the Latin American as he attempted to reach his accustomed conversation space.

Americans in their offices in Latin America tend to keep their native acquaintances at our distance—not the Latin American's distance— by taking up a position behind a desk or typewriter. The barricade approach to communication is practiced even by old hands in Latin America who are completely unaware of its cultural significance. They know only that they are comfortable without realizing that the distance and equipment unconsciously make the Latin American uncomfortable.

How class channels communication

We would be mistaken to regard the communication patterns which we observe around the world as no more than a miscellaneous collection of customs. The communication pattern of a given society is part of its culture pattern and can only be understood in that context.

We cannot undertake here to relate many examples of communication behavior to the underlying culture of the country. For the businessman, it might be useful to mention the difficulties in the relationship between social levels and the problems of information feedback from lower to higher levels in industrial organizations abroad.

There is in Latin America a pattern of human relations and union-management relations quite different from that with which we are familiar in the United States. Everett Hagen of MIT has noted the heavier emphasis upon line authority and the lesser development of staff organizations in Latin American plants when compared with North American counterparts. To a much greater extent than in the United States, the government becomes involved in the handling of all kinds of labor problems.

These differences seem to be clearly related to the culture and social organization of Latin America. We find there that society has been much more rigidly stratified that it has with us. As a corollary, we find a greater emphasis upon authority in family and the community.

This emphasis upon status and class distinction makes it very difficult for people of different levels to express themselves freely and frankly in discussion and argument. In the past, the pattern has been for the man of lower status to express deference to his superior in any face-to-fact contact. This is so even when everyone knows that the subordinate dislikes the superior. The culture of Latin America places a great premium upon keeping personal relations harmonious on the surface.

In the United States, we feel that it is not only desirable but natural to speak up to your superior, to tell the boss exactly what you think, even when you disagree with him. Of course, we do not always do this, but we think that we should, and we feel guilty if we fail to speak our minds frankly. When workers in our factories first get elected to local union office, they may find themselves quite self-conscious about speaking up to the boss and arguing grievances, Many of them, however, quickly learn to do it and enjoy the experience. American culture emphasizes the thrashing-out differences in face-to-face contacts. It de-emphasizes the importance of status. As a result, we have built institutions for handling industrial disputes on the basis of the local situation, and we rely on direct discussion by the parties immediately involved.

In Latin America, where it is exceedingly difficult for people to express their differences face to face and where status differences and authority are much more strongly emphasized than here, the workers tend to look to a third party—the government—to take care of their problems. Though the workers have great difficulty in thrashing out their problems with management, they find no difficulty in telling government representatives their problems. And it is to their government that they look for an authority to settle their grievances with management.

Status and class also decide whether business will be done on an individual or a group basis.

In the United States, we are growing more and more accustomed to working as members of large organizations. Despite this, we still assume that there is no need to send a delegation to do a job that one capable man might well handle.

In some other parts of the world, the individual cannot expect to gain the respect necessary to accomplish this purpose, no matter how capable he is, unless he brings along an appropriate number of associates.

In the United States, we would rarely think it necessary or proper to call on a customer in a group. He might well be antagonized by the hard sell. In Japan—as an example—the importance of the occasion and of the man is measured by whom he takes along.

This practice goes far down in the business and government hierarchies. Even a university professor is likely to bring one or two retainers along on academic business. Otherwise people might think that he was a nobody and that his affairs were of little moment.

Even when a group is involved in the United States, the head man is the spokesman and sets the tone. This is not always the case in Japan. Two young Japanese once requested an older American widely respected in Tokyo to accompany them so that they could "stand on his face." He was not expected to enter into the negotiation; his function was simply to be present as an indication that their intentions were serious.

Adjustment goes both ways

One need not have devoted his life to a study of various cultures to see that none of them is static. All are constantly changing and one element of change is the very fact that U.S. enterprise enter a foreign field. This is inevitable and may be constructive if we know how to utilize our knowledge. The problem is for us to be aware of our impact and to learn how to induce changes skillfully.

Rather than try to answer the general question of how two cultures interact, we will consider the key problem of personnel selection and development in two particular intercultural situations, both in Latin cultures.

One U.S. company had totally different experiences with "Smith" and "Jones" in the handling of its labor relations. The local union leaders were bitterly hostile to Smith, whereas they could not praise

Jones enough These were puzzling reactions to higher management. Smith seemed a fair-minded and understanding man; it was difficult to fathom how anyone could be bitter against him. At the same time, Jones did not appear to be currying favor by his generosity in giving away the firm's assets. To management, he seemed to be just as firm a negotiator as Smith.

The explanation was found in the two men's communcation characteristics. When the union leaders came in to negotiate with Smith, he would let them state their case fully and freely—without interruption, but also without comment. When they had finished, he would say, "I'm sorry. We can't do it." He would follow this blunt statement with a brief and entirely cogent explanation of his reasons for refusal. If the union leaders persisted in their arguments, Smith would paraphrase his first statement, calmly and succinctly. In either case, the discussion was over in a few minutes. The union leaders would storm out of Smith's office complaining bitterly about the cold and heartless man with whom they had to deal.

Jones handled the situation differently. His final conclusion was the same as Smith's but he would state it only after two or three hours of discussion. Furthermore, Jones participated actively in these discussions, questioning the union leaders for more information, relating the case in question to previous cases, philosophizing about labor relations and human rights and exchanging stories about work experience. When the discussion came to an end, the union leaders would leave the office, commenting on how warmhearted and understanding he was, and how confident they were that he would help them when it was possible for him to do so. They actually seemed more satisfied with a negative decision from Jones than they did with a hard-won concession from Smith.

This was clearly a case where the personality of Jones happened to match certain discernible requirements of the Latin American culture. It was happenstance in this case that Jones worked out and Smith did not, for by American standards both were top-flight men. Since a talent for the kind of negotiation that the Latin American considers graceful and acceptable can hardly be developed in a grown man (or perhaps even in a young one), the basic problem is one of personnel selection in terms of the culture where the candidate is to work.

The second case is more complicated because it involves much deeper intercultural adjustments. The management of the parent U.S. company concerned had learned—as have the directors of most large firms with good-sized installations overseas—that one cannot afford to have all of the top and middle-management positions manned by

North Americans. It is necessary to advance nationals up the overseas-management ladder as rapidly as their abilities permit. So the nationals have to learn not only the technical aspects of their jobs but also how to function at higher levels in the organization.

Latin culture emphasizes authority in the home, church, and community. Within the organization this produces a built-in hesitancy about speaking up to one's superiors. The initiative, the acceptance of responsibility which we value in our organizations had to be stimulated. How could it be done?

We observed one management man who had done a remarkable job of building up these very qualities in his general foremen and foremen. To begin with, he stimulated informal contacts between himself and these men through social events to which the men and their wives came. He saw to it that his senior North American assistants and their wives were also present. Knowing the language, he mixed freely with all. At the plant, he circulated about, dropped in not to inspect or check up, but to joke and to break down the great barrier that existed in the local traditions between authority and the subordinates.

Next, he developed a pattern of three-level meetings. At the top, he himself, the superintendents, and the general foremen. At the middle level, the superintendents, general foremen, and foremen. Then the general foremen, foremen, and workers.

At the top-level meeting, the American management chief set the pattern of encouraging his subordinates to challenge his own ideas, to come up with original thoughts. When his superintendents (also North Americans) disagreed with him, he made it clear that they were to state their objections fully. At first, the general foremen look surprised and uneasy. They noted, however, that the senior men who argued with the boss were encouraged and praised. Timorously, with great hesitation, they began to add their own suggestions. As time went on, they more and more accepted the new convention and pitched in without inhibition.

The idea of challenging the boss with constructive new ideas gradually filtered down to the second-and third-level meetings. It took a lot of time and gentle handling, but out of this approach grew an extraordinary morale. The native general foremen and foremen developed new pride in themselves, accepted new responsibilities, even reached out for more. They began to work to improve their capacities and to look forward to moving up in the hierarchy.

Conformity or adjustment?

To work with people, must we be just like them? Obviously not. If we try to conform completely, the Arab, the Latin American, the

Italian, whoever he might be, finds our behavior confusing and in-sincere. He suspects our motive. We are expected to be different. But we are also expected to respect and accept the other people as they are. And we may, without doing violence to our own personalities, learn to communicate with them by observing the unwritten patterns they are accustomed to.

To be aware that there are pitfalls in cross-cultural dealings is the first big step forward. An to accept the fact that our convictions are in no respect more eternally "right" than someone else's is another con-structive step.

Beyond these:

1. We can learn to control our-so-called frankness in a culture which puts a high value on maintaining pleasant surface relations.

2. We can avoid expressing quick decisions when their utterance without a long period of polite preparation would show disrespect.

3. We can be on the lookout for the conversation patterns of na-tionals of whatever country we are in and accustom ourselves to closer quarters than we are used to. (This is uncomfortable at first but under-standing the reason why it is important helps greatly.)

4. Where the situation demands it, we can learn to express our emotions more freely—most people find this rather exhilarating.

5. We can try to distinguish between the organizational practices which are really necessary to effectiveness and those that we employ from habit because they happen to be effective in the United States.

Research for organizational effectiveness

We have outlined a point of view the individual can seek to apply in order to increase his own effectiveness. Valuable as they may be, we must recognize the limitations of an individual approach. Since each family transported overseas represents an investment of between $25,-000 and $100,000 per year to the organization, the losses involved in poor selection or inadequate training can be enormous.

While no ready-made answers are now available, research can serve the organization both in *selection* and *training* of personnel.

It would be a mistake to assume that the ideal training program would fit just any administrator effectively into any given culture. We must assume that some personalties will fit more readily than others. By the time man reaches adulthood, his personality is rather solidly formed, and basic changes are difficult if not impossible to induce. It is therefore important to work to improve the selection process so that men with little chance of fitting into a foreign culture will not be sent where they are bound to fail.

Our Latin American case of Smith and Jones is relevant here. One who had observed Smith in his native setting should have been able to predict that he would not be effective in handling labor relations in Latin America. However, that statement is based upon the hindsight observation that there was a very obvious lack of fit between Smith's personality and the cultural requirements of his job. It remains for research men to devise schemes of observation and testing which will enable personnel men to base their selections upon criteria of personality *and* culture.

To what extent can training improve the effectiveness of individuals in intercultural communication? Training of men in overseas operations is going on all the time. So far as we know, little of it currently deals with the considerations outlined in this article. Until organizations are prepared to develop training along these lines—and support research on the effects of such training—we shall not know to what extent intercultural communications can be improved through training.

We do not mean to give the impression that behavioral scientists already have the knowledge regarding intercultural communication. What we have presented here is only a demonstration of the importance of the topic. We have not presented a systematic analysis of the problems of communication from culture A to culture B. We have just said in effect: "These are some of the things that are important. Watch out for them."

What more is needed? In the first place, the problem calls for a new emphasis in antropological research. In the past, anthropologists have been primarily concerned with the *internal* pattern of a given culture. In giving attention to intercultural problems, they have examined the impact of one culture upon another. Very little attention has been given to the actual communication process between representatives of different cultures.

Much could be learned, for example, if we observed North Americans in interaction with people of another culture. We would want also to be able to interview both parties to the interaction to study how A was interpreting B and how B was interpreting A. In this way we might discover points of friction and miscommunication whose existence we now do not even suspect. Such studies, furthermore, would provide systematic knowledge much more useful than the fragments provided in this article.

6

Leading:
Inspiration and Direction

Introduction

We said earlier that this second section is about communicating and influencing. Leaders are people who do a lot of communicating and influencing, so we place our chapter on leadership in this section. But we do so with some hesitancy, because leadership is still a messy construct, defined in many ways and researched from many different angles. So this chapter doesn't try for a thorough description of the role of leadership in the managing process. Instead, we have selected three papers that we think will give the reader a good picture of some of the dimensions of both the leadership process and the process of influence, as they apply to managing.

The first paper, by Douglas McGregor, is, as many readers know, one of the all-time classics of organizational behavior. McGregor was himself a leader, an influencer, of American and indeed of world attitudes toward the managing of human beings. The McGregor paper is aimed at the beliefs held by people in leadership positions. He makes the now-famous distinction between two such sets of beliefs which he labels Theory X and Theory Y. And he argues that Theory X assumptions (assumptions that humans are fundamentally lazy organisms, motivated only by states of deprivation) push one toward an authoritarian and perhaps punitive view of the managing process. While Theory Y assumptions (steeped in the notion that man is a knowing, growing, and searching organism) drive one toward much more participative practices in the leading of organizations.

The second paper, by Vroom and Yetton, goes on to try to "model" key aspects of the leadership process. Theirs is a *normative* model (a how-it-*should*-be-done model) rather than a descriptive one. Vroom and Yetton set up the following question: If you are the leader of a group, how should you go about making decisions? Under what conditions, for example, should you make your decision alone, without

consultation or participation by your subordinates? When is consulta-
tation in order? When should you try to get full participation by your
subordinates in the decision process? Vroom and Yetton follow a lot
of field research to end up with these ideas: Information is the key to
high-quality decisions; participation is the key to willing (for either)
acceptance of decisions. And both quality or acceptance may be important, depending on the problem at hand.

The third paper in this chapter switches to still another problem,
the problem of the movement of women into leadership roles in management. In her paper, Jean Lipman-Blumen argues that access to
key information (cf. Vroom and Yetton) and key people is a necessary
condition for achieving power in organizations, and that access to
such resources is often very difficult for women to attain in men's
organizations. Even if the formal organizational network officially
permits such access, the informal (what she calls the "homosocial")
male network is often inpenetrable for people who are not members of
the ingroup. Lipman-Blumen then goes on to offer some tips for
women (or for anyone on the outside looking in at the old boy network) on ways of breaking through to gain leadership and power in
organizational hierarchies.

The Human Side of Enterprise
Douglas M. McGregor

It has become trite to say that the most significant developments of the next quarter-century will take place not in the physical but in the social sciences, that industry—the economic organ of society—has the fundamental know-how to utilize physical science and technology for the material benefit of mankind, and that we must now learn how to utilize the social sciences to make our human organizations truly effective.

Many people agree in principle with such statements; but so far they represent a pious hope—and little else. Consider with me, if you will, something of what may be involved when we attempt to transform the hope into reality.

Problems and opportunities facing management

Let me begin with an analogy. A quarter-century ago basic conceptions of the nature of matter and energy had changed profoundly from what they had been since Newton's time. The physical scientists were persuaded that under proper conditions new and hitherto unimagined sources of energy could be made available to mankind.

We know what has happened since then. First came the bomb. Then, during the past decade, have come many other attempts to exploit these scientific discoveries—some successful, some not.

The point of my analogy, however, is that the application of theory in this field is a slow and costly matter. We expect it always to be thus. No one is impatient with the scientist because he cannot tell industry how to build a simple, cheap, all-purpose source of atomic energy today. That it will take at least another decade and the investment of billions of dollars to achieve results which are economically competitive with present sources of power is understood and accepted.

Reprinted from *Leadership and Motivation* by Douglas McGregor by permission of The M.I.T. Press, Cambridge, Massachusetts. © 1966, 1968, The M.I.T. Press.

It is transparently pretentious to suggest any *direct* similarity between the developments in the physical sciences leading to the harnessing of atomic energy and potential developments in the social sciences. Nevertheless, the analogy is not as absurd as it might appear to be at first glance.

To a lesser degree, and in a much more tentative fashion, we are in a position in the social sciences today like that of the physical sciences with respect to atomic energy in the thirties. We know that past conceptions of the nature of man are inadequate and in many ways incorrect. We are becoming quite certain that, under proper conditions, unimagined resources of creative human energy could become available within the organizational setting.

We cannot tell industrial management how to apply this new knowledge in simple, economic ways. We know it will require years of exploration, much costly development research, and a substantial amount of creative imagination on the part of management to discover how to apply this growing knowledge to the organization of human effort in industry.

May I ask that you keep this analogy in mind—overdrawn and pretentious though it may be—as a framework for what I have to say.

Management's task: Conventional view

The conventional conception of management's task in harnessing human energy to organizational requirements can be stated broadly in terms of three propositions. In order to avoid the complications introduced by a label, I shall call this set of propositions "Theory X":

1. Management is responsible for organizing the elements of productive enterprise—money, materals, equipment, people—in the interest of economic ends.

2. With respect to people, this is a process of directing their efforts, motivating them, controlling their actions, modifying their behavior to fit the needs of the organization.

3. Without this active intervention by management, people would be passive—even resistant—to organizational needs. They must therefore be persuaded, rewarded, punished, controlled—their activities must be directed. This is management's task—in managing subordinate managers or workers. We often sum it up by saying that management consists of getting things done through other people.

Behind this conventional theory there are several additional beliefs —less explicit, but widespread:

4. The average man is by nature indolent—he works as little as possible.

5. He lacks ambition, dislikes responsibility, prefers to be led.

6. He is inherently self-centered, indifferent to organizational needs.

7. He is by nature resistant to change.

8. He is gullible, not very bright, the ready dupe of the charlatan and the demagogue.

The human side of economic enterprise today is fashioned from propositions and beliefs such as these. Conventional organization structures, managerial policies, practices, and programs reflect these assumptions.

In accomplishing its task—with these assumptions as guides—management has conceived of a range of possibilties between two extremes.

The hard or the soft approach?

At one extreme, management can be "hard" or "strong." The methods for directing behavior involve coercion and threat (usually disguised), close supervision, tight controls over behavior. At the other extreme, management can be "soft" or "weak." The methods for directing behavior involve being permissive, satisfying people's demands, achieving harmony. Then they will be tractable, accept direction.

This range has been fairly completely explored during the past half-century, and management has learned some things from the exploration. There are difficulties in the "hard" approach. Force breeds counterforces: restriction of output, antagonism, militant unionism, subtle but effective sabotage of management objectives. This approach is especially difficult during times of full employment.

There are also difficulties in the "soft" approach. It leads frequently to the abdication of management—to harmony, perhaps, but to indifferent performance. People take advantage of the soft approach. They continually expect more, but they give less and less.

Currently, the popular theme is "firm but fair." This is an attempt to gain the advantages of both the hard and the soft approaches. It is reminiscent of Teddy Roosevelt's "speak softly and carry a big stick."

Is the conventional view correct?

The findings which are beginning to emerge from the social sciences challenge this whole set of beliefs about man and human nature and about the task of management. The evidence is far from conclusive, certainly, but it is suggestive. It comes from the laboratory, the clinic, the schoolroom, the home, and even to a limited extent from industry itself.

The social scientist does not deny that human behavior in industrial organization today is approximately what management perceives it to be. He has, in fact, observed it and studied it fairly extensively. But he is pretty sure that this behavior is not a consequence of man's inherent nature. It is a consequence rather of the nature of industrial organizations, of management philosophy, policy, and practice. The conventional approach of Theory X is based on mistaken notions of what is cause and what is effect.

"Well," you ask, "what then is the *true* nature of man? What evidence leads the social scientist to deny what is obvious?" And, if I am not mistaken, you are also thinking, "Tell me—simply, and without a lot of scientific verbiage—what you think you know that is so unusual. Give me—without a lot of intellectual claptrap and theoretical nonsense—some practical ideas which will enable me to improve the situation in my organization. And remember, I'm faced with increasing costs and narrowing profit margins. I want proof that such ideas won't result simply in new and costly human relations frills. I want practical results, and I want them now."

If these are your wishes, you are going to be disappointed. Such requests can no more be met by the social scientist today than could comparable ones with respect to atomic energy be met by the physicist fifteen years ago. I can, however, indicate a few of the reasons for asserting that conventional assumptions about the human side of enterprise are inadequate. And I can suggest—tentatively—some of the propositions that will comprise a more adequate theory of the management of people. The magnitude of the task that confronts us will then, I think, be apparent.

Man as a wanting animal

Perhaps the best way to indicate why the conventional approach of management is inadequate is to consider the subject of motivation. In discussing this subject I will draw heavily on the work of my colleague, Abraham Maslow of Brandeis University. His is the most fruitful approach I know. Naturally, what I have to say will be overgeneralized and will ignore important qualifications. In the time at our disposal, this is inevitable.

Physiological and safety needs

Man is a wanting animal—as soon as one of his needs is satisfied, another appears in its place. This process is unending. It continues from birth to death.

Man's needs are organized in a series of levels—a hierarchy of importance. At the lowest level, but preeminent in importance when they are thwarted, are his physiological needs. Man lives by bread alone, when there is no bread. Unless the circumstances are unusual, his needs for love, for status, for recognition are inoperative when his stomach has been empty for a while. But when he eats regularly and adequately, hunger ceases to be an important need. The sated man has hunger only in the sense that a full bottle has emptiness. The same is true of the other physiological needs of man—for rest, exercise, shelter, protection from the elements.

A satisfied need is not a motivator of behavior! This is a fact of profound significance. It is a fact which is regularly ignored in the conventional approach to the management of people. I shall return to it later. For the moment, one example will make my point. Consider your own need for air. Except as you are deprived of it, it has no appreciable motivating effect upon your behavior.

When the physiological needs are reasonably satisfied, needs at the next higher level begin to dominate man's behavior—to motivate him. These are called safety needs. They are needs for protection against danger, threat, deprivation. Some people mistakenly refer to these as needs for security. However, unless man is in a dependent relationship where he fears arbitrary deprivation, he does not demand security. The need is for the "fairest possible break." When he is confident of this, he is more than willing to take risks. But when he feels threatened or dependent, his greatest need is for guarantees, for protection, for security.

The fact needs little emphasis that since every industrial employee is in a dependent relationship, safety needs may assume considerable importance. Arbitrary management actions, behavior which arouses uncertainty with respect to continued employment or which reflects favoritism or discrimination, unpredictable administration of policy— these can be powerful motivators of the safety needs in the employment relationship *at every level* from worker to vice-president.

Social needs

When man's physiological needs are satisfied and he is no longer fearful about his physical welfare, his social needs become important motivators of his behavior—for belonging, for association, for acceptance by his fellows, for giving and receiving friendship and love.

Management knows today of the existence of these needs, but it often assumes quite wrongly that they represent a threat to the organization. Many studies have demonstrated that the tightly knit, cohesive work group may, under proper conditions, be far more effective than an equal number of separate individuals in achieving organizational goals.

Yet management, fearing group hostility to its own objectives, often goes to considerable lengths to control and direct human efforts in ways that are inimical to the natural "groupiness" of human beings. When man's social needs—and perhaps his safety needs, too—are thus thwarted, he behaves in ways which tend to defeat organizational objectives. He becomes resistant, antagonistic, uncooperative. But this behavior is a consequence, not a cause.

Ego needs

Above the social needs—in the sense that they do not become motivators until lower needs are reasonably satisfied—are the needs of greatest significance to management and to man himself. They are the egoistic needs, and they are of two kinds:

1. Those needs that relate to one's self-esteem—needs for self-confidence, for independence, for achievement, for competence, for knowledge.

2. Those needs that relate to one's reputation—needs for status, for recognition, for appreciation, for the deserved respect of one's fellows.

Unlike the lower needs, these are rarely satisfied; man seeks indefinitely for more satisfaction of these needs once they have become important to him. But they do not appear in any significant way until physiological, safety, and social needs are all reasonably satisfied.

The typical industrial organization offers few opportunities for the satisfaction of these egoistic needs to people at lower levels in the hierarchy. The conventional methods of organizing work, particularly in mass production industries, give little heed to these aspects of human motivation. If the practices of scientific management were deliberately calculated to thwart these needs—which, of course, they are not—they could hardly accomplish this purpose better than they do.

Self-fulfillment needs

Finally—a capstone, as it were, on the hierarchy of man's needs—there are what we may call the needs for self-fulfillment. These are the needs for realizing one's own potentialities, for continued self-development, for being creative in the broadest sense of that term.

It is clear that the conditions of modern life give only limited opportunity for these relatively weak needs to obtain expression. The deprivation most people experience with respect to other lower-level needs diverts their energies into the struggle to satisfy *those* needs, and the needs for self-fulfillment remain dormant.

The dynamics of motivation

Now, briefly, a few general comments about motivation:

We recognize readily enough that a man suffering from a severe dietary deficiency is sick. The deprivation of physiological needs has behavioral consequences. The same is true—although less well recognized—of deprivation of higher-level needs. The man whose needs for safety, association, independence, or status are thwarted is sick just as surely as is he who has rickets. And his sickness will have behavioral consequences. We will be mistaken if we attribute his resultant passivity, his hostility, his refusal to accept responsibility to his inherent "human nature." These forms of behavior are *symptoms* of illness—of deprivation of his social and egoistic needs.

The man whose lower-level needs are satisfied is not motivated to satisfy those needs any longer. For practical purposes they exist no longer. (Remember my point about your need for air.) Management often asks, "Why aren't people more productive? We pay good wages, provide good working conditions, have excellent fringe benefits, and steady employment. Yet people do not seem to be willing to put forth more than minimum effort."

The fact that management has provided for these physiological and safety needs has shifted the motivational emphasis to the social and perhaps to the egoistic needs. Unless there are opportunities *at work* to satisfy these higher-level needs, people will be deprived; and their behavior will reflect this deprivation. Under such conditions, if management continues to focus its attention on physiological needs, its efforts are bound to be ineffective.

People *will* make insistent demands for more money under these conditions. It becomes more important than ever to buy the material goods and services which can provide limited satisfaction of the thwarted needs. Although money has only limited value in satisfying many higher-level needs, it can become the focus of interest if it is the *only* means available.

The carrot and stick approach

The carrot and stick theory of motivation (like Newtonian physical theory) works reasonably well under certain circumstances. The *means* for satisfying man's physiological and (within limits) his safety needs can be provided or withheld by management. Employment itself is such a means, and so are wages, working conditions, and benefits. By these means the individual can be controlled so long as he is struggling for subsistence. Man lives for bread alone when there is no bread.

But the carrot and stick theory does not work at all once man has reached an adequate subsistence level and is motivated primarily by higher needs. Management cannot provide a man with self-respect, or with the respect of his fellows, or with the satisfaction of needs for self-fulfillment. It can create conditions such that he is encouraged and enabled to seek such satisfactions *for himself,* or it can thwart him by failing to create those conditions.

But this creation of conditions is not "control." It is not a good device for directing behavior. And so management finds itself in an odd position. The high standard of living created by our modern technological know-how provides quite adequately for the satisfaction of physiological and safety needs. The only significant exception is where management practices have not created confidence in a "fair break"— and thus where safety needs are thwarted. But by making possible the satisfaction of low-level needs, management has deprived itself of the ability to use as motivators the devices on which conventional theory has taught it to rely—rewards, promises, incentives, or threats and other coercive devices.

Neither hard nor soft

The philosophy of management by direction and control—*regardless of whether it is hard or soft*—is inadequate to motivate because the human needs on which this approach relies are today unimportant motivators of behavior. Direction and control are essentially useless in motivating people whose important needs are social and egoistic. Both the hard and the soft approach fail today because they are simply irrelevant to the situation.

People, deprived of opportunities to satisfy at work the needs which are now important to them, behave exactly as we might predict—with indolence, passivity, resistance to change, lack of responsibility, willingness to follow the demagogue, unreasonable demands for economic benefits. It would seem that we are caught in a web of our own weaving.

In summary, then, of these comments about motivation: Management by direction and control—whether implemented with the hard, the soft, or the firm but fair approach—fails under today's conditions to provide effective motivation of human effort toward organizational objectives. It fails because direction and control are useless methods of motivating people whose physiological and safety needs are reasonably satisfied and whose social, egoistic, and self-fulfillment needs are predominant.

A new perspective

For these and many other reasons, we require a different theory of the task of managing people based on more adequate assumptions about human nature and human motivation. I am going to be so bold as to suggest the broad dimensions of such a theory. Call it "Theory Y," if you will:

1. Management is responsible for organizing the elements of productive enterprise—money, materials, equipment, people—in the interest of economic ends.

2. People are *not* by nature passive or resistant to organizational needs. They have become so as a result of experience in organizations.

3. The motivation, the potential for development, the capacity for assuming responsibility, the readiness to direct behavior toward organizational goals are all present in people. Management does not put them there. It is a responsibility of management to make it possible for people to recognize and develop these human characteristics for themselves.

4. The essential task of management is to arrange organizational conditions and methods of operation so that people can achieve their own goals *best* by directing *their* own efforts toward organizational objectives.

This is a process primarily of creating opportunities, releasing potential, removing obstacles, encouraging growth, providing guidance. It is what Peter Drucker has called "management by objectives" in contrast to "management by control."

And I hasten to add that it does *not* involve the abdication of management, the absence of leadership, the lowering of standards, or the other characteristics usually associated with the "soft" approach under Theory X. Much to the contrary. It is no more possible to create an organization today which will be a fully effective application of this theory than it was to build an atomic power plant in 1945. There are many formidable obstacles to overcome.

Some difficulties

The conditions imposed by conventional organization theory and by the approach of scientific management for the past half-century have tied men to limited jobs which do not utilize their capabilities, have discouraged the acceptance of responsibility, have encouraged passivity, have eliminated meaning from work. Man's habits, attitudes, expectations—his whole conception of membership in an industrial organization—have been conditioned by his experience under these circumstances. Change in the direction of Theory Y will be slow, and it will require extensive modification of the attitudes of management and workers alike.

People today are accustomed to being directed, manipulated, controlled in industrial organizations and to finding satisfaction for their social, egoistic, and self-fulfillment needs away from the job. This is true of much of management as well as of workers. Genuine "industrial citizenship"—to borrow again a term from Drucker—is a remote and unrealistic idea, the meaning of which has not even been considered by most members of industrial organizations.

Another way of saying this is that Theory X places exclusive reliance upon external control of human behavior, while Theory Y relies heavily on self-control and self-direction. It is worth noting that this difference is the difference between treating people as children and treating them as mature adults. After generations of the former, we cannot expect to shift to the latter overnight.

Applications of the theory

Before we are overwhelmed by the obstacles, let us remember that the application of theory is always slow. Progress is usually achieved in small steps.

Consider with me a few innovative ideas which are entirely consistent with Theory Y and which are today being applied with some success:

Decentralization and delegation

These are ways of freeing people from the too-close control of conventional organization, giving them a degree of freedom to direct their own activities, to assume responsibility, and, importantly, to satisfy their egoistic needs. In this connection, the flat organization of Sears, Roebuck and Company provides an interesting example. It forces "management by objectives" since it enlarges the number of people reporting to a manager until he cannot direct and control them in the conventional manner.

Job enlargement

This concept, pioneered by I.B.M. and Detroit Edison, is quite consistent with Theory Y. It encourages the acceptance of responsibility at the bottom of the organization; it provides opportunities for satisfying social and egoistic needs. In fact, the reorganization of work at the factory level offers one of the more challenging opportunities for innovation consistent with Theory Y. The studies by A.T.M. Wilson and his associates of British coal mining and Indian textile manufacture have added appreciably to our understanding of work organization. Moreover, the economic and psychological results achieved by this work have been substantial.

Participation and consultative management

Under proper conditions these results provide encouragement to people to direct their creative energies toward organizational objectives, give them some voice in decisions that affect them, provide significant opportunities for the satisfaction of social and egoistic needs. I need only mention the Scanlon Plan as the outstanding embodiment of these ideas in practice.

The not infrequent failure of such ideas as these to work as well as expected is often attributable to the fact that a management has "bought the idea" but applied it within the framework of Theory X and its assumptions.

Delegation is not an effective way of exercising management by control. Participation becomes a farce when it is applied as a sales gimmick or a device for kidding people into thinking they are important. Only the management that has confidence in human capacities and is itself directed toward organizational objectives rather than toward the preservation of personal power can grasp the implications of this emerging theory. Such management will find and apply successfully other inovative ideas as we move slowly toward the full implementation of a theory like Y.

Performance appraisal

Before I stop, let me mention one other practical application of Theory Y which—while still highly tentative—may well have important consequences. This has to do with performance appraisal within the ranks of management. Even a cursory examination of conventional programs of performance appraisal will reveal how completely consistent they are with Theory X. In fact, most such programs tend to treat the individual as though he were a product under inspection on the assembly line.

Take the typical plan: substitute "product" for "subordinate being appraised," substitute "inspector" for "superior making the appraisal," substitute "rework" for "training or development," and, except for the attributes being judged, the human appraisal process will be virtually indistinguishable from the product inspection process.

A few companies—among them General Mills, Ansul Chemical, and General Electric—have been experimenting with approaches which involve the individual in setting "targets" or objectives *for himself* and in a *self*-evaluation of performance semiannually or annually. Of course, the superior plays an important leadership role in this process —one, in fact, which demands substantially more competence than the conventional approach. The role is, however, considerably more congenial to many managers than the role of "judge" or "inspector" which is forced upon them by conventional performance. Above all, the individual is encouraged to take a greater responsibility for planning and appraising his own contribution to organizational objectives; and the accompanying effects on egoistic and self-fulfillment needs are substantial. This approach to performance appraisal represents one more innovative idea being explored by a few managements who are moving toward the implementation of Theory Y.

Conclusion

And now I am back where I began. I share the belief that we could realize substantial improvements in the effectiveness of industrial organizations during the next decade or two. Moreover, I believe the social sciences can contribute much to such developments. We are only beginning to grasp the implications of the growing body of knowledge in these fields. But if this conviction is to become a reality instead of a pious hope, we will need to view the process much as we view the process of releasing the energy of the atom for constructive human ends—as a slow, costly, sometimes discouraging approach toward a goal which would seem to many to be quite unrealistic.

The ingenuity and the perseverance of industrial management in the pursuit of economic ends have changed many scientific and technological dreams into commonplace realities. It is now becoming clear that the application of these same talents to the human side of enterprise will not only enhance substantially these materialistic achievements but will bring us one step closer to "the good society." Shall we get on with the job?

A Normative Model of
Leadership Style
Victor H. Vroom and
Philip Yetton

Introduction

One of the most persistent and controversial issues in the study of
management concerns the issue of participation in decision making by
subordinates. Traditional models of the managerial process have been
autocratic in nature. The manager makes decisions on matters within
his area of freedom, issues orders or directives to his subordinates, and
monitors their performance to ensure conformity with these directives.
Scientific management, from its early developments in time and motion
study to its contemporary manifestations in linear and heuristic programming, has contributed to this centralization of decision making in
organizations by focusing on the development of methods by which
managers can make more rational decisions, substituting objective
measurements and empirically validated methods for casual judgments.

Most social psychologists and other behavorial scientists who have
turned their attention toward the implications of psychological and
social processes for the practice of management have called for greater
participation by subordinates in the problem-solving and decision-
making process. Pointing to evidence of restriction of output and lack
of involvement under traditional managerial systems, they have argued
for greater influence in decision making on the part of those who are
held responsible for decision execution.

The empirical evidence provides some, but not overwhelming, support for beliefs in the efficacy of participative management. Field experiments on rank-and-file workers by Coch and French,[1] Bavelas,[2]

Abridged from Victor H. Vroom and Philip Yetton, *Leadership and Decision
Making* (Pittsburgh: University of Pittsburgh Press, 1973), by permission of the
publisher and authors. © 1973 by the University of Pittsburgh Press.
1. L. Coch and J. R. P. French, Jr., "Overcoming Resistance to Change."
Human Relations 1 (1948): 512–32.
2. Reported in J. R. P. French, Jr., "Field Experiments: Changing Group

and Strauss[3] indicate that impressive increases in productivity can be brought about by giving workers an opportunity to participate in decision making and goal setting. In addition, several correlational field studies[4] indicate positive relationships between the amount of influence which supervisors afford their subordinates in decisions which affect them and individual or group performance. On the other hand, in an experiment conducted in a Norwegian factory, French et al.[5] found no significant differences in production between workers who did and workers who did not participate in decisions regarding introduction of changes in work methods; and in a recent laboratory experiment, Sales and Rosen[6] found no significant differences between groups exposed to democratic and autocratic supervision. To complicate the picture further, Morse and Reimer[7] compared the effects of two programs of change, each of which was introduced in two divisions of the clerical operations of a large insurance company. One of the programs involved increased participation in decision making by rank-and-file workers, while the other involved increased hierarchical control. The results show a significant increase in productivity under both programs, with the hierarchically controlled program producing the greater increase.

Reconciliation of these discrepant findings is not an easy task. It is made complex by different empirical interpretations of the term "participation"[8] and by great differences in the situations in which it is applied. It appears highly likely that an increase in participation of subordinates in decision making may increase productivity under some circumstances but decrease productivity under other circumstances. Identification of the situational conditions which determine the efficacy of participative management requires the specification of

Productivity," in J. G. Miller, ed., *Experiments in Social Process: A Symposium on Social Psychology* (New York: McGraw-Hill, 1950), pp. 79–96.

3. Reported in W. F. Whyte, *Money and Motivation* (New York: Harper, 1955).

4. D. Katz, N. Maccoby, and Nancy C. Morse, *Productivity, Supervision and Morale in an Office Situation* (Ann Arbor: University of Michigan, Institute for Social Research, 1950); V. H. Vroom, *Some Personality Determinants of the Effects of Participation* (Englewood Cliffs, N. J.: Prentice-Hall, 1960).

5. J. R. P. French, Jr., J. Israel, and D. As, "An Experiment on Participation in a Norwegian Factory," *Human Relations* 13 (1960): 3–9.

6. S. M. Sales and N. A. Rosen, "A Laboratory Investigation of the Effectiveness of Two Industrial Supervisory Patterns" (unpublished manuscript, Cornell University, 1965).

7. Nancy C. Morse and E. Reimer, "The Experimental Change of a Major Organizational Variable," *Journal of Abnormal Social Pschology* 52 (1956): 120–29.

8. G. Strauss, "Some Notes on Power Equalization," in H. J. Leavitt, ed., *The Social Science of Organizations* (Englewood Cliffs, N. J.: Prentice-Hall, 1963), pp. 39–84.

the decision-making processes which it entails and of the various mechanisms by which it may influence the extent to which the formal objectives of the organization are attained.

The conclusion appears inescapable that participation in decision making has consequences which vary from one situation to another. Given the potential importance of this conclusion for the study of leadership and its significance to the process of management, it appears to be critical for social scientists to begin to develop some definitions of the circumstances under which participation in decision making may contribute to or hinder organizational effectiveness. These could then be translated into guidelines of potential value to managers in choosing the leadership styles to fit the demands of the situations which they encounter.

In this chapter, one approach to dealing with this important problem will be described. A normative model is developed which is consistent with existing empirical evidence concerning the consequences of participation and which purports to specify a set of rules which should be used in determining the form and amount of participation in decision making by subordinates to be used in different classes of situations.

Basic assumptions

1. The normative model should be constructed in such a way as to be of potential value to managers or leaders in determining which leadership styles they should employ in each of the various situations that they encounter in carrying out their formal leadership roles. Consequently, it should deal with behaviors which are within their repertoire and their control.

2. There are a number of discrete social processes by which organizational problems can be translated into solutions and these processes vary in terms of the potential amount of participation by subordinates in the problem-solving process.

The term "participation" has been used in a number of different ways. Perhaps the most influential definitions have been those of French et al.[9] and Vroom,[10] who define participation as a process of joint decision making by two or more parties. The amount of participation of any individual is the amount of influence he has on the decisions and plans agreed upon. Given the existence of a property such as participation which varies from high to low, it should be possible to define leadership styles or behaviors which represent clear alterna-

9. French, Israel, and As, "An Experiment on Participation."
10. Vroom, *Some Personality Determinants.*

tive processes for making decisions which can be related to the amount of participation each process affords the managers' subordinates.

A taxonomy of leadership style created for normative purposes should distinguish among methods which are likely to have different outcomes but should not be so elaborate that leaders are unable to determine which style they are employing in any given instance. The taxonomy to be used in the normative model is shown in table 1.

It should be noted that the styles are arranged in two columns corresponding to their applicability to problems which involve the entire group or some subset of it (hereafter called group problems) or a single subordinate (hereafter called individual problems). If a problem or decision clearly affects only one subordinate, the leader would choose among the methods shown in the right-hand column; if it had potential effects on the entire group (or subset of it), he would choose among the methods shown in the left-hand column. The styles in both columns are arranged from top to bottom in terms of the opportunity for subordinates to influence the solution to the problem. (The principle behind the numbering system is as follows: The letters A, C, G, and D stand for autocratic, consultative, group, and delegation. The numerals I and II denote variations on the basic decision processes.)

3. No single leadership style is applicable to all situations; the function of a normative model should be to provide a framework for the analysis of situational requirements which can be translated into prescriptions of leadership styles.

The fact that the most effective leadership method or style is dependent on the situation is becoming widely recognized by behavorial scientists interested in problems of leadership and administration. A decision-making process which is optimal for a quarterback on a football team making decisions under severe time constraints is likely to be far from optimal when used by a dean introducing a new curriculum to be implemented by his faculty. Even the advocates of participative management have noted this "situational relativity" of leadership styles. Thus, Argyris writes:

> No one leadership style is the most effective. Each is probably effective under a given set of conditions. Consequently, I suggest that effective leaders are those who are capable of behaving in many different leadership styles, depending on the requirements of reality as they and others perceive it. I call this "reality-centered" leadership.[11]

11. C. Argyris, *Interpersonal Competence and Organizational Effectiveness* (Homewood, Ill.: Irwin-Dorsey, 1962), p. 81.

Table 1. Decision Methods for Group and Individual Problems

Group Problems		*Individual Problems*	
AI	You solve the problem or make the decision yourself, using information available to you at that time.	AI	You solve the problem or make the decision yourself, using information available to you at that time.
AII	You obtain the necessary information from subordinates, then decide on the solution to the problem yourself. You may or may not tell subordinates what the problem is in getting the information from them. The role played by your subordinates in making the decision is clearly one of providing the necessary information to you, rather than generating or evaluating alternative solutions.	AII	You obtain necessary information from the subordinate, then decide on solution to problem yourself. You may or may not tell the subordinate what the problem is in getting the information from him. The role played by the subordinate in making the decision is clearly one of providing the necessary information to you, rather than generating or evaluating alternative solutions.
CI	You share the problem with relevant subordinates individually, getting their ideas and suggestions without bringing them together as a group. Then you make the decision which may or may not reflect your subordinates' influence.	CI	You share the problem with the subordinate, getting his ideas and suggestions, then you make the decision which may or may not reflect your subordinate's influence.
CII	You share the problem with your subordinates as a group, collectively obtaining their ideas and suggestions. Then, you make the decision which may or may not reflect your subordinates' influence.		
GII	You share the problem with your subordinates as a group. Together you generate and evaluate alternatives and attempt to reach agreement (consensus) on a solution.	GI	You share the problem with your subordinate and together you analyze the problem and arrive at a mutually agreeable solution.
		DI	You delegate the problem to your subordinate, providing him with any relevant information that you possess, but giving him responsibility for solving the problem by himself. You may or may not request him to tell you what solution he has reached.

It is necessary to go beyond noting the importance of situational factors and begin to move toward a road map or normative model which attempts to prescribe the most appropriate leadership style for different kinds of situations. The most comprehensive treatment of situational factors as determinants of the effectiveness and efficiency of participation in decision making is found in the work of Tannenbaum and Schmidt.[12] They list and discuss a large number of variables including attributes of the manager, his subordinates, and the situation, which ought to enter into the manager's decision about the degree to which he should share his power with his subordinates. But they do not go beyond this inventory of variables to show how these might be combined and translated into different forms of actions.

4. The most appropriate unit for the analysis of the situation is the particular problem to be solved and the context in which the problem occurs.

While it is becoming widely recognized that different situations require different leadership methods, there is less agreement concerning the appropriate units for the analysis of the situation. One approach is to assume that the situations which interact with or condition the choice and effectiveness of different leadership styles correspond to the environment of the system. Alternatively, one might assume that the critical features of the situation concern the role of the leader, including his relations with his subordinates.

The approach taken here is to utilize the properties of the problem to be solved as the most critical situational dimensions for determining the appropriate form or amount of participation. Different prescriptions would be made for a given leader for different problems within a given role. It should be noted that constructing a normative model with the problem rather than the role or any organizational differences as the unit of analysis does not rule out the possibility that different roles and organizations may involve different distributions of problem types and which in aggregate may require different modal styles or levels of participation.

5. The leadership method used in response to one situation should not constrain the method or style used in other situations.

This assumption is necessary to make possible the construction of a normative model founded on problem differences. It may seem inconsistent with the view, first proposed by McGregor,[13] that consis-

12. R. Tannenbaum and W. H. Schmidt, "How to Choose a Leadership Pattern," *Harvard Business Review* 36 (1958): 95–101.
13. D. McGregor, "Getting Effective Leadership in the Industrial Organization," *Advanced Management* 9 (1944): 148–53.

tency in leadership style is desirable because it enables subordinates to predict or anticipate their superiors' behavior and to adapt to it. However, predictability does not preclude variability. There are many variable phenomena which can be predicted quite well because the rules or processes which govern them are understood. The antithesis of predictability is randomness and, if McGregor is correct, a normative model to regulate choices among alternative leadership styles should be deterministic rather than stochastic. The model developed here is deterministic; the normatively prescribed style for a given problem type is a constant.

Conceptual and empirical basis of the model

A model designed to regulate, in some rational way, choices among the leadership styles shown in table 1 should be based on sound empirical evidence concerning the likely consequences of the styles. The more complete the empirical base of knowledge, the greater the certainty with which one can develop the model and the greater will be its usefulness. In this section we will restrict ourselves to the development of a model concerned only with group problems and, hence, will use only the methods shown in the left-hand column of table 1. To aid in this analysis, it is important to distinguish three classes of outcomes which bear on the ultimate effectiveness of decisions. These are:

1. The quality or rationality of the decision.
2. The acceptance of commitment on the part of subordinates to execute the decision effectively.
3. The amount of time required to make the decision.

The evidence regarding the effects of participation on each of these outcomes or consequences has been reviewed elsewhere.

The results suggest that allocating problem-solving and decision-making tasks to entire groups as compared with the leader or manager in charge of the groups, requires a greater investment of man hours but produces higher acceptance of decisions and a higher probability that the decisions will be executed efficiently. Differences between these two methods in quality of decisions and in elapsed time are inconclusive and probably highly variable. . . . It would be naïve to think that group decision making is always more "effective" than autocratic decision making, or vice versa; the relative effectiveness of these two extreme methods depends both on the weights attached to quality, acceptance, and time variables and on differences in amounts of these outcomes resulting from these methods, neither of which is invariant from one situation to another. The critics and proponents of participative management would do well to direct their efforts toward identifying the properties of situations in which different decision-making approaches are effective rather than wholesale condemnation or deification of one approach.[14]

Stemming from this review, an attempt has been made to identify these properties of the situation or problem which will be the basic elements in the model. These problem attributes are of two types: (1) those which specify the importance of quality and acceptance for a particular problem (see A and D below) and (2) those which, on the basis of available evidence, have a high probability of moderating the effects of participation on each of these outcomes (see B, C, E, G, and H below). The following are the problem attributes used in the present from of the model.

A. The importance of the quality of the decision.
B. The extent to which the leader possesses sufficient information/ expertise to make a high-quality decision by himself.
C. The extent to which subordinates, taken collectively, have the necessary information to generate a high-quality decision.
D. The extent to which the problem is structured.
E. The extent to which acceptance or commitment on the part of subordinates is critical to the effective implementation of the decision.
F. The prior probability that the leader's autocratic decision will receive acceptance by subordinates.
G. The extent to which subordinates are motivated to attain the organizational goals as represented in the objectives explicit in the statement of the problem.
H. The extent to which subordinates are likely to be in disagreement over preferred solutions.

Table 2 shows the same eight problem attributes expressed in the form of questions which might be used by a leader in diagnosing a particular problem before choosing his leadership style. In phrasing the questions, technical language has been held to a minimum. Furthermore, the questions have been phrased in yes-no form, translating the continuous variables defined above into dichotomous variables. For example, instead of attempting to determine how important the deci-

14. V. H. Vroom, "Industrial Social Psychology," in G. Lindsey and E. Aronson, eds., *Handbook of Social Psychology* (Reading, Mass.: Addison-Wesley, 1970). chap. 5, pp. 239–40.

sion quality is to the effectiveness of the decision (attribute A), the leader is asked in the first question to judge whether there is any quality component to the problem. Similarly, the difficult task of specifying exactly how much information the leader possesses that is relevant to the decision (attribute B) is reduced to a simple judgment by the leader concerning whether he has sufficient information to make a high-quality decision.

Table 2. Problem Attributes

A. If decision were accepted, would it make a difference?
B. Do I have sufficient information to make a high-quality decision?
C. Do subordinates have sufficient additional information to result in a high-quality decision?
D. Do I know exactly what information is needed, who possesses it, and how to collect it?
E. Is acceptance of decision by subordinates critical to effective implementation?
F. If you were to make the decision by yourself, is it certain that it would be accepted by your subordinates?
G. Can subordinates be trusted to base solutions on organizational considerations?
H. Is conflict among subordinates likely in preferred solutions?

Expressing what are obviously continuous variables in dichotomous form greatly simplifies the problem of developing a model incorporating these attributes which can be used by leaders. It sidesteps the problem of scaling each problem attribute and reduces the complexities of the judgments required of leaders.

It has been found that managers can diagnose a situation quite quickly and accurately by answering this set of eight questions concerning it. But how can such responses generate a prescription concerning the most effective leadership style or decision process? What kind of normative model of participation in decision making can be built from this set of problem attributes?

A normative model of leadership styles

Let us assume that you are a manager faced with a concrete problem to be solved. We will also assume that you have judged that this problem could potentially affect more than one of your subordinates. Hence, it is what we have defined as a group problem, and you have to choose among the five decision processes (AI, AII, CI, CII GII) shown at the left side of table 1.

On a priori grounds any one of these five decision processes could be called for. The judgments you have made concerning the status of each of the problem's attributes can be used to define a set of feasible alternatives. This occurs through a set of rules which eliminate decision processes from the feasible set under certain specifiable conditions.

The rules are intended to protect both the quality and acceptance of the decision. In the present form of the model, there are three rules which protect decision quality and four which protect acceptance. The seven rules are presented here both as verbal statements and the more formal language of set theory. In the set theoretic formulation, the letters refer to the problem attributes as stated in question form in table 2. $\overline{A}$ signifies that the answer to question A for a particular problem is yes; A signifies that the answer to that question is no; ∩ signifies intersection; ⟹ signifies "implies"; and $\overline{AI}$ signifies not AI. Thus $A \cap \overline{B} \Rightarrow \overline{AI}$ may be read as follows; when both the answer to question A is yes and the answer to question B is no, AI is eliminated from the feasible set.

1. *The Information Rule.* If the leader does not possess enough information or expertise to solve the problem by himself, AI is eliminated from the the feasible set. (Its use risks a low-quality decision.) $(A \cap \overline{B} \Rightarrow \overline{AI})$

2. *The Trust Rule.* If the subordinates cannot be trusted to base their efforts to solve the problems on organizational goals, GII is eliminated from the feasible set. (Alternatives which eliminate the leader's final control over the decision reached may jeopardize the quality of the decision.) $(A \cap \overline{G} \Rightarrow \overline{GII})$

3. *The Unstructured Problem Rule.* If the leader lacks the necessary information or expertise to solve the problem by himself, and if the problem is unstructured, i.e., he does not know exactly what information is needed and where it is located, the method used must provide not only for him to collect the information but to do so in an efficient and effective manner. Methods which involve interaction among all subordinates with full knowledge of the problem are likely to be both more efficient and more likely to generate a high-quality solution to the problem. Under these conditions, AI, AII, and CI are eliminated from the feasible set. (AI does not provide for him to collect the necessary information, and AII and CI represent more cumbersome, less effective, and less efficient means of bringing the necessary information to bear on the solution of the problem than methods which do permit those with the necessary information to interact.) $(A \cap \overline{B} \cap \overline{D} \Rightarrow \overline{AI}, \overline{AII}, \overline{CI})$

4. *The Acceptance Rule.* If the acceptance of the decision by sub-

ordinates is critical to effective implementation and if it is not certain that an autocratic decision made by the leader would receive that acceptance, AI and AII are eliminated from the feasible set. (Neither provides an opportunity for subordinates to participate in the decision and both risk the necessary acceptance.) $(E \cap \overline{F} \Rightarrow \overline{AI}, \overline{AII})$

5. *The Conflict Rule.* If the acceptance of the decision is critical, and an autocratic decision is not certain to be accepted, and subordinates are likely to be in conflict or disagreement over the appropriate solution, AI AII, and CI are eliminated from the feasible set. (The method used in solving the problem should enable those in disagreement to resolve their differences with full knowledge of the problem. Accordingly, under these conditions, AI, AII, and CI, which involve no interaction or only "one-on-one" relationships and therefore provide no opportunity for those in conflict to resolve their differences, are eliminated from the feasible set. Their use runs the risk of leaving some of the subordinates with less than the necessary commitment to the final decision.) $(E \cap \overline{F} \cap H \Rightarrow \overline{AI}, \overline{AII}, \overline{CI})$

6. *The Fairness Rule.* If the quality of decision is unimportant, and if accepance is critical and not certain to result from an autocratic decision, AI, AII, CI, and CII are eliminated from the feasible set. (The method used should maximize the probability of acceptance as this is the only relevant consideration in determining the effectiveness of the decision. Under these circumstances AI, AII, CI, and CII which create less acceptance or commitment than GII are eliminated from the feasible set. To use them is to run the risk of getting less than the needed acceptance of the decision.) $(\overline{A} \cap E \cap \overline{F} \Rightarrow \overline{AI}, \overline{AII}, \overline{CI}, \overline{CII})$

7. *The Acceptance Priority Rule.* If acceptance is critical, not assured by an autocratic decision and if subordinates can be trusted, AI, AII, CI, and CII are eliminated from the feasible set. (Methods which provide equal partnership in the decision-making process can provide greater acceptance without risking decision quality. Use of any method other than GII results in an unnecessary risk that the decision will not be fully accepted or receive the necessary commitment on the part of subordinates.) $(E \cap \overline{F} \cup G \Rightarrow \overline{AI}, \overline{AII}, \overline{CI}, \overline{CII})$

Application of these rules to a problem is aided by their pictorial representation in the form of a decision tree. Figure 1 shows a simple decision tree which serves this purpose.

The problem attributes are arranged along the top of the figure. To apply the rules to a particular problem one starts at the left-hand side and works toward the right, asking oneself the question immediately above any box that is encountered. When a terminal node is reached, the number designates the problem type which in turn designates a set of methods which remains feasible after the rules have been applied.[15] It can be seen that this method of representing the decision tree generates fourteen problem types. Problem type is a nominal variable designating classes of problems generated by the paths which lead to the terminal nodes. Thus, all problems which have no quality requirements and in which acceptance is not critical are defined as type 1; all problems which have no quality requirement in which acceptance is critical but the prior probability of acceptance of the leader's decision is high are defined as type 2; and so on.

The feasible set for each of the fourteen problem types is shown in table 3. It can be seen that there are some problem types for which

Table 3. Problem Types and the Feasible Set of Leadership Styles

Problem Type	Acceptable Methods
1	AI, AII, CI, CII, GII
2	AI, AII, CI, CII, GII
3	GII
4	AI, AII, CI, CII, GII*
5	AI, AII, CI, CII, GII*
6	GII
7	CII
8	CI, CII
9	AII, CI, CII, GII*
10	AII, CI, CII, GII*
11	CII, GII*
12	GII
13	CII
14	CIII, GII*

*Within the feasible set only when the answer to question G is yes.

only one method remains in the feasible set, others for which two methods remain feasible, and still others for which five methods remain feasible. It should be recalled that the feasible set is defined as the set of methods which remains after all those which violate rules designated to protect the quality and acceptance of the decision have been excluded.

Choosing among alternatives in the feasible set

When more than one method remains in the feasible set, there are a number of alternative decision rules which might dictate the choice

15. Rule 2 has not been applied to problem types 4, 9, 10, 11, and 14. This rule eliminates GII from the feasible set when the answer to question G is no. Thus, we can distinguish two variants of each of these types.

among them. One, which will be examined in greatest depth, utilizes
the number of man hours used in solving the problem as the basis for
choice. Given a set of methods with equal liklihood of meeting both
quality and acceptance requirements for the decision, it chooses that
method which requires the least investment in man-hours. This is
deemed to be the method furthest to the left within the feasible set.
Thus, if AI, AII, CI, CII, and GII are all feasible as in problem types
1 and 2, AI would be the method chosen. This decision rule acts to
minimize man-hours subject to quality and acceptance constraints.

This decision rule for choosing among alternatives in the feasible
set results in the prescription of each of the five decision processes in
some situations. AI is prescribed for four problem types (1, 2, 4, and
5); AII is prescribed for two problem types (9 and 10); CI is prescribed for only one problem type (8); CII is prescribed for four
problem types (7, 11, 13, and 14); and GII is prescribed for three
problem types (3, 6, and 12). The relative frequency with which the
five decision processes would be prescribed for any leader would, of
course, be dependent on the distribution of problem types in his role.

Application of the model

To illustrate how the model might be applied in actual administrative
situations, a set of four cases will be presented and analyzed with the
use of the model. Following the description of the case, the authors'
analysis will be given, including a specification of problem type, feasible set, and solution indicated by the model. While an attempt has been
made to describe these cases as completely as is necessary to permit
the reader to make the judgments required by the model, there may
remain some room for subjectivity. The reader may wish after reading
the case to analyze it himself using the model and then to compare his
analysis with that of the authors.

Case 1

You are general foreman in charge of a large gang laying an oil pipe-
line. It is now necessary to estimate your expected rate of progress in
order to schedule material deliveries to the next field site.

You know the nature of the terrain you will be traveling and have
the historical data needed to compute the mean and variance in the
rate of speed over that type of terrain. Given these two variables it
is a simple matter to calculate the earliest and latest times at which
materials and support facilities will be needed at the next site. It is
important that your estimate be reasonably accurate. Underestimates
result in idle foremen and workers, and an overestimate results in
tying up materials for a period of time before they are to be used.

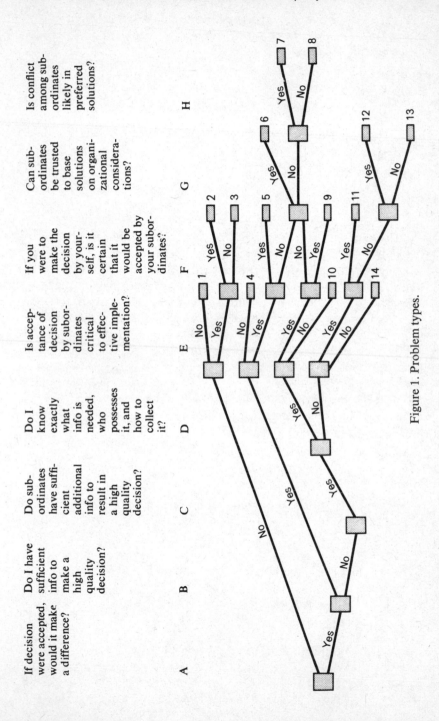

Figure 1. Problem types.

Progress has been good and your five foremen and other members of the gang stand to receive substantial bonuses if the project is completed ahead of schedule.

Analysis

Questions: A (Quality?) = Yes
            B (Manager's Information?) = Yes
            E (Acceptance?) = No

Problem type: 4

Feasible set: AI, AII, CI, CII, GII

Minimum man-hours solution: AI

Rule violations: None

Case 2

You are supervising the work of twelve engineers. Their formal training and work experience are very similar, permitting you to use them interchangeably on projects. Yesterday, your manager informed you that a request had been received from an overseas affiliate for four engineers to go abroad on extended loan for a period of six to eight months. For a number of reasons, he argued and you agreed that this request should be met from your group.

All your engineers are capable of handling this assignment and, from the standpoint of present and future projects, there is no particular reason why any one should be retained over any other. The problem is somewhat complicated by the fact that the overseas assignment is in what is generally regarded in the company as an undesirable location.

Analysis

Questions: A (Quality?) = No
            E (Acceptance?) = Yes
            F (Prior probability of acceptance?) = No

Problem type: 3

Feasible set: GII

Minimum man-hours solution: GII

Rule violations: AI and AII violate rules 4, 5, and 6
                  CI violates rules 5 and 6
                  CII violates rule 6

Case 3

You are the head of a staff unit reporting to the vice-president of finance. He has asked you to provide a report on the firm's current portfolio to include recommendations for changes in the selection criteria currently employed. Doubts have been raised about the efficiency of the existing system in the current market conditions, and there is considerable dissatisfaction with prevailing rates of return.

You plan to write the report, but at the moment you are quite perplexed about the approach to take. Your own specialty is the bond market and it is clear to you that a detailed knowledge of the equity market, which you lack, would greatly enhance the value of the report. Fortunately, four members of your staff are specialists in different segments of the equity market. Together, the possess a vast amount of knowledge about the intricacies of investment. However, they seldom agree on the best way to achieve anything when it comes to the stock market. While they are obviously conscientious as well as knowledgeable, they have major differences when it comes to investment philosophy and strategy.

You have six weeks before the report is due. You have already begun to familiarize yourself with the firm's current portfolio and have been provided by management with a specific set of constraints that any portfolio must satisfy. Your immediate problem is to come up with some alternatives to the firm's present practices and select the most promising for detailed analysis in your report.

Analysis
Questions: A (Quality?) = Yes
B (Manager's information?) = No
C (Subordinates' information?) = Yes
D (Structured?) = No
E (Acceptance?) =No
Problem type: 14
Feasible set: CII, GII
Minimum man-hours solution: GII
Rule violations: AI violates rules 1 and 3
AII violates rule 3
CI violates rule 3

Case 4

You are on the division manager's staff and work on a wide variety of problems of both an administrative and technical nature. You have been given the assignment of developing a universal method to be used in each of the five plants in the division for manually reading equipment registers, recording the readings, and transmitting the scorings to a centralized information system. All plants are located in a relatively small geographical region.

Until now there has been a high error rate in the reading and/or transmittal of the data. Some locations have considerably higher error rates than others, and the methods used to record and transmit the data vary between plants. It is probable, therefore, that part of the error variance is a function of specific local conditions rather than anything else, and this will complicate the establishment of any system common to all plants. You have the information on error rates but no information on the local practices which generate these errors or on the local conditions which necessitate the different practices.

Everyone would benefit from an improvement in the quality of the data as these data are used in a number of important decisions. Your contacts with the plants are through the quality-control supervisors who are responsible for collecting the data. They are a conscientious group committed to doing their jobs well, but are highly sensitive to interference on the part of higher management in their own operations. Any solution which does not receive the active support of the various plant supervisors is unlikely to reduce the error rate significantly.

Analysis
  Questions: A (Quality?) = Yes
              B (Manager's information?) = No
              C (Subordinates' information?) = Yes
              D (Structured?) = No
              E (Acceptance?) = Yes
              F (Prior probability of acceptance?) = No
              G (Trust?) = Yes
  Problem type: 12
  Feasible set: GII
  Minimum man-hours solution: GII
  Rule violations: AI violates rules 1, 3, 4 and 7
                    AII violates rules 3, 4, and 7
                    CI violates rules 3 and 7
                    CII violates rule 7

Short-term versus long-term models

The model described above seeks to protect, if relevant, the quality of the decision, to create any necessary acceptance of the decision, and to expend the least number of man-hours in the process. In view of its attention to conditions surrounding the making and implementation of a particular decision rather than any long-term considerations, it could be termed a short-term model.

It seems likely, however, that the leadership methods which may be optimal for short-term results may be different from those which would be optimal when executed over a longer period of time. Consider a leader who has been uniformly pursuing an autocratic style (AI or AII) and, perhaps as a consequence, has subordinates who cannot be trusted to pursue organizational goals (attribute G) and who have little additional knowledge or experience to bring to bear on the decisions to be made (attribute C). An examination of the structure of the time-minimizing model reveals that with few exceptions, the leader would be instructed by the model to continue his present autocratic style.

It appears likely, however, that the use of more participative methods would, in time, change the status of these problem attributes (i.e., increase the extent to which subordinates would have information relevant to the solution of problems in the future and increase the extent to which their goals are congruent with those of the organization) so as to develop ultimately a more effective problem-solving system. In the example given above, an autocratic approach would be indicated to maximize short-run benefits but a higher degree of participation might maximize performance aggregated over a longer period.

A promising approach to the development of a long-term model is one which places less weight on man-hours as the basis for choice of method within the feasible set. Given a long-term orientation one would be interested in the trade-off between man-hours in problem solving and team development, both of which increase with participation. Viewed in these terms, the time minimizing model places maximum relative weight on man-hours and no weight on development and hence chooses the style furthest to the left within the feasible set. A model which places less weight on man-hours and more weight on development would, if these assumptions are correct, choose a style further to the right within the feasible set.

Summary

In this chapter, a normative model of leadership style was developed. The model attempts to deal with the complexities of the processes involved in leadership by specifying (1) a set of alternatives among which a choice is to be made, (2) the general nature of the processes which they affect, (3) the principal variables governing the effects of the alternatives on each process, and (4) explicit rules for decision making based on estimates of the outcome of each process.

Some might argue that it is premature for social scientists to attempt to be prescriptive. Our knowledge is too little and the issues too complex to warrant explicit normative models dealing with matters such as leadership style. It is also true, however, that leaders are facing daily the task of selecting decision-making processes which in turn reflect their leadership style. Is it likely that a model which requires them to deal analytically with the forces impinging upon them and which is consistent with admittedly imperfect research base would produce less rational choices than those which they do make? The criterion for social ability is not perfection but improvement over present practice.

Furthermore, social scientists are increasingly having an influence not only on people's leadership style but also on such matters as job design, training methods, and compensation systems. Too frequently, in the view of the present authors, their prescriptions for action, whether it be job enrichment, sensitivity training, or group decision making, are not based on a systematic analysis of the situation in a manner which would point to the costs and benefits of available alternatives.

Perhaps the most convincing argument for the development of normative models is the fact that in developing and using them their weaknesses can be identified. Insofar as these weaknesses stem from lack of basic knowledge, this deficiency can be remedied through further research. A strong case can be made for the continued interplay between the worlds of practice and social science on the basis of their mutual contributions to one another.

Female Leadership
In Formal Organizations:
Must the Female Leader
Go Formal?
Jean Lipman-Blumen

From Machiavelli to modern times, the conundrum of leadership has tantalized the human intellect. Since the general issue of leadership is so problematical, it is hardly surprising that the conditions of female leadership are even more ambiguous (particularly since most leadership studies have focused on male subjects). And, as with other poorly understood phenomena, female leadership is overgrown with mythology. Accepted myths, as well as some research (when it is even possible to distinguish between the two), suggest that women make poor leaders, and, in recognition of this "fact," subordinates dislike working for them (Ellman 1963; Bowman et al. 1965; and Bass et al. 1971).[1] That women have not had a major share in leadership roles is seen as further proof of their shortcomings—another case of "blaming the victim." Moreover, those women who are acknowledged leaders are perceived, in a peculiar combination of denigration and·praise, as masculine. The first prime minister of Israel, Ben-Gurion, allegedly described Golda Meir as the only real man in his Cabinet.

These myths are difficult to shatter, particularly since "evidence" marshalled to support them rests upon the relatively small numbers of women leaders in both the public and private sector. Despite recent harbingers of change, the last two centuries have been a virtual wasteland for American women in the important leadership arena of public life.[2] Even in the 1970s, within the private sector, women only rarely

This paper has been abridged, with permission. It appears in full in Horner, M., ed., *Perspectives on the Patterns of an Era* (Cambridge, Mass.: Harvard University Press, forthcoming).

1. More recent evidence (Handley and Sedlacek 1977) suggests that women who work for a female supervisor are more likely to report greater job satisfaction and less sex bias than women working for male managers.
2. Between 1776 and 1976, the federal government has included 11 women vs. 1,715 men in the U.S. Senate, 87 women vs. 9,591 men in the U.S. House of Representatives, no women and 101 men in the Supreme Court, and 5 women

are found in key leadership positions.[3] But the winds of change are slowly beginning to blow.[4] Rising concern about women as leaders in the private and public sectors has been presaged by the emergence of groups specifically designed to promote female leadership.[5] At the same time, industry, government, and academia have felt the growing pressures to bring women into leadership positions.

With increasing attention focused on women as leaders in public and private arenas, it seems appropriate to reconsider the nature of female leadership. This paper addresses that question in the context of male-female relationships in contemporary organizations.

The purpose of this paper is not to present a systematic review of leadership theories, achievement literature, or even female leadership and achievement research. Rather, its aim is to examine a group of ideas related to female leadership, most of which, we shall contend, have contributed to its current condition. To that end, we shall be concerned with (a) female and male leadership in mixed-sex groups; (b) communication as authority and the homosociality of the informal structure; (c) male-female socialization as it affects formal organizations; (d) the informal organizational structure as a resource-allocation device; (e) male-female predilections for different achievement styles; and finally (f) some possibilities for change.

Female and male leadership in mixed-sex groups

The growing literature on leadership behavior in mixed-sex groups has distilled three major generalizations about the differences between

---

vs. 507 men in the president's Cabinet. At the present time (1978), two women serve in the U.S. Senate (both through widow's inheritance), and 18 of the 435 U.S. Representatives are women, constituting 3.6% of the total Congressional membership (Center for American Women and Politics 1978).

3. Among the Fortune 500 companies, only 1 (.2%) has a woman as chief executive officer, and women constitute only 1.1% of the presidents of national unions. Among four-year institutions of higher learning, 3.6% have women presidents, and 2.4% have women vice-presidents. In two-year colleges, women comprise 0.6% of the chief executive officers (Estler and Davis 1977).

4. In state legislatures, women are winning an increasing number of seats, with a 1.3% gain (8% to 9.3%) in the three-year period 1975-78. While women are gaining in areas of elective office, their record in appointed managerial or administrative roles is somewhat less vigorous. Between 1959 and 1974, among managerial and administrative workers, women increased only 3.1%, from 15.5% to 18.6%, respectively (U.S. department of Labor 1975). Nonetheless, the number of women applying to and graduating from law and business schools is on the rise, and the percentage of women seeking ordination degrees in divinity schools has increased 180.9% since 1970, offering some slight basis for optimism about their future corner on the leadership market.

5. For example, the National Women's Political Caucus was formed to assist women political candidates, and a presidential task force was appointed to consider the factors inhibiting women business owners.

male and female behavior (Hall 1972; Lockheed and Hall 1976; Lockheed 1976):

First, *men talk more than women;* that is they "initiate more verbal acts" (Lockheed and Hall 1976). The evidence contradicts the mythology which would have us believe that women talk more than men. Talking or communicating, as we shall argue later, is an important aspect of leadership, and women, in the company of men, often apparently feel inhibited about talking. Negative attitudes toward female communication have not changed much since Aristotle wrote, ". . . a woman would be thought loquacious if she imposed no more restraint on her conversation than a good man" (Jowett 1943, p. 294).

Other research on the relationship between activity levels and perceived leadership reports that those group members who are the most active—including verbally active—are most likely to be perceived as leaders by other group members (Lana et al. 1960; Marsk 1964; Zdep and Oakes 1967; Zdep 1969; Morris and Hackman 1969). The "Catch-22" situation that women face in trying to balance group behavior, verbal activity, and leadership is classic.

The second generalization that emerges from the research on leadership in mixed-sex groups is that *men's opinions are more likely than women's to influence the opinions of both male and female group members.* Testing for the extent to which subjects would acquiesce to a distorted norm, Tuddenham, et al. (1958) found that in mixed-sex groups men were less likely to acquiesce than in all-male groups, while women tended to acquiesce more than they had in all-female groups. Whittaker's (1965) experiments with judgments about autokinetic lights revealed that male opinion leaders were more readily followed by both male and female subjects, but that female opinion leaders evoked considerable resistance from subjects of both sexes. Again, the works of Strodtbeck et al. (1957), Kenkel (1957), and Zander and Van Egmond (1958) all seem to offer supportive evidence. The resistance women encounter when offering their analyses of problems presents a serious obstacle to female leadership.

The third generalization centers around Parsons' (1955) formulation that *males are more task-oriented, while females are more socioemotionally oriented.* According to Borgatta and Stimson (1963), as well as Strodtbeck and Mann (1956) and Heiss (1962), men are more likely than women to offer task-related suggestions in a group decision-making situation, while women are more likely than men to provide encouragement and support to other group members.

More recent work by Lockheed and Hall (1976) suggests that men are not necessarily more active and task-oriented than women, but that maleness represents a more highly valued status characteristic which is translated into increased opportunities for action and, therefore, leadership, within a group setting. Their research offers the possibility that intervention techniques—such as training and demonstrating competence specific to the task at hand—may offset the initial leadership advantage that males bring to groups simply on the basis of their sex.

To confound the problem, Bartol and Wortman (1975) present data that cast doubt upon the notion that the leader's sex inevitably influences the subordinates' perception of the leader's behavior or the subordinates' job satisfaction. Their findings reveal that, from the subordinates' perspective, the sex of the leader bears no relationship to the association between perceived leader behavior and satisfaction with supervision. Moreover, Bartol and Wortman's findings call attention to sex of the subordinates as a powerful variable in predicting the satisfaction levels of subordinates. Male subordinates are more likely than females to express lower levels of satisfaction, regardless of the leader's sex.

Despite the many areas of conflict among the research results to date, some useful insights still may be gained from juxtaposing certain findings that have emerged:

> If, in mixed-sex situations (as in day-to-day organizational life), the more active members are seen as leaders;
> men are given more opportunities to talk and act; men actually do talk more than women;
> men's opinions are more likely to influence the group positively and women's opinions are more likely to evoke negative or resistant reactions;
> male subordinates are more likely than female subordinates to express dissatisfaction with their leader, regardless of the leader's sex; and
> the most important informal groups consist of men (as we shall discuss below),

then the current structure of organizations serves as a serious barrier to the acceptance of female leadership.

Communication as authority and the homosociality of the informal structure

The Bartol and Wortman (1975) study is important because it begins to shift the focus beyond the behavior and characteristics of women as leaders. Much of the recent leadership and management literature has placed a disproportionate emphasis upon the personal characteristics of the leader (Hennig and Jardim 1977; Bayes and Newton 1978).

Other organizational literature, however, makes it clear that the authority of position most commonly held by men is buttressed by the symbols (e.g., corner offices, chauffered limousines) that authenticate authority.

More importantly, the decision that an act of leadership has authority "lies with the persons to whom it is addressed and does not reside in 'persons of authority' or those who issue these orders" (Barnard 1968, p. 163). The question of female leadership (or nonleadership), therefore, should be considered in terms of its acceptance or legitimation by those to whom it is directed. This is not to deny that the character of the communication (to which we shall return later) has some weight, but more to emphasize the importance of the attitudes of the subordinate group members. If (1) authority is indeed a characteristic of communication and "rests upon . . . acceptance or consent" (Barnard, p. 164), and (2) the subordinate group has a high proportion of men, then women who attempt leadership, or more modestly managerial, roles in formal organizations (other than all-female organizations) are in serious trouble.

If we recall, first, that the mixed-sex group research indicates that women talk less than men, it is clear that the issue of establishing communication, and thereby authority, is more problematical for women. One function of the myth of women's loquaciousness becomes apparent: it serves as a control mechanism for limiting women's communication in the presence of men. By inhibiting women's communications in the presence of men for fear of fulfilling a negative female stereotype, the women's leadership behavior in mixed-sex groups also is conveniently limited.

Second, mixed-group research tells us that even when women do talk, their contributions tend to have a negative effect upon group opinion. But the formal and (perhaps even more importantly) the informal systems are areas which separately generate the group opinions by which one's authority is maintained.

The individual builds a credibility base within each sphere on somewhat different grounds: official rank in the formal system; sentiment and personalities in the informal system. The personal credibility generated in the informal system influences one's authority in the formal structure, and often vice versa. From a slightly different vantage point, the leader who also is a member of the informal system (i.e., "the old boy network") is allowed an extra margin of credibility. All other things being equal, in official settings, that leader's co-workers are prepared to be receptive to his ideas. (Compare this to the common experience of high-level organizational women, excluded from the informal male system, who point out that their comments in official situations often are ignored altogether or attributed to a male member of the group.)

To add to the complexity of life in organizations, credibility associated with formal rank marks the individual as a desirable recruit for the informal structure. It is easy to see that the connection between the formal and informal bases of credibility has a Catch-22 circularity. If you're "in" in one system, you're likely to be "in" in the other system, which in turn makes you more "in" in the first. Of course, it follows that if you're "out" in one, you're more likely to be "out" in the other, and so on. Thus, for the formal and informal bases of credibility to potentiate one another, the individual must have access to both the formal and the informal. External pressures rather recently have created opening wedges for women in formal structures. Nevertheless, women in leadership positions still confront the formidable problem of gaining access to the informal structure, the greenhouse milieu for growing not only sentiment and affection so critical to public opinion, but also decisions and transactions that ultimately move the formal structure.

In addition to building supportive sentiment and affection within the informal structure, a leader must sharpen communication by an accurate assessment of events, conditions, and people. Again, there is a troublesome circularity to such information flows. To be credible, information from leaders to followers must be informed by the culture and currency of the followers' group. The leader gains credibility when s/he seems to know more than the followers know. A leader who transmits information which subordinates perceive as naive soon loses credibility. Formal information is augmented by intelligence that flows from the informal network. Such intelligence is, itself, a valuable resource.

This is not to deny that women in leadership positions receive the usual official information through formal channels, such as staff meetings, briefings, memoranda, and the like. Rather, we are suggesting that the "insider's" knowledge—offering the insider strategic advantages—is not readily available to women, who are blocked from executive level, all-male groups.

Women's exclusion from the informal network prevents them from developing an "intelligence or communication base," which then could spread a mantle of authority over their communications in the formal structure. The resulting handicap activates a vicious cycle which women managers or leaders rarely have the resources to break. The parallel all-female informal networks that ordinarily arise do not transmit executive and policy level information. This is partly the result of the sex segregation of formal organizations (Blaxall and

Reagan 1976) and the long-standing tendency for women to be confined within the lowest strata of such structures. Rarely are there sufficient numbers of executive-level women within any single formal organization to constitute an informal network. Only recently have women begun to develop interorganizational networks to offset the information barrier.[6]

Although informal networks, in general, are sex segregated, social relationships between individual men and women provide conduits for resource exchange between these structures. For example, the secretary-executive relationship historically has been the channel through which the male executives tapped into the female informal network, thereby acquiring valuable information about their male co-workers. Similarly, females in organizational settings often have had to rely on their individual relationships with male co-workers to gain access to important organizational information.

Male-female socialization and formal organizations

Male homosociality[7] has been described elsewhere as a powerful factor in the sex segregation of American social institutions (Lipman-Blumen 1976). The male homosocial ethic focuses on competition and winning—often in team settings—and operates within a context replete with complex role networks and clearly articulated hierarchies.

The team, with its formal structure of interlocking task-oriented roles, is a depersonalized world. Specialized skill is the primary, if not the only, criterion for entry into team roles; while feelings, sensitivities, understanding, and other interpersonal skills are far less relevant. No soccer team is complete without a goalie, and the goalie position is filled by the individual most adept at defending the goal, without regard to that individual's interpersonal skills.

---

6. Some recent exceptions have begun to emerge in the world of women's issues, within the public and private sectors, where strong informal networks have developed. Since women's programs commonly involve small, all-female staff within large mostly male (except for support staff) organizations, the feminist networks that have developed often cross organizational lines. These informal structures serve as avenues for policy level and other information, support, decision-making and strategy development across organizational boundaries. Thus, women managers in unrelated subdivisions of a large-scale organization, in separate but similar private institutions, and within different agencies in government have created effective feminist homosocial networks. These networks have involved coalitions not only among "insiders" in different divisions, but also between "insiders" and "outsiders." Nonetheless, because of the common segregation of women professionals within their own organizations, women leaders still have difficulty penetrating the informal male homosocial structures within their parent organizations.

7. Homosociality is defined as the "seeking, enjoyment, and/or preference for the company of the same sex."

Males learn early on that winning the game often means playing with teammates they may not like. Team spirit is the recognition of the superordinate importance of the group over the individual. Personal relationships among role occupants become the domain of the informal, not the formal, structure. The informal structure provides a necessary cushion against the impersonality of the formal structure (i.e., the team) and arises in the service of the formal structure.

The informal structure fulfills the personal needs frustrated by the formal structure. In his recent autobiography, Roethlisberger (1977), the dean of the early human relations movement in management, lucidly underscores this distinction:

> These relations of interconnectedness among persons . . . I call the strong, close, and warm relationships. They make the cheese more binding. The (formal) ones in contrast are weak, distant, and cold. . . . It seemed to me that in most organizations the employees found these informal relationships rewarding. Whenever and wherever it was possible, they generated them like crazy. . . . The two kinds of relations were in sharp contrast. Among members of (formal) relations, there were few interactions, few close friendships and seldom any small, warm, cozy groups. There was sometimes "respect" but quite often distrust, apprehension, and suspicion. Interaction was limited to what the task required. It looked as if the logic of rational management generated weak, distant, and cold relations, whereas the employees as persons generated strong, close, and warm relations. The outcome, which was often conflict, was not because anyone was deliberately trying to throw a monkey wrench in the machinery. The logic of management could do only what it was supposed to do, its business, so to speak. It could only produce those relations in which rational order existed. To ask it to produce strong, close, cozy and comfortable relations would be like asking an icicle to produce warmth for man. However, that man as man sought for these warm relations was also not being just ornery. He also was doing what his nature as man and the itch-ouch balance compelled him to do. [pp. 165-166]

Given the offsetting warmth of the informal structure, the team members can tolerate more readily the coolness of the formal structure. This formal-informal counterpoint provides the milieu for male socialization. Men learn early in childhood to distinguish and move easily between formal and informal structures.

Women grow up outside the world of large, complexly structured teams. They are socialized in small play groups of two or three individuals (Maccoby and Jacklin 1974), in which the formal is not differentiated from the informal structure. The focus is upon individual personalities and the relationships among them. Winning is not highly emphasized, relating is.

Thus socialized, women often see the formal and informal worlds as one and treat even formal roles informally. Given the emotionally positive aspects of the informal structure, as Roethlisberger has described it, the choice is a natural one, one that men, too, probably would take if the structure of their world permitted.

But women's inexperience in separating the formal from the informal structure becomes a liability. The effects can be particularly destructive when, as adults, they enter leadership roles requiring differentiation of formal and informal structures. And it is not simply a question of inexperience. Women learn to *value* personal relationships, to rank their importance above simple task-orientation and winning. The more adept females become in interpersonal relationships, the more they value this modus vivendi, and the more likely they are to incorporate this value in their managerial style (Reif, et al. 1975).

Raphaela Best (in progress), in her ethnographic study of third-graders at play, describes how little girls happily let their female friends win a race in the name of friendship. The playtime role structures of young females are not depersonalized. Personality counts. It is the individual, not the role, who has salience. An individual who docs not have certain personal characteristics will not be accepted in the playmate role, even if the role remains vacant. The emphasis is upon people as personalities and upon relationships, rather than upon the structure and coordination of goal-oriented roles. The goal *is* the relationship; the external task may even be the means. The focus is on relating, not on winning.

If it is important to women to like the person in the related role, it is equally (perhaps too) critical for them to feel that *they* are liked.[8] In fact, the early achievement studies of McClelland et al. (1953) suggested that social acceptability cues were the only cues likely to stimulate need for achievement in female subjects. The need to be liked, thus, may impede women in organizational situations which require competence and task-orientation, unalloyed with personal popularity.

Homosociality as a resource-allocation device

Like the formal structure, the informal structure is composed of numerous, segmented, and unequal parts. It reflects the hierarchy and sex

8. The reciprocal need to be liked was suggested to me in personal communication by Professor Constantiana Safilios-Rothschild in 1978.

segregation of the formal structure. Indeed, sex segregation in the informal structure is often more severe than in the formal one. This homosociality that characterized the informal structure provides a mechanism for the control and distribution of resources. Both tangible and intangible resources flow along the informal net work. Personal *autonomy,* for example, is often dispersed through its tributaries. That is, the ordinary bureaucratic controls are not applied very rigidly to those who are solid members of the informal network. Another vital resource, time, is also allocated through informal channels. Personal time, as well as official deadlines, are granted a measure of flexibility from members of the informal network. For example, such members are less likely to have their comings and going carefully scrutinized. Their organizational tethers are longer, providing greater latitude for action before being called to account. Their time, autonomy, personal and organizational freedom are thereby enlarged.

These important resources are building blocks of power which create leverage in the formal system. The leader who accrues autonomy and time can in turn provide special treatment for staff, colleagues, and clients, which eventually yields loyalty, reciprocal help, profits, and promotions.

The informal structure also distributes *loopholes,* ways around the formal requirements of the system. *Special perquisites* are distributed, as well. For example, in times of tight budgets, when travel funds supposedly are restricted, favored members of the informal network usually can manage to have their travel orders approved.

Still another resource available through the informal network is *accessibility* to people and services. While formal availability of co-workers and services is a legitimate part of every formal organizational role, approachability is enhanced or inhibited by the informal system. Thus, while the division manager has some legitimate claim on the time and help of his/her supervisor, that claim is processed quickly or lackadaisically according to the manager's informal standing. The co-member of the informal group does not "cool his heels" waiting for an appointment. Both the quality and quantity of entrée and service are influenced by the informal system. Even official resources, such as staff and budget, are influenced by the informal structure. Any seasoned observer of the organizational scene has witnessed how favored members of the informal system somehow manage to secure additional staff and increased budgets beyond whatever official allocations have been set.

Political, financial, legal, professional, and other extraorganizational help are still other resources that flow along the informal waters. The easy accessibility of the informal group allows the insiders to develop a sixth sense within the organization. They know one another well enough to sense when it is the appropriate moment to ask for or offer help. This easy access provides the context within which "understanding" about goals, values, and sentiments develops, reducing the probability of serious political or interpersonal errors that could jeopardize leadership. All these valuable resources—autonomy, freedom, time, loopholes, perquisites, accessibility to people and services, political, professional, financial, and legal help (not to mention valuable "insider's" information discussed earlier)—are distributed by the all-male executive informal system.

Of course, homosocial enclaves of women also exist and serve as control and distribution mechanisms. But the resources that flow along the channels of the women's network are likely to be interpersonal and relational in nature. The access of women to crucial organizational resources is more limited, and, thus, the largesse that can be distributed to other women often is not keyed to organizational or professional goals.

Because women rarely have access to the informal male structure, they commonly lack the resources necessary for negotiating their way through the higher levels of the formal structure. They do not participate in the transactions which allocated vital organizational resources. As a result, they have less access to executive power and limited maneuverability within the organization.

Those women who enter the formal organization with significant resources of their own (e.g., family fortunes, prior connections to powerful members of the organization, or political or professional networks) usually are better able to counter the informal male network. If such women can maintain their resources, their authority may be sustained and even acknowledged by their male colleagues.

Occasionally women with male mentors develop indirect routes to information and other key resources from the informal system. Mentors who are privy to the power centers within the organization are able to confer an impressive array of largesse, including status and support, upon their proteges. Although young, ambitious men in organizations rather easily attach themselves to successful male mentors, such a process poses greater difficulties for women and may be fraught with sexual overtones (Rowe 1977; Shapiro et al. 1978).

Male and female achievement styles

While the nature of the structures within which one seeks goals are undeniably important, how one goes about attaining those goals is probably just as crucial. Both men and women develop characteristic ways of achieving whatever goals they set for themselves. The more adept one becomes at certain achievement "styles," the more likely one is to continue to use them.

Men raised in the world of competitive teams easily focus on *direct* achievement styles, on getting things done, on winning. The early male world encourages pitting oneself against one's environment, acting directly in one's own behalf, achieving through one's own efforts. Each team player has a specific piece of direct action to contribute to the general task of winning. The reward of winning is shared among all, even though the quarterback may be seen as the key player.

Another factor contributing to this direct achievement style is the early understanding that adult men are expected to support themselves and possibly others. Men are socialized to act in their own behalf. For adult males, there are only two "escapes" from responsibility for direct action: either recurrently demonstrated failure to perform or its opposite, a substantial history of successful performance. Either of these two histories may let men off the hook. But there are many legitimate loopholes—including marriage—to channel females away from frontline responsibility.

The difference between the early socialization of boys and girls is great on this issue of self-reliance. Little boys traditionally are asked what they want to be when they grow up; little girls, whom they want to marry. Hennig and Jardim (1977) remind us of the enormity of the resulting differences in mind set. From early socialization, males expect to protect and support women; and women traditionally have accepted this arrangement without recognizing that such protection is tantamount to control.

While men are pushed into a direct achievement world, women are encouraged to become relational achievers (Lipman-Blumen and Leavitt 1976, 1978a, 1978b). For women, the relationship itself often becomes the goal. And acts that contribute to building relationships become valued means of achieving. *Relational* achievement styles are translated into certain occupational roles, often the traditional "feminine occupations" such as teaching, social work, and nursing. But other, less specific roles also include large relational components, coaching and managing. And here we begin to see the importance of such roles for organizations.

It is an interesting characteristic of formal organizations that the common reward for competent task performance as a nonsupervisor is promotion to supervisor. But supervision usually requires a large relational component. Supervisors, that is, are not just doers, but coaches, mentors, developers of their people. The shift from direct bench to supervisory work may thus be difficult for both company and supervisor. But it appears that it is precisely in this area that women can offer very strong skills. Yet present organizational reward systems frustrate the match of women to managerial roles. Nonetheless, it is clear that technical expertise without such relational skills rarely sends one to the head of the leadership line.[9]

Some possibilities for change

While many changes to ease some of these problems are possible, few are simple and feasible. For example, decentralization of large organizations into much smaller units would increase local autonomy of leaders and enhance interpersonal bonds. But few organizations are likely to pay the costs of a major decentralization program solely to gain the advantages outlined here. Similarly, rotating leadership positions could yield salutary effects. But leader rotation would also entail (or so the myth suggests) such costs that few organizations are likely to do it just to open pathways for women.

On the other hand, organizations can, as they debate structural and operational change, factor in the likely impact of proposed changes on subsequent leadership patterns. And further, women, as they search the job market, would do well to evaluate potential employers against criteria like the degree of decentralization of leadership power, the extent to which interpersonal skills are *explicitly* weighed and rewarded in personnel evaluations, and the extent to which the organization has demonstrated flexibility in the promotional policies, as well as the degree to which it *demonstrably* values employee behaviors that glue the organization together into a solid social unit.

Some other changes that organizations can make are far less costly than such major structural changes, and far more feasible. Here are some possiblities:

— Women leaders can be brought into the organizations at *high enough levels* so their positions carry adequate and unequivocal formal credibility. Unlike men, women have special difficulty in establishing credibility when they enter at lower ranks.

— The domains women leaders are asked to supervise can be made more *central* to the goals of the organization.

— Women leaders can be anointed with both *symbols of power* and the *reality of resources*. Corner offices and large budgets will lend clout to women leaders, just as they always have to men. Adequate resources and the symbols of clout will encourage male co-workers to seek the help, and even the sponsorship, of women leaders.

9. Japanese organizational structures tend to assign higher priority to interpersonal or relational skills than to technical expertise (Abegglen 1958; Johnson and Ouchi 1974; Okamoto; Vogel 1968; Lipman-Blumen and Leavitt 1978).

— Two other obvious possibilities: encourage women (1) to create their *own informal groups* and (2) to find ways of entering men's. The former may be easier than the latter.

— If a *cadre* of high-level women is brought into the organization in positions that minimize potential competition among them, they can build their own informal network, providing each other with exec-utive-level information and other resources, as well as interpersonal support. Where there are too few top-level women in an organization, women leaders can construct (and in many places they are doing so) an *interorganizational* informal network composed of top-level women in analogous positions.

— Even if the woman leader cannot enter as a bona fide member of the male informal network, she still may develop access to informa-tion transmitted through the informal system. Not only will individual ties to one or more members of the male informal network help, but particular male co-workers may be more helpful than others. For ex-ample, a *male* member of the informal system to whom the woman leader reports in the formal structure is a key linkpin to the informal structure. *Enlisting* that *male supervisor's help,* in fact, making it his *quasi-legitimate* responsibility to keep the female leader posted, is an important method for sustaining her information level (and therefore her credibility in the formal group). Obviously, this tactic must be used with special care to avoid jeopardizing the male informant's status as a trustworthy member of the informal group.

— So much has been written recently about the role of *mentors* in individual careers that it is unnecessary to dwell at length on that strat-egy. Nonetheless, the male supervisor just mentioned is one possible mentor. But other *high-status males* both in and sometimes outside the organization are likely candidates as mentors for nascent women leaders.

— Another structural possibility for enhancing women's credibility as group leaders is to pay serious attention to the *sex* and *status* com-position of the ingroups. If, as the literature tells us, male subordinates are more likely than females to express dissatisfaction regardless of the leader's sex, then initially women leaders should be given groups in which there is a *slight preponderance of women.* Once their reputations and confidence are established, they can move on to groups with higher proportions of men. It is also useful, if possible, to include at least one high-status male group member who is clearly perceived as (and, in fact, is) her ally.

— Credibility in groups, we have seen, is enhanced by active par-ticipation. Roles such as team leader, expert on a given issue, liaison person to other important groups all offer structured possibilities for unequivocal contribution to goals. As we noted earlier, individuals who contribute to group tasks, rather than to the socioemotional climate of the group, are more likely to be seen as leaders, given our current value system. As group leaders, women, at least initially, should *downplay* expressions of nurturance and emotional support, concentrating instead on task-related directions reinforcements and advice. The reciprocal of this strategy is to train males (1) to *listen* when women talk and (2) to offer *emotional and social support* to other group members.

— Training women as specialists in *short-term* tasks is an important means of refocussing the group's perceptions of her value to goal attainment. For example, a consulting group which plans to bid on a contract in a new substantive area could give a woman leader special training in that subject to ensure her claim to unique leadership eligibility.

An important caveat: specialist roles often prove to be dead-end. So if women enter organization as specialists, clear pathways toward the "generalist" ranks of leadership have to be carefully kept open. Urging women to enter organizations as specialists runs counter to the current trend in leading business schools, where managers are advised to become "generalists!" Nonetheless, entering the group as a specialist can be a useful *short-term* strategy by which women at the outset establish their leadership credibility before moving on to generalist roles.

Although women's comments often are ignored in group discussions, research findings suggest that leadership is attributed to the group members who talk frequently. *Structured opportunities* to encourage women to talk more in groups therefore make sense. For example, women can be given frequent opportunities (and should welcome them!) to make oral presentations. Placing women in roles like team leader, presenter, or discussion leader, offers structured opportunities for women to talk. If men's subsequent performance is partially dependent on information gleaned from a woman leader's presentation, this *"structured talking"* by women could be a valuable way of encouraging males' *"structured listening."*

— "Anointed analysis," in which a woman's opinions are validated by the *explicit approval* of a high-status male leader, is another means of motivating women to talk and men to listen. In official meetings, the top executive can solicit a woman executive's opinion, listen deferentially and attentively, and thus set the example for other males in the organization.

— *Closing* some of the *escape hatches* from responsibility for women, including their socially approved avoidance of mathematics and science (Aiken 1970, 1976; Fenema 1976; Sells 1973; Tobias

1978), will facilitate the development of direct achievement styles in women. Males are raised with the societal expectation that they must do for themselves; they must *directly* encounter their environment. Females are socialized to the expectation that they will *not* be directly responsible for themselves. In fact, by helping others to achieve or by providing encouragement and emotional support, they can achieve *indirectly*. As more women recognize and accept the inevitability of labor force participation, just as men do, they will value more the benefits derived from moving flexibly between direct and relational achievement styles and roles.

At the same time that we are closing some of the *escape hatches* for women, it is reasonable to think about *opening* a few for *men*. Offering men opportunities to follow less rigid career paths, to take nonorganizational roles, to feel freer to enter and leave the labor force at different points can ease the tensions many men currently feel in their occupational lives. Developing the flexibility to shift from direct to relational achievement styles may be a decided asset in this process.

— As we noted earlier, the barriers against women entering the male homosocial network have been impervious. What, if any, tactics might be useful in that realm? Some possibilities: selection of people already like present group members, training new members to be more like group members in relevant ways; training old group members to be more like the new entrants; promoting the entry of women who are *similar* to the male homosocial group in terms of education, political outlook, and professional interests. But it is clear that these approaches also carry serious limitations: (1) they downplay the special skills, qualities, and orientations that women can bring to organizations and limit the potential strength and richness that diversity brings to any group; and (2) they ignore the important imperative of affirmative action.

Conclusions

The approaches to change listed in this section cover a broad range —small, large, short-term, long-term, individual, organizational, and societal. Implementation of change is the subject of an impressive literature (Leavitt and Webb 1978) whose distillation is not possible in a few paragraphs. And clearly, the vast societal changes that are called for are beyond the scope of this chapter. But perhaps a few last cautionary words are in order.

We are *not* proposing that women should become pseudomen and men pseudowomen. The need is for greater balance and freedom for both sexes. Sex role stereotypes of active males and passive, helpful females contribute to the rigidity with which the sexes are pressed into

sex-segregated organizational roles. While changing such stereotypes
in the whole society is a longer and more arduous endeavour, altering
values and perceptions inside organizations is a far more attainable
goal. The linkages among competition, aggression, and masculinity can
be loosened. Women can work aggressively and compete without being
perceived as "defeminized." And men can, if we permit and encourage
it, behave more supportively without fearing "demasculinization." The
separation of masculinity and feminity from competition and aggressiveness on the one hand, and helpfulness and passivity on the other, is
a task which both the present managers of organizations and women
who aspire to management roles can begin to address immediately.

Bibliography

Abegglen, J. G. *The Japanese factory.* Glencoe, Ill.: The Free Press,
1958.

Aiken, L. R. Update on attitudes and other affective variables in learning mathematics. *Review of Educational Research,* 1976, *46*:293–
311.

————. Attitudes toward mathematics. *Review of Educational Research,* 1970, *40*:551–96.

Argyris, C. *Understanding organizational behavior.* Homewood, Ill.:
Dorsey Press, 1960.

Askinas, B. E. The impact of coeducational living on peer interaction.
(Doctoral dissertation, Stanford University, 1971.) *Dissertation
Abstracts International,* 1971, *32,* 1634–A.

Barnard, C. I. *Functions of the executive.* Cambridge, Mass.: Harvard
University, 1968.

Bartol, K. M., & Wortman, Jr., M. S. Male versus female leaders: Effects on perceived leader behavior and satisfaction in a hospital.
Personnel Psychology, 1975, *28*:533–47.

Bass, B. M., Krusell, J., & Alexander, R. A. Male managers' attitudes
toward working women. *American Behavioral Scientist,* 1971, *15*:
221–36.

Bayes, M., & Newton, P. M. Women in authority: A sociopsychological analysis. *The Journal of Applied Behavioral Science,* 1978, *14*
(1):7–25.

Bernard, J. *The female world,* Part IV, in progress.

Best, R. *The group, sex and learning in the primary grades,* in progress.

Blake, R. R., & Mouton, J. S. *Grid organization development.* Houston, Texas: Gulf Publishing Co., 1968.

Blaxall, M., & Reagen, B., Eds. *Women and the workplace: The implications of occupational segregation.* Chicago, Ill.: The University of
Chicago Press, 1976.

358   Leading: Inspiration and direction

Borgatta, E. F., & Stimson, J. Sex differences in interaction character-istics. *Journal of Social Psychology,* 1963, *60*:89–100.

Bowman, C. W., Worthy, N. B., & Greyser, S. A. Are women execu-tives people? *Harvard Business Review,* July-August, 1965, *43*:14–17+.

Bradford, D. L., Sargent, A. C., Sprague, M. S. The executive man and woman: The issue of sexuality. Chapter 3 in *Bringing women into management,* Eds. Gordon, F. E., & Strober, M. H. New York: McGraw-Hill, 1975, 39–58.

Couch, A. S., & Carter, L. A factorial study of the rated behavior of group members. Paper presented at Eastern Psychological Associa-tion, Atlantic City, April, 1952.

Ellman, E. S. *Managing women in business.* Waterford, Conn.: Pren-tice-Hall, Inc., 1963.

Estler, S., & Davis, C. *Women in decision-making.* Stanford University Center for Research on Women, 1977 (April).

Fenema, E. *Influences of selected cognitive, effective and educational variables in sex-related differences in mathematics learning and studying.* National Institute of Education, Grant No. P–76–0274, 1976.

Gibb, C. A. Leadership. Chapter 24 in *Handbook of social psychology,* Vol. II, Ed. Lindzey, G. Cambridge, Mass.: Addison-Wesley Pub-lishing Co., Inc., 877–920.

Hall, K. P. Sex differences in initiation and influence in decision-mak-ing among prospective teachers. (Doctoral dissertation, Stanford University, 1972.) *Dissertation Abstracts International,* 1972, *33* 8), 3952–A.

Halpin, A. W., & Winer, B. J., A factorial study in the leader-behavior descriptions. In *Leader behavior: Its description and measurement,* Eds. Stogdill, R. M., & Coons, A. E., 1957, 39–51. Columbus: Ohio State University, Bureau of Business Research, Research Mono-graph #88.

Handley, A., & Sedlacek, W. Characteristics and work attitudes of women working on campus. *National Association of Women Deans, Administrators, and Counselors,* 1977, *40*(4).

Heiss, J. Degree of intimacy and male-female interaction. *Sociometry,* 1962, *25*:197–208.

Hennig, M., & Jardim, A. *The managerial woman.* Garden City, N.Y.: Anchor Press/Doubleday & Co., Inc., 1977.

Hoffman, L. W. Early childhood experiences and women's achieve-ment motives. *Journal of Social Issues,* 1972, *28*(2), 129–55.

Jewett, B. Trans. *Aristotle's politics.* New York, N.Y.: Modern Li-brary, 1943.

Johnson, R. T., & Ouchi, W. G. Made in America (under Japanese management). *Harvard Business Review,* Sept.-Oct., 1974:61–69.

Kanter, R. M. *Men and women of the corporation.* New York, N.Y.: Basic Books, Inc., 1977.

Kenkel, W. F. Differentiation in family decision making. *Sociology and Social Research,* 1957, *42*:18–25.

Lana, R. E., Vaughan, W., & McGinnies, E. Leadership and friendship status as factors in discussion group interaction. *Journal of Social Psychology,* 1960, *52*:127–34.

Leavitt, H. J. Beyond the analytic manager. *California Management Review,* spring, 1975, *17*(3):5–12; and summer, 1975, *17*(4): 11–21.

————. Applied organization change in industry: Structural, Technical, and human approaches. Chapter 4 in *New perspectives in organization research,* Eds. W. W. Cooper, H. J. Leavitt, M. W. Shelly, 2. New York, N.Y.: John Wiley & Sons, Inc., 1964, 55–71.

Leavitt, H. J., & Lipman-Blumen, J. Achievement styles and managerial behavior: The case for the relational manager. Unpublished manuscript, 1978.

Leavitt, H. J., & Webb, E. Implementing: Two approaches. Research Paper #440, May 1978, Research Paper Series, Graduate School of Business, Stanford University.

Lipman-Bluman, J. A paradigm for the entrance of women into new occupational roles. In *Women organizing,* Eds., Cummings, B., & Schuck, V. Garden City, Long Island, N.Y.: Adelphi University Press, forthcoming, spring, 1979.

————. A crisis perspective on divorce and role change. Chapter 10 in *Women into wives: The legal and economic impact of marriage.* Sage Yearbooks in Women's Policy Studies, Vol. 2, Eds., Chapman, J. R., & Gates, M. Beverly Hills, Calif.: Sage Publications, 1977.

————. Toward a homosocial theory of sex roles: An explanation of the sex segregation of social institutions. *Signs,* spring, 1976, *1*(3), Part 2, 15–31. (Reprinted in *Women and the workplace,* Eds., Blaxall, M., & Reagan, B. Chicago, Ill.: University of Chicago Press, 1976.)

————. A crisis framework applied to macro-sociological family changes: Marriage, divorce, and occupational trends associated with World War II. *Journal of Marriage and the Family,* November, 1975, 889–902.

————. Role de-differentiation as a system response to crisis: Occupational and political roles of women. *Sociological Inquiry,* 1973, *43*(2):105–129.

Lipman-Blumen, J., & Leavitt, H. J. Socialization and achievement patterns in cross-cultural perspective: Japanese and American family and work roles. Presented at the Ninth World Congress of Sociology, Uppsala, Sweden, August 14–19, 1978.

――――. Sexual behavior as an expression of achievement orientation. In *Human sexual development: Alternative perspectives,* Ed. Katchadourian, H. Berkeley, Calif.: University of California Press, 1978.

――――. Vicarious and direct achievement patterns in adulthood. *The Counseling Psychologist,* 1976, *6*(1):26–32. (Reprinted in *Career development and counseling of women,* Eds., Hansen, J. S., & Rapoza-Blocher, R. S.) Springfield, Ill.: Charles C. Thomas Publishing Co., 1977.

Lockheed, M. E. Cognitive style effects on sex status in student work groups. *Journal of Educational Psychology,* 1977, *69*(2):158–65.

――――. The modification of female leadership behavior in the presence of males. Educational Testing Service, Princeton, New Jersey. N.I.E. Grant No. NE–G–00–3–0130, October, 1976.

Lockheed, M. E., & Hall, K. P. Conceptualizing sex as a status characteristic: Applications to leadership training strategies. *Journal of Social Issues,* 1976, *32*(3):111–23.

Maccoby, E. M., & Jacklin, C. N. *The psychology of sex differences.* Stanford, Calif.: Stanford University Press, 1974.

Marak, G. E. The evolution of leadership structure. *Sociometry,* 1964, *27*:174–82.

McClelland, D. C., Atkinson, J. W., Clark, R. A., & Lowell, E. L. *The achievement motive.* New York: Irvington Publishers, 1953.

Michels, R. Authority. In *The encyclopedia of the social sciences,* Eds. Seligman, R. A., & Johnson, A. New York, N.Y.: Macmillan, 1937.

Morris, C. G., & Hackman, J. R. Behavioral correlates of perceived leadership. *Journal of Personality and Social Psychology,* 1969, *13*: 350–61.

Okamoto, Y. Japanese business behavior and the management based on groupism. Mimeographed ms., Faculty of Economics, University of Tokyo, no date.

Parsons, T. Family structure and the socialization of the child. In *Family socialization and interaction process,* Eds. Parsons, T., Bales, R. F. Glencoe, Ill.: The Free Press, 1955.

――――. *Essays in sociological theory pure and applied.* Glencoe, Ill.: The Free Press, 1949.

Reif, W. E., Newstrom, J. W., & Monezka, R. M. Exploding some myths about women managers. *California Management Review,* summer, 1975, *7*(4):72–79.

Roethlisberger, F. J. *The elusive phenomena: An autobiographical ac-*

count of my work in the field of organizational behavior at the Harvard Business School. Ed. Lombard, G. F. F. Boston, Mass.: Division of Research, Graduate School of Business Administration, Harvard University, 1977.

Rowe, M. P. Go hire yourself a mentor. In Proceedings of the Conference on Women's Leadership and Authority in the Health Professions, U.C. Santa Cruz, June 19–21, 1977, sponsored by Program for Women in Health Sciences, University of California, San Francisco, pp. 40–42.

Safilios-Rothschild, C. Theoretical model of sex discrimination in education. April 25, 1977, Final Report, Unpublished, Wayne State University.

———. Sex role socialization patterns in selected societies. Paper presented at the American Educational Research Association Annual Meetings, April 2, 1975, Washington, D.C.

Sells, L. High school mathematics as the critical filter in the job market. In *Developing opportunities for minorities in graduate education.* Proceedings of the Conference on Minority Graduate Education at the University of California, Berkeley, May, 1973, pp. 47–59.

Shapiro, E., Haseltine, F., & Rowe, M. P. Moving up: Role models, mentors, and the 'patron system.' *Sloan Management Review,* spring, 1978, *19*:51–58.

Shaw, M. E., & Sadler, O. W. Interaction patterns in heterosexual dyads varying in degree of intimacy. *Journal of Social Psychology,* 1965, *66*:345–51.

Strodtbeck, F. L., James, R. M., & Hawkins, C. Social status in jury deliberations. *American Sociological Review,* 1957, *22*:713–19.

Strodtbeck, F. L., & Mann, R. D. Sex role differentiation in jury deliberations. *Sociometry,* 1956, *19*:3–11.

Tannenbaum, A., Kavcic, B., Rosner, M., Vianello, M., & Wieser, G. *Hierarchy in organizations: An international comparison.* San Francisco, Calif.: Jossey Bass, 1974.

Tobias, S. *Overcoming math anxiety,* 1st ed. New York, N.Y.: Norton & Co., 1978.

Tuddenham, R. D., MacBride, P., & Zahn, V. The influence of the sex composition of the groups upon yielding to a distorted group norm. *Journal of Psychology,* 1958, *46*:243–51.

U.S. Department of Labor, Women's Bureau. *1975 Handbook on women workers.* Washington, D.C.: Government Printing Office, 1975, Bulletin 297.

Vogel, E. F. *Japan's new middle class: The salary man and his family in a Tokyo suburb.* Berkeley, Calif.: University of California Press, 1968.

Vroom, V., & Yetton, P. W. *Leadership and decision-making.* Pittsburgh, Pa.: University of Pittsburgh, 1973.

Weber, Max. *The theory of social and economic organization.* (Translated by Henderson, A. M., & Parsons, T.) Glencoe, Ill.: The Free Press, 1947.

Whittaker, J. O. Sex differences and susceptibility to interpersonal persuasion. *Journal of Social Psychology,* 1965, *66*:91–92.

Zander, A., & Van Egmond, E. Relationship of intelligence and social power to the interpersonal behavior of children. *Journal of Educational Psychology,* 1958, *49*:257–68.

Zdep, S. M. Intragroup reinforcement and its effects on leadership behavior. *Organizational Behavior and Human Performance,* 1969, *4*:284–98.

Zdep, S. M., & Oakes, W. F. Reinforcement of leadership behavior in group discussion. *Journal of Experimental Social Psychology,* 1967, *3*:310–20.

7 Power: Over and Under the Table

Introduction

Power is a difficult word to define simply and operationally. But certainly one major aspect of the notion of power is the capacity of one person to influence or control the behavior of others. Power becomes a central issue in hierarchical organizations. The whole idea of the human organization is built around the notion that some people can control and directly influence many others in orderly and systematic ways. But the word "power" has other connotations. Some don't smell so sweet. Some connotations are of blackmail, manipulation, coercion. This chapter, picking up from the Lipman-Blumen article in chapter 6, digs further into issues of power and influence.

In the first article, Martin and Sims, partially tongue in cheek, make a series of recommendations to the manager on ways to behave that will maximize his or her power. They suggest that the manager calculate his power tactics carefully and that he be aware constantly of his power position within the organization. Many of the tactics Martin and Sims propose will seem ethically borderline if not downright immoral. Yet managers everywhere will acknowledge at least a partial reality of just about every one of the tactics that Martin and Sims describe. We hope the reader struggles with this one, asking how far, when, and whether he or she ought to think as a manager, in the style outlined here.

The second paper, by Salancik and Pfeffer, is much more descriptive. It describes a contingency model of power and is concerned with who in an organization achieves power and what aspects of the organization tend to maintain that power. The Salancik and Pfeffer piece is part of a rapidly building trend to model, within organizations, patterns of organizational behavior as they occur in the real world. The reader will notice a sharp difference between the Salancik and Pfeffer orientation and more classical organizational theories which were much more formalistically concerned with issues like authority and responsibility in normative "principles" of organization.

The third paper, by David Mechanic, while older than the Salancik and Pfeffer piece, is out of the same tradition. Mechanic looks descriptively at how people in lower levels of hierarchies gain power and influence in organizations. What are the routes open to them? What are the handles that one can grab onto if one does not have stars on one's shoulders? Again, however, the emphasis is descriptive. It is not advice to the junior manager on how to gain power, as the Martin and Sims piece is, but rather a description of what people at low levels in particular hierarchies have been observed to do.

From all of these papers the reader should draw at least one essential theme. Power need not be a dirty word in organizations, and it need not be a clean word either. It is a hard reality. Some people in organizations can control the means to other people's satisfactions. They can do it many ways, formally and informally, above board and under the table. Everyone who lives in organizations must deal with power, both on the receiving end and as a user of power tools over other people. The question is not whether power is good or bad, but how it can be used both ethically and effectively.

Power Tactics
Norman H. Martin and
John Howard Sims

Executives—whether in business, government, education, or the church—have power and use it. They maneuver and manipulate in order to get a job done and, in many cases, to strengthen and enhance their own position. Although they would hate the thought and deny the allegation, the fact is that they are politicians. "Politics," according to one of the leading authorities in this complex and fascinating field, "is . . . concerned with relationships of control or of influence. To phrase the idea differently, politics deals with human relationships of superordination and subordination, of dominance and submission, of the governors and the governed."[1] In this sense, everyone who exercises power must be a politician.

It is true, as many others have pointed out in different connections, that we in this country have an instinctive revulsion against the term "power." It carries immoral connotations for us, despite the definitions of men like R. H. Tawney, the economic historian, who divorces it from any ethical attributes by calling it simply "the capacity of an individual or group of individuals to modify the conduct of other individuals or groups in the manner which he desires, and to prevent his own conduct from being modified in the manner which he does not."[2]

Furthermore, though we glorify ambition in the abstract, we frown on its practice and are distressed at the steps which must be taken if ambition is to be translated into actual advancement. Thus when power is coupled with ambition, we shy away and try to pretend that neither really exists.

Reprinted from the *Harvard Business Review*, November-December 1956, pp. 25–29, by permission of the authors and the publisher. © 1956 by the President and Fellows of Harvard College; all rights reserved.
    1. V. O. Key Jr., *Politics, Parties and Pressure Groups*, 2d ed. (New York: Thomas Y. Crowell Co., 1948), p. 3.
    2. R. H. Tawney, *Equality*, 4th ed. (London: George Allen & Unwin, Ltd., 1952), p. 175.

But the fact is that we use power and exercise our ambitions just the same—troubled though we may be by the proverbial New England conscience which "doesn't prevent you from doing anything—it just keeps you from enjoying it!"

The complexity of the problem is increased when we recall that the real source of power is not the superior but the subordinate. Men can only exercise that power which they are allowed by other men—albeit their positions are buttressed by economic, legal, and other props. The ultimate source of power is the group; and a group, in turn, is made up of people with consciousness and will, with emotion and irrationality, with intense personal interests and tenaciously held values.

The human being resists being treated as a constant. Knowledge, reason, and technical know-how will not suffice as means of control but give way to the arts of persuasion and inducement, of tactics and maneuver, of all that is involved in interpersonal relationships. Power cannot be given; it must be won. And the techniques and skills of winning it are at the same time the methods of employing it as a medium of control. This represents the political function of the power-holder.

In such a light, we see why the successful functioning and advancement of the executive is dependent, not only on those aspects of an enterprise which are physical and logical, but on morale, teamwork, authority, and obedience—in a word, on the vast intricacy of human relationships which make up the political universe of the executive.

The real question then becomes: How can power be used most effectively? What are some of the political strategems which the administrator must employ if he is to carry out his responsibilities and further his career? This is an area that has carefully been avoided by both students and practitioners of business—as if there were something shady about it. But facts are facts, and closing our eyes to them will not change them. Besides, if they are important facts, they should be brought into the open for examination.

Accordingly, we present here preliminary findings of the first stage of a fairly extensive investigation of just how the executive functions in his political-power environment. We have searched the biographies of well-known leaders of history, from Alexander to Roosevelt; we have explored the lives of successful industrialists like Rockefeller and Ford; and we have interviewed a number of contemporary executives.

There follows an account of certain tactics which we have found to be practiced by most men whose success rests on ability to control and direct the actions of others—no doubt, raw and oversimplified when reduced to a few black-and-white words, but for this very reason more likely to be provocative. With further refinement, these generalizations will serve as hypotheses in the succeeding stages of our research, but in the meantime we present them to businessmen to look at openly and objectively—to ask, "Do we not use just such techniques frequently?" and, if so, to ponder, "How can we best operate in this particular area, for our own interest as managers and for the good of people under us?"

Taking counsel

The able executive is cautious about how he seeks and receives advice. He takes counsel only when he himself desires it. His decisions must be made in terms of his own grasp of the situation, taking into account the views of others when he thinks it necessary. To act otherwise is to be subject, not to advice, but to pressure; to act otherwise too often produces vacillation and inconsistency.

Throwing a question to a group of subordinates is all too often interpreted as a delegation of power, and the executive may find himself answered with a decision instead of counsel. He must remember that he, not the group under him, is the responsible party. If an executive allows his subordinates to provide advice when he does not specifically call for it, he may find himself subject, not only to pressure, but to conflicting alignments of forces within his own ranks. A vague sort of policy which states, "I am always ready to hear your advice and ideas on anything," will waste time, confuse issues, dilute leadership, and erode power.

Alliances

In many respects, the executive system in a firm is composed of complexes of sponsor-protégé relationships.[3] For the protégé, these relationships provide channels for advancement; for the sponsor, they build a loyal group of followers. A wise administrator will make it a point to establish such associations with those above and below him. In the struggles for power and influence that go on in many organizations, every executive needs a devoted following and close alliances with other executives, both on his own level and above him, if he is to protect and to enhance his status and sphere of influence.

Alliances should not be looked upon, however, merely as a protective device. In addition, they provide ready-made systems of communication, through which the executive can learn firsthand how his decisions are being carried out, what unforeseen obstacles are being encountered, and what the level of morale in the organization is at any moment.

3. See Norman H. Martin and Anselm S. Strauss, "Patterns of Mobility within Industrial Organizations," *Journal of Business,* April 1956, p. 101.

Maneuverability

The wise executive maintains his flexibility, and he never completely commits himself to any one position or program. If forces beyond his control compel a major change in company policy, he can gracefully bend with the wind and cooperate with the inevitable, thus maintaining his status.

An executive should preserve maneuverability in career planning as well. He ought never to get in a situation that does not have plenty of escape hatches. He must be careful, for instance, that his career is not directly dependent on the superior position of a sponsor. He should provide himself with transferable talents, and interfirm alliances, so that he will be able to move elsewhere if the conditions in his current organization become untenable.

Communication

During recent years emphasis has been placed on the necessity for well-dredged channels of communication which run upward, downward, and sideways. Top management should supply its subordinates with maximum information, according to this theory; subordinates, in turn, must report fully to their chiefs.

It is possible, however, that executives have been oversold on maximizing the flow of information. It simply is not good strategy to communicate everything one knows. Instead, it may often be advantageous to withhold information or to time its release. This is especially true with reference to future plans—plans which may or may not materialize; it is also valid in the case of information that may create schism or conflict within the organization; and it is prudent when another executive is a threat to one's own position. Furthermore, information is an important tactical weapon, and should be considered as such.

It would appear, then, that executives should be concerned with determining "who gets to know what and when" rather than with simply increasing the flow. Completely open communcation deprives the executive of the exclusive power of directing information which should be his.

Compromising

The executive should accept compromise as a means of settling differences with his tongue in his cheek.While appearing to alter his view, he should continue to press forward toward a clear-cut set of goals. It is frequently necessary to give ground on small matters, to delay, to move off tangents, even to suffer reverses in order to retain power for future forward movement. Concessions, then, should be more apparent than real.

Negative timing

The executive is often urged to take action with which he is not in agreement. Sometimes pressure for such action arises from the expectations of subordinates, the influence of his associates with his superiors, the demands of custom and tradition, or other sources he would be unwise to ignore.

To give in to such demands would be to deny the executive's prerogative; to refuse might precipitate a dangerous crisis, and threaten his power. In such situations the executive may find it wise to use what might be called the technique of "negative timing." He initiates action, but the process of expedition is retarded. He is considering, studying, and planning for the problem; there are difficulties to be overcome and possible ramifications which must be considered. He is always *in the process* of doing something but never quite does it, or finally he takes action when it is actually too late. In this way the executive escapes the charge of dereliction, and at the same time the inadvisable program "dies on the vine."

Self dramatization

Most vocal communication in which an executive engages—whether with his superiors, his colleagues, or his subordinates—is unpremeditated, sincere, spontaneous. His nonvocal communication—the impression projected by his posture, gestures, dress, or facial expressions —is commonly just as natural.

But executives would do well to reexamine this instinctive behavior, for many of them are overlooking an important political strategem. The skill of the actor—whose communcation is "artistic" as opposed to "natural"—represents a potential asset to an administrator. Dramatic art is a process by which selections from reality are chosen and arranged by the artists for the particular purpose of arousing the emotions, of convincing, of persuading, of altering the behavior of the audience in a *planned direction*.

The actor's purpose is no different from that of the manager who wants to activate his subordinates in certain specific directions—to secure a certain response from those with whom he communicates. The actor's peculiar gift is in deliberately shaping his own speech and behavior to accomplish his purpose. The element of chance, the variable of the unknown, is diminished, if not removed; and rehearsal with some foreknowledge of what is to occur takes place. The *how* of communicating is considered as well as the *what*.

Of course, this is no easy task. The effectiveness of the actor's performance depends on his ability to estimate what will stimulate the audience to respond. And once he makes his choices, he must be able to use them skillfully. His voice and body must be so well disciplined, so well trained, that the images he chooses may be given life. The question is, How can an executive acquire the skill of artistic communication? How can he learn to dramatize himself?

The development of sharper powers of observation is the first step. Having witnessed effective communication—whether a TV drama or an actual meeting of the board of directors—the executive should try to determine what made it effective. He should pay attention to *how* a successful man handled himself, not what he said or did. Formal classes can provide the executive with control over his voice—its pitch, tone, color, speed, diction; training can do the same for his body—gesture, posture, and mime. Most important, the executive should seize any opportunity to gain actual experience in putting such skills to work, in amateur theatricals or "role-playing" sessions.

It would be foolish to deny that such skills cannot be entirely learned; to some extent they depend on the unknowns of flair, talent, and genius. But such an acknowledgement does not excuse the executive from making an effort, for the range of possible improvement is very great.

Confidence

Related to, but not identical with, self-dramatization is the outward appearance of confidence. Once an executive has made a decision, he must look and act decided. In some instances genuine inner conviction may be lacking, or the manager may find it difficult to generate the needed dynamics. The skillful executive who finds himself in such a situation will either produce the effect of certainty or postpone any contact with his associates in order to avoid appearing in an unfavorable light.

Thus, the man who constantly gives the impression of knowing what he is doing—even if he does not—is using his power and increasing it at the same time.

Always the boss

Warm personal relations with subordinates have sometimes been considered the mark of a good executive. But in practice an atmosphere of social friendship interferes with the efficiency of an operation and acts to limit the power of the manager. Personal feelings should not be a basis for action—either negative or positive. The executive should never permit himself to be so committed to a subordinate as a friend that he is unable to withdraw from this personal involvement and regard the man objectively as an element in a given situation.

Thus, a thin line of separation between executive and subordinate must always be maintained. The situation should be one of isolation and contact—of the near and far—of marginality. No matter how cordial he may be, the executive must sustain a line of privacy which cannot be transgressed; in the final analysis, he must always be the boss. If we assume, then, that the traditional "open-door" policy of the modern executive is good strategy, we must always ask the question: "How far open?"

The foregoing discussion will undoubtedly raise questions, and even indignation, in the minds of some readers. In the last two decades, the finger of censure has often been pointed at the interpersonal relations in the management of industrial organizations, questioning whether they are harmonious with a democratic society and ideology.[4] Executives have been urged to adopt practices and programs aimed at "democratizing" their businesses. Perhaps they have even developed a sense of guilt from the realization of their own position of authority and that they cannot be completely frank, sincere, honest, and aboveboard in their interpersonal relations. We live in an era of "groupiness"; we are bombarded with admonitions which insist that everyone who is participating in an enterprise should have a part in the management of it.

In the light of such a trend even the terminology used in this article —"power," "maneuver," "tactics," "techniques"—appears disturbing when set down in black and white. But in fact it is neither immoral nor cynical to recognize and describe the actual daily practices of power. After all, sweeping them under the rug—making believe that they are not actually part of the executive's activity—does not cause them to vanish. Open and honest discussion of the political aspects in the administrator's job exposes these stratagems to the constructive spotlight of knowledge. They exist; therefore, we had better take a look at them and see what they are really like.

As we delve deeper into the study of political tactics in business management, the contrast with modern human relations theory and practice will stand out in ever-sharper relief. Mutual confidence, open communication, continuing consultation and participation by subordinates, friendship, and an atmosphere of democracy seem hard to reconcile with much of the maneuvering and power plays that go on in the nation's offices and factories every day.

Yet businessmen must develop some rationale of executive behavior which can encompass the idealism of democracy and the practicality of politics—and, at the same time, be justified in terms of ultimate values. If they do not, they will feel like hypocrites as the day-to-day operation of their offices clashes with their speeches before women's

4. See Thomas C. Cochran, "Business and the Democratic Tradition," *Harvard Business Review*, March–April 1956, p. 39.

clubs. The old cliché that "business is business" is no longer satisfying to the general public nor to the executive himself.

One way to try to fit human relations theory and political tactics together is to state that the means or ways of exercising power are neutral. In and of themselves, they have no moral value. They take on moral qualities only in connection with the ends for which they are used. Power can be used for good or ill according to this theory, and we should have the courage and knowledge to use it wisely. Conscious, deliberate, and skilled use of executive power means responsible use of power. If men in the past have employed power for evil ends, that is unfortunate; it is just as true that other men, if they had made use of business politics in an effective fashion, might have been a greater force for good.

The difficulty with this line of thought lies in the well-known pitfalls inherent in the timeless means-ends controversy. In real life, what are means and what are ends? Can you achieve good ends by bad means? If the way one man conducts his relationship with another has no moral implications, what human activity does have moral significance?

Others may take the position that "so long as my general philosophy is sound and moral, the specific actions I have to take in the course of my job don't matter." But one may question the validity of a philosophy of life that breaks down every time it comes into contact with reality.

Still another formula could be found in the statement, "The good of the company comes before that of an individual. If I have to violate moral codes and democratic principles in dealing with one man, that is too bad for him. But I cannot allow any single person to overshadow the interests of all our other employees, stockholders, and customers." The skeptical listener might then raise the issue of collectivism versus individualism, and ask whether the general welfare really overrides the worth and dignity of the individual. Can we build a society on the idea of the individual's importance if we violate the principle whenever it interferes with what we consider to be the good of the group?

There are, of course, other approaches, but they too are fraught with internal contradictions. The riddle, then, remains unsolved; the conflict between the use of power and the principles of democracy and enlightened management is unrelieved. Businessmen, who face this paradox every day in countless situations, cannot avoid the responsibility of explaining or resolving it. If a viable philosophy of management is to be developed, they must contribute their ideas—for the sake of their own peace of mind, if nothing else.

If this article succeeds in getting more businessmen to do some thinking along this line, then it will have served its purpose.

Who Gets Power—and How They Hold on to It: A Strategic-Contingency Model of Power

Gerald R. Salancik

Jeffrey Pfeffer

Power is held by many people to be a dirty word or, as Warren Bennis. has said, "It is the organization's last dirty secret."

This article will argue that traditional "political" power, far from being a dirty business, is, in its most naked form, one of the few mechanisms available for aligning an organization with its own reality. However, institutionalized forms of power—what we prefer to call the cleaner forms of power: authority, legitimization, centralized control, regulations, and the more modern "management information systems" —tend to buffer the organization from reality and obscure the demands of its environment. Most great states and institutions declined, not because they played politics, but because they failed to accommodate to the political realities they faced. Political processes, rather than being mechanisms for unfair and unjust allocations and appointments, tend toward the realistic resolution of conflicts among interests. And power, while it eludes definition, is easy enough to recognize by its consequences—the ability of those who possess power to bring about the outcomes they desire.

The model of power we advance is an elaboration of what has been called strategic-contingency theory, a view that sees power as something that accrues to organizational subunits (individuals, departments) that cope with critical organizational problems. Power is used by subunits, indeed, used by all who have it, to enhance their own survival through control of scarce critical resources, through the placement of allies in key positions, and through the definition of organizational problems and policies. Because of the processes by which power develops and is used, organizations become both more aligned and more misaligned with their environments. This contradiction is the most interesting aspect of organizational power, and one that makes administration one of the most precarious of occupations.

What is organizational power?

You can walk into most organizations and ask without fear of being misunderstood, "Which are the powerful groups or people in this organization?" Although many organizational informants may be *unwilling* to tell you, it is unlikely they will be *unable* to tell you. Most people do not require explicit definitions to know what power is.

Power is simply the ability to get things done the way one wants them to be done. For a manager who wants an increased budget to launch a project that he thinks is important, his power is measured by his ability to get that budget. For an executive vice-president who wants to be chairman, his power is evidenced by his advancement toward his goal.

People in organizations not only know what you are talking about when you ask who is influential but they are likely to agree with one another to an amazing extent. Recently, we had a chance to observe this in a regional office of an insurance company. The office had 21 department managers; we asked ten of these managers to rank all 21 according to the influence each one had in the organization. Despite the fact that ranking 21 things is a difficult task, the managers sat down and began arranging the names of their colleagues and themselves in a column. Only one person bothered to ask, "What do you mean by influence?" When told "power," he responded, "Oh," and went on. We compared the rankings of all ten managers and found virtually no disagreement among them in the managers ranked among the top five or the bottom five. Differences in the rankings came from department heads claiming more influence for themselves than their colleagues attributed to them.

Such agreement on those who have influence, and those who do not, was not unique to this insurance company. So far we have studied over 20 very different organizations—universities, research firms, factories, banks, retailers, to name a few. In each one we found individuals able to rate themselves and their peers on a scale of influence or power. We have done this both for specific decisions and for general impact on organizational policies. Their agreement was unusually high, which suggests that distributions of influence exist well enough in everyone's mind to be referred to with ease—and, we assume, with accuracy.

Where does organizational power come from?

Earlier we stated that power helps organizations become aligned with their realities. This hopeful prospect follows from what we have dubbed the strategic-contingencies theory of organizational power. Briefly, those subunits most able to cope with the organization's critical problems and uncertainties acquire power. In its simplest form, the strategic-contingencies theory implies that when an organization faces a number of lawsuits that threaten its existence, the legal department will gain power and influence over organizational decisions. Somehow other organizational interest groups will recognize its critical importance and confer upon it a status and power never before enjoyed. This influence may extend beyond handling legal matters and into decisions about product design, advertising production, and so on. Such extensions undoubtedly would be accompanied by appropriate, or acceptable, verbal justifications. In time, the head of the legal department may become the head of the corporation, just as in times past the vice-president for marketing had become the president when market shares were a worrisome problem and, before him, the chief engineer, who had made the production line run as smooth as silk.

Stated in this way, the strategic-contingencies theory of power paints an appealing picture of power. To the extent that power is determined by the critical uncertainties and problems facing the organization and, in turn, influences decisions in the organization, the organization is aligned with the realities it faces. In short, power facilitates the organization's adaptation to its environment—or its problems.

We can cite many illustrations of how influence derives from a subunit's ability to deal with critical contingencies. Michael Crozier described a French cigarette factory in which the maintenance engineers had a considerable say in the plantwide operation. After some probing he discovered that the group possessed the solution to one of the major problems faced by the company, that of troubleshooting the elaborate, expensive, and irascible automated machines that kept breaking down and dumbfounding everyone else. It was the one problem that the plant manager could in no way control.

The production workers, while troublesome from time to time, created no insurmountable problems; the manager could reasonably predict their absenteeism or replace them when necessary. Production scheduling was something he could deal with since, by watching inventories and sales, the demand for cigarettes was known long in advance. Changes in demand could be accommodated by slowing down or speeding up the line. Supplies of tobacco and paper were also easily dealt with through stockpiles and advance orders.

The one thing that management could neither control nor accommodate to, however, was the seemingly happenstance breakdowns. And the foremen couldn't instruct the workers what to do when emergencies developed since the maintenance department kepts is records of problems and solutions locked up in a cabinet or in its members' heads. The breakdowns were, in truth, a critical source of uncertainty for the organization, and the maintenance engineers were the only ones who could cope with the problem.

The engineers' strategic role in coping with breakdowns afforded them a considerable say on plant decisions. Schedules and production quotas were set in consultation with them. And the plant manager, while formally their boss, accepted their decisions about personnel in their operation. His submission was to his credit, for without their cooperation he would have had an even more difficult time in running the plant.

Ignoring critical consequences

In this cigarette factory, sharing influence with the maintenance workers reflected the plant manager's awareness of the critical contingencies. However, when organizational members are not aware of the critical contingencies they face, and do not share influence accordingly, the failure to do so can create havoc. In one case, an insurance company's regional office was having problems with the performance of one of its departments, the coding department. From the outside, the department looked like a disaster area. The clerks who worked in it were somewhat dissatisfied; their supervisors paid little attention to them, and they resented the hard work. Several other departments were critical of this manager, claiming that she was inconsistent in meeting deadlines. The person most critical was the claims manager. He resented having to wait for work that was handled by her department, claiming that it held up his claims adjusters. Having heard the rumors about dissatisfaction among her subordinates, he attributed the situation to poor supervision. He was second in command in the office and therefore took up the issue with her immediate boss, the head of administrative services. They consulted with the personnel manager and the three of them concluded that the manager needed leadership training to improve her relations with her subordinates. The coding manager objected, saying it was a waste of time, but agreed to go along with the training and also agreed to give more priority to the claims department's work. Within a week after the training, the results showed that her workers were happier but that the performance of her department had decreased, save for the people serving the claims department.

About this time, we began, quite independently, a study of influence in this organization. We asked the administrative services director to draw up flow charts of how the work of one department moved on to the next department. In the course of the interview, we noticed that the coding department began or interceded in the work flow of most of the other departments and casually mentioned to him, "The coding manager must be very influential." He said "No, not really. Why would you think so?" Before we could reply he recounted the story of her leadership training and the fact that things were worse. We then told him that it seemed obvious that the coding department would be influential from the fact that all the other departments depended on it. It was also clear why productivity had fallen. The coding manager took the training seriously and began spending more time raising her workers' spirits than she did worrying about the problems of all the departments that depended on her. Giving priority to the claims area only exaggerated the problem, for their work was getting done at the expense of the work of the other departments. Eventually the company hired a few more clerks to relieve the pressure in the coding department and performance returned to a more satisfactory level.

Originally we got involved with this insurance company to examine how the influence of each manager evolved from his or her department's handling of critical organizational contingencies. We reasoned that one of the most important contingencies faced by all profit-making organizations was that of generating income. Thus we expected managers would be influential to the extent to which they contributed to this function. Such was the case. The underwriting managers, who wrote the policies that committed the premiums, were the most influential; the claims managers, who kept a lid on the funds flowing out, were a close second. Least influential were the managers of functions unrelated to revenue, such as mailroom and payroll managers. And contrary to what the administrative services manager believed, the third most powerful department head (out of 21) was the woman in charge of the coding function, which consisted of rating, recording, and keeping track of the codes of all policy applications and contracts. Her peers attributed more influence to her than could have been inferred from her place on the organization chart. And it was not surprising, since they all depended on her department. The coding department's records, their accuracy and the speed with which they could be retrieved, affected virtually every other operating department in the insurance office. The underwriters depended on them in getting the contracts straight; the typing department depended on them in preparing the formal contract document; the claims department depended on them in adjusting claims; and accounting depended on them for billing. Unfortunately, the "bosses" were not aware of these dependences, for unlike the cigarette factory, there were no massive breakdowns that made them obvious, while the coding manager, who was a hard-working but quiet person, did little to announce her importance.

The cases of this plant and office illustrate nicely a basic point about the source of power in organizations. The basis for power in an organization derives from the ability of a person or subunit to take or not take actions that are desired by others. The coding manager was seen as influential by those who depended on her department, but not by the people at the top. The engineers were influential because of their role in keeping the plant operating. The two cases differ in these respects: The coding supervisor's source of power was not as widely recognized as that of the maintenance engineers, and she did not use her source of power to influence decisions; the maintenance engineers did. Whether power is used to influence anything is a separate issue. We should not confuse this issue with the fact that power derives from a social situation in which one person has a capacity to do something and another person does not, but wants it done.

Power sharing in organizations

Power is shared in organizations; and it is shared out of necessity more than out of concern for principles of organizational development or participatory democracy. Power is shared because no one person controls all the desired activities in the organization. While the factory owner may hire people to operate his noisy machines, once hired they have some control over the use of the machinery. And thus they have power over him in the same way he has power over them. Who has more power over whom is a mooter point than that of recognizing the inherent nature of organizing as a sharing of power.

Let's expand on the concept that power derives from the activities desired in an organization. A major way of managing influence in organizations is through the designation of activities. In a bank we studied, we saw this principle in action. This bank was planning to install a computer system for routine credit evaluation. The bank, rather progressive-minded, was concerned that the change would have adverse effects on employees and therefore surveyed their attitudes.

The principal opposition to the new system came, interestingly, not from the employees who performed the routine credit checks, some of whom would be relocated because of the change, but from the manager of the credit department. His reason was quite simple. The manager's primary function was to give official approval to the applications, catch any employee mistakes before giving approval, and arbitrate any difficulties the clerks had in deciding what to do. As a consequence of his role, others in the organization, including his superiors, subordinates, and colleagues, attributed considerable importance to him. He, in turn, for example, could point to the low proportion of credit approvals, compared with other financial institutions, that resulted in bad debts. Now, to his mind, a wretched machine threatened to transfer his role to a computer programmer, a man who knew nothing of finance and who, in addition, had ten years less seniority. The credit manager eventually quit for a position at a smaller firm with lower pay, but one in which he would have more influence than his redefined job would have left him with.

Because power derives from activities rather than individuals, an individual's or subgroup's power is never absolute and derives ultimately from the context of the situation. The amount of power an individual has at any one time depends, not only on the activities he or she controls, but also on the existence of other persons or means by which the activities can be achieved and on those who determine what ends are desired and, hence, on what activities are desired and critical for the organization. One's own power always depends on other people for these two reasons. Other people, or groups or organizations, can determine the definition of what is a critical contingency for the organization and can also undercut the uniqueness of the individual's personal contribution to the critical contingencies of the organization.

Perhaps one can best appreciate how situationally dependent power is by examining how it is distributed. In most societies, power organizes around scarce and critical resources. Rarely does power organize around abundant resources. In the United States, a person doesn't become powerful because he or she can drive a car. There are simply too many others who can drive with equal facility. In certain villages in Mexico, on the other hand, a person with a car is accredited with enormous social status and plays a key role in the community. In addition to scarcity, power is also limited by the need for one's capacities in a social system. While a racer's ability to drive a car around a 90° turn at 80 mph may be sparsely distributed in a society, it is not likely to lend the driver much power in the society. The ability simply does not play a central role in the activities of the society.

The fact that power revolves around scarce and critical activities, of course, makes the control and organization of those activities a major battleground in struggles for power. Even relatively abundant or trivial resources can become the bases for power if one can organize and control their allocation and the definition of what is critical. Many occupational and professional groups attempt to do just this in modern economies. Lawyers organize themselves into associations, regulate the entrance requirements for novitiates, and then get laws passed specifying situations that require the services of an attorney. Workers had little power in the conduct of industrial affairs until they organized themselves into closed and controlled systems. In recent years, women and blacks have tried to define themselves as important and critical to the social system, using law to reify their status.

In organizations there are obviously opportunities for defining certain activities as more critical than others. Indeed, the growth of managerial thinking to include defining organizational objectives and goals has done much to foster these opportunities. One sure way to liquidate the power of groups in the organization is to define the need for their services out of existence. David Halberstam presents a description of how just such a thing happened to the group of correspondents that evolved around Edward R. Murrow, the brilliant journalist, interviewer, and war correspondent of CBS News. A close friend of CBS chairman and controlling stockholder William S. Paley, Murrow, and the news department he directed, were endowed with freedom to do what they felt was right. He used it to create some of the best documentaries and commentaries ever seen on television. Unfortunately, television became too large, too powerful, and too suspect in the eyes of the federal government that licensed it. It thus became, or at least the top executives believed it had become, too dangerous to have in-depth, probing commentary on the news. Crisp, dry uneditorializing headliners were considered safer. Murrow was out and Walter Cronkite was in.

The power to define what is critical in an organization is no small power. Moreover, it is the key to understanding why organizations are either aligned with their environments or misaligned. If an organization defines certain activities as critical when in fact they are not critical, given the flow of resources coming into the organization, it is not likely to survive, at least in its present form.

Most organizations manage to evolve a distribution of power and influence that is aligned with the critical realities they face in the environment. The environment, in turn, includes both the internal environment, the shifting situational contexts in which particular decisions get made, and the external environment that it can hope to influence but is unlikely to control.

The critical contingencies

The critical contingencies facing most organizations derive from the environmental context within which they operate. This determines the available needed resources and thus determines the problems to be dealt with. That power organizes around handling these problems suggests an important mechanism by which organizations keep in tune with their external environments. The strategic-contingencies model implies that subunits that contribute to the critical resources of the organization will gain influence in the organization. Their influence presumably is then used to bend the organization's activities to the contingencies that determine its resources. This idea may strike one as obvious. But its obviousness in no way diminishes its importance. Indeed, despite its obviousness, it escapes the notice of many organizational analysts and managers, who all too frequently think of the organization in terms of a descending pyramid, in which all the departments in one tier hold equal power and status. This presumption denies the reality that departments differ in the contributions they are believed to make to the overall organization's resources, as well as to the fact that some are more equal than others.

Because of the importance of this idea to organizational effectiveness, we decided to examine it carefully in a large midwestern university. A university offers an excellent site for studying power. It is composed of departments with nominally equal power and is administered by a central executive structure much like other bureaucracies. However, at the same time is is a situation in which the departments have clearly defined identities and face diverse external environments. Each department has its own bodies of knowledge, its own institutions, its own sources of prestige and resources. Because the departments operate in different external environments, they are likely to contribute differentially to the resources of the overall organization. Thus a physics department with close ties to NASA may contribute substantially to the funds of the university; and a history department with a renowned historian in residence may contribute to the intellectual credibility or prestige of the whole university. Such variations permit one to examine how these various contributions lead to obtaining power within the university.

We analyzed the influence of 29 university departments throughout an 18-month period in their history. Our chief interest was to determine whether departments that brought more critical resources to the university would be more powerful than departments that contributed fewer or less critical resources.

To identify the critical resources each department contributed, the heads of all departments were interviewed about the importance of seven different resources to the university's success. The seven included undergraduate students (the factor determining size of the state allocations by the university), national prestige, administrative expertise, and so on. The most critical resource was found to be contract and grant monies received by a department's faculty for research or consulting services. At this university, contract and grants contributed somewhat less than 50 percent of the overall budget, with the remainder primarily coming from state appropriations. The importance attributed to contract and grant monies, and the rather minor importance of undergraduate students, was not surprising for this particular university. The university was a major center for graduate education; many of its departments ranked in the top ten of their respective fields. Grant and contract monies were the primary source of discretionary funding available for maintaining these programs of graduate education, and hence for maintaining the university's prestige. The prestige of the university itself was critical both in recruiting able students and attracting top-notch faculty.

From university records it was determined what relative contributions each of the 29 departments made to the various needs of the university (national prestige, outside grants, teaching). Thus, for instance, one department may have contributed to the university by teaching 7 percent of the instructional units, bringing in 2 percent of the outside contracts and grants, and having a national ranking of 20. Another department, on the other hand, may have taught 1 percent of the instructional units, contributed 12 percent to the grants, and be ranked the third best department in its field within the country.

The question was: Do these different contributions determine the relative power of the departments within the university? Power was measured in several ways; but regardless of how measured, the answer was Yes. Those three resources together accounted for about 70 percent of the variance in subunit power in the university.

But the most important predictor of departmental power was the department's contribution to the contracts and grants of the university. Sixty percent of the variance in power was due to this one factor, suggesting that the power of departments derived primarily from the dollars they provided for graduate education, the activity believed to be the most important for the organization.

The impact of organizational power on decision making

The measure of power we used in studying this university was an analysis of the responses of the department heads we interviewed. While such perceptions of power might be of interest in their own right, they contribute little to our understanding of how the distribution of power might serve to align an organization with its critical realities. For this we must look to how power actually influences the decisions and policies of organizations.

While it is perhaps not absolutely valid, we can generally gauge the relative importance of a department of an organization by the size of the budget allocated to it relative to other departments. Clearly it is of importance to the administrators of those departments whether they get squeezed in a budget crunch or are given more funds to strike out after new opportunities. And it should also be clear that when those decisions are made and one department can go ahead and try new approaches while another must cut back on the old, then the deployment of the resources of the organization in meeting its problem is most directly affected.

Thus our study of the university led us to ask the following question: Does power lead to influence in the organization? To answer this question, we found it useful first to ask another one, namely: Why should department heads try to influence organizational decisions to favor their own departments to the exclusion of other departments? While this second question may seem a bit naive to anyone who has witnessed the political realities of organizations, we posed it in a context of research on organizations that sees power as an illegitimate threat to the neater rational authority of modern bureaucracies. In this context, decisions are not believed to be made because of the dirty business of politics but because of the overall goals and purposes of the organization. In a university, one reasonable basis for decision making is the teaching workload of departments and the demands that follow from that workload. We would expect, therefore, that departments with heavy student demands for courses would be able to obtain funds for teaching. Another reasonable basis for decision making is quality. We would expect, for that reason, that departments with esteemed reputations would be able to obtain funds both because their quality suggests they might use such funds effectively and because such funds would allow them to maintain their quality. A rational model of bureaucracy intimates, then, that the organizational decisions taken would favor those who perform the stated purposes of the organization—teaching undergraduates and training professional and scientific talent—well.

The problem with rational models of decision making, however, is that what is rational to one person may strike another as irrational. For most departments, resources are a question of survival. While teaching undergraduates may seem to be a major goal for some members of the university, developing knowledge may seem so to others; and to still others, advising governments and other institutions about policies may seem to be the crucial business. Everyone has his own idea of the proper priorities in a just world. Thus goals rather than being clearly defined and universally agreed upon are blurred and contested throughout the organization. If such is the case, then the decisions taken on behalf of the organization as a whole are likely to reflect the goals of those who prevail in political contests, namely, those with power in the organization.

Will organizational decisions always reflect the distribution of power in the organization? Probably not. Using power for influence requires a certain expenditure of effort, time, and resources. Prudent and judicious persons are not likely to use their power needlessly or wastefully. And it is likely that power will be used to influence organizational decisions primarily under circumstances that both require and favor its use. We have examined three conditions that are likely to affect the use of power in organizations: scarcity, criticality, and uncertainty. The first suggests that subunits will try to exert influence when the resources of the organization are scarce. If there is an abundance of resources, then a particular department or a particular individual has little need to attempt influence. With little effort, he can get all he wants anyway.

The second condition, criticality, suggests that a subunit will attempt to influence decisions to obtain resources that are critical to its own survival and activities. Criticality implies that one would not waste effort, or risk being labeled obstinate, by fighting over trivial decisions affecting one's operations.

An office manager would probably balk less about a threatened cutback in copying machine usage than about a reduction in typing staff. An advertising department head would probably worry less about losing his lettering artist than his illustrator. Criticality is difficult to define because what is critical depends on people's beliefs about what is critical. Such beliefs may or may not be based on experience and knowledge and may or may not be agreed upon by all. Scarcity, for instance, may itself affect conceptions of criticality. When slack resources drop off, cutbacks have to be made—those "hard decisions," as congressmen and resplendent administrators like to call them. Managers then find themselves scrapping projects they once held dear.

The third condition that we believe affects the use of power is uncertainty: When individuals do not agree about what the organization should do or how to do it, power and other social processes will affect decisions. The reason for this is simply that, if there are no clear-cut criteria available for resolving conflicts of interest, then the only means for resolution is some form of social process, including power, status, social ties, or some arbitrary process like flipping a coin or drawing straws. Under conditions of uncertainty, the powerful manager can argue his case on any grounds and usually win it. Since there is no real consensus, other contestants are not likely to develop counter arguments or amass sufficient opposition. Moreover, because of his power and their need for access to the resources he controls, they are more likely to defer to his arguments.

Although the evidence is slight, we have found that power will influence the allocations of scarce and critical resources. In the analysis of power in the university, for instance, one of the most critical resources needed by departments is the general budget. First granted by the state legislature, the general budget is later allocated to individual departments by the university administration in response to requests from the department heads. Our analysis of the factors that contribute to a department getting more or less of this budget indicated that sub-unit power was the major predictor, overriding such factors as student demand for courses, national reputations of departments, or even the size of a department's faculty. Moreover, other research has shown that when the general budget has been cut back or held below previous uninflated levels, leading to monies becoming more scarce, budget allocations mirror departmental powers even more closely.

Student enrollment and faculty size, of course, do themselves relate to budget allocations, as we would expect since they determine a department's need for resources, or at least offer visible testimony of needs. But departments are not always able to get what they need by the mere fact of needing. In one analysis it was found that high-power departments were able to obtain budget without regard to their teaching loads and, in some cases, actually in inverse relation to their teaching loads. In contrast, low-power departments could get increases in budget only when they could justify the increases by a recent growth in teaching load, and then only when it was far in excess of norms for other departments.

General budget is only one form of resource that is allocated to departments. There are others such as special grants for student fellowships or faculty research. These are critical to departments because they affect the ability to attract other resources, such as outstanding faculty or students. We examined how power influenced the allocations of four resources department heads had described as critical and scarce.

When the four resources were arrayed from the most to the least critical and scarce, we found that departmental power best predicted the allocations of the most critical and scarce resources. In other words, the analysis of how power influences organizational allocations leads to this conclusion: Those subunits most likely to survive in times of strife are those that are most critical to the organization. Their importance to the organization gives them power to influence resource allocations that enhance their own survival.

How external environment influences executive selection

Power not only influences the survival of key groups in an organization, it also influences the selection of individuals to key leadership positions, and by such a process further aligns the organization with its environmental context.

We can illustrate this with a recent study of the selection and tenure of chief administrators in 57 hospitals in Illinois. We assumed that since the critical problems facing the organization would enhance the power of certain groups at the expense of others, then the leaders to emerge should be those most relevant to the context of the hospitals. To assess this we asked each chief administrator about his professional background and how long he had been in office. The replies were then related to the hospital's funding, ownership, and competitive conditions for patients and staff.

One aspect of a hospital's context is the source of its budget. Some hospitals, for instance, are run much like other businesses. They sell bed space, patient care, and treatment services. They charge fees sufficient both to cover their costs and to provide capital for expansion. The main source of both their operating and capital funds is patient billings. Increasingly, patient billings are paid for, not by patients, but by private insurance companies. Insurers like Blue Cross dominate and represent a potent interest group outside a hospital's control but critical to its income. The insurance companies, in order to limit their own costs, attempt to hold down the fees allowable to hospitals, which they do effectively from their positions on state rate boards. The squeeze on hospitals that results from fees increasing slowly while costs climb rapidly more and more demands the talents of cost accountants or people trained in the technical expertise of hospital administration.

By contrast, other hospitals operate more like social service institutions, either as government health-care units (Bellevue Hospital in New York City and Cook County Hospital in Chicago, for example) or as charitable institutions. These hospitals obtain a large proportion of their operating and capital funds, not from privately insured patients, but from government subsidies or private donations. Such institutions rather than requiring the talents of a technically efficient administrator are likely to require the savvy of someone who is well integrated into the social and political power structure of the community.

Not surprisingly, the characteristics of administrators predictably reflect the funding context of the hospitals with which they are associated. Those hospitals with larger proportions of their budget obtained from private insurance companies were most likely to have administrators with backgrounds in accounting and least likely to have administrators whose professions were business or medicine. In contrast, those hospitals with larger proportions of their budget derived from private donations and local governments were most likely to have administrators with business or professional backgrounds and least likely to have accountants. The same held for formal training in hospital management. Professional hospital administrators could easily be found in hospitals drawing their incomes from private insurance and rarely in hospitals dependent on donations or legislative appropriations.

As with the selection of administrators, the context of organizations has also been found to affect the removal of executives. The environment, as a source of organizational problems, can make it more or less difficult for executives to demonstrate their value to the organization. In the hospitals we studied, long-term administrators came from hospitals with few problems. They enjoyed amicable and stable relations with their local business and social communities and suffered little competition for funding and staff. The small city hospital director who attended civic and Elks meetings while running the only hospital within a 100-mile radius, for example, had little difficulty holding on to his job. Turnover was highest in hospitals with the most problems, a phenomenon similar to that observed in a study of industrial organizations in which turnover was highest among executives in industries with competitive environments and unstable market conditions. The interesting thing is that instability characterized the industries rather than the individual firms in them. The troublesome conditions in the individual firms were attributed, or rather misattributed, to the executives themselves.

It takes more than problems, however, to terminate a manager's leadership. The problems themselves must be relevant and critical. This is clear from the way in which an administrator's tenure is affected by the status of the hospital's operating budget. Naively we might assume that all administrators would need to show a surplus. Not necessarily so. Again, we must distinguish between those hospitals that depend on private donations for funds and those that do not. Whether an endowed budget shows a surplus or deficit is less important than the hospital's relations with benefactors. On the other hand, with a budget dependent on patient billing, a surplus is almost essential; monies for new equipment or expansion must be drawn from it, and without them quality care becomes more difficult and patients scarcer. An administrator's tenure reflected just these considerations. For those hospitals dependent upon private donations, the length of an administrator's term depended not at all on the status of the operating budget but was fairly predictable from the hospital's relations with the business community. On the other hand, in hospitals dependent on the operating budget for capital financing, the greater the deficit the shorter was the tenure of the hospital's principal administrators.

Changing contingencies and eroding power bases

The critical contingencies facing the organization may change. When they do, it is reasonable to expect that the power of individuals and subgroups will change in turn. At times the shift can be swift and shattering, as it was recently for powerholders in New York City. A few years ago it was believed that David Rockefeller was one of the ten most powerful people in the city, as tallied by *New York* magazine, which annually sniffs out power for the delectation of its readers. But that was before it was revealed that the city was in financial trouble, before Rockefeller's Chase Manhattan Bank lost some of its own financial luster, and before brother Nelson lost some of his political influence in Washington. Obviously David Rockefeller was no longer as well positioned to help bail the city out. Another loser was an attorney with considerable personal connections to the political and religious leaders of the city. His talents were no longer in much demand. The persons with more influence were the bankers and union pension fund executors who fed money to the city; community leaders who represent blacks and Spanish-Americans, in contrast, witnessed the erosion of their power bases.

One implication of the idea that power shifts with changes in organizational environments is that the dominant coalition will tend to be that group that is most appropriate for the organization's environment, as also will the leaders of an organization. One can observe this historically in the top executives of industrial firms in the United States. Up until the early 1950s, many top corporations were headed by former production line managers or engineers who gained prominence because of their abilities to cope with the problems of production. Their success, however, only spelled their demise. As production became routinized and mechanized, the problem of most firms became one of selling all those goods they so efficiently produced. Marketing executives were more frequently found in corporate boardrooms. Success outdid itself again, for keeping markets and production steady and stable requires the kind of control that can only come from acquiring competitiors and suppliers or the invention of more and more appealing products—ventures that typically require enormous amounts of capital. During the 1960s, financial executives assumed the seats of power. And they, too, will give way to others. Edging over the horizon are legal experts, as regulation and antitrust suits are becoming more and more frequent in the 1970s, suits that had their beginnings in the success of the expansion generated by prior executives. The more distant future, which is likely to be dominated by multinational corporations, may see former secretaries of state and their minions increasingly serving as corporate figureheads.

The nonadaptive consequences of adaptation

From what we have said thus far about power aligning the organization with its own realities, an intelligent person might react with a resounding ho-hum, for it all seems too obvious: Those with the ability to get the job done are given the job to do.

However, there are two aspects of power that make it more useful for understanding organizations and their effectiveness. First, the "job" to be done has a way of expanding itself until it becomes less and less clear what the job is. Napoleon began by doing a job for France in the war with Austria and ended up emperor, convincing many that only he could keep the peace. Hitler began by promising an end to Germany's troubling postwar depression and ended up convincing more people than is comfortable to remember that he was destined to be the savior of the world. In short, power is a capacity for influence that extends far beyond the original bases that created it. Second, power tends to take on institutionalized forms that enable it to endure well beyond its usefulness to an organization.

There is an important contradiction in what we have observed about organizational power. On the one hand we have said that power derives from the contingencies facing an organization and that when those contingencies change so do the bases for power. On the other hand we have asserted that subunits will tend to use their power to influence organizational decisions in their own favor, particularly when their own survival is threatened by the scarcity of critical resources. The first statement implies that an organization will tend to be aligned with its environment since power will tend to bring to key positions those with capabilities relevant to the context. The second implies that those in power will not give up their positions so easily; they will pursue policies that guarantee their continued domination. In short, change and stability operate through the same mechanism, and, as a result, the organization will never be completely in phase with its environment or its needs.

The study of hospital administrators illustrates how leadership can be out of phase with reality. We argued that privately funded hospitals needed trained technical administrators more so than did hospitals funded by donations. The need as we perceived it was matched in most hospitals, but by no means in all. Some organizations did not conform with our predictions. These deviations imply that some administrators were able to maintain their positions independent of their suitability for those positions. By dividing administrators into those with long and short terms of office, one finds that the characteristics of longer-termed administrators were virtually unrelated to the hospital's context. The shorter-termed chiefs, on the other hand, had characteristics more appropriate for the hospital's problems. For a hospital to have a recently appointed head implies that the previous administrator had been unable to endure by institutionalizing himself.

One obvious feature of hospitals that allowed some administrators to enjoy a long tenure was a hospital's ownership. Administrators were less entrenched when their hospitals were affiliated with and dependent upon larger organizations, such as governments or churches. Private hospitals offered more secure positions for administrators. Like private corporations, they tend to have more diffused ownership, leaving the administrator unopposed as he institutionalizes his reign. Thus he endures, sometimes at the expense of the performance of the organization. Other research has demonstrated that corporations with diffuse ownership have poorer earnings than those in which the control of the manager is checked by a dominant shareholder. Firms that overload their board-rooms with more insiders than are appropriate for their context have also been found to be less profitable.

A word of caution is required about our judgment of "appropriateness." When we argue some capabilities are more appropriate for one context than another, we do so from the perspective of an outsider and on the basis of reasonable assumptions as to the problems the organization will face and the capabilities they will need. The fact that we have been able to predict the distribution of influence and the characteristics of leaders suggests that our reasoning is not incorrect. However, we do not think that all organizations follow the same pattern. The fact that we have not been able to predict outcomes with 100 percent accuracy indicates they do not.

Mistaking critical contingencies

One thing that allows subunits to retain their power is their ability to name their functions as critical to the organization when they may not be. Consider again our discussion of power in the university. One might wonder why the most critical tasks were defined as graduate education and scholarly research, the effect of which was to lend power to those who brought in grants and contracts. Why not something else? The reason is that the most powerful departments argued for those criteria and won their case, partly because they were more powerful.

In another analysis of this university, we found that all departments advocate self-serving criteria for budget allocation. Thus a department with large undergraduate enrollments argued that enrollments should determine budget allocations, a department with a strong national reputation saw prestige as the most reasonable basis for distributing funds, and so on. We further found that advocating such self-serving criteria actually benefited a department's budget allotments but, also, it paid off more for departments that were already powerful.

Organizational needs are consistent with a current distribution of power also because of a human tendency to categorize problems in familiar ways. An accountant sees problems with organizational performance as cost accountancy problems or inventory flow problems. A sales manager sees them as problems with markets, promotional strategies, or just unaggressive salespeople. But what is the truth? Since it does not automatically announce itself, it is likely that those with prior credibility, or those with power, will be favored as the enlightened. This bias, while not intentionally self-serving, further concentrates power among those who already possess it, independent of changes in the organization's context.

Institutionalizing power

A third reason for expecting organizational contingencies to be defined in familiar ways is that the current holders of power can structure the organization in ways that institutionalize themselves. By institutionalization we mean the establishment of relatively permanent structures and policies that favor the influence of a particular subunit. While in power, a dominant coalition has the ability to institute constitutions, rules, procedures, and information systems that limit the potential power of others while continuing their own.

The key to institutionalizing power always is to create a device that legitimates one's own authority and diminishes the legitimacy of others. When the "Divine Right of Kings" was envisioned centuries ago it was to provide an unquestionable foundation for the supremacy of royal authority. There is generally a need to root the exercise of authority in some higher power. Modern leaders are no less affected by this need. Richard Nixon, with the aid of John Dean, reified the concept of executive privilege, which meant in effect that what the president wished not to be discussed need not be discussed.

In its simpler form, institutionalization is achieved by designating positions or roles for organizational activities. The creation of a new post legitimizes a function and forces organization members to orient to it. By designating how this new post relates to older, more established posts, moreover, one can structure an organization to enhance the importance of the function in the organization. Equally, one can dinish the importance of traditional functions. This is what happened in the end with the insurance company we mentioned that was having trouble with its coding department. As the situation unfolded, the claims director continued to feel dissatisfied about the dependency of his functions on the coding manager. Thus he instituted a reorganization that resulted in two coding departments. In so doing, of course, he placed activities that affected his department under his direct control, presumably to make the operation more effective. Similarly, consumer-product firms enhance the power of marketing by setting up a coordinating role to interface production and marketing functions and then appoint a marketing manager to fill the role.

The structures created by dominant powers sooner or later become fixed and unquestioned features of the organization. Eventually, this can be devastating. It is said that the battle of Jena in 1806 was lost by Frederick the Great, who died in 1786. Though the great Prussian leader had no direct hand in the disaster, his imprint on the army was so thorough, so embedded in its skeletal underpinnings, that the organization was inappropriate for others to lead in different times.

Another important source of institutionalized power lies in the ability to structure information systems. Setting up committees to investigate particular organizational issues and having them report only to particular individuals or groups facilitates their awareness of problems by members of those groups while limiting the awareness of problems by the members of other groups. Obviously, those who have information are in a better position to interpret the problems of an organization, regardless of how realistically they may, in fact, do so.

Still another way to institutionalize power is to distribute rewards and resources. The dominant group may quiet competing interest groups with small favors and rewards. The credit for this artful form of cooptation belongs to Louis XIV. To avoid usurpation of his power by the nobles of France and the Fronde that had so troubled his father's reign, he built the palace at Versailles to occupy them with hunting and gossip. Awed, the courtiers basked in the reflected glories of the "Sun King" and the overwhelming setting he had created for his court.

At this point, we have not systematically studied the institutionalization of power. But we suspect it is an important condition that mediates between the environment of the organization and the capabilities of the organization for dealing with that environment. The more institutionalized power is within an organization, the more likely an organization will be out of phase with the realities it faces. President Richard Nixon's structuring of his White House is one of the better documented illustrations. If we go back to newspaper and magazine descriptions of how he organized his office from the beginning in 1968, most of what occurred subsequently follows almost as an afterthought. Decisions flowed through virtually only the small White House staff; rewards, small presidential favors of recognition, and perquisites were distributed by this staff to the loyal; and information from the outside world —the press, Congress, the people on the streets—was filtered by the staff and passed along only if initialed "bh." Thus it was not surprising that when Nixon met war protestors in the early dawn, the only thing he could think to talk about was the latest football game, so insulated had he become from their grief and anger.

One of the more interesting implications of institutionalized power is that executive turnover among the executives who have structured the organization is likely to be a rare event that occurs only under the most pressing crisis. If a dominant coalition is able to structure the organization and interpret the meaning of ambiguous events like declining sales and profits or lawsuits, then the "real" problems to emerge will easily be incorporated into traditional modes of thinking and acting. If opposition is designed out of the organization, the interpretations will go unquestioned. Conditions will remain stable until a crisis develops, so overwhelming and visible that even the most adroit rhetorician would be silenced.

Implications for the management of power in organizations

While we could derive numerous implications from this discussion of power, our selection would have to depend largely on whether one wanted to increase one's power, decrease the power of others, or merely maintain one's position. More important, the real implications depend on the particulars of an organizational situation. To understand power in an organization one must begin by looking outside it—into the environment—for those groups that mediate the organization's outcomes but are not themselves within its control.

Instead of ending with homilies, we will end with a reversal of where we began. Power, rather than being the dirty business it is often made out to be, is probably one of the few mechanisms for reality testing in organizations. And the cleaner forms of power, the institutional forms, rather than having the virtues they are often credited with, can lead the organization to become out of touch. The real trick to managing power in organizations is to ensure somehow that leaders cannot be unaware of the realities of their environments and cannot avoid changing to deal with those realities. That, however, would be like designing the "self-liquidating organization," an unlikely event since anyone capable of designing such an instrument would be obviously in control of the liquidations.

Management would do well to devote more attention to determining the critical contingencies of their environments. For if you conclude, as we do, that the environment sets most of the structure influencing organizational outcomes and problems, and that power derives from the organization's activities that deal with those contingencies, then it is the environment that needs managing, not power. The first step is to construct an accurate model of the environment, a process that is quite difficult for most organizations. We have recently started a project to aid administrators in systematically understanding their environments. From this experience, we have learned that the most critical blockage to perceiving an organization's reality accurately is a failure to incorporate those with the relevant expertise into the process. Most organizations have the requisite experts on hand but they are positioned so that they can be comfortably ignored.

One conclusion you can, and probably should, derive from our discussion is that power—because of the way it develops and the way it is used—will always result in the organization suboptimizing its performance. However, to this grim absolute, we add a comforting caveat: If any criteria other than power were the basis for determining an organization's decisions, the results would be even worse.

Selected bibliography

The literature on power is at once both voluminous and frequently empty of content. Some is philosophical musing about the concept of power, while other writing contains popularized palliatives for acquiring and exercising influence. Machiavelli's *The Prince,* if read carefully, remains the single best prescriptive treatment of power and its use. Most social scientists have approached power descriptively, attempting to understand how it is acquired, how it is used, and what its effects are. Mayer Zald's edited collection *Power in Organizations* (Vanderbilt University Press, 1970), is one of the more useful sets of thoughts about power from a sociological perspective, while James Tedeschi's edited book, *The Social Influence Processes* (Aldine-Atherton, 1972) represents the social psychological approach to understanding power and influence. The strategic contingencies approach, with its emphasis on the importance of uncertainty for understanding power in organizations, is described by David Hickson and his colleagues in "A Strategic Contingencies Theory of Intraorganizational Power" (*Administrative Science Quarterly,* December 1971, pp. 216–229).

Unfortunately, while many have written about power theoretically, there have been few empirical examinations of power and its use. Most of the work has taken the form of case studies. Michel Crozier's

The Bureaucratic Phenomenon (University of Chicago Press, 1964) is important because it describes a group's source of power as control over critical activities and illustrates how power is not strictly derived from hierarchical position. J. Victor Baldridge's *Power and Conflict in the University* (John Wiley & Sons, 1971) and Andrew Pettigrew's study of computer purchase decisions in one English firm (*Politics of Organizational Decision-Making,* Tavistock, 1973) both present insights into the acquisition and use of power in specific instances. Our work has been more empirical and comparative, testing more explicitly the ideas presented in this article. The study of university decision making is reported in articles in the June 1974, pp. 135–151, and December 1974, pp. 453–473, issues of the *Administrative Science Quarterly,* the insurance firm study in J. G. Hunt and L. L. Larson's collection, *Leadership Frontiers* (Kent State University Press, 1975), and the study of hospital administrator succession appears in 1977 in the *Academy of Management Journal.*

Sources of Power of
Lower Participants in
Complex Organizations
David Mechanic

It is not unusual for lower participants[1] in complex organizations to assume and wield considerable power and influence not associated with their formally defined positions within these organizations. In sociological terms they have considerable personal power but no authority. Such personal power is often attained, for example, by executive secretaries and accountants in business firms, by attendants in mental hospitals, and even by inmates in prisons. The personal power achieved by these lower participants does not necessarily result from unique personal characteristics, although these may be relevant, but results rather from particular aspects of their location within their organizations.

Informal versus formal power

Within organizations the distribution of authority (institutionalized power) is closely if not perfectly correlated with the prestige of positions. Those who have argued for the independence of these variables[2] have taken their examples from diverse organizations and do not deal with situations where power is clearly comparable.[3] Thus when Bierstedt argues that Einstein had prestige but no power, and the policeman power but no prestige, it is apparent that he is comparing categories that are not comparable. Generally persons occupying

Reprinted from *Administrative Science Quarterly* 7, no. 3 (December 1962): 349–64, by permission of the author and the publisher.

1. The term "lower participants" comes from Amitai Etzioni, *A Comparative Analysis of Complex Organizations* (New York, 1961) and is used by him to designate persons in positions of lower rank: employees, rank-and-file, members, clients, customers, and inmates. We shall use the term in this paper in a relative sense denoting position vis-à-vis a higher-ranking participant.

2. Robert Bierstedt, "An Analysis of Social Power," *American Sociological Review* 15 (1950): 730–38.

3. Robert A. Dahl, "The Concept of Power," *Behavioral Science* 2 (1957): 201–15.

high-ranking positions within organizations have more authority than those holding low-ranking positions.

One might ask what characterizes high-ranking positions within organizations. What is most evident, perhaps, is that lower participants recognize the right of higher-ranking participants to exercise power, and yield without difficulty to demands they regard as legitimate. Moreover, persons in high-ranking positions tend to have considerable access and control over information and persons both within and outside the organization, and to instrumentalities or resources. Although higher supervisory personnel may be isolated from the task activities of lower participants, they maintain access to them through formally established intermediary positions and exercise control through intermediary participants. There appears, therefore, to be a clear correlation between the prestige of positions within organizations and the extent to which they offer access to information, persons, and instrumentalities.

Since formal organizations tend to structure lines of access and communication, access should be a clue to institutional prestige. Yet access depends on variables other than those controlled by the formal structure of an organization, and this often makes the informal power structure that develops within organizations somewhat incongruent with the formally intended plan. It is these variables that allow work groups to limit production through norms that contravene the goals of the larger organization, that allow hospital attendants to thwart changes in the structure of a hospital, and that allow prison inmates to exercise some control over prison guards. Organizations, in a sense, are continuously at the mercy of their lower participants, and it is this fact that makes organizational power structure especially interesting to the sociologist and social psychologist.

Clarification of definitions

The purpose of this paper is to present some hypotheses explaining why lower participants in organizations can often assume and wield considerable power which is not associated with their positions as formally defined within these organizations. For the purposes of this analysis the concepts "influence," "power," and "control" will be used synonymously. Moreover, we shall not be concerned with type of power, that is, whether the power is based on reward, punishment, identification, power to veto, or whatever.[4] Power will be defined as

---

4. One might observe, for example, that the power of lower participants is based primarily on the ability to "veto" or punish. For a discussion of bases of power, see John R. P. French, Jr., and Bertram Raven, "The Bases of Social

any force that results in behavior that would not have occurred if the force had not been present. We have defined power as a force rather than a relationship because it appears that much of what we mean by power is encompassed by the normative framework of an organization, and thus any analysis of power must take into consideration the power of norms as well as persons.

I shall also argue, following Thibaut and Kelley,[5] that power is closely related to dependence. To the extent that a person is dependent on another, he is potentially subject to the other person's power. Within organizations one makes others dependent upon him by controlling access to information, persons, and instrumentalities, which I shall define as follows:

a. Information includes knowledge of the organization, knowledge about persons, knowledge of the norms, procedures, techniques, and so forth.

b. Persons include anyone within the organization or anyone outside the organization upon whom the organization is in some way dependent.

c. Instrumentalities include any aspect of the physical plant of the organization or its resources (equipment, machines, money, and so on).

Power is a function not only of the extent to which a person controls information, persons, and instrumentalities, but also of the importance of the various attributes he controls.[6]

Finally, following Dahl,[7] we shall agree that comparisons of power among persons should, as far as possible, utilize comparable units. Thus we shall strive for clarification by attempting to oversimplify organizational processes; the goal is to set up a number of hypothetical statements of the relationship between variables taken two at a time, "all other factors being assumed to remain constant."

A classic example

Like many other aspects of organizational theory, one can find a classic statement of our problem in Weber's discussion of the political bureaucracy. Weber indicated the extent to which bureaucrats may have

Power," in D. Cartwright and A. Zander, eds., *Group Dynamics* (Evanston, Ill., 1960), pp. 607–23.

5. John Thibaut and Harold H. Kelley, *The Social Psychology of Groups* (New York, 1959). For a similar emphasis on dependence see Richard H. Emerson, "Power-Dependence Relationships," *American Sociological Review* 27 (1962): 31–41.

6. Although this paper will not attempt to explain how access may be measured, I feel confident that the hypotheses concerned with access are clearly testable.

7. Dahl, "The Concept of Power."

considerable power over political incumbents, as a result, in part, of
their permanence within the political bureaucracy, as contrasted to
public officials, who are replaced rather frequently.[8] Weber noted how
the low-ranking bureaucrat becomes familiar with the organization—
its rules and operations, the work flow, and so on, which gives him
considerable power over the new political incumbent, who might have
higher rank but is not as familiar with the organization. While Weber
does not directly state the point, his analysis suggests that bureaucratic
permanence has some relationship to increased access to persons,
information, and instrumentalities. To state the hypothesis suggested
somewhat more formally:

H1 Other factors remaining constant, organizational power is related to access to persons, information, and instrumentalities.
H2 Other factors remaining constant, as a participant's length of
time in an organization increases, he has increased access to
persons, information, and instrumentalities.

While these hypotheses are obvious, they do suggest that a careful
scrutiny of the organizational literature, especially that dealing with
the power or counterpower of lower participants, might lead to further
formalized statements, some considerably less obvious than the ones
stated. This kind of hypothesis formation is treated later in the paper,
but at this point I would like to place the discussion of power within a
larger theoretical context and discuss the relevance of role theory to
the study of power processes.

Implications of role theory for the study of power

There are many points of departure for the study of power processes
within organizations. An investigator might view influence in terms
of its sources and strategies; he might undertake a study of the flow of
influence; he might concentrate on the structure of organizations, seeing to what extent regularities in behavior might be explained through
the study of norms, roles, and traditions; and finally, more psychologically oriented investigators might concentrate on the recipients of
influence and the factors affecting susceptibility to influence attempts.
Each of these points of departure leads to different theoretical em-
phases. For our purposes the most important emphasis is that presented
by role theorists.

Role theories approach the question of influence and power in terms
of the behavioral regularities which result from established identities

8. Max Weber, "The Essentials of Bureaucratic Organization: An Ideal-Type
Construction," in Robert Merton et al., *Reader in Bureaucracy* (Glencoe, Ill.,
1952), pp. 18–27.

within specific social contexts like families, hospitals, and business firms. The underlying premise of most role theorists is that a large proportion of all behavior is brought about through socialization within specific organizations, and much behavior is routine and established through learning the traditional modes of adaptation in dealing with specific tasks. Thus the positions persons occupy in an organization account for much of their behavior. Norms and roles serve as mediating forces in influence processes.

While role theorists have argued much about vocabulary, the basic premises underlying their thought have been rather consistent. The argument is essentially that knowledge of one's identity or social position is a powerful index of the expectations such a person is likely to face in various social situations. Since behavior tends to be highly correlated with expectations, prediction of behavior is therefore possible. The approach of role theorists to the study of the behavior within organizations is of particular merit in that it provides a consistent set of concepts which is useful analytically in describing recruitment, socialization, interaction, and personality, as well as the formal structure of organizations. Thus the concept of role is one of the few concepts clearly linking social structure, social process, and social character.

Many problems pertaining to role theory have been raised. At times it is not clear whether role is regarded as a real entity, a theoretical construct, or both. Moreover, Gross et al. have raised the issue of role consensus, that is, the extent to which the expectations impinging upon a position are held in common by persons occupying reciprocal positions to the one in question.[9] Merton has attempted to deal with inevitable inconsistencies in expectations of role occupants by introducing the concept of role-set which treats differences in expectations as resulting, in part, from the fact that any position is differently related to a number of reciprocal positions.[10] Furthermore, Goffman has criticized role theory for its failure to deal adequately with commitment to roles[11]—a factor which Etzioni has found to be related intimately to the kind of power exercised in organizations.[12] Perhaps these various criticisms directed at role theory reflect its importance as well as its deficiencies, and despite the difficulties involved in role analysis, the concept of role may prove useful in various ways.

9. Neal Gross, Ward S. Mason, and Alexander W. McEachern, *Explorations in Role Analysis* (New York, 1958).

10. Robert Merton, "The Role-Set: Problems in Sociological Theory," *British Journal of Sociology* 8 (1957): 106–20.

11. Erving Goffman, *Encounters* (Indianapolis, Ind., 1961), pp. 85–152.

12. Etzioni, *A Comparative Analysis.*

Role theory is useful in emphasizing the extent to which influence and power can be exercised without conflict. This occurs when power is integrated with a legitimate order, when sentiments are held in common, and when there are adequate mechanisms for introducing persons into the system and training them to recognize, accept, and value the legitimacy of control within the organization. By providing the conditions whereby participants within an organization may internalize the norms, these generalized rules, values, and sentiments serve as substitutes for interpersonal influence and make the workings of the organization more agreeable and pleasant for all.

It should be clear that lower participants will be more likely to circumvent higher authority, other factors remaining constant, when the mandates of those in power, if not the authority itself, are regarded as illegitimate. Thus as Etzioni points out, when lower participants become alienated from the organization, coercive power is likely to be required if its formal mandates are to be fulfilled.[13]

Moreover, all organizations must maintain control over lower participants. To the extent that lower participants fail to recognize the legitimacy of power, or believe that sanctions cannot or will not be exercised when violations occur, the organization loses, to some extent, its ability to control their behavior. Moreover, insofar as higher participants can create the impression that they can or will exert sanctions above their actual willingness to use such sanctions, control over lower participants will increase. It is usually to the advantage of an organization to externalize and impersonalize controls, however, and if possible to develop positive sentiments toward its rules.

In other words, an effective organization can control its participants in such a way as to make it hardly perceivable that it exercises the control that it does. It seeks commitment from lower participants, and when commitment is obtained, surveillance can be relaxed. On the other hand, when the power of lower participants in organizations is considered, it often appears to be clearly divorced from the traditions, norms, and goals and sentiments of the organization as a whole. Lower participants do not usually achieve control by using the role structure of the organization, but rather by circumventing, sabotaging, and manipulating it.

Sources of power of lower participants

The most effective way for lower participants to achieve power is to obtain, maintain, and control access to persons, information, and instrumentalities. To the extent that this can be accomplished, lower

13. Ibid.

participants make higher-ranking participants dependent upon them. Thus dependence together with the manipulation of the dependency relationship is the key to the power of lower participants.

A number of examples can be cited which illustrate the preceding point. Scheff, for example, reports on the failure of a state mental hospital to bring about intended reform because of the opposition of hospital attendants.[14] He noted that the power of hospital attendants was largely a result of the dependence of ward physicians on attendants. This dependence resulted from the physician's short tenure, his lack of interest in administration, and the large amount of administrative responsibility he had to assume. An implicit trading agreement developed between physicians and attendants, whereby attendants would take on some of the responsibilities and obligations of the ward psysician in return for increased power in decision-making processes concerning patients. Failure of the ward physician to honor his part of the agreement resulted in information being withheld, disobedience, lack of cooperation, and unwillingness of the attendants to serve as a barrier between the physician and a ward full of patients demanding attention and recognition. When the attendant withheld cooperation, the physician had difficulty in making a graceful entrance and departure from the ward, in handling necessary paper work (officially his responsibility), and in obtaining information needed to deal adequately with daily treatment and behavior problems. When attendants opposed change, they could wield influence by refusing to assume responsibilities officially assigned to the physician.

Similarly, Sykes describes the dependence of prison guards on inmates and the power obtained by inmates over guards.[15] He suggests that although guards could report inmates for disobedience, frequent reports would give prison officials the impression that the guard was unable to command obedience. The guard, therefore, had some stake in ensuring the good behavior of prisoners without use of formal sanctions against them. The result was a trading agreement whereby the guard allowed violations of certain rules in return for cooperative behavior. A similar situation is found in respect to officers in the Armed Services or foremen in industry. To the extent that they require formal sanctions to bring about cooperation, they are usually perceived by their superiors as less valuable to the organization. For a good leader is expected to command obedience, at least, if not commitment.

14. Thomas J. Scheff, "Control over Policy by Attendants in a Mental Hospital," *Journal of Health and Human Behavior* 2 (1961): 93–105.
15. Gresham M. Sykes, "The Corruption of Authority and Rehabilitation," in A. Etzioni, ed., *Complex Organizations* (New York, 1961). pp. 191–97.

Factors affecting power

Expertise

Increasing specialization and organizational growth has made the expert or staff person important. The expert maintains power because high-ranking persons in the organization are dependent upon him for his special skills and access to certain kinds of information. One possible reason for lawyers obtaining many high governmental offices is that they are likely to have access to rather specialized but highly important means to organizational goals.[16]

We can state these ideas in hypotheses, as follows:

> *H3*   Other factors remaining constant, to the extent that a low-ranking participant has important expert knowledge not available to high-ranking participants, he is likely to have power over them.

Power stemming from expertise, however, is likely to be limited unless it is difficult to replace the expert. This leads to two further hypotheses:

> *H4*   Other factors remaining constant, a person difficult to replace will have greater power than a person easily replaceable.
>
> *H5*   Other factors remaining constant, experts will be more difficult to replace than nonexperts.

While persons having expertise are likely to be fairly high-ranking participants in an organization, the same hypotheses that explain the power of lower participants are relevant in explaining the comparative power positions of intermediate- and high-ranking persons.

The application of our hypothesis about expertise is clearly relevant if we look at certain organizational issues. For example, the merits of medical versus lay hospital administrators are often debated. It should be clear, however, that all other factors remaining unchanged, the medical administrator has clear advantage over the lay administrator. Where lay administrators receive preference, there is an implicit assumption that the lay person is better at administrative duties. This may be empirically valid but is not necessarily so. The special expert knowl-

16. As an example, it appears that six members of the cabinet, thirty important subcabinet officials, sixty-three senators, and two hundred thirty congressmen are lawyers (*New Yorker*, 14 April 1962, p. 62). Although one can cite many reasons for lawyers holding political posts, an important one appears to be their legal expertise.

edge of the medical administrator stems from his ability legitimately to oppose a physician who contests an administrative decision on the basis of medical necessity. Usually hospitals are viewed primarily as universalistic in orientation both by the general public and most of their participants. Thus medical necessity usually takes preference over management policies, a factor contributing to the poor financial position of most hospitals. The lay administrator is not in a position to contest such claims independently, since he usually lacks the basis for evaluation of the medical problems involved and also lacks official recognition of his competence to make such decisions. If the lay administrator is to evaluate these claims adequately on the basis of professional necessity, he must have a group of medical consultants or a committee of medical men to serve as a buffer between medical staff and the lay administration.

As a result of growing specialization, expertise is increasingly important in organizations. As the complexity of organizational tasks increases, and as organizations grow in size, there is a limit to responsibility that can be efficiently exercised by one person. Delegation of responsibility occurs, experts and specialists are brought in to provide information and research, and the higher participants become dependent upon them. Experts have tremendous potentialities for power by withholding information, providing incorrect information, and so on, and to the extent that experts are dissatisfied, the probability of organizational sabotage increases.

Effort and interest

The extent to which lower participants may exercise power depends in part on their willingness to exert effort in areas where higher-ranking participants are often reluctant to participate. Effort exerted is directly related to the degree of interest one has in an area.

> *H6*   Other factors remaining constant, there is a direct relationship between the amount of effort a person is willing to exert in an area and the power he can command.

For example, secretarial staffs in universities often have power to make decisions about the purchase and allocation of supplies, the allocation of their services, the scheduling of classes, and, at times, the disposition of student complaints. Such control may in some instances lead to sanctions against a professor by polite reluctance to furnish supplies, ignoring his preferences for the scheduling of classes, and giving others preference in the allocation of services. While the power to make such decisions may easily be removed from the jurisdiction of the lower participant, it can only be accomplished at a cost—the willingness to allocate time and effort to the decisions dealing with these matters. To the extent that responsibilities are delegated to lower participants, a certain degree of power is likely to accompany the responsibility. Also, should the lower participant see his perceived rights in jeopardy, he may sabotage the system in various ways.

Let us visualize a hypothetical situation where a department concludes that secretarial services are being allocated on a prejudicial basis as a result of complaints to the chairman of the department by several of the younger faculty. Let us also assume that, when the complaint is investigated, it is found to be substantially correct; that is, some of the younger faculty have difficulty obtaining secretarial services because of preferences among the secretarial staff. If, in attempting to eliminate discretion by the secretarial staff, the chairman establishes a rule ordering the allocation of services on the basis of the order in which work appears, the rule can easily be made ineffective by complete conformity to it. Deadlines for papers, examinations, and the like will occur, and flexibility in the allocation of services is required if these deadlines are to be met. Thus the need for flexibility can be made to conflict with the rule by a staff usually not untalented in such operations.

When an organization gives discretion to lower participants, it is usually trading the power of discretion for needed flexibility. The cost of constant surveillance is too high, and the effort required too great; it is very often much easier for all concerned to allow the secretary discretion in return for cooperation and not too great an abuse of power.

> *H7*   Other factors remaining constant, the less effort and interest higher-ranking participants are willing to devote to a task, the more likely are lower participants to obtain power relevant to this task.

Attractiveness

Another personal attribute associated with the power of low-ranking persons in an organization is attractiveness or what some call "personality." People who are viewed as attractive are more likely to gain access to persons, and, once such access is gained, they may be more likely to succeed in promoting a cause. But once again dependence is the key to the power of attractiveness, for whether a person is dependent upon another for a service he provides, or for approval or affection, what is most relevant is the relational bond which is highly valued.

> *H8*   Other factors remaining constant, the more attractive a person, the more likely he is to obtain access to persons and control over these persons.

Location and position

In any organization the person's location in physical space and position in social space are important factors influencing access to persons, information, and instrumentalities.[17] Propinquity affects the opportunities for interaction, as well as ones position within a communication network. Although these are somewhat separate factors, we shall refer to their combined effect as centrality[18] within the organization.

> *H9*   Other factors remaining constant, the more central a person is in an organization, the greater is his access to persons, information, and instrumentalities.

Some low participants may have great centrality within an organization. An executive's or university president's secretary not only has access, but often controls access in making appointments and scheduling events. Although she may have no great formal authority, she may have considerable power.

Coalitions

It should be clear that the variables we are considering are at different levels of analysis; some of them define attributes of persons, while others define attributes of communication and organization. Power processes within organizations are particularly interesting in that there are many channels of power and ways of achieving it.

In complex organizations different occupational groups attend to different functions, each group often maintaining its own power structure within the organization. Thus hospitals have administrators, medical personnel, nursing personnel, attendants, maintenance personnel, laboratory personnel, and so on. Universities, similarly, have teaching personnel, research personnel, administrative personnel, maintenance personnel, and so on. Each of these functional tasks within organizations often becomes the sphere of a particular group that controls activities relating to the task. While these tasks usually are coordinated at the highest levels of the organization, they often are not coordinated

17. There are considerable data showing the powerful effect of propinquity on communication. For summary, see Thibaut and Kelley, *The Social Psychology of Groups,* pp. 39–42.

18. The concept of centrality is generally used in a more technical sense in the work of Bavelas, Shaw, Gilchrist, and others. For example, Bavelas defines the central region of a structure as the class of all cells with the smallest distance between one cell and any other cell in the structure, with distance measured in link units. Thus the most central position in a pattern is the position closest to all others. Cf. Harold Leavitt. "Some Effects of Certain Communication Patterns on Group Performance." in E. Maccoby, T. N. Newcomb, and E. L. Hartley, eds., *Readings in Social Psychology* (New York, 1958), p. 559.

at intermediate and lower levels. It is not unusual, however, for coalitions to form among lower participants in these multiple structures. A secretary may know the man who manages the supply of stores, or the person assigning parking stickers. Such acquaintances may give her the ability to handle informally certain needs that would be more time-consuming and difficult to handle formally. Her ability to provide services informally makes higher-ranking participants in some degree dependent upon her, thereby giving her power, which increases her ability to bargain on issues important to her.

Rules

In organizations with complex power structures lower participants can use their knowledge of the norms of the organization to thwart attempted change. In discussing the various functions of bureaucratic rules, Gouldner maintains that such rules serve as excellent substitutes for surveillance, since surveillance, in addition to being expensive in time and effort, arouses considerable hostility and antagonism.[19] Moreover, he argues, rules are a functional equivalent for direct, personally given orders, since they specify the obligations of workers to do things in specific ways. Standardized rules, in addition, allow simple screening of violations, facilitate remote control, and to some extent legitimize punishment when the rule is violated. The worker who violates a bureaucratic rule has little recourse to the excuse that he did not know what was expected, as he might claim for a direct order. Finally, Gouldner argues that rules are "the 'chips' to which the company staked the supervisors and which they could use to play the game.";[20] that is, rules established a punishment which could be withheld, and this facilitated the supervisors' bargaining power with lower participants.

While Gouldner emphasizes the functional characteristics of rules within an organization, it should be clear that full compliance to all the rules at all times will probably be dysfunctional for the organization. Complete and apathetic compliance may do everything but facilitate achievement of organizational goals. Lower participants who are familiar with an organization and its rules can often find rules to support their contention that they not do what they have been asked to do, and rules are also often a rationalization for inaction on their part. The following of rules becomes especially complex when associations and unions become involved, for there are then two sets of rules to which the participant can appeal.

19. Alvin W. Gouldner, *Patterns of Industrial Bureaucracy* (Glencoe, Ill., 1954).
20. Ibid., p. 173.

What is suggested is that rules may be chips for everyone concerned in the game. Rules become the "chips" through which the bargaining process is maintained. Scheff, as noted earlier, observed that attendants in mental hospitals often took on responsibilities assigned legally to the ward physician, and when attendants refused to share these responsibilities the physician's position became extremely difficult.[21]

The ward physician is legally responsible for the care and treatment of each ward patient. This responsibility requires attention to a host of details. Medicine, seclusion, sedation, and transfer orders, for example, require the doctor's signature. Tranquilizers are particularly troublesome in this regard since they require frequent adjustment of dosage in order to get the desired effects. The physician's order is required to each change in dosage. With 150 patients under his care on tranquilizers, and several changes of dosages a week desirable, the physician could spend a major portion of his ward time in dealing with this single detail.

Given the time-consuming formal chores of the physician, and his many other duties, he usually worked out an arrangement with the ward personnel, particularly the charge (supervisory attendant), to handle these duties. On several wards, the charge called specific problems to the doctor's attention, and the two of them, in effect, would have a consultation. The charge actually made most of the decisions concerning dosage change in the back wards. Since the doctor delegated portions of his formal responsibilities to the charge, he was dependent on her good will toward him. If she withheld her cooperation, the physician had absolutely no recourse but to do all the work himself.[22]

In a sense such delegation of responsibility involves a consideration of reward and cost, whereby the decision to be made involves a question of what is more valuable—to retain control over an area, or to delegate one's work to lower participants.

There are occasions, of course, when rules are regarded as illegitimate by lower participants, and they may disregard them. Gouldner observed that, in the mine, men felt they could resist authority in a situation involving danger to themselves.[23] They did not feel that they could legitimately be ordered to do anything that would endanger their lives. It is probably significant that in extremely dangerous situations organizations are more likely to rely on commitment to work than on authority. Even within nonvoluntary groups dangerous tasks are regarded usually as requiring task commitment, and it is likely that com-

21. Scheff, "Control over Policy by Attendants."
22. Ibid., p. 97.
23. Gouldner, *Patterns of Industrial Bureaucracy.*

mitment is a much more powerful organizational force than coercive authority.

Summary

The preceding remarks are general ones, and they are assumed to be in part true of all types of organizations. But power relationships in organizations are likely to be molded by the type of organization being considered, the nature of organizational goals, the ideology of organizational decision making, the kind of commitment participants have to the organization, the formal structure of the organization, and so on. In short, we have attempted to discuss power processes within organizations in a manner somewhat divorced from other major organizational processes. We have emphasized variables affecting control of access to persons, information, and facilities within organizations. Normative definitions, perception of legitimacy, exchange, and coalitions have all been viewed in relation to power processes. Moreover, we have dealt with some attributes of persons related to power: commitment, effort, interest, willingness to use power, skills, attractiveness, and so on. And we have discussed some other variables: time, centrality, complexity of power structure, and replaceability of persons. It appears that these variables help to account in part for power exercised by lower participants in organizations.

8 Groups: Pressures and Decisions

Introduction

Everyone of us spends a large part of our lives in groups—athletic teams, classrooms, committees, families. And we all know how painful, disorderly, and unproductive groups can be. Fred Allen used to define a committee as a "group of people who individually do nothing but as a group decide that nothing can be done." Milton Berle commented that a committee "keeps minutes and wastes hours."

But we also know how powerful groups can be in pressuring and shaping the behavior of their members. The Symbionese Liberation Army's successful pressuring of Patricia Hearst is one example; the holocaust at Jonestown, Guiana, was a more dreadful one; and the "brainwashing" of U.S. prisoners by the Chinese in Korea was still another.

But group pressures are not necessarily destructive. In the "lifers group" in Rahway State Prison in New Jersey, the power of group process is turned toward socially desirable ends. Each working day, groups of juvenile offenders are brought face to face with the lifers group of convicted murderers, rapists, and thieves. The lifers verbally insult, abuse, and intimidate the juveniles. They isolate informal leaders, deprive juveniles of social support from counselors, parents, and peers, and in general destroy any illusions and stereotypes about the romantic or "cool" nature of prison life. The program costs little, is administered by volunteer inmates, and has dramatic results on juvenile behavior. At the same time, the lifers themselves are probably positively affected by doing something socially useful, and by the success of their efforts.

Edgar Schein's paper, the first in this chapter, considers just how groups influence the individual's beliefs, values, and attitudes. His interest is in looking at how people are "brainwashed," changed, socialized by groups. He then applies those recipes to the indoctrination of managers. Schein compares management development to the brain-washing techniques used by the Chinese military on American prisoners during the Korean War. Groups not only pressure people, they support their members, and hold their hands. So by depriving the individual of that support from his familiar, comfortable groups, one can better "unfreeze" his old attitudes and beliefs. And on the other end, new "model" groups for the individual to join, groups which provide social support for new attitudes, can help to "refreeze" the individual into new sets of beliefs.

While Schein's article considers the effects of groups on individuals, the next article, by Janis, looks at the whole group as a unit and at problems Janis labels "groupthink." He shows how groups can become so concerned with their own esprit de corps and their own cohesiveness that critical thinking ceases. The group lives out the prophecies of Fred Allen and Milton Berle, even though the individuals may be aware, at some level, of their own weaknesses. Janis uses the Bay of Pigs fiasco as an example of groups entrapped in "groupthink."

Finally, Boje's article on "Making a Horse out of a Camel," suggests that groupthink is but one of many potentially damaging games groups may be caught in. He points out that groups often acquire the dysfunctional habit of following a single problem-solving style regardless of the nature of the problem. For example, a group may decide to "brain storm" every problem or to make every decision by majority rule. Boje lays out a sort of computer flowchart, to allow managers to look for decision points and subroutines so that several alternative ways of managing different problems can be considered. His contingency model also helps to provide guidelines for managing the games people play in groups, to increase the chances of reasonable and useful solutions.

Management Development as a Process of Influence

Edgar H. Schein

The continuing rash of articles on the subject of developing better managers suggests, on the one hand, a continuing concerns that existing methods are not providing the talent which is needed at the higher level of industry and, on the other hand, that we continue to lack clear cut formulations about the process by which such development occurs. We need more and better managers, and we need more and better theories of how to get them.

In the present paper I would like to cast management development as the problem of how an organization can influence the beliefs, attitudes, and values (hereafter simply called attitudes) of an individual for the purpose of "developing" him, i.e., changing him in a direction which the organization regards to be in his own and the organization's best interests. Most of the existing conceptions of the development of human resources are built upon assumptions of how people learn and grow, and some of the more strikingly contrasting theories of management development derive from disagreements about such assumptions.[1] I will attempt to build on a different base: instead of starting with assumptions about learning and growth, I will start with some assumptions from the social psychology of influence and attitude change.

Building on this base can be justified quite readily if we consider that adequate managerial performance at the higher levels is at least as much a matter of attitudes as it is a matter of knowledge and specific skills, and that the acquisition of such knowledge and skills is itself in part a function of attitudes. Yet we have given far more attention to

1. An excellent discussion of two contrasting approaches—the engineering vs. the agricultural—deriving from contrasting assumptions about human behavior can be found in D. McGregor, *The Human Side of Enterprise* (New York: McGraw-Hill, 1960), chap. 14.

the psychology which underlies change in the area of knowledge and abilities than we have to the psychology which underlies change in attitudes. We have surprisingly few studies of how a person develops loyalty to a company, commitment to a job, or a professional attitude toward the managerial role; how he comes to have the motives and attitudes which make possible the rendering of decisions concerning large quantities of money, materials, and human resources; how he develops attitudes toward himself, his co-workers, his employees, his customers, and society in general which give us confidence that he has a sense of responsibility and a set of ethics consistent with his responsible position or at least which permit us to understand his behavior.

It is clear that management is becoming increasingly professionalized, as evidenced by increasing emphasis on undergraduate and graduate education in the field of management. But professionalization is not only a matter of teaching candidates increasing amounts about a set of relevant subjects and disciplines; it is equally a problem of preparing the candidate for a role which requires a certain set of attitudes. Studies of the medical profesion (Merton et al.[2] for example) have turned their attention increasingly to the unraveling of the difficult problem of how the medical student acquires those attitudes and values which enable him to make responsible decisions involving the lives of other people. Similar studies in other professions are sorely needed. When these are understaken, it is likely to be discovered that much of the training of such attitudes is carried out implicitly and without a clearly formulated rationale. Law schools and medical schools provide various kinds of experiences which insure that the graduate is prepared to fulfill his professional role. Similarly, existing approaches to the development of managers probably provide ample opportunities for the manager to learn the attitudes he will need to fulfill high-level jobs. But in this field, particularly, one gets the impression that such opportunities are more the result of intuition or chance than of clearly formulated policies. This is partly because the essential or pivotal aspects of the managerial role have not as yet been clearly delineated, leaving ambiguous both the area of knowledge to be mastered and the attitude to be acquired.

Existing practice in the field of management development involves activities such as indoctrination and training programs conducted at various points in the manager's career; systematic job rotation involving changes both in the nature of the functions performed (e.g., moving from production into sales), in physical location, and in the indi-

2. R. K. Merton, G. G. Reader, and Patricia L. Kendall, *The Student-Physician* (Cambridge, Mass.: Harvard University Press, 1957).

vidual's superiors; performance appraisal programs including various amounts of testing, general personality assessment, and counseling both within the organization and through the use of outside consultants: apprenticeships, systematic coaching, junior management boards, and special projects to facilitate practice by the young manager in functions he will have to perform later in his career; sponsorship and other comparable activities in which a select group of young managers is groomed systematically for high-level jobs (i.e., made into "crown princes"); participation in special conferences and training programs, including professional association meetings, human relations workshops, advanced management programs conducted in business schools or by professional associations like the American Management Association, regular academic courses like the Sloan programs offered at Stanford and MIT, or liberal arts courses like those offered at the University of Pennsylvania, Dartmouth, Northwestern, and so on. These and many other specific educational devices, along with elaborate schemes of selection, appraisal, and placement, form the basic paraphernalia of management development.

Most of the methods mentioned above stem from the basic conception that it is the responsibility of the business enterprise, as an institution, to define what kind of behavior and attitude change is to take place and to construct mechanisms by which such change is to occur. Decisions about the kind of activity which might be appropriate for a given manager are usually made by others above him or by specialists hired to make such decisions. Where he is to be rotated, how long he is to remain on a given assignment, or what kind of new training he should undertake is masterminded by others whose concern is "career development." In a sense, the individual stands alone against the institution where his own career is concerned, because the basic assumption is that the institution knows better than the individual what kind of man it needs or wants in its higher levels of management. The kind of influence model which is relevant, then, is one which considers the whole range of resources available to an organization.

In the remainder of this paper I will attempt to spell out these general themes by first presenting a conceptual model for analyzing influence, then providing some illustrations from a variety of organizational influence situations, and then testing its applicability to the management development situation.

A model of influence and change

Most theories of influence or change accept the premise that change does not occur unless the individual is *motivated* and *ready* to change. This statement implies that the individual must perceive some need for change in himself, must be able to change, and must perceive the influencing agent as one who can facilitate such change in a direction acceptable to the individual. A model of the influence process, then, must account for the development of the motivation to change as well as the actual mechanisms by which the change occurs.

It is usually assumed that pointing out to a person some of his areas of deficiency or some failure on his part in these areas is sufficient to induce in him a readiness to change and to accept the influencing agent's guidance or recommendations. This assumption may be tenable if one is dealing with deficiencies in intellectual skills or technical knowledge. The young manager can see, with some help from his superiors, that he needs a greater knowledge of economics or marketing or production methods and can accept the suggestion that spending a year in another department or six weeks at an advanced management course will give him the missing knowledge and/or skills.

When we are dealing with attitudes, however, the suggestion of deficiency or the need for change is much more likely to be perceived as a basic threat to the individual's sense of identity and to his status position vis-à-vis others in the organization. Attitudes are generally organized and integrated around the person's image of himself, and they result in stabilized, characteristic ways of dealing with others. The suggestion of the need for change not only implies some criticism of the person's image of himself but also threatens the stability of his working relationships because change at this level implies that the expectations which others have about him will be upset, thus requiring the development of new relationships. It is not at all uncommon for training programs in human relations to arouse resistance or to produce, at best, temporary change because the expectations of co-workers operate to keep the individual in his "normal" mold. Management development programs which ignore these psychological resistances to change are likely to be self-defeating, no matter how much attention is given to the actual presentation of the new desired attitudes.

Given these general assumptions about the integration of attitudes in the person, it is appropriate to consider influence as a process which occurs over time and which includes three phases:

1. *Unfreezing:*[3] an alteration of the forces acting on the individual, such that his stable equilibrium is disturbed sufficiently to motivate him and to make him ready to change; this can be accomplished either by

---

3. These phases of influence are a derivation of the change model developed by K. Lewin, "Frontiers in Group Dynamics: Concept, Method, and Reality in Social Science." *Human Relations* 1 (1957): 5–42.

increasing the pressure to change or by reducing some of the threats of resistance to change.

2. *Changing:* the presentation of a direction of change and the actual process of learning new attitudes. This process occurs basically by one of two mechanisms: *(a) identification*[4]—the person learns new attitudes by identifying with and emulating some other person who holds those attitudes or *(b) internalization*—the person learns new attitudes by being placed in a situation in which new atittudes are demanded of him as a way of solving problems which confront him and which he cannot avoid; he discovers the new attitudes essentially for himself, though the situation may guide him or make it probable that he will discover only those attitudes which the influencing agent wishes him to discover.

3. *Refreezing:* the integration of the changed attitudes into the rest of the personality and/or into ongoing significant emotional relationships.

In proposing this kind of model of influence we are leaving out two important cases—the individual who changes because he is *forced* to change by the agent's direct manipulation of rewards and punishments (what Kelman calls "compliance") and the individual whose strong motivation to rise in the organizational hierarchy makes him eager to accept the attitudes and acquire the skills which he perceives to be necessary for advancement. I will ignore both of these cases for the same reason—they usually do not involve genuine, stable change but merely involve the adoption of overt behaviors which imply to others that attitudes have changed, even if they have not. In the case of compliance, the individual drops the overt behavior as soon as surveillance by the influence agent is removed. Among the upwardly mobile individuals, there are those who are willing to be unfrozen and to undergo genuine attitude change (whose case fits the model to be presented below) and those whose overt behavior change is dictated by their changing perception of what the environment will reward but whose underlying attitudes are never really changed or refrozen.

I do not wish to imply that a general reward-punishment model is incorrect or inappropriate for the analysis of attitude change. My purpose, rather, is to provide a more refined model in terms of which it becomes possible to specify the differential effects of various kinds of rewards and punishments, some of which have far more significance and impact than others. For example, as I will try to show, the reward-

4. These mechanisms of attitude change are taken from H. C. Kelman, "Compliance, Identification, and Internalization: Three Processes of Attitude Change," *Conflict Resolution* 2 (1958): 51–60.

ing effect of approval from an admired person is very different in its ultimate consequence from the rewarding effect of developing a personal solution to a difficult situation.

The processes of unfreezing, changing, and refreezing can be identified in a variety of different institutions in which they are manifested in varying degrees of intensity. The content of what may be taught in the influence process may vary widely from the values of communism to the religious doctrines of a nun, and the process of influence may vary drastically in its intensity. Nevertheless, there is value in taking as our frame of reference a model like that proposed and testing its utility in a variety of different organizational contexts, ranging from Communist "thought reform" centers to business enterprises' management development programs. Because the value system of the business enterprise and its role conception of the manager are not as clear-cut as the values and role prescriptions in various other institutions, one may expect the processes of unfreezing, changing, and refreezing to occur with less intensity and to be less consciously rationalized in the business enterprise. But they are structurally the same as in other organizations. One of the main purposes of this paper, then, will be to try to make salient some features of the influence of the organization on the attitudes of the individual manager by attempting to compare institutions in which the influence process is more drastic and explicit with the more implicit and less drastic methods of the business enterprise.

Illustrations of organizational influence

Unfreezing

The concept of unfreezing and the variety of methods by which influence targets can be unfrozen can best be illustrated by considering examples drawn from a broad range of situations. The Chinese Communists in their attempt to inculcate Communist attitudes into their youth or into their prisoners serve as a good prototype of one extreme. First and most important was the removal of the target person from those situations and social relationships which tended to confirm and reinforce the validity of the old attitudes. Thus the targets, be they political prisoners, prisoners of war, university professors, or young students, were isolated from their friends, families, and accustomed work groups and cut off from all media of communication to which they were accustomed. In addition, they were subjected to continuous exhortations (backed by threats of severe punishment) to confess their crimes and adopt new attitudes and were constantly humiliated in order to discredit their old sense of identity.

The isolation of the target from his normal social and ideological supports reached its height in the case of Western civilians who were placed into group cells with a number of Chinese prisoners who had already confessed and were committed to reforming themselves and their lone Western cell mate. In the prisoner of war camps such extreme social isolation could not be produced, but its counterpart was created by the fomenting of mutual mistrust among the prisoners, by cutting off any supportive mail from home, and by systematically disorganizing the formal and informal social structure of the POW camp (by segregation of officers and noncommissioned officers from the remainder of the group, by the systematic removal of informal leaders or key personalities, and by the prohibition of any group activity not in line with the indoctrination program).[5]

The Chinese did not hesitate to use physical brutality and threats of death and/or permanent nonrepatriation to enforce the view that only by collaboration and attitude change could the prisoner hope to survive physically and psychologically. In the case of the civilians in group cells, an additional and greater stress was represented by the social pressure of the cell mates who would harangue, insult, revile, humiliate, and plead with the resistant Westerner twenty-four hours a day for weeks or months on end, exhorting him to admit his guilt, confess his crimes, reform, and adopt Communist values. This combination of physical and social pressures is perhaps a prototype of the use of coercion in the service of unfreezing a target individual in attitude areas to which he is strongly committed.

A somewhat milder, though structurally similar, process can be observed in the training of a nun.[6] The novice enters the convent voluntarily and is presumably ready to change, but the kind of change which must be accomplished encounters strong psychological resistances because, again, it involves deeply held attitudes and habits. Thus the novice must learn to be completely unselfish and, in fact, selfless; she must adapt to a completely communal life; she must give up any source of authority except the absolute authority of God and of those senior to her in the convent; and she must learn to curb her sexual and aggressive impulses. How does the routine of the convent facilitate unfreezing? Again a key element is the removal of the novice from her accustomed routines, sources of confirmation, social supports, and old relationships. She is physically isolated from the outside world, surrounded by others who are undergoing the same training as she, subjected to a

5. E. H. Schein, *Brainwashing* (Cambridge, Mass.: Center for International Studies, M.I.T., 1961); and E. H. Schein, "Interpersonal Communication, Group Solidarity, and Social Influence," *Sociometry* 23: 148–61.
6. K. Hulme, *The Nun's Story* (Boston: Little, Brown, 1957).

highly demanding and fatiguing physical regimen, constantly exhorted toward her new role and punished for any evidence of old behaviors and attitudes, and subjected to a whole range of social pressures ranging from mild disapproval to total humiliation for any failure.

Not only is the novice cut off from her social identity, but her entry into the convent separates her from many aspects of her physical identity. She is deprived of all means of being beautiful or even feminine; her hair is cut off and she is given institutional garb which emphasizes formlessness and sameness; she loses her old name and chronological age in favor of a new name and age corresponding to length of time in the convent; her living quarters and daily routine emphasize an absolute minimum of physical comfort and signify a total devaluation of anything related to the body. At the same time the threat associated with change is minimized by the tremendous support which the convent offers for change and by the fact that everyone else either already exhibits the appropriate attitudes or is in the process of learning them.

If we look at the process by which a pledge comes to be a full-fledged member of a fraternity, we find in this situation also a set of pressures to give up old associations and habits, a devaluation of the old self by humiliations ranging from menial, senseless jobs to paddling and hazing, a removal of threat through sharing of training, and support for good performance in the pledge role. The evangelist seeking to convert those who come to hear him attempts to unfreeze his audience by stimulating guilt and by devaluating their former selves as sinful and unworthy. The teacher wishing to induce motivation to learn sometimes points out deficiencies in the student's knowledge and hopes at the same time to induce some guilt for having those deficiencies.

Some of the elements which all unfreezing situations have in common are the following: (1) the physical removal of the influence target from his accustomed routines, sources of information, and social relationships; (2) the undermining and destruction of all social supports; (3) demeaning and humiliating experience to help the target see his old self as unworthy and thus to become motivated to change; and (4) the consistent linking of reward with willingness to change and of punishment with unwillingness to change.

Changing

Once the target has become motivated to change, the actual influence is most likely to occur by one of two processes. The target finds one or more models in his social environment and learns new attitudes by identifying with them and trying to become like them; or the target confronts new situations with an experimental attitude and develops for himself attitudes which are appropriate to the situation and which remove whatever problem he faces. These two processes—*identification* and *internalization*—probably tend to occur together in most concrete situations, but it is worthwhile, for analytical purposes, to keep them separate.[7]

The student or prisoner of the Chinese Communists took his basic step toward acquiring Communist attitudes when he began to identify with his more advanced fellow student or prisoner. In the group cell it was the discovery by the Western prisoner that his Chinese cell mates were humans like himself, were rational, and yet completely believed in their own and his guilt, which forced him to reexamine his own premises and bases of judgment and led him the first step down the path of acquiring the Communist point of view. In other words, he began to identify with his cell mates and to acquire their point of view as the only solution to getting out of prison and reducing the pressure on him. The environment was, of course, saturated with the Communist point of view, but it is significant that such saturation by itself was not sufficient to induce genuine attitude change. The prisoner kept in isolation and bombarded with propaganda was less likely to acquire Communist attitudes than the one placed into a group cell with more reformed prisoners. Having a personal model was apparently crucial.

In the convent the situation is essentially comparable except that the novice is initially much more disposed toward identifying with older nuns and has a model of appropriate behavior around her all the time in the actions of the others. It is interesting to note also that some nuns are singled out as particularly qualified models and given the appropriate name of "the living rule." It is also a common institution in initiation or indoctrination procedures to attach to the target individual someone who is labeled a "buddy" or "big brother," whose responsibility it is to teach the novice "the ropes" and to communicate the kinds of attitudes expected of him.

In most kinds of training and teaching situations, and even in the sales relationship, it is an acknowledged fact that the process is facilitated greatly if the target can identify with the influence agent. Such identification is facilitated if the social distance and rank difference between agent and target are not too great. The influence agent has to be close enough to the target to be seen as similar to the target, yet must be himself committed to the attitudes he is trying to inculcate.

7. Both are facilitated greatly if the influence agent saturates the environment with the new message or attitude to be learned.

Thus, in the case of the Chinese Communist group cell, the cell mates could be perceived as sharing a common situation with the Western prisoner and this perception facilitated his identification with them. In most buddy systems, the buddy is someone who has himself gone through the training program in the recent past. If the target is likely to mistrust the influence attempts of the organization, as might be the case in a management-sponsored training program for labor or in a therapy program for delinquents in a reformatory, it is even more important that the influence agent be perceived as similar to the target. Otherwise he is dismissed as a "company man" or one who has already sold out, and hence is seen as someone whose message or example is not to be taken seriously.

Internalization, the discovery of attitudes which are the target's own solutions to his perceived dilemmas, can occur at the same time as identification. The individual can use the example of others to guide him in solving his own problems without necessarily identifying with them to the point of complete imitation. His choice of attitude remains ultimately his own in terms of what works for him, given the situation in which he finds himself. Internalization is only possible in an organizational context in which, from the organization's point of view, a number of different kinds of attitudes will be tolerated. If there is a "party line," a company philosophy, or a given way in which people have to feel about things in order to get along, it is hardly an efficient procedure to let trainees discover their own solutions. Manipulating the situation in such a way as to make the official solution the only one which is acceptable can, of course, be attempted, but the hazards of creating real resentment and alienation on the part of the individual when he discovers he really had no choice may outweigh the presumed advantages of letting him think he had a choice.

In the case of the Chinese Communists, the convent, the revival meeting, the fraternity, or the institutional training program, we are dealing with situations in which the attitudes to be learned are clearly specified. In this kind of situation, internalization will not occur unless the attitudes to be learned happen to fit uniquely the kind of personal problem the individual has in the situation. For example, a few prisoners of the Communists reacted to the tremendous unfreezing pressures with genuine guilt when they discovered they held certain prejudices and attitudes (e.g., when they realized that they had looked down on lower-class Chinese in spite of their manifest acceptance of them). These prisoners were then able to internalize certain portions of the total complex of Communist attitudes, particularly those dealing with unselfishness and working for the greater good of others. The attitudes which the institution demanded of them also solved a personal problem of long standing for them. In the case of the nun, one might hypothesize that internalization of the convent's attitudes will occur to the extent that asceticism offers a genuine solution to the incumbent's personal conflicts.

Internalization is a more common outcome in those influence settings where the direction of change is left more to the individual. The influence which occurs in programs like Alcoholics Anonymous, in psychotherapy or counseling for hospitalized or incarcerated populations, in religious retreats, in human relations training of the kind pursued by the National Training Laboratories,[8] and in certain kinds of progressive education programs is more likely to occur through internalization or, at least, to lead ultimately to more internalization.

Refreezing

Refreezing refers to the process by which the newly acquired attitude comes to be integrated into the target's personality and ongoing relationships. If the new attitude has been internalized while being learned, this has automatically facilitated refreezing because it has been fitted naturally into the individual's personality. If it has been learned through identification, it will persist only so long as the target's relationship with the original influence model persists unless new surrogate models are found or social support and reinforcement is obtained for expressions of the new attitude.[9]

In the case of the convent such support comes from a whole set of expectations which others have of how the nun should behave, from clearly specified role prescriptions, and from rituals. In the case of individuals influenced by the Chinese Communists, if they remained in Communist China they received constant support for their new attitudes from superiors and peers; if they returned to the West, the permanence of their attitude change depended on the degree of support they actually received from friends and relations back home or from groups which they sought out in an attempt to get support. If their friends and relatives did not support Communist attitudes, the repatriates were influenced once again toward their original attitudes or toward some new integration of both sets.

The importance of social support for new attitudes was demonstrated dramatically in the recent Billy Graham crusade in New York

8. National Training Laboratory in Group Development, *Explorations in Human Relations Training: An Assessment of Experience, 1947–53* (Washington, D.C.: National Education Association, 1953).

9. In either case the change may be essentially permanent, in that a relationship to a model or surrogate can last indefinitely. It is important to distinguish the two processes, however, because if one were to try to change the attitude, different strategies would be used depending upon how the attitude had been learned.

City. An informal survey of individuals who came forward when Graham called for converts indicated that only those individuals who were subsequently integrated into local churches maintained their faith. Similar kinds of findings have been repeatedly noted with respect to human relations training in industry. Changes which may occur during the training program do not last unless there is some social support for the new attitudes in the "back-home" situation.

The kind of model which has been discussed above might best be described by the term "coercive persuasion." The influence of an organization on an individual is coercive in the sense that he is usually forced into situations which are likely to unfreeze him, in which there are many overt and covert pressures to recognize in himself a need for change, and in which the supports for his old attitudes are in varying degrees coercively removed. It is coercive also to the degree that the new attitudes to be learned are relatively rigidly prescribed. The individual either learns them or leaves the organization (if he can). At the same time, the actual process by which new attitudes are learned can best be described as persuasion. In effect, the individual is forced into a situation in which he is likely to be influenced. The organization can be highly coercive in unfreezing its potential influence targets, yet be quite open about the direction of attitude change it will tolerate. In those cases where the direction of change is itself coerced (as contrasted with letting it occur through identification or internalization), it is highly unlikely that anything is accomplished other than surface behavioral change in the target. And such surface change will be abandoned the moment the coercive force of the change agent is lessened. If behavioral changes are coerced at the same time as other unfreezing operations are undertaken, actual influence can be facilitated if the individual finds himself having to learn attitudes to justify the kinds of behavior he has been forced to exhibit. The salesman may not have an attitude of cynicism toward his customers initially. If, however, he is forced by his boss to behave as if he felt cynical, he might develop real cynicism as a way of justifying his actual behavior.

Management development: Is it coercive persuasion?

Do the notions of coercive persuasion developed above fit the management development situation? Does the extent to which they do or do not fit such a model illuminate for us some of the implications of specific management development practices?

Unfreezing

It is reasonable to assume that the majority of managers who are being "developed" are not ready or able to change in the manner in which their organization might desire and therefore must be unfrozen before they can be influenced. They may be eager to change at a conscious motivation level, yet still be psychologically unprepared to give up certain attitudes and values in favor of untried, threatening new ones, I cannot support this assumption empirically, but the likelihood of its being valid is high because of a related fact which is empirically supportable. Most managers do not participate heavily in decisions which affect their careers, nor do they have a large voice in the kind of self-development in which they wish to participate. It is the manager's superior or a staff specialist in career development who makes the key decisions concerning his career.[10] If the individual manager is not trained from the outset to take responsibility for his own career and given a heavy voice in diagnosing his own needs for a change, it is unlikely that he will readily be able to appreciate someone else's diagnosis. It may be unclear to him what basically is wanted of him or, worse, the ambiguity of the demands put upon him combined with his own inability to control his career development is likely to arouse anxiety and insecurity which would cause even greater resistance to genuine self-assessment and attitude change.[11] He becomes preoccupied with promotion in the abstract and attempts to acquire at a surface level the traits which he thinks are necessary for advancement.

If the decisions made by the organization do not seem valid to the manager or, if the unfreezing process turns out to be quite painful to him, to what extent can he leave the situation? His future career, his financial security, and his social status within the business community all stand to suffer if he resists the decisions made for him. Perhaps the most coercive feature is simply the psychological pressure that what he is being asked to do is "for his own ultimate welfare." Elementary loyalty to his organization and to his managerial role demands that he accept with good grace whatever happens to him in the name of his own career development. In this sense, then, I believe that the business organization has coercive forces at its disposal which are used by it in a manner comparable to the uses made by other organizations.

Given the assumption that the manager who is to be developed needs to be unfrozen, and given that the organization has available coercive power to accomplish such unfreezing, what mechanisms does it actually use to unfreeze potential influence targets?

The elements essential to unfreezing are the removal of supports for the old attitudes, the saturation of the environment with the new atti-

10. T. M. Alfred, personal communication, 1960.
11. An even greater hazard, of course, is that the organization communicates to the manager that he is not expected to take responsibility for his own career at the same time that it is trying to teach him how to be able to take responsibility for important decisions!

tudes to be acquired, a minimizing of threat, and a maximizing of support for any change in the right direction. In terms of this model it becomes immediately apparent that training programs or other activities which are conducted in the organization at the place of work for a certain number of hours per day or week are far less likely to unfreeze and subsequently influence the participant than those programs which remove him for varying lengths of time from his regular work situation and normal social relationships.

Are appraisal interviews, used periodically to communicate to the manager his strengths, weaknesses, and areas for improvement, likely to unfreeze him? Probably not, because as long as the individual is caught up in his regular routine and is responding, probably quite unconsciously, to a whole set of expectations which others have about his behavior and attitudes, it is virtually impossible for him to hear, at a psychological level, what his deficiencies or areas needing change are. Even if he can appreciate what is being communicated to him at an intellectual level, it is unlikely that he can emotionally accept the need for change, and even if he can accept it emotionally, it is unlikely that he can produce change in himself in an environment which supports all of his old ways of functioning. This statement does not mean that the man's co-workers necessarily approve of the way he is operating or like the attitudes which he is exhibiting. They may want to see him change, but their very expectations concerning how he normally behaves operate as a constraint on him which makes attitude change difficult in that setting.

On the other hand, there are a variety of training activities which are used in management development which approximate more closely the conditions necessary for effective unfreezing. These would include programs offered at special training centers such as those maintained by IBM on Long Island and General Electric at Crotonville, New York; university-sponsored courses in management, liberal arts, and/or the social sciences; and, especially, workshops or laboratories in human relations such as those conducted at Arden House, New York, by the National Training Laboratories. Programs such as these remove the participant for some length of time from his normal routine, his regular job, and his social relationships (including his family, in most cases), thus providing a kind of moratorium during which he can take stock of himself and determine where he is going and where he wants to go.

The almost total isolation from the pressures of daily life in the business world which a mountain chateau such as Arden House provides for a two-week period is supplemented by other unfreezing forces. The de-emphasis on the kind of job or title the participant holds in his company and the informal dress remove some of the symbolic or status supports upon which we all rely. Sharing a room and bath facilities with a roommate requires more than the accustomed exposure of private spheres of life to others. The total involvement of the participant in the laboratory program leaves little room for reflection about the back-home situation. The climate of the laboratory communicates tremendous support for any efforts at self-examination and attempts as much as possible to reduce the threats inherent in change by emphasizing the value of experimentation, the low cost and risk of trying a new response in the protected environment of the lab, and the high gains to be derived from finding new behavior patterns and attitudes which might improve back-home performance. The content of the material presented in lectures and the kind of learning model which is used in the workshop facilitate self-examination, self-diagnosis based on usable feedback from other participants, and rational planning for change.[12]

The practice of rotating a manager from one kind of assignment to another over a period of years can have some of the same unfreezing effects and thus facilitate attitude change. Certainly his physical move from one setting to another removes many of the supports to his old attitudes, and in his new job the manager will have an opportunity to try new behaviors and become exposed to new attitudes. The practice of providing a moratorium in the form of a training program prior to assuming a new job would appear to maximize the gains from each approach, in that unfreezing would be maximally facilitated and change would most probably be lasting if the person did not go back to a situation in which his co-workers, superiors, and subordinates had stable expectations of how he should behave.

Another example of how unfreezing can be facilitated in the organizational context is the practice of temporarily reducing the formal rank and responsibilities of the manager by making him a trainee in a special program, or an apprentice on a special project, or an assistant to a high-ranking member of the company. Such temporary lowering of formal rank can reduce the anxiety associated with changing and at the same time serves officially to destroy the old status and identity of the individual because he could not ordinarily return to his old position once he had accepted the path offered by the training program. He would have to move either up or out of the organization to maintain his sense of self-esteem. Of course, if such a training program is perceived by the trainee as an indication of his failing rather than a

12. Although, as I will point out later, such effective unfreezing may lead to change which is not supported or considered desirable by the "back-home" organization.

step toward a higher position, his anxiety about himself would be too high to facilitate effective change on his part. In all of the illustrations of organizational influence we have presented above, change was defined as being a means of gaining status—acceptance into Communist society, status as a nun or a fraternity brother, salvation, and so on. If participants come to training programs believing they are being punished, they typically do not learn much.

The above discussion is intended to highlight the fact that some management development practices do facilitate the unfreezing of the influence target but that such unfreezing is by no means automatic. Where programs fail, therefore, one of the first questions we must ask is whether they failed because they did not provide adequate conditions for unfreezing.

Changing

Turning now to the problem of the mechanisms by which changes actually occur, we must confront the question of whether the organization has relatively rigid prescribed goals concerning the direction of attitude change it expects of the young manager or whether it is concerned with growth in the sense of providing increasing opportunities for the young manager to learn the attitudes appropriate to ever more challenging situations. It is undoubtedly true that most programs would claim growth as their goal, but the degree to which they accomplish it can only be assessed from an examination of their actual practice.

Basically the question is whether the organization influences attitudes primarily through the mechanism of identification or the mechanism of internalization. If the development programs stimulate psychological relationships between the influence target and a member of the organization who has the desired attitudes, they are thereby facilitating influence by identification but, at the same time, are limiting the alternatives available to the target and possibly the permanence of the change achieved. If they emphasize that the target must develop his own solutions to ever more demanding problems, they are risking that the attitudes learned will be incompatible with other parts of the organization's value system but are producing more permanent change because the solutions found are internalized. From the organization's point of view, therefore, it is crucial to know what kind of influence it is exerting and to assess the results of such influence in terms of the basic goals which the organization may have. If new approaches and new attitudes toward management problems are desired, for example, it is crucial that the conditions for internalization be created. If rapid learning of a given set of attitudes is desired, it is equally crucial that the conditions for identification with the right kind of models be created.

One obvious implication of this distinction is that programs conducted within the organization's orbit by its own influence agents are much more likely to facilitate identification and thereby the transmission of the "party line" or organization philosophy. On the other hand, programs like those conducted at universities or by the National Training Laboratories place much more emphasis on the finding of solutions by participants which fit their own particular needs and problems. The emphasis in the human relations courses is on "learning how to learn" from the participant's own interpersonal experiences and how to harness his emotional life and intellectual capacities to the accomplishment of his goals rather than on specific principles of human relations. The nearest thing to an attitude which the laboratory staff, acting as influence agents, does care to communicate is an attitude of inquiry and experimentation, and to this end the learning of skills of observation, analysis, and diagnosis of interpersonal situations is given strong emphasis. The training group, which is the acknowledged core of the laboratory approach, provides its own unfreezing forces by being unstructured as to the content of discussion. But it is strongly committed to a method of learning by analysis of the member's own experiences in the group, which facilitates the discovery of the value of an attitude of inquiry and experimentation.

Mutual identification of the members of the group with each other and member identifications with the staff play some role in the acquisition of this attitude, but the basic power of the method is that the attitude of inquiry and experimentation *works* in the sense of providing for people valuable new insights about themselves, groups, and organizations. To the extent that it works and solves key problems for the participants, it is internalized and carried back into the home situation. To the extent that it is learned because participants wish to emulate a respected fellow member or staff member, it lasts only so long as the relationship with the model itself, or a surrogate of it, lasts (which may, of course, be a very long time).

The university program in management or liberal arts is more difficult to categorize in terms of an influence model, because within the program there are usually opportunities both for identification (e.g., with inspiring teachers) and internalization. It is a safe guess in either case, however, that the attitudes learned are likely to be in varying degrees out of phase with any given company's philosophy unless the company has learned from previous experience with a given course that the students are taught a point of view consistent with its own philosophy. Of course, universities, as much as laboratories, emphasize the value of a spirit of inquiry and, to the extent that they are successful in teaching this attitude, will be creating potential dissidents or innovators, depending on how the home company views the result.

Apprenticeships, special jobs in the role of "assistant to" somebody, job rotation, junior management boards, and so on stand in sharp contrast to the above methods in the degree to which they facilitate, indeed almost demand, that the young manager learn by watching those who are senior or more competent. It is probably not prescribed that in the process of acquiring knowledge and skills through the example of others he should also acquire their attitudes, but the probability that this will happen is very high, if the trainee develops any degree of respect and liking for his teacher and/or supervisor. It makes little difference whether the teacher, coach, or supervisor intends to influence the attitudes of his trainee or not. If a good emotional relationship develops between them, it will facilitate the learning of knowledge and skills, and will, at the same time, result in some degree of attitude change. Consequently, such methods do not maximize the probability of new approaches being invented to management problems, nor do they really by themselves facilitate the growth of the manager in the sense of providing opportunities for him to develop solutions which fit his own needs best.

Job rotation, on the other hand, can facilitate growth and innovation provided it is managed in such a way as to insure the exposure of the trainee to a broad range of points of view as he moves from assignment to assignment. The practice of shifting the developing manager geographically as well as functionally both facilitates unfreezing and increases the likelihood of his being exposed to new attitudes. This same practice can, of course, be merely a convenient way of indoctrinating the individual by sending him on an assignment, for example, "in order to acquire the sales point of view from Jim down in New York," where higher management knows perfectly well what sort of a view Jim will communicate to his subordinates.

Refreezing

Finally, a few words are in order about the problem of refreezing. Under what conditions will changed attitudes remain stable, and how do existing practices aid or hinder such stabilization? Our illustrations from the nonindustrial setting highlighted the importance of social support for any attitudes which were learned through identification. Even the kind of training emphasized in the National Training Laboratories programs, which tends to be more internalized, does not produce stable attitude change unless others in the organization, especially superiors, peers, and subordinates, have undergone similar changes and give each other stimulation and support, because lack of support acts as a new unfreezing force producing new influence (possibly in the direction of the original attitudes).

If the young manager has been influenced primarily in the direction of what is already the company philosophy, he will, of course, obtain strong support and will have little difficulty maintaining his new attitudes. If, on the other hand, management development is supposed to lead to personal growth and organizational innovation, the organization must recognize the reality that new attitudes cannot be carried by isolated individuals. The lament that we no longer have strong individualists who are willing to try something new is a fallacy based on an incorrect diagnosis. Strong individuals have always gained a certain amount of their strength from the support of others, hence the organizational problem is how to create conditions which make possible the nurturing of new ideas, attitudes, and approaches. If organizations seem to lack innovators, it may be that the climate of the organization and its methods of management development do not foster innovation, not that its human resources are inadequate.

An organizational climate in which new attitudes which differ from company philosophy can nevertheless be maintained cannot be achieved merely by an intellectual or even emotional commitment on the part of higher-ranking managers to tolerance of new ideas and attitudes. Genuine support can come only from others who have themselves been influenced, which argues strongly that at least several members of a given department must be given the same training before such training an be expected to have effect. If the superior of the people involved can participate in it as well, this strengthens the group that much more, but it would not follow from my line of reasoning that this is a necessary condition. Only some support is needed, and this support can come as well from peers and subordinates.

From this point of view, the practice of sending more than one manager to any given program at a university or human relations workshop is very sound. The Natonal Training Laboratories have emphasized from the beginning the desirability of having organizations send teams. Some organizations like Esso Standard have created their own laboratories for the training of the entire management complement of a given refinery, and all indications are that such a practice maximizes the possibility not only of the personal growth of the managers, but of the creative growth of the organization as a whole.

Conclusion

In the above discussion I have deliberately focused on a model of influence which emphasizes procedure rather than content, interpersonal relations rather than mass media, and attitudes and values rather than knowledge and skills. By placing management development into a context of institutional influence procedures which also include Chinese Communist thought reform, the training of a nun, and other more drastic forms of coercive persuasion, I have tried to highlight aspects of management development which have remained implicit yet which need to be understood. I believe that some aspects of management development are a mild form of coercive persuasion, but I do not believe that coercive persuasion is either morally bad in any a priori sense or inefficient. If we are to develop a sound theory of career development which is capable of including not only many of the formal procedures discussed in this paper but the multitudes of informal practices, some of which are more and some of which are less coercive than those discussed, we need to suspend moral judgments for the time being and evaluate influence models solely in terms of their capacity to make sense of the data and to make meaningful predictions.

Groupthink
Irving L. Janis

"How could we have been so stupid?" President John F. Kennedy asked after he and a close group of advisers had blundered into the Bay of Pigs invasion. For the last two years I have been studying that question, as it applies not only to the Bay of Pigs decision-makers but also to those who led the United States into such other major fiascos as the failure to be prepared for the attack on Pearl Harbor, the Korean War stalemate, and the escalation of the Vietnam War.

Stupidity certainly is not the explanation. The men who participated in making the Bay of Pigs decision, for instance, comprised one of the greatest arrays of intellectual talent in the history of American government—Dean Rusk, Robert McNamara, Douglas Dillon, Robert Kennedy, McGeorge Bundy, Arthur Schlesinger, Jr., Allen Dulles, and others.

It also seemed to me that explanations were incomplete if they concentrated only on disturbances in the behavior of each individual within a decision-making body: temporary emotional states of elation, fear, or anger that reduce a man's mental efficiency, for example, or chronic blind spots arising from a man's social prejudices or idiosyncratic biases.

I preferred to broaden the picture by looking at the fiascos from the standpoint of group dynamics as it has been explored over the past three decades, first by the great social psychologist Kurt Lewin and later in many experimental situations by myself and other behavioral scientists. My conclusion after poring over hundreds of relevant documents—historical reports about formal group meetings and informal conversations among the members—is that the groups that committed the fiascos were victims of what I call "groupthink."

"Groupy"

In each case study, I was surprised to discover the extent to which each group displayed the typical phenomena of social conformity that are regularly encountered in studies of group dynamics among ordinary citizens. For example, some of the phenomena appear to be completely in line with findings from social-psychological experiments showing that powerful social pressures are brought to bear by the members of a cohesive group whenever a dissident begins to voice his objections to a group consensus. Other phenomena are reminiscent of the shared illusions observed in encounter groups and friendship cliques when the members simultaneously reach a peak of "groupy" feelings.

Above all, there are numerous indications pointing to the development of group norms that bolster morale at the expense of critical thinking. One of the most common norms appears to be that of remaining loyal to the group by sticking with the policies to which the group has already committed itself, even when those policies are obviously working out badly and have unintended consequences that disturb the conscience of each member. This is one of the key characteristics of groupthink.

1984

I use the term groupthink as a quick and easy way to refer to the mode of thinking that persons engage in when *concurrence-seeking* becomes so dominant in a cohesive ingroup that it tends to override realistic appraisal of alternative courses of action. Groupthink is a term of the same order as the words in the Newspeak vocabulary George Orwell used in his dismaying world of *1984*. In that context, groupthink takes on an invidious connotation. Exactly such a connotation is intended, since the term refers to a deterioration in mental efficiency, reality testing, and moral judgments as a result of group pressures.

The symptoms of groupthink arise when the members of decision-making groups become motivated to avoid being too harsh in their judgments of their leaders' or their colleagues' ideas. They adopt a soft line of criticism, even in their own thinking. At their meetings, all the members are amiable and seek complete concurrence on every important issue, with no bickering or conflict to spoil the cozy, "we-feeling" atmosphere.

Kill

Paradoxically, soft-headed groups are often hard-hearted when it comes to dealing with outgroups or enemies. They find it relatively easy to resort to dehumanizing solutions—they will readily authorize bombing attacks that kill large numbers of civilians in the name of the noble cause of persuading an unfriendly government to negotiate at the peace table. They are unlikely to pursue the more difficult and controversial issues that arise when alternatives to a harsh military solution come up for discussion. Nor are they inclined to raise ethical issues that carry the implication that *this fine group of ours, with its humanitarianism and its high-minded principles, might be capable of adopting a course of action that is inhumane and immoral.*

Norms

There is evidence from a number of social-psychological studies that as the members of a group feel more accepted by the others, which is a central feature of increased group cohesiveness, they display less overt conformity to group norms. Thus we would expect that the more cohesive a group becomes, the less the members will feel constrained to censor what they say out of fear of being socially punished for antagonizing the leader or any of their fellow members.

In contrast, the groupthink type of conformity tends to increase as group cohesiveness increases. Groupthink involves nondeliberate suppression of critical thoughts as a result of internalization of the group's norms, which is quite different from deliberate suppression on the basis of external threats of social punishment. The more cohesive the group, the greater the inner compulsion on the part of each member to avoid creating disunity, which inclines him to believe in the soundness of whatever proposals are promoted by the leader or by a majority of the group's members.

In a cohesive group, the danger is not so much that each individual will fail to reveal his objections to what the others propose but that he will think the proposal is a good one, without attempting to carry out a careful, critical scrutiny of the pros and cons of the alternatives. When groupthink becomes dominant, there also is considerable suppression of deviant thoughts, but it takes the form of each person's deciding that his misgivings are not relevant and should be set aside, that the benefit of the doubt regarding any lingering uncertainties should be given to the group consensus.

Stress

I do not mean to imply that all cohesive groups necessarily suffer from groupthink. All ingroups may have a mild tendency toward groupthink, displaying one or another of the symptoms from time to time, but it need not be so dominant as to influence the quality of the group's final decision. Neither do I mean to imply that these is anything necessarily inefficient or harmful about group decisions in general.

On the contrary, a group whose members have properly defined roles, with traditions concerning the procedures to follow in pursuing a critical inquiry, probably is capable of making better decisions than any individual group member working alone.

The problem is that the advantages of having decisions made by groups are often lost because of powerful psychological pressures that arise when the members work closely together, share the same set of values and, above all, face a crisis situation that puts everyone under intense stress.

The main principle of groupthink, which I offer in the spirit of Parkinson's Law, is this: *The more amiability and esprit de corps there is among the members of a policy-making ingroup, the greater the danger that independent critical thinking will be replaced by groupthink, which is likely to result in irrational and dehumanizing actions directed against outgroups.*

Symptoms

In my studies of high-level governmental decision-makers, both civilian and military, I have found eight main symptoms of groupthink.

Invulnerability

Most or all of the members of the ingroup share an *illusion* of invulnerability that provides for them some degree of reassurance about obvious dangers and leads them to become over-optimistic and willing to take extraordinary risks. It also causes them to fail to respond to clear warnings of danger.

The Kennedy ingroup, which uncritically accepted the Central Intelligence Agency's disastrous Bay of Pigs plan, operated on the false assumption that they could keep secret the fact that the United States was responsible for the invasion of Cuba. Even after news of the plan began to leak out, their belief remained unshaken. They failed even to consider the danger that awaited them: a worldwide revulsion against the United States.

A similar attitude appeared among the members of President Lyndon B. Johnson's ingroup, the "Tuesday Cabinet," which kept escalating the Vietnam War despite repeated setbacks and failures. "There was a belief," Bill Moyers commented after he resigned, "that if we indicated a willingness to use our power, they [the North Vietnamese] would get the message and back away from an all-out confrontation. . . . There was a confidence—it was never bragged about, it was just there—that when the chips were really down, the other people would fold."

A most poignant example of an illusion of invulnerability involves the ingroup around Admiral H. E. Kimmel, which failed to prepare for the possibility of a Japanese attack on Pearl Harbor despite repeated warnings. Informed by his intelligence chief that radio contact with Japanese aircraft carriers had been lost, Kimmel joked about it: "What, you don't know where the carriers are? Do you mean to say that they could be rounding Diamond Head (at Honolulu) and you wouldn't know it?" The carriers were in fact moving full-steam toward Kimmel's command post at the time. Laughing together about a danger signal, which labels it as a purely laughing matter, is a characteristic manifestation of groupthink.

Rationale

As we see, victims of groupthink ignore warnings; they also collectively construct rationalizations in order to discount warnings and other forms of negative feedback that, taken seriously, might lead the group members to reconsider their assumptions each time they recommit themselves to past decisions. Why did the Johnson ingroup avoid reconsidering its escalation policy when time and again the expectations on which they based their decisions turned out to be wrong? James C. Thompson, Jr., a Harvard historian who spent five years as an observing participant in both the State Department and the White House, tells us that the policymakers avoided critical discussion of their prior decisions and continually invented new rationalizations so that they could sincerely recommit themselves to defeating the North Vietnamese.

In the fall of 1964, before the bombing of North Vietnam began, some of the policymakers predicted that six weeks of air strikes would induce the North Vietnamese to seek peace talks. When someone asked, "What if they don't?" the answer was that another four weeks certainly would do the trick.

Later, after each setback, the ingroup agreed that by investing just a bit more effort (by stepping up the bomb tonnage a bit, for instance), their course of action would prove to be right. *The Pentagon Papers* bears out these observations.

In *The Limits of Intervention,* Townsend Hoopes, who was acting Secretary of the Air Force under Johnson, says that Walt W. Rostow in particular showed a remarkable capacity for what has been called "instant rationalization." According to Hoopes, Rostow buttressed the group's optimism about being on the road to victory by culling selected scraps of evidence from news reports or, if necessary, by inventing "plausible" forecasts that had no basis in evidence at all.

Admiral Kimmel's group rationalized away their warnings, too. Right up to December 7, 1941, they convinced themselves that the Japanese would never dare attempt a full-scale surprise assault against

Hawaii because Japan's leaders would realize that it would precipitate an all-out war which the United States would surely win. They made no attempt to look at the situation through the eyes of the Japanese leaders—another manifestation of groupthink.

Morality

Victims of groupthink believe unquestioningly in the inherent morality of their ingroup; this belief inclines the members to ignore the ethical or moral consequences of their decisions.

Evidence that this symptom is at work usually is of a negative kind —the things that are left unsaid in group meetings. At least two influential persons had doubts about the morality of the Bay of Pigs adventure. One of them, Arthur Schlesinger, Jr., presented his strong objections in a memorandum to President Kennedy and Secretary of State Rusk but suppressed them when he attended meetings of the Kennedy team. The other, Senator J. William Fulbright, was not a member of the group, but the president invited him to express his misgivings in a speech to the policymakers. However, when Fulbright finished speaking the president moved on to other agenda items without asking for reactions of the group.

David Kraslow and Stuart H. Loory, in *The Secret Search for Peace in Vietnam,* report that during 1966 President Johnson's ingroup was concerned primarily with selecting bomb targets in North Vietnam. They based their selections on four factors—the military advantage, the risk to American aircraft and pilots, the danger of forcing other countries into the fighting, and the danger of heavy civilian casualties. At their regular Tuesday luncheons, they weighed these factors the way schoolteachers grade examination papers, averaging them out. Though evidence on this point is scant, I suspect that the group's ritualistic adherence to a standardized procedure induced the members to feel morally justified in their destructive way of dealing with the Vietnamese people—after all, the danger of heavy civilian casualties from U.S. air strikes was taken into account on their checklists.

Stereotypes

Victims of groupthink hold stereotyped views of the leaders of enemy groups: they are so evil that genuine attempts at negotiating differences with them are unwarranted, or they are too weak or too stupid to deal effectively with whatever attempts the ingroup makes to defeat their purposes, no matter how risky the attempts are.

Kennedy's groupthinkers believed that Premier Fidel Castro's air force was so ineffectual that obsolete B-26s could knock it out completely in a surprise attack before the invasion began. They also believed that Castro's army was so weak that a small Cuban-exile brigade could establish a well-protected beachhead at the Bay of Pigs. In addition, they believed that Castro was not smart enough to put down any possible internal uprisings in support of the exiles. They were wrong on all three assumptions. Though much of the blame was attributable to faulty intelligence, the point is that none of Kennedy's advisers even questioned the CIA planners about these assumptions.

The Johnson advisers' sloganistic thinking about "the Communist apparatus" that was "working all around the world" (as Dean Rusk put it) led them to overlook the powerful nationalistic strivings of the North Vietnamese government and its efforts to ward off Chinese domination. The crudest of all stereotypes used by Johnson's inner circle to justify their policies was the domino theory ("If we don't stop the Reds in South Vietnam, tomorrow they will be in Hawaii and next week they will be in San Francisco," Johnson once said). The group so firmly accepted this stereotype that it became almost impossible for any adviser to introduce a more sophisticated viewpoint.

In the documents of Pearl Harbor, it is clear to see that the navy commanders stationed in Hawaii had a naive image of Japan as a midget that would not dare to strike a blow against a powerful giant.

Pressure

Victims of groupthink apply direct pressure to any individual who momentarily expresses doubts about any of the group's shared illusions or who questions the validity of the arguments supporting a policy alternative favored by the majority. This gambit reinforces the concurrence-seeking norm that loyal members are expected to maintain.

President Kennedy probably was more active than anyone else in raising skeptical questions during the Bay of Pigs meetings, and yet he seems to have encouraged the group's docile, uncritical aceptance of defective arguments in favor of the CIA's plan. At every meeting, he allowed the CIA representatives to dominate the discussion. He permitted them to give their immediate refutations in response to each tentative doubt that one of the others expressed, instead of asking whether anyone shared the doubt or wanted to pursue the implications of the new worrisome issue that had just been raised. And at the most crucial meeting, when he was calling on each member to give his vote for or against the plan, he did not call on Arthur Schlesinger, the one man there who was known by the president to have serious misgivings.

Historian Thomson informs us that whenever a member of Johnson's ingroup began to express doubts, the group used subtle social pressures to "domesticate" him. To start with, the dissenter was made to feel at home, provided that he lived up to two restrictions: (1) that he did not voice his doubts to outsiders, which would play into the hands of the opposition; and (2) that he kept his criticisms within the bounds of acceptable deviation, which meant not challenging any of the fundamental assumptions that went into the group's prior commitments. One such "domesticated dissenter" was Bill Moyers. When Moyers arrived at a meeting, Thomson tells us, the president greeted him with, "Well, here comes Mr. Stop-the-Bombing."

Self-censorship

Victims of groupthink avoid deviating from what appears to be group consensus; they keep silent about their misgivings and even minimize to themselves the importance of their doubts.

As we have seen, Schlesinger was not at all hesitant about presenting his strong objections to the Bay of Pigs plan in a memorandum to the president and the secretary of state. But he became keenly aware of his tendency to suppress objections at the White House meetings. "In the months after the Bay of Pigs I bitterly reproached myself for having kept so silent during those crucial discussions in the cabinet room," Schlesinger writes in *A Thousand Days*. "I can only explain my failure to do more than raise a few timid questions by reporting that one's impulse to blow the whistle on this nonsense was simply undone by the circumstances of the discussion."

Unanimity

Victims of groupthink share an *illusion* of unanimity within the group concerning almost all judgments expressed by members who speak in favor of the majority view. This symptom results partly from the preceding one, whose effects are augmented by the false assumption that any individual who remains silent during any part of the discussion is in full accord with what the others are saying.

When a group of persons who respect each other's opinions arrives at a unanimous view, each member is likely to feel that the belief must be true. This reliance on consensual validation within the group tends to replace individual critical thinking and reality testing, unless there are clear-cut disagreements among the members. In contemplating a course of action such as the invasion of Cuba, it is painful for the members to confront disagreements within their group, particularly if it becomes apparent that there are widely divergent views about whether the preferred course of action is too risky to undertake at all. Such disagreements are likely to arouse anxieties about making a serious error. Once the sense of unanimity is shattered, the members no longer can feel complacently confident about the decision they are inclined to make. Each man must then face the annoying realization that there are troublesome uncertainties and he must diligently seek out the best information he can get in order to decide for himself exactly how serious the risks might be. This is one of the unpleasant consequences of being in a group of hardhearted, critical thinkers.

To avoid such an unpleasant state, the members often become inclined, without quite realizing it, to prevent latent disagreements from surfacing when they are about to initiate a risky course of action. The group leader and the members support each other in playing up the areas of convergence in their thinking, at the expense of fully exploring divergencies that might reveal unsettled issues.

"Our meetings took place in a curious atmosphere of assumed consensus," Schlesinger writes. His additional comments clearly show that, curiously, the consensus was an illusion—an illusion that could be maintained only because the major participants did not reveal their own reasoning or discuss their idiosyncratic assumptions and vague reservations. Evidence from several sources makes it clear that even the three principals—President Kennedy, Rusk, and McNamara—had widely differing assumptions about the invasion plan.

Mindguards

Victims of groupthink sometimes appoint themselves as mindguards to protect the leader and fellow members from adverse information that might break the complacency they shared about the effectiveness and morality of past decisions. At a large birthday party for his wife, Attorney General Robert F. Kennedy, who had been constantly informed about the Cuban invasion plan, took Schlesinger aside and asked him why he was opposed. Kennedy listened coldly and said, "You may be right or you may be wrong, but the president has made his mind up. Don't push it any further. Now is the time for everyone to help him all they can."

Rusk also functioned as a highly effective mindguard by failing to transmit to the group the strong objections of three "outsiders" who had learned of the invasion plan—Undersecretary of State Chester Bowles, USIA Director Edward R. Murrow, and Rusk's intelligence chief, Roger Hilsman. Had Rusk done so, their warnings might have reinforced Schlesinger's memorandum and jolted some of Kennedy's ingroup, if not the president himself, into reconsidering the decision.

Products

When a group of executives frequently displays most or all of these interrelated symptoms, a detailed study of their deliberations is likely to reveal a number of immediate consequences. These consequences are, in effect, products of poor decision-making practices because they lead to inadequate solutions to the problems under discussion.

First, the group limits its discussions to a few alternative courses of action (often only two) without an initial survey of all the alternatives that might be worthy of consideration.

Second, the group fails to reexamine the course of action initially preferred by the majority after they learn of risks and drawbacks they had not considered originally.

Third, the members spend little or no time discussing whether there are nonobvious gains they may have overlooked or ways of reducing the seemingly prohibitive costs that made rejected alternatives appear undesirable to them.

Fourth, members make little or no attempt to obtain information from experts within their own organizations who might be able to supply more precise estimates of potential losses and gains.

Fifth, members show positive interest in facts and opinions that support their preferred policy; they tend to ignore facts and opinions that do not.

Sixth, members spend little time deliberating about how the chosen policy might be hindered by bureaucratic inertia, sabotaged by political opponents, or temporarily derailed by common accidents. Consequently, they fail to work out contingency plans to cope with foreseeable setbacks that could endanger the overall success of their chosen course.

Support

The search for an explanation of why groupthink occurs has led me through a quagmire of complicated theoretical issues in the murky area of human motivation. My belief, based on recent social psychological research, is that we can best understand the various symptoms of groupthink as a mutual effort among the group members to maintain self-esteem and emotional equanimity by providing social support to each other, especially at times when they share responsibility for making vital decisions.

Even when no important decision is pending, the typical administrator will begin to doubt the wisdom and morality of his past decisions each time he receives information about setbacks, particularly if the information is accompanied by negative feedback from prominent men who originally had been his supporters. It should not be surprising, therefore, to find that individual members strive to develop unanimity and esprit de corps that will help bolster each other's morale, to create an optimistic outlook about the success of pending decisions, and to reaffirm the positive value of past policies to which all of them are committed.

Pride

Shared illusions of invulnerability, for example, can reduce anxiety about taking risks. Rationalizations help members believe that the risks are really not so bad after all. The assumption of inherent morality helps the members to avoid feelings of shame or guilt. Negative stereotypes function as stress-reducing devices to enhance a sense of moral righteousness as well as pride in a lofty mission.

The mutual enhancement of self-esteem and morale may have functional value in enabling the members to maintain their capacity to take action, but it has maladaptive consequences insofar as concurrence-seeking tendencies interfere with critical, rational capacities and lead to serious errors of judgment.

While I have limited my study to decision-making bodies in government, groupthink symptoms appear in business, industry, and any other field where small, cohesive groups make the decisions. It is vital, then, for all sorts of people—and especially group leaders—to know what steps they can take to prevent groupthink.

Remedies

To counterpoint my case studies of the major fiascos, I have also investigated two highly successful group enterprises, the formulation of the Marshall Plan in the Truman administration and the handling of the Cuban missile crisis by President Kennedy and his advisers. I have found it instructive to examine the steps Kennedy took to change his group's decision-making processes. These changes ensured that the mistakes made by his Bay of Pigs ingroup were not repeated by the missile-crisis ingroup, even though the membership of both groups was essentially the same.

The following recommendations for preventing groupthink incorporate many of the good practices I discovered to be characteristic of the Marshall Plan and missile-crisis groups:

1. The leader of a policy-forming group should assign the role of critical evaluator to each member, encouraging the group to give high priority to open airing of objections and doubts. This practice needs to be reinforced by the leader's acceptance of criticism of his own judgments in order to discourage members from soft-pedaling their disagreements and from allowing their striving for concurrence to inhibit critical thinking.

2. When the key members of a hierarchy assign a policy-planning mission to any group within their organization, they should adopt an

impartial stance instead of stating preferences and expectations at the beginning. This will encourage open inquiry and impartial probing of a wide range of policy alternatives.

3. The organization routinely should set up several outside policy-planning and evaluation groups to work on the same policy question, each deliberating under a different leader. This can prevent the insulation of an ingroup.

4. At intervals before the group reaches a final consensus, the leader should require each member to discuss the group's deliberations with associates in his own unit of the organization—assuming that those associates can be trusted to adhere to the same security regulations that govern the policy-makers—and then to report back their reactions to the group.

5. The group should invite one or more outside experts to each meeting on a staggered basis and encourage the experts to challenge the views of the core members.

6. At every general meeting of the group, whenever the agenda calls for an evaluation of policy alternatives, at least one member should play devil's advocate, functioning as a good lawyer in challenging the testimony of those who advocate the majority position.

7. Whenever the policy issue involves relations with a rival nation or organization, the group should devote a sizable block of time, perhaps an entire session, to a survey of all warning signals from the rivals and should write alternative scenarios on the rivals' intentions.

8. When the group is surveying policy alternatives for feasibility and effectiveness, it should from time to time divide into two or more subgroups to meet separately, under different chairmen, and then come back together to hammer out differences.

9. After reaching a preliminary consensus about what seems to be the best policy, the group should hold a "second-chance" meeting at which every member expresses as vividly as he can all his residual doubts, and rethinks the entire issue before making a definitive choice.

How

These recommendations have their disadvantages. To encourage the open airing of objections, for instance, might lead to prolonged and costly debates when a rapidly growing crisis requires immediate solution. It also could cause rejection, depression, and anger. A leader's failure to set a norm might create cleavage between leader and members that could develop into a disruptive power struggle if the leader looks on the emerging consensus as anathema. Setting up outside evaluation groups might increase the risk of security leakage. Still, inventive executives who know their way around the organizational maze probably can figure out how to apply one or another of the prescriptions successfully, without harmful side effects.

They also could benefit from the advice of outside experts in the administrative and behavioral sciences. Though these experts have much to offer, they have had few chances to work on policy-making machinery within large organizations. As matters now stand, executives innovate only when they need new procedures to avoid repeating serious errors that have deflated their self-images.

In this era of atomic warheads, urban disorganization, and eco-catastrophes, it seems to me that policymakers should collaborate with behavioral scientists and give top priority to preventing group-think and its attendant fiascos.

Making a Horse out of a Camel: A Contingency Model for Managing the Problem-Solving Process in Groups
David M. Boje

One of the familiar sayings about the work done in groups is: "A camel is a horse put together by a committee." Anyone who has led a committee, team, assembly, or other group will testify that even with the best of intentions, obtaining a decision which represents the interests and capabilities of the individual members, and at the same time effectively solves the problem at hand, is an all but impossible task. In fact, many would respond that given common group games, like one person trying to dominate the group, hidden agendas, conformity pressures, people talking without listening—managing to put together a camel is doing quite well.

While many behavioral scientists have attempted to describe the differences between productive and nonproductive groups on tasks involving creative thinking or accuracy, few have attempted to summarize those differences in a *contingency model* of group decision making.[1] While many problem-solving models abound, most advocate *one best way* to problem-solve and to make the final group decision.[2] At the same time, people who have had years of experience at handling group decision-making situations have in hindsight developed many prescriptive interventions for facilitating the decision-making process. I would like to propose a flexible model that offers several ways to attack and decide problems. This model combines the findings of behavioral science researchers and the prescriptions of practitioners.

Displayed in flowchart format are a number of decisions and courses of action open to group leaders in the problem-solving process. For

Reprinted from *Managing II,* 2d ed., Boje, Brass, Pondy, eds., © 1977, by permission of Ginn and Co. and the author.

1. Two notable exceptions are the Vroom and Yetton decision model (1973) and Delbecq et al. (1975) work on the Nominal Group technique.

2. Some of the problem-solving methods are discussed in Bales (1950), Osborn (1957), Sandberg (1973), and chapter 7 in Schmuck et al. (1972).

ease of presentation, the model is divided into five parts corresponding to the five phases in the group decision process. These consist of (1) problem identification, (2) solution generation, (3) evaluation, (4) decision, and (5) implementation. After explaining the five phases, an overall model will be presented.

In addition to presenting a contingency decision model, I will present a number of "games" which group members must avoid. Eric Berne defines a game as "an ongoing series of complementary ulterior transactions progressing to a well-defined, predictable outcome. Descriptively, it is a recurring set of transactions, often repetitious, superficially plausible, with a concealed motivation; or more colloquially, a series of moves with a snare, or 'gimmick' " (p. 48). One or more individuals in a group will from time to time engage in a game that, if left unchallenged by other members, will lead to dysfunctional consequences.

Consider the game of the "hidden agenda." Here the individual has an ulterior purpose, such as a personally beneficial decision outcome, pursuing a personality conflict with another member, wanting to leave early, or other concealed motive. Unless confronted, the "hidden agenda" game will result in any of several outcomes. A problem will be defined to yield the hidden preference, other members' alternatives will be attacked so that a pet alternative can be introduced, a hasty decision strategy will be advocated in order to push a hidden agenda through.

While the number of possible games is indeed infinite, we will focus only on dysfunctional games which repeatedly crop up in the problem-solving process. Further, the games will be introduced in the problem-solving phase where they occur most frequently. Take the hidden agenda; it is most likely to emerge in the problem-identification phase where members, for example, attempt to get the problem defined to yield their solution. This does not mean that a hidden agenda or other game will not occur in the other phases of the problem-solving process. In fact, if not resolved, a game can raise its ugly head early in the problem-identification phase and remain a recurring threat throughout the remaining four phases. The chart below lists the five problem-solving phases and the games that will be described within each phase.

Problem-Solving Process Phases	*Dysfunctional Process Games to Resolve*
1. Problem identification	"The hidden agenda" "Why don't we do it my way?" "Ain't it awful"*
2. Solution generation	"The hard sell" "Lend me your ear"

"Why don't you, yes but"*
"All talk and no listening"
"Have we been here before?"

3. Evaluation   "Love me, love my dog"
                     "Groupthink"

4. Decision   "Let's get this over with"
                     "We all agree, right?"

5. Implementation   "Avoid the monkey"
                     "Building lead balloons"

*Game originally developed by Eric Berne.

Content vs. process leaders

Let's begin by distinguishing between the content, the actual work done on the problem by the group, and the proces, *how* individuals work with each other to solve the problem.[3] Further, we can break process into two types: *functional* processes, such as the *problem-solving phases,* and *dysfunctional processes,* such as any *disruptive games* that group members play. Functional here refers to improving the effectiveness of the operating performance of the group. When the leader decides how to attack a problem, what decision strategy to use, summarizes comments, interprets comments, defines objectives, etc., the problem-solving process is being attended. Alternatively, when the leader attempts to counter game playing, keeping people from being left out of the conversation, getting talkative people to be more brief, resolving personal conflicts, he is dealing with the dysfunctional aspects of the process.

Given these three activities—(1) dealing with content affairs, (2) leading the problem-solving process phases, and (3) countering game playing—the leader does not necessarily fill all three roles in all groups. One person can contribute his expertise on a topic and lead the content activities. Another individual (say, with administrative skills) structures the problem-solving process for the group. Yet a third person may deal with game-playing situations, perhaps even countering games leaders play to get their way in groups. To simplify the discussion, we will talk of strategies leaders use to counter games. It is important to note *leaders and nonleaders play games. All group members need to be trained to handle dysfunctional games and to share responsibility for managing the process phases.*

3. The distinction of content vs. process is based on Benne and Sheets' (1948) distinction between task and maintenance functions. It should be added here that many actions can be both process and content, such as who works on and does not work on a problem and information offered to the group by a member.

For someone who is just learning about group leadership, it is advisable to lead the process levels of the group and let the other members deal with the content isues. This is also a preferred strategy for group leaders who fear that their higher status in the group will give too much weight to ideas they introduce. This does not mean that a leader should not offer his own ideas to the group. The point is that how a leader introduces an idea will have a critical impact upon the direction the group takes. You might even consider this a *functional game,* i.e., where the transactions are seen as leading to a more effective decision outcome. Further, leading the problem-solving and game-countering process levels of the group is a demanding enough task to merit a leader's full attention.

Contingency model for group problem solving

The model is meant to be a guideline for group leaders and *not* a set of hard-and-fast rules and procedures. The leader should be familiar with the model to the extent of being able to pinpoint critical decision points and the situational determinants that suggest what action to pursue in each phase. The decisions must also be made on the basis of the leader's insight into factors peculiar to the situation at hand. As each part of the model is presented, a triangle refers to a decision that the problem-solving process leader must make and the squares represent action strategies which result from each decision. Where a paragraph is numbered, this number refers to a corresponding number in the diagram. Following the discussion of each phase of the model is the set of games that tend to emerge in that phase.

1.1   The first decision to be made is: Is this an appropriate problem for group action? Too often a leader will present the group with a problem that is (1) so trivial that the leader would be making better use of the group's time by deciding it himself, (2) not within the authority of the group to decide. This may also mean a problem where the leader has a vested interest in his own strategy. If this is the case, he should not waste the group's time. He should tell them what he wants and seek their critical opinions or not involve them at all. (3) Problems which are so emotionally charged that making a group decision may be dysfunctional to the long-term functioning of the group.

1.2   The next decision is: Is it a problem or a symptom?[4] Many decision theorists have observed that groups often spend as much time looking for the underlying problem as they spend resolving the problem. Problem finding needs to be given much more attention by groups. Problems are not visually given. If a group is deciding what to

---

4. For more discussion of problems versus symptoms, read Jay (1976).

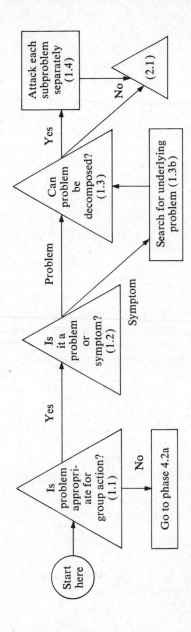

Figure 1. Problem-Identification Phase

do about a plant that is on strike, the strike itself may be a symptom of a more fundamental problem. The group will often need to wade through a number of symptoms before they will be able to identify the problem. A problem that seems clear may prove under close analysis to be the tip of the iceberg. It is the process leader's role to insure that all members have a thorough understanding of the fundamental problem before letting the group move prematurely to a phase it is unprepared for.

1.3b If what initially appeared to be a problem turns out to be a symptom, the group can share information in a way that will allow the problem to become evident. It may be advisable to gather additional information or even develop a case history to determine if the symptom is an indicator of a trend of symptoms, caused by a basic problem, such as poor communication channels, a need for a buffer between two departments, poorly trained managers, etc. Once the problem has been pinpointed and is well understood by all members the battle is all but won. A good problem definition will make solutions more obvious.

1.3 According to the decomposition principle, a problem with an underlying structure is best solved by a strategy of divide and conquer (structure is defined here as categories which are independent of one another).[5] In decompositions, the group can handle more factors to apply to each of the simpler problems (subcategories) than if the entire problem is faced head-on. Leaders can often spot a decomposition problem when the group jumps from issue to issue with little progress. Decomposition helps to structure the problem into smaller units that are more manageable. Consider the following example.

As you decompose the problem, you may want to use different methods of generating solutions to each subproblem. For example, having each person tackle a different subproblem—using a creative approach for some subproblems and a more analytic (accuracy) approach to others (to be discussed further in the next phase).

Problem: What is the estimated cost of establishing a dial-a-ride service for the elderly population in the city of Springfield?

1.4 If the problem can be decomposed, research suggests that the accuracy of the decision will be increased. The leader must decide how far to decompose a problem before diminishing returns result or whether the interrelation among problem components is too complex to decompose.

5. This section is based on the results of an empirical study of problem decomposition by Armstrong et al. (1975). They found decomposition led to increased accuracy in individual problem solving. It seems plausible that the same will hold true for group problem solving.

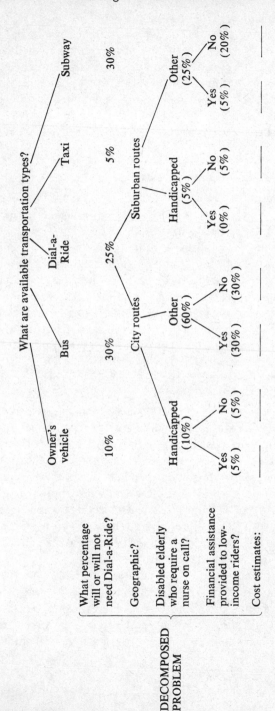

Figure 1.3

The problem-identification phase is without a doubt the most critical and most often neglected activity on the part of decision-making groups. A leader who can get the group to fully understand and analyze the problem will improve the effectiveness of the group and avoid needless time wasted by jumping too soon for solutions to poorly understood problems. It is a good idea to write a problem statement down on a wall chart, chalkboard, or flip chart with newsprint (and felt-tipped pens) to insure that everyone is in agreement and to keep the discussion on the track.[6]

Problem-identification phase games to resolve

"The hidden agenda."   As described earlier, one or more members has a hidden purpose which they are not revealing before the group. This can sometimes be spotted early in the discussion when a member attempts to get a problem defined his way in order to set the group up to later introduce a preferred alternative. One strategy to confront this game is to ask the person directly if he has something else in mind. "I heard you say . . . but I feel that you are trying to get at something else." In this way, the person is made aware that a game is occurring and others know about it. In giving such feedback, not hurting the player's feelings is crucial. It is always better to give feedback by relating how *you* interpret a person's behaviors or how *you* felt about a behavior instead of assuming you know what is going on inside their head.

"Why don't we do it my way?"   This has also been referred to as the self-authorized agenda. This game can be spotted when a member attempts to lead the group in a particular direction when other options are still being considered. The leader or other member may want to counter this game by asking the other members what they would prefer to do. A second strategy is to use the feedback approach described in the "hidden agenda" game. "I hear you saying . . . but I get the feeling you are trying to get the group to go the way you want it to go. Is that how you see it?" Again, focus on the behavioral or linguistic cues that lead you to that interpretation. Don't assume.

"Ain't it awful?"   In this game, one or more members dwell on the negative aspects of the situation. They attempt to make it sound like there is no possible way out, or that forces outside the control of the group have taken over. While things may be bad, at some point the leader needs to focus attention on what can be done to turn things around.

6. The wall chart can consist of newspapers taped to the wall. The process leader uses a magic marker to list ideas.

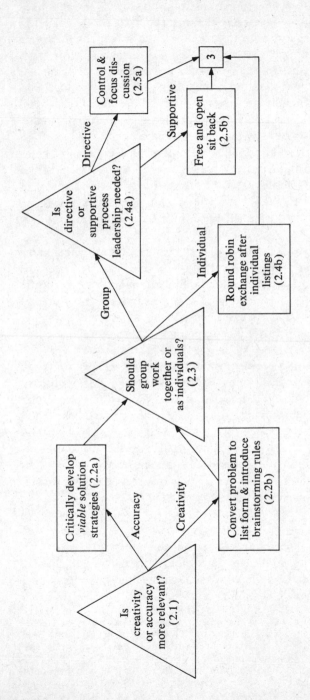

Figure 2. Solution-generation phase

2.1   In the solution-generation phase of problem solving, a number of decisions about how to structure the interaction to develop solution strategies are required of a group process leader. You should try to keep your group from getting into the "rut" of using the same technique for all problems. In this first decision, one must determine if creativity or accuracy is more relevant to the problem at hand. Problems of accuracy generally are less novel and more attention is paid to detailing well-understood search procedures. In creativity, many diverse inputs need to be integrated to resolve a novel problem or to generate a totally new solution. This does not mean accuracy and creativity are separable and distinct. Imagination is needed to generate critical details. Accuracy is needed to keep imagination from being aimless. The point is that the two involve different ways of processing group information, just as the left brain processes information differently than the right.

2.2a   If accuracy is the objective, then critically developing a number of viable solution strategies is called for.[7] Here the group attempts to combine their inputs to develop a limited number of carefully analyzed and systematically developed strategies to solve the problem. Later, a cost/benefit analysis can be used to evaluate each strategy. Many groups develop several competing strategy proposals for comparison.

2.2b   In the case of a problem suitable for more creative thinking, the use of Osborn's Brainstorming Rules has been found to improve the group's ability to generate novel solutions.[8] Sometimes one of the worst ills of a problem-solving group is developing the same "bad" solutions to the same recurring problems. The first step is to convert the wording of the problem to a statement that will cause the group to generate a long of solution alternatives. For example, convert a problem such as "how to launch a new product" to "what are all the ways we can think of to launch this new product?"

Brainstorming rules

(1) *Criticism is ruled out.* Adverse judgement of ideas must be withheld until later. (Later here refers to the evaluation phase.)
(2) *"Freewheeling" is welcomed.* The wilder the idea, the better; it is easier to tame down than to think up.

7. For a review of the parallels and differences between creativity and accuracy research, read Boje (1977). As to research on accuracy problems, Boje (1977) and Yost et al. (1977) suggest that certain problem-solving methods may be more appropriate for structured problems.
8. For a review of the creativity problem-solving research, read Bouchard (1969). See Thomas and Fink (1961), Vroom et al. (1969), and Taylor et al. (1958) as sample of the many studies in this area.

(3) *Quantity is wanted.* The greater the number of ideas, the more the likelihood of winners.

(4) *Combination and improvement are sought.* In addition to contributing ideas of their own, participants should suggest how ideas of others can be turned into better ideas, or how two or more ideas can be joined into still another idea. (This rule is not applicable when individuals work in isolation to develop lists of ideas.)

The process leader needs to familiarize members with the brainstorming rules and may want to have them tackle some commonly used brainstorming problems to develop their brainstorming skills before trying an important issue. Here are a few exercises to try:

1. *Tourist Problem:* Each year a great many American tourists go to visit Europe. But now suppose that our country wished to get many more European tourists to come to visit America during their vacations. What steps can you suggest that would get more European tourists to come to this country?

2. *Thumbs Problem:* We don't think this is very likely to happen, but imagine for a moment what would happen if everyone born after 1980 had an extra thumb on each hand. This extra thumb will be built just as the present one is but located on the other side of the hand. It faces inward so that is can press against the fingers just as the regular thumb does now. Now, the question is: What practical benefits or difficulties will arise when people start having this extra thumb?[9]

3. List as many uses as you can think up for a coathanger; for a broomstick.

2.3   With both techniques there remains disagreement as to whether having individuals work alone to generate separate lists of alternatives or together to develop a common list is better. Advocates of the individual technique argue that there are too many inhibiting factors, such as dysfunctional games, to use a joint listing approach.[10] A number of studies in this area conclude that having people develop independent lists leads to a greater quantity of ideas and more unique ideas.[11] In general, group participation using the brainstorming technique has been found to inhibit creative thinking in the solution to simple problems. In the case of accuracy problem solving, there is less agreement

9. A classic study using these two problems is Taylor et al. (1958).
10. See, for example, Maier (1967) and VandeVen and Delbecq (1971) for discussions of dysfunctional group phenomenon.
11. See Taylor et al. (1958) and Thomas and Fink (1961).

on the virtues of working independently, especially in the case of highly complex problems.[12] (Complex is defined here as many highly inter-dependent parts to a problem.) Consider, for example, problems which demand the expertise of a diverse set of specialists, no one of which could solve the problem alone. Deciding the design characteristics of a nuclear power plant (accuracy) or developing a new power source (creativity)—both require that the group attack the problem as one so that specialized information can be exchanged. Problems where one person alone could generate that new idea or handle an analysis issue can be attacked by individuals in isolation.

2.4a If you decide to work as a group, two styles of leadership you might consider, depending upon the situational requirements, are directive and supportive. The supportive approach has been found to be better suited to complex problems where information exchange is required.[13]

2.5a In the directive approach, a wall pad or blackboard can be used by the leader to list alternatives developed by the group. At this point in the problem-solving process it is advisable to actively limit evaluative comments until a number of strategies have been developed. By focusing attention on the pad or blackboard everyone will have the information before them and stay on track. If the tempo demands it, you may want to have more than one person available to do the list-ing. (This is especially true in brainstorming.) As you list ideas, try to list the ideas in as close to the member's phrasing and as fast as possible. Don't let any get away! It is important to list even far-out alternatives so that people feel free to contribute their ideas. Later in the evaluation phase a critical attitude can be emphasized to drop far-out suggestions. Don't say no to any idea at this point, just keep writing. A far-out idea can be important in jarring someone else's thinking. Finally, in the directive approach, the leader keeps central control over the communication exchanges. All comments are directed toward the process leader.

2.5b In the supportive style, the process leader temporarily aban-dons his leadership role to join the group. Here, open horizontal com-munication between all members is encouraged. With a highly complex

12. See Boje (1977) and Gustafson et al. (1973). Group techniques were not significantly better than individuals on accuracy problems. There is some indica-tion that the complexity of a problem may account for these results (Yost and Herbert [1977]).

13. Bennis (1966) attempts to apply the results of communication experi-ments on the marble experiments with problem-solving styles. Directive as used here refers to the "wheel" group network where all communication is directed toward the leader. Supportive is analagous to the "circle" or all-to-all network. The latter has been found to be better suited to complex problems.

and difficult problem, one strategy is to let the group focus on each other's comments in a nondirective fashion. The leader may also want to be silent during most of this phase if he is trying to solicit an unbiased set of alternatives from the group. An alternative strategy is to let one of the group members or a secretary do the listing on a wall pad or blackboard and for the leader to become an active group member. Here the leader has to be careful to throw his idea out the same status attached as everyone else's. You do not want an alternative to be adopted simply because it came from your lips.

In both styles the listing can be facilitated by the proper use of "silence." (This is also useful for getting less assertive members to talk.) If ideas are not forthcoming, a simple way to jar people into action is to take a chair and stare at the members eye to eye. This increases the tension level and will often get people thinking and speaking again. Some of the best ideas can evolve by not shying away from from silence. You should, however, avoid overusing the technique. When the group has generated a sufficient number of alternatives, silence may be an informal signal that it is time to move to the next phase.

2.4b   If your need is to have people develop independent lists, one way to combine the lists is in a round-robin exchange format.[14] The process leader asks each member for a single idea to place on the blackboard. Each member contributes one idea at a time in round-robin fashion until all ideas have been listed. There is no need for members to repeat an idea someone else has already introduced, unless their idea contributes significant variation to the first. Here again, the process leader must postpone evaluative comments and debates over specific alternatives until the next phase in the problem-solving process.

Solution-generation phase games to resolve

"The hard sell."   If you observe a member not only introducing an alternative, but following it up with a barrage of comments like: "This is the obvious choice," "I have here ten volumes of statistical tables in support of this alternative," "Here is how it is better than anything else presented today," "This alternative was driven by a little ol' lady," you know you are in the hard-sell game. To counter this game, inform the person that evaluative or "selling" comments belong in the next phase of the problem-solving process. At this point all you want to do is develop a number of alternative ideas on the problem.

"Lend me your ear."   How often have you been in a group where

14. For more discussion of round robins, see Delbecq et al. (1975).

you encounter the excessive talker or speech giver. A subtle way to train members to avoid this game is the use of the wall pad or blackboard. Summarize the member's comments into a short paraphrase. Then check with the member to see if the summary captures what he was trying to say. Either the member will get the point and make future comments more brief and to the point, or the member will continue to ramble. *Be careful* to avoid alienating yourself from the group by cutting the person off too soon. This will introduce unnecessary leader-versus-group conflict. At the conclusion of the second rambling ask the group for support. "Does the rest of the group see any difference between this shorter phrasing and what . . . just said?" If all else fails, you may want to ask the rest of the group what they are gaining from the person's comments. In general, to avoid leader-versus-group conflict, let the game go for awhile until others are aware of it. Shutting it off too early will make you appear the villian.[15]

"Why don't you, yes but."   In this game, one or more members will counter every solution alternative suggested with comments like: "Yes, but you have not considered . . . ," "Yes, but that will never work because of . . . ." If this game persists, members with ideas will soon become uncomfortable about introducing them into the group. This is especially true of an idea that has not been completely thought out. This is also why evaluative comments are held until the next phase. (Often this is the very idea that with a little group work could become a superior solution.) "Yes, but" may also be a symptom of a "hidden-agenda" game. The member may be attacking everyone else's ideas to protect a hidden alternative. In "yes, but," the option is to either focus on the problem-solving process ("Let's save the challenges for the evaluation phase") or to use a feedback approach (a description of the behavior cues followed by *your* feelings) as outlined in the "hidden-agenda" game ("I hear you saying . . . but I have the feeling that you have something else in mind").

"All talk and no listening."   During some moments in the problem-solving process it is a good idea to let everyone have the floor either to get some thinking started or to release tensions on topics where everyone comes to the meeting with deeply felt opinions they intend to share. This getting-it-all-on-the-table strategy can become dysfunctional when members stop listening to one another. Here, once the members are aware of the problem, the process leader can intervene to demand that the group begins listening to one another. You may even want to ask people to start building on the previous comment to get things settled down. It is important to point out that, as the process leader,

15. This solution is based on suggestions found in Sandberg (1973).

you want the *group to take its share of responsibility* for game counter-ing. Perhaps we need a game dealing with "why only me?"

"Have we been here before?" Groups frequently forget where they are going and where they have been. A group will begin solving problem "A" and end up developing totally irrelevant solutions. Mem-bers will introduce the same ideas over and over again. To counter this game, a *"recorder"* is needed. This is generally the process leader (it can be another group member or a secretary), who records the problem statement and a summary phrasing of each of the members' solution ideas. This should be in open view of all members and is a very useful way to keep the group on track.

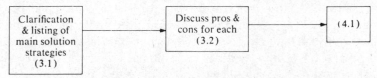

Figure 3. Evaluation phase

3.1 Whether your group has used the "critical" or the "brain-storming" problem-solving approach, it is important at this point for the process leader to list the main solution strategies, so that each one can be given careful evaluative consideration. If the group has gene-rated a large number of alternatives (e.g., greater than ten), then it is advisable to ask that the group pare the list down to the five most workable and important. This can be done by going down the list of generated alternatives and asking the group if each one should be kept. If one person wants it, leave it up. If no answer comes or if they say no, then that alternative can be scratched. Similar alternatives can be combined into overall strategies. An alternative approach is to rank order and choose the top five. Clarify each strategy to be sure everyone understands all implications. Be sure you give each alterna-tive *equal* consideration to keep the group from running off with the first one.

3.2 Here is where you can reapply brainstorming or critical anal-ysis to come up with a listing of pros and cons for each strategy. You may even want to have individuals develop separate lists and then use a round-robin format to come up with an overall analysis of the strat-egies. Whether you employ a group or individual approach, you will need to avoid debates and confrontations between proponents of vari-ous alternatives. The focus here should be to give each alternative a complete hearing so that the group does not run off with the first one. Often, in discussing the pros and cons it will become obvious that the group has overlooked some major contingencies. If this occurs, then you will need to redefine the problem and begin at phase 1 to repeat the problem-solving process. Giving the group the option of redefining the problem will keep them from implementing inappropriate strategies just to make a decision.

Evaluation-phase games to resolve

"Love me, love my dog."   A common game in the evaluation phase is where one or more members get their ego tangled up with their ideas. The result is that members feel pressured to evaluate the idea along with the person. A good analogy to tell a group about before this phase begins is poker. Once you put *your* money into the pot, it becomes the *group's* money. A bad poker player will invest in a losing hand because he fails to make this distinction. You need to emphasize the importance of such things as personal ownership of ideas and confrontations over who has the better idea as being out of place in problem-solving sessions. A caution to the group on games to avoid before each phase can save a lot of wasted energy.

"Groupthink."   Irving Janis defines groupthink as "a mode of thinking that persons engage in when concurrence seeking becomes so dominant in a cohesive ingroup that it tends to override realistic appraisal of alternative courses of action."[16] In other words, the members place such a high value on being cohesive and avoiding internal conflicts that they generate pressures against critical thinking. This can result in being overoptimistic about the risks involved in a strategy, rationalizing a strategy to the extent of ignoring negative information, or even withholding such information from the group, as well as a host of other dysfunctional consequences. To counter groupthink, you need to build some opposition into the group *before* it can take hold. Janis suggests assigning the role of critical evaluator to some members of the group, setting up independent evaluation groups to examine a problem-solving group's ideas, taking the role of "devil's advocate" to challenge the list of alternatives, and inviting in outside experts as some of the ways to combat groupthink.

5.1   It seems an obvious proposition that the type of decision strategy used by a group should depend on any number of contingent stiuational factors. Yet, groups invariably get into the rut of employing one method of decision making to the exclusion of all others. A number of decision theorists have suggested which situational factors are appropriate to which decision style, but there is still wide disagreement.[17]

16. See Janis (1971, 1972) for more on the group think phenomonen.
17. See Vroom (1973), Vroom and Yetton (1973), and Schmuck et. al. (1972) for discussion of when to use voting vs. consensus.

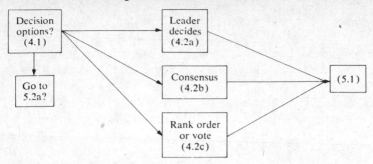

Figure 4. Decision phase

The following is an incomplete checklist of factors and the decision method which seems most appropriate. It's important to reemphasize that each group leader will need to examine his own situation to determine which method is most applicable. (If your answer to any of the following is yes, then the option indicated is probably required.)

1. Is the task trivial to the interests of the group members or is an obvious preference present?   (Leader)
2. Does the authority to make the decision rest outside the group? Does the group have a vested interest? (It may still be useful to get suggestions and criticisms.)   (Leader)
3. Is this a highly emotionally charged issue which will only serve to disrupt the long-term effectiveness of the group? (Groupthink must be avoided here.)   (Leader)
4. Is is a problem where the group does not possess adequate background information to act?   (Leader)
5. Is it a complex task where a high rate of information exchange and a critical discussion is preferred?   (Consensus)
6. Is a voting decision likely to disguise conflicts or cover up disagreements?   (Consensus)
7. Is involvement of the members needed to promote decision support and responsibility taking in implementation?   (Consensus)
8. Is it a problem which requires a high-quality decision to cope with a potentially risky consequence?   (Consensus)
9. Is it an issue where tension and disagreement is likely to be so diverse as to make consensus dysfunctional and where obtaining a group sanction is preferable to a leader-only decision?   (Voting)
10. Is it a decision where a small minority stands in opposition and is not likely to affect acceptance or implementation?   (Voting)
11. Does available time not allow for the arguments and conflicts to be fully developed and resolved?   (Voting)

By becoming familiar with the above checklist, you can match the situation at hand with the most appropriate decision method. In this way, you will avoid overuse of, for example, consensus in trivial situations, saving it instead for just those major problems where it is needed most.[18]

4.2a Even if the leader makes the decision, it may be advisable to let the group provide useful information on the likely outcomes of a proposed decision. This can be accomplished either on a one-to-one basis by interviewing each member or as a group discussion. There may also be advantages to having a group participate in implementation planning even if it is not advisable for them to participate in the actual decision, for example, when a group is given a strategy to implement by a higher authority. Even though the decision has been made, involvement and implementation problem solving will point out unforeseen obstacles and generate partial commitment.

4.2b In consensus, the leader agrees in advance to abide by the final group decision. Consensus does not require having a unanimous vote where *everyone* agrees. It does require that everyone can freely express their arguments, that no decision will be made until every member who disagrees agrees to support the final group decision. In other words, even if the decision is not a member's first choice, he agrees to stand by the decision. Consensus is generally assumed to induce the greatest degree of commitment to the final decision. Consensus also affords the most thorough treatment of a problem by insuring that disagreements are exposed and resolved, it is also the most demanding and time-consuming of the three procedures.

4.2c Rank ordering involves having the members independently rank the alternatives from the most to the least preferred. The final group decision is the result of the combined rank orderings. Some suggest that this method allows for a better representation of minority opinions than a simple voting procedure.[19] Voting, however, involves less time and is better suited where only a few alternatives are being considered. In some cases, you may want to combine the two (e.g., a rank ordering can be used to pick the two or three alternatives for final consideration in a final voting situation). At various points during the problem-solving process another type of voting that can be used is the "straw vote." This is a vote that does not count, that is useful as a nonthreatening check on how much agreement a group has.

5.2a One option that most groups overlook is the decision to reject all strategies that have been proposed on the grounds that none

18. Jean Bartunek points out that overuse of consensus as a decision option will turn people off to the technique because of the emotional stress that accompanies the strategy and the added time required.
19. See Delbecq et al. (1975) and Van de Ven and Delbecq (1973).

solve the problem at hand. In this case, the group goes back to the drawing board. This can be a particularly useful strategy when you consider that often the best ideas are the ones that the group comes up wth once they have dispensed with the obvious, but often weak, strategies.

Decision-phase games to resolve

"Let's get this over with." Some of the worst group decisions are the result of haste. If one or more members is pushing to reach a decision because of the time constraints, then it may be advisable to postpone the actual decision until members have more time. If this game is introduced because the members do not feel the issue is important enough or if they are apathetic to the issue, then maybe it was inappropriate to present that problem for group consideration in the first place. Someone may be speeding everyone down a hidden agenda or other game.

"We all agree, right?" A game introduced to save time or because of apathy is one thing, but one which is a disguised way of forcing one's solution onto the group is another story. This game, sometimes referred to as the "self-authorized agenda," involves a member who pushes for a decision when, in fact, the majority of members are actually against that strategy. Thinking that everyone else agrees (when they do not), the members give in and the result is a decision only one person wanted and no one is aware that the minority won. A good way to counter this game is to quiz each member to see if, in fact, there is a consensus among the members. This game may also be a sign of the "groupthink" phenomenon or possibly a power play on the part of a member who wants your title. Beware!

5.1 One of the more common mistakes a group will make is to make the decision without developing a set of implementation plans. The solution selected should be broken into action steps. Each action step describes a segment of the solution to be implemented by a certain date. In this way, you can assign individual responsibility to each action

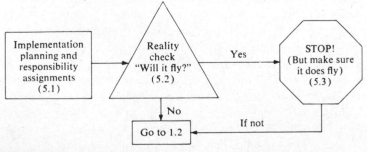

Figure 5. Implementation phase.

step and insure that something happens as a result of the problem-
solving session. You may also want to brainstorm a list of resources
that will be needed to implement each of the action steps. An alternative to jumping right into a large commitment of resources is to propose a pilot study of the selected alternatives. In this way, you can
gather information on the pitfalls of implementing the complete
strategy.

  5.2   Reality Check.   Now is the time to look back at your problem
definition and determine if the strategy plan your group has developed
solves the problem you identified. If you implemented this strategy,
would it solve that problem? If not, then you can avoid a costly mistake by going back and redefining the problem or coming up with a
more appropriate solution. One useful technique is to ask the group
to brainstorm a list of all the things that could possibly go wrong.
(According to Murphy's Law, "If something can go wrong, it will!")
Once you have tested your planned strategy against all reasonable criticisms, go to the people who will be affected by the group's strategy and
have them criticize it. In this way, you will avoid unnecessary stumbling
blocks.

  5.3   Stop.   Once you have implemented your strategy, gather feedback on its progress. By closely monitoring the strategy, you can deal
with problem areas by feeding them back through the problem-solving
model at phase *1.2.* Your strategy must be made to adapt to the contingencies that you were not able to anticipate. Don't get into the trap
of ignoring unforeseen contingencies just to keep your plan intact. Continually look at modification options to your plan in light of new
contingencies.

Implementation Phase Games to Resolve

  "Avoid the monkey."   "Monkey" refers to the acceptance of responsibility for the results of the group decision and for participating in
actual implementation.[20] Whether members avoid the monkey will depend to great extent on the kind of participation that the leader was
able to motivate on the part of the members during the entire meeting.
The highest involvement should be in a thorough problem search,
consensus decision where each member agrees to support the decision.
By not participating in the phases you can take the minority position
and later feel no responsibility for aiding in implementation. Whatever
problem-solving method, interaction scheme, or decision technique,
involvement of the members in implementation planning will generate
some opportunities for responsibility taking. In fact, throughout the
meeting you should focus on action planning and dividing the task up

20. For more on the monkey metaphor, see Oncken and Wass (1974).

among the members; then you can avoid leaving the problem-solving decision with the monkey on your shoulder.

"Building lead balloons." Oftentimes, a group will get carried away with their own ideas and propose an alternative that, while sounding like the answer to beat all answers, is in fact a lead balloon. It may be advisable to postpone implementation until the members have had a chance to reflect on the strategy and think through all the implications. At a second meeting, if everything is in order then you can proceed. Again, this game may be symptomatic of the "groupthink" phenomenon and can be avoided by building some critical thinking into your group.

The contingency model: combining all the phases

Figure 1 combines the five phases into one model. At each decision point, you will need to decide which course of action to take by examining the situational factors present. The primary thing to avoid is the assumption that there is *one best way* to analyze, solve, and implement in problem solving. The model can be extended by keeping in mind that there are many other decisions to consider besides the few presented here. As the process leader it is your responsibility to get the group to uncover those decision points so that the problem process you use matches the demands of the situation. Don't get into the rut of managing your group meeting the same "ole" way, regardless of the situation at hand.

You can begin at any point in this model. For example, if you have a firm grasp on the problem, you can start in phase 2. If your concern is with how to implement a directive assigned to your group, you can begin at phase 3. Any time you are in a phase and you discover that what you thought was a problem turns out to be a symptom, you can take your group back to phase 1. The model is meant to be a guide for you to plan and guide your group through the problem-solving process and to build some flexibility into your approach to problem solving. If enough groups in the organization become more adaptive in their ability to cope with a wider variety of problem types (e.g., from simple, to complex, to dealing with an undetermined problem), then the organization as a whole will be more adaptive. Building adaptability into an organization improves its long-term survival power.

Other games

Game analysis is a useful way to spot dysfunctional process behaviors on the part of group members. There are many more games to consider than the few listed here. Consider the following or go on to develop your own list.

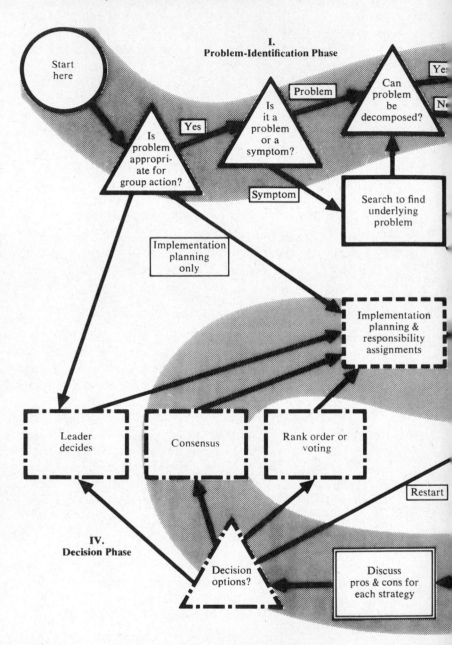

Fig. 6

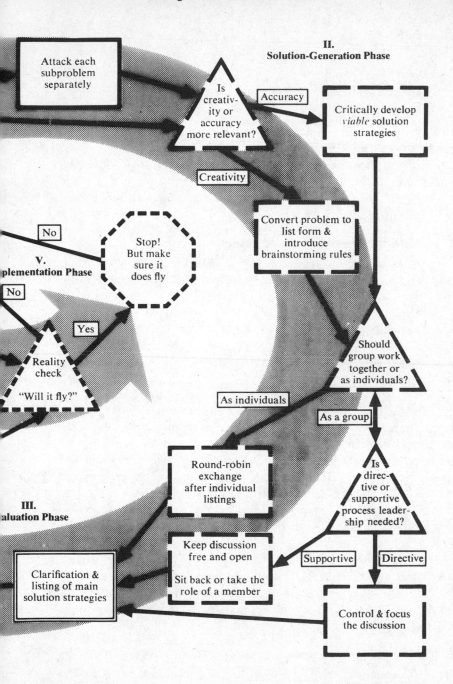

"Let's you and him fight." A member sets two members against each other for sport.

"Now I've got you, you S.O.B." A member digs a trap for one or more members to fall into.

"I'll speak if you make me." Someone uses silence as a crutch or as a way to get more psychic attention.

These games can occur anytime during the problem-solving process. In addition to dysfunctional games, there are functional games which you may want to build into your group, such as Harris' "I'm OK, You're OK." By managing the game playing in groups you can improve not only the group's problem-solving productivity, but the overall spirit and enthusiasm of the group.

Case episode: The financial aids office

It is now Tuesday and you are a director of a financial aids office. Your assistant director, responsible for counseling, has come to you several times about the nonprofessional attitudes of his staff. His concerns lie in the areas of commitment to the job and their attitudes toward assigned responsibilities. Specifically, he raises the issue of a "professional mentality" versus an "8-to-5 mentality." He sees himself as an open person with a progressive managerial style, but feels forced to begin cracking down.

On two separate occasions, members of his staff have come to you and expressed their concern about his overbearing interference in their work. The staff members preface their remarks with expressions of respect, but at the same time imply that he does not recognize their abilities nor trust them to perform up to their professional capabilities. He does not delegate work or responsibilities, fails to make assignments until issues are at a crisis stage, and supervises them as if they were blue-collar workers. They are fearful of giving him direct feedback.

It comes to a head today at your regular staff meeting. Your assistant director is absent until next Monday. Instead of pursuing the planned agenda, the counseling staff spends all morning expressing their doubts about their supervisor's ability to provide the leadership required by the unit. They are ready to walk out unless something is settled by 1 P.M. You have until the staff returns from lunch to consider the problem.

Follow the guidelines below

1. After general group discussion, appoint one person to be the process leader, while the remaining members focus on the content.

2. Reach agreement on a one-sentence definition of the underlying problem. Be sure it is a problem and not a symptom.
3. Decide if a critical or a creative problem-solving approach is more appropriate.
4. Should you, as directors, develop a list of alternatives individually or as a group?
5. Pare the final list down to the best three alternatives and clarify each.
6. Discuss the pros and cons for each alternative.
7. Which decision technique should be used? Who should be involved in the decision? Director, assistant director, staff?
8. Develop an implementation plan and action steps to get the chosen alternative into action.
9. *Reality Check.* Before going back to face the staff at 1 P.M., discuss any potential pitfalls in your chosen alternative plan and action steps.
10. *Stop!* How will you monitor your plan to be sure that it flies?

References

Armstrong, S. J., Denniston, W. B., and Gordon, M. M. "The Use of Decomposition Principles in Making Judgments," *Organizational Behavior and Human Performance,* 14 (1975): 257–63.

Bales, R. F. *Interaction Process Analysis: A Method for the Study of Small Groups.* Cambridge, Massachusetts: Addison-Wesley, 1950.

Benne, K. and Sheets, P. "Functional Roles of Group Members," *Journal of Social Issues,* 4(2) (1948): 41–49.

Bennis, W. G. *Changing Organizations.* New York: McGraw-Hill, 1966, pp. 41–55.

Berne, E. *Games People Play.* New York: Grove Press, 1964.

Boje, D. M. "Is Your First Guess Your Best? An Empirical Comparison of Individual, Nominal and Delphi Decision Techniques on Judgment Accuracy and Confidence." Mimeo, Organizational Behavior Group, University of Illinois, Urbana, May 1977.

Bouchard, T. J. "Personality, Problem-Solving Procedure and Performance in Small Groups," *Journal of Applied Psychology,* Monograph, 53 (1969): 1–29.

Delbecq, A. L., VandeVen, A. H., and Gustafson, D. H. *Group Techniques for Program Planning: A Guide to Nominal and Delphi Processes.* Glenview, Illinois: Scott Foresman, 1975.

Gustafson, D. H., Shukla, R. K., Delbecq, A., and Walster, G. W. "A Comparative Study of Differences in Subjective Likelihood Estimates Made by Individuals, Interacting Groups, Delphi Groups and

Nominal Groups," *Organizational Behavior and Human Performance,* 9 (1973): 280–91.

Harris, T. A. *I'm Okay, You're Okay: A Practical Guide to Transactional Analysis.* New York: Harper & Row, 1967.

Janis, I. L. "Groupthink," *Psychology Today,* 5(6) (1971): 43–46, 74–76.

———. *Victims of Groupthink.* Boston: Houghton Mifflin, 1972.

Jay, A. "How to Run a Meeting," *Harvard Business Review,* March–April 1976, pp. 43–57.

Maier, N. F. R. "Assets and Liabilities in Group Problem Solving: The Need for an Integrative Function," *Psychology Review,* 74(4) (1967): 239–49.

Oncken, W., Jr. and Wass, D. L. "Management Time: Who's Got the Monkey?" *Harvard Business Review,* November–December 1974, pp. 75–80.

Osborn, A. F. *Applied Imagination,* revised edition. New York: Scribner, 1957.

Sandberg, M. "Mini-Guide to Problem Solving Meetings." Mimeo, Rider College, Trenton, New Jersey, 1973.

Schmuck, R. A., Runkel, P. J., Saturen, S. L., Martell, R. T., and Derr, C. B. *Handbook of Organization Development in Schools.* Palo Alto, California: National Press, (1972), chapters 6 and 7.

Taylor, D. W., Berry, P. C., and Block, C. H. "Does Group Participation When Using Brainstorming Facilitate or Inhibit Creative Thinking?" *Administrative Science Quarterly,* 3 (1958):23–47.

Thomas, R. J. and Fink, C. F. "Models of Group Problem Solving," *Journal of Abnormal and Social Psychology,* 63 (1961): 153–63.

Van de Ven, A., and Delbecq, A. L. "Nominal Versus Interacting Group Processes for Committee Decision Making," *Academy of Management Journal,* 14(2) (June 1971): 203–13.

Vroom, V. H., Grant, L. D. and Cotton, T. S. "The Consequences of Social Interaction in Group Problem-Solving," *Journal of Applied Psychology,* 53 (August 1969): 53–54.

———. "A New Look at Managerial Decision Making," *Organizational Dynamics,* Vol. I, No. 4 (Spring 1973).

Vroom, V. H. and Yetton, P. W. *Leadership and Decision Making.* Pittsburgh: University of Pittsburgh Press, 1973.

Yost, D. B., and Herbert, T. T. "An Empirical Analysis of Nominal and Interacting Consensus Groups: Decision Quality with a Structured Problem." Paper presented at the Annual Meeting of the Midwest American Institute of Decision Sciences, Cleveland, Ohio, May 1977.

9   Conflict Management: Friends and Enemies

Introduction

If solving problems within a group can be difficult and challenging, working out problems among several groups can be even more so. All organizations are, in one sense, political coalitions of many groups, each with its own interests and objectives. Any individual is likely to find himself caught up in loyalties to different groups with conflicting demands, preferences, interdependencies, and even beliefs. Conflict among groups can occur in all of these areas. And outside the organization, there are competing organizations, consumer groups, environmental groups, governmental bodies, and special-interest groups, each trying to influence the behavior of groups within the organization. A wide range of conflicts throughout the organization and its environment must thus be "managed" if the organization is to do its work. But managing conflict does not always mean eliminating or reducing it. Sometimes conflict levels can usefully be increased. Here are some reasons why.

1. Conflict often accomplishes what cooperation cannot. Given our limited information-processing capacity, conflict is a means of sorting out issues where there is incomplete information, where several rationalizations appear equally valid, or where new actions require realignments of power and status structures.

2. Conflict releases energy. Given apathy and lack of commitment, conflict can stimulate creative and motivational forces.

3. Conflict facilitates adaptation. Via conflict, groups in the organization can realign themselves, form new coalitions, absorb some old groups, thereby adapting and surviving in changing environments.

The implication of all the above is, of course, that *levels* of conflict in organizations are important. The articles which follow conceptualize and illustrate the role of conflict and its management in organizations.

The first paper, by Pondy, treats the issue of conflict rather abstractly. He provides a comprehensive model for understanding the conflict implications of the two remaining papers. Pondy conceptualizes conflict as a five-stage episode. As a conflict escalates through these stages, a variety of options and opportunities arise for resolving the conflict.

The second article, by Love, focuses on a more specific issue, the kind of conflict which frequently occurs between subgroups and their parent organizations. Dr. Love contrasts "protest absorption" with other strategies for dealing with internal conflict, strategies like condemnation, avoidance, or expulsion of the nonconforming subgroup. The beauty of the protest absorption strategy (from the organization's perspective) is that it both encapsulates the nonconforming subgroup (thereby preventing the spread of its rebellious ideas) and harnesses the innovative energies of the nonconforming subgroup.

There are now two appendices to her original paper, which was first written in 1962. In the 1972 postscript, Dr. Love tied protest absorption of organizational subgroups to the prominent forms of social conflict that characterized our society during the middle and late 1960s. In the 1979 postscript, written especially for the current revision of this book, she has moved farther into the environment to explain how and why nonconforming subgroups emerge in organizations.

Finally, Professor Kanter's paper offers a cultural analysis of life in organizations, an analysis so rich that we shall need both Pondy's episode model and Love's absorption model to understand its implications for conflict management. The conflict episodes Dr. Kanter points to are not those generally dealt with in the conflict literature. She raises a wide variety of more subtle conflict issues, such as the changing role of women in male-dominated organizations or the executive trying to defend some small zone of privacy from the corporation's gaze.

So while this chapter begins by looking at *big* intergroup and interorganizational conflicts, it ends by looking at the little ones, the ones that really matter to each of us, the everyday conflicts of organizational life.

Organizational Conflict:
Concepts and Models
Louis R. Pondy

There is a large and growing body of literature on the subject of organizational conflict. The concept of conflict has been treated as a general social phenomenon, with implications for the understanding of conflict within and between organizations.[1] It has also assumed various roles of some importance in attempts at general theories of management and organizational behavior.[2] Finally, conflict has recently been the focus of numerous empirical studies of organization.[3]

Reprinted with permission from *Administrative Science Quarterly*, vol. 12, no. 2, 1967.

1. Jessie Bernard, T. H. Pear, Raymond Aron, and Robert C. Angell, *The Nature of Conflict* (Paris: UNESCO, 1957); Kenneth Boulding, *Conflict and Defense* (New York: Harper, 1962); Lewis Coser, *The Functions of Social Conflict* (Glencoe, Ill.: Free Press, 1956); Kurt Lewin, *Resolving Social Conflict* (New York: Harper, 1948); Anatol Rapaport, *Fights, Games, and Debates* (Ann Arbor: University of Michigan, 1960); Thomas C. Schelling, *The Strategy of Conflict* (Cambridge, Mass.: Harvard Univ., 1961); Muzafer Sherif and Carolyn Sherif, *Groups in Harmony and Tension* (Norman, Okla.: University of Oklahoma, 1953); Georg Simmel, *Conflict*, trans. Kurt H. Wolff (Glencoe, Ill.: Free Press, 1955).

2. Bernard M. Bass, *Organizational Psychology* (Boston, Mass.: Allyn and Bacon, 1965); Theodore Caplow, *Principles of Organization* (New York: Harcourt, Brace, and World, 1964); Eliot D. Chapple and Leonard F. Sayles, *The Measure of Management* (New York: Macmillan, 1961); Michel Crozier, *The Bureaucratic Phenomenon* (Glencoe, Ill.: Free Press, 1964); Richard M. Cyert and James G. March, *A Behavioral Theory of the Firm* (Englewood Cliffs, N. J.: Prentice-Hall, 1963); Alvin W. Gouldner, *Patterns of Industrial Bureaucracy* (Glencoe, Ill.: Free Press, 1954); Harold J. Leavitt, *Managerial Psychology* (Chicago: University of Chicago, 1964); James G. March and Herbert A. Simon, *Organizations* (New York: Wiley, 1958); Philip Selznick, *TVA and the Grass Roots* (Berkeley: University of California, 1949); Victor Thompson, *Modern Organization* (New York: Knopf, 1961).

3. Joseph L. Bower, The Role of Conflict in Economic Decision-making Groups, *Quarterly Journal of Economics,* 79 (May 1965), 253–257; Melville Dalton, *Men Who Manage* (New York: Wiley, 1959); J. M. Dutton and R. E. Walton, "Interdepartmental Conflict and Cooperation: A Study of Two Contrasting Cases," dittoed, Purdue University, October 1964; William Evan,

Slowly crystallizing out of this research are three conceptual models designed to deal with the major classes of conflict phenomena in organizations.[4]

1. *Bargaining model.* This is designed to deal with conflict among interest groups in competition for scarce resources. This model is particularly appropriate for the analysis of labor-management relations, budgeting processes, and staff-line conflicts.

2. *Bureaucratic model.* This is applicable to the analysis of superior-subordinate conflicts or, in general, conflicts along the vertical dimension of a hierarchy. This model is primarily concerned with the problems caused by institutional attempts to control behavior and the organization's reaction to such control.

3. *Systems model.* This is directed at lateral conflict, or conflict among the parties to a functional relationship. Analysis of the problems of coordination is the special province of this model.

Running as common threads through each of these models are several implicit orientations. The most important of these orientations follow:

1. Each conflict relationship is made up of a sequence of interlocking conflict episodes; each episode exhibits a sequence or pattern of development, and the conflict relationship can be characterized by stable patterns that appear across the sequence of episodes. This orientation forms the basis for a working definition of conflict.

2. Conflict may be functional as well as dysfunctional for the individual and the organization; it may have its roots either within the individual or in the organizational context; therefore, the desirability of conflict resolution needs to be approached with caution.

3. Conflict is intimately tied up with the stability of the organization, not merely in the usual sense that conflict is a threat to stability, but in a much more complex fashion; that is, conflict is a key variable in the feedback loops that characterize organizational behavior. These orientations are discussed before the conceptual models are elaborated.

Superior-Subordinate Conflict in Research Organizations, *Administrative Science Quarterly,* 10 (June 1965), 52–64; Robert L. Kahn, *et al., Studies in Organizational Stress* (New York: Wiley, 1964); L. R. Pondy, Budgeting and Inter-Group Conflict in Organizations, *Pittsburgh Business Review,* 34 (April 1964), 1–3; R. E. Walton, J. M. Dutton, and H. G. Fitch, *A Study of Conflict in the Process, Structure, and Attitudes of Lateral Relationships* (Institute Paper No. 93; Lafayette, Ind.: Purdue University, November 1964); Harrison White, Management Conflict and Sociometric Structure, *American Journal of Sociology,* 67 (September 1961), 185–199; Mayer N. Zald, Power Balance and Staff Conflict in Correctional Institutions, *Administrative Science Quarterly,* 7 (June 1962), 22–49.

4. The following conceptualization draws heavily on a paper by Lawrence R. Ephron, Group Conflict in Organizations: A Critical Appraisal of Recent Theories, *Berkeley Journal of Sociology,* 6 (Spring 1961), 53–72.

A working definition of conflict

The term "conflict" has been used at one time or another in the literature to describe: (1) *antecedent conditions* (for example, scarcity of resources, policy differences) of conflictful behavior, (2) *affective states* (e.g., stress, tension, hostility, anxiety, etc.) of the individuals involved, (3) *cognitive states* of individuals, i.e., their perception or awareness of conflictful situations, and (4) *conflictful behavior,* ranging from passive resistance to overt aggression. Attempts to decide which of these classes—conditions, attitude, cognition, or behavior— is really conflict is likely to result in an empty controversy. The problem is not to choose among these alternative conceptual definitions, since each may be a relevant stage in the development of a conflict episode, but to try to clarify their relationships.

Conflict can be more readily understood if it is considered a dynamic process. A conflict relationship between two or more individuals in an organization can be analyzed as a sequence of conflict episodes. Each conflict episode begins with conditions characterized by certain conflict potentials. The parties to the relationship may not become aware of any basis of conflict, and they may not develop hostile affections for one another. Depending on a number of factors, their behavior may show a variety of conflictful traits. Each episode or encounter leaves an aftermath that affects the course of succeeding episodes. The entire relationship can then be characterized by certain stable aspects of conditions, affect, perception, and behavior. It can also be characterized by trends in any of these characteristics.

This is roughly analogous to defining a "decision" to include activities preliminary to and following choice, as well as the choice itself. In the same sense that a decision can be thought of as a process of gradual commitment to a course of action, a conflict episode can be thought of as a gradual escalation to a state of disorder. If choice is the climax of a decision, then by analogy, open war or aggression is the climax of a conflict episode.

This does not mean that every conflict episode necessarily passes through every stage to open aggression. A potential conflict may never be perceived by the parties to the conflict, or if perceived, the conflict may be resolved before hostilities break out. Several other alternative courses of development are possible. Both Coleman and Aubert make these points clearly in their treatments of the dynamics of conflict.[5]

Just as some decisions become programmed or routinized, conflict

5. James S. Coleman, *Community Conflict* (Glencoe, Ill.: Free Press, 1957); Vilhelm Aubert, Competition annd Dissensus: Two Types of Conflict and Conflict Resolution, *Journal of Conflict Resolution,* 7 (March 1963), 26–42.

management in an organization also becomes programmed or institutionalized sometimes. In fact, the institutionalization of means for dealing with recurrent conflict is one of the important aspects in any treatment of the topic. An organization's success hinges to a great extent on its ability to set up and operate appropriate mechanisms for dealing with a variety of conflict phenomena.

Five stages of a conflict episode are identified: (1) latent conflict (conditions), (2) perceived conflict (cognition), (3) felt conflict (affect), (4) manifest conflict (behavior, and (5) conflict aftermath (conditions). The elaboration of each of these stages of a conflict episode will provide the substance for a working definition. Which specific reactions take place at each stage of a conflict episode, and why, are the central questions to be answered in a theory of conflict. Only the framework within which those questions can be systematically investigated is developed here.

Latent conflict

A search of the literature has produced a long list of underlying sources of organizational conflict. These are condensed into three basic types of latent conflict: (1) competition for scarce resources, (2) drives for autonomy, and (3) divergence of subunit goals. Later in the paper each of these fundamental types of latent conflict is paired with one of the three conceptual models. Briefly, competition forms the basis for conflict when the aggregated demands of participants for resources exceed the resources available to the organization; autonomy needs form the basis of conflict when one party either seeks to exercise control over some activity that another party regards as his own province or seeks to insulate itself from such control; goal divergence is the source of conflict when two parties who must cooperate on some joint activity are unable to reach a consensus on concerted action. Two or more types of latent conflict may, of course, be present simultaneously.

An important form of latent conflict, which appears to be omitted from this list, is role conflict. The role conflict model treats the organization as a collection of role sets, each composed of the focal person and his role senders. Conflict is said to occur when the focal person receives incompatible role demands or expectations from the persons in his role set.[6] This model has the drawback that it treats the focal person as merely a passive receiver rather than as an active participant in the relationship. It is argued here, that the role conflict model does not postulate a distinct type of latent conflict. Instead, it defines a

6. Kahn, et al., op. cit., pp. 11–35.

conceptual relationship, the role set, which may be useful for the analysis of all three forms of latent conflict described.

Perceived conflict

Conflict may sometimes be perceived when no conditions of latent conflict exist, and latent conflict conditions may be present in a relationship without any of the participants perceiving the conflict.

The case in which conflict is perceived when on latent conflict exists can be handled by the so-called semantic model of conflict.[7] According to this explanation, conflict is said to result from the parties' misunderstanding of each others' true position. It is argued that such conflict can be resolved by improving communications between the parties. This model has been the basis of a wide variety of management techniques aimed at improving interpersonal relations. Of course, if the parties' true positions *are* in opposition, then more open communication may only exacerbate the conflict.

The more important case, that some latent conflicts fail to reach the level of awareness also requires explanation. Two important mechanisms that limit perception of conflict are the suppression mechanism and the attention-focus mechanism.[8] Individuals tend to block conflicts that are only mildly threatening out of awareness.[9] Conflicts become strong threats, and therefore must be acknowledged, when the conflicts relate to values central to the individual's personality. The suppression mechanism is applicable more to conflicts related to personal than to organizational values. The attention-focus mechanism, however, is related more to organizational behavior than to personal values. Organizations are characteristically faced with more conflicts than can be dealt with, given available time and capacities. The normal reaction is to focus attention on only a few of these, and these tend to be the conflicts for which short-run, routine solutions are available. For organizations successfully to confront the less programmed conflicts, it is frequently necessary to set up separate subunits specifically to deal with such conflicts.

Felt conflict

There is an important distinction between perceiving conflict and feeling conflict. *A* may be aware that *B* and *A* are in serious disagreement over some policy, but it may not make *A* tense or anxious, and it

7. Bernard, Pear, Aron, and Angell, *op. cit.*

8. These two mechanisms are instances of what Cyert and March, *op. cit.*, pp. 117–118, call the "quasi-resolution" of conflict.

9. Leavitt, *op. cit.*, pp. 53–72.

may have no effect whatsoever on A's affection towards B. The personalization of conflict is the mechanism which causes most students of organization to be concerned with the dysfunctions of conflict. There are two common explanations for the personalization of conflict.

One explanation is that the inconsistent demands of efficient organization and individual growth create anxieties within the individual.[10] Anxieties may also result from identity crises or from extra-organizational pressures. Individuals need to vent these anxieties in order to maintain internal equilibrium. Organizational conflicts of the three latent types described earlier provide defensible excuses for displacing these anxieties against suitable targets. This is essentially the so-called tension-model.[11]

A second explanation is that conflict becomes personalized when the whole personality of the individual is involved in the relationship. Hostile feelings are most common in the intimate relations that characterize total institutions, such as monasteries, residential colleges, and families.[12] In order to dissipate accumulated hostilities, total institutions require certain safety-valve institutions such as athletic activities or norms that legitimize solitude and withdrawal, such as the noncommunication norms prevalent in religious orders.

Thus, felt conflict may arise from sources independent of the three types of latent conflict, but latent conflicts may provide appropriate targets (perhaps symbolic ones) for undirected tensions.

Manifest conflict

By manifest conflict is meant any of several varieties of conflictful behavior. The most obvious of these is open aggression, but such physical and verbal violence is usually strongly proscribed by organizational norms. Except for prison riots, political revolutions, and extreme labor unrest, violence as a form of manifest conflict in organizations is rare. The motivations toward violence may remain, but they tend to be expressed in less violent form. Dalton has documented the covert attempts to sabotage or block an opponent's plans through aggressive and defensive coalitions.[13] Mechanic has described the tactics of con-

10. Chris Argyris, *Personality and Organization: The Conflict Between the System and the Individual* (New York: Harper, 1957).

11. Bernard, Pear, Aron, and Angell, *op. cit.*

12. It should be emphasized that members of total institutions characteristically experience both strong positive *and* negative feelings for one another and toward the institution. It may be argued that this ambivalence of feeling is a primary cause of anxiety. See Coser, *op. cit.*, pp. 61–65; and Amitai Etzioni and W. R. Taber, Scope, Pervasiveness, and Tension Management in Complex Organizations, *Social Research,* 30 (Summer 1963), 220–238.

13. Dalton, *op. cit.*

flict used by lower-level participants, such as apathy or rigid adherence to the rules, to resist mistreatment by the upper levels of the hierarchy.[14]

How can one decide when a certain behavior or pattern of behavior or pattern of behavior is conflictful? One important factor is that the behavior must be interpreted in the context in which it takes place. If *A* does not interact with *B,* it may be either because *A* and *B* are not related in any organizational sense, or because *A* has withdrawn from a too stressful relationship, or because *A* is deliberately frustrating *B* by withdrawing support, or simply because *A* is drawn away from the relationship by other competing demands upon his time. In other words, knowledge of the organizational requirements and of the expectations and motives of the participants appears to be necessary to characterize the behavior as conflictful. This suggests that behavior should be defined to be conflictful if, and only if, some or all of the participants perceive it to be conflictful.

Should the term *manifest conflict* be reserved for behavior which, in the eyes of the actor, is deliberately and consciously designed to frustrate another in the pursuit of his (the other's) overt or covert goals? But what of behavior which is not *intended* to frustrate, but does? Should not that behavior also be called conflictful? The most useful definition of manifest conflict seems to be that behavior which, in the mind of the actor, frustrates the goals of at least some of the other participants. In other words, a member of the organization is said to engage in conflictful behavior if he consciously, but not necessarily deliberately, blocks another member's goal achievement. He may engage in such behavior *deliberately* to frustrate another, or he may do so in spite of the fact that he frustrates another. To define manifest conflict in this way is to say that the following question is important: "Under what conditions will a party to a relationship *knowingly* frustrate another party to the relationship?" Suppose *A* unknowingly blocks *B*'s goals. This is not conflictful behavior. But suppose *B* informs *A* that he perceives *A*'s behavior to be conflictful; if then *A* acknowledges the message and *persists* in the behavior, it is an instance of manifest conflict.

The interface between perceived conflict and manifest conflict and the interface between felt conflict and manifest conflict are the pressure points where most conflict-resolution programs are applied. The object of such programs is to prevent conflicts which have reached the level of awareness or the level of affect from erupting into noncooperative behavior. The availability of appropriate and effective administrative

14. David Mechanic, "Sources of Power of Lower Participants in Complex Organizations," in W. W. Cooper, H. J. Leavitt, and M. W. Shelly (eds.), *New Perspectives in Organization Research* (New York: Wiley, 1964), pp. 136–149.

devices is a major factor in determining whether conflict becomes manifest. The collective bargaining apparatus of labor-management disputes and budgeting systems for internal resource allocation are administrative devices for the resolution of interest-group conflicts. Evan and Scott have described due process or appeal systems for resolving superior-subordinate conflicts.[15] Mechanisms for resolving lateral conflicts among the parties to a functional relationship are relatively undeveloped. Transfer-pricing systems constitute one of the few exceptions. Much more common are organizational arrangements designed to *prevent* lateral conflicts, e.g., plans, schedules, and job descriptions, which define and delimit subunit responsibilities. Another alternative is to reduce the interdependence between conflicting subunits by introducing buffers, such as inventories, which reduce the need for sales and production departments in a business firm to act in perfect accord.

The mere availability of such administrative devices is not sufficient to prevent conflict from becoming manifest. If the parties to a relationship do not value the relationship, or if conflict is strategic in the pursuit of subunit goals, then conflictful behavior is likely. Furthermore, once conflict breaks out on some specific issue, then the conflict frequently widens and the initial specific conflict precipitates more general and more personal conflicts which had been suppressed in the interest of preserving the stability of the relationship.[16]

Conflict aftermath

Each conflict episode is but one of the sequence of such episodes that constitute the relationships among organization participants.[17] If the conflict is genuinely resolved to the satisfaction of all participants, the basis for a more cooperative relationship may be laid; or the participants, in their drive for a more ordered relationship, may focus on latent conflicts not previously perceived and dealt with. On the other hand, if the conflict is merely suppressed but not resolved, the latent conditions of conflict may be aggravated and explode in more

15. Evan, *op. cit.*; William G. Scott, *The Management of Conflict: Appeals System in Organizations* (Homewood, Ill.: Irwin, 1965). It is useful to interpret recent developments in leadership and supervision (e.g., participative management, Theory Y, linking-pin functions) as devices for preventing superior-subordinate conflicts from arising, thus, hopefully, avoiding the problem of developing appeals systems in the first place.

16. See Coleman, *op. cit.*, pp. 9–11, for an excellent analysis of this mechanism. A chemical analogue of this situation is the supersaturated solution, from which a large amount of chemical salts can be precipitated by the introduction of a single crystal.

17. The sequential dependence of conflict episodes also plays a major role in the analysis of role conflicts by Kahn, *et al.*, *op. cit.*, pp. 11–35. Pondy, *op. cit.*, has used the concept of "budget residues" to explain how precedents set in budgetary bargains guide and constrain succeeding budget proceedings.

serious form until they are rectified or until the relationship dissolves. This legacy of a conflict episode is here called "conflict aftermath."[18]

However, the organization is not a closed system. The environment in which it is imbedded may become more benevolent and alleviate the conditions of latent conflict, for example, by making more resources available to the organization. But a more malevolent environment may precipitate new crisis. The development of each conflict episode is determined by a complex combination of the effects of preceding episodes and the environmental milieu. The main ideas of this view of the dynamics of conflict are summarized in figure 1.

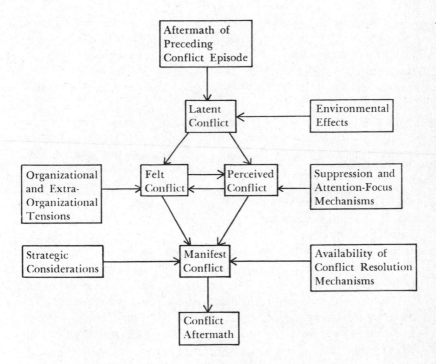

Figure 1. The dynamics of a conflict episode.

Functions and dysfunctions of conflict

Few students of social and organizational behavior have treated conflict as a neutral phenomenon to be studied primarily because of scientific curiosity about its nature and form, its causes, and its effects. Most frequently the study of conflict has been motivated by a desire

18. Aubert, *op. cit.*

to resolve it and to minimize its deleterious effects on the psychological health of organizational participants and the efficiency of organization performance. Although Kahn and others pay lip service to the opinion that, "one might well make a case for interpreting some conflict as essential for the continued development of mature and competent human beings," the overriding bias of their report is with the "personal costs of excessive emotional strain," and, they state, "the fact that common reactions to conflict and its associated tensions are often dysfunctional for the organization as an ongoing social system and self-defeating for the person in the long run."[19] Boulding recognizes that some optimum level of conflict and associated personal stress and tension are necessary for progress and productivity, but he portrays conflict primarily as a personal and social cost.[20] Baritz argues that Elton Mayo has treated conflict as "an evil, a symptom of the lack of social skills," and its alleged opposite, cooperation, as "symptomatic of health."[21] Even as dispassionate a theory of organization as that of March and Simon defines conflict conceptually as a "*breakdown* in the standard mechanisms of decision making"; i.e., as a malfunction of the system.[22]

It has become fashionable to say that conflict may be either functional or dysfunctional and is not necessarily either one. What this palliative leaves is that the effects of conflict must be evaluated relative to some set of values. The argument with those who seek uniformly to abolish conflict is not so much with their a priori assertion that conflict is undesirable, as it is with their failure to make explicit the value system on which their assertion rests.

For the purposes of this research, the effects of organizational conflict on individual welfare are not of concern. Conflict may threaten the emotional well-being of individual persons; it may also be a positive factor in personal character development; but this research is not addressed to these questions. Intraindividual conflict is of concern only insofar as it has implications for organizational performance. With respect to organizational values, *productivity,* measured in both quantitative and qualitative terms, is valued; other things being equal, an or-

19. Kahn, *et al., op. cit.,* p. 65.
20. Boulding, *op. cit.,* pp. 305–307.
21. Loren Bartiz, *The Servants of Power* (Middletown, Conn.: Wesleyan University, 1960), p. 203.
22. March and Simon, *op. cit.,* p. 112, italics mine. At least one author, however, argues that a "harmony bias" permeates the entire March-Simon volume. It is argued that what March and Simon call conflicts are mere "frictions" and "differences that are not within a community of interests are ignored." See Sherman Krupp, *Pattern in Organization Analysis* (New York: Holt, Rinehart and Winston, 1961), pp. 140–167.

ganization is "better" if it produces more, if it is more innovative, and if its output meets higher standards of quality than other organizations. *Stability* is also valued. An organization improves if it can increase its cohesiveness and solvency, other things being equal. Finally *adaptability* is valued. Other things being equal, organizations that can learn and improve performance and that can adapt to changing internal and environmental pressures are preferred to those that cannot. In this view, therefore, to say that conflict is functional or dysfunctional is to say that it facilitates or inhibits the organization's productivity, stability, or adaptabiliy.

Clearly, these values are not entirely compatible. An organization may have to sacrifice quality of output for quantity of output; if it pursues policies and actions that guarantee stability, it may inhibit its adaptive abilities. It is argued here that a given conflict episode or relationship may have beneficial or deleterious effects on productivity, stability, and adaptability. Since these values are incompatible, conflict may be simultaneously functional and dysfunctional for the organization.

A detailed examination of the functional and dysfunctional effects of conflict is more effectively made in the context of the three conceptual models. Underlying that analysis is the notion that conflict disturbs the "equilibrium" of the organization, and that the reaction of the organization to disequilibrium is the mechanism by which conflict affects productivity, stability, and adaptability.

Conflict and equilibrium

One way of viewing an organization is to think of each participant as making contributions, such as work, capital, and raw materals, in return for certain inducements, such as salary, interest, and finished goods. The organization is said to be in "equilibrium," if inducements exceed contributions (subjectivity valued) for every participant, and in "disequilibrium" if contributions exceed inducements for some or all of the participants. Participants will be motivated to restore equilibrium either by leaving the organization for greener pastures, when the disequilibrium is said to be "unstable," for by attempting to achieve a favorable balance between inducements and contributions within the organization, when it is considered "stable." Since changing organizational affiliation frequently involves sizable costs, disequilibria tend to be stable.

If we assume conflict to be a cost of participation, this inducements-contributions balance theory may help in understanding organizational reactions to conflict. It suggests that the perception of conflict by the participants will motivate them to reduce conflict either by withdrawing from the relationship, or by resolving the conflict within the context of the relationship, or by securing increased inducements to compensate for the conflict.

The assumption that conflict creates a disequilibrium is implicit in nearly all studies of organizational conflict. For example, March and Simon assume that "where conflict is perceived, motivation to reduce conflict is generated," and conscious efforts to resolve conflict are made.[23] Not all treatments of the subject make this assumption, however. Harrison White attacks the March-Simon assumption of the disequilibrium of conflict as "naive."[24] He bases his assertion on his observation of chronic, continuous, high-level conflict in administrative settings. This, of course, raises the question, "Under what conditions *does* conflict represent a disequilibrium?"

To say that (perceived) conflict represents a state of disequilibrium and generates pressures for conflict resolution is to say three things: (*1*) that perceived conflict is a cost of participation; (*2*) that the conflict disturbs the inducements-contributions balance; and (*3*) that organization members react to perceptions of conflict by attempting to resolve the conflict, *in preference to* (although this is not made explicit in the March-Simon treatment) other reactions such as withdrawing from the relationship or attempting to gain added inducements to compensate for the conflict.

1. *Conflict as a cost.* Conflict is not necessarily a cost for the individual. Some participants may actually enjoy the "heat of battle." As Hans Hoffman argues, "The unique function of man is to live in close creative touch with chaos and thereby experience the birth of order."[25]

Conflict may also be instrumental in the achievement of other goals. One of the tactics of successful executives in the modern business enterprise is to create confusion as a cover for the expansion of their particular empire,[26] or, as Sorensen observes, deliberately to create dissent and competition among one's subordinates in order to ensure that he will be brought into the relationship as an arbiter at critical times, as Franklin D. Roosevelt did.[27] Or, conflict with an out-group may be desirable to maintain stability within the in-group.

In general, however, conflict can be expected to be negatively valued; particularly if conflict becomes manifest, and subunit goals and

23. March and Simon, *op. cit.,* pp. 115, 129.
24. Harrison White, *op. cit.*
25. Quoted in H. J. Leavitt and L. R. Pondy, *Readings in Managerial Psychology* (Chicago: University of Chicago, 1964), p. 58.
26. Dalton, *op. cit.*
27. Theodore Sorensen, *Decision Making in the White House* (New York: Columbia University, 1963), p. 15. This latter tactic, of course, is predicated and the fact that, *for the subordinates,* conflict is indeed a cost!

actions are blocked and frustrated. Latency or perception of conflict should be treated as a cost, only if harmony and uniformity are highly valued. Tolerance of divergence is not generally a value widely shared in contemporary organizations, and under these conditions latent and perceived conflict are also likely to be treated as costly.

2. *Conflict as a source of disequilibrium.* White's observation of *chronic* conflict creates doubt as to whether conflict represents a dis-equilibrium.[28] He argued that if conflict *were* an unstable state for the system, then only transient conflict or conflict over shifting foci would be observable. Even if organizational participants treat conflict as a cost, they may still endure intense, chronic conflict, if there are compensating inducements from the organization in the form of high salary, opportunities for advancement, and others. To say that a participant will endure chronic conflict is not to deny that he will be motivated to reduce it; it is merely to say that if the organization member is unsuccessful in reducing conflict, he may still continue to participate if the inducements offered to him exceed the contributions he makes in return. Although conflict may be one of several sources of disequilibrium, it is neither a necessary nor a sufficient condition of disequilibrium. But, as will be shown, equilibrium nevertheless plays an important role in organizational reactions to conflict.[29]

3. *Resolution pressures a necessary consequence of conflict.* If conflicts are relatively small, and the inducements and contributions remain in equilibrium, then the participants are likely to try to resolve the conflict within the context of the existing relationship.[30] On the other hand, when contributions exceed inducements, or when conflict is intense enough to destroy the inducements-contributions balance and there is no prospect for the reestablishment of equilibrium, then

28. Harrison White, *op. cit.*

29. Conflict may actually be a source of equilibrium and stability, as Coser, *op. cit.*, p. 159, points out. A multiplicity of conflicts internal to a group, Coser argues, may breed solidarity, provided that the conflicts do not divide the group along the same axis, because the multiplicity of coalitions and associations provide a web of affiliation for the exchange of dissenting viewpoints. The essence of his argument is that some conflict is inevitable, and that it is better to foster frequent minor conflicts of interest, and thereby gradually adjust the system, and so forestall the accumulation of latent antagonisms which might eventually disrupt the organization. Frequent minor conflicts also serve to keep the antagonists accurately informed of each other's relative strength, thereby preventing a serious miscalculation of the chances of a successful major conflagration and promoting the continual and gradual readjustment of structure to coincide with true relative power.

30. For example, labor unions, while they wish to win the economic conflict with management, have no interest in seeing the relationship destroyed altogether. They may, however, choose to threaten such disruptive conflict as a matter of strategy.

conflict is likely to be reduced by dissolving the relationship. Temporary imbalances, of course, may be tolerated; i.e., the relationship will
not dissolve if the participants perceive the conflicts to be resolvable
in the near future.

What is the effect of conflict on the interaction rate among participants? It depends on the stability of the relationship. If the participants
receive inducements in sufficient amounts to balance contributions,
then perception of conflict is likely to generate pressures for *increased*
interaction, and the content of the interaction is likely to deal with resolution procedures. On the other hand, if conflict represents a cost to
the participant and this cost is not compensated by added inducements,
then conflict is likely to lead to *decreased* interaction or withdrawal
from the relationship.

To summarize, conflict is frequently, but not always, negatively
valued by organization members. To the extent that conflict *is* valued
negatively, minor conflicts generate pressures towards resolution without altering the relationship; and major conflicts generate pressures to
alter the form of the relationship or to dissolve it altogether. If inducements for participation are sufficiently high, there is the possibility of
chronic conflict in the context of a stable relationship.

Three conceptual models of organizational conflict

As Ephron points out, only a very abstract model is likely to be applicable to the study of all organizational conflict phenomena.[31] To be
useful in the analysis of real situations, a general theoretical framework
must at least fit several broad classes of conflict, some or all of which
may occur within the same organization. This suggests that different
ways of abstracting or conceptualizing a given organization are required, depending on what phenomena are to be studied. The three
models of organization described at the beginning of this paper are the
basis of the general theory of conflict presented here.

Bargaining model

A reasonable measure of the potential conflict among a set of interest
groups is the discrepancy between aggregated demands of the competing parties and the available resources. Attempts at conflict resolution
usually center around attempting either to increase the pool of available resources or to decrease the demands of the parties to the conflict.
Because market mechanisms or elaborate administrative mechanisms
have usually evolved to guarantee orderly allocation of scarce resources, bargaining conflicts rarely escalate to the manifest level, ex-

31. Ephron, *op. cit.*, p. 55.

cept as strategic maneuvers.[32] Walton and McKersie describe such conflicts as complex relationships which involve both integrative (cooperative and distributive (competitive) subprocesses.[33] Each party to the conflict has an interest in making the total resources as large as possible, but also in securing as large a share of them as possible for itself. The integrative subprocess is largely concerned with joint problem solving, and the distributive subprocess with strategic bargaining. A major element of strategy in strategic bargaining is that of attitudinal structuring, whereby each party attempts to secure the moral backing of relevant third parties (for example, the public or the government).

An important characteristic of interest-group conflicts is that negotiation is frequently done by representatives who face the dual problems of (1) securing consensus for the negotiated solution among respective group members, and (2) compromising between the demands for flexibility by his opposite number and the demands for rigidity by his own group.[34] The level of perceived conflict will increase as the deadline for a solution approaches; and interest-group conflicts are invariably characterized by deadline pressures.

Most of Walton and McKersie's framework has been developed and applied within the context of labor-management relations. But the interest-group model is not limited to this sphere of activity. Pondy has described the process of capital budgeting as a process of conflict resolution among departments competing for investment funds.[35] Wildavsky has described government budgeting as a political process involving the paraphernalia of bargaining among legislative and executive interest groups.[36] Just as past labor agreements set precedents for current labor agreements, budgeting is an incremental process that builds on the residues of previous budgetary conflicts. But, whereas the visible procedures of bargaining are an accepted part of labor-management relations, there are strong pressures in budgeting (particularly *business* budgeting) to conceal the bargaining that goes on and to attempt to cloak all decisions in the guise of rationality.[37]

32. However, the Negro demonstrations of the 1960's and the labor riots of the early twentieth century testify to the futility of managing interest-group conflicts when mechanisms for resolution are not available or when the parties in power refuse to create such mechanisms.

33. R. E. Walton and R. B. McKersie, *A Behavorial Theory of Labor Negotiations* (New York: McGraw-Hill, 1965).

34. These two negotiator problems are termed "factional conflict" and "boundary conflict" by Walton and McKersie, *op. cit.,* p. 283 ff.

35. Pondy, *op. cit.*

36. Aaron Wildavsky, *The Politics of the Budgetary Process* (Boston: Little, Brown, 1964).

37. March and Simon, *op. cit.,* p. 131.

Bureaucratic model

The bureaucratic model (roughly equivalent to Ephron's "political" model) is appropriate for the analysis of conflicts along the *vertical* dimension of a hierarchy, that is, conflicts among the parties to an authority relation. Vertical conflicts in an organization usually arise because superiors attempt to control the behavior of subordinates, and subordinates resist such control. The authority relation is defined by the set of subordinate activities over which the subordinate has surrendered to a superior the legitimacy to exercise discretion.[38] The potential for conflict is thus present when the superior and subordinate have different expectations about the zone of indifference. The subordinate is likely to perceive conflict when the superior attempts to exercise control over activities outside the zone of indifference; and the superior perceives conflict when his attempts at control are thwarted. Superiors are likely to interpret subordinate resistance as due to resentment of the exercise of *personal* power. A typical bureaucratic reaction to subordinate resistance is therefore the substitution of impersonal rules for personal control. As numerous students of bureaucracy are quick to point out, however, the unanticipated reaction to rules is more conflict, not less. The usual reasoning goes as follows: The imposition of rules defines the authority relation more clearly and robs the subordinate of the autonomy provided by ambiguity. Replacing supervision with control by rules invariably narrows the subordinate's freedom of action, makes his behavior more predictable to others, and thus weakens his power position in the organization. Control over the conditions of one's own existence, if not over others', is highly valued in organizations, particularly in large organizations. The subordinate therefore perceives himself to be threatened by and in conflict with his superiors, who are attempting to decrease his autonomy.

But why should autonomy be so important? What is the drawback to being subject to a benevolent autocrat? The answer, of course, is that autocrats seldom are or seldom remain benevolent. There is no assurance that the superior's (the organization's) goals, interests, or needs will be compatible with those of the subordinate, especially when: (*1*) organizations are so large that the leaders cannot identify personally with the rank and file; (*2*) responsibilities are delegated to organizational subunits, and subunit goals, values, etc. become differentiated from those of the hierarchy; and (*3*) procedures are formal-

---

38. This set of activities is usually called the "zone of indifference" or "zone of acceptance." See Chester Barnard, *The Functions of the Executive* (Cambridge, Mass.: Harvard University, 1960), pp. 168–170, and Herbert A. Simon, *Administrative Behavior* (New York: Macmillan, 1960, pp. 11–13.

ized, and the organization leaders tend to treat rank and file members as mere instrumentalities or executors of the procedures.

In short, numerous factors influence goals and values along the vertical dimension of an organization; therefore, because subordinates to an authority relation can not rely on superiors to identify with their goals, autonomy becomes important. This leads to resistance by subordinates to attempts by superiors to control them, which in turn generates pressures toward routinization of activities and the institution of impersonal rules. This may lead to relatively predictable, conflict-free behavior, but behavior which is rigid and largely immune to personal persuasion. It is ironic that these very factors provide the potential for conflict when the organization must adapt to a changing environment. Rigidity of behavior, which minimizes conflict in a stable environment, is a major source of conflict when adaptability is required.

Research on leadership and on role conflict also provides important insights into vertical conflict. Whereas bureaucratic developments have sought to minimize conflict by altering the *fact* of supervision (for example, the use of impersonal rules and emphasis on procedure), leadership developments have sought to alter the *style* of supervision (for example, Likert's "linking pin" proposal and the various techniques of participative management).[39] Instead of minimizing dependence and increasing autonomy, leadership theorists have proposed minimizing conflict by using personal persuasion and group pressures to bring subordinate goals more closely into line with the legitimate goals of the organization. They have prescribed solutions which decrease autonomy and increase dependence. By heightening the individual's involvement in the organization's activities, they have actually provided the basis for the intense personal conflict that characterizes intimate relations.[40]

Both the bureaucratic and the leadership approaches to vertical conflict, as discussed here, take the superior-subordinate dyad as the unit of analysis. The role-conflict approach opens up the possibility of examining the conflicts faced by a man-in-the-middle between the demands of his subordinates and the demands of his superiors. Blau and Scott have suggested that effective leadership can occur only on alternative levels of a hierarchy.[41] The "man-in-the-middle" must align himself with the interests of either his superior or his subordinate, and

39. Rensis Likert, *New Patterns of Management* (New York: McGraw-Hill, 1961); See, for example, Chris Argyris, *Interpersonal Competence and Organizational Effectiveness* (Homewood, Ill.: Dorsey, 1962), or Douglas McGregor, *The Human Side of Enterprise* (New York: McGraw-Hill, 1960).

40. Coser, *op. cit.,* pp. 67–72.

41. Peter Blau and Richard Scott, *Formal Organizations* (San Francisco: Chandler, 1962), pp. 162–163.

in so doing he alienates the other. Of the three conceptual models of conflict, the bureaucratic model has probably received the most attention from researchers from a wide variety of disciplines. Partly because of this diversity, and partly because of the ease with which researchers identify with values of efficiency or democracy, this model is the least straight-forward of the three.

Systems model

The systems model, like Ephron's "administrative" model, derives largely from the March-Simon treatment of organizational conflict.[42] It is appropriate for the analysis of conflicts among the parties to a functional relationship. Or to use Walton's terminology, the systems model is concerned with "lateral" conflicts or conflicts among persons at the same hierarchial level.[43] Whereas the authority-structure model is about problems of control, and the interest-group model is about problems of competition, the systems model is about problems of coordination.

The dyad is taken as the basic building block of the conceptual system. Consider two individuals, each occupying some formal position in an organization and playing some formal role with respect to the other. For example, A is the production manager and B the marketing manager of the XYZ company. The production manager's position is defined by the responsibility to use resources at his disposal (for example, raw materials, workers, machines) to manufacture specified products within certain constraints of quantity, quality, cost, time, and perhaps procedure. The marketing manager's position is defined by the responsibility to use resources at his disposal (for example, promotional media, salesmen, salable goods) to market and sell the company's products within certain constraints, and so on. The constraints under which each manager operates and the resources at his disposal may be set for him by himself, by the other manager, or by someone else either in or outside of the company. The role of each with respect to the other is specified by the set of directions, requests, information, and goods which he minimally must or maximally may give to or receive from the other manager. The roles may also specify instances of and procedures for joint selection of product mix, schedules, and so on. These *formal* specifications of position and role are frequently described in written job descriptions, but may also form part of a set of unwritten, stable, widely shared expectations legitimized by the appropriate hierarchial

42. March and Simon, *op. cit.*, pp. 112–135.

43. R. E. Walton, "Theory of Conflict in Lateral Organizational Relationships," (Institute Paper No. 85; Lafayette, Ind.: Purdue University, November 1964).

authorities. If certain responsibilities and activities are exercised without legitimization, that is, without the conscious, deliberate recognition and approval of the appropriate authorities, then they constitute *informal* positions and roles. Such expectations may still be widely shared, and are not necessarily illegitimate, i.e., specifically proscribed by the hierarchial authorities.

The fundamental source of conflict in such a system arises out of the pressures toward suboptimization. Assume first that the organization is goal-oriented rather than procedure-oriented. The subunits in a goal-oriented system will, for various reasons, have different sets of active goals,[44] or different preference orderings for the same set of goals. If in turn, two subunits having differentiated goals are functionally interdependent, then conditions exist for conflict. Important types of interdependence matter are: (*1*) common usage of some service or facility, (*2*) sequences of work or information flow prescribed by task or hierarchy, and (*3*) rules of unanimity or consensus about joint activity.

Two ways of reducing conflict in lateral relationships, if it be desirable to do so, therefore, are to reduce goal differentiation by modified incentive systems, or by proper selection, training, or assignment procedures; and to reduce functional interdependence. Functional interdependence is reduced by (*1*) reducing dependence on common resources; (*2*) loosening up schedules or introducing buffers, such as inventories or contingency funds; and (*3*) reducing pressures for consensus. These techniques of preventing conflict may be costly in both direct and indirect costs. Interpersonal friction is one of the costs of "running a tight ship."

If the parties to the conflict are flexible in their demands and desires,[45] the conflict is likely to be perceived only as a transient disturbance. Furthermore, the conflict may not be perceived, if alternative relationships for satisfying needs are available. This is one of the persuasive arguments for building in redundant channels of work and information flow.

Some relationships may be traditionally conflictful (e.g., administration-faculty, sales-production, and others). The parties to such a relationship have a set to expect conflict, and therefore may perceive conflict when none exists.

44. Following Simon, we treat a goal as any criterion of decision. Thus, both purposes and constraints are taken to be goals. See Herbert A. Simon, On the Concept of Organizational Goal, *Administrative Science Quarterly,* 9 (June 1964), 1–22.

45. Such flexibility is one of the characteristics of a problem-solving relationship. Conversely, a bargaining relationship is characterized by rigidity of demands and desires.

As to the forms of manifested conflict, it is extremely unlikely that any violent or aggressive actions will occur. First, strongly held norms proscribe such behavior. Secondly, the reaction of other parties to the relationship is likely to be that of withdrawing all cooperation. A much more common reaction to perceived conflict is the adoption of a joint decision process characterized by bargaining rather than problem solving. Walton, Dutton, and Fitch have described some of the characteristics of a bargaining style: careful rationing of information and its deliberate distortion; rigid, formal, and circumscribed relations; suspicion, hostility, and disassociation among the subunits.[46] These rigidities and negative attitudes, of course, provide the potential for conflict over other issues in future episodes of the relationship.

Summary

It has been argued that conflict within an organization can be best understood as a dynamic process underlying a wide variety of organizational behaviors. The term conflict refers neither to its antecedent conditions, nor individual awareness of it, nor certain affective states, nor its overt manifestations, nor its residues of feeling, precedent, or structure, but to all of these taken together as the history of a conflict episode.

Conflict is not necessarily bad or good, but must be evaluated in terms of its individual and organizational functions and dysfunctions. In general, conflict generates pressures to reduce conflict, but chronic conflict persists and is endured under certain conditions, and consciously created and managed by the politically astute administrator.

Conflict resolution techniques may be applied at any of several pressure points. Their effectiveness and appropriateness depends on the nature of the conflict and on the administrator's philosophy of management. The tension model leads to creation of safety-valve institutions and the semantic model to the promotion of open communication. Although these may be perfectly appropriate for certain forms of imagined conflict, their application to real conflict may only exacerbate the conflict.

A general theory of conflict has been elaborated in the context of each of three conceptual models: (1) a bargaining model, which deals with interest groups in competition for resources; (2) a bureaucratic model, which deals with authority relations and the need to control; and (3) a systems model, which deals with functional relations and the need to coordinate.

46. Walton, Dutton, and Fitch, *op. cit.*

The Absorption of Protest
Ruth Leeds Love

Introduction: The nonconformist and the enclave

The usual fate of the nonconformist who occupies a position of some responsibility in a complex organization has been established: the cleric who wavers from the true path goes on retreat; the maverick army officer is appointed to an innocuous position; the recalcitrant political party deputy is temporarily suspended.[1] If temporary suspension or relegation to an insignificant position does not suffice to curb the nonconformist, he is gradually eased out of the organization. But what happens when an organization is faced with not just a single nonconformist but with several who form a cohesive enclave in its midst? The organization—specifically incumbents of positions superordinate to the nonconformists—must now check not just one individual but many who could potentially divert organization resources from their current commitments, undermine organizational effectiveness, or form a front capable of capturing control of the organization.

To control a nonconforming enclave, the organization has to employ techniques other than those typically used to check a single nonconformist. An individual's nonconformity often as not stems primarily from personality factors, although structural determinants do contribute to it. The nonconformity of an enclave, which is shared by all its members, stems primarily from structural determinants rather than personality factors. Hence, different techniques are called for to check nonconforming enclaves.

There is one organizational technique—the subject of this chapter—

Reprinted (except for postscript) from *New Perspectives in Organization Research,* ed. W. W. Cooper, H. J. Leavitt, and M. W. Shelly (New York: John Wiley & Sons, 1964), by permission of the publisher.

1. Amitai Etzioni, *A Comparative Analysis of Complex Organizations* (Glencoe, Ill.: The Free Press, 1961), pp. 241–44. This paper represents an expansion of an idea briefly discussed by Etzioni, pp. 245–48.

that is particularly suited for controlling wayward groups. It consists of integrating the protest of the nonconforming enclave into the organization by converting it into a new legitimate subunit. Through conversion, the nonconforming enclave obtains a legitimate outlet for its nonconformity, and thereby contributes to the attainment of legitimate goals of the organization. The conversion from nonconforming enclave to legitimate subunit will be called the protest-absorbing process. Protest absorption might take as little as a year or as long as a generation. Regardless, by the end of the process, the nonconforming enclave and the top authorities of the organization reach an accommodation such that the enclave is given some autonomy to pursue a specific activity (usually the activity which was the focus of the nonconformity), but, at the same time, it is expected to abide by the regulations and restrictions to which all legitimate subunits adhere.

Protest absorption is a structural "weapon" available to the organization. It is a weapon insofar as it is used to control nonconforming groups. It is a structural weapon insofar as its effectiveness rests on formal changes in the organizational structure, that is, on the formal positions of subunits vis-à-vis each other. As will be seen, the weapon is unleashed through the exercise of *authority,* although *power* is a variable in the protest-absorption process. Protest absorption should not be confused with co-optation which comes about through power differentials between the co-opters and the co-opted regardless of the authority structure.[2] Although reductionist concepts like power and charisma are variables in the protest-absorption process, they are not the major explanatory concepts. Structure and authority are the key concepts to an understanding of protest absorption, although these terms will be used only rarely to avoid awkward phrasing.

Organizational analyses which generate theories about the organization as if all structures were cut from the same cloth must be qualified when applied to specific organizations, e.g., a prison, an army, or a factory. The development of a comparative approach permits the enrichment of organizational theories by adding statements of regularities within one type of organization to statements of universal uniformities. Given this consideration, the first step is to delineate the type of organization in which protest absorption is expected to be an effective weapon. Then we can characterize the nonconforming enclave and the process by which it is converted into a legitimate and quiescent unit. The appendix presents an outline of cases which *illustrate* the protest-absorption model. Since this paper represents both an exploratory

2. Philip Selznick, *TVA and the Grass Roots* (Berkeley: University of California Press, 1949).

study and a preliminary report, we are not concerned here with the frequency with which the model is approximated.

Normative Organizations and the distribution of charisma[3]

Organizations can be characterized by the nature of the primary power that is used to control its lowest ranking participants. *Coercive* organizations, e.g., prisons, keep order through the use of physical force (or the threat of it); *utilitarian* organizations, e.g., factories, keep order primarily through monetary rewards; *normative* organizations, e.g., churches, elicit compliance through the allocation and manipulation of symbolic rewards. For reasons to be evident shortly, protest absorption is expected to occur most frequently in normative organizations.

Two other major characteristics distinguish the normative from the coercive and utilitarian organizations. First, a normative organization tends to demand a high degree of commitment and loyalty from its members, often to the point that members are expected to give their primary allegiance to the organization. The priest is symbolically wedded to the church; in those organizations where secular marriage is permitted, the wife is drawn into the structure and is known by its name, e.g., a navy wife.[4] Voluntary exiting from the organization is perceived as a sign of insufficient loyalty; for example, resignation from academic departments tends to precipitate feelings of resentment and rejection among the professors who remain.[5] Criticism of the organization's institutionalized norms and methods is also taken as a sign of insufficient loyalty.

Second, most offices in normative organizations have charisma ascribed to them. The performances associated with the position of priest or military officer are charismatic and are symbolized by such devices as special dress, badges of office, and ritual courtesies. The charismatic elements of a particular office enrich the organization's symbols and rituals with additional meaning, and increase their reward value for the loyalty and discipline which lowest-ranking members exhibit. Moreover, personal contact with an incumbent of a charismatic office is itself perceived as a reward by members. Thus charismatic power in its routinized form reinforces the normative power of the organization.

At the same time that charisma helps to generate loyalty and disci-

3. Based on Etzioni, *A Comparative Analysis.*
4. Arthur K. Davis, "Bureaucratic Patterns in the Navy Officers Corps," in R. K. Merton et al., eds., *Reader in Bureaucracy* (Glencoe, Ill.: The Free Press, 1952).
5. Theodore Caplow and R. J. McGee, *The Academic Marketplace* (New York: Basic Books, 1958), p. 66.

pline among the personnel, it also is a potential disrupter of discipline and loyalty to the organization itself. The problem is present in latent form when the lower participants of the organization attribute the functionally specific charisma of office to a *particular* incumbent, and, in so doing, generalize the charisma so that it takes on diffuse characteristics. Where this occurs, the participants make personal commitments to the particular individual who occupies a charismatic office rather than to the office itself. If the charismatic officer uses these particularistic commitments for purposes that are functional to the organization as a whole (or for purposes that do not generate dysfunctions), then the problem remains latent. The case might be, however, that the charismatic employs these commitments to challenge organizational hegemony and integration, and to compete against regular subunits (sometimes laterally related) for resources, thereby undermining the organization's allocation and reward system. (That such a situation might occur indicates both the desirability and the apparent impossibility of routinizing charisma.)

The potential strain between charisma and discipline is greatest in those organizations where the gift of grace parallels the formal organizational chart, being characteristic of many offices as well as the top ones, and yet where formal authority is centralized. The Catholic church and wartime military organizations are the major examples of organizations that have charisma distributed throughout their lines combined with a strong, centralized authority structure. Protest absorption is more likely to be used in these organizations to control nonconforming enclaves than in normative structures which have the potential for strain between charisma and discipline but lack a strong central authority (e.g., Protestant denominations and the early Catholic church).

The process of protest absorption

The potential strain between charisma and discipline erupts into a tempest in a tepid teapot with the formation of a nonconforming enclave. More often than not, the enclave is led by a charismatic who is concerned with devising new ways for carrying out his responsibilities more effectively. The leadership of the enclave is strengthened by able lieutenants. The enclave itself is endowed with a militant spirit; its members are eager to undertake large-scale tasks and to execute them with novel strategies. The organization, grown weak internally in one or several respects, either cannot or prefers not to initiate change (although from some objective perspective change might be functionally required if the organization is to continue being effective). Protest absorption has two major consequences for the organization; it checks the nonconforming enclave by turning it into a legtimate subunit which remains loyal to the organization and it permits the introduction of change. The descriptive model of protest absorption contains three parts: (1) the characteristics of the nonconforming enclave, (2) the state of the organization, and (3) the process of absorbing protest.

The Nonconforming Enclave

Two conditions are basic to the emergence of a nonconforming enclave. First, some members of a normative organization must attribute personal charisma to an official. This provides the official with an opportunity to lead a loyal following over which diffuse influence and control can be exercised Second, the official must have tendencies toward nonconformity and unorthodoxy, and must disregard at least some traditional norms and strategies. Once the official has proved his capacity to acquire a personal following, he may be referred to as the enclave leader; once he leads in unorthodox directions, the enclave becomes a nonconforming group.

The leader's nonconformity stems in large measure from his position in the organization. Assume that the leader is in unit C_4 (fig. 1). Assume further that C_4 is not functioning effectively with regard to its

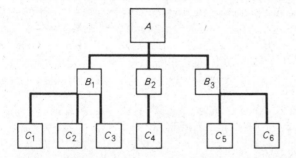

Figure 1. Boxes denote units in organization.

subunit goals. Lack of effectiveness could stem from one or several factors. For example, the unit is functionally peripheral and so does not receive the optimum quantity and quality of inputs; or the unit is a long-established one which has become more concerned with self-maintenance than with attainment of goals; or changes in the unit's environment have occurred which make present methods and procedures obsolete; or contingencies have emerged for which there is no formal provision. In short, the unit's responsibility for goals far exceeds its capacity for attainment of goals, thereby making it relatively ineffective.[6] One response to lack of effectiveness is to exercise trained in-capacity, that is, to continue conforming to rules and procedures which have become inappropriate.[7] A second response is to search for new rules and procedures which would permit increased unit effectiveness. The first response is symptomatic of functional rationality and the second of substantive rationality.[8] The leader, either in his capacity as head of C_4 or as a member of it, exercises some degree of substantive rationality and assumes responsibility for devising methods which will make the unit more effective. Increased unit effectiveness would permit him to fulfill his own particular position more adequately.

In large measure, one's position determines whether one perceives the discrepancy between responsibility and control, and whether one chooses to respond functionally or substantively to it. The greater the responsibility for goal attainment or the greater the environmental contact associated with a given position, the more likely is the incum-bent to respond substantively rather than functionally. In our simpli-fied organization chart, the A level has overall responsibility for organization goals; the C level is responsible for subunit goals. More-over, both A and C levels have some contact with the environment. The B level serves internal coordination and communication functions. On a probability basis, then, the enclave leader is more likely to occupy a position in A or C than in B. To simplify presentation of our model, we assume that the enclave leader is located in C.

The leader's nonconformity is not to be confused with deviancy. Un-like a deviant, a nonconformist does not hide his dissent from the pre-vailing norms. He publicly challenges the efficacy of the existing norms and their applicability to specific situations in the hope of changing them without destroying the organization. The nonconformist justifies his challenge of the status quo by appealing to what the organization recognizes as its highest morality or its ultimate set of values.[9] The offi-

6. See Etzioni. *A Comparative Analysis,* pp. 77–79, for a discussion of effec-tiveness.

7. R. K. Merton, *Social Theory and Social Structure,* rev. ed. (Glencoe, Ill.: The Free Press, 1957), p. 198.

8. Karl Mannheim. Ideology and Utopia (New York: Harcourt, Brace and Co., 1936), pp. 112–17.

9. If the leader appeals to a morality or values not recognized by the organi-zation, the likelihood of protest absorption is reduced and the organization will resort to other means to check him. Orde Wingate was able to organize and arm Jews to quell Arab raids on the British pipelines in Palestine in the late 1930s, despite British policy not to give arms to Jews. Wingate also hoped that his Special Night Squad would form the basis for a Jewish army which would help to pave the way for Palestine's independence. Wingate's advocacy of a cause which ex-tended beyond military purlieus led to his recall from Palestine, and probably helps to account for the rapid de-judification of the Special Night Squad. See Christopher Sykes. *Orde Wingate* (London: Collins. 1959).

cial who emerges as a leader of a nonconforming enclave is justified in saying, in the area of his specific responsibility, "It is written . . . but I say unto you . . ." on two counts. First, because he has charisma attributed to him, and second, because as a nonconformist he is oriented to existing rules only in a negative sense—to challenge them.[10]

Concomitant with his personal charisma and tendency toward nonconformity, the leader also has a flair for originality which permits him to create new strategies, ideologies, and symbols to counter those of the organization.[11] The development and implementation of new strategies come to represent the goal of the enclave. The new ideology and symbols serve as extensions to the leader's charisma in welding the enclave into a cohesive, dynamic group.

The charismatic rarely leads the enclave by himself.[12] He is usually assisted by lieutenants who support his unorthodox tactics and innovations, and spearhead the enclave with their own missionary fire and ability to influence others. The leader, by granting his lieutenants some autonomy in a specialized area like procuring supplies, insures that they will remain subservient to him. Since the lieutenants are likely to promulgate their own ideas, a limited amount of autonomy may prevent rival ideas and methods from disrupting the unity of the enclave.

The energy and zeal of the nonconforming enclave are focused on innovations, which often assume the form of techniques intended to facilitate attainment of organizational goals. New techniques might be more effective in attaining existing goals by permitting higher output or they might revitalize goals which have grown fallow. (Later we shall have more to say about the enclave's objectives and their bearing on the protest-absorption process.) In essence, the enclave maintains a high commitment to the basic goals of the organization, and desires to display this commitment through recognition of its innovations. The commitment inspiring the nonconformists is frequently viewed as higher than that possessed by others in the organization. The perceived

10. R. K. Merton. "Social Problems and Sociological Theory," in R. K. Merton and R. A. Nisbet, eds., *Contemporary Social Problems* (New York: Harcourt, Brace and World, 1961). pp. 725–26; and Max Weber, *The Theory of Social and Economic Organization,* trans. A. M. Henderson and T. Parsons (New York: Oxford University Press: Glencoe, Ill.: The Free Press, 1947), p. 361.

11. Dorothy Emmet, *Function, Purpose and Powers* (London: Macmillan, 1958), p. 258. The problem of what an administrator should do with the single nonconformist, the "creative genius," the person with a flair who is "beyond good and evil," receives excellent treatment by Professor Emmet. She feels that a solution might develop if the administrator has the capacity to comprehend different roles; with such understanding the administrator might create a special role in the organization for the nonconformist. In the present context, protest absorption would require the administrator to have some understanding of structure. Emmet does not deal with the problems presented by a group of nonconformists.

12. See Weber. *The Theory of Social and Economic Organization,* p. 360.

or alleged discrepancy between the extremely high degree of loyalty to basic organizational values exhibited by the nonconforming enclave and the moderate degree of loyalty exhibited by other organization participants is likely to provoke conflict. Other participants have little tolerance for the enthusiasm of the enclave, for, by comparison, they appear less diligent and less loyal to the organization.

The nonconforming enclave is further distinguished by an unorthodox atmosphere which permeates many aspects of its life. This atmosphere varies from extreme austerity and asceticism to romance, adventure, and heroic sacrifice. The unorthodox behavior of the enclave, whether reflected in the wearing of special clothing or in reckless courage, not only sets the enclave apart from the rest of the organization but also contributes to its cohesiveness and strength. A member can readily identify with a group symbolized by noticeable objects or mannerisms. If the group merits esteem from outsiders, it can be bestowed on easily recognized members. The symbols of unorthodoxy also facilitate recruitment in that they help publicize the group to potential members who share similar values and similar tendencies toward nonconformity.

In summary, the nonconforming enclave is characterized by a leader whose charisma of office has become personal. He pursues a course of action or cause which is perceived as unorthodox, and for which he creates symbols and an ideology. His immediate lieutenants are nonconformers in their own right, although less influential and original than the leader. The cause served is usually a means to revive allegedly neglected organizational goals or to achieve present organizational goals more effectively. Lastly, a peculiar aura, either of asceticism or of romance, envelops the enclave, contributing to its integration and highlighting its dedication to its cause.

The state of the organization

Although nonconformity can erupt at all times, a cohesive nonconforming enclave is likely to emerge in a context in which one or a combination of the following variations of organizational weakness is prevalent. If, over time, the legitimacy of the organization procedures decreases generally or within any subunit, charisma tends to shift from office to person among those dedicated to the ultimate purposes of the organization. If an organization is insensitive to potential nonconformity (due to such factors as inadequacies of communication networks), control mechanisms might not be activated in time to forestall a nonconforming official before he gains a personal following.[13] If an

13. In some instances the "following" emerges first and then casts about for a leader. According to Erle Wilson's less romantic account of the *Bounty* mutiny,

organization's internal authority is weak, owing to the corruption of officers responsible for enforcing conformity or owing to the lack of (or limited) control over enforcement facilities, then whatever control mechanisms the organization might employ are ineffectual. Finally, resources diverted outside the organization to meet an external challenge, or stoppage of inputs, limit the availability of the means needed to combat nonconformity.

Once the enclave emerges, mild checks to contain the nonconformity are no longer adequate. If the organizational elite ousts the leader, his immediate lieutenants could assume control of the enclave, or members of the enclave might follow their leader and form the beginnings of a competing structure. Such a possibility is particularly threatening when the organization enjoys a monopoly or duopoly position. If the organization is one of several of its kind, then one more similar structure in the environment makes little difference. Finally, if both the leader and the members of the enclave are dispersed throughout the organization, in an effort to disband the group, nonconformity might be spread rather than eliminated.

Given the inadequacy of control techniques which are typically applied to single nonconformists, the organizational elite must choose between several alternatives: condemnation, avoidance, expulsion, or protest absorption. The first three alternatives are not effective in containing the nonconformity unless the enclave itself is quite weak to begin with. Condemnation contains the danger of widening the rift between the enclave and the rest of the organization by forcing a polarization of issues.[14] Avoidance, which means consciously taking little account of the existence of the enclave, sidesteps the danger of polarization.[15] During the period that the organization elite obstensibly ignores the enclave, however, the enclave might grow in size and strength instead of drying out. Expulsion of the enclave represents a costly loss of resources which might yet be channeled to serve organizational goals.[16] Also, expulsion could lead to the emergence of a rival

---

the potential mutineers were ship's sailors, who, on becoming cognizant of each other's discontents, recruited Fletcher Christian to be their leader. Subsequent events indicated that the choice was not entirely fortunate, for Christian lacked the capacity to live up to the charisma which his followers attributed to him. See Erle Wilson, *Adams of the* Bounty (New York: Popular Library, 1959).

14. Z. Brzezinski, "Deviation Control: A Study in the Dynamics of Doctrinal Conflict." *American Political Science Review* 56 (1962): 9–10.

15. Ibid., pp. 11–12.

16. A recent report of the AFL-CIO council stated: "It is obvious that expulsion as such does not cure the offending practices. And, what is more important, once outside the federation the membership of such an organization is no longer accessible to corrective influences from the parent body through education and persuasion." (Quoted in the *Reporter,* 26 October 1961, p. 18.)

structure (albeit it does permit tightening of organizational ranks). The negative consequences which might result from attempting to control the enclave through condemnation, avoidance, or expulsion are particularly dysfunctional to the organization when it displays one or more signs of weakness. Although protest absorption also entails some dangers, it is a more promising way of checking nonconformity on several counts.

If protest absorption is successful, it not only eliminates the pocket of nonconformity but also strengthens the organization by providing it with the services of an energetic, devoted group. Moreover, the process permits the legitimation of innovation which better equips the organization to face external challenges or to attain its own goals more effectively. Protest absorption can also lead to the elimination of nonconformity without the emergence of a devoted group or the introduction of innovation. This form results when the organization provides the enclave with an "opportunity to fail." When the enclave protests about matters beyond its ken or original bailiwick, and it is accorded legitimacy in the area of protest, it is likely to fail because it lacks the skills and knowledge to carry out the now-legitimate activity. Any nonconformity which survives outright failure is expected to be sufficiently weakened so as to be eliminated easily. Should the enclave succeed despite its opportunity to fail, then the organization can reap the benefits. The risk accompanying protest absorption is that the nonconforming enclave may, during the time that the organization attempts to check it, gain access to the key power positions and, subsequently, assume control of the total structure.

The process of protest absorption

Once the nonconforming enclave has been converted into a new legitimate subunit, the organization is strengthened. During the protest-absorption process, however, the organization, especially that sector of it in which the enclave has erupted, faces a series of internal battles involving several levels of its hierarchy. The charismatic leader and his followers oppose those persons who formally are their immediate superiors. These shall be called the middle hierarchy and represent the enemy in the battles. Insofar as the organization has a centralized top hierarchy which can exercise authority over the middle hierarchy, these battles tend not to be fought to the death of one or the other set of combatants. Instead, the top hierarchy intercedes and more or less arbitrarily terminates the conflict. Protest absorption essentially is a process whereby the top hierarchy attempts to balance the two opposing forces—members of the nonconforming enclave against members of the middle hierarchy who are the immediate superiors of the former.

In some instances, units which are laterally related to the nonconforming enclave will also be aligned with the middle hierarchy in opposing the enclave. In other cases, the opposition will be made up only of heads of laterally related units and an opposing middle hierarchy will be absent. The varying composition of the "enemy" depends upon the location of the enclave in the organizational structure. The general pattern, however, might be diagrammed as shown in fig. 2.

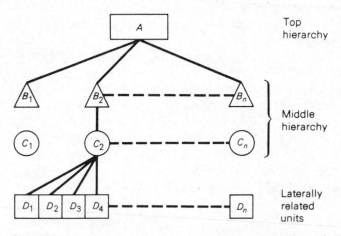

Figure 2

Assume that the enclave erupts in D_4. If the leader is the head of D_4, the enclave will encompass the entire unit. If the leader is only a member, the enclave will set itself up as D_4. In either case, the enclave will have to contend with C_2, who is responsible for D_1–D_4. Directly, or indirectly, the enclave will also have to contend with the other D units. The emergence of the nonconforming enclave creates increased competition for resources among the D units. In addition, they perceive themselves as being cast in an unfavorable light by the enthusiasm and heightened activity of the enclave. Hence, the D units will pressure C_2 to suppress the enclave. The D units do not always form part of the opposition to the enclave; another variation is that C_2 might also be directly in charge of one D unit as well as having general responsibility for the entire D section. Such structural variations in the formation of the opposition to the nonconforming enclave do not affect the general pattern of protest absorption, although they help to explain slight variations from case to case, Hence, for simplicity's sake, in describing the process we shall limit the opposition to the middle hierarchy, although the reader should bear in mind that the opposition can vary in its composition.

Incumbents of positions constituting the middle hierarchy are more likely to exhibit "trained incapacity" than incumbents of other levels.

Hence, they are usually incapable of comprehending the significance of the enclave's protest. Furthermore, their positions are threatened by the enclave, both because it reveals that their loyalty to basic values of the organization is not as strong as it could be and because it indicates that they cannot make use of the authority vested in them to maintain order in their own bailwicks. Their response to the enclave is to attempt to suppress it through such means as closing the communication links between the charismatic leader and the top hierarchy, restricting the enclave members' freedom of movement, and reducing the resources available to them. From the perspective of the middle hierarchy, the use of such techniques represents the full exercise of their rights of office.[17] From the perspective of the nonconforming enclave, such techniques are obstructions which indicate that the organization is against it, and hence, to carry out its cause, the enclave must try to be even more dynamic and more cohesive.

If the charismatic leader is to demonstrate his basic loyalty to organizational values and if he is to gain recognition and legitimation for his cause, he must have access to the top hierarchy. When such access via regular channels is barred, the leader develops his own routes to the top. Frequently this is done through an intermediary who is outside the organization but has legitimate access to the top echelon. Insofar as the charismatic leader is able to establish a particularistic relationship with such in intermediary which is beyond organizational control, he has relatively easy access to the top.

The particularistic communication line gives the nonconforming enclave some leverage in an attempt to have its cause recognized and legitimized. That the hierarchy is willing to use his power over the top hierarchy in behalf of the enclave is regarded by its members as a significant step forward and as a sign of incipient legitimation.

At the same time that a particularistic communication line gives the enclave hope that its cause will be successful, it also produces potential instability and unreliability. First, the communication line is maintained at the will—or the whim—of the intermediary, which means that it can be opened and closed arbitrarily. Second, a particularistic request to the top hierarchy in behalf of the nonconforming enclave might elicit informal instructions to the middle hierarchy which it can easily overlook in its continued attempts to obstruct the enclave.

In some instances the charismatic leader need not resort to particularistic communication channels for he might be able to go to the top

17. When legitimate techniques fail to quell the enclave, the middle hierarchy might resort to illegitimate or nonlegitimate ones. Paradoxically, it is at such times that the middle hierarchy overcomes its "trained incapacity."

directly;[18] or the attention of the top hierarchy might be drawn to the nonconforming enclave as a result of the conflict between it and the middle hierarchy, especially if the conflict has affected task performance adversely.

Regardless of the means by which the attention of the top hierarchy is directed to the enclave, the leader who has gained this attention can demonstrate his basic loyalty to organizational values and communicate his ideas for their more effective realization in the hope of gaining official approval. Concerned with blocking such approval, the middle hierarchy urges the top to suppress the enclave. The top hierarchy is interested in enhancing general organizational effectiveness, and, by extension, is concerned with maintaining internal order. With its broader, more substantive, perspective, the top is more amenable to innovation than the middle hierarchy, especially when faced with internal weakness or external challenge. Hence, the top is more likely to accede to some demands of the nonconforming enclave, especially if its leader is backed by a powerful intermediary, than to the insistence of the middle hierarchy that the enclave be thoroughly curbed or eliminated.

The first round in the protest-absorption process is completed when the top hierarchy recognizes the nonconforming enclave and gives it a modicum of autonomy to pursue its advocated innovation. This is followed by several more rounds of obstruction by the middle hierarchy, unorthodox communication to the top by the nonconforming enclave, and a gradually increasing grant of resources, autonomy, and legitimacy to the enclave by the top hierarchy. With each round the enclave comes closer to approximating a new legitimate subunit.

In exchange for autonomy and legitimacy from the top hierarchy, the enclave must agree to accept certain stabilizers. The stabilizers are mechanisms to insure the loyalty of the new unit to the organization and its conformity to organization regulations. First, the protest-absorbing unit is expected to develop rules, subject to approval by the top echelon, to guide its conduct; any changes in these rules are also subject to approval by the top. Second, the unit must accept a regular source of finance through which it will acquire all or most of its inputs. In this way, unauthorized appropriations of resources and competition with existing units for available resources are minimized, and the frustrations of an irregular source of income, typical of a group during its nonconformist period, are avoided. Third, and most important, the

18. The leader's ability to communicate with the top hierarchy directly is determined in large part by other capacities, roles, and statuses which he might have within or outside of the organization.

unit's activity is limited to a particular sphere of operation, usually that for which the leader and his followers advocated their innovation.[19]

With the introduction of stabilizers, the leader's personal charisma becomes attenuated. The personal charisma is reconverted to charisma of office as the leader (or his successor) assumes legitimate control of the protest-absorber unit. Furthermore, the most radical members of the former enclave perceive the leader as bowing to the dictates of the top hierarchy, thereby betraying the cause; they cease to accept the leader as a charismatic figure, leave the unit, and, where possible, even the organization. The more visible to his followers are the leader's negotiations with the top hierarchy, the more likely is this to be the case. In fact, the top hierarchy could reduce the leader's personal charisma considerably by sending a representative directly to the members of the enclave to grant it legitimacy. By circumventing the leader, the top hierarchy gives the impression that it has been wise enough to recognize the value of the enclave's cause of its own accord and so no credit need be given to the leader who has spearheaded the cause. Circumvention of the leader does present certain dangers, however. Such a procedure is most likely to be successful only if the representative has instructions to grant all or the most important of the enclave's demands. Otherwise, enclave members are likely to perceive the visitation of the representative as an attempt by the top hierarchy to sabotage the cause. Since, in most cases, the top is unlikely to grant major concessions in one fell swoop, this danger is almost always present and serves to strengthen the enclave. A second danger is that the representative himself might be affected by the leader's charisma and join the enclave rather than fulfill his orders.

Occasionally other stabilizers are also introduced, e.g., limiting the size of the protest-absorber unit, appointing a special supervisor to watch for and check any excessive enthusiasm which the unit might display, and restricting the use it may make of its particularistic communication channel. Generally, these particular stabilizers are instituted if the newly legitimized unit still remains somewhat recalcitrant in its adherence to organization rules.

The conformity of the unit is further enhanced through pressures arising within it to replace the instability of its charismatic nature with the stabilizing characteristics which accompany routinization. The

19. The nature of the task limitation imposed on the protest-absorber unit is in part determined by the form of the organization's division of labor, i.e., whether it is structured along geographic lines such that each unit engages in the same task but in a different locality, or around functionally specific lines where each unit engages in its own speciality, or is a combination of geography and functional specificity. See C. I. Barnard, *The Functions of the Executive* (Cambridge, Mass.: Harvard University Press, 1938), p. 129ff.

nonconforming enclave, like the large-scale charismatic movement, faces "everyday" problems of economic and administrative organization. For example, the unit at some point must provide for the selection of a successor to replace its charismatic leader. (The criteria for selection may be established either by the enclave or by the organization.)

The external pressures toward protest absorption and the internal pressures toward routinization eventually tame the nonconforming enclave and convert it into a quiescent unit concerned with maintaining order in its own bailiwick.[20] The unit may show signs of quiescence simultaneously with its legitimation through protest absorption, or after a period of dynamism during which it expands and gives devoted service to the organization. Its concern with expansion and innovation is replaced by one of self-maintenance. The zeal and energy of the unit are dissipated in legitimized action without being replenished. Once the original members of the unit are gone, or have become concerned with preserving their newly legitimized positions within the organization, the verve that sparked the unit when it was a nonconforming enclave cannot be sustained. Successors to key positions in the unit most likely have been socialized by the organization, and tend to resemble the middle hierarchy more than the original members of the enclave.

The unit's agreement to restrict itself to a specialized sphere of operation is itself another contributing factor to the emerging quiescent period. The agreement helps to preclude the possibility that the unit will attempt innovation beyond its allotted sphere; and whatever success the unit has in its speciality also drains it of further nonconformity. Success is its own detriment when the question of new risks arises: members of the unit prefer to maintain rather than gamble their resources and status on a new venture.

Another factor in the elimination of nonconformity from the unit is time itself. Norms which the enclave had revitalized once again become eroded through increasing lack of strict adherence to them. Members of the unit remain committed to their once-new methods even though they have become outmoded and ineffectual. The unit as a whole is no longer dedicated to the ultimate values of the organization but rests content with the sinecure provided it through protest absorption.

The factors that contribute to quiescence—cessation of innovation, dissipation of zeal and energy, emergent conservative tendencies, modification of norms, and the obsolescence of methods—also set the stage for new protest and new forms of nonconformity, which are likely

20. Robert Michels, *Political Parties* (New York: Dover Publications, 1959), pp. 174–75.

to erupt because the unit legitimized through protest absorptions is more vulnerable to the strains between charisma and discipline than are other units. Its history of nonconformity remains unforgotten and lends it an aura of prestige, thereby distinguishing the former enclave from ordinary units. It is further distinguished by having institutionalized a more arduous socialization period for its recruits. Finally, its standards tend to be more strict and demanding than those of the organization as a whole, even with the corroding effects of time. These factors not only militate against the complete integration of the unit into the organization but also make it extremely attracive to recruits, particularly to those who tend to be strongly or rigidly committed to its original values. In short, the unit, limited to its own sphere of action, tamed by stabilizers, concerned with its own well-being, and yet, endowed with the aura of its unorthodox past which facilitates recruitment of potential nonconformers, nurtures a fertile field for the regeneration of a nonconforming enclave and another cycle of protest absorption.

In summary, the process of protest absorption follows several steps. A nonconforming enclave is able to gain some power within the organization because the latter is internally weak or faced with an external crisis. To check the internal threat without further weakening itself, the organization form a new administrative unit to absorb the enclave, based on the institutionalization of new norms. The emergence of the unit represents a *Sturm und Drang* period: the enclave demands more autonomy and resources so that it can pursue its course of action while the organization reluctantly grants some autonomy and resources, and permits some innovation, in order to maintain peace and overcome the crisis confronting it. The *Sturm und Drang* begins to subside when the enclave achieves the status of a more or less legitimate unit within the organization, and is virtually quelled as the unit loses its initial élan, no longer taking on new ventures and becoming concerned with its own maintenance. From the perspective of the top hierarchy of the organization, protest absorption is a process of encapsulation. The nonconforming enclave becomes encased in a network of stabilizers which limits its freedom of action.

Implications of protest absorption for the organization

In large measure, the significance of protest absorption for the organization as a whole depends upon the bearing which the enclave's cause has on the core policies and practices of the organization. From the standpoint of its proponents, the cause usually has a greater degree of significance for core policies than the top hierarchy is willing to acknowledge.

It is convenient to formalize what is generally involved here by means of a continuum in which the cause advocated by an enclave is scaled relative to the degree with which it is likely to affect core policies and practices. Then, as in fig. 3, the enclave can be characterized as to where it *aspires to be* on the continuum, and where it is *willing to be placed*. The organization can be characterized as to where it would *like* to locate the enclave, and where it is *willing to place it*. The shaded area indicates the range of acceptability for an enclave and its organization; in this instance there is an overlap, although this is not always the case. Moreover, the ranges of acceptability can shift in the course of the protest-absorption process.

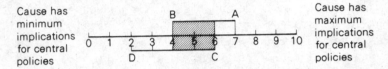

Cause has minimum implications for central policies

Cause has maximum implications for central policies

Figure 3. *A*, enclave desires cause to have value of 7. *B*, enclave willing to accept value of 4. *C*, organization willing to permit value of 6. *D*, organization prefers value of 2.

Once these ranges are known, further statements can be made about protest absorption. Where there is an overlap in ranges, protest absorption should prove more successful in controlling the enclave's nonconformity than where such an overlap does not exist. In the case where an overlap is absent (or in the case where the organization makes strong attempts to place the enclave below its minimum acceptable position—in fig. 3 this would be below 4), the enclave will retain its zeal and unorthodoxy in order to attempt to achieve its cause in the face of control measures. For as the enclave is forced toward the lower end of the continuum, its cause becomes more attenuated, and its chances are lessened for realizing the goals which sparked it in the first place.

Furthermore, by locating the ranges of acceptability, we can predict approximately the number of rounds the protest-absorption process is likely to undergo. More rounds can be anticipated as the overlap between the two ranges is lessened. For the organization will usually try to check the enclave by locating it as low on the continuum as it can, while the enclave will continue its nonconformist activity until it is located as high on the continuum as it can be.

The more that protest absorption takes place at the higher end of the continuum, the more likely it is that an organization's central policies and practices will undergo a change. This is likely, if only for the reason that the more central the protest-absorber unit is to the organization, the more probable it is that its members will be promoted upward in the hierarchy until they reach the top.[21] The variables which determine where, on the continuum, the enclave will ultimately be absorbed are those involved in the protest-absorption process itself: the degree of weakness of the organization, the strength of the nonconforming enclave, the power of the intermediary, the nature of the stabilizers, and so on. Thus the protest-absorption process can lead to a long-term chain reaction of major changes in the organization, as well as check nonconformity and introduce a particular innovation.

Finally, protest absorption can have implications for organizational policy for dealing with nonconformity. An organization which has had long experience with nonconformity, e.g., the Catholic church, might institutionalize the rounds of protest absorption. This means that, as a nonconforming enclave emerges, it "automatically" will be converted into a new subunit over several stages, as it is able to meet criteria specified by the top hierarchy. If the adoption of protest absorption as a conscious organization policy is carried out effectively, an organization will strengthen its ability to cope with nonconformity and to implement changes flowing upward from the bottom.

Appendix

Some historical examples

Following a presentation of a middle-range theory model, ideally, one should develop indicators for the variables that make up the model, and then collect a sample of cases to test the model. Traditional limitations of time and space prevent the realization of the ideal. To facilitate comprehension of the protest-absorption model, however, the history of two nonconforming enclaves is presented in table 1. One enclave emerged within the Carmel Order in sixteenth-century Spain under the leadership of St. Teresa. The second enclave began when Claire Chennault was faced with the problem of developing a Chinese Air Force in the late 1930s.

Space does not permit even a skeleton consideration of other enclaves. Examples abound however. To name a few: Orde Wingate's Special Night Squad, his Gideon Force which fought in Ethiopia, and his long-range penetration unit known as the Chindits; the Cistercian Order which began as an enclave within the Benedictine Order, and the Trappist Order which emerged from the Cistercian Order, and so

21. The most cogent illustration of this process can probably be found in the history of the United States Air Force and of the submarine and aircraft carrier units in the United States Navy.

on. Our examples have been limited to military groups and to the cenobitic structures of the Catholic church, not only because these are normative organizations with strong centralized authorities but also because of availability of data. The reader should bear in mind, however, that nonconforming enclaves and their containment through protest absorption can occur in other normative organizations. An example is the Fund for the Republic which has been described as "Paul Hoffman's severance pay." In his unofficial biography of the Ford Foundation, Dwight MacDonald writes:[22]

> The Foundation's trustees decided that (the program) should be implemented by a new agency, which finally emerged in December, 1952 as the Fund for the Republic. . . . Hoffman originally supported Hutchins in proposing it, and its establishment coincided with Hoffman's extrusion from the Foundation. . . . The Fund's elephantine gestation is perhaps explained by the dilemma of the Ford trustees . . . who found themselves being chivied by Hoffman and Hutchins into doing something that was as "controversial" as it was logical on the basis of the program they themselves had adopted.

Postscript 1972

After this working paper was completed in 1962, no systematic effort was undertaken to test the hypothesis implicit in the description of the protest absorption process. But other research endeavors, and the militant, and at times violent, protest that has permeated many American institutions in recent years have stimulated some additional thoughts about protest absorption. I shall describe these briefly here.

Protest absorption in competitive organizations

Protest absorption is almost always shrouded with uncertainty, because it depends on the charismatic strength of the leader as he pursues his cause, among other reasons. His charisma might only be adequate through one round of absorption. But there is one structural characteristic that might compensate for the leader's deficiency and assure the establishment of a new legitimate subunit, and that is competition.

Among a set of organizations competing within the same market, either for resources or for clientele, the process of absorbing protest in one unit may have implications for structural change within a competing unit. Let us assume that organization A has, after much strife, converted a nonconforming enclave into a new legitimate subunit, with a delimited amount of autonomy to pursue its innovative ideas. Fur-

22. Dwight MacDonald, *The Ford Foundation* (New York: Reynal & Co., 1956), p. 71.

Table 1.   History of Two Nonconforming Enclaves

	Discalced Carmelities, 1562–93	Flying Tigers, 1941–60
Organization	Catholic church	United States Army
Leader	St. Teresa	General C. L. Chennault
Lieutenants	St. John of the Cross	Colonel C. V. Haynes Colonel R. L. Scott
Cause	Greater concern with salvation. Revive asceticism of early Carmelites. Concern with action as well as contemplation, eg., praying for the souls of others. This was to lead to emphasis on missionary work.	Develop and put into action fighter pilot tactics. Train American pilots in the use of fighter planes. Furnish air support for Chinese land forces and fight delaying action against Japanese.
Symbols	Alpargatas (hemp and rope sandals). Rough material for clothing.	Flying Tiger sharks painted on planes. Cowboy boots instead of regulation military boots.
State of organization	Carmel Order had its strict rule modified in 1432. By the sixteenth century, adherence to the modified rule had become lax. Nuns spent time in gossip rather than in prayer. Spanish church beginning to seethe with reform to meet challenge of Reformation.	Tactics for use of planes not developed at pace commensurate with technological progress. Tendency by military to view planes as auxiliary to infantry and artillery. Lack of preparation to deal with onset of World War II.
Middle hierarchy	Officials of Carmel Order in Spain and Italy	Generals Bissell and Stilwell
Top hierarchy	The pope	President Roosevelt
Intermediary	Philip II of Spain	Madame Chiang Kai-shek
Obstruction techniques	Teresa assigned for three-year period to head of a Carmel convent to halt her activities. Excommunication of nuns who voted for Teresa when her three-year term was concluded. Assigning Calced confessors to Discalced houses. Kidnapping and imprisoning friars loyal to Teresa.	Limiting allocation of supplies and personnel. Detaining Flying Tiger recruits in India, enroute to China, to indoctrinate them against Chennault. Attempting to select Chennault's chief of staff for him.
Stabilizers	Constitution for Discalced providing for a centralized government.	Induction of Flying Tigers into U.S. Army which meant that group would have to adhere to military regulations.

Origin of enclave and rounds of protest absorption	Within convent at Avila, Teresa gained small following. Permission granted to start her own house.	Chennault invited to China by Madame Chiang Kai-shek to develop Chinese Air Force. From 1936 to 1940, Chennault fought Japanese with whatever pilots and equipment drifted to China. From 1940 to 1941, American Volunteer Group organized; group commanded by Chennault and paid by Chinese government.
	1. Discalced established as separate province. 1579. Free to establish religious houses. Subject to General of Order of Spain.	1. AVG transformed into China Air Task Force and inducted into USAAF, July 1942, subject to Bissell as head of parent 10th Air Force.
	2. Established as separate congregation, 1587. Subject to General of entire Carmel Order but elected its own Vicar-General.	2. CATF converted into 14th Air Force, March 1943, subject to Stilwell's command as head of China-Burma-India theater.
	3. Established by papal bull as separate order, 1593, subject only to pope.	3. No further rounds of protest absorption occurred, for General Marshall felt that Chennault should continue under Stilwell's command, but Stilwell was instructed to give Chennault all that he asked for.
	4. In succeeding centuries Discalced Order engaged in missionary work and spread beyond the boundaries of Spain.	4. 14th Air Force deactivated in 1960.

Note: For references pertaining to table I, see the following:

Discalced Carmelites:

Nigg, Walter, *Warriors of God*, New York: Alfred A. Knopf, 1959.

Peers, E. A., *Handbook to the Life and Times of St. Teresa and St. John of the Cross*, Westminster, Maryland: Newman Press, 1954.

———, *Spirit of Flame*, New York: Morehouse-Gorham, 1945.

St. Teresa, *Life of St. Teresa* (trans. by Rev. John Dalton), New York: P. J. Kennedy & Sons, N.D.

Zimmerman, B., *Carmel in England*, London: Burns & Oates, 1899.

Flying Tigers:

Romanus, C. F. and Sunderland, R., *Stilwell's Mission to China*, Washington, D.C.: Office of the Chief of Military History, Dept. of the Army, 1953.

Scott, R. L., *God is my Co-Pilot*, New York: Ballantine, 1959.

———, *Flying Tiger: Chennault of China*, New York: Doubleday, 1959.

Wedemyer, A. C., *Wedemyer Reports*, New York: Henry Holt, 1958.

ther, assume that the new subunit is visible to competing organizations. It may be the case that competing organization B is already faced with a similar nonconforming enclave. In this instance, B might convert the enclave into a legitimate subunit without as much conflict as occurred in A, to assure the maintenance of its competitive position. And this might occur regardless of the energies that the leader of the enclave brings to his cause, a particularistic link to the top leader of B, or the presence of other conditions that contribute to the protest-absorption process.[23]

Finally, organization C may not have a nonconforming enclave, but in response to protest absorption in A, it may introduce a new unit in order to maintain its competitive position. In this way protest absorption within one organization may have implications for structural change, if not protest absorption, for other organizations that compete in the same environment.

Protest and organizational learning

What has just been hypothesized about competing organizations implies that they learn from each other. The question that might be asked now is to what extent organizations which are functionally similar, such as universities, but are not competitive in the unual market sense, learn from each other in controlling nonconformity. Specifically, to what extent did the demand for and the institutionalization of such innovations as Black Studies programs or coed dormitories in one university affect the institutionalization process in other universities? The question is pertinent insofar as on some campuses such innovations emerged from the efforts of university officials to control nonconforming student enclaves. Probably a key explanatory variable for answering the question is the degree to which institutions of higher learning see themselves as similar to the university that is absorbing student protest by developing a new specialized curriculum.

The same types of questions about protest absorption could be raised vis-à-vis public school systems. Within the last five years some of the larger urban systems have been experimenting with innovative learning centers which replace the traditional public school for some students. Did these centers emerge from the efforts of school officials to control nonconforming enclaves or through other avenues?

23. This hypothesis about the effects of competition on protest absorption emerged from a review of the histories of the news units within CBS and NBC. See Mitchell V. Charnley, *News by Radio* (New York: Macmillan, 1948); A. A. Schechter, *I Live on Air* (New York: Frederick A. Stokes, 1941); Francis Chase, Jr., *Sound and Fury* (New York: Harper & Bros., 1942); Eric Sevareid, *No So Wild a Dream* (New York: Alfred Knopf, 1946), and other memoirs by broadcasters.

Separation as an alternative to absorption

Certainly not all conforming enclaves are absorbed by their parent organizations. The history of Protestantism is, in large measure, the history of nonconforming sects that separated from their parent religions. The history of western political parties details the rise of splinter groups that either died out or established themselves as separate parties. Voluntary organizations also tend to produce splinter groups. A recent example is the Friends of the Earth, a conservation organization that arose soon after the more radical leaders of directors, and resigned. A full account of the conditions leading to separation rather than absorption cannot be undertaken here, but a brief listing of them may serve to highlight the protest absorption process.

These conditions will be presented in the form of separate hypotheses. First, separation of the enclave, rather than its absorption, is more likely to occur when the parent organization lacks a long span of control. Where the middle hierarchy is short or absent the enclave is likely to pose a direct threat to the authority of the top leadership. Second, separation is more likely to occur when the enclave's cause directly challenges the premises underlying the organization's central policies. In both of these instances there is little room for arriving at solutions that would be acceptable both to the enclave and the top leadership. Third, separation is more likely when the organization feels it is sufficiently strong that it can afford to lose its protesting members, and face them as a part of its environment. (A small liberal arts college let the dissident members of its faculty go, to form a new type of college, at a time when Ph.Ds were beginning to be a glut on the market. The rift in the Sierra Club became complete as its membership was expanding rapidly.) Fourth, separation is more likely when an individual can easily obtain and shed member status in the organization. Fifth, separation rather than absorption is more likely to occur when the organization does not have a monopoly or partial monopoly on means and rewards. These last two conditions tend to be interrelated, and when they obtain, the enclave is more likely to believe that it can survive on its own.

Absorption and the content of protest

In view of the varieties of protest that institutions have sustained in recent years, the phrase of "protest absorption," which refers to the process by which a nonconforming enclave is checked through conversion into a new legitimate subunit, may be unfortunate. Even though the phrase is broader than the process it denotes, it shall be retained.

At least two types of protest within organizations have been evident in recent years, where protest absorption would not be feasible. The first type occurs when the protestors are advocating something for another party rather than for themselves. A case in point would be student objection to university actions such as research contracts with the Department of Defense. A university might create a new college that would have no defense contracts, for protesting students to attend. But since these students are not likely to be involved in activities relating to such contracts in the first place, it is unclear how a new subcampus would dampen their protest.

The second type occurs when the protestors are advocating a change in the organization's central policies. Pertinent examples are the pressures within the Catholic church to change its position on the rule of clerical celibacy and on the use of contraceptives. Logically, protests on both matters could be handled through the creation of new subunits. For the former there could be a cenobitic order whose members would be permitted to marry. For the latter, subparishes could be established whose members would be permitted to use contraceptives. But the creation of such subunits would mean institutionalizing actions that contravene central beliefs (see figure 3 in the main text of the article).

All this suggests that the incidence of protest absorption within organizations broadly bears some kind of curvilinear relationship to societal change in general. When a society is extremely stable some of the conditions that produce a nonconforming enclave are probably absent, so the incidence of protest absorption would be very low. When a society has been accumulating extensive changes, nonconforming enclaves within organizations abound, but their protests are not always amenable to absorption through the creation of new subunits. Consequently, the incidence of protest absorption would be much smaller than the incidence of nonconforming enclaves. Between these extremes of stability and change, when conditions are present to produce nonconforming enclaves but the types of change that generate extreme pressures on an organization's central policies are absent, one might anticipate a much higher incidence of protest absorption.

Postscript 1979

Many observers of the American scene (e.g., Gary Trudeau in Doonesbury) see the 1970s as a formless decade, in contrast to earlier ones, not lending itself to easy symbolization. But from the perspective of protest absorption, the 1970s can be viewed as a decade in which many organizations were (and still are) faced with absorbing and institutionalizing changes stimulated by the 1960s social movements.

These processes invite further reflection on the protest absorption theory. Here I shall elaborate on two points of the theory as they pertain to one outcome of the environmental movement. The two points are (1) that dispersal of the leader and members of the non-conforming enclave throughout the organization, in an effort to disband the group, might spread rather than eliminate the nonconformity; (2) that the protest of nonconforming enclaves is less amenable to absorption through the creation of new legitimate subunits the closer the subject of protest is to the organization's central beliefs and policies.

The environmental movement led to the passage of the National Environmental Policy Act of 1969 (NEPA), requiring federal agencies to address the latent as well as manifest consequences of their proposed construction projects, and resource extraction and utilization plans. Findings are to be published in environmental impact statements (EISs). The law requires that an agency publish a draft EIS which is to be reviewed by other agencies, citizen groups, and individuals during a sixty to ninety-day public review period. The agency then prepares a final EIS which includes comments submitted during the review period, the agency's responses to the comments, and any revisions of the draft EIS stimulated by public review.

NEPA, in effect, is a mandate to have agencies improve their decision-making processes. Decisions about large construction projects and resource utilization are to be based on a more thorough understanding of the likely effects of a proposed undertaking on natural and social environments. The EIS process is intended to broaden an agency's vision, to make it more sensitive to public concerns about its activities and their effects, to have it seriously contemplate alternative approaches for fulfilling its objectives, to make it more responsive to public concerns in choosing among alternative proposals, and to have an agency develop mitigation plans to dampen at least some of the anticipated unavoidable, adverse consequences of the alternative it has chosen to implement.

To comply with NEPA, federal agencies, in effect, had to permit the emergence of nonconforming enclaves within their organizations. Enclaves evolved through the hiring of relatively young, somewhat idealistic and very energetic persons with degrees in a variety of natural and social sciences, who were charged with preparing EISs, and with other responsibilities relating to the implementation of an "environmental sensitivity" in day-to-day affairs. For agencies whose professional positions were staffed almost exclusively by engineers, foresters, planners, or architects, the hiring of professionals in quite different disciplines marked a major new thrust. Typically, an agency would hire two or three "environmental specialists" at the outset, placing them in a subsection of the planning branch. Although the characteristics of the enclaves and the degree of cooperation they received from their organizations vary considerably from agency to agency, and from district office to district office within any one agency, in general they resemble the model of the nonconforming enclave. Enclave staffs had to be expanded rapidly to keep pace with court interpretations of what constituted legally acceptable impact statements. Some enclaves have as many as twenty to twenty-five members. Charismatic leaders have emerged in a number of them; in some enclaves, where the leader never emerged or where he was "exiled" to another unit of the organization, enclave members regarded themselves as committed to a charismatic idea, namely bringing about more "environmentally and socially sensitive" decisions.[24]

In the district offices of some agencies, middle management has used several bureaucratic tactics to check the enclaves and force them to produce EISs that discuss only the benign consequences of the proposed action and stress the adverse aspects of alternatives to it. By the same token, the enclaves have developed tactics to produce "full disclosure" EISs despite the censuring efforts of middle management. Also, some enclaves have sought to permeate a wide array of agency activities to stimulate "environmental sensitiviey" in day-to-day actions. Such permeation is particularly important in agency planning branches where ideas for future construction and resource utilization projects are initiated. It is much easier to develop "environmentally sensitive" plans if such an orientation is considered throughout the planning process rather than tacked on after several years of planning, during which time the project planning staff has developed a commitment to a particular course of action.

In some agency district offices, the enclaves experienced several rounds of protest absorption, often from subsections to sections within planning branches, and in a few instances to fullfledged branch status

24. For a discussion of chrismatic ideas and their dependency on leaders for transmission see Peter Berger, "Charisma, Religious Innovation, and the Israelite Prophecy," *American Sociological Review* 28 (1963): 940–50 and Edward Shils, "Charisma, Order and Status," *American Sociological Review* 30 (1965): 199–212. In the context of a highly differentiated society with many voluntary organizations, the structure and networks are there for an idea without aid of a charismatic leader in the enclave itself. Enclave members can sustain commitment to the idea, and keep up with reinterpretations of it through memberships in professional and citizen organizations, through reading the literature published by these groups, and through nonwork activities allowing reaffirmation to the charismatic idea. In fact, such activities may bring enclave members in contact with charismatic leaders in nonwork settings like club activities and professional meetings.

with their own sections. Several factors prompted these rounds: (1) increasing pressure from external sources like citizen groups to prepare comprehensive EISs, which required more labor; (2) increasing pressure from external sources to prepare EISs for a wide variety of agency undertakings, which also required more labor; (3) arguments presented by enclave leaders to higher management levels that work could be performed with greater quality and less delay if the environmental specialists had more autonomy, including developing their own budgets and schedules, and letting their own research contracts.

Meanwhile, the chiefs of nonplanning branches began to recognize the need for the permeation of "environmental sensitivity" in their areas of responsibility. They observed that failure to exercise such sensitivity led to delays in implementing actions and programs beyond the planning stage, or their cancellation or modification as citizen groups or other agencies used various legal tools (administrative appeals, court injunctions, etc.) to have environmentally insensitive actions halted.

This recognition had its own effect on the environmental enclaves. Generally, the enclaves worked most closely with planning branches, preparing EISs to accompany planning documents. But as other branches, in particular, those charged with construction and resource extraction supervision, and issuance of permits for activities to be engaged in by the private sector, developed the recognition, they turned to the environmental enclaves for assistance. (Prior informal contact with the environmental specialists helped encourage this recognition.) The enclaves responded to requests for help by working overtime, which was consistent with the youth and idealism of its members, and by hiring additional staff.

These responses, however, were usually not adequate for the increasing demands placed on the enclaves. As a result, work priorities shifted almost daily, and it became increasingly difficult to meet deadlines for the preparation of EISs. The need to cross department lines and go through time-consuming chains of command to obtain environmental assistance led to other solutions. Branch chiefs (other than planning) created new environmental positions within their units, often filling them by recruiting from the environmental enclaves. (In several instances, movement to these positions constituted promotions for the environmental specialists.)

Planning-branch heads also began to recognize the need for closer integration between various aspects of planning and environmental sensitivity, which led to further inroads on the environmental enclaves. Senior natural and social scientists were dispersed to different sections of planning branches. If the environmental enclave had achieved branch status, it was once again reduced to section or subsection status within the planning branch, with a smaller staff and lesser responsibility. Its main responsibility would be to coordinate all components of an EIS with other sections of the planning branch, and to rewrite a variety of study and planning documents into a relatively short and readable EIS. (The latter is consistent with new Council of Environmental Quality guidelines stipulating that EISs should summarize key research findings but should not present detailed studies.)

In summary, the passage of NEPA required federal construction and resource management agencies to bring an "environmental" orientation to their central policies which necessitated the utilization of training and skills the agencies had heretofore not found necessary. Initially, they responded to the law through establishing nonconforming enclaves of environmental specialists; some enclaves sustained several rounds of protest absorption. As pressures continued in the larger society to have "environmental" considerations influence decision and activities, agency managers created environmental positions within a variety of branches, often filling these with personnel from the enclaves, in an effort to institutionalize an environmental orientation throughout the agencies. (However, early in the history of some enclaves, some particularly zealous environmental specialists were ordered out of the enclaves into other sections in efforts to check them. Such transfers occurred after particularly abrasive incidents between enclave members and "old-time" agency members and were clearly regarded as "punishment.") Such dispersals, brought about partly because enclave members voluntarily applied for the new positions on a competitive basis, led to the devolution of the enclaves. Further devolution occurred when other members were transferred. With each type of dispersal, enclave members took with them many of the same responsibilities they had within the enclaves.

From the standpoint of the protest absorption theory, when external pressures are brought to bear on an organization's central policies which require the use of different skills and training, the organization may respond initially by developing a nonconforming enclave in its midst. Recruitment to the enclave is based on possession of the requisite skills to allow the organization to be responsive, to some degree, to pressures for change. For a while, the relationship between the enclave and the organization will follow the protest absorption model. But if external pressure for change in the organization's central policies continues, even an enclave that has undergone several rounds of protest absorption—becoming a new legitimate subunit—will not be able to handle all the demands placed on it. At this juncture, the organization will begin dispersing enclave specialists to new positions throughout the organization (or recruiting specialists from outside if necessary) in an effort to have its central policies change in a manner responsive to external pressure.

In conclusion, when the type of changes being demanded in an organization's central policies require skills and training that the organization has not used in the past, the formation of nonconforming enclaves and several rounds of protest absorption can be expected, followed by enclave devolution as positions based on the new skills are created throughout the organization.

How the Top Is Different
Rosabeth Moss Kanter

Corporate headquarters of the company I have called Indsco, occupied many floors in a glass and steel office building in a large city. The surroundings were luxurious. At ground level was a changing art exhibit in glass cases with displays of awards to Indsco executives for meritorious public service or newspaper clippings about the corporation. There might be piles of company newspapers on a nearby table or special publications like the report by foreign students who spent the summer with Indsco families. Such public displays almost always stressed Indsco's contributions to the welfare of the larger community. Across from gleaming chrome elevators and a watchman's post were doors leading into the employees' dining room. In the morning a long table with coffee, sweet rolls, and bagels for sale was set up outside the dining room; during the day coffee carts were available on each floor. Inside, the dining room was divided into two parts; a large cafeteria for everyone and a small area with already set tables, hostess seating, menus, and waitress service. Those tables were usually occupied by groups of men; the largely female clerical work force tended to eat in the cafeteria. Special luncheon meetings arranged by managers were held in the individual executive dining rooms and conference areas on the top floor; to use these rooms, reservations had to be made well in advance by someone with executive status.

Indsco executives were also likely to go out for lunch, especially if they were entertaining an outside visitor, to any of the numerous posh restaurants in the neighborhoods. At these lunches a drink was a must; at one time it was two extra-dry martinis, but more recently it became a few glasses of wine. However, despite the fact that moderate social drinking was common, heavy drinking was frowned upon. A person's

Excerpted from LIFE IN ORGANIZATIONS: Workplaces As People Experience Them, edited by Rosabeth Kanter and Barry A. Stein, Basic Books, Inc., Publishers, New York.

career could be ruined by the casual comment that he or she had alcoholic tendencies. Stories told about men who cavorted and caroused in bars, staying up all night, were told with the attitude that "that was really crazy."

The office floors were quietly elegant, dominated by modern design, white walls, and beige tones. At one end, just off the elevators, sat a receptionist who calls on a company telephone line to announce visitors. A secretary would then appear to escort a visitor to his or her appointment. Offices with windows were for higher status managers, and their secretaries were often proud of having drapes. Corner offices were reserved for the top. They were likely to be larger in size, with room for coffee tables and couches, and reached through a reception area where a private secretary sat. Inside offices went to assistants and other lower-status salaried personnel; conference rooms were also found along the inside rim. Secretaries and other hourly workers occupied rows of desks with banks of cabinets and files in the public spaces between. There were few signs of personal occupancy of space, except around the secretaries' desks. Managers might put up a painting or poster on the wall, and they usually had a small set of photographs of their families somewhere on or near their desk. Rarely would more than a few books or reports be visible, and the overall impression was one of tidiness, order, and uniformity from office to office. In fact, it was often true that the higher the status of an executive, the less cluttered was his desk. Office furnishings themselves reflected status rather than personality. There was a clear system of stratification. As status increased, desks went from a wood top with steel frame through solid wood to the culmination in a marble-top desk. Type of ashtray was also determined by the status system; and a former executive secretary, promoted into a management position herself, reported that her former peers were upset that she took her stainless steel file trays with her because a secretary working for her would not be entitled to such luxurious equipment. The rational distribution of furniture and supplies was thought to make the system more equitable and to avoid competition for symbols of status. . . .

The secretary also contributed in minor ways to the boss's status. Some people have argued that secretaries function as "status symbol" for executives, holding that the traditional secretarial role is developed and preserved because of its impact on managerial egos, not its contribution to organizational efficiency. Robert Townsend, iconoclastic former president of Avis, claimed in *Up the Organization* that the existence of private secretaries was organizationally inefficient, as proven by his experience in gaining half a day's time by giving up what he called "standard executive equipment." One writer was quite explicit about the meaning of a secretary: "In many companies a secretary outside your door is the most visible sign that you have become an executive; a secretary is automatically assigned to each executive, whether or not his work load requires one. . . . When you reach the vice-presidential level, your secretary may have an office of her own, with her name on the door. At the top, the president may have two secretaries. . . ." A woman professional at Indsco agreed with the idea that secretaries were doled out as rewards rather than in response to job needs, as she talked about her own problems in getting enough secretarial help.

At Indsco, the secretary's function as a status symbol increased up the ranks as she became more and more bound to a specific boss. "It's his image, his status, sitting out in front," a personnel administrator said. "She's the sign of how important he is." . . .

Physical height corresponded to social height at Indsco, like other major corporations. Corporate officers resided at the very top on the forty-fifth floor, which was characterized by many people in Indsco as "a hospital ward." The silence was deafening. The offices were huge. According to one young executive who had served as an assistant to an officer, "One or two guys are sitting there; there's not much going on. It's the brain center, but there is no activity. It's like an old folks' home. You can see the cobwebs growing. A secretary every quarter mile. It's very sterile." An executive secretary told the story of her officer boss's first reaction to moving onto the forty-fifth floor. "He was the one human being," she said, "who was uncomfortable with the trappings of status. When he moved up, he had to pick an office." She wouldn't let him take anything but a corner—it was the secretary who had to tell him that. Finally he agreed for the sake of the corporate image, but he was rarely there, and he set up the office so that everything was in one corner and the rest was useless space.

Some people felt that the physical insulation of top executives also had its counterpart in social insulation. Said a former officer's assistant, "There are courtiers around the top guys, telling them what they want to hear, flattering them. For example, there was a luncheon with some board members. The vice-chairman mentioned that he was looking for a car for his daughter. A courtier thought, 'We'll take care of it.' He went down the line, and someone in purchasing had to spend half a day doing this. The guy who had to do it resented it, so he became antagonistic to the top. The vice-chairman had no idea this was going on, and if he had known, he would probably have stopped it; but you can't say anything at the top without having it be seen as an order. Even ambiguous remarks may get translated into action. At the top you have to figure out the impact of all of your words in advance because an innocent expression can have a major effect. A division president says, 'It might be a good idea to _____.' He's just ruminating, but that gets sent down to the organization as an ultimatum, and everyone scrambles around to make sure it gets done. He looks down and says, 'What the hell is happening?' "

At the same time, officers could also be frustrated by their distance from any real action. One remarked, "You get into a position like mine, and you think you can get anything done, but I shout down an order, and I have to wait years for any action. The guy in the plant turns a valve and sees the reaction, or the salesman offers a price, but I may never live to see the impact of my decisions." For this reason, it was known that once in a while officers could be expected to leave their protected environment and try to get involved in routine company activities. Some would go down and try to do something on the shop floor. Once in a while one would make a sales call at a very high level or make an appearance at a customer golf outing. It was also a legend that an early president had his own private laboratory outside of his office—his own tinkering room. As a manager put it, "He would close the door and go play. It was almost as though he was babied. He was given a playroom." . . .

Conformity pressures at the top: Uncertainty and the growth of inner circles

Leaders who already have power seek as new recruits those they can rely upon and trust. They demand that the newcomers to top positions be loyal, that they accept authority, and that they conform to a prescribed pattern of behavior.

Unlike a more communal environment, where eccentrics can be lovingly tolerated because trust is based on mutual commitments and deep personal knowledge, those who run the bureaucratic corporation often rely on outward manifestations to determine who is the "right sort of person." Managers tend to carefully guard power and privilege for those who fit in, for those they see as "their kind." Wilbert Moore was commenting on this phenomenon when he used the metaphor of a "bureaucratic kinship system" to describe the corporation—but a kinship system based on homosocial reproduction in which men reproduce themselves in their own image. The metaphor is apt. Because of the *situation* in which managers function, because of the position of managers in the corporate structure, social similarity tends to become extremely important to them. The structure sets in motion forces leading to the replication of managers as the same kind of social individuals. And people at the top reproduce themselves in kind.

Conformity pressures and the development of exclusive management circles closed to "outsiders" stem from the degree of uncertainty surrounding managerial positions. Bureaucracies are social inventions that supposedly reduce the uncertain to the predictable and routine. Yet much uncertainty remains—many situations in which individual people rather than impersonal procedures must be trusted. "Uncertainty," James Thompson wrote in a recent major statement on organizations, "appears as the fundamental problem for complex organizations, and coping with uncertainty as the essence of the administrative process." Thompson identified three sources of uncertainty in even the most perfect of machinelike bureaucracies; a lack of cause-effect understanding in the culture at large (limiting the possibility for advance planning); contingencies caused by the fact that the bureaucracy is not alone, so that outcomes of organizational action are in part determined by action of other elements in the environment; and the interdependence of parts, the human interconnections inside the organization itself, which can never fully be reduced to predictable action. The requirements for a perfectly technically "rational" bureaucracy that never has to rely on the personal discretion of a single individual can never be met; complete knowledge of all cause-effect relationships plus control over all of the relevant variables. Thus, sources of uncertainty that are inherent in human institutions mean that some degree of reliance on individual persons must always be present.

It is ironic that in those most impersonal of institutions the essential communal problem of trust remains. For wherever there is uncertainty, *someone* (or some group) must decide, and thus, there must be personal discretion. And discretion raises not technical but human, social, and even communal questions: trust, and its origins in loyalty, commitment, and mutual understanding based on the sharing of values. It is the uncertainty quotient in managerial work, as it has come to be defined in the large modern corporation, that causes management to become so socially restricting: to develop tight inner circles excluding social strangers; to keep control in the hands of socially homogeneous peers; to stress conformity and insist upon a diffuse, unbounded loyalty; and to prefer ease of communication and thus social certainty over the strains of dealing with people who are "different."

If conditions of uncertainty mean that people have to be relied on, then people fall back on social bases for trust. The greater the uncertainty, the greater the pressures for those who have to trust each other to form a homogeneous group. At different times in an organization's history, and at different places in its structure, a higher degree of uncertainty brings with it more drive for social similarity. . . .

Uncertainty can stem from either the time-span of decisions and the amount of information that must be collected, or from the frequency with which nonroutine events occur and must be handled. The impossibility of specifying contingencies in advance, operating procedures for all possible events, leaves an organization to rely on personal discretion. (It is also this pressure that partly accounts for the desire to centralize responsibility in a few people who can be held accountable for discretionary decisions.) Commented a sales manager at Indsco, "The need for flexibility is primary in my job. The situation changes from minute to minute. One minute it's a tank truck that collapsed. Another it's a guy whose wife just had a hysterectomy and is going to die. . . . I'm dealing with such different problems all the time."

The importance of discretion increases with closeness to the top of a hierarchical organization. Despite the institutionalization and routinization of much of the work of large organizations and despite the proliferation of management experts, uncertainty remains a generic condition, increasing with rank. Jobs are relatively unstructured, tasks are nonroutine, and decisions must be made about a variety of unknown elements. Issues such as "direction" and "purpose" cannot be reduced to rational formulae. Organizational improvement, or even maintenance, is not a simple matter that can be summarized in statements about "the ten functions of managers" or techniques of operation. If the "big picture" can be viewed from the top, it also looks bigger and fuzzier. Computers have not necessarily reduced the uncertainty of decisions at the top; in some cases, they have merely increased the amount of information that decision-makers must take into account. A major executive of Indsco confessed in a meeting that "we don't know how to manage these giant structures; and I suspect no one does. They are like dinosaurs, lumbering on of their own accord, even if they are no longer functional."

Criteria for "good decisions" or good management performance also get less certain closer to the top. The connection between an upper management decision and a factor such as production efficiency several layers below or gross sales is indirect, if it is even apparent. (An Indsco division president said, "In the 1960s we thought we were really terrific. We patted ourselves on the back a lot because every decision was so successful. Business kept on expanding. Then came the recession, and we couldn't do anything to stop it. We had been lucky before. Everything turned to gold in the 1960s. But it became clear that we don't know the first thing about how to make this enterprise work.")

Financial measures of performance are sometimes even artifactual because of the juggling of figures; for example, when and how a loss is recorded. There are also a variety of dilemmas in trying to evaluate the success of managers: qualitative versus quantitative measures, short-run versus long-run outcomes. Decisions that look good in the short-term might be long-term diasters, but by that time the failure can be blamed on other factors, and those responsible for the decisions might be so entrenched in power that they now call the shots anyway. A former public relations manager at DuPont formulated what he called the Law of Inverse Certainty: "The more important the management decision, the less precise the tools to deal with it . . . and the longer it will take before anyone knows it was right." One example was a rigid cost cutter who helped increase profits by eliminating certain functions; by the time the company began to feel the loss of those functions, he had been promoted and was part of the inner power group. Someone else picked up the pieces.

The uncertainty up the ranks, like the uncertainty of beginnings, also puts trust and homogeneity at a premium. The personal loyalty normally demanded of subordinates by officials is most intense at the highest levels of organizations, as others have also noted. The lack of structure in top jobs makes it very important for decision-makers to work together closely in at least the harmony of shared understanding and a degree of mutual trust. Since for an organization to function at all requires that, to some extent, people will pull together around decisions, the solidarity that can be mustered through common membership in social networks, and the social control this provides, is a helpful supplement for decision-makers. Indeed, homogeneity of class and ethnic background and prior social experiences is one important "commitment mechanism" found to build a feeling of communion among members of viable utopian communities. Situational pressures, then, place a great emphasis on personal relations and social homogeneity as functional elements in the carrying out of managerial tasks. And privilege is also kept within a small circle.

The social homogeneity of big business leaders from the early-to-middle twentieth century has been noted frequently by critics such as C. Wright Mills as well as business historians. Their class background and social characteristics tended to be similar: largely white, Protestant men from elite schools. Much attention has also been paid to the homogeneity of type within any particular company. In one industrial organization, managers who moved ahead needed to be members of the Masonic Order and the local yacht club; not Roman Catholic; Anglo-Saxon or Germanic in origin; and Republican.

At Indsco, until ten years ago, top executives in the corporation were traceable to the founders of the company or its subsidiaries—people who held stock or were married to people who did. There was a difference between who did well in the divisions, where performance tended to account for more, and who got into top positions in the corporation itself. To get ahead in the corporation, social connections were known to be very important. Indeed, corporate staff positions became a place to put people who were nonmovers, whose performance was not outstanding, but were part of the "family." The social homogeneity of corporate executives was duly noted by other managers. One asked a consultant, "Do all companies have an ethnic flavor? Our top men all seem to be Scotch-Irish." (But as management has become more rationalized, and the corporation has involved itself more heavily in divisional operations, there has also been a trend, over the past five years, toward more "objective" criteria for high-level corporate positions.)

We expect a direct correlation, then, between the degree of uncertainty in a position—the extent to which organizations must rely on personal discretion—and a reliance on "trust" through "homosocial reproduction"—selection of incumbents on the basis of social similarity. . . .

Management becomes a closed circle in the absence of better, less exclusionary responses to uncertainty and communication pressures. Forces stemming from organizational situations help foster social homogeneity as a selection criterion for managers and promote social conformity as a standard for conduct. Concerned about giving up control and broadening discretion in the organization, managers choose others that can be "trusted." And thus they reproduce themselves in kind. Women are occasionally included in the inner circle when they are part of an organization's ruling family, but more usually this system leaves women out, along with a range of other people with discrepant social characteristics. Forces insisting that trust means total dedication and nondiffuse loyalty also serve to exclude those, like women, who are seen as incapable of such a single-minded attachment.

There is a self-fulfilling prophecy buried in all of this. The more closed the circle, the more difficult it is for "outsiders" to break in. Their very difficulty in entering may be taken as a sign of incompetence a sign, that the insiders were right to close their ranks. The more closed the circle, the more difficult it is to share power when the time comes, as it inevitably must, that others challenge the control by just one kind. And the greater the tendency for a group of people to try to reproduce themselves, the more constraining becomes the emphasis on conformity. It would seem a shame, indeed, if the only way out of such binds lay in increasing bureaucratization—that is, in a growth in routinization and rationalization of areas of uncertainty and a concomitant decline in personal discretion. But somehow corporations must grapple with the problem of how to reduce pressures for social conformity in their top jobs. . . .

Conformity reaches home

It is one of the prevailing ironies of modern corporate life that the closer to the top of the organization, the more traditional and non-"modern" does the system look. As Max Weber noted, at this point more charismatic, symbolic, and "non-rational" elements come into play. At the top—and especially in interaction with its environment—the organization is most likely to show strong elements of a personal, familistic system imbued with ritual, drawing on traditional behavior modes, and overlaid with symbolism. The irony stem from the fact that it is the top level that prescribes routine and impersonality—the absence of particularism and familism—for the rest of the organization. The modern organization formally excludes the family from participation in organizational life and excludes family ties as a basis for organizational position, even to the extent of antinepotism rules. Yet, at the top the wife may come into the picture as a visible member of the husband's "team"; she may be given a position and functions (and, in some cases, may even jump over qualified employees in taking on an official, paid, executive position). The wife who is excluded below may be included at the top, as part of the diplomatic apparatus of the corporation. And she has little freedom to refuse participation.

The dilemma that can confront people at this level is the issue of publicness/privateness. Both husband and wife can be made into public figures, with no area of life remaining untinged with responsibilities for the company. Here, as Wilbert Moore said, "The man, and his wife, simply cannot divest themselves of corporate identification. Their every activity with persons outside the immediate family is likely to be tinged with a recognition of the man's position. He represents the company willy-nilly. His area of privacy, and that of his wife, is very narrowly restricted." One rising young Indsco executive felt that the following had to be considered the "modern risks" of corporate vice-presidential and presidential jobs: traveling 80 percent of the time, getting shot at or kidnapped by radicals, prostituting yourself to customers, and opening your private life to scrutiny.

The higher executive's work spills over far beyond the limits of a working day. There may be no distinction between work and leisure. Activities well out of the purview of the organization's goals and defined as pleasure for other people (golf club memberships, symphony attendance, party-giving) are allowable as business expenses on income tax returns because the definition of what is "business" becomes so broad and nonspecific. People entertain one another on yachts or over long, lavish lunches—all in an attempt to mutually obligate, to create personal relations that will give someone an inside track when

it comes to more formal negotiations. Whenever "selling" is a part of
the organization's relations with its environment and sufficient sums of
money rest on each deal, those who sell tend to offer gifts (tickets to a
sports event, dinners at fancy restaurants, expensive pen and pencil
sets) to those who buy, trying to bind the others beyond the limits of a
rational contractural relationship. Entertaining in the home with the
wife as hostess is especially binding, since it appears to be a more personal offering not given to all, sets up a social obligation, implicates
others, and also calls on ancient and traditional feelings about the
need to reward hospitality.

Fusion of business and private life also occurs around longer-term
relationships. At the top, all friendships may have business meaning.
Business relations can be made because of social connections. (One
unlikely merger between two companies in very different fields was
officially said to result from one company's need for a stock exchange
listing held by the other, but off the record it was known to have been
brought about by the friendship of the two presidents and their wives.)
Charitable and community service activities, where the life's role is
especially pivotal, may generate useful business and political connections. Wives may meet each other through volunteer work and bring
their husbands into contact, with useful business results. Stratification
of the volunteer world paralleling class and ethnic differentiation in
the society ensures that husbands and wives can pinpoint the population with which they desire connections by an appropriate choice of
activity. As one chief executive wife wrote, "Any public relations man
worth his salt will recognize the corporate wife as an instrument of communication with the community far more sincere and believable than
all the booze poured down the press to gain their favor."

The importance of the wife stems not only from her own skills and
activities (which could be, and are, performed by paid employees)
but also from the testimony her behavior provides, its clue to the character and personal side of her husband. The usefulness of this testimony, in turn, is derived from unique aspects of top leadership. Image,
appearance, background, and likability are all commodities traded at
the top of the system, where actors are visible and where they put pressure on one another to demonstrate trustworthiness. . . . Farther down
a hierarchy, jobs can be broken down into component skills and decisions about people and jobs made on the basis of ability to demonstrate
those skills. At the top, decisions about people are not so easy or
mechanical; they rest on personal factors to a degree perhaps much
greater than systems themselves officially admit. The situations that a
corporation president or a president of a country face are not routine
and predictable; indeed, constituents are less interested in their

handling of routine matters than in their capacities for the unexpected. So there is no test except a vague one: Is this person trustworthy? Even questions about philosophy and intelligence are proxies for trust.

Furthermore, the capacities of an organization itself are unknown and cannot be reduced precisely either to history or to a set of facts and figures. Thus, the character of its leaders can become a critical guide to making a decision about a future relationship with it: whether to invest, to donate funds, to allow it into the community, to provide some lee-way in the regulation of its activities. Indsco was always concerned about character in its managers. Company newspapers from field loca-tions routinely stressed church leadership in articles about individual managers, and "integrity" and "acceptance of accountability" appeared on the list of eleven traits that must be possessed by candidates for officer-level jobs. Disclosures of corrupt practices by other companies in the mid-1970s enhanced Indsco's concerns about public respect-ability. Whereas, at lower levels of the organization, there was a ten-dency to formalize demands, to create routinized job descriptions, to ensure continuity of functioning by seeing to it that the occupant did not make over the job in his own image, and to exclude as much as possible of the personal and emotional life of the worker, close to the top, opposite pressure prevailed. Those with whom leaders entered into relationships looked for the private person behind the role and for the qualities and capacities that could not be encompassed by a job descrip-tion but on which they must bet when deciding to trust the leader or the organization. Here's where the wives are important.

One way leaders can offer glimpses of their private beings is by bringing along their wives, by inviting others into their homes, and by making sure that their wives confirm the impression of themselves they are trying to give. By meeting in social circumstances, by throwing open pieces of private life for inspection, leaders try to convey their taste and their humanity. Wives, especially, are the carriers of this humanity and the shapers of the image of the private person. Of course, to the extent that social events and "informal" occasions are known to communicate an image for the purposes of making appropriate rela-tionships, they may come to be as carefully managed and rationally calculated as any production task within the organization. The public relations department might even stage-manage the performance of the leader and his wife; when Dollie Ann Cole, wife of a General Motors president, wrote that PR departments no longer tell the wife what to wear and what to say, she made it explicit that they once did: ". . . a new day has dawned. Corporate wives no longer ask the public rela-tions office what charity they should work with or whether they can debate for a cause on a local or national radio or television show— or even who is coming to dinner."

The wife is thus faced with an added task at the boundary of the public and the private: to make an event seem personal that is instead highly ritualized and contrived. She must recognize also the meanings conveyed by small acts (who sits next to whom, how much time she and her husband spend with each person, the taste implied by objects in the home, how much she drinks, who seem to be the family friends) and manage even small gestures with extreme self-consciousness, as one high-level wife at Indsco recalled she did at managers' meetings: "I had to be very careful to be invariably cordial, friendly, to remember everyone's names—and then to stay away. If I was too involved with someone, it would look like I was playing favorites; that would set up waves in highly inappropriate ways. Some of the young wives were terrified, but there was only so much I could do because I had other things to worry about."

Private life thus becomes penetrable and not very private at the top. Wives face the demand to suppress private beliefs and self-knowledge in the interest of public appearance. As an instrument of diplomacy and a critical part of her husband's image, the corporate wife must often hide her own opinions in order to preserve a united front, play down her own abilities to keep him looking like the winner and the star. The women's intelligence and superior education—assets when the men looked for wives—give way to other, more social traits, such as gregariousness, adaptability, attractiveness, discretion, listening ability, and social graces.

Thus, unless serving as a surrogate for the husband, voicing opinions was not easily allowed of corporate wives at Indsco, like those political wives who must beware of outshining their husbands. An aide to Eleanor McGovern spoke of the contradictory pressures on a candidate's wife: to be able to give the speech when he can't make it but to shut her mouth and listen adoringly when he is there. Indeed, Eleanor was told to stop looking so good when she started getting better press notices than George. Abigail McCarthy recalled the anxiety she felt about how words would affect her husband's prospects: "After every interview, I lay awake in a black nightmare of anxiety, fearful that I had said something which would do Gene irreparable harm." Betty Ford became an object of controversy (and of admiration) precisely because she violated these rules of the game and refused to distort her private life. Yet, wives of upper management at Indsco felt they did not have that luxury, even though they characterized the pressure to suppress independent opinions as "nonsense" and frustrating. Not everyone complained. One wife reported that she was proud of never having unburdened herself, even to a confidante, and never having forgotten her public role throughout her husband's career.

Stresses, choices, and dilemmas in the top leadership phase, then, center around the tension between the public and the private. If men and their wives at the top gained public recognition, they also lost private freedoms. The emotional pressure this entailed was too much for some wives, as literature in the corporate-wives-as-victims tradition made clear; but it should be pointed out, too, that emotional breakdowns and secret deviances could also reflect defiant independence, unobtainable in any other way under constraining role definitions. The wishes expressed by wives in this position were of two kinds. Some women said that if they were going to be used by the company anyway, they would like the opportunity to do a real job, exercise real skills— by which they meant take on official areas of responsibility. Others wanted merely to be able to carve out more areas of privacy and independence in an otherwise public existence.

Power and its prices

The top leadership of an organization has all of the privileges of office: the signs of status, the benefits and perquisites, the material advantages their position is seen to warrant. They play ball in a large field, and the scope of their decisions is vast and far-reaching. They have, on occasion, gigantic power which does not even have to be used; a mere wish on their part is translated into action, with full cooperation and without the show of force.

But such power exists in a vise of checks and constraints; it comes out of a system, and the system, in turn, exacts its price. What if a top leader tries to exercise power that violates the expectations of other top leaders and organization members—if he or she steps out of line, out of character, or out of role? Would obedience be so easily forthcoming? Power at the top is contingent on conformity. Pressures to "fit in" also mean restraints on the unbridled exercise of power.

Furthermore, power which in some respects is contingent on trust for its effective exercise also, ironically, breeds suspicion: Can people at the top trust what they hear? Can they trust each other? What, beyond social appearance, can they use as keys to trust? Sometimes cut off from the "real action," they are seen by the organization's rank and file as remote from the daily events which truly constitute the organization—as once potent actors who now make whimsical decisions with little real understanding of organizational operations. And, as the final price of power, top leaders have to acknowledge the organization's ownership of that ultimate piece of property, their own private lives and beings. Life at the top is life in a goldfish bowl, an existence in which all the boundaries can be rendered transparent at the twitch of the public's curiosity.

The room at the top is all windows.

10

Organizational Decision Making: Analysis, Intuition, Judgment

Introduction

This chapter is about how choices are made in large organizations. Consider such decisions as new product selections, acquisitions, budget allocations, impact reports, new technologies, or layoffs. For a single individual, such decisions seem almost overwhelming. One person has little to say about the definition of the problem, almost no impact on the criteria for selecting alternatives, and little control over how the ultimate decision will be implemented. There just seem to be too many units, preferences, political and power issues, traditions, and controversies for any individual—even the individual sitting in a position of power—to make much of a difference. But decisions of this scale *can* be managed. Human and machine intelligence *can* be put together to produce pretty good (if not perfect) choices, at least most of the time.

In the first paper in this chapter, Perrow argues that the choice processes of large organizations may be too lumbering and too politically complex to be influenced *directly* by anyone. But one can use powerful secondary controls for directing the broad flow of decisions while leaving the narrow particulars to others. It follows that many committees, task forces, and commissions spend their time, money, and energy "making decisions" that have already been framed, blocked, or even abandoned. Such unreal choice making may serve necessary emotional functions of venting hostilities or providing the illusion of participation. Or the public decision-making process may serve to camouflage more sub-rosa processes and networks of decision making.

Note that Perrow argues from a behaviorist posture for managing the reinforcers that affect behaviors. At the same time, he ties many of the bureaucratic and structural aspects of organization to the more microissues of choice making. If you control the contextual environment of the choice makers, you also control the choices.

The second paper, by Mintzberg, considers what managers actually do. Do they sit at their desks and make command decisions? Do they rubber-stamp other people's decisions? Where do the problems they worry about come from? This rather refreshing look at the reality of managerial behavior (obtained by careful observation of a sample of managers over an extended period) will help the reader to see what a messy combination of logic, intituiton, manipulation, and faith go into the process of making the organization go.

And the third article, by March, goes a step further, emphasizing the role of nonrational factors in organizational decision making and goal setting. He uses metaphors of "play" and "foolishness" to derive some quite unusual insights into the choice-making process in organizations. By postponing our nationality and legitimating the playful experimental attitudes of children, March proposes we may discover interesting goals, nontrivial alternatives, and pathways that traditional rationality would never open up. Just as in small groups, premature and limited evaluation of ideas and alternatives may curb effective decision making in large organizations, too. And, as in the earlier article by Ornstein on two sides of the brain, both reasoning and intuition may be needed for fully intelligent choice making.

So, the key point of this chapter is that context, rational analysis, and also intentionally nonrational behavior can all contribute to effective choice making in large organizations.

The Bureaucratic Paradox: The Efficient Organization Centralizes in Order to Decentralize
Charles Perrow

A large organization felt the pinch of a contracting economy at the same time that new ways of processing its materials were being developed. To help in adjusting to the change, and to help in identifying areas of low productivity, a management consultant was called in. In the course of his study, the consultant looked at the management information services department, which was responsible for processing large amounts of information from the major divisions on sales, market trends, production, inventory control, costs, internal pricing, and so on. The department produced standard reports for the divisions as well as special reports for division heads and top management as needed. The department had grown steadily to meet the increased demand for its services. It now had 20 people reporting directly to Mr. Able, the manager, in addition to key-punchers and other hourly personnel.

Able worked hard, knew his job, and made himself accessible to his people, who filed through his office during the day seeking help with problems. The consultant sensed a bottleneck. The information coming in was piling up, and the reports going out were being held up. Able agreed that there was indeed a problem and asked for additional staff. The consultant instead recommended that he pick two of his present staff, promote them, and put them in charge of two groups of workers, one a processing section of ten, the other, an analysis section of eight, The consultant argued that Able was handling too many routine matters and not delegating enough authority, and that he should revise his procedures for dealing with the input resources of information and the uses of the reports.

Able resisted. He asserted that he was personally responsible for errors, that he would not know what was going on, that he would lose control over his staff. No one had as much information and skill as he had, and his expertise was badly needed in handling the data that went through the departments. Besides, adding another layer of supervision would only increase the degree of bureaucracy and slow the processing of information.

What Able prided himself on, the division heads resented. They never really liked Able that much—he was always too well informed, too ready to give an exhaustive answer to any query, too obviously working nights and weekends to keep up. "Something must be wrong with people like that. Too eager," one said. "A workaholic," said another.

Top management made the change anyway. Mr. Baker and Mr. Charles were made assistant supervisors, and in the course of the next year they made some changes. They met with their groups and went over the most frequent problems until they reached the point at which they were able to reduce the number of contacts their subordinates had with them. Baker and Charles themselves met regularly, coordinating their efforts, and as a result gradually reduced the amount of daily information that went to Able.

Fretting about the loss of direct information on problems, Able set up regular meetings with his two assistants to keep tabs on what they were doing. However, they presented him with only those problems that involved the input sources (the divisions that supplied the information) and the output sources (the divisions that received the reports). Baker and Charles were not authorized to deal with these outside sources.

Able, as always energetic, began to work on these problems with the divisions, altering the form of the material they received, finding out what happened to the reports his department sent out, and reducing the amount of special requests by making frequent ones a standard output. The efficiency of the unit, as a consequence, improved considerably; turnaround time was reduced, and the overall number of reports was reduced through consolidation while some new ones were added. The divisions were happy. Staff morale increased. Turnover and absenteeism declined.

Lessons from the case

What does this little case study illustrate? First, to put a positive construction on it, we have an increase in the delegation of decision making. Able had not delegated authority to any of his people. With the promotion of Baker and Charles, however, he was forced to delegate some authority to them. They, in turn, delegated to their subordinates. They did not have to; they could have replicated Able's style of supervision. But fortunately, it was in some disrepute.

They found that by working with small groups they could better appraise the strengths of their former co-workers and give them more say over routine matters. Furthermore, with a reduction in direct supervision, the groups were not just supervisory units, but problem-solving units. The distinction is subtle, but a supervisory unit is defined in terms of the tasks performed under the supervision of a manager. The supervised tasks determined its activities. A problem-solving unit has a manager, but it is defined in terms of the problems it receives. It then proceeds to develop tasks designed to solve those problems.

The crux of the matter is that a problem-solving unit can change its tasks. It can even change its definition of the problem. The problem is no longer a report on the number of below-standard units produced by Department A, but a report on the number of below-standard units by scrap value, by inventory sizes, or by the possibility of developing an acceptable substitute. The problem is the varying consequences of rejects, not the total number of rejects.

But let us use some negative labels that are also appropriate. We had added to all the key elements of bureaucracy: Formalization (rules and regulations) increased somewhat as the contact between employees and their section leader was reduced and replaced by regulations; specialization appeared with the two groups and the two new section leaders; standardization appeared when the total unit achieved more control over the inputs it received and the outputs it produced by standardizing some of theirs; and hierarchical levels increased as another level was interposed between Able and his subordinates.

But how can we have an increase in delegation of authority at the same time as we have an increase in bureaucratization? Burcaucracy is assumed to involve the centralization of authority. How can rules, standardization, specialization, and hierarchy produce more decentralized decision making? That is the problem this article addresses.

In brief, the answer is that the unit simultaneously experienced both a centralization and a decentralization of decision making, or power. This was accomplished by minimizing some first-order controls, thus decentralizing, and imposing some second-order controls at the same time, thus centralizing some others. If you felt there was something to be said for both the consultant's position (Able would not let go of his authority) and Able's position (chaos might result if he did not maintain control, keep in touch, use his skills, and so on), your instincts were correct. But the present state of organizational theory does not allow us to accommodate these instincts for delegation and control simultaneously. We are in a bind that insists that the idea of a centralized-decentralized bureaucracy is a contradiction in terms. Yet the fact is that our terms are about a half-century out of date.

Organizations have changed, but changes in terminology to reflect those changes in organizations have not been forthcoming and are long overdue.

First-order controls

When the factory system first appeared, it was necessary, as Frederick W. Taylor emphasized some decades later, to separate the workers from the skills of their work and make the required work skills the responsibility of their supervisors. The most common form of production had involved gangs of workers headed by a contractor who was given a fixed sum by the owner for turning out a specified amount of work. The owner had little control over the contractor and none at all over the workers.

Later the owner dispensed with the contractor, installed his own supervisor, put him in charge of the gangs, paid him at a fixed rate, and made the workers employees of the owner. Becoming the employer gave the owner the power to discipline workers, introduce new techniques, pay wages that varied with the skill of each job, and teach new hands. Direct orders and direct surveillance were probably the primary forms of control at the turn of the century.

Able relied heavily upon direct, obtrusive controls as staff members filed past his desk asking him what to do whenever there was an exception, or when they forgot the correct procedures or were unclear about them. Such an approach is common today in most employee-supervisor relationships in all organizations, and it probably always will be. But it is expensive. Able had to know every job himself. He often thought he could do the job himself almost as fast as he could tell someone else how to do it. Also, he had to spend a lot of time watching the work in progress to make sure that the people did just what they were told. The expense mounts when direct controls are applied to repetitive tasks, because the controls must be employed repeatedly. Unfortunately, this was the primary basis for Able's close contact with his staff.

Specific and direct surveillance is necessary and proper in some situations, such as those that involve a change in procedures, a new task, or a new employee. But it need not be used continually, as Able had used it. And it may be necessary in other situations where management itself has become inefficient, as in a crisis it did not avoid, or in handling an employee who has over time been made recalcitrant and unwilling to work effectively on his own initiative.

Rules and regulations were also used by Able, by early organizations, and by all organizations today. In terms of control, rules constitute a sizable advance over orders, because rules hang there, omnipresent, telling employees what to do, while the supervisor can attend to other matters.

The rule is slightly less direct and more remote. It is also more impersonal, an advantage because that makes it less obtrusive and less offensive to many employees—"Sorry, it's the rule." The rule is more efficient because it is always in effect—we hope. But it also loses the flexibility of direct orders. If situations are subject to change, if the raw materials come in odd shapes and sizes, if the skills of employees vary, rules and regulations have to proliferate.

Even if the employee is well intentioned, the proliferation of rules (and forms, procedures, instructions, regulations, and so on) alone will sometimes produce errors—or requests for direct instruction. If the employee is not particularly interested in increasing his output so that his bosses can enjoy more returns (and why should he?), the rule that causes him the least trouble will be selected. Able probably reflected this phenomenon in his complaints to the consultants that "it's hard to get good people nowadays for these jobs; they just don't care." It is quite possible that with poor management, they simply gave up and "did their job"—in other words, let Able and the least inconvenient rule make the decision.

Think of direct orders and surveillance and rules and regulations as first-order controls, appropriate perhaps for disciplining a labor force in low-complexity organizations existing in a favorable labor market. Still used, and still necessary, they remain primitive forms of control. The need for them has been reduced by the development of more sophisticated forms, but many managers—even dedicated, knowledgeable, tireless ones such as Able—lack the sophistication to use them.

Second-order controls

Though Able was not aware of it, a lack of awareness shared with many managers and even organization theorists, two second-order controls actually were making his job easier: standardization and specialization. We think of these concepts as having technical origins and rationales. If the inputs can be of standard shapes, sizes, complexity, and importance—whether they be things, problems, symbols, or people— there are economies of scale to be realized, less setup time, and a steeper learning curve for the employee.

But standardization and specialization also control people because they limit the variety of stimuli a person has to attend to, thus limiting an employee's opportunities to score off his boss when selecting an alternative. What if the employee has the interests of his boss fully at heart—a fairly unlikely event in most organizations? Even so, standardization and specialization limit the chance of his making a decision he thinks is good for other departments (which he doesn't really understand), or one that he thinks is what higher management wants (when he doesn't really understand the preferences of higher management). Standardization and specialization channel behavior, and if the channel is well constructed by the organization, more predictable and efficient behavior is emitted, as the operant psychologists put it. As organizations grew in size and complexity, efficient control grew to mean standardization and specialization.

In Able's case, his unit already was specialized, and many of its inputs, processes, and outputs were standardized. The unit processed only data that came from computerized systems, not all data, and the format was quite standardized. The divisions expected summaries and analyses in set forms. But there was not enough specialization and standardization. Much of the computerized data stayed with the divisions anyway, for their direct use, so the management information system outputs were sometimes redundant as well as out of date.

Baker and Charles realized even before they were promoted that any one of the staff might work on processing and analyzing for any division depending on informal priorities set under overload conditions. So they specialized the workforce by type of task and, within that specialization, by division—and then rotated people every few months. This made it apparent that small variations in division requirements limited standardization, as did variations in the format for incoming material.

It was a small task for Able to negotiate these changes with the several divisions, thereby producing large economies for the department. In a sense, Able had not been sufficiently specialized before. Because he did everything else, he could not attend to such systems changes. At that he got around to investigating the way reports were used. It soon became clear that the divisions and top management either ignored many of them because they did not deal with important variables— reject rate per departmental unit, rather than rate in terms of subsequent usage of the item, for example—or performed laborious analyses of the data on their own. Able's salesmanship for the work performed in his department was in terms of his willingness to work long hours and drive his staff; it was not in terms of determining the needs of his clients. Nor was it salesmanship conceived in terms of getting clients to adjust their needs so as to make the work of his own unit more efficient. (But then, few sales departments adopt this second conception.) When he found he was not needed for daily direction and surveillance, he turned to these more appropriate tasks—and performed them well.

With these changes, the range of stimuli the staff had to respond to was reduced. In turn, this reduced their opportunities to maximize their own interests when these conflicted with the interests of their superiors.

Did the employees feel that they were subject to greater control? Probably not. In fact, with less ambiguity, fewer exceptions that needed decisions from above, fewer occasions when they said, "Oh, well, I guess we should send it there, but who knows," they probably felt that they had more control over their jobs. Paradoxically, they did. But there was less for them to control.

Did they feel they were robots? No. They were given more discretion. How could that be when their options were more limited? They felt that they hadn't been given legitimate discretion before; now they knew when they could legitimately make a choice. Large areas of ambiguity and uncertainty didn't give them a feeling of having options, only a feeling of fear and anxiety over potential repercussions from a possible error.

Were the choices they made under the new system appropriate ones? Very likely. After all, they worked continually with the inputs, gathered experience their supervisors did not have, knew more about the problems, and probably had shortcuts they could use if they were given legitimate discretion.

The paradox of bureaucracy

So, far, we have described a bureaucracy: formalization (rules and regulations), specialization, standardization, and hierarchy. The latter three we consider to be second-order controls. We have said that the more bureaucratized an organization, the more possibilities there are for decentralization of decision making. Is there any empirical evidence to support this paradoxical assertion? Yes; several studies have now found that the greater the degree of bureaucracy, the greater the decentralization of certain kinds of decisions.

In his first study of this sort, Peter Blau was understandably surprised to find it in a variety of organizations, having believed that the narrower the span of control, the closer the supervision and the less the direction. Able at times argued that he did decentralize—he had to, with 20 people under him. It makes some sense—if you have 20 people to watch, you presumably can't watch them too closely, so in effect you have decentralized. This is the argument that James Worthy used in his study of Sears back in the early 1950s, and it has been repeated many times. But Able didn't realize that they were queuing up to ask him about small things because he had allotted no time for giving them guidance in big things.

After examining his data on state and local finance agencies, Blau made the following argument: Whenever spans of control were narrow, and the personnel were well qualified, and there were labor-saving devices such as computers to handle the routine work, these small groups probably engaged in problem-solving tasks, designing new routines, making more efficient use of the computers—and probably, we might add, generated a more efficient output. But whenever spans of control were broad, the personnel turned out not to have as many qualifications, and computers were not in evidence, employees were probably engaged in routine work with little discretion and performed an inferior service. Before the reorganization, Able appeared to operate in this second way. Thus Blau concluded, the efficient modern bureaucracy has more levels of hierarchy than the inefficient old-fashioned bureaucracy did. You decentralize, we might say, by centralizing. Other and later independent studies in England reached similar conclusions.

You may be skeptical at this point, recalling situations in which specialization meant tunnel vision, standardization involved crushing routine, rules were something to be evaded if anything was to be accomplished quickly and well, and hierarchies meant that ideas, requests, and information were delayed, distorted, disemboweled, and denigrated as they followed their tortuous route up and down the hierarchy. All too true. It happens all the time. We are frequently not very good at making bureaucracy work. But the answer is not to debureaucratize (unless the task is so nonroutine that standardization, specialization, and rules are not possible—which is true only for a relatively few exotic organizations or parts of them). Nor is the answer to revert to direct, obtrusive controls. The answer is better rules, more appropriate supervision to forestall tunnel vision, and mechanization or restructuring of tasks whenever we encounter crushing routine. When things go wrong, we blame bureaucracy instead of blaming the misuse of rules, specialization, and so on. And when things go right, we talk about good leadership, never about good bureaucratcy. But, as we shall see, good leadership may be a synonym for good bureaucracy.

Third-order controls

But we haven't quite finished with Able and his crew. Note that Baker and Charles exercised some controls over him. They couldn't use first-order or second-order controls, so what did they do? First, they changed the channels of communication, channeling information to each other rather than to Able. Having divided the functions of the unit between them, they became the coordinating mechanism, something Able had done previously. Without these inputs, Able found it hard to make the decisions he used to.

Second, in their meetings with him they were vague and slightly impatient with his questions about the work they were supervising and coordinating; instead they asked questions about coordination with other units, to which they had no formal access. (Had they unofficially communicated with these other units, bypassing the bureaucratic chain of command, Able would have legitimately fought back with everything he had.)

They did not tell Able what to do about these interfaces (it is even worse for subordinates to tell a superior what to do than for a superior to give direct orders to a subordinate); they changed the *premises* of his behavior, of his decisions. He "saw things in a different light"; he applied a different set of priorities. Of course, Able put it differently; he now "had time" to work on these problems. Baker put it differently still: Able had begun finally to fill his key role, which was not primarily that of a supervisor of a unit, but that of a manager who had to deal with other managers, to work with them in problem solving that would make his own unit more efficient.

Baker was right and so was Able. But I prefer a different emphasis still, because Able had not received a lecture on good management anymore than his available time had expanded. Someone, in this case his two subordinates, had altered the premises of his behavior. Since he was experienced and competent, he could rise to the challenge that Baker and Charles had presented to him. The premises had changed, however, not the man.

Changing the premises of decision making

What does it mean to change or control premises? A premise is a largely unexamined set of assumptions that directs our attention to some stimuli out of the welter that assail us, and evokes particular sets of responses to those stimuli. We become so accustomed to particular premises that it is hard to be conscious of them. Whenever a manager moves from one company to another or, particularly, from one industry to another, for a short time he is acutely aware of the different style, atmosphere, preoccupations, hangups, culture, or milieu of the new setting. But after a time he stops being aware of it, and only if a new employee talks about it will he recall that, oh yes, he had some of the same reactions when he first came on board. But otherwise, he lets the premises of his situation guide him unobtrusively.

A change in jobs is a fairly radical change. What were Baker and Charles doing to change Able's premises? First, they had reduced the amount of information he had in one area—the daily functioning of the unit—thus giving him fewer stimuli to respond to. Second, they had selected other stimuli to replace the ones he had formerly responded to —problems with other units. They were ambiguous or mildly impatient when he made certain inquiries—thus conveying subtle signals to him —but they were interested and enthusiastic whenever he responded to their inquiries about the activity of the other units.

There is a presumably apocryphal tale about a class of psychology students that decided to put their instructor's theories to a test. He was a pacer, walking back and forth across the room. They agreed among themselves to look interested and take notes whenever he approached the window side of the room, but to look bored whenever he came near the center of the room. Without being aware of why he did it, the instructor soon found himself pacing uncomfortably, confined within a six-foot area next to the window. In addition, there was an unanticipated consequence: The students found themselves showing more interest and taking more notes. In order to change the instructor's behavior they had to change their own behavior too!

For two subordinates to change the behavior of their superior is somewhat unusual. Superiors have vastly more resources with which to change the behavior of their subordinates. Let me at last leave the Able–Baker–Charles example and talk about much more typical ways of using third-order controls—from the top down.

Top management directs attention; it functions as a traffic cop deciding which of the stimuli that bombard us will get through. Signs, posters, speeches, memos, and performance reviews are obvious examples, telling us to pay attention to this but not to that. Their effectiveness is limited, however, because their official nature may put us on guard. Once they are heard or read, their effect decays quickly. Bluepenciling words in a memo is more effective; frowns and ـmiles in the context of ordinary interaction is even more effective; and repeated use of key words in ordinary contacts is more powerful still. The effect is unobtrusive, creating and changing assumptions through repetition.

As a result of a market or product shift, for example, the distinction between high- and low-volume customers may no longer be worth the energy it takes to make the distinction and act on it. Salesmen may be told of this in a memo, if the sales manager is that conscious of it himself, but it is hard to extinguish firmly rooted behavior through proscriptions, especially ones expressed in writing. We know that managers attend to the spoken word more than the written one—partly, I suspect, because it reveals more of the underlying premises. But if the distinction is not reinforced by the superior—that is, not responded to and not used by him—salesmen will gradually learn that the vocabulary used to make the distinction is no longer in favor. They will concentrate, it is hoped, on other distinctions.

If you want to know whether a particular policy is really important to your superiors, examine the vocabulary that surrounds it; if it is rich, full of synonyms and active verbs and new phrases, the policy is alive—and will float. If the policy is conveyed only by set phrases, with no distinctive context of supporting words—let it sink; it is not an active premise for decisions. Where snow is only an occasional inconvenience, as it is for Londoners, there is only one word for it; by contrast, when people's lives or recreation depend on it, as with Eskimos and skiers, there are many words for snow. By controlling the number of words, we can shape the premises for action.

We are only beginning to realize the extent to which natural leaders use subtle controls. The clever administrator probably intuits, without being conscious of it, that reinforcements for behavior are best intermittent, even irregular, and should be administered as soon as possible after the desirable behavior has been "emitted." We know that the goals set for subordinates should be raised in gradual increments so that success can be achieved after each increase. The leader intuits that devices that provide immediate feedback on performance are powerful correctors of behavior and potentially powerful stimulants of desired behavior.

This may be one reason why the full assembly and testing mode in job enrichment programs is so effective. Generally, the reduction of routine is given credit. Certainly it plays a role. But there is usually not much reduction in routine. The employee still does the same operations —on his part of the pacemaker or whatever—day in and day out. One would still consider as routine a job that consists of assembling and testing 20 identical units a day, five days a week, month after month. What may be different is that 20 times a day there is immediate feedback on the quality of the work—a powerful reinforcement indeed. Its effect can atrophy, of course, and readers presumably would not for a minute consider such a job acceptable for themselves or for their offspring. But it appears to have meant a lot to assembly workers.

Management by objectives, positive goal setting, and so on are occasionally successful devices in organizations. They are viewed as a means of keeping the employee's eyes on the ball and reinforcing the organization's goals. I suspect that the successful programs have a quite different impact. For many tasks there are no positive reinforcements, not even self-administered reinforcements as in full assembly and testing, because of three widespread conditions. First, expectations are unclear, because no one bothers to think about them except when crises occur, and then they are unattainable. Second, expectations are unrealistic, because they were established in some simpler time, or generated by wishful thinking, or laid out to allow for selective disciplining for the reason that no one can fulfill them successfully. Third, expectations are simply unremarked and unrewarded when they are fulfilled and unnoticed and unpunished when they aren't fulfilled.

Inquiring into this in a public agency, we were surprised to find out that most people checked the category "nothing will happen" when asked the consequence of meeting targets and of failing to meet targets!

No reinforcements, no shaping of premises, is possible in such situations. When control systems are so poorly designed, orders must replace acceptable premises for behavior. Reinforcements, especially positive ones, build a strong honeycomb of premises, of operating assumptions that direct attention and evoke the proper responses. Most of us are no better, alas, at performing these functions than we are at handling our own children—where, for example, we do not focus on the behavior that has just occurred, but generalize instead with the threatening, immobilizing statement, "You are always doing this." Premises are shaped by patient, repeated attention to the matter at hand. If it were otherwise, our children would be docile angels and our organizations obedient servants.

Third-order controls—the shaping of premises—operate at all levels, of course, but they become much more crucial at the upper levels because tasks are less routine, making rules applicable; outputs are less standardized; the raw material is less tractable and comes in odd sizes and shapes such as crises, breakdowns, expectations, pressure from banks and owners and unions, and so on. Top management hopes that those selected for upper-management positions will come equipped with the proper point of view. But something special is required at this level, and it is perhaps one of the most powerful of all control devices—indoctrination into the values of the larger systems that sustain the particular organization. A personnel test won't disclose this; an interview hardly does much better. Instead, top management relies on a host of scattered traces of the employee's life and values—social background, speech patterns, lifestyle, spouse, house, ability to drink or graciously decline, imagery and allusion in speech, and so on. Sheer technical competence is not enough, perhaps not even very important —such people can be on one's staff—whenever these general premises are at stake. Remember, the delegation of authority will be immense, surveillance minimal, directives unformulated; the premises upon which those decisions are made must be secure.

Melville Dalton in his by-now classic *Men Who Manage* captured the essence of much of what we are talking about in describing what a top officer faces in resolving a problem of organizational succession:

Nevertheless higher officers must consider the capacity of competing candidates to utilize and aid necessary cliques, control dangerous ones, etc. Too often the search for men who combine formal competence with this unspecified skill throws a top officer into despair. He is likely to put a premium on "loyalty" in terms of the candidate's seeing the job as he does. Wittingly or not, he begins to look for attitudes like his own as assuring a basis for understanding and cooperation. But he knows the difficulty of getting at the disposition and probable behavior of untried and artful people, however overwhelming their credentials. Hence at varying levels of conscious purpose, the appointing chief gropes for more valid marks of loyalty. This does not of course mean that he does not value subordinates who on occasion differ with him.

With considerable scientific support, his search moves on the assumption that those with qualities and interests like his own will think as he does. Hence in his quandary he finds it good that the prospective candidate is also Irish, went to such-and-such a school, came from a "good" family (socioeconomically similar to his own), and has civic activities and recreational tastes similar to his own. These likenesses would naturally not be advanced as proofs of fitness in general discussion, but tacitly or unconsciously they predispose judges to see the prospect as one with a "good job outlook" and readiness to act jointly on critical issues. Moved by these pleasing characteristics, the desperate personnel assessor may easily overlook other qualities.

Conclusion

Perhaps now we can see why it is only when premises can be controlled that extensive decentralization or delegation can take place. But if they are controlled, it should *take* place. Centralization and decentralization should go hand in hand. The problem with most organizations, I believe, is that at every level management is not aware of the potential it possesses for extensive control, so it is afraid to delegate. But the very failure to delegate erodes that control. Whenever the rules are vague, standardization limited, and specialization undeveloped, search behavior cannot be channeled. For a small number of nonroutine tasks this is unfortunately necessary, and the emphasis upon third-order controls is correspondingly greater; inefficiencies and redundancies occasioned by the absence of many first- and second-order controls are expensive, but recoverable in the price of the product if the organization is successful. Whenever premises are not carefully established, third- and even second-order controls are minimized. Excessive use of rules and direct orders alienates, limiting the chances of effective second- and third-order controls.

My message to managers is to delegate; *you have far more control than you think*. The efficient organization is both centralized and decentralized. This is the assumption, largely unrecognized and unexamined, that underlies much of the work in participative management, sensitivity training, and related techniques that serve to make the manager aware of the amount of power he does have, as well as how he misuses it. This in turn—a benevolent development—helps to make him less fearful of delegation.

Selected bibliography

The notion of premise control in organizations was first raised by James March and Herbert Simon in the second half of their classic, *Organizations* (John Wiley, 1958). I would modestly recommend the discussion of the book in my own volume, *Complex Organizations: A Critical Essay* (Scott, Foresman, 1972, pp. 145–158). Further application of the notion and especially an early statement of the paradox of centralization with decentralization, using Alfred Sloan's revolutionary work at General Motors as the example, appears in a section of my article "Is Business Really Changing?" *Organizational Dynamics* (Summer 1974, pp. 31–44).

The work of Peter Blau is most accessible in his early articles on the subject rather than in his massive tome. See Peter Blau, et al., "The Structure of Small Bureaucracies," *American Sociological Review* (April 1966, pp. 179–192); and "The Hierarchy of Authority in Organizations," *American Journal of Sociology* (January 1968, pp. 453–467). The tome is by Peter Blau and Richard Schoenherr, *The Structure of Organizations* (Basic Books, 1971). The English studies in this area, directed by Derek Pugh, are accurately summarized in John Child's "Predicting and Understanding Organization Structure," *Administrative Science Quarterly* (June 1973, pp. 168–185).

A good discussion of reinforcement theory and job enrichment is Curt Tausky and E. Lauck Parke's "Job Enrichment, Need Theory and Reinforcement Theory," in Robert Dubin, ed., *The Handbook of Work, Organization and Society* (Rand McNally, 1976, pp. 531–566). For a shorter version see their article, "The Mythology of Job Enrichment: Self-Actualization Revisited," in *Personnel* (September-October 1975, pp. 12–22).

Managerial Work:
Analysis from Observation
Henry Mintzberg

What do managers do? Ask this question and you will likely be told that managers plan, organize, coordinate, and control. Since Henri Fayol (1) first proposed these words in 1916, they have dominated the vocabulary of maangement. (See, for example, Drucker [2], Gulick [3] and Kelly [4]). How valuable are they in describing managerial work? Consider one morning's work of the president of a large organization:

> As he enters his office at 8:23, the manager's secretary motions for him to pick up the telephone. "Jerry, there was a bad fire in the plant last night, about $30,000 damage. We should be back in operation by Wednesday. Thought you should know."
>
> At 8:45, a Mr. Jamison is ushered into the manager's office. They discuss Mr. Jamison's retirement plans and his cottage in New Hampshire. Then the manager presents a plaque to him commemorating his thirty-two years with the organization.
>
> Mail processing follows: An innocent-looking letter, signed by a Detroit lawyer, reads: "A group of us in Detroit has decided not to buy any of your products because you used that antiflag, antiAmerican pinko, Bill Lindell, on your Thursday night TV show." The manager dictates a restrained reply.
>
> The 10:00 meeting is scheduled by a professional staffer. He claims that his superior, a high-ranking vice-president of the organization, mistreats his staff, and that if the man is not fired, they will all walk out. As soon as the meeting ends, the manager rearranges his schedule to investigate the claim and to react to this crisis.

Which of these activities may be called planning, and which may be called organizing, coordinating, and controlling? Indeed, what do words such as "coordinating" and "planning" mean in the context of

Reprinted by permission from Henry Mintzberg, "Managerial Work: Analysis from Observation," *Management Science,* October 1971. B97–B110. Copyright 1971 The Institute of Management Sciences.

real activity? In fact, these four words do not describe the actual work of managers at all; they describe certain vague objectives of managerial work." They are just ways of indicating what we need to explain" (5, p. 537).

Other approaches to the study of managerial work have developed, one dealing with managerial decision-making and policy-making processes, another with the manager's interpersonal activities. (See, for example, Braybrooke and Lindblom [6] and Gibb [7]). And some empirical researchers, using the "diary" method, have studied, what might be called, managerial "media"—by what means, with whom, how long, and where managers spend their time.* But in no part of this literature is the actual content of managerial work systematically and meaningfully described.† Thus, the question posed at the start— what do managers do?—remains essentially unanswered in the literature of management.

This is indeed an odd situation. We claim to teach management in schools of both business and public administration; we undertake major research programs in management; we find a growing segment of the management science community concerned with the problems of senior management. Most of these people—the planners, information and control theorists, systems analysts, etc.—are attempting to analyze and change working habits that they themselves do not understand. Thus, at a conference called at M.I.T. to assess the impact of the computer on the manager; and attended by a number of America's foremost management scientists, a participant found it necessary to comment after lengthy discussion (14, p. 198):

> I'd like to return to an earlier point. It seems to me that until we get into the question of what the top manager does or what the functions are that define the top management job, we're not going to get out of the kind of difficulty that keeps cropping up. What I'm really doing is leading up to my earlier question which no one really answered. And that is: Is it possible to arrive at a specification of what constitutes the job of a top manager?

His question was not answered.

*Carlson (8) carried out the classic study just after World War II. He asked nine Swedish managing directors to record on diary pads details of each activity in which they engaged. His method was used by a group of other researchers, many of them working in the United Kingdom. (See Burns (9, 10), Horne and Lupton (11), and Stewart (12).

†One major project, involving numerous publications, took place at Ohio State University and spanned three decades. Some of the vocabulary used followed Fayol. The results have generated little interest in this area. (See, for example, Hemphill (13).

Research study on managerial work

In late 1966, I began research on this question, seeking to replace Fayol's words by a set that would more accurately describe what managers do. In essence, I sought to develop by the process of induction a statement of managerial work that would have empirical validity. Using a method called "structured observation," I observed for one-week periods the chief executves of five medium to large organizations (a consulting firm, a school system, a technology firm, a consumer goods manufacturer, and a hospital).

Structured as well as unstructured (i.e., anecdotal) data were collected in three "records." In the *chronology record,* activity patterns throughout the working day were recorded. In the *mail record,* for each of 890 pieces of mail processed during the five weeks, the purpose, format, and sender, the attention it received, and the action it elicited were recorded. And, recorded in the *contact record,* for each of 368 verbal interactions, were the purpose, the medium (telephone call, scheduled or unscheduled meeting, tour), the participants, the form of initiation, and the location. It should be noted that all categorizing was done during and after observation so as to ensure that the categories reflected only the work under observation. Mintzberg's study (15) contains a fuller description of this methodology and a tabulation of the results of the study.

Two sets of conclusions are presented below. The first deals with certain characteristics of managerial work, as they appeared from analysis of the numerical data (e.g., How much time is spent with peers? What is the average duration of meetings? What proportion of contacts are initiated by the manager himself?). The second describes the basic content of managerial work in terms of ten roles. This description derives from an analysis of the data on the recorded *purpose* of each contact and piece of mail.

The liberty is taken of referring to these findings as descriptive of managerial, as opposed to chief executive, work. This is done because many of the findings are supported by studies of other types of managers. Specifically, most of the conclusions on work characteristics are to be found in the combined results of a group of studies of foremen (16, 17), middle managers (9–12), and chief executives (8). And although there is little useful material on managerial roles, three studies do provide some evidence of the applicability of the role set. Most important, Sayles' empirical study of production managers (18) suggests that at least five of the ten roles are performed at the lower end of the managerial hierarchy. And some further evidence is provided by comments in Whyte's study of leadership in a street gang (19) and Neustadt's study of three U.S. presidents (20). (Reference is made to these findings where appropriate.) Thus, although most of the illustrations are drawn from my study of chief executives, there is some justification in asking the reader to consider when he sees the terms "manager" and his "organization" not only "presidents" and their "companies," but also "foremen" and their "shops," "directors" and their "branches," "vice-presidents" and their "divisions." The term *manager* shall be used with reference to all those people in charge of formal organizations or their subunits.

Some characteristics of managerial work

Six sets of characteristics of managerial work derive from analysis of the data of this study. Each has a significant bearing on the manager's ability to administer a complex organization.

Characteristic 1. The manager performs a great quantity or work at an unrelenting pace

Despite a semblance of normal working hours, in truth managerial work appears to be very taxing. The five men in this study processed an average of thirty-six pieces of mail each day, participated in eight meetings (half of which were scheduled), engaged in five telephone calls, and took one tour. In his study of foremen, Guest (16) found that the number of activities per day averaged 583, with no real break in the pace.

Free time appears to be very rare. If by chance a manager has caught up with the mail, satisfied the callers, dealt with all the disturbances, and avoided scheduled meetings, a subordinate will likely show up to usurp the available time. It seems that the manager cannot expect to have much time for leisurely reflection during office hours. During "off" hours, our chief executives spent much time on work-related reading. High-level managers appear to be able to escape neither from an environment which recognizes the power and status of their positions nor from their own minds which have been trained to search continually for new information.

Characteristic 2. Managerial activity is characterized by variety, fragmentation, and brevity

There seems to be no pattern to managerial activity. Rather, variety and fragmentation appear to be characteristic, as successive activities deal with issues that differ greatly both in type and in content. In effect the manager must be prepared to shift moods quickly and frequently.

A typical chief executive day may begin with a telephone call from a director who asks a favor (a "status request"); then a subordinate calls to tell of a strike at one of the facilities (fast movement of information, termed "instant communication"); this is followed by a relaxed scheduled event at which the manager speaks to a group of visiting dignitaries (ceremony); the manager returns to find a message from a major customer who is demanding the renegotiation of a contract (pressure); and so on. Throughout the day, the managers of our study encountered this great variety of activity. Most surprisingly, the significant activities were interspersed with the trivial in no particular pattern.

Furthermore, these managerial activities were characterized by their brevity. Half of all the activities studied lasted less than nine minutes and only ten percent exceeded one hour. Guest's foremen averaged 48 seconds per activity, and Carlson (8) stressed that his chief executives were unable to work without frequent interruption.

In my own study of chief executives, I felt that the managers demonstrated a preference for tasks of short duration and encouraged interruption. Perhaps the manager becomes accustomed to variety, or perhaps the flow of "instant communication" cannot be delayed. A more plausible explanation might be that the manager becomes conditioned by his workload. He develops a sensitive appreciation for the opportunity cost of his own time. Also, he is aware of the ever-present assortment of obligations associated with his job—accumulations of mail that cannot be delayed, the callers that must be attended to, the meetings that require his participation. In oher words, no matter what he is doing, the manager is plagued by what he must do and what he might do. Thus, the manager is forced to treat issues in an abrupt and superficial way.

Characteristic 3. Managers prefer issues that are current, specific and ad hoc

Ad hoc operating reports received more attention than did routine ones; current, uncertain information—gossip, speculation, hearsay—which flows quickly was preferred to historical, certain information; "instant communication" received first consideration; few contacts were held on a routine or "clocked" basis; almost all contacts concerned well-defined issues. The managerial environment is clearly one of stimulus-response. It breeds not reflective planners, but adaptable information manipulators who prefer the live, concrete situation, men who demonstrate a marked action orientation.

Characteristic 4. The manager sits between his organization and a network of contacts

In virtually every empirical study of managerial time allocation, it was reported that managers spent a surprisingly large amount of time in horizontal or lateral (nonline) communication. It is clear from this study and from that of Sayles (18) that the manager is surrounded by a diverse and complex web of contacts which serves as his self-designed external information system. Included in this web can be clients, associates, and suppliers, outside staff experts, peers (managers of related or similar organizations), trade organizations, government officials, independents (those with no relevant organizational affiliation), and directors or superiors. (Among these, directors in this study and superiors in other studies did *not* stand out as particularly active individuals.)

The managers in this study received far more information than they emitted, much of it coming from contacts, and more from subordinates who acted as filters. Figuratively, the manager appears as the neck of an hour-glass, sifting information into his own organization from its environment.

Characteristic 5. The manager demonstrates a strong preference for the verbal media

The manager has five media at his command—mail (documented), telephone (purely verbal), unscheduled meeting (informal face-to-face), scheduled meeting (formal face-to-face), and tour (observational). Along with all the other empirical studies of work characteristics, I found a strong predominance of verbal forms of communication.

Mail

By all indications, managers dislike the documented form of communication. In this study, they gave cursory attention to such items as operating reports and periodicals. It was estimated that only thirteen percent of the input mail was of specific and immediate use to the managers. Much of the rest dealt with formalities and provided general reference data. The managers studied initiated very little mail, only twenty-five pieces in the five weeks. The rest of the outgoing mail was sent in reaction to mail received—a reply to a request, an acknowledgment, some information forwarded to a part of the organization. The managers appeared to dislike this form of communication, perhaps because the mail is a relatively slow and tedious medium to use.

Telephone and unscheduled meetings

The less formal means of verbal communication—the telephone, a purely verbal form, and the unscheduled meeting, a face-to-face form—were used frequently (two-thirds of the contacts in the study) but for brief encounters (average duration of six and twelve minutes, respectively). They were used primarily to deliver requests and to transmit pressing information to those outsiders and subordinates who had informal relationships with the manager.

Scheduled meetings

These tended to be of long duration, averaging sixty-eight minutes in this study, and absorbing over half the managers' time. Such meetings provided the managers with their main opportunities to interact with large groups and to leave the confines of their own offices. Scheduled meetings were used when the participants were unfamiliar to the manager (e.g., students who request that he speak at a university), when a large quantity of information had to be transmitted (e.g., presentation of a report), when ceremony had to take place, and when complex strategy-making or negotiation had to be undertaken. An important feature of the scheduled meeting was the incidental, but by no means irrelevant, information that flowed at the start and end of such meetings.

Tours

Although the walking tour would appear to be a powerful tool for gaining information in an informal way, in this study tours accounted for only three percent of the manager's time.

In general, it can be concluded that the manager uses each medium for particular purposes. Nevertheless, where possible, he appears to gravitate to verbal media since these provide greater flexibility, require less effort, and bring faster response. It should be noted here that the manager does not leave the telephone or the meeting to get back to work. Rather, communication is his work, and these media are his tools. The operating work of the organization—producing a product, doing research, purchasing a part—appears to be undertaken infrequently by the senior manager. The manager's productive output must be measured in terms of information, a great part of which is transmitted verbally.

Characteristic 6. Despite the preponderance of obligations, the manager appears to be able to control his own affairs

Carlson suggested in his study of Swedish chief executives that these men were puppets, with little control over their own affairs. A cursory examination of our data indicates that this is true. Our managers were responsible for the initiation of only thirty-two percent of their verbale contacts and a smaller proportion of their mail. Activities were also classified as to the nature of the managers' participation, and the active ones were outnumbered by the passive ones (e.g., making requests vs. receiving requests). On the surface, the manager is indeed a puppet, answering requests in the mail, returning telephone calls, attending meetings initiated by others, yielding to subordinates' requests for time, reacting to crises.

However, such a view is misleading. There is evidence that the senior manager can exert control over his own affairs in two significant ways: (1) It is he who defines many of his own long-term commitments, by developing appropriate information channels which later feed him information, by initiating projects which later demand his time, by joining committees or outside boards which provide contacts in return for his services, and so on (2) The manager can exploit situations that appear as obligations. He can lobby at ceremonial speeches; he can impose his values on his organization when his authorization is requested; he can motivate his subordinates whenever he interacts with them; he can use the crisis situation as an opportunity to innovate.

Perhaps these are two points that help distinguish successful and unsuccessful managers. All managers appear to be puppets. Some decide who will pull the strings and how, and they then take advantage of each move that they are forced to make. Others, unable to exploit this high-tension environment, are swallowed up by this most demanding of jobs.

The manager's work roles

In describing the essential content of managerial work, one should aim to model managerial actvity, that is, to describe it as a set of programs. But an undertaking as complex as this must be preceded by the development of a useful typological description of managerial work. In other words, we must first understand the distinct components of managerial work. At the present time we do not.

In this study, 890 pieces of mail and 368 verbal contacts were categorized as to purpose. The incoming mail was found to carry acknowledgments, requests and solicitations of various kinds, reference data, news, analytical reports, reports on events and on operations, advice on various situations, and statements of problems, pressures, and ideas. In reacting to mail, the managers acknowledged some, replied to the requests (e.g., by sending information), and forwarded much to subordinates (usually for their information). Verbal contacts involved a variety of purposes. In 15% of them activities were scheduled, in 6% ceremonial events took place, and a few involved external board work. About 34% involved requests of various kinds, some insignificant, some for information, some for authorization of proposed actions. Another 36% essentially involved the flow of information to and from the manager, while the remainder dealt specifically with issues of strategy and with negotiations. (For details, see Mintzberg [15].)

In this study, each piece of mail and verbal contact categorized in this way was subjected to one question: Why did the manager do this? The answers were collected and grouped and regrouped in various ways (over the course of three years) until a typology emerged that was felt to be satisfactory. While an example, presented below, will partially explain this process to the reader, it must be remembered that (in the words of Bronowski (21, p. 62): "Every induction is a speculation and it guesses at a unity which the facts present but do not strictly imply."

Consider the following sequence of two episodes: A chief executive attends a meeting of an external board on which he sits. Upon his return to his organization, he immediately goes to the office of a subordinate, tells of a conversation he had with a fellow board member, and concludes with the statement: "It looks like we shall get the contract."

The purposes of these two contacts are clear—to attend an external board meeting, and to give current information (instant communication) to a subordinate. But why did the manager attend the meeting? Indeed, why does he belong to the board? And why did he give this particular information to his subordinate?

Basing analysis on this incident, one can argue as follows: The manager belongs to the board in part so that he can be exposed to special information which is of use to his organization. The subordinate needs the information but has not the status which would give him access to it. The chief executive does. Board memberships bring chief executives in contact with one another for the purpose of trading information.

Two aspects of managerial work emerge from this brief analysis. The manager serves in a "liaison" capacity because of the status of his office, and what he learns here enables him to act as "disseminator" of information into his organization. We refer to these as *roles*—organized sets of behaviors belonging to identifiable offices or positions (22). Ten roles were chosen to capture all the activities observed during this study.

All activities were found to involve one or more of three basic behaviors—interpersonal contact, the processing of information, and the making of decisions. As a result, our ten roles are divided into three corresponding groups. Three roles—labelled *figurehead, liaison,* and *leader*—deal with behavior that is essentially interpersonal in nature. Three others—*nerve center, disseminator,* and *spokesman*—deal with information-processing activities performed by the manager. And the remaining four—*entrepreneur, disturbance handler, resource allocator,* and *negotiator*—cover the decision-making activities of the manager. We describe each of these roles in turn, asking the reader to note that they form a *gestalt,* a unified whole whose parts cannot be considered in isolation.

The interpersonal roles

Three roles relate to the manager's behavior that focuses on interpersonal contact. These roles derive directly from the authority and status associated with holding managerial office.

Figurehead

As legal authority in his organization, the manager is a symbol, obliged to perform a number of duties. He must preside at ceremonial events, sign legal documents, receive visitors, make himself available to many of those who feel, in the words of one of the men studied, "that the only way to get something done is to get to the top." There is evidence that this role applies at other levels as well. Davis cites the case of the field sales manager who must deal with those customers who believe that their accounts deserve his attention.

Leader

Leadership is the most widely recognized of managerial roles. It describes the manager's relationship with his subordinates—his attempts to motivate them and his development of the milieu in which they work. Leadership actions pervade all activity—in contrast to most roles, it is possible to designate only a few activities as dealing exclusively with leadership (these mostly related to staffing duties). Each time a manager encourages a subordinate, or meddles in his affairs, or replies to one of his requests, he is playing the *leader* role. Subordinates seek out and react to these leadership clues, and, as a result, they impart significant power to the manager.

Liaison

As noted earlier, the empirical studies have emphasized the importance of laterial or horizontal communication in the work of managers at all levels. It is clear from our study that this is explained largely in terms of the *liaison* role. The manager establishes his network of contacts essentially to bring information and favors to his organization. As Sayles notes in his study of production supervisors (18, p. 258), "The one enduring objective [of the manager] is the effort to build and maintain a predictable, reciprocating system of relationships. . . ."

Making use of his status, the manager interacts with a variety of peers and other people outside his organization. He provides time, information, and favors in return for the same from others. Foremen deal with staff groups and other foremen; chief executives join boards of directors, and maintain extensive networks of individual relationships. Neustadt notes this behavior in analyzing the work of President Roosevelt (20, p. 150):

> His personal sources were the product of a sociability and curiosity that reached back to the other Roosevelt's time. He had an enormous acquaintance in various phases of national life and at various levels

of government; he also had his wife and her variety of contacts. He extended his acquaintanceships abroad; in the war years Winston Churchill, among others, became a "personal source." Roosevelt quite deliberately exploited these relationships and mixed them up to widen his own range of information. He changed his sources as his interests changed, but no one who had ever interested him was quite forgotten or immune to sudden use.

The informational roles

A second set of managerial activities relates primarily to the processing of information. Together they suggest three significant managerial roles, one describing the manager as a focal point for a certain kind of organizational information, the other two describing relatively simple transmission of this information.

Nerve Center

There is indication, both from this study and from those by Neustadt and Whyte, that the manager serves as the focal point in his organization for the movement of nonroutine information. Homans, who analyzed Whyte's study, draws the following conclusions (19, p. 187):

> Since interaction flowed toward [the leaders], they were better informed about the problems and desires of group members than were any of the followers and therefore better able to decide on an appropriate course of action. Since they were in close touch with other gang leaders, they were also better informed than their followers about conditions in Cornerville at large. Moreover, in their positions at the focus of the chains of interaction, they were better able than any follower to pass on to the group decisions that had been reached.

The term *nerve center* is chosen to encompass those many activities in which the manager receives information.

Within his own organization, the manager has legal authority that formally connects him—and only him—to *every* member. Hence, the manager emerges as *nerve center* of internal information. He may not know as much about any one function as the subordinate who specializes in it, but he comes to know more about his total organization than any other member. He is the information generalist. Furthermore, because of the manager's status and its manifestation in the *liaison* role, the manager gains unique access to a variety of knowledgeable outsiders including peers who are themselves *nerve centers* of their own organizations. Hence, the manager emerges as his organization's *nerve center* of external information as well.

As noted earlier, the manager's nerve center information is of a special kind. He appears to find it most important to get his information quickly and informally. As a result, he will not hesitate to bypass formal information channels to get it, and he is prepared to deal with a large amount of gossip, hearsay, and opinion which has not yet become substantiated fact.

Disseminator

Much of the manager's information must be transmitted to subordinates. Some of this is of a *factual* nature, received from outside the organization or from other subordinates. And some is of a *value* nature. Here, the manager acts as the mechanism by which organizational influencers (owners, governments, employee groups, the general public, etc., or simply the "boss") make their preferences known to the organization. It is the manager's duty to integrate these value positions, and to express general organizational preferences as a guide to decision made by subordinates. One of the men studied commented: "One of the principal functions of this position is to integrate the hospital interests with the public interests." Papandreou describes his duty in a paper published in 1952, referring to management as the "peak coordinator" (24).

Spokesman

In his *spokesman* role, the manager is obliged to transmit his information to outsiders. He informs influencers and other interested parties about his organization's performance, its policies, and its plans. Furthermore, he is expected to serve outside his organization as an expert in its industry. Hospital administrators are expected to spend some time serving outside as public experts on health, and corporation presidents, perhaps as chamber of commerce executives.

The decisional roles

The manager's legal authority requires that he assume responsibility for all of his organization's important actions. The *nerve center* role suggests that only he can fully understand complex decisions, particularly those involving difficult value trade-offs. As a result, the manager emerges as the key figure in the making and interrelating of all significant decisions in his organization, a process that can be referred to as *strategy-making*. Four roles describe the manager's control over the strategy-making system in his organization.

Entrepreneur

The *entrepreneur* role describes the manager as initiator and designer of much of the controlled change in his organization. The manager looks for opportunities and potential problems which may cause him to initiate action. Action takes the form of *improvement projects*—the marketing of a new product, the strengthening of a weak department, the purchasing of new equipment, the reorganization of formal structure, and so on.

The manager can involve himself in each improvement project in one of three ways: (1) He may *delegate* all responsibility for its design and approval, implicitly retaining the right to replace that subordinate who takes charge of it. (2) He may delegate the design work to a subordinate, but retain the right to *approve* it before implementation. (3) He may actively *supervise* the design work himself.

Improvement projects exhibit a number of interesting characteristics. They appear to involve a number of subdecisions, consciously sequenced over long periods of time and separated by delays of various kinds. Furthermore, the manager appears to supervise a great many of these at any one time—perhaps fifty to one hundred in the case of chief executives. In fact, in his handling of improvement projects, the manager may be likened to a juggler. At any one point, he maintains a number of balls in the air. Periodically, one comes down, receives a short burst of energy, and goes up again. Meanwhile, an inventory of new balls waits on the sidelines and, at random intervals, old balls are discarded and new ones added. Braybrooke and Lindblom (6) and Marples (25) touch on these aspects of strategy-making, the former stressing the disjointed and incremental nature of the decisions, and the latter depicting the sequential episodes in terms of a stranded rope made up of fibers of different lengths, each of which surfaces periodically.

Disturbance Handler

While the *entrepreneur* role focuses on voluntary change, the *disturbance handler* role deals with corrections which the manager is forced to make. We may describe this role as follows: The organization consists basically of specialist operating programs. From time to time, it experiences a stimulus that cannot be handled routinely, either because an operating program has broken down or because the stimulus is new and it is not clear which operating program should handle it. These situations constitute disturbances. As generalist, the manager is obliged to assume responsibility for dealing with the stimulus. Thus, the handling of disturbances is an essential duty of the manager.

There is clear evidence for this role both in our study of chief executives and in Sayles' study of production supervisors (18, p. 162):

The achievement of this stability, which is the manager's objective, is a never-to-be-attained ideal. He is like a symphony orchestra conductor, endeavoring to maintain a melodious performance in which contributions of the various instruments are coordinated and sequenced, patterned and paced, while the orchestra members are having various personal difficulties, stagehands are moving music stands, alternating excessive heat and cold are creating audience and instrument problems, and the sponsor of the concert is insisting on irrational changes in the program.

Sayles goes further to point out the very important balance that the manager must maintain between change and stability. To Sayles, the manager seeks "a dynamic type of stability" (p. 162). Most disturbances elicit short-term adjustments which bring back equilibrium; persistent ones require the introduction of long-term structural change.

Resource Allocator

The manager maintains ultimate authority over his organization's strategy-making system by controlling the allocation of its resources. By deciding who will get what (and who will do what), the manager directs the course of his organization. He does this in three ways:

(1) *In scheduling his own time,* the manager allocates his most precious resource and thereby determines organizational priorities. Issues that receive low priority do not reach the *nerve center* of the organization and are blocked for want of resources.

(2) In designing the organizational structure and in carrying out many improvement projects, the manager *programs the work of his subordinates.* In other words, he allocates their time by deciding what will be done and who will do it.

(3) Most significantly, the manager maintains control over resource allocation by the requirement that he *authorize all significant decisions* before they are implemented. By retaining this power, the manager ensures that different decisions are interrelated—that conflicts are avoided, that resource constraints are respected, and that decisions complement one another.

Decisions appear to be authorized in one of two ways. Where the costs and benefits of a proposal can be quantified, where it is competing for specified resources with other known proposals, and where it can wait for a certain time of year, approval for a proposal is sought in the context of a formal *budgeting* procedure. But these conditions are most often not met—timing may be crucial, nonmonetary costs may predominate, and so on. In these cases, approval is sought in terms of an *ad hoc request for authorization.* Subordinate and manager meet (perhaps informally) to discuss one proposal alone.

Authorization choices are enormously complex ones for the manager. A myriad of factors must be considered (resource constraints, influencer preferences, consistency with other decisions, feasibility, payoff, timing, subordinate feeling, etc.). But the fact that the manager is authorizing the decision rather than supervising its design suggests that he has little time to give to it. To alleviate this difficulty, it appears that managers use special kinds of *models* and *plans* in their decision-making. These exist only in their minds and are loose, but they serve to guide behaviors. Models may answer questions such as, "Does this proposal make sense in terms of the trends that I see in tariff legislation?" or "Will the EDP department be able to get along with marketing on this?" Plans exist in the sense that, on questioning, managers reveal images (in terms of proposed improvement projects) of where they would like their organizations to go: "Well, once I get these foreign operations fully developed, I would like to begin to look into a reorganization," said one subject of this study.

Negotiator

The final role describes the manager as participant in negotiation activity. To some students of the management process (2, p. 343), this is not truly part of the job of managing. But such distinctions are arbitrary. Negotiation is an integral part of managerial work, as this study notes for chief executives and, as that of Sayles made very clear for production supervisors (18, p. 131): "Sophisticated managers place great stress on negotiations as a way of life. They negotiate with groups who are setting standards for their work, who are performing support activity for them, and to whom they wish to 'sell' their services."

The manager must participate in important negotiation sessions because he is his organization's legal authority, its *spokesman,* and its *resource allocator.* Negotiation is resource trading in real time. If the resource commitments are to be large, the legal authority must be present.

These ten roles suggest that the manager of an organization bears a great burden of responsibility. He must oversee his organization's status system; he must serve as a crucial informational link between it and its environment; he must interpret and reflect its basic values; he must maintain the stability of its operations, and he must adapt it in a controlled and balanced way to a changing environment.

Management as a profession and as a science

Is management a profession? To the extent that different managers perform one set of basic roles, management satisfies one criterion for becoming a profession. But a profession must require, in the words of the *Random House Dictionary,* knowledge of some department of learning or science." Which of the ten roles now requires specialized learning? Indeed, what school of business or public administration teaches its students how to disseminate information, allocate resources, perform as figurehead, make contacts, or handle disturbances? We simply know very little about teaching these things. The reason is that we have never tried to document and describe in a meaningful way the procedures (or programs) that managers use.

The evidence of this research suggests that there is as yet no science in managerial work—that managers do not work according to procedures that have been prescribed by scientific analysis. Indeed, except for his use of the telephone, the airplane, and the dictating machine, it would appear that the manager of today is indistinguishable from his predecessors. He may seek different information, but he gets much of it in the same way—from word-of-mouth. He may take decisions dealing with modern technology but he uses the same intuitive (that is, nonexplicit) procedures in making them. Even the computer, which has had such a great impact on other kinds of organizational work, has apparently done little to alter the working methods of the general manager.

How do we develop a scientific base to understand the work of the manager? The description of roles is a first and necessary step. But tighter forms of research are necessary. Specifically, we must attempt to model managerial work—to describe it as a system of programs. First, it will be necessary to decide what programs managers actually use. Among a great number of programs in the manager's repertoire, we might expect to find a time-scheduling program, an information-disseminating program, and a disturbance-handling program. Then, researchers will have to devote a considerable amount of effort to studying and accurately describing the content of each of these programs—the information and heuristics used. Finally, it will be necessary to describe the interrelationships among all of these programs so that they may be combined into an integrated descriptive model of managerial work.

When the management scientist begins to understand the programs that managers use, he can begin to design meaningful systems and provide help for the manager. He may ask: Which managerial activities can be fully reprogrammed (i.e., automated)? Which cannot be reprogrammed because they require human responses? Which can be partially reprogrammed to operate in a man-machine system? Perhaps scheduling, information-collecting, and resource-allocating activities lend themselves to varying degrees of reprogramming. Management will emerge as a science to the extent that such efforts are successful.

Improving the manager's effectiveness

Fayol's fifty-year-old description of managerial work is no longer of use to us. And we shall not disentangle the complexity of managerial work if we insist on viewing the manager simply as a decision-maker or simply as a motivator of subordinates. In fact, we are unlikely to over-estimate the complexity of the manager's work, and we shall make little headway if we take overly simple or narrow points of view in our research.

A major problem faces today's manager. Despite the growing size of modern organizations and the growing complexity of their problems (particularly those in the public sector), the manager can expect little help. He must design his own information system, and he must take full charge of his organization's strategy-making system. Furthermore, the manager faces what might be called the *dilemma of delegation*. He has unique access to much important information but he lacks a formal means of disseminating it. As much of it is verbal, he cannot spread it around in an efficient manner. How can he delegate a task with confi-dence when he has neither the time nor the means to send the neces-sary information along with it?

Thus, the manager is usually forced to carry a great burden of re-sponsibility in his organization. As organizations become increasingly large and complex, this burden increases. Unfortunately, the man can-not significantly increase his available time or significantly improve his abilities to manage. Hence, in the large, complex bureaucracy, the top manager's time assumes an enormous opportunity cost and he faces the real danger of becoming a major obstruction in the flow of decisions and information.

Because of this, as we have seen, managerial work assumes a num-ber of distinctive characteristics. The quantity of work is great; the pace is unrelenting; there is great variety, fragmentation, and brevity in the work activities; the manager must concentrate on issues that are current, specific, and ad hoc, and to do so, he finds that he must rely on verbal forms of communications. Yet it is on this man that the burden lies for designing and operating strategy-making and information-processing systems that are to solve his organization's (and society's) problems.

The manager can do something to alleviate these problems. He can learn more about his own roles in his organization, and he can use this information to schedule his time in a more efficient manner. He can recognize that only he has much of the information needed by his or-ganization. Then, he can seek to find better means of disseminating it into the organization. Finally, he can turn to the skills of his management scientists to help reduce his workload and to improve his ability to make decisions.

The management scientist can learn to help the manager to the extent he can develop an understanding of the manager's work and the manager's information. To date, strategic planners, operations researchers, and information system designers have provided little help for the senior manager. They simply have had no framework available by which to understand the work of the men who employed them, and they have had poor access to the information which has never been documented. It is folly to believe that a man with poor access to the organization's true *nerve center* can design a formal management information system. Similarly, how can the long-range planner, a man usually uninformed about many of the *current* events that take place in and around his organization, design meaningful strategic plans? For good reason, the literature documents many manager complaints of naïve planning and many planner complaints of disinterested managers. In my view, our lack of understanding of managerial work has been the greatest block to the progress of management science.

The ultimate solution to the problem—to the overburdened manager seeking meaningful help—must derive from research. We must observe, describe, and understand the real work of managing; then and only then shall we significantly improve it.

References

1. Fayol, Henri. *Administration industrielle et générale,* Dunods, Paris, 1950 (first published 1916).
2. Drucker, Peter F. *The Practice of Management,* Harper and Row, New York, 1954.
3. Gulick, Luther H. "Notes on the Theory of Organization," in Luther Gulick and Lyndall Urwick (eds.), *Paper on the Science of Administration,* Columbia University Press, New York, 1937.
4. Mackenzie, R. Alex. "The Management Process in 3D," *Harvard Business Review* (November-December 1969), pp. 80–87.
5. Braybrooke, David. "The Mystery of Executive Success Reexamined," *Administrative Science Quarterly,* Vol. 8 (1964), pp. 533–60.
6. Braybrooke, David, and Lindblom, Charles E. *A Strategy of Decision,* Free Press, New York, 1963.
7. Gibb, Cecil A. "Leadership," chapter 31 in Gardner Lindzey and Elliot A. Aronson (eds.), *The Handbook of Social Psychology,* Vol. 4, second edition, Addison-Wesley, Reading, Mass., 1969.
8. Carlson, Sune. *Executive Behavior,* Strömbergs, Stockholm, 1951.

9. Burns, Tom. "The Directions of Activity and Communications in a Departmental Executive Group," *Human Relations,* Vol. 7 (1954), pp. 73–97.

10. Burns, Tom. "Management in Action," *Operational Research Quarterly,* Vol. 8 (1957), pp. 45–60.

11. Horne, J. H., and Lupton, Tom. "The Work Activities of Middle Managers: An Exploratory Study," *The Journal of Management Studies,* Vol. 2 (1965), pp. 14–33.

12. Stewart, Rosemary. *Managers and Their Jobs,* Macmillan, London, 1967.

13. Hemphill, John K. *Dimensions of Executive Positions,* Bureau of Business Research Monograph Number 98, Ohio State University, Columbus, 1960.

14. Myers, Charles A. (Ed.). *The Impact of Computers on Management,* MIT Press, Cambridge, Mass., 1967.

15. Mintzberg, Henry. "Structured Observation as a Method to Study Managerial Work," *The Journal of Management Studies,* Vol. 7 (1970), pp. 87–104.

16. Guest, Robert H. "Of Time and the Foreman," *Personnel,* Vol. 32 (1955–56), pp. 478–86.

17. Kelly, Joe. "The Study of Executive Behavior by Activity Sampling," *Human Relations,* Vol. 17 (1964), pp. 277–87.

18. Sayles, Leonard R. *Manageral Behavior: Administration in Complex Enterprises,* McGraw-Hill, New York, 1964.

19. Whyte, William F. *Street Corner Society,* second edition, University of Chicago Press, 1955.

20. Neustadt, Richard E. *Presidential Power: The Politics of Leadership,* The New American Library, New York, 1964.

21. Bronowski, J. "The Creative Process," *Scientific American,* Vol. 199 (1958), pp. 59–65.

22. Sarbin, T. R., and Allen, V. L. "Role Theory," in Gardner Lindzey and Elliot A. Aronson (eds.), *The Handbook of Social Psychology,* Vol. I, second edition, Addison-Wesley, Reading, Mass., 1968, pp. 488–567.

23. David Robert T. *Performance and Development of Field Sales Managers,* Division of Research, Graduate School of Business Administration, Harvard University, Boston, 1957.

24. Papandreou, Andreas G. "Some Basic Problems in the Theory of the Firm," in Bernard F. Haley (ed.), *A Survey of Contemporary Economics,* Vol. II, Irwin, Homewood, Illinois, 1952, pp. 183–219.

25. Marples, D. L. "Studies of Managers: A Fresh Start?" *The Journal of Management Studies,* Vol. 4 (1967), pp. 282–99.

The Technology of Foolishness

James G. March

I

The concept of choice as a focus for interpreting human behavior has rarely had an easy time in the realm of ideas. It is beset by theological disputations over free will, by the dilemmas of absurdism, by the doubts of psychological behaviorism, by the claims of historical, economic, social, and demographic determinism. Nevertheless, the idea that humans make choices has proven robust enough to become a major matter of faith in important segments of contemporary Western civilization.

The major tenets of this faith run something like this: Human beings make choices. They do this by evaluating their alternatives in terms of their goals on the basis of information available to them. They choose the alternative that is most attractive in terms of the goals. The process of making choices can be improved by using the technology of choice. Thorugh the paraphernalia of modern techniques, we can improve the quality of the search for alternatives, the quality of information, and the quality of the analysis used to evaluate alternatives. Although actual human choice may fall short of this ideal in various ways, it is an attractive model of how choices should be made by individuals and organizations.

Whatever the merits of such a faith within the academic worlds of philosophy, psychology, economics, history, and sociology, it is, I believe, a dominant view among businessmen, politicians, engineers, educators, scientists, and bureaucrats. It qualifies as a key part of the current conception of intelligence. It affirms the efficacy and possibility of intelligent human action.

These articles of faith have been built upon, and have stimulated,

Previously published in *Civiløkonomen* (Copenhagen) 18, no. 4 (May 1971): 7–12. Reprinted with permission of the author.

some scripture. It is the scripture of theories of individual and organizational decision making. The scripture is partly a codification of received doctrine and partly a source for that doctrine. As a result, our cultural ideas of intelligence and our theories of choice bear some substantial resemblance. In particular, they share three conspicuous interrelated ideas:

The first idea is the *preexistence of purpose*. We find it natural to base an interpretation of human choice behavior on a presumption of human purpose. We have, in fact, invented one of the most elaborate terminologies in the professional literature: "values," "needs," "wants," "goods," "preferences," "utility," "objectives," "goals," "aspirations," "drives." All of these reflect a strong tendency to believe that a useful interpretation of human behavior involves defining a set of objectives that (*a*) are prior attributes of the system, and (*b*) make the observed behavior in some sense intelligent vis-à-vis those objectives.

Whether we are talking about individuals or about organizations, purpose is an obvious presumption of the discussion. An organization is often defined in terms of its purpose. It is seen by some as the largest collectivity directed by a purpose. Action within an organization is justified (or criticized) in terms of the purpose. Individuals explain their own behavior, as well as the behavior of others, in terms of a set of value premises that are presumed to be antecedent to the behavior. Normative theories of choice begin with an assumption of a preexistent preference ordering defined over the possible outcomes of a choice.

The second idea is the *necessity of consistency*. We have come to recognize consistency both as an important property of human behavior and as a prerequisite for normative models of choice. Dissonance theory, balance theory, theories of congruency in attitudes, statuses, and performances have all served to remind us of the possibilities for interpreting human behavior in terms of the consistency requirements of a limited capacity information-processing system.

At the same time, consistency is a cultural and theoretical virtue. Action should be made consistent with belief. Beliefs should be consistent with each other, and stable over time. Actions taken by different parts of an organization should be consistent with each other. Individual and organizational activities are seen as connected with each other in terms of their consequences for some consistent set of purposes. In an organization, the structural manifestation of the dictum of consistency is the hierarchy with its obligations of coordination and control. In the individual, the structural manifestation is a set of values that generates a consistent preference ordering.

The third idea is the *primacy of rationality*. By rationality I mean a

procedure for deciding what is correct behavior by relating consequences systematically to objectives. By placing primary emphasis on
rational techniques, we implicitly have rejected—or seriously impaired
—two other procedures for choice: (*a*) the processes of intuition, by
means of which people may do things without fully understanding why,
and (*b*) the processes of tradition and faith, through which people do
things because that is the way they are done.

Both within the theory and within the culture we insist on the ethic
of rationality. We justify individual and organizational action in terms
of an analysis of means and ends. Impulse, intuition, faith, and tradition are outside that system and viewed as antithetical to it. Faith may
be seen as a possible source of values. Intuition may be seen as a possible source of ideas about alternatives. But the analysis and justification of action lies within the context of reason.

These ideas are obviously deeply embedded in the culture. Their
roots extend into ideas that have conditioned much of modern Western history and interpretations of that history. Their general acceptance is probably highly correlated with the permeation of rationalism
and individualism into the style of thinking within the culture. The
ideas are even more obviously embedded in modern theories of choice.
It is fundamental to those theories that thinking should precede action;
that action should serve a purpose; that purpose should be defined in
terms of a consistent set of preexistent goals; and that choice should
be based on a consistent theory of the relation between action and its
consequences.

Every tool of management decision that is currently a part of management science, operations research, or decision theory assumes the
prior existence of a set of consistent goals. Almost the entire structure
of microeconomic theory builds on the assumption that there exists a
well-defined, stable, and consistent preference ordering. Most theories
of individual or organizational choice behavior accept the idea that
goals exist and that (in some sense) an individual or organization acts
on those goals, choosing from among some alternatives on the basis of
available information.

From the perspective of all of man's history, the ideas of purpose,
consistency, and rationality are relatively new. Much of the technology
currently available to implement them is extremely new. Over the past
few centuries, and conspicuously over the past few decades, we have
substantially improved man's capability for acting purposively, consistently, and rationally. We have substantially increased his propensity to
think of himself as doing so. It is an impressive victory, won—where
it has been won—by a happy combination of timing, performance,
ideology, and persistence. It is a battle yet to be concluded, or even en-

gaged, in many cultures of the world; but within most of the Western world, individuals and organizations see themselves as making choices.

II

The tools of intelligence as they are fashioned in modern theories of choice are necessary to any reasonable behavior in contemporary society. It is difficult to see how we could, and inconceivable that we would, fail to continue their development, refinement, and extension. As might be expected, however, a theory and ideology of choice built on the ideas outlined above is deficient in some obvious, elementary ways, most conspicuously in the treatment of human goals.

Goals are thrust upon the intelligent man. We ask that he act in the name of goals. We ask that he keep his goals consistent. We ask that his actions be oriented to his goals. But we do not concern ourselves with the origin of goals. Theories of individual and organizational choice assume actors with preexistent value systems.

Since it is obvious that goals change over time and that the character of those changes affects both the richness of personal and organizational development and the outcome of choice behavior, a theory of choice must somehow justify ignoring the phenomena. Although it is unreasonable to ask a theory of choice to solve all of the problems of man and his development, it is reasonable to ask how something as conspicuous as the fluidity of objective can plausibly be ignored in a theory that is offered as a guide to human choice behavior.

There are three classic justifications. The first is that goal development and choice are independent processes, conceptually and behaviorally. The second is that the model of choice is never satisfied in fact and that deviations from the model accommodate the problems of introducing change. The third is that the idea of changing goals is so intractable in a normative theory of choice that nothing can be said about it. Since I am unpersuaded of the first and second justifications, my optimism with respect to the third is somewhat greater than most of my fellows.

The argument that goal development and choice are independent behaviorally seems clearly false. It seems to me perfectly obvious that a description that assumes goals come first and action comes later is frequently radically wrong. Human choice behavior is at least as much a process for discovering goals as for acting on them. Although it is true enough that goals and decisions are "conceptually" distinct, that is simply a statement of the theory. It is not a defense of it. They are conceptually distinct if we choose to make them so.

The argument that the model is incomplete is more persuasive. There do appear to be some critical "holes" in the system of intelligence as described by standard theories of choice. There is incomplete information, incomplete goal consistency, and a variety of external processes impinging on goal development—including intuition and tradition. What is somewhat disconcerting about the argument, however, is that it makes the efficacy of the concepts of intelligent choice dependent on their inadequacy. As we become more competent in the techniques of the model, and more committed to it, the "holes" become smaller. As the model becomes more accepted, our obligation to modify it increases.

The final argument seems to me sensible as a general principle, but misleading here. Why are we more reluctant to ask how human beings might find "good" goals than we are to ask how they might make "good" decisions? The second question appears to be a relatively technical problem. The first seems more pretentious. It claims to say something about alternative virtues. The appearance of pretense, however, stems directly from the theory and the ideology associated with it.

In fact, the conscious introduction of goal discovery as a consideration in theories of human choice is not unknown to modern man. We have two kinds of theories of choice behavior in human beings. One is a theory of children. The other is a theory of adults. In the theory of childhood, we emphasize choices as leading to experiences that develop the child's scope, his complexity, his awareness of the world. As parents, or psychologists, we try to lead the child to do things that are inconsistent with his present goals because we know (or believe) that he can only develop into an interesting person by coming to appreciate aspects of experience that he initially rejects.

In the theory of adulthood, we emphasize choices as a consequence of our intentions. As adults, or economists, we try to take actions that (within the limits of scarce resources) come as close as possible to achieving our goals. We try to find improved ways of making decisions consistent with our perceptions of what is valuable in the world.

The asymmetry in these models is conspicuous. Adults have constructed a model world in which adults know what is good for themselves, but children do not know what is good for themselves. It is hard to react positively to the conceit. Reaction to the asymmetry has, in fact, stimulated a rather large number of ideologies and reforms designed to allow children the same moral prerogative granted to adults—the right to imagine that they know what they want. The efforts have cut deeply into traditional child-rearing, traditional educational policies, traditional politics, and traditional consumer economics.

In my judgment, the asymmetry between models of choice for adults and models of choice for children is awkward; but the solution we have adopted is precisely wrong-headed. Instead of trying to adapt the model of adults to children, we might better adapt the model of children to adults. For many purposes, our model of children is better. Of course, children know what they want. Everyone does. The critical question is whether they are encouraged to develop more interesting "wants." Values change. People become more interesting as those values and the interconnections made among them change.

One of the most obvious things in the world turns out to be hard for us to accommodate in our theory of choice: A child of two will almost always have a less interesting set of values (yes, indeed, a *worse* set of values) than a child of twelve. The same is true of adults. Although one of the main natural arenas for the modification of human values is the arena of choice, our theories of adult and organizational decision making ignore the phenomenon entirely.

Introducing ambiguity and fluidity to the interpretation of individual and organizational goals obviously has implications for behavioral theories of decision making. The main point here, however, is not to consider how we might describe the behavior of individuals and organizations that are discovering goals as they act. Rather it is to examine how we might improve the quality of that behavior, how we might aid the development of interesting goals.

We know how to advise an organization or an individual if we are first given a consistent set of preferences. Under some conditions, we can suggest how to make decisions if the preferences are only consistent up to the point of specifying a series of independent constraints on the choice. But what about a normative theory of goal-finding behavior? What do we say when our client tells us that he is not sure his present set of values is the set of values in terms of which he wants to act?

It is a question familiar to many aspects of ordinary life. It is a question that friends, associates, students, college presidents, business managers, voters, and children ask at least as frequently as they ask how they should act within a set of consistent and stable values.

Within the context of the normative theory of choice as it exists, the answer we give is: First determine the values, then act. The advice is frequently useful. Moreover, we have developed ways in which we can use conventional techniques for decision analysis to help discover what our value premises are and to expose value inconsistencies for resolution. These techniques involve testing the decision implications of some successive approximations to a set of preferences. The object is to find a consistent set of preferences with implications that are acceptable to the person or organization making the decisions. Variations on such techniques are used routinely in operations research, as well as in personal counseling and analysis.

The utility of such techniques, however, apparently depends on the assumption that a primary problem is the excavation of preexistent values. The metaphors—"finding oneself," "goal clarification," "self-discovery"—are metaphors of search. If our value premises are to be "constructed" rather than "discovered," our standard procedures may be useful; but we have no a priori reason for assuming they will.

Perhaps we should explore a somewhat different approach to the normative question of how we ought to behave when our value premises are not yet (and never will be) fully determined. Suppose we treat actions as a way of creating interesting goals at the same time as we treat goals as a way of justifying action. It is an intuitively plausible and simple idea, but one that is not immediately within the domain of standard normative theories of intelligent choice.

Interesting people and interesting organizations construct complicated theories of themselves. In order to do this, they need to supplement the technology of reason with a technology of foolishness. Individuals and organizations need ways of doing things for which they have no good reason. Not always. Not usually. But sometimes. They need to act before they think.

III

In order to use the act of intelligent choice as a planned occasion for discovering new goals, we apparently require some idea of sensible foolishness. Which of the many foolish things that we might do now will lead to attractive value consequences? The question is almost inconceivable. Not only does it ask us to predict the value consequences of action, it asks us to evaluate them. In what terms can we talk about "good" changes in goals?

In effect, we are asked either to specify a set of supergoals in terms of which alternative goals are evaluated, or to choose among alternatives now in terms of the unknown set of values we will have at some future time (or the distribution over time of that unknown set of future values). The former alternative moves us back to the original situation of a fixed set of values—now called "supergoals"—and hardly seems an important step in the direction of inventing procedures for discovering new goals. The latter alternative seems fundamental enough, but it violates severely our sense of temporal order. To say that we make decisions now in terms of goals that will only be knowable later is nonsensical—as long as we accept the basic framework of the theory of choice and its presumptions of preexistent goals.

I do not know in detail what is required, but I think it will be substantial. As we challenge the dogma of preexistent goals, we will be forced to reexamine some of our most precious prejudices: the strictures against imitation, coercion, and rationalization. Each of those honorable prohibitions depends on the view of man and human choice imposed on us by conventional theories of choice.

Imitation is not necessarily a sign of weak blood. It is a prediction. It is a prediction that if we duplicate the behavior or attitudes of someone else, the chances of our discovering attractive new goals for ourselves are relatively high. In order for imitation to be normatively attractive we need a better theory of who should be imitated. Such a theory seems to be eminently feasible. For example, what are the conditions for effectiveness of a rule that you should imitate another person whose values are in a close neighborhood of yours? How do the chances of discovering interesting goals through imitation change as the number of other people exhibiting the behavior to be imitated increases?

Coercion is not necessarily an assault on individual autonomy. It can be a device for stimulating individuality. We recognize this when we talk about parents and children (at least sometimes). What has always been difficult with coercion is the possibility for perversion that it involves, not its obvious capability for stimulating change. What we require is a theory of the circumstances under which entry into a coercive system produces behavior that leads to the discovery of interesting goals. We are all familiar with the tactic. We use it in imposing deadlines, entering contracts, making commitments. What are the conditions for its effective use?

Rationalization is not necessarily a tricky way of evading morality. It can be a test for the feasibility of a goal change. When deciding among alternative actions for which we have no good reason, it may be sensible to develop some definition of how "near" to intelligence alternative "unintelligent" actions lie. Effective rationalization permits this kind of incremental approach to changes in values. To use it effectively, however, we require a better idea of the kinds of metrics that might be possible in measuring value distances. At the same time, rationalization is the major procedure for integrating newly discovered goals into an existing structure of values. It provides the organization of complexity itself becomes indistinguishable from randomness.

There are dangers in imitation, coercion, and rationalization. The risks are too familiar to elaborate. We should, indeed, be able to develop better techniques. Whatever those techniques may be, however, they will almost certainly stress the superstructure of biases erected on purpose, consistency, and rationality. They will involve some way of thinking about action now as occurring in terms of a set of unknown future values.

IV

A second requirement for a technology of foolishness is some strategy for suspending rational imperatives toward consistency. Even if we know which of several foolish things we want to do, we still need a mechanism for allowing us to do it. How de we escape the logic of our reason?

Here, I think, we are closer to understanding what we need. It is playfulness. Playfulness is the deliberate, temporary relaxation of rules in order to explore the possibilities of alternative rules. When we are playful, we challenge the necessity of consistency. In effect, we announce—in advance—our rejection of the usual objections to behavior that does not fit the standard model of intelligence.

Playfulness allows experimentation. At the same time, it acknowledges reason. It accepts an obligation that at some point either the playful behavior will be stopped or it will be integrated into the structure of intelligence in some way that makes sense. The suspension of the rules is temporary.

The idea of play may suggest three things that are, in my mind, quite erroneous in the present context. First, play may be seen as a kind of Mardi Gras for reason, a release of the emotional tensions of virtue. Although it is possible that play performs some such function, that is not the function with which I am concerned. Second, play may be seen as part of some mystical balance of spiritual principles: fire and water, hot and cold, weak and strong. The intention here is much narrower than a general mystique of balance. Third, play may be seen as an antithesis of intelligence, so that the emphasis on the importance of play becomes a support for simple self-indulgence. Without prejudicing the case for self-indulgent behavior, my present intent is to propose play as an instrument of intelligence, not a substitute.

Playfulness is a natural outgrowth of our standard view of reason. A strict insistence on purpose, consistency, and rationality limits our ability to find new purposes. Play relaxes that insistence to allow us to act "unintelligently" or "irrationally," or "foolishly" to explore alternative ideas of possible purposes and alternative concepts of behavioral consistency. And it does this while maintaining our basic commitment to the necessity of intelligence.

Although play and reason are in this way functional complements, they are often behavioral competitors. They are alternative styles and alternative orientations to the same situation. There is no guarantee that the styles will be equally well developed. There is no guarantee that all individuals or all organizations will be equally adept in both styles. There is no guarantee that all cultures will be equally encouraging to both.

Our design problem is either to specify the best mix of styles or, failing that, to assume that most people and most organizations most of the time use an alternation of strategies rather than persevere in either one. It is a difficult problem. The optimization problem looks extremely difficult on the face of it, and the learning situations that will produce alternation in behavior appear to be somewhat less common than those that produce perseveration.

Consider, for example, the difficulty of sustaining playfulness as a style within contemporary American society. Individuals who are good at consistent rationality are rewarded early and heavily. We define it as intelligence, and the educational rewards of society are associated strongly with it. Much of the press from social norms is in the same direction, particularly for men. Many of the demands of modern organizational life reinforce the same abilities and style preferences.

The result is that many of the most influential, best educated, and best placed citizens have experienced a powerful overlearning with respect to rationality. They are exceptionally good at maintaining consistent pictures of themselves, of relating action to purposes. They are exceptionally poor at a playful attitude toward their own beliefs, toward the logic of consistency, or toward the way they see things as being connected in the world. The dictates of manliness, forcefulness, independence, and intelligence are intolerant of playful urges if they arise. The playful urges that arise are weak ones.

The picture is probably overdrawn, but not, I believe, the implications. Both for organizations and for individuals reason and intelligence have had the unnecessary consequence of inhibiting the development of purpose into more complicated forms of consistency. In order to move away from that position, we need to find some ways of helping individuals and organizations to experiment with doing things for which they have no good reason, to be playful with their conception of themselves. It is a facility that requires more careful attention than I can give it, but I would suggest five things as a small beginning:

First, we can treat *goals as hypotheses*. Conventional decision theory allows us to entertain doubts about almost everything except the thing about which we frequently have the greatest doubt—our objectives. Suppose we define the decision process as a time for the sequential testing of hypotheses about goals. If we can experiment with alternative goals, we stand some chance of discovering complicated and interesting combinations of good values that none of us previously imagined.

Second, we can treat *intuition as real*. I do not know what intuition is, or even if it is any one thing. Perhaps it is simply an excuse for doing something we cannot justify in terms of present values or for refusing to follow the logic of our own beliefs. Perhaps it is an inexplicable way of consulting that part of our intelligence that is not organized in a way anticipated by standard theories of choice. In either case, intuition permits us to see some possible actions that are outside our present scheme for justifying behavior.

Third, we can treat *hypocrisy as a transition*. Hypocrisy is an inconsistency between expressed values and behavior. Negative attitudes about hypocrisy stem from two major things. The first is a general onus against inconsistency. The second is a sentiment against combining the pleasures of vice with the appearance of virtue. Apparently, that is an unfair way of allowing evil to escape temporal punishment. Whatever the merits of such a position as ethics, it seems to me distinctly inhibiting toward change. A bad man with good intentions may be a man experimenting with the possibility of becoming good. Somehow it seems to me more sensible to encourage the experimentation than to insult it.

Fourth, we can treat *memory as an enemy*. The rules of consistency and rationality require a technology of memory. For most purposes, good memories make good choices. But the ability to forget, or overlook, is also useful. If I do not know what I did yesterday or what other people in the organization are doing today, I can act within the system of reason and still do things that are foolish.

Fifth, we can treat *experience as a theory*. Learning can be viewed as a series of conclusions based on concepts of action and consequences that we have invented. Experience can be changed retrospectively. By changing our interpretive concepts now, we modify what we learned earlier. Thus, we expose the possibility of experimenting with alternative childhoods. The usual strictures against "self-deception" in experience need occasionally to be tempered with an awareness of the extent to which all experience is an interpretation subject to conscious revision. Personal histories, like national histories, need to be rewritten rather continuously as a base for the retrospective learning of new self-conceptions.

11

Organizational Design:
Size, Shape,
Function, and Beauty

Introduction

The dream home you or I have often designed is a lot more than just a place to eat and sleep. We design that home as some expression of ourselves, a place that "fits" us, "reflects" us, is "in harmony" with us. But that home also will have a roof and plumbing that we hope will work. How much should the practical functions like plumbing determine the design of our home? And what proportion should be dictated by those more subjective issues of personal expression? Perhaps it is even feasible to do both to their fullest. Shouldn't the design of organizations pay attention to the same issues? To aesthetics as well as efficiency?

This chapter is about balancing the practical design of organizational technology and structure with the "aesthetic" design of meanings; it is about balancing pragmatic issues like job specialization, hierarchies, and assembly operations with the softer stuff of philosophies, ideologies, myths, purposes, and even missions. While meanings can frequently be created by the contexts in which they occur, the causality can also run in just the reverse direction. Charismatic leaders, for example, can often design intricate meaning systems which then generate new contexts in the form of new social and technical structures. Similarly, two leaders managing equivalent subordinates may generate very different meanings. One leader may cause his subordinates to perceive great significance and quality in their working life, while the other initiates only interpretations of gloom, tedium, and despair.

Leavitt's article considers two basic approaches to organizational design, a pragmatic/rational approach and an imaginative/purposive approach. By the rational approach, General Motors would be designed to use advanced technologies, social structures, and information networks in ways that are congruent with existing (or expected) social, political, economic, and physical environments. By the purposive approach, General Motors would be designed to fulfill some combination of economic or social or other purposes desired by its designers. The rational approach directs our attention to very different attributes and general problem areas than the purposive approach. In the real world, of course, both orientations are required. The problem, Leavitt argues, is that our educational system, if not our society in general, stamps in rational analysis, while wiping out or ignoring imaginative, "problem-finding" approaches to design. Students are taught to be solution oriented rather than more question oriented.

One critical assumption made in most organizational design and redesign efforts is that organizations are stable units; thus, they can be loosened up, changed, and retightened like the wheels of a car. Most consultants employ the imagery of unfreezing, moving, and refreezing as if organizations were as solid as ice cubes. Weick, in the second paper of this chapter, describes organizations as self-designing systems, where the ice-cube metaphor is given a novel twist. Weick suggests that we consider the design strategies of "chronically frozen systems" and "chronically unfrozen systems." In the first, the designer builds in suspicion and doubt of the initial design with an emphasis on constantly modifying the original elements. In the second strategy, the design begins with fluidity and minimal constraints, temporary coalitions are preferred, and the habit of self-design becomes institutionalized. Weick's main point is that organizational designs usually do not give enough attention to building in processes which are tuned in to the adaptive needs of the organization's changing environmental niche.

Weick's article also reveals more clearly the role of meaning in organizational design. For example, one would expect that in self-designing systems individuals would compensate for the ambiguity of their situations by constructing elaborate systems of belief about social realities. Such designing of systems of meaning is more fully explored in the third article of this chapter.

Clark, in that third piece, tackles the role of belief and sentiment in large organizations. Leaders and members of organizations design intricate sagas or legends about their organizations. Stories about an organization's history, origin, and mission are repeated to strangers, new recruits, and publics in order to teach them the traditions, behavioral prescriptions, and even moral character of the organization. Charismatic leaders, skillful entrepreneurs, and social movements can often modify, bend, revise, and otherwise manipulate an organization's "fabric of meaning," with dramatic results. Clark describes how leaders in several colleges were able to change the whole orientation of the organization by careful redesigns of meaning. College staff and faculty were led to feel meaningfully unique, innovative, and intellectually elite. Commitment of time and energy, loyalty, and pride all emerged from the process.

So organizational design is far more than simply laying out a logical organization chart; it is a complex set of social and psychological processes.

On the Design Part of Organizational Design
Harold J. Leavitt

This conference is about organizational design. It is not just about organizational analysis or organizational change or organizational structure. All of those are relevant, but the emphasis is on *design*. Design implies the future, the not-yet. It implies creation, from nonexistence to existence. It implies divergence—a multiplicity, perhaps an infinite multiplicity of possible alternatives.

In this short paper I will argue that most of us, practitioners and scholars alike, don't know much about design, that indeed we have been taught to avoid it. I will also argue that in order to learn more about it, we could usefully do two things: first, we could use different models of problem solving than those we have characteristically used; and second, we could look for help and ideas in some rather far-out places, in the world of artists, philosophers, gurus, developmental psychologists, and neurologists; as well as in certain parts of our own more familiar worlds.

To get back to design, it seems to me that the uniqueness of the notion of design (as contrasted with, say, problem solving or analysis) lies in the divergent and creative aspects of the process. Designers don't just make things, they think up new ones. There seems to be no limit to the possibilities for designing anything from toilets to shoes. This is not to say that the design process is entirely free and unconstrained. Presumably the toilets should work and the shoes should be wearable. But the constraints will vary depending on the client-designer relationship and several other states of the world. If an architect is confronted by his client with a preselected site, a predetermined set of materials, some very precise space requirements, and a host of other limitations, then the design phase of his activities will be sharply limited. But, if he

Harold J. Leavitt "On the Design Part of Organizational Design" in *The Management of Organizational Design,* Kilman, Pondy, and Slevin, eds., © 1976. Reprinted by permission of Elsevier North-Holland, Inc., New York.

can design first, and then search for a site and for materials and for a client who will like the space use that he has sketched out, he becomes that much more of a designed and that much less of a traditional problem solver.

I think organizational design is like that. We can preconstrain organizational design so tightly that there is very little room left for design. If the tasks that the organization is to perform are clearly prespecified, if the technology is predetermined, if the structural options are narrowly limited by tradition or by client preference, then design becomes a small piece of the total; the rest consisting essentially of logical analytic problem solving, of working out a satisfactory alternative to fit the constraints. We can do that problem-solving kind of job by cutting and trying, or by modelling alternatives and checking out their fits, or in more traditional deductive analytic ways, working from the task backward.

Looked at this way, design becomes one phase of a larger, perhaps tripartite problem working process (Pounds 1969). Part I is the problem-*finding* or problem-*making* part of the process—and that is the design part. Part II is problem *solving* in the analytic, decompositional sense—breaking the problem into subparts and finding sensible and efficient ways of putting them together again. Part III becomes *solution implementing*—the action, getting-it-done part of the process, laying the bricks, influencing the people, ironing out the bugs.

The weight we choose to give to part I is the weight we give to design. But this design part is the most slippery part. It raises questions about what is inside the problem solver; what he values, wants, and loves; and questions of imagination, of dreams and fancies. It's the most loose, ill-understood, ill-structured part of the larger process.

It may be worth pointing out that we social science types know a lot (and fight a lot among ourselves) about the importance of the second and third phases in this model. Management scientists value phase II most of all. Good problem solving is just about equatable with good analysis. For management scientists the joy seems to be in working out the decision rule; finding the better way; solving the given puzzle. The third phase, implementation, is often perceived by hard-nosed analytic organizational theorists as both ancillary and serially subsequent to the analytic process. For example, in the very last sentence of Harvey Wagner's now-classic text in operations research, he says:"To enhance the adoption of these technical and technological advances by industry and government, management and behavioral scientists together will have to find ways by which executives can deal effectively with computerized systems as beneficial change agents" (p. 937).

In contrast, behavioral scientists—applied ones, that is—are implementation lovers. For them the joy of problem solving lies mostly in getting people to do things. It doesn't matter that the answer be elegant or even right, as long as people are with it. Management scientists want to analyze first and then let others implement the solution. Behavioral scientists want to bring the analysis to the implementers, to combine planning and doing in order to get the doers committed to the plans. If the plans aren't very good, too bad. Who needs good plans if no one will carry them out?

Those debates, as we all know, go on endlessly in every business school in the country—usually not in simple English, but in the holy jargons of the two churches.

So we fight among ourselves, while neither group pays much more than peripheral attention to phase I: How do we find what to plan and what to implement?

One of the real curiosities about these phase I design problems, when they are presented to people like us, is that we seem to avoid them, often positively demanding those tighter constraints that will reduce the design phase of the process to a trivial level. The first questions we are likely to raise with clients are question like: "What's your problem? What are your goals? Just what products do you want to make? How many and what kind of people do you want to employ? Where do you plan to locate your new establishment?" And if the other party won't give us clear answers to those questions, we are apt, privately, to denigrate this damn fool who doesn't know what he wants.

If that's true, and I assert that it is, it's worth a little analysis. One of the reasons we like to solve rather than create problems is, I propose, simply because most of us have been taught, formally and by experience, how to do the one and how not to do the other. We have received positive reward and reinforcement for correct analyses and right answers, not for right questions. There are good psychological reasons for why people learn to love what they do at least as much as they learn to do what they love. As students or as academics or as practitioners, we have seldom been asked to design organizations in an unconstrained, creative sense. What we have been asked to "design," typically, is methods for researching a given problem, or ways of remodelling an existing organization to accomplish a particular set of goals. The examination questions that we were given as students included such tight constraints that design meant mostly applying a set of measurement methods to a predetermined problem, or analyzing a problem into its significant parts. Even the idea of examination questions implicitly includes some predefinition of "the" problem. We have learned a lot about how to answer a Ph.D. question asking us how to test the hypothesis that increased wage rates will increase the per capita consumption of food in the company cafeteria. And we like such questions. We know little about how to answer questions like: "Design an interesting piece of research," or "What kind of organization would you just love to build?"

The story about Robert Benchley's handling of an exam question when he was an undergraduate seems apropos here. He was given a question about the economics of the fisheries of Alaska. His answer started out about like this: "I don't know much about the fisheries of Alaska, but I can give you the fishes' point of view. . . ." And he did.

Indeed, a related reason that we are lousy designers is because we have been actively, albeit unconsciously, trained to avoid such issues. For design as I have defined it is part of the softheaded, nonlogical artsy-craftsy world. And those kinds of people don't make it in our society. Those sorts of skills are for women and artists and other lesser creatures who have no real power in our culture. The norms, in business, in education, and in science, favor the steel-trap logical analytic thinker and the man of action. They do not favor the imaginer, the dreamer, the introspector.

And it goes beyond that. As students, as managers, as professors we not only get positive brownie points for sophisticated methodology and analytic viruosity, we get *negative* brownie points for thinking "loosely" or "intuitively." We are—at least most highly educated people are—socialized *into* valuing analysis and action, and socialized *out of* valuing imagination and intuition. When we learn our profession we learn not only the content and method of the field, we also learn an ideology, a religion. We become true believers, and to venture across the ideological boundaries is something of a sin, at least until one becomes an old theologian.

But perhaps I can even make a more analytic case for the same point. Much of what we call progress in the Western world is a consequence of skill in phases II and III: analytic problem solving and active implementing. We have become good at both. Which means that we have methods which we know to be useful if they are followed. So we teach our young managers to use those rules, not to violate them. Back when I was in Pittsburgh at Carnegie Tech, one of our graduate students, Bob Altemeyer (1966), did a nice doctoral thesis showing just that. Engineering and science students as freshmen were pretty good at analytic tests; sophomores were better still; juniors even better; and seniors were great. But on tests of imagination, the seniors were worst, and the juniors were worse than the sophomores, and the freshmen engineers were the most imaginative of all. It looked as though the engineering education process was not only stamping in analysis, but wiping out imagination. Fine-arts students went precisely the other way—except architects, who improved somewhat in both dimensions.

Please note that I am not arguing that design is unrelated to analysis, nor that designers need not understand structure nor technology nor people. Design without analysis or implementation doesn't look very interesting or very useful. But I am arguing that design implies, for me at least, a much greater and a prior concern for problem finding over problem analysis or implementation. Design is relatively more concerned with what would be interesting or exciting or novel than with what is correct or efficient or even feasible. One can ask the latter set of questions after something has been designed, or even during the process of spinning out a design; but such questions as a *precursor* to design serve only to evade the heart of the design or at least better at phase I? I wish I knew. Three very unclear ideas seem to me to distinguish this part of the process from the others.

The first is love. You have probably noticed my frequent use of that word thus far in the context of phase I. But it seems to me to be real. Design seems to require an idea that we love, that we are hooked on. An idea that actively comes up out of the inside of us rather than as a response to some environmental press. And where such ideas come from, how we find them, is, at this time at least, an unclear, uncontrollable, perhaps a nonrational process. Movies and novels are full of artists who can't paint for extended periods because the right idea won't come, or writers who can't write for the same reason. Maybe we can learn to understand creativity and regulate this part of the process. But one more reason most of us may avoid it is precisely because we can't control and regulate it. We live in a scheduled world. Finding ideas we love is thus far an unscheduled process.

The second notion involves some kind of escape from "normal" routines. Many of us have developed little heuristics that we feel will help us along in finding ideas. Some of us talk about needing the stimulation of other similar people. We need open communication to kick off ideas. Or time off the job. Don Marquis, who knew an awful lot about industrial research organizations, once told me that one thing that always seemed to pay off in ideas was time off the job—any kind of time off—meetings, sabbaticals, seminars. And in direct contrast to the communication-stimulation heuristic is the isolation heuristic. Give me a year on a desert island and I'll come up with the great idea.

Most of us in academia also ask ourselves why, in certain fields, certain schools, for certain periods, have been seminally productive. In my field, MIT had some gloriously productive years in the late 40s and early 50s. So did Carnegie Tech in the late 50s and early 60s. And we ask ourselves (and can't answer the question), "How one can recreate such climates?" That's a phase I-type question and we still don't know much about it. We think about the leadership of great people (which may mean people who are both smart and have ideas they love) or atmospheres of openness, but we haven't done much research on such settings. I would argue observationally that a lot of high IQs are not sufficient for such seminal atmospheres, and that analytic and implementational virtuosity are not sufficient either. In most cases I have seen, there also is some kind of new ball game: new rules, a fresh start, a new setting. But I'm sure that isn't sufficient either.

The third unclear thought I would offer about phase I follows from the first. Phase I seems to be somewhat more of an inductive activity than deductive; what I would call a "local process" rather than a general one. If we've got the beginnings of an idea we love, where can we go with it? Phase I questions are questions like: What might the relevant world look like if we started with this idea? What if we, in Lindblom's (1959) terminology, "muddled through"? Phase I, that is, requires something like the architect's sketches: divergent dry runs to get an idea of what things might look like. But architects can only do *sketches* that way; they can't build the finished building that way. They are constrained by the realities of phases II and III.

What I'm suggesting is that the design phase seems to include a large amount of local activity; cutting and trying; spinning out possibilities. And that's just where phase I activities bump into phases II and III. For the architect, the interface with phase II probably comes fairly early, and he must somehow shift from a divergent, local design mode into the more analytic mode; at which point he becomes much less an artist and much more a plumber. We don't know much about that transitional process in architecture or anywhere else, but I'll take long odds that it creates serious problems both for the architect and his client. For it requires a major shift in cognitive style. And I'm sure the same kind of phase I-phase II interface causes trouble between "creative" people and line managers in many organizations.

I wish I felt more confident about the next part of this paper but I don't. For now comes the tough issue: Where shall we search for possible leads to phase I-type questions? How do we learn to become better designers? How do we understand what we love?

I've already argued elsewhere (Leavitt 1974) that it might be useful to go hunting in other fields—even some far-out ones like the arts.

Another place to look may be among the brainstormers, the lateral thinkers (deBono 1970), the conceptual blockbusters (Adams 1974); that is, among the practitioners of creativity. Most of them have been treated by us academicians as only peripherally legitimate, as too gimmicky and atheoretical. But they may have something to teach us about how to loosen up our idea-generating mechanisms.

Another place, farther out, is in the realm of altered states of consciousness (Tart 1969; Ornstein 1972). Zen (Herrigel 1953), transcendental mediation (Naranja and Ornstein 1971), and other perspectives on understanding may just have something to offer. My own cursory overview, particularly of Eastern perspectives, suggests that many of the variants on meditation share at least one common notion, the idea that "normal" thinking processes obscure and interfere with the search for the core of self-insight, or understanding, or peace of mind, or whatever it is that these people feel is hiding inside there. So the techniques of meditation seem always to start with enabling devices, ways of getting rid of interference from normal thought, getting rid of language, logic, and so on. Presumably by so doing inner truth will be let out. In his introduction to Herrigel's *Zen and the Art of Archery* (1953), Suzuki describes the nature of Zen this way:

> Zen is the "everyday mind." This "everyday mind" is not more than "sleeping when tired, eating when hungry." As soon as we reflect, deliberate, and conceptualize, the original unconsciousness is lost and a thought interferes. We no longer eat while eating, we no longer sleep while sleeping. . . . Man is a thinking reed but his great works are done when he is not calculating and thinking. "Childlikeness" has to be restored with long years of training in the art of self-forgetfulness. When this is attained, man thinks yet he does not think. [P. 11]

That view begins to make sense if one couples it with the recent research on the two hemispheres of the brain (Sperry 1969; Gazanniga 1970). That research, carried on with patients in whom the cerebral hemispheres have been surgically isolated from one another, suggests the presence of quite different thinking styles in the left and right lobes, with essential dominance (in normal persons) of the left brain (controlling the right side of the body) over the right. The left hemisphere seems to be good at verbal, numerical, logical, serial tasks. But the right is visual, affective, and holistic. Maybe the meditators (and the artists?) are trying to get the left brain to relax so the right can do its imaginative stuff. And maybe we analytic types need a little right-brain training.

A third place to look, closer in, is at the research of people like Jim March (1974), who has argued that organizations don't really know their goals; that may of the analytic rules of consistency and logic obscure goal setting more than they help it; and that better alternatives may emerge by temporarily abrogating these rules through play or other kinds of foolishness.

Finally, cognitive styles research (Altemeyer 1966; Leavitt and Doktor, 1967) may give us some leads. How do we learn our thinking styles? How can we unlearn them? How do we get socialized into our beliefs about the "right" and the "wrong" ways to think? How is women's thinking different from men's, and is women's thinking, for design purposes, more useful than men's? Can we do better at design if

we diversify our organizations to bring in people who think differently
—women, blacks, artists—and then exploit their styles of thought
instead of training them to think like us?

Maybe some of this will help, maybe it won't. But to design organizations, it seems reasonable to try to understand design itself, as well
as organizations. And some of these far-out territories look like moderately rich turf on which to learn more about design. In any case,
the intent of this paper is to argue that we may currently be obscuring
the design process rather than clarifying it. And that clarifying it may
require us, uncomfortably, to put aside, temporarily at least, some of
our analytic and implementational prejudices.

References

Adams, J., *Conceptual Blockbusting.* Stanford, Calif.: Stanford
Alumni Association, 1974.

Altemeyer, R., "Education in the Arts and Sciences: Divergent Paths."
Doctoral dissertation, Carnegie Institute of Technology, 1966.

DeBono, E., *Lateral Thinking: Creativity Step by Step.* New York:
Harper, 1970.

Gazanniga, M. S., *Bisected Brain.* New York: Appleton, 1970.

Herrigel, E., *Zen and the Art of Archery.* London: Pantheon, 1953.

Leavitt, H. J., "Beyond the Analytic Manager," *California Management Review,* forthcoming May–June 1975.

Leavitt, H. J., and R. Doktor, "Personal Growth, Laboratory Training,
Science and All That: A Shot at a Cognitive Clarification," *Journal
of Applied Behavioral Science,* Vol. 6, No. 2, 1967, pp. 173–179.

Lindblom, C. E., "The Science of Muddling through," *Public Administrative Review,* Vol. 19, No. 2, 1959, pp. 78–88.

March, J., "The Technology of Foolishness", in Leavitt, H. J., L. Pinfield, and E. J. Webb (eds.), *Organization of the Future.* New York:
Praeger, 1974.

Naranjo, C., and R. Ornstein, *On the Psychology of Meditation.* New
York: Viking, 1971 (an Esalen book).

Ornstein, R. E., *The Psychology of Consciousness.* San Francisco:
Freeman, 1972.

Pounds, W. F., "The Process of Problem Finding," *Industrial Management Review,* Vol. 11, No. 1, Fall 1969, pp. 1–19.

Sperry, R. W., "A Modified Concept of Consciousness," *Psychological
Review,* Vol. 76, 1969, pp. 532–536.

Tart, C. T. (ed.), *Altered States of Consciousness.* New York: Wiley,
1969.

Wagner, H., *Principles of Operations Research.* Englewood Cliffs,
N.J.: Prentice-Hall, 1969.

Organization Design:
Organizations as
Self-designing Systems
Karl E. Weick

On Friday, December 27, 1973, the Apollo 3 astronauts conducted the first daylong sit-down strike in outer space. Their grievance concerned a problem of self-design.

To get the most information from this final trip in the Apollo program, ground control in Houston had removed virtually all the slack from the astronauts' schedule of activities and had treated the men as if they were robots. To get everything in, ground control shortened meal times, reduced setup times for experiments, and made no allowance for the fact that previous crews aboard Skylab had stowed equipment in an unsystematic manner. The astronauts' favorite pastimes—watching the sun and earth—were forbidden.

As Neal Hutchinson, flight director of the mission said, "We send up about six feet of instructions to the astronauts' teleprinter in the docking adapter every day—at least 42 separate sets of instructions—telling them where to point the solar telescope, which scientific instruments to use, and which corollaries to do. We lay out the whole day for them, and the astronauts normally follow it to a 'T.' What we've done is we've learned how to maximize what you can get out of a man in one day."

Not quite. Here's where the issue of self-design entered the picture. Edward Gibson, the civilian physicist in the Apollo 3 crew, made the following plea to ground control shortly before the strike: "I think in the future the ground should give the astronauts the bare framework of a schedule, together with a shopping list of things for them to do, and then let the guys on board figure out the best way of doing them."

This had already been done with one activity—making solar observations. Shopping lists had been designed "to allow the crewmen to

Reprinted by permission of the publisher, from *Organizational Dynamics*, Autumn 1977. Copyright © 1977, AMACOM, a division of American Management Associations. All rights reserved.

work independently of ground advice in selecting targets and objectives for solar observations. These lists were originally devised to suggest to the crewmen a variety of short objectives that could be met if an extra five or ten minutes of observing time should become available. The data collected in these intervals were found to be so useful that soon the ground team was requesting specific allotments of time to be used entirely at crewmen option. Because the crewmen had the current sensor outputs . . . [they were] in the best position to select the most interesting features and programs for study. In this activity the crewmen truly performed as the alter ego of the science community."

Despite the reasonableness of general frameworks and shopping lists, mission control saw things differently. "So many jobs interfere with one another!" Hutchinson said, after the third crew had returned to earth. "What if a guy gets an instrument focused on a star and just then his buddies in the docking adapter maneuver the vehicle around to look at the earth? Or what if a guy starts riding the bicycle ergometer, jiggling the space station, while another guy is taking a long film of the solar flare? Now, say that I gave the crew a rough framework of a schedule that said, for example, 'Do five orbits of solar work followed by two orbits of earth resources passes over Africa.' They might get so super-interested in the sun that they didn't get ready in time for the earth resources passes and miss an important target on the ground! With so many constraints, I'd say they're bound to screw something up!"

The problem of disturbing authority for the Skylab activities between the ground and the sky has classical overtones. We can analyze the situation using such concepts as autonomy, discretion, perceived control, self-determination, job enrichment, delegation, power, time span of discretion, or role conflict. To this already lengthy list I want to add the proposition that there are features of Skylab that the preceding concepts overlook, and these oversights require us to invent still another way of thinking—namely, the concept of a self-designing system.

Skylab as a problem in self-design

Several naunces of the Skylab situation are thrown into relief when we think about it as a problem in self-design.

• If the astronauts *had* received a bare framework and a shopping list, and if they did screw up and miss the earth-resources pass as Hutchinson feared, *the three-man Skylab crew, acting alone,* might still have been capable of restructuring their ways of combining the framework and the shopping list. One means of restructuring potentially available to the Skylab crew would be for them, not ground control, to decide that frameworks and laundry lists were not useful and then to request that a greater portion of their activities be suggested by mission control.

• In response to missed experiments, space station jiggles, or pure fascination, the astronauts might redefine the mission and alter the priorities of assignments. This is not as heretical as it may sound; it happened anyway. The original mission of Apollo 3 was to see if men could really live in space for long periods of time, and living meant to live decently with regular shifts and time off for relaxation. Given the somewhat precarious position of the NASA program and of this series of flights, this aim disappeared and relaxation time became the occasion for just one more experiment.

• If they had a self-designing system, the astronauts could have modified their resources by lengthening or shortening the mission, asking for other persons to join them, or starting a Skylab-to-earth rest and relaxation cycle with people shuttling back and forth. They could have shut off the teleprinter while they were doing a set of tasks and restarted it only when they were ready for a new batch. They could have requested that a second crew be sent aloft and treated this second crew as robots; or the original crew could have built actual robots out of junk on board so that commands from the ground that assumed robots at the other end could in fact have been assigned to robots.

Throughout Henry Cooper's (1976) analysis of Skylab, and in the material quoted here, there is the suggestion that ground control defined itself as *the* planners and defined the astronauts as *the* implementers. While planning, designing, and implementing are distinct activities, frequently the implementation undertaken before the designs have been formed serves to create the design. After implementing the first steps of the "design," the designers discover what that design was in the first place. Similarly, as the design unfolds, this development actually amounts to implementation in progress. Although seemingly separate activities, design and implementation provide the opportunity to improve and learn more about their counterparts. Implementation clarifies design; design clarifies implementation.

The concept of self-designing systems

The astronauts' world may appear specialized. In fact, it mirrors design problems that are found in all kinds of organized relationships that span long distances or large differences: headquarters and branches, ships controlled partly from the shore, superiors and subordinates, control towers and pilots, sales managers and salesmen, teachers and pupils, superintendents and teachers.

The concept of self-design is so new that concrete illustrations of it in business organizations are rare. Furthermore, since self-design is as much a strategy as it is an object, it's not obvious what it would look like or where it would be visible.

Nevertheless, it's easy to spot organizations that are incapable of self-design and therefore vulnerable. They value forecasts more than improvisation, they dwell on constraints rather than opportunities, they borrow solutions rather than invent them, they defend past actions rather than devise new ones, they cultivate permanence rather than impermanence, they value serenity more highly than argument, they rely on accounting systems as their sole means to assess performance rather than use more diverse measures, they remove doubt rather than encourage it, they search for final solutions rather than continuously experimenting, and they discourage contradictions rather than seek them.

Any organization that shows this pattern will make the same mistakes mission control did and will show the same inability to devise and insert new ways of acting. In the face of swift changes in the environment, such organizations will do too little, too late—and will fail.

To become more self-designing, organizations must reverse many of the patterns and preferences we have just listed. People must look at their organization in a different way and begin to value features of it and begin to value features of it that they used to disparage. The remainder of this article suggests some ways to initiate that rethinking and revaluing.

The essential problem in self-design is to make a teacher out of the learner—that is, to have the same people performing both functions. When an organization finds a present design inadequate, it avoids having someone from the outside come in to rewrite the organization; it does the rewiring itself.

At the most elementary level, self-design involves generating alternatives and testing them against the requirements and constraints perceived by people in the organization. The old design may provide some of the pieces for the new design or be used as one criterion to select among various alternatives, but unless it serves in this subsidiary role, the organization is merely introducing variations on the old theme. In self-design, the new design is underdetermined in the sense that fortuitous, arbitrary, sometimes even random elements are added to portions of old designs and in the interaction between them new forms are generated.

Principles of self-design

Self-design involves a different way of thinking about what is valuable and what is worthless in organizations. Four principles will illustrate some of the ways in which a preoccupation with self-design alters what you notice about organizations. These principles, not intended to exhaust the possibilities of self-design, deal with how to generate and select alternative designs and what it takes for an organization to make itself capable of implementing them.

Self-design is more than unfreezing

Most organization watchers have encountered what they assume to be design issues when they interact with organizational development specialists or change agents who believe in the formula "unfreeze, change, refreeze." That litany has its merits, but it glosses over several issues of self-design.

Failures of self-design occur quite as often because too little is frozen as because too much is frozen. A designer should not automatically assume that he's got to build in a capacity for systems to unfreeze themselves in order for them to be self-designing. The incipient model of a self-designing system that we're beginning to develop in this article is one in which there is considerable fluidity and modest amounts of anarchy. The last thing organized anarchy needs is unfreezing.

The designer of self-designing systems considers freezing in at least two distinct ways. He designs either chronically frozen or chronically unfrozen entities.

With a *chronically frozen system* the designer freezes the system, initially into a set of job descriptions, assigned tasks, rules, structures, and so on. Having done this, he knows that self-design invokes orchestrating how to loosen and modify the elements he originally built into this system. The designer needs to put into the system both respect for and suspicion about implanted structures. This sanctioned ambivalence is not easy to create on a sustained basis, but it is a necessity when freezing is used as a design principle. Essentially, the trick is to educate system participants in the art of decommitting themselves from concepts in which they have made considerable investments.

The designer says basically, "I'll build a system and spend most of my design time educating participants in ways to unfreeze what I gave them." Notice that this form of indoctrination can weaken the initial commitments—"If he's spending all this time lecturing me about the virtues of unfreezing, why did he implant this in the first place?"—so building chronically frozen systems is not as simple as it may sound. The designer has the tough task of saying to people, "Take this system seriously enough to operate it with gusto, but don't take it so seriously that you can't imagine any other way of running it or even the prospect of not running it any more." With this strategy the designer can create belief and solidity by building a substantial structure, by freezing some portion of a process, and by trying to lengthen the life of the system by simultaneously incorporating doubts about its solidity.

The opposite strategy, building a *chronically unfrozen system,* involves cultivating enthusiasm for improvisation, fluidity, minimal constraints, and a chronically protean existence. Self-design under these conditions requires members to be trained to trust structures and distrust anarchies, since self-design will require unfrozen systems to engage in selective freezing.

In the chronically unfrozen system, people may coalesce temporarily when some crisis occurs so that they can resolve the problem successfully. But once they have agreed on what changes are necessary, people can continue to go about their autonomous ways secure in the knowledge that they have workably consistent views about the organization and the directions in which it should be going. In the chronically unfrozen system, people negotiate less often about less consequential events because their continuing improvisation and short memories make them update themselves more often. They make a habit of self-design.

It's probably easier in the short run to build structures and instill irreverence for them than it is to foster pattern-free improvisation and qualify it by inserting the occasional need for collective action and constraints. Improvisation and anarchies are costly in time, costly in coordination costs, expensive in dollars, and costly in terms of the demands they make on people's attention. In an organized anarchy, people have to watch more things for longer periods to make any sense out of them. If we assume that people prefer certainty to uncertainty and programmed tasks to unprogrammed ones, then the strategy of starting with tangible structures makes immediate sense. The problem with this strategy is that we have merely postponed our troubles with design.

Chronically unfrozen systems are deceptive. They cause immediate problems because of their uncertainty, fluid job descriptions, occasional overlapping assignments, and healthy amounts of improvisation, but their redesign problems are relatively minor since this redesign can take the form of imposing some minor constraints, a relatively easy exercise given the comforts conferred by orderliness. The real subtlety in a chronically unfrozen system is that it may never have to redesign itself. With its steady diet of improvisation, its continual rearrangements of structure, its continual updating to meet changing realities, it may never need a major redesign.

Chronically unfrozen systems may appear to use more energy than frozen systems because everything is treated as problematic, past learning doesn't count for much, and the efficiencies produced by memory are sacrificed. However, if we compare this large expenditure of energy with the amount of energy consumed by structures that organize specific activities plus the energy needed to dismantle former structures, and develop new loyalties, then the drains on energy called for by the two systems might in fact be similar.

In summary, if a designer of self-designing systems uses the metaphor of "freezing" to guide his design efforts, he does considerably more with it than a typical change agent does. He either unfreezes the chronically frozen system or freezes the chronically unfrozen system. The designer has to implant the idea that structures are to be trusted or mistrusted depending on what the participants in the system start with.

Beginning a system with structure brings about a smoother start but rougher ending—when the structure in which people have a substantial investment needs to be dissolved and replaced. Unfrozen systems start roughly. Things never settle down, but they seldom get worse either. Self-design becomes less of a problem in the unfrozen system because it subsists on a steady diet of self-design. When the unfrozen system does find a problem requiring self-design, it can meet this problem by the relatively easier solution of imposing structure than the more difficult task of dissolving the structure. And the structure momentarily imposed by the unfrozen systems may be more readily dissolved at any time, since it consists of shared meanings rather than altered patterns of interdependence or more substantial structural arrangements.

Quantities don't generate designs; discrediting does

Psychologists have established that as stress and arousal increase, people pay less attention to what is going on around them. As stress increases and our vision narrows, our views of the world become more simplified and more impoverished. We neglect more and more important variables. We see the same old things even less imaginatively than we did before. Whenever this happens, managers respond by urging people to continue doing what they have done before but to do it with more vigor.

Whenever managers tell people to solve their problems by redoubling their efforts, they make a fatal mistake. They assume that quantities can *change* patterns. They can't. If, for example, you pour money into a system that's defective, all you're doing is reinforcing the defects. Pouring money, which is a quantity, into a system that has a shape will not generate a new shape.

All quantities can do is to help you discover the pattern that already exists. For example, if you increase the tension on a chain you can break it at its weakest link, and you then know which the weakest link was. But the tension didn't create the weakest link. If you want to change something, pouring money into it won't do it. Something *else* will have to change the pattern first. *Then* you can use an infusion of money to lock the new pattern into place.

The demise of the *Saturday Evening Post* is a perfect example of pouring money into a defective system and merely reinforcing the defects. For years the *Saturday Evening Post* used the rule of thumb in the publishing industry that the number of editorial pages should match the number of advertising pages. The tight coupling between these two elements means that when advertising shrinks, the magazine's editorial coverage also shrinks. A thinner magazine that attracts fewer readers is generated, making advertisers even more reluctant to purchase ads. Eventually profits vanish. But when the ads and editorial pages increase, printing expenses also increase. In fact, the costs of the enlarged magazine rise faster than the revenues, and profits again disappear. Whether publishers try to cope with this vicious circle by increasing promotional expenditures, cutting advertising costs, or buying more high-priced, sensational articles, the outcome is the same.

One way to break this pattern and to insert a *qualitative* change is by controlling the number of pages in the magazine. And one way to accomplish this, of course, is to control the price of advertising. In the old days, advertising was priced on a per-page basis. When the readership increased, the advertiser got more people for the same price. Consequently, the cost per reader went down for him. Changing this pricing method so that the advertising rate per 1,000 readers is kept constant removes the lethal linkage and publishing becomes more stable.

Hypocrisy often makes sense in self-design. The *Saturday Evening Post* failed to raise questions about a publisher's rule of thumb. They failed to realize that frequently "ambivalence is the optimal compromise." Doing what you have always done is necessary in short-term adaptations. Doing what you have never done is necessary in longer-term adaptations, and both need to be done simultaneously.

If words and deeds are contradictory, if one of them perpetuates past wisdom while the other discredits that past wisdom, then our current functioning should be effective and we should be able to preserve our ability to adapt to future contingencies. It is not simply that an organization should doubt what it knows for certain. It should also treat as certain the very things it doubts. If to doubt is to discredit clear information, then to act decisively is to discredit ambiguous information. Therefore, if you want to act on the point that ambivalence is the optimal compromise, when things are clear, you should doubt those things; when they are unclear, you should treat them as if they're clear. That's the meaning of discrediting.

We can observe discrediting in numerous organizational problems. The failure of watchmakers to entertain the possibility that watches could be made without gears left many of them close to bankruptcy when digital watches caught on. Banks "know" that it is good for people to save money, but unless they discredit that knowledge and successfully get people to borrow money, they fail. Albert Speer noted, ironically, that Allied bombing raids frequently helped the cause of the Third Reich during World War II. The raids destroyed files that contained information about past procedures used to run bureaucracies, and this automatic discrediting led to developing newer, more streamlined administrative procedures. Many city libraries are in trouble, for example, because they have failed to discredit procedures that are geared to service a white, middle-class population that has fled to the suburbs. The center city now contains groups who have neither a tradition of book learning nor a strong desire to adopt the values of the white majority, which are the values librarians are well suited to inculcate. Another example: The failure of *The New York Times* to doubt its skill at investigative reporting led it to overlook clues that, if noticed, would have enabled it to break the Watergate story two months before *The Washington Post*.

Discrediting the hard-won lessons of experience may seem silly in generating designs. However, we have to remember that the lessons from experience are always dated. The world in which they were learned changes chronically and discontinuously. Discrediting means that all past experience has lots of surplus meanings and there is no reason to think that we have exhausted the meanings of that experience by how we currently process it. So if we look back at that experience and alter it by new kinds of crediting and discrediting. If we rewrite portions of our history, new designs should be generated and the selections among them should be more intelligent.

Self-design requires inefficient acting

Many people argue that design isn't much of a problem because when an old design falters or fails we can always borrow a new design. I think that's naive. If responses become standardized when organizations merge, if people show strong tendencies to praise their own groups and downgrade other groups, and if people are less willing to run the risk of appearing frivolous, from whom are we going to borrow these elegant designs? We seem to have plenty of parasites, but where's the host?

One way to sponsor experimental-designs inside an organization is to encourage "galumphing." Galumphing is the "patterned voluntary elaboration or complication of process, where the pattern is not under the dominant control of goals." Stephen Miller argues that play or galumphing preserves adaptability because it provides a way to develop novel designs. Play "makes us flexible and gives us exercise in the control of means that we are capable of using which are superfluous right now. . . . [When people play] they are using their capacity to combine pieces of behavior that would have no basis for juxtaposition in a utilitarian framework."

From this standpoint, play is not a direct means to an end; instead it is a crooked line to the end. It gets around obstacles put there by the player in order to complicate his life. Deliberate complication, if it gives a person experience in combining elements in novel ways, could be potentially important in generating new design. Notice that in the case of galumphing, means activities are given much more leeway to unfold. No longer are they dominated by goals. What play basically does is "unhook behavior from the demands of real goals." The person gains experience in combining pieces of behavior that he would never have thought of combining given the practical problems that confront him.

Several possibilities are implicit in this line of analysis. Less efficient organizations could retain more adaptability than more efficient organizations. The assumption would be that less efficient organizations, which use more complicated means to achieve ends, might actually learn to recombine their repertoire. This would hold true only if they continually reshuffled their ways of being inefficient.

A further benefit of galumphing might be that people would discover capabilities they had overlooked before. When people build new activities and recombine acts, they may learn more about what's being recombined. Therefore, one of the possible benefits when people deliberately complicate themselves is that they learn more about the elements in their repertoire as well as the way in which these elements can be recombined.

Many contemporary organizations should find self-design next to impossible because they live in a climate of accountability. Within such climates, variability is treated as noise, significant changes are a nuisance, and unjustified variation is prohibited. The unfortunate effects of these practices may be reversed if people learn more about the activity of combining elements.

Self-design benefits from superstitious acting

As we have just seen, intentionally complicating action through galumphing can provide a means of generating alternative designs. Alternative designs can also be generated through superstitious acts that unwittingly complicate the life of the actor and his designs. We can out-

line the argument by analyzing divination as practiced by a group of
hunters in Labrador called the Naskapi Indians.

Every day the Naskapi face the question: "What direction should
the hunters take to locate game?" They answer this question by holding dried caribou shoulder bones over a fire. As the bones become
heated they develop cracks and smudges that are then "read" by an
expert. These cracks indicate the direction in which the hunter should
go to look for game. The Naskapi believe that this practice involves
the gods in their hunting decisions.

The interesting feature of these practices is that they work. To realize
why they work, think about the characteristics of this decision process.
First, the final decision about where to hunt is not a purely personal or
group choice. If no game are found, the gods, not the group, are to
blame. Second, the final decision is not affected by the outcomes of
past hunts. If the Indians were influenced by the outcomes of past
hunts, they would run the definite risk of depleting the stock of animals.
Prior success would induce subsequent failure. Third, the final decision
is not influenced by the inevitable patterning of choice and preferences
that holds true for all human beings. These very patterns enable the
hunted animals to take evasive action and to develop sensitivity to the
presence of human beings.

Given these general characteristics of bone reading, we can say
something about the utility of the practice. The use of scapuae (bones)
is a very crude way of randomizing human behavior under conditions
in which fixed patterns of behavior could be used advantageously by
adversaries. Thus, if people want to avoid regularities that can be exploited, they need something like a table of random numbers to generate their behavior.

My impression is that using tables of random numbers to make decisions may be effective in a broader range of settings than those involving adversaries. For example, one reason adaptation may preclude adaptability is that people remember only those practices that
are currently useful. Memory may preclude innovation.

It's conceivable that if groups used randomizing devices more frequently, they would forget what enables them to function in the here
and now and would be positioned to generate better designs. For example, if an executive burned caribou bones to decide how to tackle
his in-basket, where to relocate his factory, what territory to move into,
or what product to market next, it's not clear to me that his organization would be any worse off than if he used a highly rational approach
as his basis for decision making. The use of randomizing is equivalent
to discrediting retained wisdom and treating memory as an enemy,

and there are occasions when this type of intentional forgetting makes sense.

Conclusion

Self-design involves some difficult managerial actions, including the management of anarchy, the encouragement of doubt, the fostering of inefficiency, and the cultivation of superstition. If an organization wants to take control of its own destiny and designs, the changes necessary to pull this off are substantial. But those changes aren't impossible. The likelihood of pulling them off, however, depends heavily on the attitudes of the managers committed to self-design.

The best example I can find of the proper attitude for engaging in successful self-design was the poet W. H. Auden's speculations about what he would like his last words to be before he passed away. "In these days when it has become the medical convention, firstly, to keep the dying people in ignorance of their condition and, secondly, to keep them under sedation, how are any of us to utter what could be legitimately called our 'last' words? Still, it's fun to imagine what one would like them to be. The best proposed comment I know of is that of my friend Chester Kalman who said: 'Well, I've never done this before.' "

Now that's self-design!

The Organizational Saga in Higher Education
Burton R. Clark

Saga, originally referring to a medieval Icelandic or Norse account of achievements and events in the history of a person or group, has come to mean a narrative of heroic exploits, of a unique development that has deeply stirred the emotions of participants and descendants. Thus a saga is not simply a story but a story that at some time has had a particular base of believers. The term often refers also to the actual history itself, thereby including a stream of events, the participants, and the written or spoken interpretation. The element of belief is crucial, for without the credible story, the events and persons become history; with the development of belief, a particular bit of history becomes a definition full of pride and identity for the group.

Introduction

An *organizational saga* is a collective understanding of unique accomplishment in a formally established group. The group's definition of the accomplishment, intrinsically historical but embellished through retelling and rewriting, links stages of organizational development. The participants have added affect, an emotional loading, which places their conception between the coolness of rational purpose and the warmth of sentiment found in religion and magic. An organizational saga presents some rational explanation of how certain means led to certain ends, but it also includes affect that turns a formal place into a beloved institution, to which participants may be passionately devoted. Encountering such devotion, the observer may become unsure of his own analytical detachment as he tests the overtones of the institutional spirit or spirit of place.

The study of organizational sagas highlights nonstructural and non-

Revised version of paper presented at the 65th Annual Meeting of the American Sociological Association, September, 1970, Washington, D.C. Reprinted from *Administrative Science Quarterly*, vol .17, no. 2, June 1972, by permission of the author and the publisher.

rational dimensions of organizational life and achievement. Macro-organizational theory has concentrated on the role of structure and technology in organizational effectiveness (Gross 1964; Litterer 1965; March 1965; Thompson 1967; Price 1968; Perrow 1970). A needed corrective is more research on the cultural and expressive aspects of organizations, particularly on the role of belief and sentiment at broad levels of organization. The human-relations approach in organizational analysis, centered largely on group interaction, showed some awareness of the role of organization symbols (Whyte 1948, chapter 23), but this conceptual lead has not been taken as a serious basis for research. Also, in the literature on organizations and purposive communities, "ideology" refers to unified and shared belief (Selznick 1949; Bendix 1956; Price 1968, pp. 104–110; Carden 1969); but the concept of ideology has lost denotative power, having been stretched by varying uses. For the phenomenon discussed in this paper, "saga" seems to provide the appropriate denotation. With a general emphasis on normative bonds, organizational saga refers to a unified set of publicly expressed beliefs about the formal group that (a) is rooted in history, (b) claims unique accomplishment, and (c) is held with sentiment by the group.

To develop the concept in this paper, extreme cases and exaggerations of the ideal type are used; but the concept will be close to reality and widely applicable when the phenomenon is examined in weak as well as strong expression. In many organizations, even some highly utilitarian ones, some segment of their personnel probably develop in time at least a weak saga. Those who have persisted together for some years in one place will have had, at minimum, a thin stream of shared experience, which they elaborate into a plausible account of group uniqueness. Whether developed primarily by management or by employees, the story helps rationalize for the individual his commitment of time and energy for years, perhaps for a lifetime, to a particular enterprise. Even when weak, the belief can compensate in part for the loss of meaning in much modern work, giving some drama and some cultural identity to one's otherwise entirely instrumental efforts. At the other end of the continuum, a saga engages one so intensely as to make his immediate place overwhelmingly valuable. It can even produce a striking distortion, with the organization becoming the only reality, the outside world becoming illusion. Generally the almost complete capture of affect and perception is associated with only a few utopian communities, fanatical political factions, and religious sects. But some formal rationalized organizations, as for example business and education, can also become utopian, fanatical, or sectarian.

Organizational sagas vary in durability. They can arise quickly in relatively unstructured social settings, as in professional sports organizations that operate in the volatile context of contact with large spectator audiences through the mass media. A professional baseball or football team may create a rags-to-riches legend in a few months' time that excites millions of people. But such a saga is also very fragile as an ongoing definition of the organization. The story can be removed quickly from the collective understanding of the present and future, for successful performance is often unstable, and the events that set the direction of belief can be readily reversed, with the great winners quickly becoming habitual losers. In such cases, there seems to be an unstable structural connection between the organization and the base of believers. The base of belief is not anchored within the organization nor in personal ties between insiders and outsiders, but is mediated by mass media, away from the control of the organization. Such sagas continue only as the organization keeps repeating its earlier success and also keeps the detached followers from straying to other sources of excitement and identification.

In contrast, organizational sagas show high durability when built slowly in structured social contexts; for example, the educational system, specifically for the purposes of this paper, three liberal arts colleges in the United States. In the many small private colleges, the story of special performance emerges not in a few months but over a decade or two. When the saga is firmly developed, it is embodied in many components of the organization, affecting the definition and performance of the organization and finding protection in the webbing of the institutional parts. It is not volatile and can be relegated to the past only by years of attenuation or organizational decline.

Since the concept of organizational saga was developed from research on Reed, Antioch, and Swarthmore, three distinctive and highly regarded colleges (Clark 1970), material and categories from their developmental histories are used to illustrate the development of a saga, and its positive effects on organizational patricipation and effectiveness are then considered.[1]

Development of saga

Two stages can be distinguished in the development of an organizational saga, initiation and fulfillment. Initiation takes place under varying conditions and occurs within a relatively short period of time, fulfillment is related to features of the organization that are enduring and more predictable.

1. For some discussion of the risks and tensions associated with organizational sagas, particularly that of success in one period leading to later rigidity and stagnation, see Clark (1970, pp. 258–261). Hale (1970) gives an illuminating discussion of various effects of a persistent saga in a theological seminary.

Initiation

Strong sagas do not develop in passive organizations tuned to adaptive servicing of demand or to the fulfilling of roles dictated by higher authorities (Clark 1956, 1960). The saga is initially a strong purpose, conceived and enunciated by a single man or a small cadre (Selznick 1957) whose first task is to find a setting that is open, or can be opened, to a special effort. The most obvious setting is the autonomous new organization, where there is no established structure, no rigid custom, especially if a deliberate effort has been made to establish initial autonomy and bordering outsiders are preoccupied. There a leader may also have the advantage of building from the top down, appointing lieutenants and picking up recruits in accord with his ideas.

Reed College is strongly characterized by a saga, and its story of hard-won excellence and nonconformity began as strong purpose in a new organization. Its first president, William T. Foster, a thirty-year-old, highminded reformer, from the sophisticated East of Harvard and Bowdoin, went to the untutored Northwest, to an unbuilt campus in suburban Portland in 1910, precisely because he did not want to be limited by established institutions, all of which were, to his mind, corrupt in practice. The projected college in Oregon was clear ground, intellectually as well as physically, and he could there assemble the people and devise the practices that would finally give the United States an academically pure college, a Balliol for America.

The second setting for initiation is the established organization in a crisis of decay. Those in charge, after years of attempting incremental adjustments (Lindblom 1959), realize finally that they must either give up established ways or have the organization fail. Preferring that it survive, they may relinquish the leadership to one proposing a plan that promises revival and later strength, or they may even accept a man of utopian intent. Deep crisis in the established organization thus creates some of the conditions of a new organization. It suspends past practice, forces some bordering groups to stand back or even to turn their backs on failure of the organization, and it tends to catch the attention of the reformer looking for an opportunity.

Antioch College is a dramatic example of such a setting. Started in the 1860s, its first sixty years were characterized by little money, weak staff, few students, and obscurity. Conditions worsened in the teens under the inflation and other strains of World War I. In 1919 a charismatic utopian reformer, Arthur E. Morgan, decided it was more advantageous to take over an old college with buildings and a charter than to start a new one. First as trustee and then as president, he began in the early 1920s an institutional renovation that overturned everything. As president he found it easy to push aside old, weak organizational structures and usages. He elaborated a plan of general education involving an unusual combination of work, study, and community participation; and he set about to devise the implementing tool. Crisis and charisma made possible a radical transformation out of which came a second Antioch, a college soon characterized by a sense of exciting history, unique practice, and exceptional performance.

The third context for initiation is the established organization that is not in crisis, not collapsing from long decline, yet ready for evolutionary change. This is the most difficult situation to predict, having to do with degree of rigidity. In both ideology and structure, institutionalized colleges vary in openness to change. In those under church control, for example, the colleges of the more liberal Protestant denominations have been more hospitable than Catholic colleges, at least until recently, to educational experimentation. A college with a tradition of presidential power is more open to change than one where the trustees and the professors exert control over the president. Particularly promising is the college with a self-defined need for educational leadership. This is the opening for which some reformers watch, the sound place that has some ambition to increase its academic stature, as for example, Swarthmore College.

Swarthmore began in the 1860s, and had become by 1920 a secure and stable college, prudently managed by Quaker trustees and administrators and solidly based on traditional support from nearby Quaker families in Pennsylvania, New Jersey, and Maryland. Such an organization would not usually be thought promising for reform, but Frank Avdelotte, who became its president in 1920, judged it ready for change. Magnetic in personality, highly placed within the élite circle of former Rhodes scholars, personally liked by important foundation officials, and recommended as a scholarly leader, he was offered other college presidencies, but he chose Swarthmore as a place open to change through a combination of financial health, liberal Quaker ethos, and some institutional ambition. His judgment proved correct, although the tolerance for his changes in the 1920s and 1930s was narrow at times. He began the gradual introduction of a modified Oxford honors program and related changes, which resulted in noteworthy achievements that supporters were to identify later as "the Swarthmore saga" (Swarthmore College Faculty 1941).

Fulfillment

Although the conditions of initiation of a saga vary, the means of fulfillment are more predictable. There are many ways in which a unified sense of a special history is expressed; for example, even a patch of sidewalk or a coffee room may evoke emotion among the believers;

but one can delimit the components at the center of the development of a saga. These may center, in colleges, on the personnel, the program, the external social base, the student subculture, and the imagery of the saga.

Personnel

In a college, the key group of believers is the senior faculty. When they are hostile to a new idea, its attenuation is likely; when they are passive, its success is weak; and when they are devoted to it, a saga is probable. A single leader, a college president, can initiate the change, but the organizational idea will not be expanded over the years and expressed in performance unless ranking and powerful members of the faculty become committed to it and remain committed even after the initiator is gone. In committing themselves deeply, taking some credit for the change and seeking to ensure its perpetuation, they routinize the charisma of the leader in collegial authority. The faculty cadre of believers helps to effect the legend, then to protect it against later leaders and other new participants who, less pure in belief, might turn the organization in some other direction.

Such faculty cadres were well developed at Reed by 1925, after the time of its first two presidents; at Antioch, by the early 1930s, after Morgan, disappointed with his followers, left for the board of directors of the new TVA; and at Swarthmore, by the 1930s, and particularly by 1940, after Aydelotte's twenty years of persistent effort. In all three colleges, after the departure of the change agent(s), the senior faculty with the succeeding president, a man appropriate for consolidation, undertook the full working out of the experiment. The faculty believers also replaced themselves through socialization and selective recruitment and retention in the 1940s and 1950s. Meanwhile, new potential innovators had sometimes to be stopped. In such instances, the faculty was able to exert influence to shield the distinctive effort from erosion or deflection. At Reed, for example, major clashes between president and faculty in the late 1930s and the early 1950s were precipitated by a new change-oriented president, coming in from the outside, disagreeing with a faculty proud of what had been done, attached deeply to what the college had become, and determined to maintain what was for them the distinctive Reed style. From the standpoint of constructing a regional and national model of purity and severity in undergraduate education, the Reed faculty did on those occasions act to create while acting to conserve.

Program

For a college to transform purpose into a credible story of unique accomplishment, there must be visible practices with which claims of distinctiveness can be supported; that is, unusual courses, noteworthy requirements, or special methods of teaching. On the basis of seemingly unique practices, the program becomes a set of communal symbols and rituals, invested with meaning. Not reporting grades to the students becomes a symbol, as at Reed, that the college cares about learning for learning's sake; thus mere technique becomes part of a saga.

In all the three colleges, the program was seen as distinctive by both insiders and outsiders. At Swarthmore it was the special seminars and other practices of the honors program, capped by written and oral examination by teams of visiting outsiders in the last days of the senior year. At Antioch it was the work-study cycle, the special set of general education requirements, community government, and community involvement. At Reed it was the required freshman lecture-and-seminar courses, the junior qualifying examination, and the thesis in the senior year. Such practices became central to a belief that things had been done so differently, and so much against the mainstream, and often against imposing odds, that the group had generated a saga.

Social base

The saga also becomes fixed in the minds of outside believers devoted to the organization, usually the alumni. The alumni are the best located to hold beliefs enduringly pure, since they can be as strongly identified with a special organizational history as the older faculty and administrators and yet do not have to face directly the new problems generated by a changing environment or students. Their thoughts can remain centered on the past, rooted in the days when, as students, they participated intimately in the unique ways and accomplishments of the campus.

Liberal alumni, as those of Reed, Antioch, and Swarthmore here, seek to conserve what they believe to be a unique liberal institution and to protect it from the conservative forces of society that might change it—that is, to make it like other colleges. At Reed, for example, dropouts as well as graduates were struck by the intellectual excellence of their small college, convinced that college life there had been unlike college life anywhere else, and they were ready to conserve the practices that seemed to sustain that excellence. Here too, conserving acts can be seen for a time as contributing to an innovation, protecting the full working out of a distinctive effort.

Student subculture

The student body is the third group of believers, not overwhelmingly important but still a necessary support for the saga. To become and remain a saga, a change must be supported by the student subculture over decades, and the ideology of the subculture must integrate with the central ideas of the believing administrators and faculty. When the students define themselves as personally responsible for upholding the image of the college, then a design or plan has become an organizational saga.

At Antioch, Reed, and Swarthmore, the student subcultures were powerful mechanisms for carrying a developing saga from one generation to another. Reed students, almost from the beginning and extending at least to the early 1960's, were great believers in the uniqueness of their college, constantly on the alert for any action that would alter it, ever fearful that administration or faculty might succumb to pressures that would make Reed just like other colleges. Students at Antioch and Swarthmore also offered unstinting support for the ideology of their institution. All three student bodies steadily and dependably transferred the ideology from one generation to another. Often socializing deeply, they helped produce the graduate who never quite rid himself of the wish to go back to the campus.

Imagery of saga

Upheld by faculty, alumni, and students, expressed in teaching practices, the saga is even more widely expressed as a generalized tradition in statues and ceremonies, written histories and current catalogues, even in an "air about the place" felt by participants and some outsiders. The more unique the history and the more forceful the claim to a place in history, the more intensely cultivated the ways of sharing memory and symbolizing the institution. The saga is a strong self-fulfilling belief; working through institutional self-image and public image, it is indeed a switchman (Weber 1946), helping to determine the tracks along which action is pushed by men's self-defined interests. The early belief of one stage brings about the actions that warrant a stronger version of the same belief in a later period. As the account develops, believers come to sense its many constituent symbols as inextricably bound together, and the part takes its meaning from the whole. For example, at Antioch a deep attachment developed in the 1930s and 1940s to Morgan's philosophy of the whole man and to its expression in a unique combination of work, study, community participation, and many practices thought to embody freedom and nonconformity. Some of the faculty of those years who remained in the 1940s and 1950s had many memories and impressions that seemed to form a symbolic whole: personnel counselors, folk dancing in Red Square, Morgan's towering physique, the battles of community government, the pacifism of the late 1930s, the frequent dash of students to off-campus jobs, the dedicated deans who personified central values. Public image also grew strong and sharp, directing liberals and radicals to the college and conservatives to other places. The symbolic expressions themselves were a strong perpetuating force.

Conclusion

An organizational saga is a powerful means of unity in the formal place. It makes links across internal divisions and organizational boundaries as internal and external groups share their common belief. With deep emotional commitment, believers define themselves by their organizational affiliation, and in their bond to other believers they share an intense sense of the unique. In an organization defined by a strong saga, there is a feeling that there is the small world of the lucky few and the large routine one of the rest of the world. Such an emotional bond turns the membership into a community, even a cult.

An organizational saga is thus a valuable resource, created over a number of years out of the social components of the formal enterprise. As participants become ideologues, their common definition becomes a foundation for trust and for extreme loyalty. Such bonds give the organization a competitive edge in recruiting and maintaining personnel and helps it to avoid the vicious circle in which some actual or anticipated erosion of organizational strength leads to the loss of some personnel, which leads to further decline and loss. Loyalty causes individuals to stay with a system, to save and improve it rather than to leave to serve their self-interest elsewhere (Hirschman, 1970). The genesis and persistence of loyalty is a key organizational and analytical problem. Enduring loyalty follows from a collective belief of participants that their organization is distinctive. Such a belief comes from a credible story of uncommon effort, achievement, and form.

Pride in the organized group and pride in one's identity as taken from the group are personal returns that are uncommon in modern social involvement. The development of sagas is one way in which men in organizations increase such returns, reducing their sense of isolation and increasing their personal pride and pleasure in organizational life. Studying the evocative narratives and devotional ties of formal systems leads to a better understanding of the fundamental capacities of organizations to enhance or diminish the lives of participants. The organization possessing a saga is a place in which participants for a time at least happily accept their bond.

References

Bendix, R. 1956. Work and Authority in Industry. New York: John Wiley.

Carden, M. L. 1969. Oneida: Utopian Community to Modern Corporation. Baltimore: The Johns Hopkins Press.

Clark, B. R. 1956. Adult Education in Transition: A Study of Institutional Insecurity. Berkeley: University of California Press.

———. 1960. The Open Door College. A Case Study. New York: McGraw-Hill.

———. 1970. The Distinctive College: Antioch, Reed, and Swarthmore. Chicago: Aldine.

———. 1971. "Belief and loyalty in college organization." Journal of Higher Education, XLIII, 6: 499–515.

Gross, B. M. 1964. The Managing of Organizations. (2 vols.) New York: Free Press.

Hale, J. R. 1970. The Making and Testing of an Organizational Saga: A Case-Study of the Lutheran Theological Seminary at Gettysburg, Pennsylvania, with Special Reference to the Problem of Merger, 1959–1969. Unpublished Ed.D. dissertation, Columbia University.

Hirschman, A. O. 1970. Exit, Voice, and Loyalty. Cambridge, Mass.: Harvard University Press.

Lindblom, C. E. 1959. "The Science of 'muddling through.'" Public Administration Review 19: 79–88.

Litterer, J. A. 1965. The Analysis of Organizations. New York: John Wiley.

March, J. G. (ed.) 1965. Handbook of Organizations. Chicago: Rand McNally.

Perrow, C. 1970. Organizational Analysis. Belmont, California: Wadsworth.

Price, J. L. 1968. Organizational Effectiveness: An Inventory of Propositions. Homewood, Illinois: Richard D. Irwin.

Selznick, P. 1949. TVA and the Grass Roots. Berkeley: University of California Press.

———. 1957. Leadership in Administration. New York: Harper & Row.

Swarthmore College Faculty 1941. An Adventure in Education: Swarthmore College Under Frank Aydelotte. New York: Macmillan.

Thompson, J. D. 1967. Organizations in Action. New York: McGraw-Hill.

Weber, M. 1946. From Max Weber: Essays in Sociology. Translated and edited by H. H. Gerth and C. Wright Mills. New York: Oxford.

Whyte, W. F. 1948. Human Relations in the Restaurant Industry. New York: McGraw-Hill.

12

Organizational Change: Moving the Mountain

Introduction

The people in organizations change; their relationships to one another change; the technologies the organization uses change; the environments surrounding and permeating the organizations change; and even the tools used to adjust the rates and directions of change are themselves changing. Each article in this chapter has something to say about how organizations change, and particularly about the nature of the tools we can use to change them.

Organizational change bears a close resemblance to its twin, organizational design. When Weick described ways to promote self-designing systems, he emphasized that organizations are always self-designing, and that they need help in improving their capacity for redesign.

The first article, by Beckhard comes from a now-classic tradition of helping organizations to change themselves—a tradition based in "team building." The heart of many change efforts rests on getting groups to work as teams. If you get the team to work, the individual is activated; and if you can get the many teams within an organization to align themselves in an even partially coordinated fashion, the organization is activated to change in directions desired by their members.

In the second article, Alderfer builds further on the team as a tool of organizational change. He suggests that a communications group be implanted in the organization to serve as a pressure valve between the organization and its environments. The communication group becomes a miniature of the organization itself, but one in which it is possible more clearly to perceive underlying organization-wide and organization-to-environment issues.

The final two articles of this chapter move from small-group interventions to the role of meaning in organizational change efforts. Indeed, the paper by Peters argues that many currently valued change tools are largely ineffective. He reviews the methods used by a number of chief

615   Introduction

executives to promote change in their organizations, and he suggests
that a barrage of small nudges is a useful device for moving the organization along. Most of these nudges involve the manipulation of meanings to shape actions. For example, the executive provides cues about
his preferred futures, or anoints certain new ideas, or reinterprets historical events, any of which refocuses the attention of the organization
an inch at a time. Peters calls his tools "mundane," but perhaps attention to the mundane side of organizations can generate significant organizational change.

In the final article by Mitroff and Kilmann, we focus more directly
on a tool aimed directly at altering the meaning side of organizations;
storytelling. As we change jobs and routines, as we experience crises,
stories are passed from one member to the other. Change the stories
and you change the images to which new and old alike orient their
decisions and actions. Stories are one way to socialize newcomers into
the accepted practices and behavioral codes of the organization. This
storytelling emphasis also takes us back to Clark's description of organizational sagas. The main point is that when one changes the cues
and loci of attention, as Peters suggests, and when one changes the
patterns of communication, as Alderfer and Beckhard intend, then the
meanings of the organization to its members are also changed. And we
can turn the whole idea around. Let's change meanings and interpretations, and perhaps we can change the organization practices and
decisions.

Optimizing Team-building Efforts
Richard Beckhard

The problem of energy

A tremendous amount of human energy in organizations is expended by participation in groups. In addition to the time spent in meetings exchanging necessary operating information, most management groups and work teams also spend a significant amount of time on issues such as future planning or improvement planning.

In the truly effective organization, most of the energy of the work force is available for *doing* and *improving* the *work* of the organization, and a minimum amount of energy is needed to maintain the human organization.

In trying to achieve this state, organizations devote considerable effort to improving the effectiveness of work teams. For example, such efforts form one of the major foundations in the Blake and Mouton Grid Organization Development Program. The programs of laboratory training are designed to help people improve the effectiveness of their collaborative work in group settings. Many team-building efforts conducted by internal and external organization development consultants are aimed at improving the effectiveness and working relationships of work groups.

The purpose of team-building

In recent years I have observed a number of team-development efforts and have lately come to the realization that there may be a discrepancy in priorities between those people in charge of teams engaging in such efforts and those people who are facilitating them. Team leaders often consider their objectives to be improving work, setting priorities, or solving problems. Consultants, trainers, and helpers often see the prime purpose of the effort to be improving the workings of the group and/or the relationships of its members.

Reprinted from Richard Beckhard, "Optimizing Team Building Efforts" in The Journal of Contemporary Business *1* (1972), no. 3, pp. 23–32.

To help understand this more fully, I have developed a classification, in order of importance, of the reasons why teams or groups meet other than for the sharing of information. These are:

To set goals and/or priorities;

To analyze or allocate the way work is performed;

To examine the way a group is working: its processes (such as norms, decision-making, communications);

To examine relationships among the people doing the work.

These purposes are usually operating in any team-development effort; but unless *one* purpose is defined as *the* primary purpose, there tends to be considerable misuse of energy. People then operate from their own hierarchy of purposes and, predictably, these are not always the same for all members.

In looking at the disenchantment of some managers and leaders regarding the amount of time spent on team improvement activities in their organizations, I have noted that organization development consultants and trainers frequently are perceived by "clients" or team leaders as having a "universal" rank-order of the four purposes, as follows:

The relationships among people,

The way the group works together,

The work,

The goals and priorities.

This perception is too often correct because the "orientation" of the organizational development (OD) consultant—his value system and much of his competence—probably is built around helping people work together in groups and is probably less related to the specific goal of an organization. However, if the perception is there on the part of the team leader, there probably will be a discrepancy between *his* preferred rank-ordering of priorities and his perceptions regarding preferences of the consultant.

It has also become clear that team leaders often tend to be inexplicit about their own rank-ordering. Therefore, the rank-ordering of the consultant may well be the controlling factor in a team-development effort. This is reinforced by the "client's" perception that the OD specialist is the *expert*. In such cases, the team leader tends to lean on the consultant for expert guidance and, in some cases, to give up his own responsibility for the effort.

Some conditions for effective team-building

From the observations, I have developed a set of guidelines for team development:

The primary goal of a team development meeting must be explicit and well articulated.

This primary goal must be owned by the leader of the group and understood (hopefully, agreed to) by the work group members.

The leader's goal should be the condition within which third parties (consultants) work (i.e., the primary purpose is defined by the leader who sets the agenda and activities of the meeting).

If the consultant is working with a team, he should help the leader be explicit in *defining* and sharing the primary purpose.

The four goal categories probably will be dealt with in a particular activity, but only as appropriate in relation to a primary purpose.

A model for team-building activities

The following model examines for each of the four primary purposes (setting goals or priorities, the work, the way the group works, relationships within the group) four dimensions which would be considered:

Leader behavior,

Member behavior,

Outcomes,

Third-party or consultant behavior.

I will describe each of these dimensions in relation to *each* of the primary purposes, and follow the description with a case illustration.

Primary purpose—setting goals or priorities

Leader behavior issues

Are the work goals "given" (the leader's), or are they to be decided by the group?

Are the priorities a "given" or are they to be decided by the group?

How much freedom does the leader *wish* others to have in determining the agenda?

To what organization conditions, other goals, policies, etc., must these goals or priorities be related?

What preparation is necessary to optimize use of the resources of the members at the activity?

What are the leader's specific hoped-for outcomes for the meeting?

Member behavior issues

What behavior around the task is expected from members—i.e., Understanding? Decision-making? Agreement to implement? Action plans?

What data are needed during the meeting—i.e., effects of alternative goals or priorities on members' work and the work of suborganizations?

Outcomes possible

What is required from the meeting—i.e., a new statement of goals or priorities? Agreement to develop one?

What action plans and responsibilities for carrying out meeting outputs should be developed?

How will assignments of responsibilities be made?

What kind of feedback and checkpoints are or should be available?

Third-party behavior issues

Some of the "processes" questions that might be asked by a facilitator concern:

Clarity of the goal—i.e., agreement on priorities;

To what degree people are understanding each other;

Clarity of the ownership of the goals;

Awareness of consequences;

Commitment to action.

Case

In a large consumer organization there were a number of departments with computer and information systems capabilities. These departments were combined into a new Management Methods Department, which was to provide leadership in applying the various technologies to requirements of the organization. It also was to provide support and assistance to a variety of users with respect to methods and hardware. A third mission was to provide an educational effort to increase the internal market of users.

The membership of the management team of this group comprised a variety of bases—some had worked together before, others had not. Each member had headed a specialty or specialists' group and had had his own "technological empire." The management group was asked to combine all these resources and develop a new kind of service organization.

The leader of the group wanted to introduce some new technologies which he knew would provide significant savings to some parts of the organization. He also was concerned with centralizing some hardware installations; with communicating the new department's capabilities and services to the rest of the organization; with upgrading both the amounts and the quality of services provided; with developing some major new applications; and with creating a new image of *helpfulness* to the line managements of the business.

Having defined the primary purpose of the meeting as setting goal and mission priorities, the leader now needed to clarify his expectations around the first issue—were the priorities *given* or to be decided by the group? It became clear, by discussion, that the leader had preferences, but he really wanted *consensus* from this group on priorities and goals. He felt that all of his goals were interdependent; thus, it did not matter which one was worked first. Therefore, his first effort at the meeting was to convince the members that relative to *their* role expectations, *he expected* that this group would, as a group, determine the priorities of the various goals, set programs, and provide the resource management for carrying out the programs necessary to achieve the goals. The leader wanted a great deal of freedom to be shared among subordinates.

In the course of a couple of meetings, it became clear from discussions that there was also a need for exploration of the way the work was going to be done. Issues arose about how the group would handle decisions around priorities, how the information should flow between sections, and how the group norms regarding openness or leveling would be decided.

Some people were unclear about the leader's position on these issues but when his attitudes were shared, their confusion ended. He wanted all to have freedom to challenge goals and priorities.

Relationship problems surfaced which, after discussion, turned out to be goal problems. For example, one person in the group had held a job now held by another person in the group. Because they had different work priorities for that subsection, there was concern about the relationship between them. Discussion quickly cleared this up.

By treating the "how we work" and "relationship" questions as agenda matters to be dealt with as they got in the way of the *goal-setting* issues, the group was able to move quite rapidly toward actual setting of goals and priorities and to make action plans for following up.

Primary purpose—analyzing and assigning work

Leader behavior issues

Defining areas of work to be studied;

Defining the *current* situation—i.e., where work and responsibility are located;

Defining boundaries of his willingness to change;

Defining roles he wants others to take in the meeting—i.e., suggestions, decisions, actions.

Member behavior issues

An understanding of the areas of work to be allocated, the alternative possibilities, and the parameters of freedom to relocate work;

Clear role expectations—what behavior is expected of them in the decision-making?

Awareness of implications and *costs* of changing work;

Payout for subordinates or members of changing allocations of work.

Outcomes possible

New work distribution;
An action plan for communicating changes to others;

Answers on costs, effects on compensation and rewards, effects on roles, titles, etc.;

Action plan for follow-up evaluation of the changes.

Third-party behavior issues

Providing a method for working the issues—e.g., providing methods of analyzing work;

Helping to clarify work boundaries;

Getting the group to face action implications and to plan;

Helping people understand each other;

Raising issues of openness of communication within the group.

Case

The top management of a division of a large chemical organization is managed by a board composed of a chairman, two deputy chairmen, and ten members of the management board. The group functions as an executive board. Each member of the team except the chairman and deputy chairmen have functional responsibilities, such as manufacturing, engineering, personnel; they also are responsible at the division level for some business area; e.g., serving as chairman of a wholly owned subsidiary.

Officially, the power of decisions rests centrally with the chairman. The remainder of the group had been perceived by its members as being mostly advisory. Actual functioning of the upper management of the organization was somewhat unclear; there were questions about the responsibilities of management board members acting in their functional capacities as opposed to their responsibilities as board members. There was considerable dissatisfaction with this ambiguity.

The chairman suggested having a team meeting to analyze realistically the tasks that needed to be performed by the board as a board; the tasks that were not getting performed; and the possibilities of delegating some tasks below board level to operating managers.

The method used was a review of the board agendas for the previous 6 months and an analysis of these agendas. This analysis provided three lists:

> Things that the group did which absolutely must be done by them as a group;

> Work that was not being done that should be done by this group—e.g., long-range planning.

> Work that was being done by this group that could be done as well or almost as well by the same members operating in other roles or by other people.

The analysis showed that between 25 and 30 percent of the work being done by this group could be done by others. There was a roughly similar amount of work that needed to be done that was not getting done.

The group examined its own *attitudes* and *commitment* toward turning over some major areas of work to other people. It explored the training, development, and changes of procedure that would be required for the transfer of work—it identified what this would mean in terms of rewards (who would be held accountable and responsible). The discussion also identified areas of personal development that the board or executive committee members needed in order to take on some of the work that they were not doing. It also provided some clarification of what the chairman expected of them. This discussion produced the need for further examination of some of the relationships between roles, particularly the roles between the deputy chairmen and the junior board members.

Outputs involved (1) a minor structural reorganization, (2) the delegation of a considerable amount of work, with full responsibility and accountability for its disposition, to the operating manager level, (3) the organization of a planning group within the board, and (4) a change of many of the practices of their board meetings.

Primary purpose—how the group works

Leader behavior issues

Dissatisfaction with the status quo as a reason for wanting to change;

Willingness to look at all data, styles, attitudes, titles, rewards, and processes;

Willingness to be influenced;

Self-realization by the leader that he is probably part of the relevant data;

Methods for working the problem.

Member behavior issues

The need for clear ground rules on "voting"; how much openness is allowed and the punishments or consequences of deviant behavior;

The need to know what the boss's feelings are regarding present practices and possible changes;

The need for a set of parameters of possibilities for change;

The need for some readiness to work the problems.

Outcomes possible

Some new norms are possible;

Action plans regarding change procedures can emerge;

Some changed "ownership" in the management of certain processes, such as agenda planning, structure, decision-making, and leadership.

Third-party behavior issues

Process interventions around issues are relevant, such as communication, decision-making, norms, and leadership;

He can provide methods for working the problems;

He can help work issues such as those on listening, problem-solving, role distortion, and projection.

Case

In a large, diversified organization, the personnel function had previously been managed by a director and several department heads, each of whom heads a function, such as employment, compensation, salary administration, benefits, training and development, industrial relations, and employee relations.

The heads of these groups were specialists. Their departments functioned as relatively independent staffs handling the particular function for which they were responsible. For general information-sharing—updating company policies and priorities and providing liaison with top management—there were "cabinet" meetings of the heads of departments with the director. However, there was no shared responsibility for or commitment to total management of the personnel function by the heads of the specific functions.

A new director moved in who believed that the personnel organization should be reorganized and redirected to focus around *organization issues* and *human resources management issues* rather than along the strict functional lines previously followed. For example, relations with employees involved not only the head of industrial relations, but also the training and development people and the employment people. He also wanted to develop a management *team* in the personnel function that could *locate* the priority issues in the organization, and *mobilize* the *total resources* of the personnel staff and others in the organization to manage these priorities.

In his early weeks of the organization, he communicated these desires and priorities and received responses ranging from outright resistance to "lip service" approval. In most cases, people responded in a "subordinate" way to what they perceived to be commands.

The director really wanted to change the mode of working. He convened a meeting with the specific purpose of "taking a look at how we're working together"—what processes and procedures are used, what processes, procedures, and systems will be necessary to move toward the kind of management of human resources that he required and desired. At the meeting, his statement of wishes immediately led to a discussion of how these decisions *had been made* and how they were now being made by him, and how people hoped they would be made.

A second issue developed around communication and influence; a third issue was the director's leadership style and the differences between his style and that of the previous leadership. A fourth issue was what were the rewards and punishments for acting one way or another in this new situation?

As the group worked, it was able to examine thoroughly the various processes, procedures, roles, norms, etc., within which they worked, and to relate these to the defined goal of a coordinated management of the human resources function. This was a case where the goal was clearly to work on *how* we work, and specific plans for changing the way work was done in the organization became the *case material* and the validating point for the work on the primary purpose of the meeting.

Primary purpose—relationships among the group members

Leader behavior issues

A willingness to expose his own attitudes and biases;

A willingness to be nonpunitive;

Some assurance that group members see this activity as relevant;

A willingness to change or to be influenced.

Members behavior issues

Enough personal security to take some risks;

A knowledge and belief that the leader has real interests in the process;

Some confidence in the process and/or the third party;

Some feelings of relevance of the activity;

Some feelings of potency;

Some willingness to expose feelings.

Outcomes possible

Increased understanding and acceptance of each other;

Better listening;

Some new norms—e.g., leveling, more information-based decisions;

More feelings of ownership;

More willingness to take risks;

More willingness to confront conflict and work to resolve it.

Third-party behavior issues

Interventions in this mode are most helpful around process issues.

Intervention process—i.e., communications, decision-making;

Protection of parameters of openness, confrontation, etc.;

Modeling behavior—e.g., feedback;

Objectivity as applied to the group's work;

Nonjudgmental feedback;

Resolution of interpersonal difficulties.

Case

A management group in a division of an organization had developed norms of openness, problem-solving, and goal direction. The organization climate was quite open and free. The division was a high technology group with a number of extremely capable scientists whose whole background was entrepreneurial and professional. The management group was committed intellectually to building a participative, democratic organization. Obstacles toward achievement of this generally shared goal and value system were (1) their own personal styles, and (2) the interaction among them. The group was able to be very open around technical problems, intergroup problems within the organization, and role problems. However, they were not able to deal with each other as people with different biases, interests, and styles. The norm of "nonconfronting" this kind of material was reinforced by the president, a brilliant executive, greatly admired by all the members of the team. He was a rational, sensible, analytically minded person who could keep the discussions rational and data-based. He managed, simultaneously, though inadvertently, to suppress much of the emotional data which were crucial and with which they needed to deal.

After a considerable amount of time working as a team—including outside developmental experiences by many individual members—a subgroup emerged which had a common goal of facing these relationship questions. It had enough potency to deal with both the president and colleagues. They suggested an extended meeting to have a thorough review of where they stood as *people* managing this business. The suggestion was accepted by all the members and the meeting was held.

At this meeting each individual received some feedback from all of his colleagues about his strengths and weaknesses as they perceived them, what bothered or pleased them about his behavior. Each individual could use this feedback any way he wished—there was no requirement for change. The feedback surfaced some historic issues that had been affecting the work of the group; for example, two people who had been competing throughout their careers maintained this competition in the group. They were perceived by all the others as sometimes robbing the group of their technical resource capability on the tasks because of their interpersonal relationship. It was agreed that the group would try to draw this to their attention whenever it arose in the future.

The feedback to the president by the team was accepted and generally understood by him. He acted on it to some degree; however, the main benefit of *this* feedback was that it freed the group to produce this kind of information in the future as needed. This became a norm of the group and was perhaps the single most significant result.

Here is a case in which interpersonal relationships of a group of responsible adults were impeding their doing what they all really wanted to do: effective work on goals and plans and effective management of their scientific capability in a humanized setting.

Summary

Work groups and teams spend a significant amount of man-hours, in addition to their administrative information meetings, on group activities aimed at one of the following goals:

—establishing goals or priorities
—analyzing and distributing the work
—examining how the group works (procedures, processes, norms)
—examining the relationship among the group members as they work.

There is a need for criteria for sorting out the rank-ordering of these purposes and for selecting *one* of them as a primary purpose.

The team leader must take responsibility for setting the specific core purpose of a meeting.

Third parties can make a major contribution in facilitating the work of such groups. Their help should be as process consultants within the core purpose defined by the client or team leader.

Managers can more or less systematically relate the primary purpose —goal setting, work planning, work relationships, to issues of leader behavior, member behavior, outcomes, and third-party or consultant behavior.

These options can help group leaders determine the goal of an improvement activity, the information needed to work the activity, an understanding of the kind of facilitation which might be helpful by a third party, and a clear commitment to some appropriate outcomes.

Conscious management of such team-building efforts can do much to utilize the human energy in organizationally and personally profitable ways.

Improving Organizational Communication through Long-term Intergroup Intervention
Clayton P. Alderfer

This article applies open-systems theory and method to an organization development intervention for improving intergroup communications. The theory involves an attempt to relate properties of system and subsystem *boundaries* to qualities of *relationships* among systems and subsystems. The OD intervention consists of a "Communications Group" or microcosm group—a structural innovation designed to increase information flow vertically and horizontally among differentiated units within a division of a large corporation. This is an action research project, in which theory was influencing action from the outset and in which the outcomes have implications for developing new theory as well as for improving professional practice.

Theoretical constructs and hypotheses

Organizations may be conceptualized as open systems of interacting groups coordinated by some common goal(s) and differentiated by hierarchy of authority, division of labor, and the collective histories of individual members. Each person in the system contributes to the performance of certain tasks, occupies a rank in the hierarchy, and identifies with certain historically determined demographic groups (Alderfer 1976c). The behavior of individuals, small groups, and organizations may be explained in part by the use of open-systems concepts concerning *boundaries* and *relationships* (Alderfer 1976b).

Boundaries

Open systems—from the individual through the small group to the large organization—are separated from their external environments by

Reproduced by special permission from *The Journal of Applied Behavorial Science,* "Improving Organizational Communication through Long-Term Intergroup Intervention," by Clayton P. Alderfer, vol. 13, no. 2, 1977, pp. 193–210, NTL Institute.

physical and psychological boundaries which define what is inside and what is outside. Boundaries regulate the flow of matter, energy, and information inward and outward for open systems. This regulatory property of boundaries is called permeability. Highly *permeable boundaries* permit extensive flows inward and outward, while comparatively *impermeable boundaries* restrict exchange among systems.

The vitality of a human system refers to its capacity to survive in a malevolent environment and to grow in benevolent surroundings. It is hypothesized that there is a curvilinear relationship between boundary permeability and system vitality. At very low levels of permeability an "overbounded" system is in danger of being closed off from necessary exchanges with its environment. At very high levels of permeability an "underbounded" system may be hard to distinguish from its environment and therefore may cease to exist entirely. "Optimal" boundary permeability occurs at some moderate level where a system is able to carry out needed interactions with its environment while retaining its organization and identity (Alderfer 1976a).

To be useful in an intervention, a concept must be "operationalized for action," a process that is directly analogous to operationalizing a concept for measurement. In the case of optimal boundary permeability, a consultant thinking in terms of this concept must have a series of actions designed to increase or decrease boundary permeability. In the project I am about to describe—the creation and maintenance of an effective "Communications Group"—there were a variety of such actions employed.

The first task of any system is to survive in relation to its environment (Rice 1969). Therefore any new system or subsystem must be distinguished from its environment; elements of the system must be differentiated from nonelements. Since the major elements of the system were individuals and groups, there had to be a means for determining who (in terms of individuals and groups) was and was not a member of the "Communications Group." Actions to establish the group helped to determine its boundaries and to prevent it from becoming "underbounded." Once the group was formed, additional actions were necessary to strengthen its boundaries.

But if the concept of optimal boundary permeability is valid, another set of actions was also needed to prevent the group from becoming closed off from the larger system in which it was embedded. Procedures were needed to encourage individuals and groups who were not formal members of the "Communications Group" to interact regularly with it, and thereby prevent the group from becoming "overbounded." In other words, the group needed a set of values and procedures to encourage and to manage regular interaction with nonmembers.

Relationships

Relationships among systems and subsystems consist of a regular exchange of matter, energy, and information. A critical property of relationships is the quality of that exchange, which here is called *mutuality*. The degree of mutuality in a relationship is determined by the extent that the relevant parties express their own and accept others' ideas and feelings (Alderfer al. 1974).

Relationships between systems and subsystems imply some degree of boundary permeability. Members of one system must join another—at least temporarily—to engage in any kind of exchange. This paper starts with the following hypothesis. *There is a relationship between boundary permeability and relationship mutuality. Optimal boundary permeability is associated with highly mutual relationships, while overbounded and underbounded systems typically show lower degrees of mutuality.*

There were a number of ways to operationalize this concept of mutuality for an intervention such as the Communications Group. The hypothesized relationship suggests that different tactics are needed depending on whether the objective is to increase the mutuality of an underbounded system or an overbounded system. In an underbounded system, the predominant condition is that people do not perceive significant bases for positive relationships. To increase mutuality under these circumstances, interventions are needed to permit participants to *discover* whatever bases of attraction exist and then to determine whether there is enough commonality to bring a group together. In overbounded systems departures from high levels of mutuality take a different form. Here limitations to high levels of mutuality arise from lack of tolerance for disagreement and differences. Under these circumstances interventions should be aimed toward letting conflict emerge. Issues that can be resolved should be identified and differentiated from those that cannot; the latter should be constrained in order not to prevent work on areas where resolution is possible.

Internal and external linkages

If, as hypothesized, there is a connection between boundary properties and relationship qualities, there should also be linkages between internal and external relationships in open systems. Indeed, boundaries mediate the influence between internal and external affairs in social systems. The internal and external relationships of a system are linked because each is partially determined by properties of the system's external boundary.

The external boundary of the larger system influences the relations among subsystems by partially determining how the external environment impacts on the internal working of the system. People are generally members of many systems, and their relationships with each other *inside* a particular system are partially influenced by the relations among the other systems in the *outside* environment. Specifically in the case of the Communications Group, *individual* members' *interpersonal* relationships with each other were hypothesized to be influenced by the *intergroup* relationships among the departments, hierarchical level, and demographic groups within the division.

Underbounded and overbounded systems in the extreme are not nearly the opposite conditions that the terms may suggest. In practice the build-up of suppressed conflict in a severely overbounded system may lead to internally generated emotional crises that result in the system "blowing apart" and becoming overbounded. And the chaos characteristic of underbounded systems may provoke external intervention that creates substantially impermeable external boundaries.

In numerous settings I have found that neither underbounded nor overbounded systems establish relationships high in mutuality. Optimally bounded systems tend to form highly mutual relationships in general; therefore, the links between internal and external relationships in systems imply that the degree of mutuality in internal relationships is directly related to the degree of mutuality in external relationships. In specific qualities, however, the exact way that lower mutuality is characteristic of underbounded and overbounded systems differs. Underbounded systems are notable for the low levels of observable positive affect in either internal or external relationships, and overbounded systems tend to deemphasize internally expressed negative reactions (Alderfer 1976*a*).

The hypothesized link between internal and external relationships in social systems provides a powerful lever for social intervention, especially with intergroups. It suggests that *changes in the internal relationships of a group can influence external relationships—and vice versa*. The general approach for intervening with the Communications Group was heavily influenced by this hypothesis.

The Group was designed to be a microcosm of the division in which it was created. Membership in the Group was to represent the major hierarchical and functional differences in the system. Implicitly, the demographic differences among members in the division would also be carried into Communications Group deliberations. Interventions that increased mutuality among members *within the Group,* according to the internal-external linkage hypothesis, could be expected to increase mutuality *between groups* in the division. In some instances the mutuality interventions within the Group were to help members discover common bonds and thereby enhance mutuality by allowing more positive affect to emerge within the Group. In other cases the mutuality interventions were to permit significant differences to emerge, either to be contained or worked through by the group members.

Start-up of the group

First thoughts and intervention team

The idea of a "Communications Group" originated with the division manager before there was a commitment to any specific type of intervention by consultants. The manager was troubled by discrepancies between what his immediate subordinates reported about events in the work units and the accounts he obtained from people throughout the division as he talked informally with them. He was unsure how to interpret these information differences, but he was certain that their existence signaled some substantial need for improved communications throughout the division. In his own mind he had imagined forming a group of employees in order to help with this task but was not entirely sure how to proceed. As part of regular discussions he was having with an internal OD consultant he brought up the subject. (At the time the author was serving as an external OD consultant and had indicated that he was especially interested in participating in interventions having to do with intergroup relations.) The internal consultant asked the division manager whether the external consultant might become part of the intervention team, and the manager responded favorably. The internal consultant's immediate supervisor, who occupied a position equal in rank to the division manager, also became a member of the intervention team in its earliest phases.

First events in the life of the group: Establishing the boundary

The intervention officially began when the division manager and his immediate subordinates established procedures for selecting the pioneer members of the Communications Group. Existing tradition within the division was followed: three management members were appointed to the Group, and eight nonmanagement members were elected by peers from their workgroups. It was understood from the outset, however, that once constituted, the Group would determine its own methods of operating, including the selection and replacement of members. When first constituted the Group had at least one member from all the major workgroups in the division; it was demographically representative and included five women and six men, two blacks and nine whites. The previously mentioned internal consultant and external consultant (author) were ex-officio members.

Interviews

After membership in the group had been determined, the consulting team arranged to interview all the members plus the division manager and his immediate subordinates. The purpose of these interviews was twofold: (1) to learn what members of the system believed to be the major communication problems in the division, and (2) to begin to establish a relationship high in mutuality between members of the consulting team and people in the division. Because issues of inclusion and exclusion are especially acute in the formation of any new group, the consultants invited members of the Communications Group to nominate other members of the division whose views would be crucial to understanding communication problems. In total, six additional people were identified and interviewed.

Tasks to increase mutuality: Hopes-and-fears day

The initial interviews provided the consulting team with the information and relationships to help continue the process of psychologically establishing the group for its members and for the division as a whole. An entire workday was set aside for the next step in this process, establishing a formal charter for the group. In attendance were the top five members of the division management, whose enthusiasm for the idea of the group ranged from nil to very high, and the eleven newly selected members of the Communications Group, who were uncertain about their mission. Two internal consultants and the external consultant/author were present to conduct the session, whose stated purpose was to reexamine jointly whether the idea of a Communications Group was viable and, if so, to determine its goals.

To this end Group members and management representatives were asked to go into separate rooms to work on a common task; to prepare two lists which expressed their hopes and fears about the Communications Group. This intervention legitimized the expression of positive and negative reactions to the Communications Group from inside and outside. If there were widely disparate concerns about the Group at the outset, confronting these differences might lead to a decision not to proceed with the Group or to modifications in its basic structure and design. But it might also turn out that both the management team and the Group members had similar hopes and fears. Then such an exploration would let both parties see that they were not alone in the nature of their mixed feelings. Regardless of whether the ultimate decision was to form the Group, the day was designed to promote high levels of mutuality.

When the top management group and the Communications Group

members reconvened, the atmosphere was electric. Sheets containing the lists made by each group were hung on the walls for all to see. Much to their surprise both groups discovered that their fears and hopes about the Communications Group were very similar. After all in attendance had viewed this spontaneous convergence of ideas, it was relatively easy for the senior internal consultant to work with the total group to reach a consensus about a common list of hopes and fears, which is presented in Table 1.

In summary, start-up activities included relationship building and boundary development. Initially the consultants established relationships with top management in the division, and the managers established procedures for determining initial Communications Group membership. After the relevant people were determined, the consultants began the process of establishing highly mutual relationships among the top management team, the Communications Group members, and themselves. Methods included a series of one-on-one interviews and the subsequent hopes-and-fears day. The hopes-and-fears day brought the Communications Group together to perform a particular communications task, and, while doing so, explicitly increased the mutuality among group members and between the Group and top management.

Major communication work of the group

Charter and operating procedures

The first task undertaken by the Group alone was to revise the hopes and fears list into a formal charter and to add to that a set of operating procedures for the group. This work commenced shortly after the hopes-and-fears day. It actualized the twelfth hope while plunging the Group into the first of several struggles arising from relations among the members and between the group and the rest of the division. Group members themselves were battered by the long discussions needed to agree upon wording of their documents. Top management was upset because they felt that the material generated during the hopes-and-fears day was very close to being a completed charter. And, finally, the rest of the division was disturbed because it appeared that a group which offered so much promise for the division as a whole was preoccupied with its own internal affairs.

The charter and election procedures specified the major intergroups which the Group would attempt to integrate. Representation was divided according to the four major functional groups in the division, where the numbers were roughly proportional to size, and between labor and management, where there were to be eight labor and three

Table 1.   Initial Hopes and Fears about the Communications Group Held in Common by Group Members and Management

Hopes	Fears
1. The group will be an effective channel of communications upward, downward, and laterally.	1. There will be conflict between the group and the union regarding contractual obligations.
2. Timely feedback and/or action will follow when an area of concern is identified.	2. The group could "come between" superior and subordinate inappropriately.
3. The group will have the right to pursue information about issues that fall within its charter.	3. A failure by the group could increase management-nonmanagement polarization.
4. People in the division will have confidence in the group.	4. People in the division could misunderstand the purpose of the group.
5. The group will regularly educate people about its mission.	5. Resources given to the group could jeopardize the division's production.
6. People in the division will feel free to initiate contact with the group without fearing that they will damage their careers.	6. Negative feeling by management could keep the group from being effective.
7. The group will promote problem solution through increased communication within and between groups.	7. Differences among group members as a result of their varying work assignments could lead to an ineffective group.
8. The group will promote mutual understanding inside and outside the division.	8. Good suggestions generated by the group could be lost because of lack of understanding.
9. The group will encourage management and nonmanagement to contribute new ideas.	9. If the group fails, disenchantment with organization development will arise.
10. The group will assist in the communication of personnel policies and practices and provide feedback to reduce undesirable affects.	10. Individuals will use the group inappropriately to deal with personal issues.
11. The group will help to develop administrative guidelines for the whole division.	11. The group will try to be all things to all people.
12. The group will determine its own mode of operating.	12. The group will not be too oriented toward the larger functional groups in the division at the expense of the smaller groups.
	13. The group will not have sufficient resources to carry out its charter.

management members. The Group decided to have three officers: chairperson, vice-chairperson, and secretary. And the first set of officers consisted of a white male nonmanagement person from the largest functional group as chairperson, a black male manager from one of the smaller functional groups as vice-chairperson, and a white female from one of the larger functional groups as secretary. The Group decided that all members, both management and nonmanagement, should be elected, and the first phase in each election was to call for interested volunteers among those categories of people who needed a representative. The Group also determined that its meetings would have "open chairs," which could be filled by nonmembers of the Group who wished to participate with the Group on certain subjects or who simply wanted to observe the Group in action.

When the Group had completed the work of developing documents about its own operation, it then had the task of communicating this information to the rest of the division. A decision was made to form pairs to conduct meetings in each functional area. Each session was led by the Communications Group member from that functional area, who was assisted by a member from another section of the division. The sessions had two classes of agenda: (a) reporting and discussing the charter and operating procedures for the group, and (b) soliciting items for Communications Group business from division members.

Completing the charter, determining operating procedures, and communicating these documents throughout the division completed the process of establishing the Communications Group. The charter and its supplement stated affirmatively that the Group existed, while explicitly recognizing the hazards of such an activity. Further confirmation of the Group's boundaries came from a letter of support signed by the division manager which stated time boundaries for member involvement. By means of formalized operating procedures the Group had determined its own degree of boundary permeability. In the short run, nonmembers were encouraged to attend meetings by taking "the open chair." In the longer run the membership would "turn over" through election of new members. The process of communicating these documents to the rest of the division increased the degree of mutuality between the Group and the division as a whole.

During the sessions when "items of business" were solicited from members of the division who did not belong to the Communications Group, four issues were identified: (1) the regular and frequent use of group meetings between supervisors and subordinates; (2) the method by which employees were informed of new job openings within the division and outside; (3) the orientation of new employees who entered the division; and (4) the process by which employees were rotated from job to job throughout the division. These issues defined the Group's major work for the next months. The Group's decision to work on these particular issues was communicated to the division as a whole by publication of an exchange of letters between the Group chairman and the division manager.

Issue I: Group meetings

On this issue, the Communications Group consulted with management. Among the management group, one man was especially known for using group meetings effectively. He prepared a set of suggestions on how to conduct a group meeting and shared the results of a "survey" taken among people who regularly used group meetings, which consisted of 12 benefits a workgroup could obtain as a result of meeting regularly. This material was circulated to the whole division with Communications Group and top management endorsements. Establishing a regular practice of group meetings was an intervention to strengthen the boundaries of work teams. The description of the kinds of discussion that could occur in effectively functioning meetings expressed a preference for high mutuality among members of a team.

Issue 2: Job postings

The Group had difficulty in reaching a consensus about the second item which it addressed: the subject of posting job openings. A split in the Group reflected the different degrees of identification that nonmanagement members felt with the union. Those highly committed to the union wanted the Group to do nothing that might appear as though the Group could get benefits for employees quicker than the union. Those less central in union affairs felt that the Group's work referred to the division, while union activities pertained to the company as a whole. Management views were also sought, and the charter supplement, which cautioned against the Group's coming into conflict with the union, was invoked. In the end, the Group decided not to act on that issue—"in view of the fact that the transfer and upgrade policies are currently being reviewed by both the company and the union. . . ."

Several weeks later the union became explicitly interested in Communications Group activities and requested a meeting with management to clarify the Group's role. Prior to the meeting the division manager provided a complete set of the materials that had been produced by the Group to date for the union leaders. These included the charter, the election procedures, and the copies of various items distributed by the Group. The meeting was attended only by management members of the Communications Group because the company-union contract specified that only management members could be present at such a session requested by union leadership. At the outset of the meeting, union officials thanked management for the completeness of the information transmitted to them and indicated that they judged that management had been sincere because the documents they had obtained "from our own sources" perfectly matched those management had provided. The rules of "information meetings" provided that the union would write the minutes, which had to be approved by management before they were deemed official. Shortly after the meeting, the consultant—who had obtained labor and management's permission to attend—provided a detailed set of notes, written in complete sentences and paragraphs, to the division manager and the highest-ranking labor official. The document attempted to *describe without interpretation* all the issues discussed in the meeting and portray accurately the views expressed by both parties. Both groups seemed pleased to receive the notes, thus indicating acceptance of the consultant's behavior in this volatile situation.

Although many specific issues were discussed in that meeting, the basic concern of the union seemed to be that the Group's charter supplement did not clearly state that "the Union is the exclusive bargaining agency for all nonmanagement employees . . . and the company will not negotiate as to matters within the provisions of this contract with individual employees or groups of employees. . . ." The union representatives asked management to request that the Communications Group amend their charter to make this point explicit. Minutes of the information meeting prepared by the union affirmed the union's role for nonmanagement employees, expressed no objection to the formation of units like the Communications Group, asked management to keep the union informed about such matters, and asked management to request the Communications Group to make some changes in the wording of their charter. Later, when the Communications Group discussed the outcome of the information meeting, they agreed to make the changes asked for, although not without some conflict among the members.

The union minutes essentially approved the existence of the Group, while they also helped to clarify further the *limits* on Group activities. Although this specific happening was not anticipated, the manner of working through this relationship and setting up of boundaries for the Group was started when the charter was being written. The charter supplement alerted the Group and all members of the division, including the union, to potential conflicts between the Group and the union. When the Group discussed the subject of job postings, they confronted *within* their own membership the dispute that was later to arise *between* the Group and the union. Working through this issue inside the Group, leading to a decision to stay away from the subject of job posting, facilitated a successful resolution of the conflict outside the Group in relation to the union and management.

Issue 3: New employee orientation

Closer adherence to guidelines for new employee orientation proceeded relatively uneventfully. The manager who was asked to prepare information on this subject found what was sought by the Communications Group in the Personnel Handbook, a document prepared for all managerial-level employees. But apparently many managers, especially those who did not regularly face an influx of new employees, were unaware of the guidelines available to them. Working with the Communication Group, the manager prepared "a package," which called this fact to the attention of all members of the division. A minor jurisdictional problem arose when some managers became upset on learning that nonmanagement members of the Communications Group were studying the Personnel Handbook—in some managers' eyes the Personnel Handbook was not a document to be seen by nonmanagement employees.

Issue 4: Careers and promotions

More effective dissemination of information about career development, evaluation, and promotion was a most difficult issue. Secrecy, deception, ambivalence, and poor communication around this topic abounded in this organization as in most. When the Communications Group decided to investigate this topic and management agreed to help, the parties were only vaguely aware of the difficult terrain they were about to enter.

Eventually a dialogue between top management and the Communications Group was transcribed from tape recordings and shared with the whole division. The response to this dialogue was quite positive throughout the division. For the first time people felt as though they were told the truth. For many the news conveyed by the questions and answers was not good. But regardless of whether or not they liked the information conveyed, employees' "needs to know" were being satisfied.

Taken together, the four issues tackled by one Group cover the complete life cycle of an employee's experience with a job in the division. The concerns follow a person from her/his entry into the division (orientation), through day-to-day work activities (group meetings), to exit through promotion or lateral transfer (job posting, career and promotion concerns). Communication on each of these issues was influenced by interventions based on boundary and relationship theory.

The division attitude survey

Another role for the Group arose in connection with the design, administration, and feedback of an attitude survey taken by all members of the division and fed back to all members. Communications Group members played significant parts at each phase of this diagnostic process. Data from the survey were also useful in assessing the Group's impact on the division and provided the Group with an opportunity to obtain feedback about its work.

The survey confirmed the validity of the Communication Group's efforts to increase division-wide knowledge about specific areas of organizational life. Forty-four percent of the people in the division reported that they held group meetings "often" or "very often," while 31 percent said they had meetings with their own workgroups "never" or "rarely." Yet 74 percent reacted "positive" or "very positive" to the idea of such meetings. Thirty-seven percent of the division disagreed with the statement that "Division training programs effectively equip people to do their jobs." And 47 percent of the respondents disagreed with the assertion, "The organization structure of the division has been clearly explained to me." The need for training and orientation was confirmed.

Division-wide concern over careers and performance evaluation also showed up. Only 20 percent of the employees agreed with the statement that, "We have a promotion system that helps the best person rise to the top." Only 27 percent of the respondents agreed that "My supervisor makes every effort to talk with me about my career aspriations." These findings assured the Communications Group, top management, and the division as a whole that the various issues that the Group was working on were not the private agendas of a few vocal individuals.

Somewhat to the surprise of many members of the Group, feelings and judgments about the Group were quite positive. Only 19 percent of respondents "resent[ed] the time given to Communications Group activities." Sixty-five percent affirmed that "The Communications Group is doing a good job responding to issues raised by division members." These data were collected after the Group had been in action only three months. At the conclusion of the survey feedback sessions, when the Group had been functioning for eight months, the items pertaining to the Group were administered again as part of a brief questionnaire evaluating the survey feedback meetings. On the whole, division-wide reactions to the Communications Group were more positive on this later administration.

Working through negative reactions to the group

But not all employees were equally positive about the Group. The subgroup that differed most notably from division-wide trends of acceptance was the middle managers. On some items their responses showed no change from earlier measures, and on other items their responses to the group became more negative. After reviewing these data with both division management and the Communications Group, the consultants decided to meet with the middle management group to discuss the nature of their questionnaire responses.

During the first of two meetings there was no doubt that the middle managers were unhappy with their relationship to the Communications Group and the consultants. Some felt as though the recently completed feedback sessions had undermined their authority and influenced their performance evaluations negatively. Others reported that they were uninformed about Communications Group meeting times, agenda, and open-chair policy. In the second meeting the consultants presented an analysis of the situation as they saw it. This included recognition and acceptance of the sense of powerlessness expressed by the managers in relation to the Group. It also focused on the covert resistance exhibited by some from the outset of the Group's life. Some managers, for example, had been specifically invited to attend the group as "open-chair guests" but always managed to be occupied with another meeting when the time came. After the consultants presented their views, the meeting took on a problem-solving orientation, and a number of suggestions for improving the effectiveness of the Communications Group emerged. As a result of these sessions, middle managers began to attend meetings to observe or to discuss issues of interest with the Group. Sometime later the Group decided to expand its membership to include a fourth member from management.

The attitude survey confirmed the significance of problems chosen for work by the Communications Group and helped to identify problems in the relationship between middle managers in the division and the Communications Group, which ultimately led to changes in how the Group operated and in how the managers behaved in relation to it. The survey feedback was also associated with 17 other specific changes in the division. They ranged from informing a workgroup that they had been exceeding performance expectations for some time in settling responsibility for a particular assignment between two workgroups after, as one manager put it, "10 years of searching for a solution."

Evaluation of theory in relation to practice

Consultant interventions into Communications Group activities were designed to follow from the theoretical constructs presented at the outset of this paper. In this sense, results of the Group's work might be viewed as an "action test" of the theoretical propositions. Outcomes consistent with theoretical predictions might be viewed as support for the theory. Unexpected consequences suggest places where the theory is in need of improvement.

There were three major ways that interventions derived from the theory were used to help the Group accomplish its communication tasks. The first pertained to direct efforts to achieve optimal boundary permeability. The second was concerned with the interdependence between boundary permeability and relationship mutuality. The third was based on the hypothesized linkages between internal and external relations in the group.

Optimal boundary permeability as an objective of group functioning was sought directly through the ways that the Communications Group arranged for members to be selected and for nonmembers to interact with the Group. During the time in which I observed the Group, these procedures seemed to work remarkably well. The Group had developed a structure that determined clearly who members were and provided a means by which new members could be added periodically over the life of the Group. On a meeting-by-meeting basis the open-chair policy provided a means by which nonmembers could interact with the Group.

In addition to direct attempts to adjust boundary permeability, this dimension of group life was also hypothetically susceptible to change by altering the degree of mutuality in key relationships. This principle was most dramatically employed when the survey instrument indicated that middle managers in the division were having difficulties with the Communications Group. After the consultants spent two intensive sessions with the managers to identify and work through their feelings about the Group, their behavior with respect to interacting with the Group increased markedly. The Group's boundary in relation to the managers had become more permeable.

The linkage between internal and external relations in the Group was crucial in determining how the Group came to terms with the union. When members of the Group who identified strongly with the union raised questions about whether the Group was infringing on contract issues by dealing with the subject of job posting, there were others inside the Group who were ready to dispute the seriousness of these concerns. By attempting to promote greater mutuality between these subgroups *within* the Group, the consultants—unknowingly at the time —were helping start the process of developing increased mutuality *external* to the group with respect to the union.

As an "action test" for the theory, the Communications Group activities provide substantial support for the theoretical propositions on which the interventions were based. Moreover, as a strategy for improving communications among the multiple groups where it was employed, there can be little doubt that the Communications Group had the intended effects. But there were also unanticipated outcomes which suggest ways that the theory might be altered and identify limitations of the Communications Group as a change strategy.

All people who participated in this intervention experienced significant degrees of stress. Individuals central to the process such as the division manager and the Communications Group chairpersons were subject to a significant number of cross-pressures. A disproportionate share of the efforts to develop and maintain optimal boundary permeability falls to group leaders, whose role in part is boundary management (Rice 1969). While no one imagined that the kind of change set in motion by the Communications Group would be easy, the amount of effort by all parties needed to make this intervention work was also probably underestimated at the outset.

The theory and practice of this intervention was most limited with respect to ways to conceptualize and act upon long-term developmental issues. The Group did not develop methods to teach new members much of what the "pioneers" had learned through the enormously rich start-up processes. When the division manager who had started the Communications Group moved to a new assignment his successor chose to continue the Group. But the consultants were at a loss about how to help this man learn in a short time who his successor had assimilated over months. The advent of the new division manager corresponded in time with decreasing involvement by the consultants, who were reducing their involvement with this Group in order to meet other commitments and to avert prolonged dependency. It is likely that the management succession and the consultant withdrawal were experienced by some members as a loss of support for the Group, although these concerns were not voiced.

In sum, despite the impressive gains the Communications Group intervention provided in terms of its major objective to improve communication in the division, the theory and methods were incomplete with respect to transferring some learning from one generation to the next.

Relationship to other approaches

The Communications Group as a social intervention may be better understood if it is compared to related approaches that involve efforts to ameliorate intergroup conflict in organizations or to introduce new group structures to compensate for dysfunctions of traditional pyramidal systems.

As an intergroup intervention, the Communications Group can be compared to the well-known intergroup problem-solving approach described by Burke (1974), based on earlier work by Blake et al. (1964) and by Sherif and Sherif (1969). This technique brings together *two* related groups who have been engaged in unproductive conflict and who wish to improve their relationship and problem-solving capability. Reports about outcomes from using this technique suggest that it works very well with groups of approximately equal power but is less effective with groups of unequal power (Blake et al. 1964, Burke 1974). Another limitation of the approach is that it is designed to deal with only two groups at a time. While expanding the number of groups participating in the intervention is theoretically possible, that kind of change rapidly increases intervention complexity. Another possible limitation of the model is that it relies upon intensive short-term intervention to diagnose problems and plan action. This approach is functional for certain types of problems but not for others. The Communications Group intervention deals with representatives from many organizational groups—not just two—and is based on an extensive rather than intensive design in order to deal with communication problems that arise intermittently in turbulent organizational environments.

As a new group structure to correct problems arising from pyramidal structures, the Communications Group might also be compared to the collateral organization proposed by Zand (1974). There are marked theoretical differences between the two approaches, but there are definite similarities with respect to the group structure in relation to the organization. The concepts on which the collateral organization is based do not explicitly recognize the existence of intergroup tensions in organizations. The major thrust of the collateral organization is to provide appropriate structures for solving problems facing managers. Neither of the examples provided by Zand (1974) involve other than management members of the system. The collateral strategy has more in common with group brainstorming than with intergroup problem solving. It is more suited to solving problems uniquely faced by managers than to dealing with system-wide communication difficulties, especially those between management and nonmanagement or arising from differences in ethnicity, race, or sex. Both approaches feed their results back into the formal system, require unusual flexibility by the top manager in the unit where the intervention is being implemented, and may be experienced as threatening by middle managers. There is nothing in the collateral strategy to deal with problems arising from groups external to the collateral system such as middle managers or labor unions.

Because boundary and relationship theory places a major emphasis on connections between internal and external events in groups and organizations, it includes a way of understanding such happenings and suggests an approach for dealing with them.

References

Alderfer, C. P. Boundary relations and organizational diagnosis. In H. Meltzer and F. R. Wickert (Eds.). *Humanizing organizational behavior*. Springfield, Ill.: Charles C. Thomas, 1976*a*.

————. Change processes in organizations. In M. D. Dunnette (Ed.).

Handbook of industrial and organizational psychology. Chicago: Rand McNally, 1976*b*.

————. Group and intergroup design. In J. R. Hackman and J. L. Suttle (Eds.). *Improving life at work.* Pacific Palisades, Calif.: Goodyear, 1976*c*.

Alderfer, C. P., Kaplan, R. E., and Smith, K. K. The effects of variations in relatedness need satisfaction on relatedness desires. *Administrative Science Quarterly,* 1974, **19,** 507–532.

Blake, R. R., Mouton, J. S., and Sloma, R. I. An actual case history of resolving intergroup conflict in union-management relations. In R. R. Blake, H. A. Shepard, and J. S. Mouton, *Managing intergroup conflict in industry.* Houston: Gulf Publishing, 1964, pp. 155–195.

Blake, R. R., Shepard, H. A., and Mouton, J. S. *Managing intergroup conflict in industry.* Houston: Gulf Publishing, 1964.

Burke, W. W. Managing conflict between groups. In J. D. Adams (Ed.). *Theory and method in organization development: An evolutionary process.* Arlington, Va.: NTL, 1974.

Rice, A. K. Individual, group, and intergroup processes. *Human Relations.* 1969, **22,** 565–584.

Sherif, M. and Sherif, C. *Social psychology.* New York: Harper & Row, 1969.

Zand, D. E. Collateral organization: A new change strategy. *Journal of Applied Behavioral Science,* 1974, **10,** 63–89.

Symbols, Patterns, and Settings: An Optimistic Case for Getting Things Done
Thomas J. Peters

*The most important decisions are often the
least apparent.*   Karl Weick

What tools come to mind when you think about changing an organization? If you came up through the ranks in the 1950s and 1960s, the answer is quite likely to be divisionalizing and developing a strategic planning system. Shifting the organizational structure and inventing new processes are still options for change. But increasingly thorny and overlapping international, competitive, and regulatory problems call for increasingly complex responses—and such responses are getting increasingly difficult to devise and problematical in their application.

It is reasonable to propose, however, that an effective set of change tools is actually embedded in senior management's daily message sending and receiving activities, and that these tools can be managed in such a way as to energize and redirect massive, lumbering business and government institutions. The tools will be characterized as symbols (the raw material), patterns (the systematic use of the raw material), and settings (the showcase for the systematic use).

It is not suggested that these tools merely be added to the traditional arsenal of formal change instruments—primarily structure and process. Rather, it will be argued that historically effective prescriptions are losing some of their impact, and their formal replacements—such as the matrix structure—have comparatively little leverage. Moreover, the typical top management is seldom around for much more than five or six years—too little time in which to leave a distinctive and productive stamp on a large, history-bound institution solely by means of the available formal change alternatives. Hence effective change may increasingly depend on systematic use of the informal change mechanisms, derived from coherent daily actions.

Some speculations

My thesis in this article is that there are a variety of practical controlled change tools appropriate to today's complex and ambiguous organization settings. Most have been around a long time and need only to be consciously packaged and managed. Some are rather new. Few have been thought of as major instruments for achieving organizational redirection. Almost all are associated with the informal organization.

Figure 1 arrays some of these change tools along the previously noted dimensions of controllability and speed of change, and figure 2 presents some mundane change tools. By briefly assessing the reasons for the failure or obsolescence of the conventional tools and their successors (shown here as having drifted to the low-control, low-speed category), a very general rationale for the nature of the new change-tool candidates can be developed. Then each new category of tools can be assessed in turn.

There are at least two reasons why the conventional solutions have failed to achieve their full promise or have declined in effectiveness. One is that none of them takes time explicitly into account. In the case of structural solutions, management typically miscalculates in two different ways. On the one hand, it grossly underestimates the growing time lag between changed structure and changed behavior. On the other hand, it overestimates their durability under growing environmental pressures and consequently tends to leave them in place long after they have outlived their effectiveness.

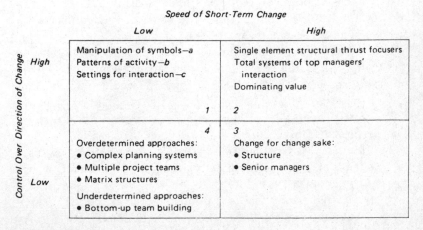

Figure 1. Speculation about current change tools.

a—Symbols:	Calendars
	Reports
	Agenda
	Physical settings
	Public statements
	Staff organization
b—Patterns:	Positive reinforcement
	Frequency and consistency of behavior
	Implementation/solution bias
	Experimenting mode
c—Settings:	Role of modeling
	Location
	Agenda control
	Presentation format
	Questioning approaches
	Deadline management
	Use of minutes

Figure 2. Mundane tools.

The second reason for the weakness of conventional solutions is over- or underdetermination. Several solutions seem to rest on an overestimation of managers' ability to determine the best way to accomplish great purposes—overdetermination. For example, complex planning systems, multiple project teams, and the matrix structure proceed from the implicit assumption that effective organizing flows from figuring out the correct wiring diagram—an assumption increasingly at odds with today's organizational tasks. Kopper's chief executive officer, Fletcher Byrom, recently remarked, "Of all the things that I have observed about corporations, the most disturbing has been a tendency toward over-organization, producing a rigidity that is intolerable in an era of rapidly accelerating change."

At the other end of the spectrum—underdetermination—bottom-up team building has been based on the opposite presumption: Overall organizational purposes can be largely ignored; seeding effective new behavior patterns at the bottom of the organization or in ranks of middle management will somehow eventuate in desirable organizational performance levels.

The proposed "new" change tools partially address both issues. First, they explicitly take time into account, recognizing both that change typically comes slowly as the result of the application of many tools and that the organizational focus of prime importance today is temporary and will almost certainly have changed substantially four or five years hence. Second, they are tools of the experimenter: That is, they neither assume an ability to fix organizational arrangements with much precision—the failing of overdetermination—nor do they ignore purposiveness—the failing of underdetermination.

Obsession with the mundane

Cell 1 of figure 1 (high-control, low-speed change), the realm of what my colleagues and I have come to call "mundane tools," reflects the notion that the management of change—small or large—is inextricably bound up with the mundane occurrences that fill an executive's calendar.

By definition, managing the daily stream of activities might be said to consist of the manipulation of symbols, the creation of patterns of activity, and the staging of occasions for interaction. The mundane tools are proposed as direct alternatives to structural manipulation and other grand solutions to strategic organization needs. Conscious experimentation with these tools can provide a sound basis for controlled, purposive change.

Manipulation of symbols

Because they have so often been applied by the media to the performances of politicians intent on reshaping or repairing an image, the terms *symbolic behavior* and *symbol manipulation* have lately acquired something of a perjorative connotation: symbol vs. substance. In a much more basic sense, however, symbols are the very stuff of management behavior. Executives, after all, do not synthesize chemicals or operate lift trucks; they deal in symbols. And their overt verbal communications are only part of the story. Consciously or unconsciously, the senior executive is constantly acting out the vision and goals he is trying to realize in an organization that is typically far too vast and complex for him to control directly.

What mundane tools might best aid the executive interested in effecting change through symbol manipulation? To signal watchers, which includes nearly everyone in his organization, there is no truer test of what he really thinks is important than the way he spends his time. As Eli Ginsberg and Ewing W. Reilley have noted: "Those a few echelons from the top are always alert to the chief executive. Although they attach importance to what he says, they will be truly impressed only by what he does."

Is he serious about making a major acquisition? The gossip surrounding his calendar—Has he seen the investment banker?—provides clues for senior and junior management alike.

As reported in *Fortune,* Roy Ash's early activities after assuming the reins at Addressograph-Multigraph suggest mastery of the calendar and other mundane tools:

> Instead of immediately starting to revamp the company, Ash spent his first several months visiting its widely scattered operations and politely asking a lot of searching questions. . . . His predecessors had always summoned subordinates to the head-quarters building, which had long lived up to its official name, the Tower. Rather than announcing his ideas, Ash demonstrated them. He left his office door open, placing his own intercom calls to arrange meetings, and always questioned people in person, not in writing. Then he removed some of the company's copying machines "to stop breeding paperwork." Spotting a well-written complaint from an important customer in Minneapolis, Ash quickly flew off to visit him. As he now explains, "I wanted the word to get around our organization that I'm aware of what's going on." Ash's next dramatic step to reshape company attitudes will be moving its headquarters to Los Angeles . . . he justifies the move primarily on psychological grounds. "We must place ourselves in a setting where —partly through osmosis—we get a different idea of our future." For much the same reason, he wants to change the corporation's name, too.

Calendar behavior includes review of reports and the use of agenda and minutes to shape expectations. What kinds of questions is the executive asking? Does he seem to focus on control of operating costs, quality, market share? How is his memory about what was "assumed" last month? Last quarter? What kinds of feedback is he giving? What sorts of issues get onto his agenda?

Other symbolic actions include the use of physical settings and public statements. By attending operating meetings in the field, the top man can provide vital evidence of his concerns and the directions he wants to pursue. By touching or ignoring a particular theme, a public statement—boilerplate to a skeptical outsider—can lead to a rash of activity. In a talk to investment bankers, a president devoted a paragraph to new departures in an R&D area that had previously been underfunded. Almost overnight, a wealth of new proposals began bubbling up from a previously disenchanted segment of the labs.

Last, his use of his personal staff—its size, their perquisites, how much probing he allows them to do—will indicate, not only the chief executive's style of doing business, but the direction of his substantive concerns as well.

The executive's ability to manage the use of symbols is at the heart of the case for optimism. Laterally at his fingertips, he has powerful tools—his day-timer and phone—for testing the possibilities of change and, over time, substantially shifting the focus of the organization.

Patterns of activity

Success or failure in exploiting these simple tools is seen in the pattern of their use. Richard E. Neustadt in *Presidential Power* maintained:

> The professional reputation of a President in Washington is made or altered by the man himself. No one can guard it for him; no one saves him from himself. . . . His general reputation will be shaped by signs of pattern in the things he says and does. These are the words and actions he has chosen, day by day.

In short, the mundane tools that involve the creation and manipulation of symbols over time have impact to the extent that they reshape beliefs and expectations. Frequent, consistent, positive reinforcement is an unparalleled shaper of expectations—and, therefore, inducer of change.

Patterns of positive reinforcement can be applied in at least two ways: (1) using praise and designing positive reinforcement schemes for individuals or groups), and (2) allowing the bad to be displaced by the good, instead of trying to legislate it out of existence.

The White House, for example, has historically made meticulous use of the tools of praise. Selecting the attendees for major events and controlling the use of various classes of presidential letters of praise is a key activity controlled by very senior staff and the president himself.

Along the same lines, a research vice-president, responsible for about 2,000 scientists, has his executive assistant provide him with a sample of about 50 reports produced each month. He sends personal notes to the authors, often junior, of the best half-dozen or so.

Without touching on the complex ramifications of reinforcement theory, these instances merely support the point that senior managers are signal transmitters, and signals take on meaning as they are reiterated. Moreover, there is ample evidence that giving prominence to positive efforts and exposing them to the light of day induces constructive change far more effectively than trying to discourage undesired activities through negative reinforcement. As an associate of mine succinctly observed, "It's a hell of a lot easier to add a new solution than attack an old problem." An example illustrates the point in a broader context:

> The information system unit of a multibillion-dollar conglomerate had a disastrously bad reputation. Rather than "clean house" or

develop better procedures, the vice-president/systems installed, with some fanfare, "Six Programs of Excellence." Six reasonably sizable projects—out of an agenda of over 100—were singled out for intensive management attention. The effort was designed to build, from the inside out, a reputation for excellence that would gradually increase user confidence and group motivation alike.

Frequency and consistency are two other primary attributes of effective pattern shaping. A pattern of frequent and consistent small successes is such a powerful shaper of expectations that its creation may be worth the deferral of ambitious short-term goals:

> In one large company, the top team wished to establish a climate in which new product development would be viewed more favorably by all divisional managers. Rather than seeking an optimal product slate the first year—with the attendant likelihood of a high failure rate—the top team instead consistently supported small new product thrusts that gradually "made believers out of the operators."

Since consistency becomes a driving force in inducing major change over time, the executive committed to change ought to be constantly on the lookout for opportunities to reinforce activities, even trivial activities, that are congruent with his eventual purpose. He scours his in-basket for solutions—bits of completed action—to be singled out as exemplars of some larger theme. Support of completed actions typically generates further actions consistent with the rewarded behavior. The executive who keeps on testing tools to produce this result will find that by varying his patterns of reinforcement he can substantially influence people's behavior over time, often several levels down in the organization. (Figure 3 offers advice to pattern shapers based on my research.)

Settings for interaction

The third class of mundane tools is settings. Senior management's development of a symbolic pattern of activities occurs somewhere. These are some of the setting-variables that can directly reinforce or attenuate the impact of the symbolic message:

Presence or absence of top managers

Psychologists now agree on the high impact of modeling behavior—the most significant finding of the last decade, according to many. The senior executive's presence and his minor actions can bring to life and rather precisely shape an institutional point of view—about investment, competitive response, the importance of tight controls. The careers of top executives abundantly reflect their intuitive awareness of this point.

Figure 3. Guiding assertions for the pattern shaper.

The world is a stream of problems that can be activated, bound in new ways, or bypassed.

His associates are pattern watchers and are acutely aware of his and their impact, over time, on each other.

Above all, timing is important.

An early step an analyzing a situation is careful assessment of the levers he does or does not control.

Most change occurs incrementally, and major change typically emerges over a long period of time.

Much of the change induced in subordinates results from consciously acting as a model himself.

Frequent rewards—directed at small, completed actions—effectively shape behavior over time.

Good questioning, focusing on the short term, helps him and his subordinates learn about system responses to small nudges one way or another.

Creating change in organizations is facilitated by unusual juxtaposition of traditional elements with small problem-making subunits that seed changes.

Long-term goals are of secondary importance since control of change follows from learning about multiple, small, real-time adjustments.

Consistency in delivering small, positive outcomes is an efficient and effective way to manipulate others' perceptions when attempting to induce change.

Patience, persistence, self-control, and attention to the mundane are often keys to achieving small, consistent outcomes.

Surprise should usually be avoided in an attempt to present stable expectations to peers, subordinates, and bosses.

It is possible approximately to calculate the opportunity value of others' and one's own time, thus substantially increasing the ability to pick change opportunities.

Adding new solutions is often better than tackling old problems; that is, as much or more change and learning can ensue from the effective implementation of new solutions as from time-consuming efforts to overcome typically deep-seated resistance to old problems.

Location of groups and meetings

Moving a meeting or a staff unit or a new activity is often a dramatic signal that something new is afoot. At one company, the previously isolated top team began holding meetings in the field, thus signaling a sincere intent to make decentralization work after three previous failures.

Agenda control

Since agenda directly symbolize priorities, agenda management can be a potent tool. A division's top team changed its basic approach to management by suddenly devoting more than half its meeting time to issues of project implementation, previously a relatively minor item on its agenda. To cope with the new questions they were getting from the top, managers throughout the organization were soon following suit.

Attendance

Who attends which meetings, and who presents material, can signal new approaches to management and new substantive directions. When one company president decided to force his vice-presidents, instead of junior staff, to present reviews and proposals, the atmosphere of his meetings perceptibly changed. All at once, heated battles between analytic guns-for-hire over numerical nuances were replaced by sober discussion of the issues.

Presentation/decision memorandum formats

Format control can shift managers' focus to new issues and fundamentally reshape the process of organizational learning. One management team vastly improved its approach to problem solving by meticulously starting every decision presentation with a historical review of "the five key assumptions." At a second major corporation, the chief executive brought to life his major theme—focus on the competition—by requiring all decision documents to include much greater depth of competitive analysis.

Questioning approaches

Among the clearest indicators of the direction or redirection of interest are the sorts or questions the top team consistently asks. Accounts of the working methods of Roy Ash, Harold Geneen, and others stress their unique questioning style and its pervasive effect on the issues the organization worries about. For instance, *Forbes* describes how A. W. Clausen of the Bank of America shifted concern from revenue to profit: "Ask an officer, 'How's business,' and you'd immediately hear how many loans he's made. I tried to leave my stamp by making everyone aware of profit."

Approaches to follow-up

Effective use of minutes, ticklers, and history can become the core of top management's real control system. Genuine accountability was introduced into a lax management organization by introducing a "blue blazer" system that made follow-up a way of life. In tracking issues, whenever operating executives' proposals had been modified by staff, the impact of the changes was explicitly noted. This put the staff and its contribution on stage. Accountability was further substantially sharpened by revamping a previous forecast-tracking procedure to highlight assumptions and outcomes.

Professor Serge Muscovici has asserted that:

> Social status, leadership, majority pressure . . . are not decisive
> factors in social influence. A minority can modify the opinions and
> norms of a majority, irrespective of their relative power or social
> status, as long as, all other things being equal, the organization of
> its actions and the expression of its opinions and objectives obey the
> conditions . . . of consistency, autonomy, investment, and fairness.

Fairness takes on added meaning on the context of mundane management tools, intended as they are to shape expectations, over time,
through minor shifts of emphasis. To be effective, the management
of expectations must be unfailingly honest, realistic, and consistent.
Violation of this property, especially if perceived as intentional, automatically destroys the effectiveness of patterned symbolic manipulation.

Richard Neustadt captures the essence of the use of mundane tools:

> [Franklin D. Roosevelt] had a strong feeling for a cardinal fact in
> government: That Presidents don't act on policies, program, or
> personnel in the abstract; they act in the concrete as they meet
> deadlines set by due dates, act on documents awaiting signatures,
> vacant posts awaiting appointees, officials seeking interviews,
> newsmen seeking answers, audiences waiting for a speech.

Note that the tools he mentions are all at hand. Though rarely disruptive or threatening, they have the potential to revolutionize an organization's ways of thinking and doing over time—particularly if, instead
of being used intuitively and implicitly, they are consciously packaged
and managed.

Major change via temporary focus

Big bureaucracies are run largely on inertia. Salesmen make their calls,
products roll off the line, and checks get processed without any intervention by senior management. The task of today's slate of top managers, then, might well be viewed as time-bound: "How do we make a
distinctive, productive difference over the next four years?" Or, "How
do we leave our mark?"

It has been suggested above that certain prescriptions—undertaking
structural shake-ups or introducing new formal processes—are less
effective than they once were in altering corporate perspectives. Constructing temporary systems to redirect the organization's attention
and energies may be a better way to coax along institutional change.
The high-impact devices proposed for this purpose are a natural extension of the mundane tools just discussed, in that in and of them-

selves they act as strong signals (or accumulations of symbols) of attention to new corporate directions.

Major—but limited—shifts in emphasis have been accomplished by public and private bureaucracies through three kinds of temporary focusing mechanisms: single-element focusers, systems of interaction, and dominating values. Each of these focusing mechanisms is discussed below.

Single-element focusers

To begin with, single-element focusers have been used time and again as a strategic signaling and implementing device. Consider how General Motors, a massive bureaucracy by any definition, recently adapted more swiftly than any other major automobile maker to the need to downsize its entire product line:

> The project center [says *Fortune*] was probably GM's single most important managerial tool in carrying out that bold decision. . . . It has eliminated a great deal of redundant effort, and has speeded numerous new technologies into production. Its success . . . rests on the same delicate balance between the powers of persuasion and coercion that underlines GM's basic system of coordinated decentralization.

Some other business examples of single-element focusers similarly wrested the attention of major organizations—temporarily—to something new:

> Harris Corporation created an interdivisonal technology manager to oversee transfer of technology—Harris's "main strategic thrust" —between previously isolated groups.
>
> Product family managers—three to five senior men with small staffs—were introduced as a means of wrenching the attention of two huge functional bureaucracies toward the marketplace; the creation of these high-visibility positions was thought to be a clearer, more efficient signal of strategic redirection than a major structural shift. Similarly, the establishment of just one job, executive vice-president for marketing, at White Consolidated is credited with sprucing up the long-stagnant sales of White's newly acquired Westinghouse appliance group.
>
> ITT's product group managers are a free-wheeling band of central staff problem solvers and questioners who have brought a common market-based orientation to a highly diversified conglomerate.
>
> An oil company's central technology staff (a roving group of top-

ranking geologists and engineers) has markedly upgraded exploration and production quality.

In surveying these and other instances of success, some common threads can be identified (see figure 4). Most important of these is

Figure 4. Attributes of single-element focusing devices.

Success Characteristic	Related Failure Mode
Focus: Limited number of "devices," no more than two and preferably one.	Use — usually simultaneously — of many devices (e.g., teams, meetings) dilutes attention and can become just a bureaucratic encumbrance.
Focus within focus: The limited device must, moreover, have a limited agenda and not take on everything at once.	Limited devices charged with turning the world around in 12 months are likely to fail (i.e., a failure of expectation).
Incumbent: Manned with a very senior contender(s) for the top.	Selection of good men, but not those recognized as members of "the top ten" or surefire top ten contenders.
Start-up: Either a pilot element (e.g., one product family manager of an eventual set of five) or a "pilot decision," (e.g., a visible output—perhaps a decision—by the new event/process) will affect acceptance.	Groups/processes invented, but no clear sign of early progress or shift of emphasis.
Need: A clear-cut, agreed-upon business need for the element exists.	The new element's agenda is not clear and/or is not viewed as urgent.
CEO role: CEO is reinforcer of project *and* lets it make its mark.	CEO nonsupporter or a supporter but preempts the new role by continuing to play the game by the old rules.
Conscience: Systems—formal or informal—to "watch" the top team and ensure that actions are being taken consistent with the purpose of the shift.	Element "implemented," but top team regularly takes decisions inconsistent with purpose.
Implementation duration: Even though single device, implementation should be expected to take a couple of years at least.	Since it is only a simple new element, put it in place and let it go.

singleness of focus. That is, the single-element focuser should not be confused with multiple-team project management. Its effectiveness rests on achieving a limited, temporary focus on one, or at most two, major new items. Note, also, that the structural manifestations tend to be about half staff, half line. On one hand, the focusing element often has the look of a traditional staff unit, but its manager, as the unmistakable agent of the top team's highest priority, visibly intrudes on operating managers' territory.

Kenneth Arrow, the Nobel laureate economist, describes an analogous approach to galvanizing massive government institutions into acting on new agenda: "Franklin D. Roosevelt . . . saw the need of assigning new tasks to new bureaus even though according to some logic [such a task] belonged in the sphere of an existing department." Congressional Budget Office Deputy Director Robert Levine summarizes the thesis this way:

> Since it seems impossible . . . to change overall public bureaucratic systems substantially either by changing their direction at the top by devices like program budgeting, or by changing their culture à la organization development, it may be useful to look for a third class of solutions . . . specifically, trying to treat bureaucratic units as if they were competing business units. . . . Even if it worked very well, this would be less well than program budgeting or organization development if they worked well. But the contention here is that in the real world this alternative concept is substantially more likely to work.

System of interaction

Attention-directing organization elements are only the first of the three high-impact focusing mechanisms to be considered here. The second is the construction of a coherent system of senior management interaction, again with the purpose of shifting management attention either to some new direction or to some new method of reaching overall consensus. Under some circumstances, this second mechanism might even be preferred to the first. On the one hand, a system of forums has perhaps less symbolic impact than a single high-visibility element. On the other hand, however, such a system does directly manipulate the agenda of senior managers.

Systems of forums designed to turn top management's eyes to new horizons range from one company's five "management forums"—a formal system of interaction designed to force regular discussion of strategic issues—to a president's regular informal breakfast meetings where senior executives, free of their staffs and the attendant bureaucratic insulation, engage in untrammeled discussion of key issues.

One particularly striking class of forums is special operating or strategic review sessions. Texas Instruments, ITT, and Emerson Electric, among others, focus top-management direction setting in regular sessions where—as everyone in the organization knows—"things get done" or "the buck stops." Another notable example is cited by *Fortune:*

One of the enduring questions of management, a subject of constant concern and endless analysis, is how a large corporation can best monitor and direct operations spread over many industries and throughout many parts of the world. A number of companies have sought the answer in ponderous and elaborate management mechanisms. . . . But there is at least one large company whose top management continues to rely on plain, old-fashioned, face-to-face contact. Richard B. Loynd, the president and chief operating officer of Eltra Corp. . . . visits each of Eltra's thirteen divisions as many as eight times a year, and puts managers through formal grillings that last several hours at a time. The people at Eltra call this the "hands-on" management technique. Loynd says: "I think I spend more time with our operating people than the president of any other major company."

Invariably, like the single-element focusers, these systems are temporary in nature. Since most of them tend to become rigid and lose their unique value in the course of time, they need to be modified at intervals. One executive reports:

The monthly breakfast meeting finally got the chairman and his operating presidents away from staff. For two years these sessions, preliminary to the regular monthly review, became the real decision-making/enervating forum. But then the staffs caught on. One by one, *they* began coming to breakfast.

Dominating value

The discussion of change mechanisms has had a consistent undercurrent. The three classes of mundane tools have been presented as apparently trivial signaling devices for redirecting organizational attention and energy over time toward a theme, while the first two major change tools have been characterized as just larger-scale or agglomerated devices for the same purpose.

One final tool, which may be labeled the *dominating* value, addresses the role and utilization of the theme itself. It is, on the one hand, more delicate than the other tools, in that its use demands consummate political commitment-building skills and a shrewd sense of timing. In another sense it is more robust than the others, in that, if handled effectively, it can generate substantial, sustained energy in large institutions. For the senior manager, therefore, thinking about and acting on the value management process is, although imprecise, extremely practical.

Business researchers have coined various terms for an effective, predominant institutional belief. Richard Normann calls it a business idea or growth idea. He devotes an entire book, *Management and Statesmanship,* to documenting a case for the power of an effective, simply articulated business idea and describing the unique role and leverage of top management in indirectly guiding the process of belief establishment and change. He argues that "the interpretation of ongoing and historical events and the associated adjustment and regulation of the dominating idea is probably the most crucial of the processes occurring in the company."

Some other recent scholarly work, well grounded in the leading edge of social science findings, provides a corroborating point of view. Andrew Pettigrew's anthropological study of the creation of organization culture is representative:

> One way of approaching the study of the entrepreneur's relationship with his organization is to consider the entrepreneur as a symbol creator, an ideologue, a formulator of organizational vocabularies, and a maker of ritual and myth. Stylistic components of a vision, which may be crucial, might include the presence of a dramatically significant series of events, rooting the vision back into history, and thus indicating the vision was more than a fad. Visions with simple, yet ambiguous content expressed in symbolic language are not only likely to be potent consciousness raisers, but also flexible enough to sustain the ravages of time and therefore the certitude of events. Visions contain new and old terminology perhaps organized into metaphors with which it is hoped to create new meanings. Words can move people from a state of familiarity to a state of awareness. Some people have the capacity to make words walk. I suspect this is one of the unexplored characteristics of successful entrepreneurs.

Louis Pondy, in "Leadership is a Language Game," quite similarly equates leadership effectiveness with the capacity to achieve what he calls "language renewal."

Roy Ash puts the same notion in more concrete terms:

> At a sufficiently high level of abstraction, he says, "all businesses are the same." Ash's plans for testing that theory are summed up in the notes that he continually pencils on yellow legal pads. One of the most revealing of these notes says: "Develop a much greater attachment of everybody to the bottom line—more agony and ectasy." As he sees it, the really important change in a company is a process of psychological transformation.

If one combs the literature for the lessons extracted by business leaders, the crucial role of a central belief emerges. The biographies of Cordiner at GE, Vail at AT&T, Greenewalt at Du Pont, and Watson at IBM all stress the quest to give operational force and meaning to a dominant, though imprecise, idea. Such accounts may be dismissed as self-serving, but it would seem a bit more cynical than even these times call for to write off the extraordinary consistency of so many closing statements.

Among active business leaders, the pattern of evidence is repeated. Richard Pascale, for example, has described the management style of several particularly effective chief executive officers. He notes the recurrence of a simple, overarching theme captured in a few words: for example, Harold Geneen's ceaseless "search for the unshakable facts," reflected in all kinds of organizational arrangements from structural contrivances—his controllers reporting to the chief executive and his intrustive product group managers—through interaction mechanisms —the famed ITT monthly review sessions. Further examples dot the business press:

A. W. Clausen at Bank of America: "Stay around Tom Clausen for about 15 minutes and he'll talk about laying pipe," says *Forbes.* "That's his shorthand for anticipating events and readying a response. Subordinates lay pipe to Clausen when they tell him about potential problems; he lays the pipe the other way when he sketches his expectations. The expression isn't especially catchy, the process isn't particularly glamorous. But it does help to explain why Bank of America isn't facing huge loan losses—and this big, slow-moving tortoise seems perfectly able to keep up with the flashier, more dynamic hares."

John DeButts at AT&T incessantly uses the term "the system is the solution." The concept, professed by DeButts in every setting from management meetings to television commercials, is aimed at starting the process of shifting the massive million-person Bell System's focus to the marketplace.

Tom Jones at Northrup, Fortune notes, has been particularly successful at gaining more than a fair share of defense contracts—largely, he believes, by bringing to life the theme "Everybody at Northrup is in marketing."

Walter Spencer at Sherwin Williams, according to *Forbes,* spent his five years as CEO working to introduce a "marketing orientation" into a previously manufacturing-dominated institution. Says Spencer: "When you take a 100-year old company and change the culture of the organization, and try to do that in Cleveland's traditional business setting—well, it takes time; you just have to keep hammering away at everybody. . . . The changeover to marketing is probably irreversible now. It's not complete, but we've brought along a lot of young managers with that philosophy, and once you've taken a company this far, you can't go back."

When the scholarly research and the anecdotal evidence are drawn together, some characteristic attributes of an effective dominating value can be discussed:

It is both loose and tight. That is, it connotes a clear directional emphasis—focus on the competition, stand for quality, become low-cost producer—but ample latitude for supporting initiatives.

It must, almost always, emerge rather than be imposed. Though it may be crystallized in a succinct phrase, it usually represents the end product of time-consuming consensus-building processes that may have gone on for a year or more.

Just as it cannot be impoved by fiat, it cannot be changed at will. Typically, a major shift in the dominant belief can be brought about only when an important change is perceived to be at hand. The process of gaining commitment requires so much emotional commitment and institutional energy that it can be repeated only infrequently.

It has a reasonably predictable life cycle. Beginning with a great deal of latitude, it becomes progressively less flexible over time—though never approaching the rigidity of a quantified goal.

It may be a definition or characterization of the past, meant primarily to mark the end of a period and provide the energy to start a search for new modes of organizational behavior. For example, one might choose to label the past five years as "the era of tight control" in order to suggest that something now coming to an end should be replaced with something new, as yet unspecified.

It imposes choices. Despite the general nature of most effective beliefs, they do require management to face up to the limits of the organization's capacities. Of course, any huge enterprise does a bit of everything, but, for example, a choice to stress controls, if effectively implemented, is likely also a choice not to push harder for new products.

It can be anything from a general management principle to a reasonably specific major business decision. At the management-principles end, it can become a commitment to something like "fact-based analysis." At the business-decision end, it can be a commitment to a revised position for a key product line. In the middle are hybrids such as "enhanced focus on competition."

It suggests movement (e.g., toward becoming the industry quality leader or dominating a particular market niche), thus implying some sort of tension or imbalance. Few leaders have been noted for achieving balance. Most have been known for going from somewhere to somewhere else.

Figure 5 gives a graphic portrayal of the essentials of the process I have been discussing. It depicts a five- to nine-year cycle of strategic transition marked by the tightening, executing, loosening, and redirecting search for an operational dominating value.

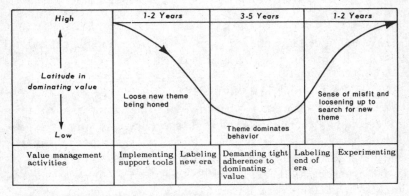

Figure 5. Five- to nine-year cycle of strategic transition.

Change for change's sake

At least one significant tool remains to be considered: namely, change for its own sake.

This is the device assigned, in figure 1, to cell 3 (low-control, high-speed change). Sometimes things are such a muddle that significant change for its own sake is a good bet to produce, on balance, a more desirable outcome than any directionally managed program.

In *The Economist,* Norman McRae recently observed:

> ... the most successful companies have been those restless enough to be unsure what their management styles should be. Successful big American corporations today will often centralize their policy making, and get a significant initial gain in effectiveness; but then, as time passes, will find that this does not work because the central planners do not know what is really going on out in the field. So these corporations will then decentralize, and get a significant initial gain in effectiveness. This constant reorganization is in fact very sensible, and is a main reason why I judge that big American corporations are still the most efficient day-to-day business operators in the world.

A somewhat less radical dose of the same medicine is the rather arbitrary reshuffling of top team member responsibilities, even when it results in a seemingly less rational match of skills to tasks. A fresh juxtaposition of perspectives, per se, is often of value.

At least one word of warning about high-early impact, low-control prescriptions in in order. The secret of their success is novelty. Routine reorganizing or all-too-regular shake-ups of top team assignments all too readily evoke the sense of déjà vu. "Nobody on the top team has been in the same job for more than 15 months," remarks an executive of a high-technology company. "Of course, all they do is trade bureaucratic barbs. That's all they've got. No one sees the results of his own initiatives."

Although it certainly merits much more discussion, the analysis of this last class of tools must necessarily be cut short at this point.

In conclusion: Limits and optimism

The purpose of this essay has been twofold: first, to provide a simple classification of change tools and some speculative hypotheses in support of the case for pessimism about the old favorites among them; second, to suggest that for the alert senior manager, today's organizational garbage cans are still full of powerful change tools—tools that he uses intuitively, and therefore not systematically, but which nevertheless are numerous and potentially powerful enough to justify a measure of optimism.

A limited measure, to be sure. Even with a mastery of all the change tools reviewed here, today's senior manager is unlikely to be able to develop real consensus, commitment, and change in more than a single direction. Richard Nelstadt's metaphor captures the essence of his role:

> Presidential power is the power to persuade. Underneath our images of Presidents-in-boots, astride decisions, are the half-observed
> · realities of Presidents-in-sneakers, stirrups in hand, trying to induce particular department heads . . . to climb aboard.

As he tries to coax his senior colleagues aboard, the senior executive has at his command a variety of settings—settings in which he can experiment, implement, and build patterns to provide a general conception of what's possible. He can, with luck and to a limited extent, grasp control of the signaling system to point a general direction and mark out limited areas of expected new institutional excellence. By adroitly managing agenda, he can nudge the day-to-day decision-making system, thus simultaneously imparting new preferences and testing new initiatives.

And some day, in retrospect, he may be able to see himself as an experimenter who attempted to build consensus on a practical (and flexible) vision of what was possible over a five-year horizon, and through incessant attention to the implementation of small, adaptive steps, eventually made that vision a reality.

If so, he should be well content.

Selected bibliography

Richard Pascale in "Three Chief Executives: The Effect of Style on Implementation" (Research Paper 357, Stanford Graduate School of Business) developed, with the subjects' cooperation, detailed case studies of Harold Geneen, Roy Ash, and Ed Carlson. He meticulously describes the links between their everyday behavior patterns, supporting organizational systems, and effectiveness.

John Kotter and Paul Lawrence in *Mayors in Action* (Wiley, 1974) discuss in a series of case studies the relationship, for example, between mayoral agenda setting and implementation success.

Four studies of bureaucratic politics offer particularly detailed analyses of the mundane attributes of influence accumulation and exercise: Graham Allison's *Essence of Decision* (Little, Brown, 1971); Edward Banfield's *Political Influence* (Free Press, 1961); Robert Caro's *The Power Broker* (Knopf, 1974); and Richard Neustadt's *Presidential Power* (Wiley, 1960).

Henry Mintzberg's unique observational study of senior executives, *The Nature of Managerial Work* (Harper & Row, 1973), vividly portrays the fragmented nature of real senior-management activity. If one finds his analysis credible, then presumably the kinds of change levers discussed in this article are of particular importance.

H. Edward Wrapp's "Good Managers Don't Make Policy Decisions" (*Harvard Business Review,* September-October 1967) and James Quinn's "Strategic Goals: Process and Politics" (*Sloan Management Review,* Fall 1977) provide good examples of effective muddling-about processes that typically attend development of what is called a "dominating value" in this paper.

The notion of organizations as temporary systems discussed in the paper is treated at length by E. J. Miller and A. K. Rice in *Systems of Organization* (Tavistock, 1967).

Last, James March and Johan Olsen's *Ambiguity and Choice* (Universitelforlaget: Norway, 1976) proposes and supports a novel, complex model of organizational choice. The decision-making environment they describe clearly calls for radically different management prescriptions. The tools offered in this paper seem, to me, to be reasonably consistent with their view of the world.

Stories Managers Tell:
A New Tool for
Organizational
Problem Solving
Ian I. Mitroff
Ralph H. Kilmann

If accounting and finance are the backbone of organizations, then the stories which permeate all organizations of any size are their lifeblood. Stories are so central to organizations that not only do organizations depend on them, but stronger still, they couldn't function without them. Big or small, every organization is dependent upon countless stories for its functioning.

While organizations typically generate stories of all kinds, there is one type that is of special interest, what we call "epic myths of the organization." While the purposes such myths serve are many and varied, if there is a central purpose, it is to define the unique quality of a particular organization.

Countless biographies and autobiographies attest to the power that stories play within modern corporations. These autobiographies retell, in a form strikingly similar to the great epic myths of the past, the life of the organization and that of the individual within it. They describe in heroic terms, more dramatic than life itself, the difficult circumstances under which the organization was born, the tremendous struggle that was necessary to keep it alive in the early perilous years of its existence, how those involved made great personal sacrifices born out of intense dedication, how the organization slowly began to grow, and finally, how in later years it achieved a success far greater than anybody had ever dared dream. The story becomes the corporate myth, the basic transcript that establishes and perpetuates corporate traditions. In short, it gives basic meaning to the corporation. It is recalled and recounted at formal occasions and at coffee break bull sessions. It is used to indoctrinate new employees. It helps to define "what this place is really like, what makes it tick, and finally, what's so special about it."

The corporate myth is the "spirit of the organization," and as such, it is infused into all levels of policy and decision making.

Through the systematic study of managerial autobiographies, countless interviews, and behavioral exercises with managers, we have evolved a technique for eliciting organizational myths or stories. More to the point, we have developed a technique for showing the practical implications of such stories for day-to-day corporate decision making. The outcome is a new approach to problem solving and planning.

The ideal organization—different stories from different managers

One reason why organizational stories have been so little studied is that most managers are only dimly aware of their existence, let alone their importance. Stories are like dreams. Most of us have to be trained not only to recognize them, but also to appreciate their significance. For this reason, it is almost impossible to get at the stories that govern organizations directly. Like dreams they have to be gotten at indirectly. Direct approaches only drive them further underground. Asking a manager to sit down and talk about this organization's "story" makes as much sense as asking someone to sit down and talk about his unconscious. Little wonder, then, why insightful organizational autobiographies are so rare. Only the most reflective managers can perceive the stories that guide their organizations and make them run.

We have found that it is much easier for managers to talk or write a story about their *ideal* organization than about their current (or real) organization. In fact, we have found that managers can more readily make up or recall a characteristic story about their real organization *after* they have first described their ideal. The reason is that ideal stories or images are not constrained by the countless number of complex details that go into the history of any real organization.

In comparison to real stories, stories about an ideal organization are relatively unconstrained. The tellers of stories about ideal situations are not obliged to stick to reality or to account for it. Their images of the ideal are purer and simpler than their images of the real could ever be. In addition, images of the ideal are often easier to get at than are images of the real because everyone has some notion of an ideal. It is often easier to describe what one would like to have than it is to say precisely what's wrong with one's current environment. Finally, asking managers to write a story about their ideal organization has the effect of opening them up and freeing their creative talents, whereas asking them to write about their real organization often has the effect of constraining their creative potential. And if ideals more readily reveal the hopes, dreams, and aspirations of people, then they also more readily reveal their fears and anxieties. For these reasons, we have asked managers to write about their ideal organization, and we have studied their stories in detail.

One of the most striking findings of our investigations is that different managers tend to have very different concepts of an ideal organization: Different managers produce very different kinds of organizational stories. To gain understanding of the basis for these differences, we have studied the personalities of different managers. We have found that:

> Managers of the same personality type tend to tell the same kind of story, that is, they have the same concept of an ideal organization.

> Managers of opposing personalities have drastically different concepts of an ideal organization. The ideal organization of one type is literally the living hell of an opposing type.

To get at these personality differences, we have administered a relatively short test to hundreds of managers. After the managers have taken the personality test, they are asked to write a short story on the concept of their ideal organization. They are instructed that the content and structure of the story is completely up to them. The stories need not be of any particular length or form. After this is done, the managers are put into various groups, and each group is then asked to come up with a story that best expresses the group's concept of an ideal organization. The groups are formed on the basis of the personality test: All the managers of the same personality type are put into the same group. We do this because we have generally found that such homogeneous groups tend to strengthen the effect of personality differences. That is, the groups—different from each other in the personality characteristics of their members, but each composed of managers with similar personalities—accentuate the differences in the concepts of an ideal organization held by managers with different personalities.

A personality framework for classifying managers

The personality framework that we have used to classify managers is that of C. G. Jung. The Jungian structure was chosen for two main reasons: (1) the dimensions of the framework are directly related to different managerial and organizational styles, and hence the classifications are of direct relevance to management; (2) the Jungian framework does not prescribe any one of its four major personality types as being superior to or better than any of the others. Instead, each type is seen as having major strengths and weaknesses. The framework can help managers to see that their personal style has certain costs or limitations as well as benefits, and that as a result, they need their managerial counterparts, with markedly different personal styles, to compensate for their weaknesses—and vice versa.

Two particular dimensions of the Jungian framework are of particular importance. The first dimension corresponds to the way in which a manager typically takes in data from the outside world. This is the *input-data dimension.* The second dimension corresponds to the way in which a manager typically makes a decision based on the data. This is the *decision-making dimension.*

According to Jung, individuals can take in data from the outside world by either *sensation or intuition;* most individuals tend to use one kind of data-input process rather than the other. Sensing, or sensation, types typically take in information via their senses. Sensing types are most comfortable when attending to the details, the specifics, of any situation. That is, sensing types tend to break every situation down into isolated bits and pieces; further, they feel most comfortable when they have gathered some "hard facts" that pertain to the situation. In contrast, intuitive types typically take in information by looking at the whole of a situation. They concentrate their attention on the hypothetical possibilities in a situation rather than getting bogged down and constrained by details and an endless array of hard facts. All individuals perceive the world with both of these functions at different times. But as Jung repeatedly argued, individuals tend to develop a habitual way of perceiving a situation and, in fact, cannot apply both types of perceiving or data input at the same time.

Also, Jung posited that there are two basic ways of reaching a decision with regard to any situation: *thinking* and *feeling.* Thinking types base their decisions on impersonal, logical modes of reasoning. That is, thinking types don't feel comfortable unless they have a logical or an analytical (for example, mathematical) basis for making a decision. Feeling types on the other hand make their decisions based on extremely personal considerations, for example, how they feel about the particular person or situation, whether they like the person, value the situation, and so forth. Thinking types want to depersonalize every situation, object, and person by "explaining" them. Feeling types on the other hand want to personalize every situation, object, and person by stressing their individual uniqueness.

Thinking is the psychological function that generalizes; feeling, the function that individuates. Thinking takes two objects that are inherently dissimilar and seeks to find what they have in common. Feeling on the other hand takes two objects, or people, or situations, that are inherently alike and emphasizes or seeks to find what is distinctly dissimilar about them. In short, thinking emphasizes sameness; feeling, characteristic differences or uniqueness—for example, that no two people are exactly alike, that each person is unique.

In summary, however an individual takes in data, by intuition or sensation, he may come to some conclusion about the data by either a logical, impersonal analysis—thinking—or by a subjective, personal process—feeling.

Combining the two data-input modes—sensation and intuition— with the two decision-making modes—feeling and thinking—in all possible ways allows us to talk about the following four Jungian personality types:

Sensing-thinking types (STs)
Sensing-feeling types (SFs)
Intuition-thinking types (NTs)
Intuition-feeling types (NFs)

The stories these four types tell are, in general, very different.

Sensing-thinking managers

The stories of STs typically contain an extreme emphasis and concentration on specifics, on factual details. STs are extremely sensitive to the physical features of their work environment. For example, the stories of STs display an extreme preoccupation with environments that are neither "too hot" nor "too cold" but "just right." The ideal organization of STs is characterized by complete control, certainty, and specificity. In their ideal organization, everybody knows exactly what his or her job is. There is no uncertainty as to what is expected in any circumstance. Further, ST organizations are impersonal: The emphasis is on work, and work roles, not on the particular individuals who fill the roles. The ideal organization of STs is authoritarian, if not the epitome of bureaucracy. There is a single leader at the top and a well-defined hierarchical line of authority that extends from the very top down to all of the lower rungs of the organization. In an ST organization, the individuals exist to serve the goals of the organization, not the organization to serve the goals of the individuals. The goals of an ST organization are realistic, down-to-earth, limited, and more often than not, narrowly economic. Finally—and it should come as no surprise— the heroes of STs are tough-minded individuals who know how "to step on people to get the job done." The greatest achievement of the heroes of STs is that they were available when the firm needed what they had to offer most: They brought "order and stability out of extreme chaos; they gave the firm a specific, well-defined sense of direction."

Intuition-thinking managers

The stories of NTs are marked by an extreme emphasis on broad, global issues. In describing their ideal organization, NTs do not specify the detailed work rules, roles, or lines of authority but focus instead on general concepts and issues. To put it somewhat differently, if the organizational goals of STs are concerned with well-defined, precise *micro*economic issues—"We need to make X dollars by September to stay solvent"—then the goals of NTs are concerned with fuzzy, ill-defined, *macro*economic issues—"There ought to be an equitable wage for all workers." NT organizations are also impersonal like ST organizations. However, where STs focus on the details of a specific impersonal organization, NTs focus on impersonal concepts and global theories of organization. For example, they are concerned with concepts of efficiency in the abstract. Likewise, whereas in an ST organization individuals exist to serve the present and specific needs of their particular organization, in an NT organization individuals exist to serve the intellectual and theoretical concepts of organizations in general. In a word, if ST organizations are impersonally realistic, then NT organizations are impersonally idealistic.

The heroes of NTs are broad conceptualizers. If the heroes of STs are problem solvers, then the heroes of NTs are problem formulators, that is, the finders, if not the creators, of new problems. The heroes of NTs take an organization designed to accomplish a very specific, limited set of goals (for example, turn out a specific product) and create new goals. They envision new products, horizons, and businesses in their firm.

Intuition-feeling managers

The stories of NFs are also marked by an extreme preoccupation with broad, global themes and issues. NFs also show an extreme disdain toward getting down to specifics. NFs are similar to NTs in that both take a broad view of organizations. However NFs differ from NTs in that where the emphasis of NTs is on the general *theory* or *theoretical* aspects of organizations, the emphasis of NFs is on the most general *personal* and *human* goals of organizations. Thus NF organizations are concerned with "serving humanity," with "making a contribution to mankind." NFs differ from both STs and NTs in that for both STs and NTs the individual exists to serve the organization, where for NFs the organization exists to serve the personal and social needs of people. Since in Jungian personality theory the NF type is the extreme opposite of the ST type—as the SF type is the extreme opposite of the NT—it is not surprising to find that the ideal organization of NFs is the exact opposite of STs. Thus, if an ST organization is authoritarian and bureaucratic with well-defined rules of behavior, then an NF organization is completely decentralized with no clear lines of authority, no central leader, and with no fixed, prescribed rules of behavior. The stories of NFs incessantly talk about "flexibility" and "decentralization." As a matter of fact, many of the stories of NFs contain diagrams of their ideal organization that show them to be circular or wheel-like in structure rather than hierarchical. NF organizations are also idealistic as opposed to realistic. In essence, NF organizations are the epitome of organic, adaptive institutions.

The heroes of NFs are not only able to envision new lines of direction, that is, new goals, objectives, and so forth, for their organization —in this sense they are like the heroes of NTs—but they are also able to give the organization a new sense of direction in the human or personal sense.

Sensing-feeling managers

If the ideal organizations of STs and NFs are extreme opposites, then the organizations of NTs and SFs are also extreme oppposites. If NTs are concerned with the general theory of all organizations but not with the details of any particular organization, then SFs don't care about theory or issues in general at all. SFs are instead concerned with the detailed human relations in their particular organization. SFs are like STs in that both are concerned with details and facts. However, SFs differ from STs in that the latter are concerned with detailed *work rules* and *roles* whereas the former are concerned with the *human qualities of the specific people* who fill the roles. SFs are in this sense similar to NFs. Both SFs and NFs are concerned with the people in the organization. SFs differ from NFs in the sense that where NFs are concerned with people in general, SFs are concerned with individuals in particular. SF organizations are also realistic as opposed to idealistic. Like STs, SFs are also concerned with the detailed work environment although, where for STs the environment of concern is physical, for SFs it is the interpersonal environment that is of concern. The heroes of SFs are those very special people who are able to create a highly personal, very warm human climate in their organization. They make you want to come to work. Indeed, the organization becomes just like home, like being one of the family.

Unfortunately, it would take too much space to give an illustration of every one of these four kinds of stories. However, the following typical example of an SF story may help to convey the spirit of what we've been talking about:

Utopia in the Business World

The day had been a particularly harrowing one at the office with more than the normal amount of frustrations with the administration, the workers, and even the public. I went home and fell exhausted into bed.

Suddenly I awoke and looked around. Where was I? What was this strange place? Who were these people? At that moment I was approached by a smiling person with hand extended who said, "Welcome to our organization. We are glad to have you with us. My name is ————. I will take you around to meet the rest of the staff."

Everyone I met was very friendly and in the days to come proved to be most helpful. My duties were explained to me quite clearly and thoroughly. The procedure with which I had to work was written in such a way that there was very little chance of misinterpretation.

All of the staff worked quite well with each other with a minimum of disagreements. The separate department heads would meet once a week with the Administrator who would keep them informed of new developments. The department heads would then keep the workers informed. Once a month the Administrator would address the entire staff. There was a free and easy exchange of ideas. There was no CIA atmosphere nor was there always a lot of rumors floating around. No one ever said, "I hear by the grapevine." There was no need to "hear by the grapevine." Everyone was fully informed as to the opportunities available to them.

A door slammed and suddenly I was transported from the ideal organization back to the world from which I came.

Implications for organizational problem solving

It has been our experience that the phenomenon of storytelling has a tremendous impact on managers. This is especially the case where managers of different psychological types are able to share their stories in an atmosphere of freedom and trust, that is, without fear or ridicule. The biggest value of such experiences is that they make managers aware, as perhaps never before, of basic differences that have always existed but that are obscured in everyday life. One rarely has the chance to witness in as explicit and systematic a way the operation of fundamental psychological differences.

The greatest value in sharing organizational stories lies in the fact that it sensitizes managers to other realities—to the fact that there are other ways of perceiving and analyzing organizational disturbances and problems. In this sense, the value of such an experience extends far beyond the seemingly trivial exercise of storytelling.

We would contend that the kinds of real problems that organizations face have aspects of every one of the psychological viewpoints we have been discussing. Almost by definition, *real* problems do not fit neatly into one and only one slice of psychological space. Rather, real problems, as opposed to idealized problems, change drastically in character —they look vastly different—as we view them from different perspectives. If we associate (1) the ST viewpoint, with its emphasis on day-to-day specifics and details, with the operational phase of organizational problem solving, (2) the NT view with long-range strategic planning, (3) the NF orientation with the setting of long-range human goals, and (4) the SF view with day-by-day human relations, then all problems of any importance not only have features that involve every one of these aspects, but organizational problems ought to be conceptualized as such. We would argue that the failure to view problems as involving all four viewpoints can be disastrous to an organization. By ignoring one or more of these viewpoints an organization can fail to recognize and hence to treat an important side of its problems.

Method of application

The implications of the approach we have been describing can be summarized as follows: We start by assuming that one or more subunits in an organization are identified as experiencing some conflict or problem. Our first step is to bring together all of the individuals concerned with the problem or their representatives if there is a large number of individuals. Each individual is asked to write out his view of the problem—what he sees as the objectives of the problem, the issues involved, the value assumptions made, and so forth. Alternatively, we ask each individual to write a story describing how the problem arose, the individuals who were involved, what got them to see the problem in a particular way, how they approached the problem, and what an ideal resolution of the problem would look like. The individuals are then formed into a Jungian group, that is, an ST, NT, SF, and NF group, and are asked to develop a group statement by combining or integrating their individual statements or stories. When the group statements have been prepared, each group shares with the others their view of the problem as indicated by their group discussions. This typically results in four very different perspectives.

The next stage in the process explicitly examines the four differentiated group products and attempts to integrate them into some new form or synthesis. The process involves having two or more individuals from each of the four Jungian groups meet as an integrated group.

This group then is asked to discuss their different perspectives, their assumptions, values, stories, and so forth. A lively debate usually develops in which the different perspectives are exaggerated, challenged, examined, denied, projected, and so forth. During this process, each individual is encouraged and pushed as much as possible to critically question and address the strengths and weaknesses of his own perspective. Once each individual in the integrated group has achieved this objective, the process moves toward a synthesis stage. The atmosphere changes, and each member of the group attempts to provide innovative solutions, capitalizing on the strengths of each position while minimizing or subduing the weaknesses. Finally, this group proposes some integrated solution that addresses the issues developed by the different perspectives.

The essential point to be emphasized is that this problem-solving process can be designed and applied to any organizational problem, whether the problem is one of macroorganization design—that is, how to organize to address the variety of task environments that the organization faces—or arises within a given organization design—for example, how to integrate two already-existing subunits. This conclusion springs from the consistently favorable results we have achieved in applying the Jungian framework to a broad range of concepts and issues in a number of organizations. It seems to us that a wide variety of organizational phenomena have their roots in the basic differences between Jungian personality types, that is, in the fact that different types see things differently. Consequently, regardless of the substantive issue at hand, the methodology is useful in addressing itself to the underlying dimensions of the issue.

This kind of problem-solving process needs to be a recurring component of any management system; it needs to be institutionalized in a form similar to the one we have described. We are suggesting that a major issue for organization design is that *organizations need to design a problem-solving system* in order to adapt successfully to different problems and different task environments. Such a system has to have the objective of *continually* addressing itself to the different sources of conflicts and value issues in the organization—that is, different people, different problems, different designs—and of providing a design mechanism to coordinate and integrate the different perspectives that are so necessary if innovative solutions are to arise. In fact, we see that the ability of an organization to confront needed changes and different problems is heavily based on the organization's ability to design itself for the possibility of taking advantage of such confrontations—organizations must ensure that these various confrontations do not occur by chance, by the dictates of a few individuals, or via a reactive as opposed to a proactive stance. Rather, how to realize the stimulus to growth that is implicit in confrontations is an organization design problem that must be approached explicitly—one that requires the organization to allocate resources to implement a system for using confrontations.

We do not mean to suggest, however, that organizations have not instituted problem-solving systems, but rather that within present problem-solving systems, organizations have not made use of the unique information and perspectives that result from storytelling—whether these are stories about ideal or real organizations. Most efforts at problem solving and decision making rely on typical accounting data. And while contemporary management information systems have begun to include broader and more varied sources of information, this information is still consciously derived and highly quantitative. The use of organizational stories, however, taps the unconscious, qualitative phenomena that pervade organizations. From our research and consulting experience we have found that for appreciating and analyzing complex problems, this latter type of information is as important or even more important than rigorous accounting data. Storytelling, when applied in a problem-solving framework as we have described, can thus be an extremely important source of data for the organization—data that would otherwise be ignored or overlooked. As such, storytelling procedures do become a new tool for organizational problem solving.

13

Organizations and Their Environments: There's a Real World Out There

Introduction

This chapter's purpose is to remind the reader that organizations do not exist in a vacuum. Three related aspects of the organization's interdependence with its surrounding environment are considered here: (1) the cultural setting of the organization, (2) the strategic relationships and interdependencies of the organization with other organizations, and (3) the people who constitute the primary linking mechanism between (*a*) the organization and its cultural surroundings and (*b*) the organization and other organizations.

Two trends in American society seem to be closely related to this. The first, summarized in our first selection by Ouchi and Jaeger, is the continuing cultural tradition of individual independence, self-reliance, and high mobility. Accompanying that emphasis has been a decline in social institutions like the extended family, the community, and local neighborhoods. One implication, Ouchi and Jaeger argue, is that organizations must fill the vacuum and meet human needs for affiliation and cultural socialization. They describe how some organizations, much more than others, are doing just that—developing strong internal cultures reminiscent of the family and the church.

A second major trend, represented by the remaining articles in this chapter, is the increasing interdependency of organizations on one another, along with an increasing pressure on managers to turn their attention from *intra*organizational to *inter*organizational issues. So managers must find new tactics and strategies for managing their growing dependency on other organizations.

There is a curious anomaly in all this: while the old institutions supporting the individual seem to be eroding and loosening up, the interorganizational culture seems to be growing more dense and interdependent.

Ouchi and Jaeger's paper casts some light on these issues by comparing Japanese and American organizations. One main difference seems to be that the individual's affiliation needs are more carefully tended in Japan. The authors then forecast (and recommend) that American organizations move in the same direction, but American-style. They propose a kind of compromise, "type Z organization," retaining the American ethic of individuality and self-reliance, but including the Japanese emphasis on building strong affiliative ties among co-workers.

As Organ points out, in the second article on interorganizational relationships, it is not organizations but people who interact. As a person begins to work closely with several organizations, he or she is pressed to adopt some of the values and cultural perspectives of each of the organizations. Such "linking" or "boundary-spanning" people can both communicate and distort information because of their needs to balance different sets of goals, values, and beliefs.

Developing more effective boundary roles is nevertheless one of many strategies an organization can employ to gain power over other organizations. Upper-level managers and executives, according to Pfeffer, in the third selection, enact a number of strategies to manage interdependencies by making interorganizational relationships more predictable. When interorganizational relationships cannot be effectively negotiated through boundary spanners, the organization may attempt, for example, to create interlocking directorates, or joint ventures, or mergers to resolve critical interdependencies. One strategy suited to the current mobility levels of American culture is to encourage personnel to move among organizations. Executive movements among firms may serve to control or limit competitive behavior. For instance, movements between a regulatory agency and a regulated organization may lessen the impact of that regulation.

In the last article, Leavitt et al. introduce several additional strategies an organization can employ to react to and act upon the world around it. As with Ouchi and Jaeger, several of these examples point to the growing importance of the culture the organization inhabits. This last article draws together a number of major points of organization-environment relations made by previous authors in this book. And, perhaps fittingly, Leavitt et al. end with some comments about some major directions in which the organizational world seems to be heading.

Type Z Organization: Stability in the Midst of Mobility
William G. Ouchi
Alfred M. Jaeger

Now all the evidence of psychiatry . . . shows that membership in
a group sustains a man, enables him to maintain his equilibrium
under the ordinary shocks of life, and helps him to bring up children
who will in turn be happy and resilient. If his group is shattered
around him, if he leaves a group in which he was a valued member,
and if, above all, he finds no new group to which he can relate
himself, he will, under stress, develop disorders of thought, feeling
and behavior. . . . The cycle is vicious; loss of group membership in
one generation may make men less capable of group membership
in the next. The civilization that, by its very process of growth,
shatters small group life will leave men and women lonely and
unhappy (1, p. 457).

Society traditionally has relied upon kinship, neighborhood church,
and family networks to provide the social support and normative
anchors which made collective life possible. As Mayo (2) pointed
out, the advent of the factory system of production and the rapid
rate of technological change produced high rates of urbanization, mobility, and division of labor. These forces weakened the community,
family, church, and friendship ties of many Americans. Social observers point to this weakening of associational ties as the basic cause of
increasing rates of alcoholism, divorce, crime, and other symptoms of
mental illness at a societal level (3–5).

While worrying over the disappearance of family, church, neighborhood, and the friendship network, predispositions can blind us to the
most likely alternative source of associational ties or cohesion: the
work organization. The large work organization which brought about
urbanization and its consequent social ills can also provide relief from
them. Donham notes:

Reprinted with permission from *Academy of Management Review,* April 1978.

Mayo shows us for the first time in the form of specific instances that it is within the power of industrial administrators to create within industry itself a partially effective substitute for the old stabilizing effect of the neighborhood. Given stable employment, it might make of industry (as of the small town during most of our national life) a socially satisfying way of life as well as a way of making a living (2).

Employment already defines many aspects of people's lives: socioeconomic status, their children's education, kinds and length of vacations, frequency and severity with which they can afford to become ill, and even the way in which pension benefits allow them to live their retirement years. From childhood to the grave, the work organization plays a central role in identifying people and molding their lives. Japan (6), Poland (7) and China (8), provide models of work systems which organize life and society, but we have been unwilling to borrow these models, because they do not permit the individual freedom that is valued in American life.

With memories of the totalitarian paternalism of the mines and plantations still not healed by time, Americans have been reluctant to even consider the work organization as the social umbrella under which people can life free, happy, and productive lives. The ideology of independence that is part of the basic fabric of the American persona recoils at the thought of individual freedom subordinated to collective commitment. American idols are the rough, tough individualists, the John Waynes, the Evel Knievals, the Gloria Steinems. Our most pitiable figures are those who lose their individuality in some larger, corporate entity and become "organization men," faceless persons "in gray flannel suits."

We must discover that ideologically unique American solution which allows individual freedom while using the work organization to support and encourage the stability of associational ties.

The beginnings of this solution were found in a study by one of the authors (9). Interviews were conducted with employees of all level of Japanese and American firms which had operations in both the United States and Japan. In Japanese companies in Japan were found the now-familiar characteristics first reported by Abegglen (6): almost total inclusion of the employee into the work organization so that the superior concerns himself or herself with the personal and family life of each subordinate; a collective, nonindividual approach to work and responsibility; and extremely high identification of the individual with the company. These characteristics are largely the result of the lifetime employment system which characterizes large companies in Japan (5, 6, 10–12).

The surprising finding was that Japanese companies with operations in the United States are applying a modified form of the pure Japanese type with some success. While they do not provide company housing or large bonuses as in Japan, they attempt to create the same sort of complete inclusion of the employee into the company. Supervisors are taught to be aware of all aspects of an employee's life; extrawork social life is often connected to other employees; corporate values are adjusted to reflect employee needs as well as profit needs, and high job security is protected above all else. The American employees expressed liking for this "atmosphere" or "climate," with the managerial staff in particular noting the difference from their previous employers.

The study gave evidence that, while Americans probably do not want a return to old-style paternalism, they favor a work organization which provides associational ties, stability, and job security. The Japanese-American mixed form suggested the model which may simultaneously permit individual freedom and group cohesion.

Some American companies, by reputation, have many of the characteristics of this mixed model. Best known are Kodak, Cummins Engine Company, IBM, Levi Strauss, National Cash Register, Proctor and Gamble, and Utah International. Their historical rates of turnover are low; loyalty and morale are reputed to be very high, and identification with the company is reputed to be strong. In addition, each company has been among the most successful of American companies for many decades, a record which strongly suggests that something about the form of organization, rather than solely a particular product or market position, has kept the organization vital and strong. It is widely believed that these companies have been co-opted by their employees; they do not express goals of short-term profitability but rather pay some cost in order to maintain employment stability through difficult times. These work organizations may have created the alternative to village life to which Mayo referred.

Compare persons associated with this mixed model to the "ideal type" of bureaucrat described by Toennies (13), Weber (14), and Merton (15)—a person involved in the limited, contractual, only partially inclusive relationships that characterize traditional American organizations. In a sense, the scheme being proposed here is an organizational analogue of Toennies' *Gemeinschaft* and *Gesellschaft* (13). Just as societies suffer from poor mental health as a result of size, density, and heterogeneity which lead to contractualism and segmentalism in life, work organizations also can become segmented and contractual as they grow. This is what Weber (14) expected. He advocated development of a contractual *Gesellschaft* in work organizations to shield the meritocracy from outside ascriptive values and ties (16, 17). In a stable society, individuals can develop ties outside work to complement the impersonal nature of participation in a contractual organization. But in a mobile and changing society, societal values and outside ties are weaker, posing less threat to the efficiency of the organization. More individuals are less likely to have developed personal ties outside of work which satisfactorily complement the impersonal interactions engaged in at work. Thus, organizations whose goals and philosophy are in tune with today's general societal values can survive and even thrive by being more "personal."

The ideal types: type A, type J, and type Z

This section describes three ideal types of work organization. It is argued that each type is an integrated system and will yield either positive or negative outcomes for the society depending on certain environmental conditions. Type A represents the Western organization, especially the North American and Western European forms. Type J represents the Japanese and mainland Chinese forms, and Type Z is an emergent form which is particularly suited to the United States of America today.

Each ideal type contains seven dimensions (table 1). Length of em-

Table 1. Characteristics of Two Familiar Organizational Ideal Types: A and J

Type A (American)	Type J (Japanese)
Short-term employment	Lifetime employment
Individual decision-making	Consensual decision-making
Individual responsibility	Collective responsibility
Rapid evaluation and promotion	Slow evaluation and promotion
Explicit, formalized control	Implicit, informal control
Specialized career path	Nonspecialized career path
Segmented concern	Holistic concern

ployment refers to the average number of years served within the corporation, considering all employees. This is important in two respects. First, if mean number of years of tenure is high, employees will be more familiar with the workings of the organization and more likely to have developed friendships among their co-workers; second, if the new employee anticipates a long career within one organization, he or she will be willing to incur greater personal costs in order to become integrated into the culture of the organization.

The mode of decision-making refers to typical ways of dealing with nonroutine problems. Individual decision-making is a mode by which the manager may or may not solicit information or opinion from others, but he or she expects and is expected by others to arrive at a decision without obligation to consider the views of others. Under consenual decision-making, the manager will not decide until others who will be affected have had sufficient time to offer their views, feel they have been fairly heard, and are willing to support the decision even though they may not feel that it is the best one (18).

Although responsibility is not easily distinguished from decision-making style in all cases, it represents an important, independent dimension. Individual responsibility as a value is a necessary precondition to conferring rewards upon individuals in a meritocracy. A manager possibly could engage in consensual decision-making while clearly retaining individual responsibility for the decision. Indeed, the Type Z organization exhibits just this combination. In the J organization, responsibility for overseeing projects and for accepting rewards or punishments is borne collectively by all members of a subunit. American companies in Japan which have attempted to introduce the notion of individual responsibility among managers and blue-collar workers have found strong resistance from their employees. But in the United States individual responsibility is such a central part of the national culture that no organization can replace it with the colective value of the J type.

The speed of evaluation and promotion category is self-explanatory, but its effects are subtle. If promotion is slow, managers have time to become acquainted with the people and the customs which surround their jobs. Workers will be shaped by and ultimately assimilated into the corporate culture. For better or worse, the maverick will not be promoted until he or she has learned to abide by local customs. An organization with a history of rapid promotion will not have as unified a culture as an organization with slower rates of upward mobility.

Speed of evaluation also has significant effects upon the character of interpersonal relationships. In an achievement-oriented organization, evaluations of performance must be free of dimensions such as friendship or kinship. The only solution open to an evaluator is an impersonal relationship. If evaluations occur rapidly, for example once each six months, the subject of the evaluation will typically be known only to the direct supervisor, who will be charged with the responsibility of rendering the evaluation. The supervisor is thus blocked from forming personal, friendship ties with the subordinate. But if major evaluations occur only once every five or ten years (as is common in Japanese firms), the evaluation is no longer explicitly rendered by one superior but emerges through a nonexplicit process of agreement between the many superiors who know the subordinate. Being one among many judges, the direct superior is freed from the need to preserve an "objective" attitude toward the subordinate and thus can take a personal interest in him or her.

The dimension of control is represented in an oversimplified manner. In a sense, the whole ideal type represents a form of social control, and each ideal type achieves this social control in a different manner. But we can identify in Type A organizations the use of explicit standards, rules and regulations, and performance measures as the primary technique of ensuring that actual performance meets desired performance. In Type Z, expectations of behavior or output are not explicitly stated but are to be deduced from a more general understanding of the corporate philosophy.

For example, during one of the author's visits to a Japanese bank in California, the Japanese president and the American vice-presidents of the bank accused each other of being unable to formulate objectives. The Americans meant that the Japanese president could not or would not give them explicit, quantified targets to attain over the next three or six months, while the Japanese meant that the Americans could not see that once they understood the company's philosophy, they would be able to deduce for themselves the proper objective for any conceivable situation.

The degree to which a career path is typically specialized according to function differs greatly between organizational types. In the A organization, an upwardly mobile manager typically remains within a functional specialty, for example going from bookkeeper to clerical supervisor to assistant department head of accounting to head of the accounting department. In the J organization, the typical career path is not specialized by function, but may go from bookkeeper to supervisor of the planning department.

A specialized career path yields professionalization, decreases organizational loyalty, and facilitates movement of the individual from one firm to another. A nonspecialized career path yields localism, increases organizational loyalty, and impedes interfirm mobility. Career specialization also increases problems of coordination between individuals and subunits, while nonspecialization eases the coordination problem. Career specialization also yields the scale economies of task specialization and expertise, whereas nonspecialized career paths often sacrifice these benefits. A and J organizations may be the same in formal structure—having equal divisional separation, for example— but individuals will move through those subunits in quite different patterns.

Concern refers to the holism with which employees view each other and especially to the concern with which the supervisor views the subordinate. In the A organization, the supervisor regards the subordinate in a purely task-oriented manner and may consider it improper to inquire into her or his personal life. In comparison to this segmented view of people, the J organization manager considers it part of the managerial role to be fully informed of the personal circumstances of each subordinate.

Each ideal type represents a set of interconnected parts, each dependent on at least one other part. The systematic nature of each type is best understood by putting it in an environmental context.

The Type A has developed in a society characterized by high rates of individual mobility, in a culture which supports norms of independence, self-reliance, and individual responsibility. A work organization in such a setting must contend with high rates of interfirm mobility and a short average tenure of employment. It reduces interdependence between individuals, avoiding the start-up costs of replacing one part of a team. Individual decision-making and individual responsibility provide an adaptive response to rapid change of personnel. If interfirm mobility is high, it becomes impossible to integrate new members into the organization on a large number of dimensions. It is simpler to attend to only the one or two necessary task dimensions of the new member and integrate those. Thus a segmented concern evolves, because a concern for the whole person presents an impossible problem to an organization with high turnover. But as a result, the employee has only limited, contractual ties to the organization, has not internalized its values, and must be dealt with in a compliant relationship, in which control is explicit and formalized.

The A type organization has a relatively short time in which to realize productive benefits from the necessary investment in an individual employee (costs of search and training). It can best realize these benefits by having the person follow a highly specialized career path in which necessary learning can occur rapidly and scale economies are soon achieved. Finally, rapid turnover requires replacement of managers and thus rapid promotion of those at lower levels. Because promotion must be preceded by evaluation, to preserve the impression if not the fact of a meritocracy, evaluation also will occur rapidly.

Ideal Type J organizations evolved in a society in which individual mobility has been low in a culture which supported norms of collectivism. Through historical accidents which preserved a feudal society in Japan into the 19th century and then, after the Meiji restoration, rushed Japan into full-blown industrialism (19), feudal loyalties were transferred to major industrial institutions, with owners and employees taking the appropriate historical roles of lord and vassal. Because employees are expected to be in the same firm for a lifetime, control can be implicit and internalized rather than explicit and compliant (as in the A type). This form of control evolves because it is more reliable and can account for a wide variety of task and personally oriented actions, whereas no explicit system of rules and regulations could be sufficiently comprehensive to encompass that range of behavior.

Type J employees need not follow specialized career paths, because the organization can invest in them for a long period of time and be assured of repayment in later years. By following nonspecialized career paths, they become experts in the organization rather than experts in some function. They are no longer interchangeable with other organizations, since their particular set of skills and values is unique to one firm, but that is not a cost to them or to the firm. Rather, their loyalty to the firm has increased and the firm need no monitor them closely, thus saving managerial overhead.

Furthermore, coordination problems are reduced, since employees have the information and inclination to accommodate each other in jointly taking action. Since they are to spend a lifetime together, they have an interest in maintaining harmonious relationships and engaging in consensual decision-making. The larger culture supports norms of collectivism which are mirrored in the organization. No individual can properly take credit or blame for actions, since organizational action by its very nature is a joint product of many individuals. Given joint responsibility, rapid evaluation would be difficult, since the task would be like that of performing a multivariate analysis with a sample of one observation. But since turnover and promotion occur slowly, evaluation need not proceed quickly. Many observations of the individual are accumulated over a period of years before the first major evaluation is made. This slow evaluation takes the pressure off a single superior and frees him or her to take a holistic concern for the employee.

The complex relationships between elements of the ideal types are not yet completely specified; that is one task of the present research, which will be aided through empirical analysis. But clearly, the major driving force behind development of the ideal types is the rate of inter-firm mobility, which is closely related to the cultural values which aid or inhibit mobility. It can be argued that the A type is an adaptive response to high rates of social mobility while the J type is a response to low rates of social mobility, both forms fitting naturally with their environments. The work organization in this view represents just one way in which members of a society are integrated; it is both influenced by and influences the structure of its surrounding society.

Having concluded that each ideal type represents a natural adaptation to a particular environment, how is it that the J type apparently has succeeded in the United States (9)? The United States provided the social environment in which the A type evolved. Americans are highly urbanized, move about, lead segmented lives, and thus have created a situation in which a work organization must be able to rely on people who are strangers to each other and still get coordinated effort out of them. The answer was the A type, which is contractual, formalized, and impersonal. How can a very different type, the J, flourish in this same social environment?

Interviews with managers from a large number of companies over the past two years were focused on companies which, by reputation, have many characteristics of Type J. Out of these interviews came a conception of a third ideal type, which initially appeared to be the J but differs from it in some essential characteristics.

The ideal Type Z (table 2) combines a basic cultural commitment to individualistic values with a highly collective, nonindividual pattern of interaction. It simultaneously satisfies old norms of independence and present needs for affiliation. Employment is effectively (although not officially) for a lifetime, and turnover is low. Decision-making is consensual, and there is often a highly self-conscious attempt to preserve the consensual mode.

Table 2. Characteristics of Organizational Type Z

Type Z (Modified American)
Long-term employment
Consensual decision-making
Individual responsibility
Slow evaluation and promotion
Implicit, informal control with explicit, formalized measures
Moderately specialized career path
Holistic concern, including family

But the individual still is ultimately the decision-maker, and responsibility remains individual. This procedure puts strains on the individual, who is held responsible for decisions singly but must arrive at them collectively. These strains are mitigated by the fact that evaluation and promotion take place slowly and that the basic control is implicit and subtle. Thus the complexities of collective decision-making are taken into account in rendering personal evaluations, but there are explicit measures of performance as in Type A. In the Z organization, although there are lots of formal accounting measures of performance, the real evaluation is subjective and highly personal. No one gets rapidly promoted or punished solely because their performance scores are good or bad. In an A organization, by contrast, people's careers often succeed or fail solely on explicit performance measures, as must be the case in any purely formalized system.

Career paths in the Z organization tend to be moderately specialized, but quite nonspecialized by comparison with the Type A organization. The slowness of evaluation and the stability of membership promote a holistic concern for people, particularly from superior to subordinate. This holism includes the employee and his or her family in an active manner. Family members regularly interact with other organization members and their families and feel an identification with the organization.

Implications for society at large

Why is the Z type useful in thinking about American organizations if the A type is the natural adaptation to a society and culture? If a second ideal type can be accommodated, social conditions must have changed.

The critical aspect of the environment is its ability to provide stable affiliations for individuals. Traditional sources of affiliation in American society (family, church, neighborhood, voluntary association, and long-term friendship) have been weakened by urbanization and geographical mobility. Figure 1 represents the combination of societal and organizational sources of affiliation. It includes only ideal Types A and Z; ideal Type J, the pure adaptation to a Japanese society, is not useful as a representation of American organizations.

Affiliation in the Organization	Affiliation in Society	
	High	Low
High (Type Z)	I Overloaded	II Integrated
Low (Type A)	III Integrated	IV Underloaded

Figure 1. Societal and organizational sources of affiliation.

Throughout most of its history, this nation has been high in sources of affiliation outside of the workplace. Under this condition, Type A organizations evolved, creating a stable, integrated state in which most people devoted most of their energies to affiliative networks away from the workplace and were only partially included in the work organization. Had the work organization been Type Z, each employee would have been torn between two mistresses and in an overloaded state (Cell I). In the past few decades, much of American society has moved from the "High" to the "Low" affiliation state (20–23). High mobility has broken the traditional patterns of interaction, but the values which supported those patterns will change more slowly. Those values support the notion of partial inclusion, of individuality, of the Type A organization. Thus many find themselves largely in the Underloaded cell (Cell IV), with society unable to provide affiliation and work organizations not organized to do so. To return to a balanced state, affiliation will have to come mostly from the organization and not from society at large.

Because not all people need the same level of affiliation (or achievement or power), each person will respond differently to being in each of the cells I through IV. According to Maslow (24), all people have a need for affiliation, belongingness, or love, which can be satisfied through feeling that they are part of a group or company. On the average, people in Cell IV ("Underloaded") will have unfulfilled needs for affiliation. They will experience "anomie," the sensation that there are no anchors or standards, and thus a feeling of being lost.

All these elements can be combined in one model which describes how the organization interacts with its social environment and with the needs of its individual members to produce high or low loyalty for the organization and high or low mental health for the employees (see figure 2).

Figure 2. A model of organizational and individual affiliation needs.

If American society is moving from high to low affiliation, people who are employed in a Type Z organization should be better able to deal with stress and should be happier than the population at large. Certainly the Type Z organization will be more appropriate for that segment of society which lacks stable and strong affiliative ties. That is not to suggest that the work organization will in any way replace or compete with other national institutions. Quite the opposite: if the company provides a strong basic stability in people's lives, then the family, church, and neighborhood can all flourish.

Some may object that they will never support a Type Z approach in their company or that it would never work in their industry. They may be right. Society contains a range of people and environments; some prefer an employer who leaves them alone, evaluates them purely on objective measures, and recognizes achievement through rapid promotion even over the heads of others. There will always be organizations for such people and such tastes. Stability of employment is not possible in some industries. Aerospace is one example of an industry where a Type Z organization woud be harmful; if people built rich ties with each other and a control system based on personal knowledge, both would be wrenched and destroyed when the contract came to an end and massive layoffs became necessary. The Type Z form will not be for everyone.

Due to chance, some models of the Type Z organization are available to study and learn from. Until recently, the Type A organization was the most successful form in American society. When people had relatives, neighbors, and churches, they did not need Dr. Spock to tell them why the baby was purple, and they did not need a company that provided them with a rich network of social contacts. But in a few cases, companies grew up in small towns, or in places like California that were populated by emigrants, or in industries which required frequent relocation of employees. In all three cases, one side effect was that people had no immediate form of social contact available except through their employer. The extreme case is the military base, which looks, feels, and smells the same whether it is in Hawaii, Illinois, or New York. To make life possible under conditions of high geographical mobility, the military has developed a culture which is immediately familiar and secure no matter where its employees go. These organizations, public and private, created a social vacuum for their employees and then had to develop internal sources of support to replace what had been taken away. Now the rest of the country is "catching up" with them as stable sources of support disappear elsewhere. One can look to such models for ideas about how to cope with the new society.

The future problem confronting the work organization seems relatively clear. American society, which has been in a constant process of change during its turbulent 200 years, has reached a critical point. Church membership is declining; violent crimes increasingly involve a victim who is completely unknown to the assailant; workers feel less commitment to employers; all of us long for stability and structure in our lives. These changes signify a decline in belongingness and suggest the fate assigned by Homans (1) to societies which lose the feeling of membership; we will become, "a dust heap of individuals without links to one another."

References

1. Homans, G. C. *The Human Group* (New York: Harcourt, Brace and World, 1950).
2. Mayo, E. *The Social Problems of an Industrial Civilization* (Boston: Harvard Business School, 1945).
3. Angell, R. C. *The Moral Integration of American Cities* (Chicago: University of Chicago Press, 1951).
4. Angell, R. C. "The Moral Integration of American Cities, Part II," *American Journal of Sociology,* Vol. 80 (1974), 607–29.
5. Form, W. H. "The Social Construction of Anomie: A Four Nation Study of Industrial Workers," *American Journal of Sociology,* Vol. 80 (1975), 1165–91.
6. Abegglen, J. C. *The Japanese Factory: Aspects of its Social Organization* (Glencoe, Ill.: Free Press, 1958).
7. Kolarska, L. "Interorganizational Networks and Politics: The Case of Polish Industry." Unpublished MS (1975).
8. Whyte, M. K. "Bureaucracy and Modernization in China: The Maoist Critique," *American Sociological Review,* Vol. 38 (1973), 149–63.
9. Johnson, R. T., and W. G. Ouchi. "Made in America (under Japanese Management)," *Harvard Business Review,* Vol. 52, No. 5 (1974), 61–69.
10. Cole, R. Japanese Blue Collar: The Changing Tradition (Berkeley: University of California Press, 1971).
11. Cole, R. "Functional Alternatives and Economic Development: An Empirical Example of Permanent Employment in Japan," *American Sociological Review,* Vol. 38 (1973), 424–38.
12. Dore, R. British Factory—Japanese Factory (Berkeley: University of California Press, 1973).
13. Toennies, Ferdinand. *Gemeinschaft und Gesellschaft,* trans. by Loomis (New York: American Book Company, 1940).

14. Weber, Max. *The Theory of Social and Economic Organization,* trans. by A. M. Henderson and T. Parsons (Glencoe, Ill.: Free Press and Falcon's Wing Press, 1947).
15. Merton, Robert K. *Social Theory and Social Structure,* 2d ed. Glencoe, Ill.: Free Press, 1957).
16. Udy, S. "Bureaucracy and Rationality in Weber's Organization Theory: An Empirical Study," *American Sociological Review,* Vol. 24 (1959).
17. Udy, S. "Administrative Rationality, Social Setting, and Organizational Development," *American Journal of Sociology,* Vol. 68 (1962), 299–308.
18. Schein, E. *Process Consultation* (Reading, Mass.: Addison-Wesley, 1969).
19. Nakane, C. *Japanese Society,* rev. ed. (Middlesex, England: Penguin Books, 1973).
20. Kasarda, J. D., and M. Janowitz. "Community Attachment in a Mass Society," *American Sociological Review,* Vol. 39 (1974), 328–39.
21. Reissman, L. *The Urban Process* (Glencoe, Ill.: Free Press, 1964).
22. Short, J. F. *The Social Fabric of the Metropolis* (Chicago: University of Chicago Press, 1971).
23. Warren, R. L. *The Community in America* (Chicago: Rand McNally, 1972).
24. Maslow, A. H. *Motivation and Personality* (New York: Harper, 1954).

Linking Pins between Organizations and Environment (Individuals do the interacting)
Dennis W. Organ

Management circles in recent years have returned again and again to the environment theme with the regularity of a Greek chorus. The term is used to mean different things by different people, and sometimes it is not clear if it really means anything at all. Nevertheless, it is perhaps reasonable to assume that most people who use the word with reference to organizations have in mind something like the definition suggested by Churchman: the environment of an organization is composed of those agencies or forces that affect the performance of the organization, but over which the organization has little or no direct control.[1]

The development and popularization of open-systems theory and its application to organization and management have undoubtedly contributed greatly to the environmental theme, at least in academic writings. The recent attention given to ecology in the mass media has perhaps generalized the popular concern over environment beyond that of physical environment to broad classes of external constraints and forces. However, underlying the pervasive emphasis of management practitioners on organizations' environments is, most likely, simply a heightened awareness of the complex interdependence among elements of modern society.

Thus, more than ever before, leaders of organizations realize their dependence upon other organizations and other parts of society for the recruitment of new members; acquisition of raw materials, technology, knowledge, and money; the disposal of finished products (whether they be goods and services, or, in the case of universities, trained and educated personnel); and, perhaps most important, the legitimacy and so-

Reprinted, by permission of the publisher, from *Business Horizons,* December 1971, © 1971 by the Foundation for the School of Business at Indiana University.
1. C. W. Churchman, *The Systems Approach* (New York: Dell Publishing Co., 1968), p. 36.

cial support attached to the organization's existence and objectives.

Furthermore, it is acknowledged that the environments of many organizations are maelstroms of accelerating change, or, in the apt words of Emery and Trist, "turbulent fields."[2] Consequently, there is a growing suspicion that the more relevant criterion of organizational effectiveness is not, as it used to be, that of efficiency, but rather that of adaptability to changes in the environment.

Role of the "Boundary Agent"

This increased awareness of organizational dependency on other elements of the social matrix has, in turn, suggested the strategic importance of interaction with the environment. To the extent that organizations depend on other organizations for survival and growth, they must establish linkages, or mechanisms of some kind, with those organizations in order to reduce the threats of uncertainty posed by dependence. Ultimately, of course, such linkages take the form of organizational roles, acted out by "boundary agents" who fill these roles. It is not really organizations that interact—it is people. It is such roles as those of salesman, purchasing agent, labor negotiator, credit manager, liaison personnel, lobbyist, and so forth that constitute the interorganizational linkages.

More important, it is through the behavior of these boundary agents that the organization adapts (or fails to adapt) to changes in the environment. It is through the reports of boundary agents that other organization members acquire their knowledge, perceptions, and evaluations of organization environments. It is through the vigilance of boundary agents that the organization is able to monitor and screen important happenings in the environment. To use a very strained analogy, it is the organization's boundary agents that function as sensory organs for the organization.

Given the strategic importance of the functions performed by these linkages (roles), one must presume that leaders of organizations would have considerable interest in the type of person who is best suited for these roles. The question is no idle one, because, as will be shown, there is evidence that these roles are qualitatively different from those that are strongly internal to the organization.

The evidence suggests that the positions considered here are best manned by persons with rather distinctive profiles of abilities, traits, and values. Kahn and his associates, who have made significant contributions to the study of these positions, have called them boundary

2. F. E. Emery and E. L. Trist, "The Causal Texture of Organizational Environments," *Human Relations,* XVIII (August, 1968), pp. 20-26.

positions.[3] Obviously, specific kinds of boundary positions (such as purchasing agent or industrial relations spokesman) require job-specific knowledge and skills. However, to the extent that they share the feature of important transactions with outsiders, they seem to share also the need for certain personal attributes of individuals in those positions.

Nature of boundary positions

Role conflict

Kahn and his associates have gathered evidence that documents the distinctive nature of boundary positions. First of all, people in such positions are susceptible to a high degree of role conflict—that is, they frequently get caught in the cross fire between people who expect different things of them.

This is not too surprising, since the boundary agent has to maintain interaction with, and owes allegiance to, two different kinds of people: those constituents in his own organization plus those agents representing other constituencies on whom his organization depends. The management spokesman in collective bargaining must contend not only with the expectations and pressures of his management colleagues, but also with those of the union spokesmen. The manager of the foreign subsidiary must take into account both the directives issuing from U.S. headquarters and those from the government and pressure groups in the host country. The industrial salesman must balance customer demands for quality, price, and custom-made features against his constituents' needs for unit profit, balanced production lines, low setup cost, and so forth.

In short, the boundary agent has to grapple with at least two different—sometimes contradictory—sets of goals, values, and beliefs. Therefore, the performance of the boundary agent is likely to be a key variable in the prevention, mitigation, and resolution of interorganizational conflict. If he is skillful in the judicious bending to pressures, compromising between conflicting demands, and balancing off some issues against others, he may be able to ward off serious conflict between organizations. On the other hand, if he is impulsive, rigid, or insensitive to others' beliefs and values, he may engender conflict even where it is not inherent in relationships between organizations.

Perhaps less obvious is the finding that the boundary agent fre-

3. R. L. Kahn, D. Wolfe, R. Quinn, J. D. Snock, and R. Rosenthal, "System Boundaries," in *Organizational Stress* (New York: John Wiley & Sons, Inc., 1964), pp. 99–124.

quently gets caught in cross fires even among his own constituents. He is likely to find that his constituents have varying, biased conceptions of his role. The credit officer's role may be viewed by financial people as that of minimizing losses due to bad debts (calling for a stringent credit policy), while marketing managers conceive his task to be that of facilitating the growth of sales and new customers (using flexible, lenient credit procedures). Strauss conducted a study of purchasing agents and found that different departments (such as engineering, production scheduling, and manufacturing) tried to impose their own goals on the purchasing agent's office.[4]

The point is that large organizations seldom have explicit, concrete overall goals; rather, each specialized department has its own goal because different functional divisions or sections are evaluated by different criteria. Therefore, any important transaction between the boundary agent and the environment will have differential effects on the "track records" of various departments. Thus, the boundary agent will often find himself caught in the middle between conflicting expectations of his own organizational kinsmen.

Lack of authority

Second, the boundary agent, by virtue of the fact that he has to interact with outsiders, must operate in situations where he does not have formal authority. He cannot solve his problems by "pulling rank" on persons who owe no allegiance to his organization. He must, therefore, use other and more subtle means of influence. He may be able to use expertise as power, as in the case of industrial salesmen who have encyclopedic technical knowledge about customers' products and the constraints imposed by their production methods.

In many cases, however, he must use the power of friendship or even the tactic of ingratiation. In short, he must be able to increase his attractiveness as a person to outsiders, even if it involves such acts as gently deriding his own organization, projecting an image of himself as an understanding ally of outsiders, making concessions to their beliefs and values, compromising on "principles," and "talking their language."

Unfortunately, it is precisely these tactics that his constituents may frown upon, if they are aware of them, even though they are of strategic value to the boundary agent for securing more substantive benefits for his organization. Such tactics may be interpreted by his constituents as reflecting disloyalty.

4. G. Strauss, "Tactics of Lateral Relationship: The Purchasing Agent," *Administrative Science Quarterly* (No. 7, 1962), pp. 161–86.

It should also be pointed out that the boundary agent often has to use these same informal methods of influence (such as friendship power or ingratiation) with his constituents. For example, the field salesman is adversely affected by low product quality, but he probably has no direct authority over quality control personnel.

Of course, informal modes of influence are often used also by persons in internal organization positions. Few organization officials use formal authority exclusively; certainly most officers would at least prefer to avoid the explicit invocation of the authority of their office, and much important communication is lateral rather than vertical. Still, a common ingredient of all intraorganizational interactions is the implicit obligation of all participants to follow standard procedures, policies, and traditions. This backdrop is lacking in typical interchanges between boundary agents and the environment.

The boundary agent's job is made doubly difficult simply because of his greater exposure to the organization's environment. Because of his frequent interaction with outsiders and his susceptibility to being influenced by them, his constituents may withhold their trust and support, granting him only a narrow range of discretion and decision making.

Agent of change

Because the boundary agent has to listen to outsiders' criticisms and attempt to view his own organization through outsiders' eyes, he is apt to feel more keenly than his constituents the defects in his organization and the need for change. The advocacy of change then initiates protracted struggles with organization officials who simply do not see the organization from the vantage point of the boundary agent and defend the status quo.

These struggles may generate further suspicions about the boundary agent's commitment to the organization's values and objectives. The boundary agent in a sense becomes an activist broker between the viewpoints, criticisms, values, and information of outsiders, on the one hand, and the values, objectives, policies, and attitudes of his constituents. Not only must he represent the organization to its environment, but he must also represent the environment to his constituents.

The preceding considerations produce an overall picture of the nature of boundary agents' jobs. These persons are often caught between conflicting pressures, both between constituents and outsiders and even among constituents. They often have to become agents of organizational change by modifying the beliefs and attitudes of constituents. They have to represent the organization—with all of its faults—to outsiders, and they have to negotiate the resolution of conflicts of interest. Their jobs are further complicated by their lack of authority over important persons, an inevitable violation of the classic principle that authority must be sufficient to carry out responsibility.[5]

The need to modify constituents' attitudes, to enhance and maintain their support and trust so as to preserve ample discretion for his own decision making, coupled with the need to make himself attractive to outsiders, puts the boundary agent in the position of having to be two-faced and to lead something of a double life.

The boundary agent's profile

Given a description of the nature of boundary positions, can we draw any tentative conclusions about the kind of persons who should fill such positions? That is, what type of person—in terms of his abilities, traits, and values—would probably be most effective in this role for attaining substantive benefits for his organization and avoiding needless conflicts with important other parties? What type of person would experience greater job satisfaction and less strain in these positions?

General abilities and intelligence

Probably more important than any measure of overall intelligence are the verbal and memory skills of the boundary agent. The boundary agent must represent the norms and values of his organization to outsiders in a way that does not offend or alienate them. Therefore, he must "watch his language." He must avoid the use of words that have unpleasant emotional connotations for other parties. The manager of the overseas subsidiary is perhaps well advised not to use the word "capitalism" indiscriminately in certain underdeveloped nations because of the term's historic connotations. The bargaining spokesman for management, in negotiation with union officials, uses such terms as "management prerogatives" with some risk.

Legislative lobbyists probably do not get very far if their active vocabulary is confined to such emotional symbols as "free enterprise," "corporate sovereignty," or "bureaucratic flunkies." The choice of relatively sterile, even awkward, terminology is less likely to conjure up specters of demons and ideological straw men that only impede the process of communication and negotiation.

The boundary agent must also be sensitive to the values of the parties with whom he deals, and those values are probably manifested in their selective use of certain words and phrases. He must be careful that semantics does not inflate the true differences of interests. He must be able to decode the positions taken by other parties and then encode them into the customary verbal repertoire of his own constituents; in

5. Kahn et al., *Organizational Stress*, p. 106.

a sense, he must be bilingual, at least with regard to the connotative dimensions of words.

Especially important, he can ingratiate himself with outsiders if he is sensitive to the symbols and words they use, and judiciously uses these words in his dealings with outside parties. Walton and McKersie tell of a labor official who was able to win the favor of high-ranking management people with the use of such businesslike language as "the policy of our organization" and "the decisions of our executive board."[6] This technique can also act as a cue to outsiders that the boundary agent understands, and appreciates the reasons for, their positions.

The above requirements place a premium on facility in manipulating words and symbols. Note that it is not vocabulary size that is important, although that may help, but a type of verbal skill represented by sensitivity to the connotations of words and the subtleties of semantics.

Good memory is important because it increases the potential of the boundary agent for ingratiating. A mind that holds onto otherwise trivial facts, dates, names, and so on about people can be used to project the impression that he is really interested in those people. We assume that people with average memories remember only those things they understand, like, or are interested in. Thus, the boundary agent who readily recalls isolated details about an outsider's place of birth, accomplishments, previous occupations, public statements, and so on has an advantage in establishing a viable relationship with that outsider. The outsider, for his part, feels subtle obligations to reciprocate in some way that may be of importance to the boundary agent's task.

Personality traits

It would seem that the boundary agent must be, above all, a person of flexibility, as opposed to rigidity. The rigid person strives for consistency in thought and behavior, has a distaste for ambiguity, commits himself strongly to beliefs and values, and tends to structure his behavior according to internally programmed rules rather than external situational factors.

These characteristics might be desirable for organizational members in many internal positions, but they would probably be dysfunctional for boundary role performance. The rigid person might easily allow his internally programmed rules to warp his perception of trends in the organization's environment, imputing structure to those trends where structure or certainty do not exist. He might forgo long-run organizational benefits for the sake of abstract principles.

6. R. E. Walton and R. B. McKersie, *A Behavioral Theory of Labor Negotiations* (New York: McGraw-Hill Book Company, 1965), pp. 226–27.

The flexible person would find it easier to vary his behavior according to the audience, the situation, or the issues. He would likely concede minor principles if the substantive outcomes were worth it. His thinking would be guided more by the criteria of feasibility and opportunity than by the norms and traditions of his constituency.

Unfortunately, these same characteristics may cause his constituents to view him as "wishy-washy" and deficient in his commitment to the organization. They may, therefore, deny him the support and discretion he needs for transactions with outsiders. This dilemma almost inevitably leads the effective boundary agent to be a little two-faced; he must be flexible when carrying out his job at the boundary (when interacting with outsiders and assessing environmental trends), yet he must project an image of staunch commitment and steadfastness before his constituents in order to preserve the flexibility of action which he needs.

The boundary agent is also likely to be more effective if he is more of an extrovert than an introvert. The extrovert, according to Kahn and his associates, is "extremely responsive to changes in external stimuli" and enjoys the company of other people. For this reason, the extrovert would probably be more skillful at establishing and using friendship power with outsiders, and he would probably be more sensitive to outsiders' norms and values. The introvert, on the other hand, has difficulty maintaining interpersonal relationships under conditions of stress and tends to be unrealistic in his assessments of external constraints on his behavior.

Values

Here the Allport-Vernon-Lindzey framework of six basic value categories—theoretical, economic, aesthetic, social, political, and religious —will serve as a basis for discussion. (The social and theoretical values will not be included because they yield less obvious predictions than the other four.) Economic and political values would seem to be desirable for the boundary agent. Economic values reflect a pragmatic style of thought and behavior, and a preference for solutions that work, even if they are not logical, elegant, internally consistent, or even unqualifiedly ethical if considered out of context. The person with strong political values would have the habit of forecasting the effects of his statements and behavior on the attitudes of outsiders, as well as his own constituents. He would appreciate the importance of personal and group persuasion as substitutes for formal authority and rigidly specified rules and obligations.

Macauley, in his study of noncontractual relationships between business organizations, found that such officials as financial officers and controllers desired written contracts with buyers and vendors, while industrial salesmen and purchasing agents preferred the flexible give-and-take of informal understanding.[7]

On the other hand, a person with strong aesthetic or religious values might balk at using ingratiation as an influence tactic or shrink from the concession of principles that might be necessary in order to effect substantive benefits for the organization. Such a person might also be repelled by the "hypocrisy" required of the boundary agent as he moves from one audience to another.

It may seem to the reader that an unnecessarily dark portrait has been drawn of the "ideal" boundary agent—that what is called for is a person without convictions, courage, or principles. But that is not the case. It is simply suggested here that the boundary agent, because of his concern for the organization's dependence on other agencies and the larger set of forces and constraints within which the organization exists, must necessarily evaluate his behavior within a larger framework than is true of internal organization members. Organizational morality, if that term must be used, must have a much more relativistic dimension, as Machiavellian as that may sound.

The reader may also respond with the query, "Are not the personal attributes suggested here simply desirable qualities for *any* organizational member? Wouldn't these traits be able to predict superior individual performance in any position?"

To some extent, the answer to the above question is "yes." For example, a number of studies have demonstrated a positive correlation between various measures of verbal ability and managerial performance.[8] However, it is difficult to imagine how extroversion or political values would be essential for the job effectiveness of a cost accountant or production engineer. Furthermore, the position taken in this article is that the attributes discussed—even though some of them are perhaps desirable for people in a variety of organizational offices—are of greater importance for the performance of the boundary agent.

A social role orientation in selection and placement

Essentially, what is at issue here is the need for a social role orientation for the analysis of organizational positions and the placement of persons in those positions. Boundary positions constitute only one class of organization offices along the social-psychological role dimension,

7. S. Macauley, "Non-contractual Relations in Business: Preliminary Study," *American Sociological Review*, XVIII, pp. 55-67.

8. See, for example, J. P. Campbell, M. D. Dunnette, E. E. Lawler, III, and K. E. Weick, Jr., *Managerial Behavior, Performance, and Effectiveness* (New York: McGraw-Hill Book Company, 1970), p. 130, 181–88.

and even this one class could perhaps be further divided. Division might be based, for example, on the importance of the interaction with outsiders, the degree of conflict with outsiders, whether the outside party is dealt with in a one-shot episode or in a continuing relationship, the degree of status or authority the boundary agent has among his own constituents by virtue of his position, or by the percentage of working time that must be allocated to dealing with outside parties.

For the most part, the development and use of selection and placement techniques have ignored the implications of social role dynamics for individual attributes. Yet, if a unifying framework for the prediction of managerial performance is to emerge, there must be more emphasis on the social roles inherent in various kinds of organizational positions. For the manager's role is largely defined by the different groups of persons he must interact with, the congruence and/or conflict among those persons' expectations of him, and the need for "shifting gears" in his behavioral style as he confronts different social situations. The variations in managerial social roles, it would seem, call for corrsponding variations in the abilities, personality traits, and values among the people needed to carry out those roles.

Furthermore, if the role analysis of an organizational position seems to call for certain individual attributes, one can specify how those attributes would be reflected in biographical data. If, as has been argued, boundary agents should have above-average memory and verbal skills, political and economic values, and a personality profile marked by extroversion and flexibility, then one can go a bit further and suggest how these would be manifested in a person's previous life experience. One would, for example, look for numerous college courses and good marks in the humanities, social sciences, or other disciplines rich in verbal content. Such a finding would probably reflect a sensitivity to semantics, a good memory for the trivia that help make impressive essay exam answers, and an ability and willingness to use "buzz" words for ingratiation purposes.

Another relevant biographical item would be membership in numerous social organizations of a nonideological character, reflecting extroversion, political values, the use of friendship power, and practice in ingratiation. On the other hand, one would hope to find that the person is not a member of organizations demanding ideological purity. Membership in these groups might indicate rigidity in thought and behavior. In fact, the use of biographical items such as these could lead to an operational program to test the validity of the arguments put forth here.

We have heard much about the importance of organizational environments and related issues of how different departments and divisions should be structured to match the demands of their particular environments. We should not forget that organizations, as such, do not interact with the environment.

Individuals do the interacting, and they do it within a greater or less detailed framework of role demands, role expectations, role conflicts, and resultant role stress. What is needed now is a program for identifying persons with the requisite skills and attributes which enable them to cope with the problems confronting the organization boundary agent.

Beyond Management and the Worker: The Institutional Function of Management
Jeffrey Pfeffer

Theory, research, and education in the field of organizational behavior and management have been dominated by a concern for the management of people *within* organizations. The question of how to make workers more productive has stood as the foundation for management theory and practice since the time of Frederick Taylor. Such an emphasis neglects the institutional function of management. While managing people within organizations is critical, managing the organization's relationships with other organizations such as competitors, creditors, suppliers, and governmental agencies is frequently as critical to the firm's success.

Parsons (1) noted that there were three levels in organizations: (*a*) the technical level, where the technology of the organization was used to produce some product or service; (*b*) the administrative level, which coordinated and supervised the technical level; and (*c*) the institutional level, which was concerned with the organization's legitimacy and with organization-environment relations. Organization and management theory has primarily concentrated on administrative-level problems, frequently at very low hierarchical levels in organizations.

Practicing managers and some researchers do recognize the importance of the institutional context in which the firm operates. There is increasing use of institutional advertising, and executives from the oil industry, among others, have been active in projecting their organizations' views in a variety of contexts. Mintzberg (2) has identified the liaison role as one of ten roles managers fill. Other authors explicitly have noted the importance of relating the organization to other organizations (3, 4).

Saying that the institutional function is important is different from developing a theory of the organization's relationships with other organizations, a theory which can potentially guide the manager's strategic actions in performing the function of institutional management. Such a theory is needed, and data are accumulating to construct such a theory.

The purposes of this article are (*a*) to present evidence of the importance of the institutional function of management, and (*b*) to review data consistent with a model of institutional management. This model argues that managers behave as if they were seeking to manage and reduce uncertainty and interdependence arising from the firm's relationships with other organizations. Several strategic responses to interorganizational exchange, including their advantages and disadvantages, are considered.

Institutional problems of organizations

Organizations are open social systems, engaged in constant and important transactions with other organizations in their environments. Business firms transact with customer and supplier organizations, and with sources of credit; they interact on the federal and local level with regulatory and legal authorities which are concerned with pollution, taxes, antitrust, equal employment, and myriad other issues. Because firms do interact with these other organizations, two consequences follow. First, organizations face uncertainty. If an organization were a closed system so that it could completely control and predict all the variables that affected its operation, the organization could make technically rational, maximizing decisions and anticipate the consequences of its actions. As an open system, transacting with important external organizations, the firm does not have control over many of the important factors that affect its operations. Because organizations are open, they are affected by events outside their boundaries.

Second, organizations are interdependent with other organizations with which they exchange resources, information, or personnel, and thus open to influence by them. The extent of this influence is likely to be a function of the importance of the resource obtained, and inversely related to the ease with which the resource can be procured from alternative sources (5, 6). Interdependence is problematic and troublesome. Managers do not like to be dependent on factors outside their control. Interdependence is especially troublesome if there are few alternative sources, so the external organization is particularly important to the firm.

Interdependence and uncertainty interact in their effects on organizations. One of the principal functions of the institutional level of the firm is the management of this interdependence and uncertainty.

The importance of institutional management

Katz and Kahn (7) noted that organizations may pursue two complementary paths to effectiveness. The first is to be as efficient as possible, and thereby obtain a competitive advantage with respect to other firms. Under this strategy, the firm succeeds because it operates so efficiently that it achieves a competitive advantage in the market. The second strategy, termed "political," involves the establishment of favorable exchange relationships based on considerations that do not relate strictly to price, quality, service, or efficiency. Winning an order because of the firm's product and cost characteristics would be an example of the strategy of efficiency; winning the order because of interlocks in the directorates of the organizations involved, or because of family connections between executives in the two organizations, would illustrate political strategies.

The uses and consequences of political strategies for achieving organizational success have infrequently been empirically examined. Hirsch (8) has recently compared the ethical drug and record industries, noting great similarities between them. Both sell their products through gatekeepers or intermediaries—in the case of pharmaceuticals, through doctors who must write the prescriptions, and in the case of records, through disc jockeys who determine air time and, consequently, exposure. Both sell products with relatively short life cycles, and both industries place great emphasis on new products and product innovation. Both depend on the legal environment of patents, copyrights, and trademarks for market protection.

Hirsch noted that the rate of return for the average pharmaceutical firm during the period 1956-1966 was more than double the rate of return for the average firm in the record industry. Finding no evidence that would enable him to attribute the striking differences in profitability to factors associated with internal structural arrangements, Hirsch concluded that at least one factor affecting the relative profitability of the two industries is the ability to manage their institutional environments, and more specifically, the control over distribution, patent and copyright protection, and the prediction of adoption by the independent gatekeepers.

In a review of the history of both industries, Hirsch indicated that in pharmaceuticals, control over entry was achieved by (a) amending the patent laws to permit the patenting of naturally occurring substances, antibiotics, and (b) instituting a long and expensive licensing procedure required before drugs could be manufactured and marketed, administered by the Food and Drug Administration (FDA). In contrast, record firms have much less protection under the copyright laws;

as a consequence, entry is less controlled, leading to more competition and lower profits. While there are other differences between the industries, including size and expenditures on research and development, Hirsch argued that at least some of the success of drug firms derives from their ability to control entry and their ability to control information channels relating to their product through the use of detail personnel and advertising in the American Medical Association journals. Retail price maintenance, tariff protection, and licensing to restrict entry are other examples of practices that are part of the organization's institutional environment and may profoundly affect its success.

Managing uncertainty and interdependence

The organization, requiring transactions with other organizations and uncertain about their future performance, has available a variety of strategies that can be used to manage uncertainty and interdependence. Firms face two problems in their institutional relationships: (a) managing the uncertainty caused by the unpredictable actions of competitors; and (b) managing the uncertainty resulting from noncompetitive interdependence with suppliers, creditors, government agencies, and customers. In both instances, the same set of strategic responses is available: merger, to completely absorb the interdependence and resulting uncertainty; joint ventures; interlocking directorates, to partially absorb the interdependence; the movement and selective recruiting of executives and other personnel, to develop interorganizational linkages; regulation, to provide government enforced stability; and other political activity to reduce competition, protect markets and sources of supply, and otherwise manage the organization's environment.

Because organizations are open systems, each strategy is limited in its effect. While merger or some other interorganizational linkage may manage one source of organizational dependence, it probably at the same time makes the organizations dependent on yet other organizations. For example, while regulation may eliminate effective price competition and restrict entry into the industry (9–11), the regulated organizations then face the uncertainties involved in dealing with the regulatory agency. Moreover, in reducing uncertainty for itself, the organization must bargain away some of its own discretion (6). One can view institutional management as an exchange process—the organization assures itself of needed resources, but at the same time, must promise certain predictable behaviors in return. Keeping these qualifications in mind, evidence on use of the various strategies of institutional management is reviewed.

Merger

There are three reasons an organization may seek to merge—first, to reduce competition by absorbing an important competitor organization; second, to manage interdependence with either sources of input or purchasers of output by absorbing them; and third, to diversify operations and thereby lessen dependence on the present organizations with which it exchanges (12). While merger among competing organizations is presumably proscribed by the antitrust laws, enforcement resources are limited, and major consolidations do take place.

In analyzing patterns of interorganizational behavior, one can either ask executives in the organizations involved the reasons for the action, or alternatively, one can develop a hypothetical model of behavior which is then tested with the available data. Talking with organizational executives may not provide the real reasons behind interorganizational activity since (*a*) different persons may see and interpret the same action in different ways, (*b*) persons may infer after the fact the motives for the action or decision, and (*c*) persons may not be motivated to tell the complete truth about the reasons for the behavior. Much of the existing literature on interorganizational linkage activity, therefore, uses the method of empirically testing the deductions from a hypothetical model of interorganizational behavior.

The classic expressed rationale for merger has been to increase the profits or the value of the shares of the firm. In a series of studies beginning as early as 1921, researchers have been unable to demonstrate that merger active firms are more profitable or have higher stock prices following the merger activity. This literature has been summarized by Reid (13), who asserts that mergers are made for growth, and that growth is sought because of the relationship between firm size and managerial salaries.

Growth, however, does not provide information concerning the desired characteristics of the acquired firm. Under a growth objective, any merger is equivalent to any other of the same size. Pfeffer (12) has argued that mergers are undertaken to manage organizational interdependence. Examining the proportion of merger activity occurring within the same 2-digit SIC industry category, he found that the highest proportion of within-industry mergers occurred in industries of intermediate concentration. The theoretical argument was that in industries with many competitors, the absorption of a single one did little to reduce competitive uncertainty. At the other extreme, with only a few competitors, merger would more likely be scrutinized by the antitrust authorities and coordination could instead be achieved through more informal arrangements, such as price leadership.

The same study investigated the second reason to merge: to absorb the uncertainty among organizations vertically related to each other, as in a buyer-seller relationship. He found that it was possible to explain 40 percent of the variation in the distribution of merger activity over industries on the basis of resource interdependence, measured by estimates of the transactions flows between sectors of the economy. On an individual industry basis, in two-thirds of the cases a measure of transactions interdependence accounted for 65 percent or more of the variation in the pattern of merger activity. The study indicated that it was possible to account for the industry of the likely merger partner firm by considering the extent to which firms in the two industries exchanged resources.

While absorption of suppliers or customers will reduce the firm's uncertainty by bringing critical contingencies within the boundaries of the organization, this strategy has some distinct costs. One danger is that the process of vertical integration creates a larger organization which is increasingly tied to a single industry.

The third reason for merger is diversification. Occasionally, the organization is confronted by interdependence it cannot absorb, either because of resource or legal limitations. Through diversifying its activities, the organization does not reduce the uncertainty, but makes the particular contingency less critical for its success and well-being. Diversification provides the organization with a way of avoiding, rather than absorbing, problematic interdependence.

Merger represents the most complete solution to situations of organizational interdependence, as it involves the total absorption of either a competitor or a vertically related organization, or the acquisition of an organization operating in another area. Because it does involve total absorption, merger requires more resources and is a more visible and substantial form of interorganizational linkage.

Joint ventures

Closely related to merger is the joint venture: the creation of a jointly owned, but independent organization by two or more separate parent firms. Merger involves the total pooling of assets by two or more organizations. In a joint venture, some assets of each of several parent organizations are used, and thus only a partial pooling of resources is involved (14). For a variety of reasons, joint ventures have been prosecuted less frequently and less successfully than mergers, making joint ventures particularly appropriate as a way of coping with competitive interdependence.

The joint subsidiary can have several effects on competitive interdependence and uncertainty. First, it can reduce the extent of new competition. Instead of both firms entering a market, they can combine some of their assets and create a joint subsidiary to enter the market. Second, since joint subsidiaries are typically staffed, particularly at the higher executive levels, with personnel drawn from the parent firms, the joint subsidiary becomes another location for the management of competing firms to meet. Most importantly, the joint subsidiary must set price and output levels, make new product development and marketing decisions and decisions about its advertising policies. Consequently, the parent organizations are brought into association in a setting in which exactly those aspects of the competitive relationship must be jointly determined.

In a study of joint ventures among manufacturing and oil and gas companies during the period 1960-71, Pfeffer and Nowak (15, 16) found that 56 percent involved parent firms operating in the same two-digit industry. Further, in 36 percent of the 166 joint ventures studied, the joint subsidiary operated in the same industry as *both* parent organizations. As in the case of mergers, the proportion of joint venture activities undertaken with other firms in the same industry was related to the concentration of the firm's industry being intermediate. The relationship between concentration and the proportion of joint ventures undertaken within the same industry accounted for some 25 percent of the variation in the pattern of joint venture activities.

In addition to considering the use of joint ventures in coping with competitive interdependence, the Pfeffer and Nowak study of joint ventures examined the extent to which the creation of joint subsidiaries was related to patterns of transaction interdependence across industries. While the correlations between the proportion of transactions and the proportion of joint ventures undertaken between industry pairs were lower than in the case of mergers, statistically significant relationships between this form of interorganizational linkage activity and patterns of resource exchange were observed. The difference between mergers and joint ventures appears to be that mergers are used relatively more to cope with buyer-seller interdependence, and joint ventures are more highly related to considerations of coping with competitive uncertainty.

Co-optation and interlocking directorates

Co-optation is a venerable strategy for managing interdependence between organizations. Co-optation involves the partial absorption of another organization through the placing of a representative of that organization on the board of the focal organization. Corporations frequently place bankers on their boards; hospitals and universities offer trustee positions to prominent business leaders; and community action agencies develop advisory boards populated with active and strong community political figures.

As a strategy for coping with interdependence, co-optation involves some particular problems and considerations. For example, a representative of the external organization is brought into the focal organization, while still retaining his or her original organizational membership. Co-optation is based on creating a conflict of interest within the co-opted person. To what extent should one pursue the goals and interests of one's organization of principal affiliation, and to what extent should one favor the interests of the co-opting organization? From the point of view of the co-opting organization, the individual should favor its interests, but not to the point where he or she loses credibility in the parent organization, because at that point, the individual ceases to be useful in ensuring that organization's support. Thus, co-optation requires striking a balance between the pressures to identify with either the parent or co-opting institution.

Furthermore, since co-optation involves less than total absorption of the other organization, there is the risk that the co-opted representative will not have enough influence or control in the principal organization to ensure the desired decisions. Of course, it is possible to co-opt more than a single representative. This is frequently done when relationships with the co-opted organization are particularly uncertain and critical. Co-optation may be the most feasible strategy when total absorption is impossible due to financial or legal constraints.

Interlocks in the boards of directors of competing organizations provide a possible strategy for coping with competitive interdependence and the resulting uncertainty. The underlying argument is that in order to manage interorganizational relationships, information must be exchanged, usually through a joint subsidiary or interlocking directorate. While interlocks among competitors are ostensibly illegal, until very recently there was practically no prosecution of this practice. In a 1965 study, a subcommittee of the House Judiciary Committee found more than 300 cases in which direct competitors had interlocking boards of directors (17). In a study of the extent of interlocking among competing organizations in a sample of 109 manufacturing organizations, Pfeffer and Nowak (3) found that the proportion of directors on the board from direct competitors was higher for firms operating in industries in which concentration was intermediate. This result is consistent with the result found for joint ventures and mergers as well. In all three instances, linkages among competing organizations occurred more frequently when concentration was in an intermediate range.

Analyses of co-optation through the use of boards of directors have not been confined to business firms. Price (18) argued that the principal function of the boards of the Oregon Fish and Game Commissions was to link the organizations to their environments. Zald (19) found that the composition of YMCA boards in Chicago matched the demography of their operating areas, and affected the organizations' effectiveness, particularly in raising money. Pfeffer (20) examined the size, composition, and function of hospital boards of directors, finding that variables of organizational context, such as ownership, source of funds, and location, were important explanatory factors. He also found a relationship between co-optation and organizational effectiveness. In 1972, he (21) found that regulated firms, firms with a higher proportion of debt in their capital structures, and larger firms tended to have more outside directors. Allen (22) also found that size of the board and the use of co-optation was predicted by the size of the firm, but did not replicate Pfeffer's earlier finding of a relationship between the organization's capital structure and the proportion of directors from financial institutions. In a study of utility boards, Pfeffer (23) noted that the composition of the board tended to correlate with the demographics of the area in which the utility was regulated.

The evidence is consistent with the strategy of organizations using their boards of directors to co-opt external organizations and manage problematic interdependence. The role of the board of directors is seen not as the provision of management expertise or control, but more generally as a means of managing problematic aspects of an organization's institutional environment.

Executive recruitment

Information also is transferred among organizations through the movement of personnel. The difference between movement of executives between organizations and co-optation is that in the latter case, the person linking the two organizations retains membership in both organizations. In the case of personnel movement, dual organizational membership is not maintained. When people change jobs, they take with themselves information about the operations, policies, and values of their previous employers, as well as contacts in the organization. In a study of the movement of faculty among schools of business, Baty et al. (24) found that similar orientations and curricula developed among schools exchanging personnel. The movement of personnel is one method by which new techniques of management and new marketing and product ideas are diffused through a set of organizations.

Occasionally, the movement of executives between organizations has been viewed as intensifying, rather than reducing, competition. Companies have been distressed by the raiding of trade secrets and managerial expertise by other organizations. While this perspective must be recognized, the exchange of personnel among organizations is a revered method of conflict *reduction* between organizations (25). Personnel movement inevitably involves sharing information among a set of organizations.

If executive movement is a form of interfirm linkage designed to manage competitive relationships, the proportion of executives recruited from within the same industry should be highest at intermediate levels of industrial concentration. Examining the three top executive positions in twenty different manufacturing industries, the evidence on executive backgrounds was found to be consistent with this argument (26). The proportion of high-level executives with previous jobs in the same industry but in a different company was found to be negatively related to the number of firms in the industry. The larger the number of firms, the less likely that a single link among competitors will substantially reduce uncertainty, but the larger the available supply of external executive talent. The data indicated no support for a supply argument, but supported the premise that interorganizational linkages are used to manage interdependence and uncertainty.

The use of executive movement to manage noncompetitive interorganizational relationships is quite prevalent. The often-cited movement of personnel between the Defense Department and major defense contractors is only one example, because there is extensive movement of personnel between many government departments and industries interested in the agencies' decisions. The explanation is frequently proposed that organizations are acquiring these personnel because of their expertise. The expertise explanation is frequently difficult to separate from the alternative that personnel are being exchanged to enhance interorganizational relationships. Regardless of the motivation, exchanging personnel inevitably involves the transfer of information and access to the other organization. It is conceptually possible to control for the effect of expertise—in other words, taking expertise into account, is there evidence that recruiting patterns reflect the influence of factors related to institutional management?

Regulation

Occasionally, institutional relationships are managed through recourse to political intervention. The reduction of competition and its associated uncertainty may be accomplished through regulation. Regulation, however, is a risky strategy for organizations to pursue. While regulation most frequently benefits the regulated industry (9, 10), the industry and firms have no assurance that regulatory authority will not be used against their interests. Regulation is very hard to repeal. Successful use of regulation requires that the firm and industry face little or no powerful political opposition, and that the political future can be accurately forecast.

The benefits of regulation to those being regulated have been extensively reviewed (11, 27). Regulation frequently has been sought by the regulated industry. Currently, trucking firms are among the biggest supporters of continued regulation of trucking. Since the Civil Aeronautics Board was created in 1938, no new trunk carriers have been started. Jordan (28) found that air rates on intrastate (hence not regulated by the CAB) airlines within California are frequently 25 percent or more lower than fares on comparable routes of regulated carriers. Estimates of the effects of regulation on prices in electric utilities, airlines, trucking, and natural gas have indicated that regulation either increases price or has no effect.

The theory behind these outcomes is still unclear. One approach suggests that regulation is created for the public benefit, but after the initial legislative attention, the regulatory process is captured by the firms subject to regulation. Another approach proposes that regulation, like other goods, is acquired subject to supply and demand considerations (11). Political scientists, focusing on the operation of interest groups, argue that regulatory agencies are "captured" by organized and well-financed interests. Government intervention in the market can solve many of the interdependence problems faced by firms. Regulation is most often accomplished by restriction of entry and the fixing of prices, which tend to reduce market uncertainties. Markets may be actually allocated to firms, and with the reduction of risk, regulation may make access to capital easier. Regulation may alter the organization's relationships with suppliers and customers. One theory of why the railroads were interested in the creation of the Interstate Commerce Commission (ICC) in 1887 was that large users were continually demanding and winning discriminatory rate reductions, disturbing the price stability of railroad price fixing cartels. By forbidding price discrimination and enforcing this regulation, the ICC strengthened the railroads' position with respect to large customers (29).

Political activity

Regulation is only one specific form of organizational activity in governmental processes. Business attempts to affect competition through the operation of the tariff laws date back to the 1700's (30). Epstein (31) provided one of the more complete summaries of the history of corporate involvement in politics and the inevitability of such action. The government has the power of coercion, possessed legally by no other social institution. Furthermore, legislation and regulation affect most of our economic institutions and markets, either indirectly through taxation, or more directly through purchasing, market protection, or market creation. For example, taxes on margarine only recently came to an end. Federal taxes, imposed in 1886 as a protectionist measure for dairy interests, were removed in 1950, but a law outlawing the sale of oleo in its colored form lasted until 1967 in Wisconsin.

As with regulation, political activities carry both benefits and risks. The risk arises because once government intervention in an issue on behalf of a firm or industry is sought, then political intervention becomes legitimated, regardless of whose interests are helped or hurt. The firm that seeks favorable tax legislation runs the risk of creating a setting in which it is equally legitimate to be exposed to very unfavorable legislation. After an issue is opened to government intervention, neither side will find it easy to claim that further government action is illegitimate.

In learning to cope with a particular institutional environment, the team may be unprepared for new uncertainties caused by the change of fundamental institutional relationships, including the opening of price competition, new entry and the lack of protection from overseas competition.

Conclusion

The institutional function of management involves managing the organization's relationships with other organizations. Table 1 presents strategies of institutional management with their principal advantages and disadvantages. From observation of organizational activities, the most common response to interdependence with external organizations seems to be the attempt to develop some form of interorganizational linkage to ensure the continuation of favorable relationship with important organizations in the environment.

All such interfirm linkages have costs, with the most fundamental being the loss of the organization's autonomy. In return for the certainty that one's competitors will not engage in predatory price cutting, one must provide assurances about one's own behavior. For example, cooptation involves the possibility of acquiring the support of an external organization, but at the same time the firm gives up some degree of privacy over its internal information and some control over its operations and decisions.

Variables affecting responses to the organization's environment can be specified. Actions taken to manage interdependencies are related to the extent of the interdependence and its importance to the organi-

Table 1. Advantages and Disadvantages of Strategies of
Institutional Management

Strategy	Advantages	Disadvantages
Merger	Completely absorbs interdependence	Requires resources sufficient to acquire another organization May be proscribed by antitrust laws, or infeasible for other reasons (e.g., a governmental unit cannot be absorbed by a firm)
Joint ventures	Can be used for sharing risks and costs associated with large, or technologically advanced activities Can be used to partially pool resources and coordinate activities	Is available only for certain types of organizations, though less restricted than merger (COMSAT, for instance, brings together government and business)
Co-optation	Relatively inexpensive	May not provide enough coordination or linkage between organizations to ensure performance Co-opted person may lose credibility in original organization
Personnel movement	Relatively inexpensive Almost universally possible	Person loses identification with original organization, lessening influence there Linkage is based on knowledge and familiarity, and on a few persons at most, not on basic structural relationships
Regulation	Enables organization to benefit from the coercive power of the government	Regulation may be used to harm the organization's interests
Political activity	Enables organization to use government to modify and enhance environment	Government intervention, once legitimated, may be used against the organization as well as for its benefit

zation. The response to competitive interdependence is related to measures of industry structure, and particularly to the necessity and feasibility of developing informal, interorganizational structures. Two important issues remain. First, is effective institutional management associated with favorable outcomes to the organization? Second, given the importance of institutional management, why are some organizations more successful than others at this task?

The effect of institutional management on firm performance is difficult to measure, and seldom has been examined. To examine the effect of successful institutional management, an outcome measure is needed.

Profit is only one possibility, because there is evidence that the reduction of uncertainty may be sought regardless of its effect on profit (32). Whatever criterion is chosen is affected by many factors. To attribute a result to institutional management, other causes must be controlled. Nevertheless, institutional management receives a great deal of management attention in some firms and a firm's interorganizational relationships may be important to its success and survival.

Of even more fundamental interest is the question of why some firms are able to develop more effective strategic responses to their institutional environments. It is possible that effective institutional management requires fundamentally different structures of top management, or the development of excess managerial capacity, or the development of particular types of information systems. It is easier to find successful institutional management than to identify critical variables enabling it to develop in the first place. For example, some universities have better relationships with their state legislatures than do others. It is possible to retrospectively infer explanations as to why this is so. What remains to be done is to explain those factors that could be designed into an organization initially to ensure effective institutional management in the future.

Considering its probable importance to the firm, the institutional function of management has received much less concern than it warrants. It is time that this aspect of management receives the systematic attention long reserved for motivational and productivity problems associated with relationships between management and workers.

References

1. Parsons, Talcott. *Structure and Process in Modern Societies* (Glencoe, Illinois: Free Press, 1960).
2. Mintzberg, Henry. *The Nature of Managerial Work* (New York: Harper and Row, 1973).
3. Pfeffer, Jeffrey, and Phillip Nowak. "Organizational Context and Interorganizational Linkages Among Corporations." Unpublished MS. (Berkeley: University of California).
4. Whyte, William F. *Street Corner Society* (Chicago: University of Chicago Press, 1955).
5. Jacobs, David. "Dependency and Vulnerability: An Exchange Approach to the Control of Organizations," *Administrative Science Quarterly,* Vol. 19 (1974), 45–59.
6. Thompson, James D. *Organizations in Action* (New York: McGraw Hill, 1967).
7. Katz, Daniel, and Robert L. Kahn. *The Social Psychology of Organizations* (New York: John Wiley, 1966).

8. Hirsch, Paul M. "Organizational Effectiveness and the Institutional Environment," *Administrative Science Quarterly,* Vol. 20 (1975), 327–44.

9. Jordan, William A. "Producer, Protection, Prior Market Structure and the Effects of Government Regulation," *Journal of Law and Economics,* Vol. 15 (1972), 151–76.

10. Pfeffer, Jeffrey. "Administrative Regulation and Licensing: Social Problem or Solution?" *Social Problems,* Vol. 21 (1974), 468–79.

11. Posner, Richard A. "Theories of Economic Regulation," *Bell Journal of Economics and Management Science,* Vol. 5 (1974), 335–58.

12. Pfeffer, Jeffrey. "Merger as a Response to Organizational Interdependence," *Administrative Science Quarterly,* Vol. 17 (1972), 382–94.

13. Reid, Samuel R. *Mergers, Managers, and the Economy* (New York: McGraw-Hill, 1968).

14. Bernstein, Lewis. "Joint Ventures in the Light of Recent Antitrust Developments," *The Antitrust Bulletin,* Vol. 10 (1965), 25–29.

15. Pfeffer, Jeffrey, and Phillip Nowak. "Joint Ventures and Interorganizational Interdependence," *Administrative Science Quarterly,* in press.

16. Pfeffer, Jeffrey and Phillip Nowak. "Patterns of Joint Venture Activity: Implications for Antitrust Policy," *The Antitrust Bulletin,* in press.

17. House of Representatives, Staff Report to the Antitrust Subcommittee of the Committee on the Judiciary. *Interlocks in Corporate Management* (Washington, D.C.: U.S. Government Printing Office, 1965).

18. Price, James L. "The Impact of Governing Boards on Organizational Effectiveness and Morale," *Administrative Science Quarterly,* Vol. 8 (1963), 361–78.

19. Zald, Mayer N. "Urban Differentiation, Characteristics of Boards of Directors and Organizational Effectiveness," *American Journal of Sociology,* Vol. 73 (1967), 261–72.

20. Pfeffer, Jeffrey. "Size, Composition and Function of Hospital Boards of Directors: A Study of Organization-Environment Linkage," *Administrative Science Quarterly,* Vol. 18 (1973), 349–64.

21. Pfeffer, Jeffrey. "Size and Composition of Corporate Boards of Directors: The Organization and its Environment," *Administrative Science Quarterly,* Vol. 17 (1972), 218–28.

22. Allen, Michael Patrick. "The Structure of Interorganizational Elite Co-optation: Interlocking Corporate Directorates," *American Sociological Review,* Vol. 39 (1971), 393–406.

23. Pfeffer, Jeffrey. "Co-optation and the Composition of Electric Utility Boards of Directors," *Pacific Sociological Review,* Vol. 17 (1974), 333–63.

24. Baty, Gordon B., William M. Evan, and Terry W. Rothermel. "Personnel Flows as Interorganizational Relations," *Administrative Science Quarterly,* Vol. 16 (1971), 430–43.

25. Stern, Louis W., Brian Sterthal, and C. Samuel Craig. "Managing Conflict in Distribution Channels: A Laboratory Study," *Journal of Marketing Research,* Vol. 10 (1973), 169–79.

26. Pfeffer, Jeffrey, and Huseyin Leblebici. "Executive Recruitment and the Development of Interfirm Organizations," *Administrative Science Quarterly,* Vol. 18 (1973), 449–61.

27. Stigler, George J. "The Theory of Economic Regulation," *Bell Journal of Economics and Management Science,* Vol. 2 (1971), 3–21.

28. Jordan, William A. *Airline Regulation in America: Effects and Imperfections* (Baltimore: Johns Hopkins University Press, 1970).

29. MacAvoy, Paul W. *The Economic Effects of Regulation* (Cambridge, Mass.: MIT Press, 1965).

30. Bauer, Raymond A., Ithiel de Sola Pool, and Lewis Anthony Dexter. *American Business and Public Policy* (New York: Atherton Press, 1968).

31. Epstein, Edwin M. *The Corporation in American Politics* (Englewood Cliffs, New Jersey: Prentice-Hall, 1969).

32. Caves, Richard E. "Uncertainty, Market Structure, and Performance: Galbraith as Conventional Wisdom," in J. W. Markham and G. F. Papanek (eds.), *Industrial Organization and Economic Development* (Boston: Houghton Mifflin, 1970), pp. 283–302.

Strategies for Survival: How Organizations Cope with Their Worlds
Harold J. Leavitt
William R. Dill
Henry B. Eyring

The relationhip between an organization and the world is much like the relationship between an individual and the world. We can learn a great deal about an individual without knowing anything at all about his world. We can understand his nervous system, his digestive system, his respiratory system, and the ways in which they articulate. But if we want to extend our understanding, we must find out how he copes with his environment. We must understand not only the structure of his nervous system but how it responds to external stimuli, not only the nature of his respiratory system but how it is affected by the atmosphere in which he breathes. We must understand the environmental limits of survival.

We must also understand how the individual copes with *changes* in his environment. Somehow organisms do manage to adjust to change, and sometimes they even manage to change the world so that it adjusts to them. When the world turns cold, they learn to build igloos, to insulate themselves from unpleasant environments to which they cannot or will not adapt. They even learn to create environments that they positively prefer. They condition and purify the air—usually after they have polluted it.

This complex relationship between the organism and its environment has a counterpart in the exchange between the organization and its environment. Sometimes the adaptation is inadequate; when the organization meets an environment it cannot cope with, it dies. What are the points at which an organization comes into contact with its environment? The list is long, but finite. Consider, for example, a small retail store. It lives at a location, an address. This address, this shop, is in a neighborhood in a town in a nation. It is made of brick and mortar.

That means it has been in contact with neighbors and plumbers and carpenters. The shop presumably sells something it has brought from someone else. So there is always the interface with the community of suppliers at one end and customers at the other.

Those are some obvious points of environmental contact, the proximate ones. But there are others. How about municipal services? The policeman on the beat and the fire department? Insurance companies? The PTA that claims the retail shop is selling dirty books to teen-agers? The black community that claims it sells racist books? There are employees, too, who are citizens of the community. They want shorter hours and higher pay.

In a multitude of ways even the small shop finds itself in a complex exchange with its environment, not just passively but in critically active ways. Its survival and growth depend on its ability to maintain and build those relationships in ways that provide the shop with what it needs. If it is a white-owned shop in a black ghetto, or a psychedelic shop in a straight, middle-class town, it may not survive. In certain areas, if it is a shop that refuses to pay off the cops, it may not survive even if it obeys all the laws. So if it *has* survived, it has perforce been shaped, perhaps brainwashed, by the forces that its particular environment exerts upon it.

But the shop can also shape its environment—to some extent. The books it sells—including the dirty ones—may influence the community. The style and design of its storefront may influence the architecture of neighboring stores. Its entrepreneurial activities may bring in all sorts of people from other areas.

Sense organs and survival

First, a generalization: the less sensitive an organization is to its environment, the less likely it is to survive. The dress shop that doesn't understand the style preferences or budgets of local women is not likely to flourish. The shop owner cannot assume that the dresses that sell in Istanbul will sell just as well in Fort Wayne.

That generalization seems obvious enough. But the converse does not. It does *not* follow that the greater an organization's capacity to sense its environment, the *more* likely it is to survive. For an organization with good sensors can survive only if it *also* possesses the capacity to modify its behavior in response to the information it receives. Indeed, if it has no mechanism for adapting to that information, its fine sensors may become downright destructive. Suppose, for example, that I am very sensitive to pain but I am paralyzed. If a pin is stuck into me I cannot move away. I would be better off if I weren't sensitive to pain at all.

Consider some recent developments in the Catholic church. Ritual texts have been translated from Latin into the language of the local community as a means of bringing church and community closer together. Priests have been encouraged to show more awareness of the problems of their communities. The church, as it were, is trying to improve its capacity to sense what is going on at the interface between its parishes and its parishioners.

But let us suppose—only for the sake of supposition—that no other changes take place within the structure of the church. Suppose that the new information now entering the system through the parish priest has nowhere to go, that the people "upstairs" either don't listen to it or don't know what to do with it. Is the church better off than it was before? In one way it is. The local priest can deal with some problems he failed to sense before. But organizationally, the church may be in trouble. For now it is faced with priests sensitive to urgent problems but frustrated by their inability to prompt responsive action at higher levels.

Internal communication, muscle, and survival

To be effective, then, a sensing mechanism must be tied into an internal mechanism for communicating and processing what is sensed, and a set of "muscles" for responding to what it processes. Without those mechanisms, a good sensing system may make the organization *less* capable of survival than an organization that is sealed off in its own shell, unaware of what is going on around it. The slow, insensitive, hard-shelled turtle can cope with its environment by closing itself off. A sensitive, but still slow, soft-shelled turtle would be vulnerable indeed.

This is another way of saying that an organization needs to be internally coherent to deal with its environment. The system needs to be a full system, with all its parts sensibly related to one another. Good sensors need to be connected to a brain and accompanying muscles. Several different systems may be coherent in their own ways and may work reasonably well, but some work better than others in particular environments.

Some alternative designs for survival

Let's consider four internally coherent ways in which organizations can sense and respond to environments.

Imperviousness: The withdrawal model

Some organizations deal with the world by shutting it out—by rolling up into a spiny ball and hoping their unattractive exterior will discourage enemies. Many religious and utopian groups, and some communes, have tried to drop out of the world. To a lesser degree withdrawal has also been the route of some government agencies, and in a less extreme way the route of some American railroads.

They try actively to eliminate any sense of the world around them. Some companies, for example, discourage their people from joining professional groups by suggesting that such activities are disloyal and that the time thus wasted might better be spent within the company. Such organizations are more concerned with sheer survival than with growth or adaptation. Their primary reaction to a changing environment is to find better ways of *not* responding to it—harder shells, tighter restrictions.

Why should any organization want to insulate itself from the world? For much the same reason that ancient cities walled themselves in— to protect what they valued from predators *who valued different things*. For the same reason that many youth communes are hidden in the woods—to permit their members to do their thing without persecution or attack. And for the same reason that the early Mormons settled in Salt Lake City.

Organizations build shells when they want to protect, in their existing forms, their values, their possessions, their beliefs, their people. But there is another reason, too. An organization that is impervious to its environment is not easily shaken from its routines; it is not "distracted" from its objectives, because it does not pay attention to things that might be distracting. It does no push panic buttons, because it does not hear the cries of fire. So an impervious exterior also helps provide for single-minded concentration.

Today, universities are active places, more active than they used to be. Professors are out consulting and carrying on field research. Students, no longer the hub of the university's universe, complain simultaneously of the "irrelevance" of their courses and of the university's multiple connections with other power groups in the environment. Are they asking for a return to isolation? If so, would "relevance" to the current world still be possible?

Or consider the diplomatic services of most nations. Diplomats act as organizational sense organs as well as muscles. One of their functions is to send home relevant intelligence about their host country. To do that, they must really get to know the host country. Yet almost all the world's diplomatic services carefully rotate their people every few years. One reason is the fear that their diplomats will become too sensitive, too understanding, and therefore too sympathetic with the host's problems, and hence may become more representational of the host than reportorial about it. Don't such rotation schemes contribute, in a mild way, to imperviousness from certain types of information?

In many companies salesmen serve as important sense organs. They work outside the organization, spending their time with customers. But they are sometimes reluctant to report back unpleasant information about the company's products or behavior because they know that home-office executives prefer not to hear such news.

And consider the old model of the mental hospital. It was a model of isolation. Get the patients out into the woods, into a walled asylum. Let few visitors in and few patients out. Minimize contact between patient and the world. And how about the model of the convent?

Selective impreviousness

So far we have considered the organization that closes off *all* environmental inputs. In the long run, especially in a changing environment, such complete imperviousness is disastrous for most organizations in the modern world.

Suppose we are the managers of an organization that foresees the danger of such isolation and wants to avoid it. But we are understandably concerned lest our people be seduced into immorality or disloyalty by exposure to the temptations of the world. And we also want to act upon our environment, to sell our product or to proselytize our religion or to enrich the coffers of our native country. How can we act intelligently upon an environment that we dare not let our people sense too well? We cannot. So we compromise. We sense, but we keep what we sense from penetrating too deeply into our organization. We hold the world at arm's length, in a gingerly fashion, and perhaps distastefully; but at least we look at it, and then act upon it.

Consider English colonialism. The English trained their men in England, in English schools and English universities. They trained them long and well so that their colonial officers would be true Englishmen. Then they sent them off to India with English manners and English dinner jackets to govern the heathen. Those officers carried England with them. They drank tea and dressed for diner as though they were in London—and to that degree they remained impervious to their environment. They were little concerned about the inappropriateness of English evening dress to the Indian climate.

But they did not *ignore* their environment. They even learned a bit of the local language. They identified local leaders. They trained local people. They set up an intelligence network to learn about local affairs. And, being English, they were polite. They learned local protocol and respected it. Yet never for a moment did they consider going native. Never did they identify with their environment, blend into it, participate in it. No snake charmers for them. They sensed the world they were in, but because they were strongly socialized into their home culture, they remained outside it.

Japanese businessmen working abroad are masters of selective imperviousness. They learn the local ways quickly, designing and marketing their products to fit local practices, but they remain culturally and organizationally Japanese.

For an organization to ensure that its people will sense well and yet not be shaken by what they sense requires a very high level of socialization of its members—high loyalty, high commitment. And the organization must police the whole process, for even strong company men may backslide. One major British company used to check up on its field managers periodically to make sure they were maintaining their British identity. "We know there's a problem," one executive said, "when a manager in Borneo stops dressing for dinner. Then it's time to bring him back to London."

Adaptiveness: The organizational chameleon

As the world changes, it becomes more difficult for organizations to sense their environment an still remain independent of it. The British could remain British in India as long as India remained a colony. It is much more difficult for them to remain British and also effective in an economically expanding, independent India, where Indian, American, Japanese, and Russian competitors abound; where the environment is active, turbulent, and differentiated rather than passive and submissive.

One alternative for the organization confronting such an active environment is the opposite of imperviousness. It is to *adapt* to the local environment, to develop good sense organs and to use the information that comes in to make the organization as much a part of the local scene as possible. The adaptive organization, in effect, goes native. It becomes part of the environment. In Rome it is Roman. In Thailand it is Thai. It joins the local clubs, hires local people, and behaves in the approved local way.

There is something seductively attractive about this alternative. It seems to be respectful of local culture, polite, nonintrusive.

But there are many dangers for the organization in such behavior. Your people in Thailand may become so understanding of the Thais' needs and problems that they show more concern for Thai welfare than for your own. Or your people may be rejected by the host for trying to be what they are not. And adaptive behavior is mostly responsive rather than active, forever modifying itself to fit the world. In a volatile, rapidly changing world, an adaptive organization may find itself trying to change its behavior from day to day, blown about by political and social winds.

An ethical danger also arises for the organization that tries too hard to adapt. Should it be adaptive to *any* environment regardless of the conditions that exist there? Should it offer bribes where bribes are commonplace? Should it be racist where the society is racist? Should it treat employees as slaves because that is the societal model? The British colonialists carried not only their tea but their British standards of morality, justice, decency, fair play. Old-fashioned as those standards may now seem, they were high standards around which the organization could stand proud and honorable, whatever the local behavior.

So beware the siren of extreme organizational adaptiveness—your organization may become a chameleon.

Action-adaptation

The impervious organization shuts itself off, neither permitting change within itself nor creating change in its environment. The selectively impervious organization rejects any stimuli that may induce change in itself but tries actively to modify the environment. The adaptive organization accepts its environment and changes itself to meet it.

But there is still another alternative. An organization may be *both* adaptive *and* active. It may change itself to live with its environment and at the same time alter its environment.

For many organizations, altering the environment is part of their normal work. Public health organizations would be of little use if they did not erase malaria and reduce infantile mortality and thereby significantly alter their environment. Agricultural agencies would be of little use if they did not change the behavior of farmers and the nature of farming.

The prime purpose, after all, of many organizations is to change their worlds. There is a story about two shoe salesmen who were sent to open up a remote African market. The first salesman cabled home: "No one here wears shoes. Sales situation hopeless. Cancel all shipments." The second salesman cabled: "No one here yet wears shoes. Ship all you can."

But a dilemma arises. How can an organization be *of* its environment and still change it? Clearly the first place to look for an answer is in the environment itself. In some environments, like Los Angeles, change is a normal attribute of the environment. A Tibetan organization can move into Los Angeles to sell mothers on the idea of feeding their infants curdled yak's milk, and few will think it very strange. The Tibetan salesmen could easily, if they were sensitive, make themselves quite at home in that turbulent, competitive, shifting environment. The complexity and rapidity of change make almost anything possible. But let the same salesmen try to peddle their yak milk in stable, traditional Charleston, South Carolina, and things will be different.

But can we also adapt to a passive, relatively unchanging environment, and simultaneously change it? That seems almost a logical contradiction.

One possibility, however, may be to try a *sequential* process. First, adapt to the environment, then change it from within. The problem here, of course, is that once the organization has adapted, it may no longer be interested in creating the change it had originally wanted.

One of the great problems for many organizations in the next few years will be to devise some appropriate blend of action with adaptation—a blend that allows the organization to maintain its own identity, to effect change in its environment, and yet to "belong" to that environment. The issues involved in working out such a path are not just issues of efficiency. They are also ethical, ecological, and human issues.

Organizational tuning

An adult organization, again like an adult person, is not infinitely flexible. It is limited in what it can do, limited by its tasks, its personality, and its history. It may wish to be adaptive and yet be unable to adapt without undertaking major internal redesign. It needs to be "tuned."

Some organizations are appropriately tuned to their environment; some are overtuned; some undertuned. A delicately tuned automobile may be great for the racetrack but not for day-to-day city driving. A highly sensitive organization, alert to every change around it, may do very well in a subtle environment where small news items create large public response and casual remarks portend large changes, where minor shifts in consumer tastes can kill an unresponsive product line. But put such a highly sensitive organization into a stolid, stable, noncompetitive environment and it may be paralyzed by its own sensitivity, overresponding to noise that is fundamentally irrelevant to the organization's activities. Organizations with a strong marketing orientation sometimes get into trouble in foreign environments for that very reason. Marketing people generally are highly sensitive to consumer signals. University faculties sometimes overrespond to local signals, too, even when the cost of responding fully to *all* those signals may be much too great for the university to bear. But organizations dominated by production people or technological people are apt to err in the opposite direction.

Overcentralized and undercentralized organizations

Consider, also, the relationship between the degree of centralization in an organization and its ability to cope with its environment. In some settings a high degree of centralization, as in a field army, is a major source of the organization's power. The centralization of control may permit a small force to overcome a larger, loosely organized enemy force with poor internal communication and no central decision points.

But that same centralized organizational design may be a source of weakness in other settings. For one thing, a lucky shot at the brain of a highly centralized organization can kill it. The Norman abbeys in England suffered such a fate. They were excellently, tightly organized communities. But they had single, identifiable heads—the abbots. When Henry VIII decided to get rid of the abbeys, he did so very easily by getting rid of the abbots. And the rest of the organization fell apart.

Conversely, some historical reports indicate that General de Gaulle advocated a *federal* rather than a central form of government for postwar Germany, because—it is said—he believed that decentralized federalism would *prevent* Germany from rapidly regaining its strength. France, after all, had a strong centralist tradition. In fact, Germany came back very fast, probably in large part because of its multiple, relatively loose federal form. It is much harder to chop off the many heads of a federalized government than to chop off the one head of a highly centralized one.

Centralized organizations, as we suggested in the chapter on organizations abroad, have other weaknesses in certain environments. Communication lines are long, for one thing. If issues must go all the way to the top for decision, reaction may be too slow in a rapidly changing environment.

On the other hand, units of highly decentralized organizations may be too adaptive, too ready to take on local color and local loyalty. Such organizations may collapse for lack of controlling bonds from the top.

The strategies of imperviousness, adaptation, and action

Viewed historically, which of these strategies has worked best, under what conditions?

Imperviousness has tended to work when the goals of the organization either do not require much interaction with the environment, or when the environment is very stable. The scholarly monk can do his work quite well if he is left alone. But as interdependence and change increase, imperviousness becomes less useful. The plumbing-fixture manufacturers of France can go on making obsolete toilets as long as the French maintain their existing attitudes toward toilets. But when tourists start fussing, and Hilton hotels start appearing, and Frenchmen come back from abroad, the pressure for change builds up.

But, since impervious organizations are, by definition, insensitive, we should not expect them to change steadily in response to steadily

mounting pressures. It is only when the temperature reaches the boil-
ing point that the turtle may decide to stick its head and feet out of its
shell and move. And then it may be too late.

When does selective imperviousness work? First, when the organization succeeds in indoctrinating its members deeply into its organizational beliefs and standards. Selective imperviousness requires a kind
of absolute faith, an ardor, a commitment to carry one's message out
to the world, to get others to do things our way. And that seems to be
getting harder to do each year.

Selective imperviousness also works well in relatively undifferenti-
ated, placid, noncompetitive environments. British colonialists and
the early Jesuits had a sort of monopoly over the environments in which
they worked. But now there are the Russians and the Cubans and the
Chinese, and, oddly enough, the locals, all in the same place.

To take the distant, formal, standoffish role implied by such selective
imperviousness becomes very risky in turbulent settings. Not only was
that true for the early British; the same is true for the contemporary
American company that insists on operating in the American way in
Latin America, or in the urban way in a rural setting. It must offer an
extraordinary product or service if it expects to remain unsullied in the
intricate networks of a briskly moving but foreign environment.

Adaptation, as we have seen, is a fine strategy—for survival. Taking
on the local coloring, going native, will usually help an organization
to stay locally alive; but it is not likely to produce innovation or to
influence the environment. Indeed, it may generate serious *internal*
problems for the organization's members. For most of us are not perfectly adaptive. We cannot become one with our environments even
if we want to. Our history, our education, our values don't permit it.

Some form of an active-adaptive strategy appears almost a necessity
for contemporary organizations, both because of the nature of the
modern organization and the nature of the modern environment. G.E.
cannot be French, but it must be quasi-French if it is to build and sell
computers in France. Certainly France cannot be suborned into the
G.E. way; but on the other hand, G.E. had better not be fully suborned
into the French way.

Redesigning oneself

So what is left? Interaction rather than isolation. Patience rather than
precipitousness. Modification rather than conversion. A world, that is
to say, of talk and compromise; of incremental changes on the outside
accompanied by incremental adaptive changes on the inside; of both
sensitivity and identity.

That is a difficult task, but organizations can work at it. To succeed, they need a good sensing apparatus with which to learn about their environment, good action apparatus with which to respond to and influence their environment, and, most of all, good internal communication and decision apparatus with which to do two things: (1) to convert what they sense into appropriate action, and (2) to modify and redesign themselves.

One important difference between man and organization is that man is born with sense organs, brain, and muscles. Organizations must make their own. They can choose to be blind or to see with many eyes, to build lots of action muscle or little, and to devise an effective internal communication and decision mechanism or a faulty one.

Yet most organizations do not treat these problems as a conscious part of their self-design. Their sense organs, especially, tend to develop helter-skelter as an ancillary product of trying to buy or sell or lobby. Their internal mechanisms for processing what they sense are often highly dependent on personalities and prejudices. Organizations hire salesmen to sell, not to listen. And often what the salesman hears, he cannot successfully transmit back into the organization. Sales meetings typically include little listening. The communication is one way, from company to salesman. Similarly, organizations hire scientists to do R&D, not to keep up with their profession. But the scientist who listens to his profession often produces highly useful work for the organization.

Only in recent years has the issue of organizational sensing begun to be examined consciously. Unfortunately, "organizational intelligence" is the phrase often used to describe this process; but that phrase, adapted from the diplomatic and military worlds, connotes spying on an enemy. That is not the central problem. The central problem is knowing one's world.

Summary

Organizations use several different strategies for coping with their environments. All those strategies involve sensing the environment, processing what is sensed, and acting.

Some organizations use a strategy of "imperviousness," sensing little and acting little. This strategy is useful for organizations that want to isolate themselves from change, but it is increasingly difficult to implement in a volatile world.

Other organizations are "selectively impervious." They try to sense the environment and act in response to it, but they also make sure they do not enter into it. Such organizations presocialize their people and require strong commitment and loyalty.

Still other organizations try to sense their environment and to become one with it. That "adaptive" strategy has some limited use for survival, but it does little to foster growth or innovation.

The strategy of "action-adaptation" involves changing both oneself and one's environment interactively. But it is easier to adapt to and to change active, volatile environments than passive ones.

In any strategy, however, one central problem is the tuning of the organization's behavior to the particular state of its particular environment. Appropriate tuning means organizational responsiveness that is neither too strong nor too weak for the organization's environment.

The degree of centralization in an organization affects its tuning. Organizations too centralized for their environment become rigid and slow to respond. Overly decentralized organizations may become too locally adaptive, too hard to control.

Organizations have a distinct advantage over individuals in coping with this problem: they can redesign their own sense organs, brains, and muscles into a system consistent with the strategies they choose.

Notes and References

A good background for this chapter may be found in works on "open-systems theory," such as E. Trist and F. E. Emery, "The Causal Texture of Organizational Environments," *Human Relations,* XVIII (1965), pp. 21–32, in which the authors categorize environments into the types we have used in our discussion. This article is also reprinted in F. E. Emery, ed., *Systems Thinking* (London: Penguin Books, 1969).

On the ways in which organizations try to cope, we have borrowed liberally from J. D. Thompson, *Organizations in Action* (New York: McGraw-Hill, 1967).

On the problems of trying to understand foreign environments, we suggest W. J. Lederer and E. Burdick, *The Ugly American* (New York: Norton, 1958).

Tom Wolfe's facinating piece on the naiveté of white officialdom in understanding black culture is also useful: *Radical Chic and Mau-Mauing the Flak Catchers* (New York: Bantam Books, 1970).

On organizational intelligence, see H. L. Wilensky, *Organizational Intelligence* (New York: Basic Books, 1967).